A Concise American History

Expertly steering readers through the often tumultuous and exhilarating history of the United States, from its early modern Native American roots to twenty-first-century neoliberalism and the shifting political climate of the past decade, this highly readable textbook provides a compelling overview of American development over the last five centuries.

This book avoids either celebratory or condemnatory rhetoric to present a critical examination of domestic America and its interaction with the rest of the world. Balancing coverage of political, social, cultural, and economic history, each chapter also includes a wealth of features to facilitate learning:

- Timelines situating key events in their wider chronology
- Lists of topics covered within each chapter for easy reference
- Concept boxes discussing selected issues in more detail
- Historiography boxes exploring key debates
- Chapter summaries offering condensed outlines of the main themes of each chapter
- Further reading lists guiding readers to additional resources
- Maps and images bringing to life important events and figures from America's history

Clearly and engagingly written and positioning America's narrative within the wider global context, this textbook is particularly accessible for non-US students and is the perfect introduction for those new to US history.

This textbook is also supported by a companion website offering interactive content including a timeline, multiple-choice quizzes, and links to selected web resources.

David Brown is Senior Lecturer in American Studies at the University of Manchester, UK.

Thomas Heinrich is Associate Professor in US Business History at Baruch College, City University of New York, USA.

Simon Middleton is Associate Professor in History at the College of William & Mary, USA.

Vivien Miller is Professor of American History at the University of Nottingham, UK.

"*A Concise American History* is an impressive achievement. It is wide-ranging in scope, rigorous but accessible, and attentive to complexity and nuance without sacrificing clarity or narrative drive. Each chapter covers a great deal of ground in an insightful way, but the reader benefits from helpful chapter summaries and 'concept boxes' to aid understanding. The book successfully places US economic, social, and political development from colonial times to the present in wider global context."

–Jonathan Bell, *University College London, UK*

"This book provides an excellent introduction to US history. Its authors, distinguished scholars in their fields, bring to bear a unique global perspective on the subject since they were themselves educated abroad or teach abroad. The text sweeps aside the myths often still taught in American schools, avoids hagiography of national political figures, and provides careful analysis of the major events and developments."

–Carol Berkin, *City University of New York, USA*

"This authoritative and fast-paced text, admirably attentive to global connections, introduces readers to the turbulent history of the United States from the colonial era to the present day. Highly recommended to anyone seeking a reliable and readable account of the restless American Republic and its formative role in the making of the modern world."

–Robert Cook, *University of Sussex, UK*

"*A Concise American History* offers a compelling account of the highly indeterminate, four-century-long formation of 'what we know today as the United States.' It is compelling precisely *because* it is indeterminate, steering clear of both progressivist and declensionist narratives to instead provide readers with an account woven of 'continuity and change . . . development and destruction.' It does so through a commitment to multiple historical approaches – including social, cultural, and transnational explanatory frameworks—and a carefully conceived thematic framework. With clarifying timelines, organizational roadmaps, discussion questions, and helpful lists of further reading accompanying the text and images, this accessibly written text paints for students a picture of a country predicated on ambition and conflict, on achievement and suffering, on plurality and power, in equal measure . . . a national history not, if we are honest with ourselves, easily summarized, but one that is all the more fascinating when we accept its complexity.

ACAH distinguishes itself from many other U.S. History textbooks particularly in its agile selection of interpretive emphases. At moments, we see events through prevailing notions of identity or human difference – as in passages describing the course of European colonialization of North America, Native American genocide, slavery, women's suffrage, immigrant experiences, and the long Civil Rights era. In other historical episodes, political and economic ideologies are highlighted – we follow the nineteenth-century rise of industrial capitalism and the discontent of reformers, for example, while later the authors trace conflicting conceptions of what shall constitute just labor systems and representative government, into our own neoliberal era. The roles played by racial ideologies, imperialism, and nationalism, alongside commitments to democracy and liberation, over many generations will be inescapable for readers.

Crucially, with such through-lines, the dramatic turning points of U.S. history – settlement, emancipation, wars both domestic and foreign, elections, depressions, legal landmarks, and environmental disaster – are placed firmly in context, losing none of their customary chronological centrality, but finding deeper explanatory resonance. When students can follow the emergence of value systems through time, rather than simply a sequence of significant events, specific historical incidents become far more instructive; when readers can readily associate influential individuals with their historical milieus, a world and not just its exceptional actors comes into focus. With these priorities and an abundance of well-chosen factual detail throughout, *A Concise American History* promises to provide students with a platform for exceptionally rich engagement with the nation's past, and even more welcome perhaps, with its present."

–Amy E. Slaton, *Drexel University, USA*

"This textbook accomplishes something highly distinctive in its field – it introduces students to the huge breadth of American History (from 1492 to the present) while directing them toward an appreciation of interdisciplinary and interlinking concepts of the subject. Students will find it a highly accessible text that gives them a firm basis for understanding the USA, both in domestic policy and foreign relations. Indeed, this text should also establish itself as an essential teaching tool in American survey courses."

–Lee Sartain, *University of Portsmouth, UK*

"This ambitious, highly accessible book is essential reading for anyone teaching or studying introductory-level courses on US history. Exploring chronologically the last five centuries of America, it deftly weaves in a range of themes and perspectives, positioning the US within a wider global context throughout. Avoiding overly simplistic narratives, the book includes helpful analytical boxes where complex themes and historiographies are elaborated in a clear and comprehensive fashion."

–Emily West, *University of Reading, UK*

A Concise American History

David Brown, Thomas Heinrich,
Simon Middleton, and Vivien Miller

Routledge
Taylor & Francis Group

LONDON AND NEW YORK

First published 2021
by Routledge
2 Park Square, Milton Park, Abingdon, Oxon OX14 4RN

and by Routledge
52 Vanderbilt Avenue, New York, NY 10017

Routledge is an imprint of the Taylor & Francis Group, an informa business

© 2021 David Brown, Thomas Heinrich, Simon Middleton, and Vivien Miller

British Library Cataloguing-in-Publication Data
A catalogue record for this book is available from the British Library

Library of Congress Cataloging-in-Publication Data
A catalog record for this book has been requested

ISBN: 978-0-415-67716-5 (hbk)
ISBN: 978-0-415-67717-2 (pbk)
ISBN: 978-1-003-03367-7 (ebk)

Typeset in Sabon
by Apex CoVantage, LLC

Visit the companion website: www.routledge.com/cw/brown

Contents

Figures

Acknowledgements

The authors would like to thank the Routledge production team, especially Eve Setch, Amy Welmers, and Autumn Spalding for all their help and support in bringing this book project to completion, and the anonymous reviewers for their diligent reading of each chapter, instructive commentaries, and helpful suggestions for improvement. All four contributors would very much like to thank colleagues, families, and friends for their support and encouragement throughout the project.

Introduction

A Concise American History traces the history of what we know today as the United States from fifteenth-century beginnings in the European occupation of the New World through to the present time and the 2016 election of President Donald Trump. Historians are a finicky lot: they frequently disagree about how to interpret the fragmentary and sometimes contradictory evidence of the past, or over who and what we should study, and even how we should write about our findings. It's easy to understand why Arthur Schopenhauer, a German philosopher, defined history as an argument without end. In the case of the history of the United States, his characterisation is particularly pertinent: even the briefest of summaries – for example, the opening sentence above – raises controversy. Does American history commence with European maritime endeavour and plucky colonists settling New World farms and villages? Surely we should start with ancient indigenous civilisations that were disrupted and in some cases destroyed by these European incomers and colonisers? Alternatively, one could begin in Africa and with the enslavement of hundreds of thousands, ultimately millions, of people whose forced labour built the empires and wealth which produced the modern world. Thereafter, a history of the United States could focus on the progress of liberty and opportunity or the manifest, and linked, growth of economic inequalities and racial injustice? Does one emphasise the rise of civil rights struggles, feminism, and environmentalism in the mid to late twentieth centuries, or the continued prevalence of white supremacism, attacks on women's reproductive rights, and anti-intellectualism in American life? All are part of the continuing stories of North America and United States' development and are woven into a longer and complex narrative that continues to move in unpredictable directions: who would have forecast the victory of the first African American president of the United States in 2008, still less his successor?

Any attempt to offer a synthetic and summative account will face criticism for its approach, nomenclature, inclusions, and omissions. This account, written by four Europeans who are specialists in colonial, nineteenth- and twentieth-century American history, is no different. We do not claim to cover every important topic and event, to do so would require a book at least double in size. Instead, we set out with object of introducing our students and readers to the peoples of North America and the continental United States and the more than four centuries of continuity and change, development and destruction, and regeneration that has characterised their history.

We do not prioritise a particular methodological approach, but combine elements of political, social, economic, and cultural history within the thematic concentrations and narrative arcs of each of the 17 chapters. Each chapter begins with a short introduction that signposts the key themes, a timeline of key events, and a list of the topics covered. Throughout our survey we focus on the importance of shifting modes of historical inquiry from the progressive to consensus historians and scholarship focused on the intersection of race, class, and gender to more recent scholarly concerns with language and culture as historical forces and the significance of various and continuing geographical turns. White concept boxes and grey historiography boxes in each chapter provide additional discussion points that students and teachers might consider further. A particular idea or issue or event is discussed or explained in more detail in a concept box. A key debate or disagreement among historians is identified in a historiography box. The chapters conclude with a summary of key themes and topics, questions for further discussion, and a reading list to get students started on developing their inquiries for essay, seminar, and exam assessments.

The primary aim is to present a concise and readable history suitable for undergraduate students, particularly those students from outside the United States who are not familiar with American themes and concepts. This distinctive emphasis pays careful attention to American history within wider transnational and global contexts at critical points in its development.

1 In Indian Country

Topics covered

- New World encounters
- New Spain
- The background to northern European colonisation
- English colonisation in Virginia and New England
- The American colonies at mid-century
- Form the English Republic to the Restoration
- Colonial crises and imperial authority

Introduction

This chapter begins by surveying Native American and European societies prior to the sustained contact initiated by Columbus's 1492 voyage in search of a sea passage to the Indian Ocean. Then it considers Spanish colonisation and the consequences of an Iberian empire for the emerging European state system. The chapter pays particular attention to the religious and philosophical background to colonisation: Catholic debates concerning Native American humanity and natural rights; the Reformation and crisis in Christian churches that prompted some to migrate to America and generated new arguments concerning political rights and resistance; and the influence of humanist ideals and philosophies derived from study of the ancient world. Thereafter the chapter compares French, Dutch, and English approaches to colonisation, the beginnings of plantation slavery, and the rise of distinctive colonial communities in North America and the Caribbean. It considers the deterioration of relations between the colonists and Native Americans, as the newcomers grew in numbers and confidence, and why the English emerged ahead of other European nations in the competition for the settlement of North America. In closing, the chapter covers the colonists' reaction to James II's efforts to rein in colonial autonomy culminating in resistance and rebellions following the 1688 Glorious Revolution in England.

New World encounters

The Eastern Woodland Indians occupied a vast swathe of land, roughly the area comprising the modern-day Eastern United States and Canada. Imagine walking into one of their many villages sometime in the spring of 1450. What would one see? Not the tall white teepees of countless Hollywood westerns, but small, squat huts made of saplings, woven mats, bark strips, and mud plaster. In some villages, especially those inhabited by the inland people called the Iroquois, there would be longhouses: large, single chamber constructions of 100 or more feet accommodating as many as 20 families around communal fires. Walking around the village we would note the absence of brightly coloured objects and shiny or reflective surfaces that might gleam or glint in the light. The Woodland Indian world was dominated by timber, skins, and smoky fire pits which provided for cooking, heating, repelling insects, and the hollowing out of canoes. Women and children gathered firewood most days, and when supplies were exhausted the village moved – maybe every 15 to 20 years in fortified Iroquois communities. Village sounds were limited to voices, laughter, sports and games, and the yelping of animals; dogs were the largest domesticated creatures in the Americas prior to contact. Before gun fire, the loudest sound the villagers heard was likely the rumble of thunder. There would also be the pounding of maize in a pedestal and mortar to make the flour needed for bread, the hammering of stones into arrow heads for hunting, and drumming and singing on social occasions. Skins and furs provided practical and simple clothing, but this did not mean that the Native Americans had no interest in design or style. In 1585, an English artist, John White, accompanied an early voyage to the area around Virginia and North Carolina and painted the people he met. These early glimpses of Algonquian society show enthusiasm for jewelry and tattoos, and the sinew and strength of a people who survived by hunting, fishing, and gathering.

Figure 1.1 Watercolour by John White of a Native American man, entitled "The Manner of Their Attire and Painting Themselves," from sometime between 1585 and 1593.

Source: Courtesy of Science History Images/Alamy

Estimates put the native population of the New World in 1450 at approximately 40 to 70 million, of whom somewhere between 7 to 18 million lived in the area comprising modern-day North America. This latter population were descended from the Paleo-Indians who inhabited the continental land mass for some 15,000 years. Attempts to identify discrete peoples from the thousands of different communities who spoke thousands of different languages is difficult. But historians and archaeologists have identified key cultural and linguistic civilisations on the eve of Christopher Columbus's voyage to what Europeans came to know as the New World. For example, in the far south the Incas dominated Andean civilisation centred around modern-day Peru. Further north, in the area that became known as Mesoamerica and particularly in what we know today as Mexico, the Aztecs held sway over neighbouring populations. In the territory that became the modern United States, only a handful of communities achieved the elaborate social organisation of Incas and Aztecs. In the west, Mississippian peoples lived in communities as large as 30,000 and built large and elaborate burial mounds. A century or so before Columbus's landfall, however, more mobile, semi-sedentary groups began to supplant these large communities. The village we imagined entering one spring day in 1450 was one of a hundred similar scenes in the Eastern Woodlands, in an area extending from the Atlantic Ocean to the Mississippi River, and from the Great Lakes region to the Gulf of Mexico. The Eastern Woodlanders were divided, again broadly speaking, into Algonquians, who lived between the St Lawrence River and Chesapeake Bay, and Iroquois or the Five Nations – Mohawk, Oneida, Onondaga, Cayuga, and Seneca – who dominated the region between the Hudson River and the Great Lakes. In the South West, straddling Arizona, Texas, and New Mexico, lived a people the Spanish named the Pueblo, after the villages of mud and stone houses.

Thus, in the two centuries preceding sustained European contact, indigenous peoples lived in diverse communities, ranging from sedentary populations numbering

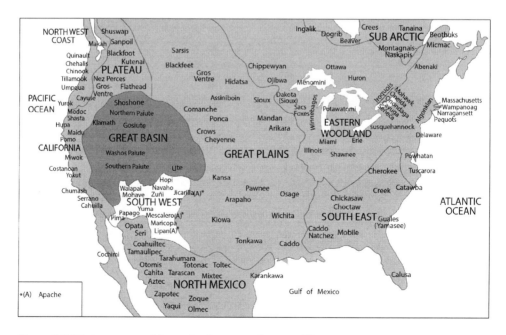

Figure 1.2 Native communities and cultures on the eve of European contact.

tens of thousands to mobile bands of as few as half a dozen family groups. Inca and Aztec civilisations flourished by subduing their neighbours and building large city states based around hierarchies of nobles, priests, warriors, peasants, and slaves. They also developed complex and productive systems of agriculture, art and letters, and architecture. At its zenith, in the fifteenth century, the Aztec city of Tenochtitlan (the site of modern day Mexico City) covered some eight square miles with 100 religious structures, around 4,000 domestic buildings, and a population of 100,000. In North America, the demise of the Mississippians produced distinctive communities divided by language and local variations of custom and mores, but united by a commitment to subsistence agriculture and hunter-gathering. Harsh conditions prompted a commitment to mutually supportive social relations and balance evident throughout native societies. Leaders, known as sachems, secured support by organising a fair distribution of food and providing for community harmony and protection, necessarily governing by consensus rather than coercion. Trade between Indians was not conducted for the sake of simple accumulation, but to secure locally unavailable items, settle disagreements, celebrate friendships, and strengthen alliances. To maintain the delicate balance between human habitation and available natural resources, some communities resorted to captive taking to sustain population numbers and comfort those in mourning. Concerns for balance and survival also governed relationships between different Native American communities. Neighbouring groups might be friends – bound by ties of language or culture, marriage and kin, or trade. Or they might be enemies – rivals for hunting or fishing grounds, blamed for illness or community disaster, provokers of family feuds or political factions. But although conflicts were often bloody and might involve toe-curling torture and even ritualistic cannibalism, they were also infrequent and limited to symbolic victories, rather than aimed at the absolute extermination of an enemy.

Eastern Woodlanders also subscribed to broadly shared beliefs concerning the interconnections between the natural and supernatural worlds. Indians inhabited both worlds equally, believing that dreams and visions – sometimes induced by fasting or eating of hallucinogenic plants – could bridge the two and provide signs and insights to be reckoned with in daily life. They also subscribed to the notion that every being and object, from people and deer to trees and mountains, had a soul, spirit, or life force. Native Americans called this spirit Manitou, and for good or for bad it figured in workings of the complex web of natural and supernatural orders that governed their lives and fates. For example, if approached properly and with respect, the deer might allow themselves to be hunted for food just as beavers would give up their fur. Some Indians, known as shamans, were gifted with special powers and insight into the spirit world. They might be consulted about illness, family troubles, or the likely fortunes of a hunt. A few daring or desperate individuals sometimes tried to fool or challenge the spirits, deploying magical powers for their own selfish purposes. But most aimed to live in harmony with the natural and supernatural worlds, respecting and fearing the power of both in equal measure.

Just as in their material and social arrangements, Indian beliefs nurtured the reciprocities necessary to live within and as a part of their surroundings, rather than separate from and in domination of them. Native Americans lacked European technologies and lived in ways that looked primitive and strange to the colonizers who came after Columbus: their settlements scarcely qualifying as towns, as the Europeans knew them, and their trade more akin to "treating" or "gifting" than self-aggrandising commerce. Indian beliefs acknowledged many deities and influences rather than one powerful God, and gender relations were also characterized by reciprocities: men hunted, fished, and engaged in warfare and external diplomacy, but women managed the land and produced the crops that sustained the community. The social and economic significance of women's roles granted them a voice in public decisions, ranging from daily household management to selection of leaders and whether or not to go to war. In some communities family identity and property descended down the female rather than male line. Indian life ways and sensibilities struck Europeans as outlandish, but in the context of their needs and the demands of the environment, they were appropriate, intelligent, and highly developed. One thing is certain: the earliest European colonists would never have survived without Native know-how and support.

In the mid fifteenth-century, European societies were also emerging from centuries of change and conflict that had generated diverse kinship-based societies. Assessed in terms of the development of agricultural, commerce, cities, arts, and religious beliefs there were as many resemblances as differences between pre-contact Native American and European communities. One major distinction, however, was the early and pan-European allegiance to the Roman Catholic Church and the consequent emergence of expansionist and militaristic royal dynasties. For centuries prior to Columbus's voyage the Church and its royal acolytes sponsored crusades aimed at securing the holy city of Jerusalem, settling hundreds of thousands of Christians in crusader states, and converting or expelling Muslims they considered infidels. These conflicts nurtured European notions of lordship, honor, and valor, inspiring many to devote their lives to religious orders dedicated to the war against Islam. This was particularly the case on the Iberian Peninsula, modern day Spain and Portugal, the southern portion of which Muslims had controlled since around 700 AD.

United as Catholics, Europeans were divided as dynasties who struggled to better their neighbours and achieve regional prominence. The turmoil of the Hundred Years' War (1337–1453), between England and France, and dynastic struggles in England and Spain produced powerful monarchs – Louis XI in France, Ferdinand and Isabella in Spain, Henry VII in England – who thereafter engaged in military and trade contests. Wartime interruptions in overland trade running from central Asia through the Italian city states to northern Europe motivated ambitious dynasties to look for an alternate, maritime route to the rich lands of Asia and China. In the service of these Catholic and dynastic aims, a fifteenth-century Portuguese prince, Henry the Navigator, developed links with the North African Arab traders to gain access to supplies of spices, salt, slaves, and most of all sugar. In the 1450s, local demand for sugar encouraged the Portuguese to establish plantations on the Canary Islands worked by slaves they brought from Africa.

Global medieval Europe

Historians have traced the roots of what we call globalisation back to the sixteenth century, but scholars are increasingly arguing that New World colonisation grew out of the earlier expansion of Latin Christianity and the activities of the nobility and merchants on European peripheries that resulted in increasing cross-cultural connections with the Near East, Africa, and Asia.

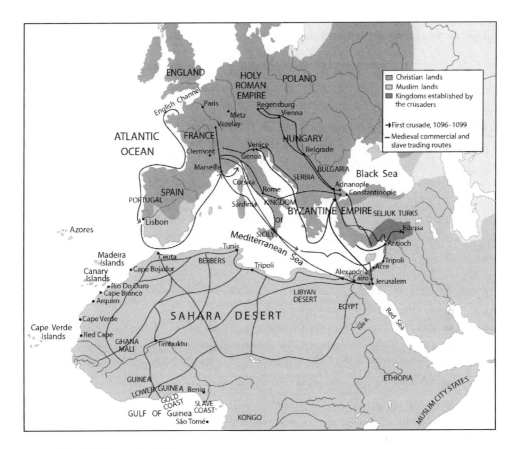

Figure 1.3 Global medieval Europe.

This was the context into which news of Christopher Columbus's reports of vast and strange new lands in the west came early in 1492, initiating a new era of European competition and expansion. Columbus learned his maritime and map making skills in the service of the Portuguese trade between the Canaries and Africa's northwestern coast. Convinced that the earth was a quarter the size of the contemporary, and correct, estimation of 12,000 miles, Columbus believed a western route to the rich East Indian and Asian trade offered investors access to riches and honor. In 1488, a Portuguese nobleman, Bartholomew Diaz, had rounded the Cape of Good Hope at the tip of Africa. Consequently, the Portuguese court could not be persuaded to back a new and risky venture. In Spain, Columbus received a more eager hearing, from Ferdinand and Isabella the monarchs in Castile, whose ambition and opportunism made up for any lack of confidence in the mariner's geographic insights.

On 3 August 1492, Columbus sailed out of the Spanish port of Palos with a flotilla of three ships, the *Nina*, the *Pinta*, and the *Santa Maria*. Thirty-three days later, on 12 October, the crew sighted the Bahamas. Convinced he had arrived in India by a western route, Columbus named the inhabitants Indians and set out to explore the other islands of these "West Indies" – modern day Cuba, Haiti, and the Dominican

Republic – which he claimed for Spain. In 1494, the Spanish, Portuguese, and Pope Alexander VI moved to secure the discoveries for the Church in Rome and signed the Treaty of Tordesillas (1494). This confirmed Portugal's dominance in Africa and Brazil in exchange for Spanish domination in the rest of the New World.

European colonisation signalled a dramatic and calamitous change of fortunes for the indigenous peoples of what now became known as New Spain and those yet to encounter the newcomers. Native Americans were no strangers to war, violence, and the blood-curdling practice of human sacrifice. However, the disruption and brutality that followed the arrival of Europeans was on a scale none had previously experienced. The spread of germs for which Native Americans had no natural immunity was the greatest single factor in undermining indigenous social organisation and civilisations. If correct, the upper figure of 70 million for the population of pre-Columbian American would mean that Native Americans comprised approximately one-seventh of the global population of roughly 500 million – 20 million more than the contemporary European population. Of this 70 million, perhaps 10 million lived in the Caribbean, 20 million in Mexico and 8 to 12 million in Peru. By the mid-sixteenth century, 60 or 70 years later, the Carib Indians had been decimated and estimates for the population of Mexico and Peru plummet to 700,000 and 600,000, respectively.

The catastrophic spread of pathogens such as small pox and measles clearly advantaged the Europeans, both sides interpreting the collapse of Native populations and their social organisations as a supernatural advantage favouring of colonisation. Commentators and scholars continue to debate the ethical implications of this incalculable human tragedy: can we "blame" Europeans and characterise their ventures as genocidal? The spread of disease was just one part of broader and largely unintentional Columbian Exchange, which brought together cultures and ecosystems that had previously existed in isolation of each other, with far-reaching consequences. New World vegetables such as squash, corn, beans, and potatoes enriched European diets, and the introduction of new agricultural methods and intensification of cultivation, not least with slave labour, increased productivity. Similarly, the introduction of European cattle, sheep, pigs, goats, and horses to the Americas seemingly limitless grazing provided the colonisers with a means of survival and further enriched the diets of both societies. Over the ensuing 300 years, the exploitation of the New World and the expansion of the global economy, especially in foodstuffs, led to a trebling of the global population, providing a healthy workforce which, in time, entered factories and constructed the modern manufacturing and industrial societies in which we live today.

New Spain

Columbus sailed to the New World three more times following his initial voyage, eventually reaching Central and South America. However, he died believing that he had reached a landmass attached to China and the west coast of the Indies rather than a new continent. His voyages fueled interest in maritime exploration in pursuit of trade and dynastic power. In 1498, Vasco de Gama consolidated Portuguese influence in the east by travelling round Africa to India and back. In 1519, Ferdinand Magellan began the voyage that resulted in the first circumnavigation of the globe. Spanish interest in the New World possessions quickly shifted from navigation to conquest and exploitation. In the same year that Columbus first sailed to America, an eight-century-long struggle between Christian and Muslim forces in southern Iberia, the

Reconquista, ended in Spanish victory. With its southern frontier secure from Muslim attack, the Spanish Crown encouraged now-underemployed noblemen, adventurers, and militant Catholics to extend Spanish power and faith in the New World. After subduing the native Arawak and Carib Indians on the islands discovered by Columbus, these Spanish conquistadores penetrated the North American continent in search of new sources of booty, often fighting amongst themselves for the richest pickings. The two most famous expeditions took place within a few years of each other: in 1519 Hernan Cortes began the incursion that ended with the subjugation of the mighty Aztecs and their city at Tenochtitlan; and in 1524 Francisco Pizarro's exploration of Peru indicated the beginning of the end for the Incas.

After the initial years of conquest and plunder, the governors in New Spain settled towns and colonies. The Spanish settlements were intended to extract mineral and other wealth, rather than establish stable Euro-American communities. The Crown maintained tight controls over hierarchical governments that allowed little autonomy to the New World jurisdictions. Most of the colonists, who were predominantly men, married Indian and later African women establishing the racially mixed population of modern day Latin America. Colonial elites governed select areas of territory granted them in return for the service to the Spanish Crown. They exacted labour and tributes from the enslaved Indians who toiled on estates or *encomienda* and who died in droves from overwork, malnutrition, and disease. Indian slavery, often carried on with indigenous participation, provided the necessary labour for colonising ventures, destabilising regions and preparing the way for the future enslavement and forced importation of African men and women to the New World.

The other major force in New Spain was the Catholic Church and missionary orders such as the Franciscans, Jesuits, and Dominicans, who came seeking to convert the Indians. The church considered the Indians ignorant of the true faith. Conversion saved Indian souls and counted as "good works" for the missionaries, thereby increasing their store of credit with the almighty and thus their chances of entry into heaven. The missionaries clashed with the landlords over their use and abuse of Indian slaves, resulting in divisive colonial power struggles. Both sides appealed to the crown for support, adding to the work of the already unwieldy colonial bureaucracy. One particularly fierce critic of the *encomienda* system and outspoken advocate for the natural rights of Indians was Bartolomé de las Casas, a Dominican friar and the first Bishop of Chiapas. His book, *A Short Account of the Destruction of the Indies* published in 1552, provided vivid descriptions and images of the atrocities committed by the conquistadors in the Americas. Claiming that Indians, like any other Christian convert, had natural rights, De Las Casas challenged the justice of Spanish plunder and warned of the potential for divine retribution against the Spanish Empire. De Las Casas and other critics won support from Philip II (1527–98), and secured some protection against the enslavement of Indians. Unfortunately, this contributed to a shift towards the use of African slaves to provide for the labour needs of New World plantations, prompting the transformation of a previously more limited African into a larger, Atlantic slave trade.

The rise of Iberian New World empires shifted the balance of power between European states and stimulated economic and political processes that dominated the early modern world. At the height of its powers in the mid-sixteenth century, the Spanish empire under Charles I – who was also heir to four other European dynasties and Holy Roman Emperor (1519–56) – comprised four million square miles ranging from

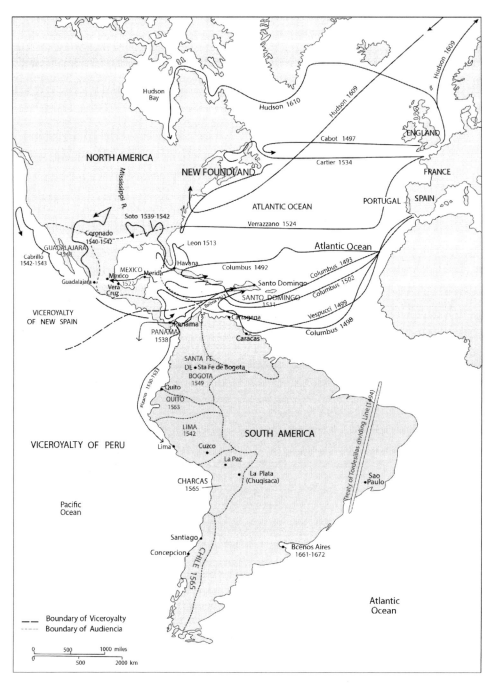

Figure 1.4 Columbus's voyages stimulated further voyages of navigation and ventures to colonise and exploit the material resources and population of what the Europeans considered an exotic New World.

Figure 1.5 Image of the burning Hatuey, a Taino chief who led a rebellion against the Spanish in 1512 and whose execution was later commemorated by Bartolomé De Las Casas, *A Short Account of the Destruction of the Indies* (1552).

Source: Courtesy of Science History Images/Alamy

Europe to the Americas, North Africa and the Philippines. Other European dynasties feared Spanish power, not least because of the writings of critics such as De Las Casas, whose book was widely read and contributed to a notorious "Black Legend" of Spanish tyranny in the Americas. The English and French both financed early voyages of exploration: in 1496 Henry VII of England backed John Cabot's voyage to America, and in 1524 the French sponsored Giovanni Verrazano's expedition down the coast from Newfoundland to modern-day North Carolina. These and other voyages sought maritime routes to the Asian trade, and the opportunity to trade furs with indigenous peoples and fish the rich stocks in colder North American latitudes. The French were early leaders in the fur trade, establishing a colony in the Gulf of the St Lawrence River in 1530s and making alliances with local Montagnais and Micmac Indians, some of whom they captured to show off back home. French merchants soon realised that the new territory offered access to valuable furs, especially beaver, which were dwindling in Europe but remained in demand for the manufacture of fashionable felt hats. Early French settlements established a pattern for the future in which European ventures depended on local Native American support for defence and the supply of furs, in return offering Indians access to European metals, cloth, alcohol, weaponry, and, when needed, military support.

The background to Northern European colonisation

A familiar combination of dynastic rivalry, geopolitical ambitions, and trading companies seeking private gain prompted Northern European colonial ventures. But Spanish power and the parlous condition of state finances and capacity stalled French and English colonisation. Northern Europeans were also pre-occupied with domestic turmoil generated by the Reformation, a widespread and far-reaching conflict within the Christian Church. For centuries, the Roman Catholic doctrine of reward for good works had promised salvation to those who adhered to the sacraments and supported the Church through their activities as well as by paying taxes and charitable giving. Thus, Catholic missionaries went to the New World to save Indian souls in order to earn themselves a place in paradise. By the late fifteenth century, the Church was a wealthy and powerful organisation, maintaining a presence throughout Europe in monastic orders and parishes and governed by popes and cardinals who lived in sumptuous palaces and cathedrals defended by powerful papal armies. There had long been those who were uncomfortable with the doctrine of works and the Church's focus on wealth and power. In 1517, a German monk, Martin Luther, visited Rome and was shocked by the corruption and depravity he witnessed. Luther became convinced that the doctrine of works had perverted the Christian message, concentrating too much on earning a place in heaven and robbing God of his majesty and omnipotence. Returning home Luther wrote a critique of the doctrine of works and Catholic government, and nailed them to the door of a local church. Declaring that the Roman Church no longer offered a path to true salvation, Luther and similarly disaffected others inspired the spread of dissent across much of Northern Europe.

These protestors, or Protestants as they became known, broke with the Roman Church arguing that its sacraments and mysteries, such as baptism with holy water and the transformation of bread and wine into the body and blood of Jesus Christ in the mass, were no more than superstitions maintained by priests and church leaders who styled themselves as God's representatives on earth. Protestants challenged the emphasis on Latin prayer, decoration of churches, and use of gold chalices that Catholics claimed edified religious worship and the worshipper thereby enhancing their connection to the almighty. For Protestants these ornamentations were, at best, misleading and at worst diverted believers from the authentic core of Christian piety: individual contemplation of one's sinfulness and relationship to God through study of the Bible; the revealed word of the Lord and the only authority that counted. In the 1540s, a French protestant living in Geneva, Jean Calvin, argued that salvation was in fact predestined by God's will and that no earthly activity could affect an individual's fate for better or worse in the hereafter. A church did not need grand buildings and princely popes. Faith alone provided a basis for salvation. True churches were congregations of believers who dedicated themselves to introspection and godly lives in the hope that they might receive assurance that they were one of the very few whom God considered the elect and had chosen to save. As protestant sects spread across Europe they often disagreed concerning the finer points of Calvinism: had Jesus died on the cross for all sinners, or only those God had chosen to be saved? Once chosen to be saved by God, was it possible for an individual to fall from grace because of their actions and thereby pervert divine ordination?

However, much they disagreed the Protestants shared a fundamental commitment to reformed principles and cohered as a pan-European movement in opposition to the Roman Church. During the remainder of the sixteenth century protestant divines drew up and debated an alternative, reformed theology, shattering the catholic consensus and prompting violent conflicts between supporters and critics of the Roman Church. In several Northern European states, the protestant challenge found support amongst monarchs and princes, some motivated by reformed religious doctrines others by the opportunity to challenge the power of Rome. With this support came new, national denominations – the French Reformed, Dutch Reformed, and Anglican Church. Wherever it took hold the Reformation fostered new thinking about crucial philosophical questions. For example, what were the limits of political authority in matters of individual religious conscience and when could resistance to sovereign authority be justified? In France, protestant and catholic conflicts were bound up with aristocratic rivalries worked out in 30 years of bloody religious wars beginning in the 1560s. In the infant Dutch Republic, formed out of a 1579 revolt by the seven provinces in the Hapsburg Netherlands governed by Charles I, Protestantism became identified with the resistance and the struggle for Dutch liberty from tyrannical and Catholic Spain.

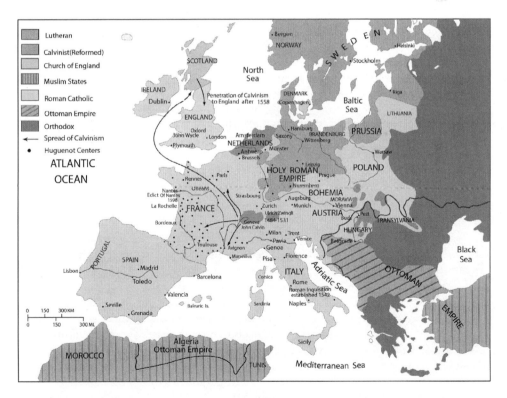

Figure 1.6 The Reformation sponsored the spread of Protestant challenges to Catholic orthodoxy which many had come to believe was a corrupt and, at best, misleading threat to the ideal of a pure and Christian church on earth.

In England, Henry VIII – a lifelong catholic whose marriage to Catherine of Aragon was intended to connect the emerging Tudor dynasty to Spanish power – used the popular force of Protestantism to secure a divorce and remarry, on five occasions. He also seized monastic lands and established the Church of England with himself and his appointees at its head.

Unfortunately for Henry and later Tudor and as in early Stuart monarchs, the English Protestants who challenged the Catholic Church hierarchy were no more ready to accept similar structures in new, national churches. In their view, true churches were first and foremost gatherings of true believers, and these congregants were also best placed to decide who should minister to their spiritual needs. When Henry died, England was plunged into a succession crisis, beginning with the short-lived reign of his 15-year-old son, Edward VI, followed by Mary I – the Catholic daughter of Catherine of Aragon – who persecuted Protestants as heretics. Following the accession of Elizabeth I – daughter of Henry's second wife, Anne Boleyn – in 1558, secular and religious authorities compromised: the monarchy would support a Protestant settlement while retaining the right to restrain more radical elements and rejecting the calls to take the fight to Rome, for example by openly supporting the Dutch rebellion against Spain.

Humanism

Humanism is often identified with the drift away from medieval supernaturalism and towards interest in secular, human affairs in the work of key European thinkers such as Francesco Petrarch (1304–74), Niccolo Machiavelli (1469–1527), and Desiderius Erasmus (1466–1536). The humanist interest in pagan classics and worldly possibilities and pleasures generated a diffuse and increasingly predominant influence in political, economic, and literary contexts that informed the development of later Enlightenment and modern political and aesthetic philosophies.

Catholic debates concerning the natural rights of New World Indians and Protestant political theorists provided two major intellectual influences on early American settlements. A third and equally significant strain of thought, which drew particular interest from Northern European Protestants, was the civic humanist tradition with roots in Renaissance urban culture of Italian city states such as Venice and Florence. Fascinated by the learning and achievements of the ancient and classical worlds, humanists argued that Greece and Rome provided a repository of examples against which contemporary practices and feats should be measured. Spreading north from Italy in the late fifteenth century via the new medium of print, this humanism informed northern European educational and cultural practice. Thus sixteenth-century English women and men cultivated skills in conversation and political persuasion. They also ruminated on the tension between self-interest and communal duty, and stressed the importance of honesty and civility in social life. These themes came to dominate contemporary arts and letters, for example in the plays of William Shakespeare which frequently addressed humanist themes of rhetoric and courtliness, often in Italian settings.

Europeans studied ancient empires and began to imagine similar possibilities for themselves, increasingly thinking of the New World and its peoples as theirs to seize, control, and improve. For humanists, the Americas took on the appearance of a virgin land: a vast and to European sensibilities mostly uninhabited territory that offered the potential for new estates, evoking the glories of Europe's feudal past. The Indians were primitive and uncivilised, much as the warlike Picts had been when first they encountered the Roman legions. Just as the Romans had subdued and civilised the ancient Britons, sixteenth-century Englishmen imagined themselves helping and uplifting the Indians. Instead of terrorising the Native Americans, like the Spanish, the English and Dutch expected, initially at least, to win Indian friendship and grateful service. With its emphasis on introspection, self-control and government, and idealistic reform there were clear connections between humanism and Protestantism. In the early seventeenth century, an English compound of Christian and humanist principles, given the derogatory title of puritanism by its critics, inspired thousands of Protestants to abandon England for America hoping to build there the godly and harmonious communities that eluded them at home.

These were the ideas and influences that percolated through Northern Europe as the power of Spain grew on the back of its New World wealth and possessions through the sixteenth century. In 1564, an early French venture to establish a settlement to in Florida as a haven for French Protestants, known as Huguenots, was sacked by nearby Spanish forces. French and English colonial ventures were pushed northwards, to the areas beyond Spanish concern. By the 1580s, French traders in the Saint Lawrence Valley and modern-day Canada were securing a steady stream of furs from Huron and Montagnais Indian suppliers. Early English colonisation plans were limited to state-sponsored monopolies granted to seafaring adventurers or privateers, such as Walter Raleigh, Francis Drake, and Humphrey Gilbert. These men, mostly from the West Country, were zealous Protestants and veterans of England's subjugation of Ireland. They used New World settlements as bases from which to plunder Spanish treasure ships bound for home from the Caribbean. These English conquistadores lacked the organisation, capital, and arguably imagination to establish and provision a colony. Their only attempt to do so, at Roanoke Island in 1585, ended in disaster when the desperate colonists clashed with local Indians and then disappeared never to be seen again.

In 1588, the defeat of the Spanish Armada (a failed attempt to invade England) convinced the English and others that Spain was no longer invincible and prepared the way for more ambitious colonial ventures. French endeavours succeeded thanks to leadership of Samuel de Champlain, who solidified earlier alliances with the Huron and Montagnais by assisting them in their war against the Iroquois to the south. Dutch colonisation remained intimately connected to their ongoing struggle against Spanish rule. In 1602, the States General, the governing body of the infant republic, established an East India Company with a monopoly of the Dutch trade in the East. The Company was a private military force, backed by the emerging Dutch state and charged with taking the fight to the Spanish even as it earned profits for the shareholders. Twenty years later, and following the navigation of the waters around modern-day New York, the States General established a West India Company to compete for trade and combat the Spanish in the Atlantic. The West India Company's monopoly, which it endeavoured to defend against all comers, included all the trade from Brazil through the Caribbean to a small and insignificant fur colony at New Netherland on North America's eastern seaboard.

English colonisation in Virginia and New England

It soon became clear that the northern latitudes held no store of riches to match the Inca and Aztec empires. The climate was too cold for sugar production and the semi-sedentary Indians were too mobile, locally advantaged, and fierce to easily subjugate. The northern American shores did offer plentiful supplies of fish and furs, and the potential for timber, salt, iron ore, and other desirable commodities. Gradually English colonial promoters conceived a different and ultimately far more successful approach centred on settlement and trade. In his *Principal Navigations, Voyages, Traffiques and Discoveries of the English Nation* (1589), Richard Hakluyt Jr. argued that colonies could end England's dependence on foreign commodity producers while simultaneously developing maritime power and providing a market for domestic manufactures. When these commercial plans were combined with humanist ambitions for colonial projects as new and virtuous commonwealths, the prospect of honor and glory idealised self-interested motives and ensured additional investment even in the face of early failures.

To encourage the enterprises the English Crown granted its royal authority to private companies to establish and govern colonies and benefit from trade monopolies. One of the earliest of these joint-stock ventures, the Virginia Company established in 1606, dispatched a group of 105 men and boys to establish a settlement called Jamestown; the first English women arrived a couple of years later as part of a "second supply" of colonists. The settlers forged friendly relations with Wahunsonacock a local Indian sachem whom the English called Powhatan, mistaking the individual for the name of Indian peoples he headed. Wahunsonacock befriended the newcomers thinking he could use them to consolidate his own regional authority. Unfortunately, it was not long before things took a turn for the worse. Settlers sickened and died from malaria and typhoid or starved for want of food, stealing from the Indians and turning allies into enemies. The cultivation of tobacco after 1610 saved the colony by providing a cash crop and return on shareholders' investments. In 1618, the Company introduced a "headright" system, allocating land to those who brought others with them in an effort to increase population. They offered free passage and the promise of land and tools for any who agreed to work as servants for seven years. The granting of private land and establishment of local representation, with the establishment of the Virginia House of Burgesses in 1619, diminished the Company's monopoly rights and author-ity, but attracted sufficient male and female settlers to ensure the colony's survival. As more women arrived, the colonists endeavored to recreate the patriarchal families and households familiar from their Old World origins. However, conditions in the colonial Chesapeake undermined idealized gender roles and disrupted patriarchal authority: labor shortages required women as well as men to work in the fields, and the uneven sex ratio and high mortality rate made multiple remarriage common amongst women, many of whom outlived their husbands. This latter trend increased the numbers of widows and children who grew up without their biological fathers, introducing uncer-tainties surrounding the traditional transfer of inherited property down the male line.

While the Virginia Company struggled on at the mouth of the James River, a very different colonial enterprise connected to the fallout from the Reformation was taking shape to the north. In 1620, a small group of English Protestants, the Pilgrims, sailed to Massachusetts Bay aboard the *Mayflower*. They were drawn from respectable, middling families who had fled England in 1610 and settled in Leiden, in the Dutch Republic, before deciding to build a new life in America. Prior to disembarking the Pilgrims drew up an agreement in which the passengers, which included unruly mariners and adventurers, agreed to be subject to the collective will. This Mayflower Compact is often considered a foundational document in the establishment of democratic government in America. Although for the Pilgrims it was more likely drawn up as an insurance policy against anti-social behavior by those on board the *Mayflower* who were not committed Protestants. Upon landing, the Pilgrims befriended a local Wampanoag sachem, Massasoit, who saw the same potential in the newcomers as had Wahunsonacock in the Virginia Company settlers. What brought this hardy band of English men and women and their families to America was the fate of the English Reformation since the death of Elizabeth I in 1602.

When Elizabeth, the "virgin queen," died without a successor the throne passed from Tudors to the Stuarts, specifically James VI of Scotland who now became also James I of England. The reformed Protestant doctrine and Calvinism had made good progress in late sixteenth-century Scotland and English puritans looked to the new monarch to purge lingering Romanish tendencies from the Anglican Church. These included practices such as making the sign of the cross at prayer and the central administration of what should have been congregational affairs – especially in the appointment of ministers. However, James disappointed his new English subjects. He placated the puritans with a new, King James, Bible translation, but instead of pushing on with more thorough reform he tolerated crypto-Catholics in senior church posts and maintained Anglican practices. The attempt at compromise satisfied neither side and religious contention continued. The zealous puritans who had been disappointed by James I were positively enraged by his son, Charles I, who came to the throne in 1626. Charles had married a French Catholic Princess, Henrietta Marie, and offered secret aid to Catholic forces fighting Protestants in Europe. Moreover, in the interminable debates between reformed theologians, Charles favoured the more liberal views of the Dutch divine, Jacob Arminius, who challenged key Calvinist principles by arguing that Christ had died on the cross for all sinners, rather than just for those predestined to become the elect. He also maintained that all true believers received God's saving grace and thereafter it was up to them to retain or lose this grace by choosing to live by God's laws. This struck many Protestants as dangerously close to the connections drawn by Catholicism between the completion of sacraments and worldly practices and guarantees of an eternal afterlife in paradise. Some, such as the Pilgrims, became convinced that the English Church was a lost cause and left for the Dutch Republic and then America in the hope of establishing their own, separate and pure churches.

Beginning in 1629 a second group of puritans led by a Suffolk squire and lawyer, John Winthrop, established a colony near to the Pilgrims at nearby Massachusetts Bay. Winthrop was a moderately wealthy and prominent member of the East Anglian gentry who decided to leave England only after much painful soul searching. He and his fellow colonists also feared that reform had stalled under Charles I, but they hoped to rescue the English church from its errors. Thus they came to America to build an exemplary community, what Winthrop memorably described as a "Citie upon a Hill," which might serve as a beacon for the wayward Anglican and other European churches. As one minister had it, they had come on an "errand into the wilderness."

Figure 1.7 Jacob Arminius, a Dutch theologian whose rejection of Calvin's notion of predestination and support for clerical authority repelled English puritans but informed the moderate Protestantism favoured by James I and Charles I and their Anglican bishops.

Source: Courtesy of Chronicle/Alamy

The Pilgrims were religious refugees, but the second and much larger group of Protestants came with a royal charter granted to the Massachusetts Bay Company. Just as with the Virginia Company, the charter granted authority to the Massachusetts Bay freemen and shareholders, expecting that they would direct operations from England. However, puritan merchants secured control of the Company and arranged for the relocation to Massachusetts, in effect giving a handful of Company freeman and the governor, John Winthrop, a chartered authority over the colony and its settlers. Shortly after arriving, however, and in part in response to local protests, the colony's leaders opened up the government, somewhat, by granting an annual vote for local representatives to the colony's General Court to all property-owning, male church members.

The New Englanders enjoyed a number of advantages over the Virginians. The Pilgrims helped clear the way for settlement by infecting, albeit unintentionally, a native population already weakened by an epidemic in 1616–19. The climate was healthier, and puritans migrated in congregations, companies, and families – quickly establishing sustainable communities. Their common purpose was evident in the distribution of land and settling of farming communities: a year after arriving New England had nine towns inhabited by over a thousand people; by 1636 the puritans had established Harvard College to train religious ministers. There were also divisions, especially concerning qualification for church membership. Just as in England, everyone in Massachusetts was required to attend church and pay taxes to support the minister. However, full membership and a right to vote in church matters was restricted to those who had testified to their experience of assurance of divine grace, or sanctification, before ministers and leading lay members. Once approved these members of the congregation were acknowledged as members of the elect or "visible saints." Winthrop and his supporters believed that by supervising the distribution of land and admission of church members they were providing for future stability. However, others resented the presumptive authority of the General Court and its tests for faith or sanctification, likening them to priestly interventions and the Catholic doctrine of achieving grace through worldly recognition and good works. Roger Williams, a brilliant scholar and friend of Winthrop's, also questioned the legality of puritan occupation of Indian lands. New Englanders migrated in family groups, sometimes whole congregations, and established patriarchal households: women did not participate in town meetings and, unless widowed, they could not own property or sign contracts. They had to dress modestly and watch what they said and did in public; breaches of stern moral codes could quickly lead to community censure and even a whipping. Puritans believed Eve's part in the tempting of Adam was indicative of women's sinful nature; women could become full church members, but had no say in running of church affairs. In the mid-1630s, with hundreds of newcomers arriving every couple of months, a protest led by a woman, Anne Hutchinson, pushed back against the colony's religious and gendered conventions by claiming independent assurance of sanctification, or "free grace" through a direct revelation from God. Others broke away from the community gathered around the mouth of the Charles River to seek land and greater autonomy in new towns and settlements which developed into the colonies of Rhode Island, New Hampshire, and Connecticut.

The colonies at mid-century

Like the French in the sixteenth and early seventeenth centuries, the first English and Dutch colonies relied on Indian alliances and support. But in each case, after an initial period of collaboration, relations soured. Europeans wanted land, trade, and defensive alliances. The Indians coveted highly prized and spiritually powerful trade goods, including cloth, cooking pots, alcohol, axes, and guns; they also saw an opportunity to bind the new and potent European allies into existing native diplomacy. These interests ensured the development of webs of European-Indian relations: the Virginians and the Powhatan Confederacy, the Pilgrims and the Wampanoags, the Rhode Islanders and Narragansetts, the New Netherlanders and the Munsee and Mohawks.

However, these mutual interests and relationships proved unsustainable over the longer term. In Virginia, the spread of tobacco plantations and intermittent conflict between the English and Indians developed into full scale war following the death of Wahunsonacock and the accession of his brother, Opechancanough, whose attacks wiped out more than a third of the settlements. In New Netherland, the Dutch came to trade for furs, never intending to settle a colony. To guarantee the supply of pelts, the newcomers were drawn into Indian rivalries, first between the Mohegans and the Mohawks and later between the Narragansetts and the Pequots – the most powerful Indian community in southern New England. Pequot regional predominance placed them directly in the path of puritan expansion into the Connecticut River Valley. In 1636–37 the colonists went to war against the Pequots. The English victory and the spread of puritan settlement to Long Island convinced the Dutch West India Company to give up its commercial monopoly in New Netherland. Opening up the fur trade to private enterprise encouraged immigration from the Dutch Republic leading to increased tensions and a further disastrous round of Indians conflicts in 1639–45. By mid-century, many Europeans viewed the Indians more as enemies than friends and, at best, as inferior and dependent subjects required to do the colonists' bidding or face the consequences.

While small settlements struggled to get established in the north, the Caribbean colonies boomed. The richest New World returns, other than the gold and silver of Mesoamerica, came not from furs and tobacco but sugar grown on plantations worked by enslaved people. Beginning in the 1620s and 1630s English and French planters nibbled around the edges of the Spanish empire, establishing plantations in the Bahamas in 1624–25 and the islands of the Lessor Antilles, the English at Nevis, Antigua, and Montserrat and the French at Guadeloupe and Martinique. The Caribbean offered quick riches, and many more investors flocked to the sugar islands than went to the North American colonies. Producing sugar required a combination of expert knowledge of extraction processes and back-breaking toil in the fields and refineries. Initial labour needs were met by indentured servants and political prisoners taken in England's civil wars. But as sugar production and competition for land increased, diminishing numbers of white servants and the availability of Africans fostered a shift to enslaved labour. Since the mid-fifteenth century the Portuguese and Spanish, and latterly the Dutch, predominated in a trade that enslaved approximately four million people in Africa and the New World. In the next century and a half, European traders, predominantly English, participated in the enslavement of approximately eight million more. Seventy per cent of the enslaved and transported were used to cultivate sugar for which the return was four times the value of Chesapeake tobacco imported to London. This at a time when the tobacco trade on its own was worth more than the rest of the combined mainland American trade. By 1660, Caribbean planters could buy servants who worked for four years for £12, and the enslaved who worked for life for £20. In Barbados the governor noted that "since people have found out the convenience and cheapness of slave labour they no longer keep the white men who used to do all the work on the plantations."

Once through the early, difficult decades, the English colonies in North America and the Caribbean thrived in comparison to New France and New Spain. Early on the piecemeal settlement of early English ventures – which depended on private companies, voluntary migration, and small-scale distribution of land – looked precarious, not least because of Indian power. Over time, however, this approach demonstrated several key advantages. Firstly, it was cheap and easy for the emerging and still limited English state. The incremental settlement of colonial land also produced sustainable communities which secured England's title and sovereignty in the face of indigenous and competing European claims. The downside, as far as central authorities and imperial planners were concerned, was that colonial communities reflected the diverse backgrounds and ambitions of those who settled. In Virginia and Maryland (established in 1634), the planters demand for land and labour encouraged a shift towards a enslavement and a plantation economy governed by a hierarchical, provincial authority modelled on an English county. The unsettled nature of family life continued to threaten male authority, which depended on reputations that were susceptible to challenge by female gossip. The courts tried to curb unruly female speech, providing for the ducking, or plunging into water, of "brabling" women. Legislators also used gender conventions to establish racial distinctions and then affirm enslavement as an inherited condition. The provincial authorities first made a distinction between African and European women, treating former as field hands and a taxable asset and the latter as non-taxed domestic workers. Then, in 1662, the Virginia authorities stipulated that "all children borne in this country shall be held bond or free only according to the condition of the mother." Children born to enslaved women would remain enslaved in perpetuity.

In New England, the idealism of a godly commonwealth was tempered by land speculation and merchant participation in the Atlantic and West Indies trade, without the profits from which the colony might have failed. Families and servants provided most of the labour for family farms and fisheries, producing supplies to be shipped to the plantation colonies. Sons worked long and hard in the hope of inheriting land and coveted status as a head of household from aging fathers. Daughters worked with their mothers in household economies that, in addition to the cooking, cleaning, nurturing, gardening, animal husbandry and whatever else was necessary to sustain the family, also soap, textiles, and food products for sale. In the West Indies a small, rich, and powerful planter elite and a marginal population of poor whites created a creole society based on the sugar wealth produced by the enslaved. Political institutions and procedures differed marginally from place to place, for example depending on their original status as a chartered or royal colony, such as Massachusetts and New York, or a proprietary concern, such as Pennsylvania. However, in each case ordinary colonists supported provincial administrations which they felt regulated public and commercial life and protected fundamental rights to property and, in general, concerned themselves with the common good.

Far away from England's shores the settlers were creating colonial communities which, if they were not yet sufficiently distinctive to be described as American, were increasingly unrecognisable as straightforwardly English. Moreover, during the century's middle decades the colonists were largely left to themselves while a continuing crisis in European monarchical authority generated unprecedented political turmoil. The seventeenth century was much troubled by disputes concerning the rights and obligations of monarchs and their subjects. Many of the disputes developed out of Reformation arguments concerning the freedom and sanctity of individual religious conscience. In essence, dissenters argued that divine authority and allegiance trumped monarchs' worldly power. In 1642, the four-year-old, Catholic Louis XIV acceded to the throne he occupied as absolute monarch for the next 72 years, making France a beacon for European sovereigns with similar ambitions. In 1648, after a struggle lasting 80 years, Catholic Spain finally acknowledged the Protestant Dutch Republic, a state whose very existence challenged the idea of monarchy's divine right to govern. In England, Scotland, and Ireland, civil wars provoked by disputes concerning religious freedom and the security of the Protestant church, as well as the personality and absolutist ambitions of Charles I, culminated with the execution (regicide) of the king in 1649. Thereafter a republican government – headed, early on, by a minority administration in parliament and, after 1654, by Oliver Cromwell – ruled England.

Across Europe these conflicts generated novel and far-reaching debates concerning radical principles, increasingly circulated in printed pamphlets and tracts: was resistance to the king justified in the name of religious conscience and, if so, what was the basis for government without a monarch? If political rights rested on humanity and were equal, then what of the relationship between poor and rich men, masters and servants, or even women and men? How could government without constitutional certainty guarantee the fundamental rights to life, liberty, and property that differentiated freemen from slaves? For many, these were more than mere abstract debates: between 1645–55 England shipped 12,000 political captives to work the plantations in Barbados, where the increasing use of enslaved people committed the emerging English empire to a form of bound labour not seen in England since the fourteenth century. In 1641, Massachusetts introduced the first colonial law defining slavery, addressing the status not of Africans, but Indian captives taken in the Pequot War. By denying some the right of property in their own labour, New World slavery intensified metropolitan and colonial debates concerning the rights and liberty of free subjects and called forth clearer definitions of the racial characteristics that some argued suited Africans to bondage.

The Restoration and proprietary colonies

At the height of his power Cromwell aimed to secure the English Revolution by offering to unite with the Dutch Republic in the face of opposition from European monarchical states. When the Dutch refused his overtures, Cromwell went on the offensive: he introduced new Navigation Acts which aimed to shut Dutch shippers out of the English colonial trade prompting the First Anglo-Dutch War (1652–54). Cromwell also launched a "western design" or expedition against the Spanish in the Caribbean, culminating in the 1655 capture of Jamaica. A new class of English merchants, envious of the Dutch and interested in the colonial trade, supported Cromwell's imperial ambitions. Unlike earlier investors in trading companies who benefited from royal charters and privileges, these merchants pursued independent opportunities in the colonial and slave trade. They opposed Spanish maritime dominance in the New World, resented Charles's pro-Catholic foreign policy, and supported the puritan and parliamentary opposition in the civil wars. Displacing the earlier monopolists, such as the shareholders in the Levant and Virginia companies, the new merchants increasingly predominated in the City of London and England's overseas trade. Hoping to emulate Dutch success the new merchants also called for the protection and encouragement of English free trade and interests. While the English were distracted by civil war, the Dutch gained an upper hand in the slave and tobacco trade to and from England's Chesapeake colonies. In 1658, Cromwell died and the tide turned against the English republic. Fearing a return to disorder and bloodletting of the civil wars, Parliament invited Charles II to return from exile in France and restored the Stuarts to the throne.

Charles promised to govern with the approval of Parliament and to tolerate independent religious views. In London and elsewhere, English colonial merchants now looked to the king to secure their overseas interests.

Mercantilism

Historians continue to debate whether mercantilism described a settled, early modern economic orthodoxy or changing and contested view of the relationship between trade, empire, and the state. In general terms, mercantilism promoted government regulation of domestic and international trade to maximise the accumulation of wealth thereby strengthening the state. Early on in the seventeenth century the focus was primarily on accumulating finite supplies of gold and silver, such that one state could only increase wealth if another state's store of bullion diminished. By the turn of the eighteenth century, however, merchants and states realised that investment and market activity promoted the expansion and trade and consumption, thereby increasing tax revenues and wealth. Thereafter different strategies and divisions appeared. Mercantilists continued to favour regulations that drew wealth and power to the domestic state. However, some favoured investing in land and control of overseas territory and slave plantations, while others advocated investment in manufacturing and trade and increasing consumption amongst the labouring population.

From early on in his reign Charles demonstrated his determination to build on existing imperial initiatives, take firmer control of England's overseas colonies and trade, and assert monarchical authority. Civil War reforms to local government and tax collection, introduced to take on the Stuarts, now enriched and strengthened the restored monarchical state. With increased revenues Charles and his advisors built up English naval power, introduced a new round of Navigation Acts, and fought a second, and largely unsuccessful, war with the Dutch Republic (1665–67). The restored monarchy also established new colonies in America, granting lands to single beneficiaries or groups of men who had supported the Stuarts during the interregnum. These colonial proprietors held title to the land and controlled the government, styling themselves as lords and evoking England's feudal past.

In the spring of 1664, Charles granted the vast territory between New England and the Chesapeake, containing the Dutch colony of New Netherland, to his younger brother, James Duke of York. The Duke promptly regranted the land between the Hudson and Delaware River to two loyal friends, Sir George Carteret and Lord Berkeley. That summer royal forces led by Colonel Richard Nicolls seized New Netherland, ending Dutch rule in the region and establishing the colonies of New York and New Jersey. Charles and his circle directed these colonies towards monarchical, aristocratic, and if necessary militaristic forms of government. This was a conscious move away from semi-independent administrations such as in New England, which imperial officials associated with the radical anti-monarchism of the English republic. Writing to his patron from New York, after reorganising the colony's administration Colonel

Richard Nicolls reported his intention to establish "the foundations of Kingly Government" in the colony where "Democracy hath taken so deepe a Roote" and noting that his reforms were "truly [is] grievous to some Republicans."

These proprietary "middle colonies" attracted diverse migrants from within and beyond America's shores. In New York City, the population remained predominantly Dutch or Dutch-identified for a generation. English military governors worked with existing Dutch civic leaders and merchants in an effort to maintain city trade and earn the Duke a revenue. After 1674, and a Third Anglo-Dutch War (1672–74) disputing control of the Atlantic trade, English merchants took a greater interest in the colony. Over time, and through commercial partnerships and intermarriage, a polyglot Anglo-Dutch, French, and Scottish merchant and landed elite came to dominate New York's trade and politics.

Early New Jersey was populated by puritan migrants from New England and English Quakers, to whom Berkeley sold his share of the province in 1673. The Quakers were one of the most radical Protestant sects in seventeenth-century England. They maintained that everyone had an "inner light" and the potential for direct and life-changing divine revelation. The manifestation of this "inner light" was often accompanied by trembling and quaking, hence the name; the sect acknowledged no church authorities or hierarchies – affording equal status even to women. Quakers were persecuted for their views, leading a wealthy and well-connected convert, William Penn,

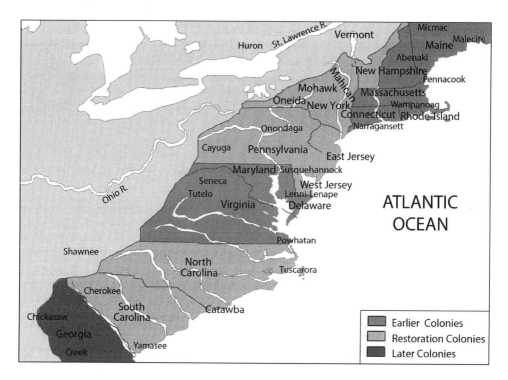

Figure 1.8 Following the 1660 Restoration of the English monarchy, Charles II favoured past and current supporters with large land grants – in particular Pennsylvania and Carolina – launching a new era of English interest in what the crown considered their colonial possessions.

to establish a colonial refuge. Penn's father had assisted Charles II while he was in exile. In 1681, the king repaid this loyalty, and a money debt borrowed from the Penns, with a tract of land that became Pennsylvania. Learning from the mistakes of others, William Penn attracted colonists by providing for religious toleration and political representation. He also tried to deal fairly with the local Delaware Indians, negotiating the purchase of land rather than seizing territory in expensive and destructive conflicts. From early on, however, the settlers challenged the authority of the Quaker proprietors and demanded enhanced local rights, leading Penn to plead, "For the love of God, me, and the poor country, be not so governmentish; so noisy and open in your disaffection." In the years to come, the settlers would also betray Penn's vision of harmonious settler-Indian relations.

In the south, the Carolinas offered perhaps the clearest example of efforts to create a colony according to monarchical and aristocratic ideals. In 1663, Charles granted the land to eight English aristocrats and supporters led by Anthony Ashley-Cooper, a prominent politician and later the Earl of Shaftesbury. As Lords Proprietors these eight men claimed an absolute right to rule over the colony that none of them ever visited, subject only to the king's command. Eager to secure and develop a territory the Lords relied on agents from Barbados who offered migrants inducements such as religious toleration, tax exemptions, and large grants of land; a generous headright provision granting 150 acres of land to each member of a settler's family. The incentives drew white farmers and artisans from Chesapeake and West Indies. There was particular interest from Barbadian sugar planters whose Caribbean lands were either exhausted or already claimed. These planters saw the new colony as a likely prospect for the cultivation of slave products. The Lords set out their plans for government in the Fundamental Constitutions of Carolina, which divided the colony into two provinces, Clarendon and Albemarle, and then county subdivisions in each of which the proprietors held large estates. The plan deliberately aimed to "avoid erecting a numerous democracy," and a provincial parliament dominated by the Lords, their representatives, and other large landowners was to govern the colony. However, like other absentee proprietors the Lords soon faced challenges form the settlers who looked to fur trading rather than farming and, in the north, built ties with Virginia and Maryland tobacco economies. In the south, around the port settlement at Charleston, relocated Barbadian planters envied the proprietors' landholdings and authority over the colony and its trade. The result was political factionalism, instability, and the growth of provincial divisions which led to the separation of the two colonies of North and South Carolina in the early eighteenth century.

Colonial crises and imperial authority

In the final quarter of the seventeenth century, England's North American colonies were divided by conflicts and endangered by brief but bloody Indian wars that threatened the future of key settlements. In Virginia frontier colonists, including many landless one-time indentured servants, protested (and provoked) attacks by Doeg and Susquehannock Indians, and called on the eastern authorities to support a war and secure new land for tobacco cultivation. The eastern planter elite, led by the governor William Berkeley, was not keen to escalate expensive conflicts that might lead to an increase in tobacco production and a further lowering of already falling in prices. When Berkeley vacillated, the frontier farmers followed a disaffected member of the gentry, Nathanial Bacon, into rebellion. Seizing the seat of provincial government at Jamestown, the rebels denounced the governor for corruption and his failure to defend the frontier. Then they torched the capital and went to war against the Susquehannocks. When Bacon fell ill and died, the rebellion fizzled out. Berkeley regained control, with the help of an English naval force, and executed the rebel leaders.

In New England, a loose coalition of Native Americans led by Metacom, a Wampanoag sachem the English called King Philip, rose up in 1675–78 after years of resentment at puritan dominance. In the decades since the Pequot War natives and colonists had lived side-by-side, sharing economic, legal, and diplomatic exchanges governed, in theory, by reciprocal duties of subjects and rulers: if Indians accepted English law and treaty obligations, the colonists promised them fair and equitable treatment. In reality, the Indians faced a far more difficult choice: remain independent and be cut off from the benefits of English protection and trade goods; or become puritan dependents and accept subordination and, in some cases, relocation to "praying towns" and the adoption of English styles of living and beliefs. All of this created resentment, especially amongst younger warriors eager to prove themselves in battle. When a court at Plymouth tried and executed three Wampanoag Indians for the murder of a praying town Indian, their infuriated supporters struck at isolated settlements. Puritan counterattacks, often on previously neutral groups, provoked further hostilities. Before the Indians ran out of ammunition and supplies, and the conflict quieted, more than half of New England's 90 towns were attacked. Terrified settlers fled their farms and puritan ministers pondered the source and depths of the divine fury that had permitted such a catastrophic conflict.

In each of these crises arguments over provincial authority, political rights, and a recasting of colonial social divisions emerge as common and intersecting themes. In Virginia the frontiersmen invoked their rights to land and protection and objected to the self-regarding administration of Berkeley and his cronies. In the generation after Bacon's Rebellion the frontier settlers won concessions, but it was African slaves and Indians who bore the cost. As late as 1675 the plantation colonies in North America had fewer than 5,000 slaves, compared to 100,000 in the English West Indies. Following the rebellion, slave numbers in the Chesapeake began to climb, partly in response to market conditions, but also as a substitute for troublesome indentured servants who might one day claim the status and rights of free men. Thus the codification of slavery and its identification with African workers created a racial and economic bond between wealthy and poor whites who encroached ever further onto Indian land.

In New England, conflict was provoked by Indian struggles on behalf of their rights, but the consequence was a more unified puritan identity and increasingly virulent anti-Indian sentiment. The seventeenth-century puritan colonies had been far from united: orthodox Massachusetts congregationalists, separatists at Plymouth and Rhode Island, and land-hungry Connecticut farmers had long competed with one another for territory, Indian alliances, and parliamentary favour. Metacom's War united these erstwhile divided puritans against a common enemy whose strength many interpreted as divine judgement of earlier colonial ambitions and divisions and a turning from godly ways. This conviction inspired an outpouring of printed rumination on the puritans and the fate of their "errand into the wilderness," even giving birth to a new literary genre – the captivity narrative. In the most famous example, Mary Rowlandson was seized on the morning of 10 February 1675 by war party of Narragansett, Wampanoag, and Nipmuc Indians and held for 11 weeks before being ransomed and returned. Rowlandson wrote a narrative describing her ordeal which she interpreted as symbolic of the journey of individual believers and the colony as a whole from sinfulness to sanctification. The clearer the puritans' sense of their destiny became, the starker the line they drew between whites and neighbouring Indians, whom they increasingly lumped together as savages. The war halved New England's Indian population to fewer than 9,000 persons and the centre of gravity of European-Indian relations shifted west, to the Iroquois Confederacy, with whom the English colonies concluded treaties known as the Covenant Chain in 1676 and 1677. The treaties addressed longstanding European and Indian differences and provided for Iroquois neutrality, first in King Philip's War and later in conflicts between the English and French to the north. For the next 80 years or so the Iroquois and others used their neutrality and offers of military aid to bargain for concessions with competing European powers.

In Virginia, New England, and around the colonies the settlers asserted their rights as individual freeborn Englishmen and as communities established over the preceding two generations. In the 1680s, this colonial resolve clashed with Stuart ambitions to enhance royal and imperial rule. In 1685, Charles II died leaving no heir and so the throne passed to his younger brother the Duke of York, henceforth James II. James was a committed catholic and controversial figure. He particularly admired his cousin the absolute monarch, Louis XIV, and how the French had supplanted the Spanish as Europe's superpower state. James was widely suspected of harboring similar ambitions for monarchical supremacy. He intervened in religious matters to secure toleration for Catholics and Protestant dissenters, asserting, some believed, the claim of monarchical authority over all matters, including religion. In the early1680s, before his accession, rumours implicated James in a plot to assassinate Charles, prompting a constitutional and Exclusion Crisis to keep James from the throne. The crown responded to this and other challenges by reforming the municipal and borough charters which had long provided a base of support for lobbies in and out of Parliament that were critical of the monarchy. When colonial patents and original deeds became embroiled in this campaign, Massachusetts refused to accept amendments and had its charter suspended. This was a prologue to a wider campaign for reform of colonial rights.

James and his circle believed that imperial consolidation and expansion were essential if his three kingdoms were to compete in the vanguard of European states. In Europe, he deferred to Louis XIV. But abroad he adopted a more militant approach, favouring continued war with the Dutch as England's major colonial competitor and establishing the Royal Africa Company to monopolise the slave trade. In the colonies, he bundled the puritan New England settlements, New York, and the Jerseys into a single Dominion of New England overseen by a trusted military commander, matching similar structures set up in the West Indies and Bombay, India. The new authorities showed scant regard for existing rights and land claims, provoking dismay and disillusionment among many. In Parliament, the opposition that emerged during the Exclusion Crisis feared for the security of the Restoration's constitutional settlement and the Protestant succession. These Whigs – a pejorative title derived from the name of Scottish opponents of earlier Stuart religious reforms – counted among their supporters many colonial merchants who were opposed to expensive wars with the Dutch. The merchants favoured support for English manufacturing at home and free trade abroad, opposing royal monopolies and the French as the enemies of both.

English Protestants and critics of the crown comforted themselves that James was in his mid-fifties and childless, apart from two daughters: Mary, who had been safely married off to the Protestant Dutch prince William of Orange, and Ann. Thus it was widely believed that James' absolutist and pro-catholic sentiments would die with him. The negotiations with William and Mary concerning a likely future succession were underway, when news came that James second wife, another Mary, had given birth to a male heir. The prospect of an heir to the pro-catholic and French Stuart dynasty prompted more urgent and secret parliamentary negotiations with William, who agreed to invade and take the throne. James fled to France and the court of Louis XIV. The end of the Stuarts was greeted with consternation in the colonies. What remained of the royal authority claimed by colonial governors and placemen? Would James's allies join with the French to north and seek to control the English colonies in America. Rebellions in Boston, Maryland, and New York turned out royal appointees and the colonists declared themselves for the Protestant succession and William and Mary; few were sure what the future held. In the otherwise undistinguished Massachusetts village of Salem, fears of French and Indian attacks fed into embittered family and religious feuds leading to a spate of witchcraft accusations and trials that would become the most infamous event in seventeenth-century American history. In the spring and summer of 1692 the Salem villagers had no sense of their future notoriety. More importantly for them, and many of their fellow settlers up and down the eastern seaboard, was the likely fate of their still fragile colonial ventures in a land that remained to all intents and purposes an Indian Country.

Chapter summary

This chapter began with a brief survey of Native American and European societies prior to Columbus's 1492 voyage and the era of European-Native contact. Thereafter it considered the rise of Spanish empire in the New World and the implications for the balance of power between early modern European states. It also examined the religious and intellectual background to Europe's colonisation ventures, particularly the Reformation and debates concerning natural rights and civic humanism. The chapter compared the Spanish experience with French, Dutch, and English approaches to colonisation the beginnings of plantation slavery and the rise of distinctive colonial communities. It also considered relations between the colonists and Native Americans and how they changed over time, as faltering and perilous early colonial ventures were transformed into more populous and permanent settlements. This led to a discussion of why the English emerged ahead of other European nations in the competition for land and influence in North America. In closing, the chapter pondered relations between the emerging English imperial centre and its colonial periphery towards the end of the seventeenth century. In particular the efforts of the restored Stuart monarchy to rein in colonial autonomy after 1680 and the colonists' reactions culminating in intermittent if widespread unrest and even rebellion. As late as the outbreak of the Glorious Revolution, it remained unclear whether the North American were best characterised as colonies of far-flung European empires or outposts in an Indian Country. In the next chapter, we will consider how the expansion of the slave trade, plantation production, and Atlantic commerce transformed the struggling European New World colonies into populous, prosperous, and expansionist settlements. In time, these settlements stretched from New France to the Caribbean in the east and pushed into the interior of North America and towards the south and west and areas long claimed by Spain, in the process encountering and clashing with powerful indigenous communities.

Discussion questions

- How would you characterise the encounter between Native Americans and Europeans in the century after 1580?
- What were the different approaches to European colonisation and why did the English colonies thrive?
- How difference in social and economic conditions influence colonial gender relations?
- What were the relative importance of ideas and/or interests in European colonisation?
- To what extent was early colonisation managed by distant imperial authorities and/or driven by those on the ground in the New World?
- How secure was the English empire in North America at the end of the seventeenth century?

Further reading

Bremer, Francis J. *John Winthrop: America's Forgotten Founding Father* (New York, 2003). A comprehensive biography of Massachusetts's first governor.

Bunker, Nick. *Making Haste from Babylon: The "Mayflower" Pilgrims and Their World* (Bodley Head, 2010). The gripping story of the pilgrims flight from England to Holland and thence to America.

Burnard, Trevor G. *Mastery, Tyranny, and Desire: Thomas Thistlewood and His Slaves in the Anglo-Jamaican World* (Chapel Hill, 2004). A biographical study of a brutal slave overseer and life on a Caribbean plantation.

Canny, Nicholas P., William Roger Louis, Alaine M. Low, and P. J. Marshall. *The Oxford History of the British Empire* (Oxford, 1998). An excellent collection of summative essays dealing with major themes and topics.

Carpenter, Roger M. *The Renewed, the Destroyed, and the Remade: The Three Thought Worlds of the Huron and the Iroquois, 1609–1650* (East Lansing, 2004). A moving account of Iroquois "thought worlds" and how they changed after European contact.

Drake, James David. *King Philip's War: Civil War in New England, 1675–1676* (Amherst, 1999). The best analysis we have of the background to King Philip's War.

Elliott, John Huxtable. *Empires of the Atlantic World: Britain and Spain in America, 1492–1830* (New Haven, 2006). A major synthesis comparing Spanish and English Atlantic empires.

Eltis, David. *The Rise of African Slavery in the Americas* (New York, 2000). A recent study of origins and growth of Atlantic slave system.

Fitzmaurice, Andrew. *Humanism and America: An Intellectual History of English Colonisation, 1500–1625* (Cambridge, 2007). A study of the importance of humanist ideas in the colonization and the establishment of Virginia.

Kupperman, Karen Ordahl. *Indians and English: Facing Off in Early America* (London, 2000). A study focusing the earliest Indian and English encounters and impressions.

Kupperman, Karen Ordahl. *The Jamestown Project* (Cambridge, MA, 2007). A revisionist look at Virginia's earliest colony which turns out to be not quite the fiasco it has sometimes been considered.

Levy, Barry. *Town Born. The Political Economy of New England From Its Founding to the American Revolution* (Philadelphia, 2009). A recent look at the importance of civic culture in early New England government and economy.

MacCulloch, Diarmaid. *Reformation: Europe's House Divided, 1490–1700* (London, 2003). A magisterial account of the European Reformation.

Merrell, James H. *The Indians' New World: Catawbas and Their Neighbors from European Contact Through the Era of Removal* (Chapel Hill, 1989). An account of the encounter and transformation of New World lives from the Native American perspective.

Morgan, Edmund S. *American Slavery, American Freedom: The Ordeal of Colonial Virginia* (New York, 1995). Classic account of the establishment of Virginia and the "paradox" of slavery and freedom in early America.

Pestana, Carla Gardina. *The English Atlantic in an Age of Revolution, 1640–1661* (Cambridge, MA, 2007). A study of the impact of the English civil wars in the wider Atlantic world.

Richter, Daniel K. *Before the Revolution: America's Ancient Pasts* (Cambridge, 2011). Recent and excellent survey of early American history from first settlements and before to the eve of the American Revolution.

Richter, Daniel K. *Facing East from Indian Country: A Native History of Early America* (Cambridge, MA, 2001). A consideration of the Native perspective on the encounter.

Rountree, Helen C. *The Powhatan Indians of Virginia: Their Traditional Culture* (Norman, 1989). One of many studies by leading historian of the Powhatan confederacy whose work also inspired the opening to this chapter.

Schwartz, Stuart. *Early Latin America: A History of Colonial Spanish America and Brazil* (Cambridge, 1983). A good introduction to early Latin American history.

Thornton, J. *Africa and Africans in the Making of the Atlantic World, 1400–1800* (New York, 1998).

Tomlins, Christopher L. *Freedom Bound: Law, Labor, and Civic Identity in Colonizing English America, 1580–1865* (New York, 2010). Prize-winning account of the connections between law and labour in the making of early America.

Withington, Phil. *Society in Early Modern England: The Vernacular Origins of Some Powerful Ideas* (Cambridge, 2011). Great introduction to key themes relating to early modern English and American history.

Zacek, Natalie. *Settler Society in the English Leeward Islands, 1670–1776* (New York, 2011). Recent study of English society in the West Indies.

Zahedieh, Nuala. *The Capital and the Colonies: London and the Atlantic Economy, 1660–1700* (Cambridge, 2010). Recent study of the emergence of powerful lobby of colonial merchants in the late seventeenth century.

2 A provincial society in an Atlantic World

Timeline

Topics covered

- The development of provincial society in an Atlantic World
- The West Indies and slavery, 1660–1770
- Eighteenth-century political culture
- Sources of colonial division and discontent
- The Seven Years' War
- The challenge of settlement in the West

Introduction

This chapter opens with the 1741 slave conspiracy in New York City and closes with the Seven Years' War (1756–63) and the challenge presented by western expansion and settlement. The chapter considers this conflict and settlement in the context of the north eastern colonies' adjustment to their position within the British empire in the decades following the 1688 Glorious Revolution. In particular, the expansion of the slave trade and plantation production which stimulated Britain's colonial and domestic commerce and underpinned its rise as a global superpower over its Spanish and French rivals. The prosperity generated by the Atlantic trade in people and commodities – and in people *as* commodities – provided for compromises regarding earlier troublesome disputes concerning imperial authority and colonial rights. The colonists embraced consumption of new products and household goods as an affirmation of their Englishness; increasing trade produced profits and taxes that financed English geopolitical influence and a series of great power wars. Colonies developed interdependent and competitive regional political economies, differentiated by demography, use of contract and enslaved labour systems, and associated social practices. For many, the colonies offered opportunities to acquire skills and land and to enjoy a life of comfort, relative to European living conditions. For many more, however – including but not limited to the enslaved, Native Americans, landless labourers, and the indigent – colonial life was a dull round of hard labour, scant comfort, routine violence, and periodic terror. In the wake of the Seven Years' War, imperial stresses and strains and the colonists' determination to possess and settle land in the west threatened the North American colonies' internal stability and imperial coherence. It was in this context that remote, London-based politicians and officials decided to introduce a series of ill-conceived reforms with disastrous consequences for England's empire in North America.

A provincial society in an Atlantic World

One night in February 1741, towards the end of the coldest winter anyone could remember, three enslaved workers robbed Rebecca Hogg's New York City dockside shop. The workers had heard from a sailor that the shop was stocked with silver coins, fine cloth, and luxury goods such as tea and snuff boxes. The sailor told them that they "might have a fine booty, if they could manage cleverly to come at it." Two of the robbers, Prince and Cuffee, took their loot home, but the third man – known to his enslaver as Caesar, but to his associates as John Quinn – brought his share to a dockside tavern run by two whites, John and Sarah Hughson. The Hughsons had a reputation for selling rum to slaves and fencing stolen goods. The following day, acting on a tip-off, the constables picked up Prince and Quinn. Both denied their part in the robbery and the constables could not find the loot. A little while later, the Hughson's servant, Mary Burton, hinted that she knew something about her master's part in the robbery. The constables returned to the tavern and arrested a young Irish woman, Peggy Kerry, rumoured to be Quinn's mistress and the mother of his illegitimate child.

Two weeks later, as the magistrates prepared to try the robbers of Rebecca Hogg's shop, the fort containing the governor's mansion and a garrison of English soldiers caught fire. In the next few days, several more buildings were set alight, and some people reported seeing slaves sprinting away from the blazes. In 1741, England was at war with Spain and rumours circulated that perhaps Spanish agents had set the fires. Called to testify, and tempted by a hefty reward, Mary Burton shocked the court by implicating the Hughsons in not only receiving stolen goods, but also a diabolical, biracial conspiracy to fire the town and hand it over to Catholic Spain. Under torture, and just before being burned at the stake, Prince and Quinn also named dozens of co-conspirators. Panic gripped the town and more trials and executions followed. Over the course of the summer, 160 enslaved people and 21 whites were jailed. Magistrates identified John Ury, a recently arrived teacher and suspected Catholic, as the ring leader. Seventeen blacks and four whites were convicted and hanged; 13 blacks were burned at the stake and 70 more were banished. The brutalised bodies of key conspirators were left to dangle and rot on wooden gibbets erected around the town.

Historians continue to debate the meaning of New York's 1741 slave conspiracy. Some argue that it was nothing more than a frenzied outburst of wartime paranoia: nervous imperial officials and enslavers, fearful of Spanish attack and panicked by news of recent slave revolts in South Carolina and the Caribbean, relieved their anxieties by turning on innocent enslaved city residents and a handful of marginal characters. One contemporary commentator even compared events in New York to the by then infamous Salem witchcraft trials a generation earlier. However, others argue that the plot was real and demonstrated a growing and deep-seated resentment felt by the lower and labouring sort towards better off New Yorkers: witnesses testified to hearing the accused muttering darkly about how "a great many people had too much and others had too little" and of their plans to "murder everyone that had money."

For our purposes the real or imagined character of the conspiracy is not as important as what the events reveal about the changing face of the British American colonies: by the mid-eighteenth century, they had grown to encompass a string of populous settlements stretching from the northern Great Lakes region to the Caribbean with growing populations pushing ever westward. A prosperous and global trade sustained the colonies, but French and Spanish rivals contested Britain's dominance. Rebecca Hogg's shop and the Hughsons' tavern bore the imprint of this prosperous British empire and its developing divisions. Hogg met the desires of middling and elite consumers for hats and fabrics from England, tea from India, silks and porcelain from China, and took payment in coins made from silver extracted by Indian slaves from Spanish mines in Peru. The tavern served Caribbean rum, and locally brewed beer and cider, to disaffected immigrants and a multi-ethnic and rebellious population of sailors, labourers, servants, and especially the enslaved who provided the backbreaking toil that sustained the empire its growing commerce and wealth.

There has been some controversy concerning the extent to which the development of British power and prosperity in the nineteenth century depended on the earlier enslavement and transportation of tens of thousands of men, women, and children to

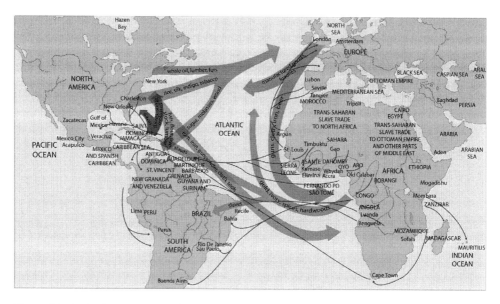

Figure 2.1 In the later seventeenth century, the English emerged as leaders in highly profitable Atlantic trade – combing the exchange of people, commodities, and manufactured goods – fostered by state mercantilism and, in particular, multinational and innumerable merchants.

work in the plantations of the Caribbean and southern colonies. In 1944, Eric Williams argued that the profits gained from the Atlantic slave trade and West Indian plantations provided the capital necessary for British imperial expansion and later industrialisation. Since then others have challenged this claim, arguing that wealth from the empire in India and other colonial investments were sufficient for British rise to global prominence without the capital earned in the slave trade and plantation production. A reasonable compromise points to three considerations. First, American plantation wealth began flowing to England at a vital time in its development as a world power, motivating and funding its defeat of the Dutch maritime empire in the late seventeenth century and thereby securing its international position on a par with France and Spain. Second, eighteenth-century plantation profits provided considerable stimulus to economic activity and consumer demand, expanding merchant trade, enriching a growing class of British and American providers of manufactured and luxury goods, inspiring technological innovation, and the growth of crucial commercial services such as banking and insurance. Third, plantation wealth enriched members of the British establishment charged with managing and investing in the future national and imperial potential. In short, wherever one looks in the upper echelons of eighteenth-century English society one finds wealth and influence tied in one way or another to the profits from slavery and the plantations, especially in the West Indies. In this respect, the trade in enslaved people and the product of their decades of unrewarded toil was essential to the development of British economic prosperity and imperial power.

The transition to capitalism debate

The arguments concerning the Williams' thesis form part of a wider controversy regarding the historical development of capitalism and its relationship to slavery. Some commentators concentrate on the rise of free enterprise and market relationships and, in particular the shift to wage labour from earlier forms of bound servitude. This suggests the development of a capitalist society based on rights to liberty and private property, increasing manufacturing and wealth creation, and opportunities for investors, workers, and consumers. In this view, slavery was an ancient and increasingly aberrant labour system that could not survive in a modern world of market relations. Others, however, consider capitalism as a less voluntary and natural development and more as compelled and often violent transition that favoured, in particular, the interests of the wealthy owners of productive resources and capital. In places this historical transition was accompanied by brutal social change, such as the enclosure common land and clearance of peasant cultivators, dispossession of indigenous peoples, or employment of child labour. In general, the transition broke down earlier community and family orientated relations of production in favour of the unending pursuit of economic growth and increased value, mostly to the advantage of the ruling capitalist class and its agents. In this account, New World slavery played a key role in producing the raw materials and surplus value that allowed for the development of far reaching capitalist markets and investment. Far from obsolete and aberrant, slavery was the major example of many forms of non-waged and compelled labour – for example, gendered domestic and caring work – upon which capitalism depended and still relies to sustain so-called voluntary market relationships.

Slavery and the West Indies, 1660–1770

English and French occupation of the Caribbean began as raids by sixteenth-century adventurers, such as Francis Drake and Walter Raleigh, on Spanish treasure ships making their way home from the New World. These privateers, meaning state-sponsored pirates, introduced English and French colonial investors to the Spanish islands of Cuba, Hispaniola, and Jamaica. By the 1620s, the opportunities presented by plantation production had encouraged English settlement on Barbados. The French matched these efforts, establishing plantations elsewhere in the Lessor Antilles on Martinique and Guadeloupe. In each place, early planters experimented with tobacco and servant labour before shifting to sugar and slavery, transforming tiny and obscure islands into the richest prizes in Europe's emerging American empire. Elsewhere the transition to large scale slave and plantation production took longer: in Virginia and Maryland enslaved workers did not predominate until after the 1670s and in Jamaica not until the early 1700s. We know from early ships' records that Virginia planters bought the enslaved as early as they could afford to and not, as was once thought, only following a downturn in the white servant migration in the later seventeenth century. But if plantations were profitable and enslavers were keen to exploit slave workers from early on, then what accounts for the time lag in the development of a plantation economy?

Part of the reason concerned geography and start-up costs. In Virginia, tobacco production rapidly exhausted the soil and nutrients, requiring the clearing and cultivating of new land. Land clearing for large-scale production was laborious, expensive, and given clashes with Indian inhabitants sometimes dangerous work. In the mid-to-late seventeenth century most Jamaican plantations were still worked by small planters who combined cotton and indigo cultivation with livestock farming assisted by a handful of indentured servants. They lacked the capital and inclination for large-scale operations requiring land clearance, often in rocky and mountainous terrain, and investment in expensive boiling vessels and enslaved labourers. Jamaica was also occupied by pirates who were welcomed by small planters as defenders against possible Spanish attack, but also discouraged major financial investments. The disruption to international shipping and trade caused by conflicts – such as the three Anglo-Dutch Wars, 1652–74 – and also drove up the costs of slaves and transportation and discouraged investment. Finally, there is evidence of general skepticism and suspicion concerning the advantages and morality of bound labour amongst ordinary colonists for whom "plantations" summoned up images of the semi-feudal bondage of Irish workers forced to cultivate land owned by absentee English landlords. The men and women of "small means" who settled the early American colonies were fiercely protective of their personal and community autonomy, a sensibility heightened by the radical arguments on behalf of religious belief and republicanism by the early puritans and the English Civil Wars.

The situation began to change following the 1660 Restoration of the Stuarts. The end of a long period of domestic conflict and rising economic prospects discouraged servant migration just as defeat of the Dutch secured the seas and England's leadership in the Atlantic trade. Understandably eager to guarantee their financial position and avoid the kind of difficulties that befell their father, Charles II and then his brother James II adopted a more interventionist approach to imperial management. They began by establishing a Royal African Company to monopolise the West African trade in gold and slaves and earn a revenue for the royal purse. Between 1672 and 1689 a group of favoured merchants working out of forts on the African coast transported 100,000 enslaved men, women, and children to the colonies, routinely branding them with the Company's logo or the King's initials to certify their monopoly right. During the same period declining mortality rates amongst whites and blacks in Virginia and Maryland encouraged settlement and the opening up of new land. Enslaved people who lived longer were a better investment, especially given the growing competition for servants and free labourers who were drawn to available land in the Jerseys and Pennsylvania, which was established in 1682. Between 1650 and 1700 the number of enslaved people in the Chesapeake increased from 300 to 13,000. The Royal African Company was unable to meet demand and faced competition from independent merchants, who challenged the legitimacy of crown monopolies and argued for their right to engage freely in the slave trade. In 1698, parliament ended the Company's monopoly and following a brief but effective campaign against piracy the slave trade boomed. By 1713, Jamaica's white population of 7,000 was dwarfed by its enslaved labour force of 55,000 men, women, and children who produced more sugar than Barbados. By mid-century, there were 150,000 enslaved people working in the Chesapeake, 40 per cent of the population. To meet demand British slave traders transported a further 40,000 people each year to work in the Caribbean and other plantation colonies.

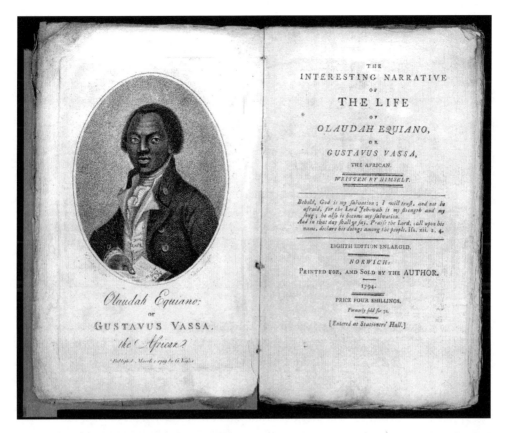

Figure 2.2 Title page from *The Interesting Narrative of the Life of Olaudah Equiano, or Gustavus Vassa, the African*, published 1789.

Source: Courtesy of the Library of Congress Prints and Photographs Division Washington

Middle passage

An enslaved person's journey from Africa to the New World was known as the middle passage. The voyage took three to four months during which time hundreds of people were chained and packed together on cramped shelves below deck. Olaudah Equiano, who experienced a voyage first hand, later recalled that the ship he sailed on was so crowded "that each had scarcely room to turn himself" and the "shrieks of women, and the groaning of the dying, created a scene of horror almost unbelievable."

Eighteenth-century plantation societies were characterised by small, very wealthy and politically powerful planter elites, larger and sometimes marginal communities of poor whites, and large and often majority populations of enslaved blacks. The shift to slave labour did not only benefit the wealthy and powerful. Beginning in the late seventeenth and early eighteenth centuries it also provided employment for former servant white workers and army and navy veterans as overseers of brutal plantation regimes. By stimulating commerce and increasing local revenues, plantation production also created demand for larger communities, better infrastructure, and local artisanal services such as blacksmiths, shipwrights, bakers, coopers, tailors and other trades. Bound and forced labour also influenced political relations between whites: by subjugating and cruelly exploiting an underclass of black workers, slavery alleviated the potential for division and discord between wealthy and impoverished whites and the kinds of disputes that had led to Bacon's Rebellion, 1676. Slavery established a foundation for political solidarity based on the shared advantages of whiteness. As slave populations increased, colonial legislatures introduced codes defining and regulating the lives of the enslaved and differentiating them from whites. In 1662 and 1664, Virginia and Maryland introduced laws affirming that slaves had to serve for the term of their natural lives and that children of enslaved mothers were born into bondage. Slave workers toiled for longer hours and under stricter supervision; laws prescribed whippings for blacks who struck or even threatened a white colonist; whatever property an enslaved workers managed to gain was subject to confiscation and sale to poor whites. Over time whites came to consider blacks as inferior, suited to their enslavement, and available for their personal enrichment and in some cases sexual gratification.

By 1770, nine out of ten African Americans lived as enslaved people in North America, approximately 278,000 people or 10 per cent of the overall population. Slave conditions varied greatly depending on location, work, and the possibilities for social interaction. Historians estimate that the enslaved in Jamaica worked approximately 4,000 hours a year, three times the workload of a modern factory worker. If employed in one of the seaport towns – Charleston, Philadelphia, or New York – an enslaved worker might avoid the brutalities of plantation labour, learn a skilled trade, and even earn a little money during precious moments of free time granted by their enslaver. Living and working closely with the white population provided for mixed race unions, like Quinn and Peggy Kerry in mid-century New York City. However, limited social contact with other enslaved workers diminished chances of establishing families and participating in cultural activities.

In the Chesapeake and Lower South, by contrast, large and even majority enslaved populations were routinely supplemented by new arrivals from Africa and the West Indies. By the 1730s, the population of 20,000 black enslaved workers in South Carolina outnumbered whites by a ratio of two to one, providing those in bondage with opportunities to settle families and established wider kin networks. Large slave populations also provided for the maintenance of African languages and culture, ranging from modes of dress and hairstyle to spiritual beliefs and working practices, for example in the cultivation of rice. Work, and the kinds of crops grown – mainly tobacco, grain, rice, or indigo, was a major influence on the life of plantation slaves. Working under close supervision was more limiting than working in self-managed gangs which might allow for some free time once designated tasks were completed. Given that all the enslaved inhabited a hostile terrain policed by every white planter and their servants, large scale resistance was limited. However, enslaved people also knew when to absent themselves from the plantation to achieve maximum disruption in work plans and thereby gain a sympathetic hearing from the enslavers who was eager to get on with the job at hand. Over time close contact between whites and blacks generated a

Figure 2.3 Stages in tobacco production.

Source: Courtesy of Universal Images Group North America LLC/Alamy

segregated society in which enslavers considered themselves as paternalists and a force for good in the lives of the enslaved men and women, whom they counted as not only their property but also dependents within an extended plantation household.

Adjustment to empire

The expansion of the slave trade that accompanied Britain's emergence onto the global stage was part of a wider colonial adjustment to empire following the Glorious Revolution. Britain's American colonies had been established haphazardly across the seventeenth century, some by chartered companies of private investors and royal prerogatives granted to proprietors, others by force backed by great power diplomacy. This piecemeal development, and the offer of available land, had drawn free migrants and motivated the transportation of servants and slaves, providing for British predominance in comparison to the more limited French and Spanish settlements. Over time, colonial communities of independent householders and farms claimed legal and administrative rights based on their original charters, their efforts in settling and cultivating the land, and their status as freeborn subjects. In the 1680s, these rights claims clashed with the James II's attempts to extend imperial control culminating in his flight from the throne. On the eve of the Glorious Revolution, John Locke, a notable Whig political theorist and radical, proposed that the consent of free subjects – albeit given in the dim and distant past and implied for future generations – provided the only legitimate basis for sovereign authority. If government, even monarchs, acted contrary to this consent and the common good, free subjects retained a right to resist and, if need be, change the government.

Locke's ideas were part of a broader intellectual transformation known as the Enlightenment in which scientists, mathematicians, and philosophers questioned long-established presumptions concerning the divine order and direction of human affairs, and addressed new findings concerning science and nature. In the case of Locke and likeminded critics of monarchy, this meant exploring the idea of natural law and natural rights theories, inherited from sixteenth-century Catholic theologians and reworked by the Dutch jurist, Hugo Grotius. These theories challenged the unquestioning obedience claimed by absolute monarchs and argued that legitimate governments were based on some form of representation and consent. Contemporary understandings of terms such as representation and consent differed greatly from our, modern-day usage. Even for Locke a person's right to a fair government meant equal protection before the law; this right did not extend to ordinary men – still less women, servants, or the enslaved – participating in the business of governing or even electing those who did. Nevertheless, Locke's ideas gave the Revolution a radical edge and informed views thereafter of the mixed constitution which combined the authority of the king with parliament, and rival political parties. These Whigs and Tories were driven by ideological and self-interested agendas and competed for the support of wealthy and influential social and political interests, while all the while claiming to represent the popular will and govern in the common good.

In 1696, the Whig administration established a Board of Trade staffed by parliamentary appointees to oversee colonial affairs. Unlike previous, ad hoc royal committees the Board sat in continuous session. This improved oversight of the sugar and tobacco trade, naval matters, the collection of customs, and communications concerning real or potential threats to Britain's interests. This enhancement of central control in London was counterbalanced by the recognition of provincial administration and a role for elected colonial assemblies. Parliament, and the Board as its representative, claimed absolute authority over the colonies, but they were also routinely preoccupied with European affairs and lacked the initiative or budget to micro-manage American government. The colonists, even those who had rebelled against the Stuarts and their appointees, could not imagine themselves apart from the empire, not least because they required protection during the Nine Years' War (1688–97) and the War of the Spanish Succession (1701–14): European conflicts, fought in part in the colonies.

A marriage of convenience developed between imperial officials and the emerging colonial gentry. The first needing local supporters if they were to have any chance of securing a revenue and governing the colony. The second eager to assure their individual and provincial rights and take advantage of attractive land and imperial trade opportunities. To broker the relationship between imperial centre and colonial periphery, the crown and proprietors appointed colonial governors, often former military men. The governors took advice from handpicked councils drawn from local landowners, merchants, and imperial appointees. Together they introduced legislation and levied taxes, with the support of a popularly elected provincial assembly, also drawn from the provincial elite. In theory, governors enjoyed more power in the colonies than the king in England: they could veto colonial legislation, suspend the assembly and jury courts, even declare martial law. In practice, they depended on the support of provincial councilors and assemblymen to maintain the public peace and agree taxes necessary for costs of administration, not least their salaries.

Eighteenth-century colonial political culture developed as a combustible combination of loyalty to Britain and equally zealous commitments to provincial rights and interests. The colonists participated in a festive culture organised around occasions such as Pope's Day (5 November) and the king's birthday: on these occasions, the colonists affirmed their virulent anti-Catholicism and hostility towards France and Spain and celebrated their inclusion in an empire that was Protestant, maritime, and free. These bonds of common identity were thickened by white colonists' self-regarding sense of their superiority over enslaved blacks and the Indian "savages." Stability was also assured by continuing assumptions concerning the divine and natural origins of inequality and social hierarchy. Although increasingly populist, colonial politics remained committed to the view that the gentry or "better sort" possessed the necessary talents and virtue for leadership and government. Virtue was a complex term implying not only education, refinement, and sophistication, but also personal morality and the ability to act in the public rather than purely self-interest.

When colonial governors played their part, distributing offices and influence and building alliances with key individuals and lobbies, provincial councilors and assemblymen remained more or less united and delivered popular support and necessary taxes. However, should governors adopt a heavy hand and fall out with the local leadership the provincial elite could stir up popular protest, posing as defenders of colonial rights against arbitrary and overbearing imperial authorities. Probably the most infamous example was Daniel Parke, governor of the Leeward Islands, who in 1710 assembled his troops to intimidate the assembly only to be dragged from his home and murdered by a mob. At other times disputes could divide colonial elites into supporters and opponents of the governor drawing ordinary colonists into politics as voters or mobs and raising questions about the singularity of the public good and gentry unanimity and virtue.

Becoming British America, 1700–1770

The expansion of Atlantic commerce and the prosperity of a growing population of colonial producers and consumers also sustained colonial allegiance. In 1700, there were 167,000 free settlers in the British mainland and Caribbean colonies, roughly 3 per cent of England's population. By 1770, there were more than 2.7 million – half the size of England's owns. Much of this growth came from new sources of non-English immigration: French Protestants, also known as Huguenots, escaping renewed religious persecution by Catholic Louis XIV; Scots encouraged by the 1707 Act of Union that conjoined England and Scotland and opened up the colonies for Scottish settlers; 80,000–100,000 Germans and Scots-Irish, pushed by economic hardship and drawn by the prospect of religious toleration to settle in Pennsylvania. As William Penn noted, it seemed to have become "the interest of England to improve and thicken her colonies with people not her own." The new immigrants expanded religious diversity, adding Lutherans, Mennonites, Presbyterian and Amish congregations to the existing mix of Calvinists, Quakers, Dutch Reformed and others all of whom implicitly challenged the Anglican Church establishment. Population growth from natural increase exceeded immigration. Americans, like Europeans, had large families of five to ten children, but in healthier New World conditions more children survived to adulthood. After 1690 colonial population doubled approximately every 25 years, producing a youthful and vigorous society of dominated by teenagers: in 1770 about half the colonial population was under 16 years old. Even the slave population grew. Only about 6 per cent of eighteenth-century slave imports went directly to British North America, the majority were bound for the Caribbean and South America. Yet, by the early nineteenth century, a quarter of African Americans in the New World lived in the continental United States.

Population growth and ethno-religious diversity produced stresses and strains as well as benefits. In 1715, the New York Assembly passed a Naturalization Act granting citizenship to aliens, including the right to bequest land, in part to retain Palatine German immigrants and encourage them to settle on the upriver frontier. Five years later in Pennsylvania, faced with a German migration that accounted for one-third of the colony's population, assemblymen instituted a loyalty oath for new arrivals and considered barring further incomers. Immigration and population growth also increased pressure on the availability of land. Nine out of ten American colonists lived and worked in the countryside. Owning and cultivating land was essential for family formation and the ambitions of middling men and women to establish independent households. However, as eastern areas filled up and farms were divided between third and fourth generation families, later generations and newcomers had to choose between becoming tenant farmers on lands owned by others or move west and take on the hardships of life on the frontier. The growth of colonial population and agriculture provided for the emergence of distinctive regional economies that bound colonies together and to the Atlantic trade. Whatever their fortunes, the European colonists' cultural ties and economic lives created a sense of their interdependence within an empire which they supposed protected their individual and collective rights and prosperity in a contested and often dangerous world.

Nowhere was this imperial contest clearer than in the Europeans' determination to control the richest of colonial prizes, the plantation islands in the Caribbean. Beginning in the mid-seventeenth century England's Navigation Acts sought to exclude enemies and competitors from the colonial trade, in particular the Dutch upon whom the colonists depended for access to well-priced trade goods and European sugar and tobacco markets. The Board of Trade also established restrictions on colonial manufacturing to ensure demand for English goods, and levied customs duties on colonial imports and exports. Following the disruption of the Nine Years' War (1688–97), as the market for sugar and slaves grew, West Indian planters committed their crops to metropolitan speculators ahead of the harvest and came to see the empire more as a guarantor rather than restrictor of trade and prosperity. Plantation masters built up stores of coin and paper credits from London merchants in the form of bills of exchange given for their sugar and tobacco which they used to settle debts with European and northern colonial suppliers. Between 1700 and 1770 total colonial exports to Britain – of which sugar and then tobacco claimed the lion share – increased more than tenfold to five million pounds. American imports of British manufactures and trade goods, mostly to the populous northern colonies, quadrupled to almost 40 per cent of national trade. This was without counting the lively and illicit trade in smuggled goods between the British colonies and the Caribbean which continued throughout the eighteenth century. The French matched and then bettered British expansion in the Caribbean, challenging the Spanish whose empire was crippled inflation, following the flood of New World gold and silver, and decades of warfare in defence of its territory and Catholic causes. In 1697, Spain ceded the western end of Hispaniola to the French who established what became their richest colony, Saint Domingue (modern day Haiti).

Bills of exchange

Bills of exchange dated back to the fourteenth century and were used to settle debts without having to transport gold and silver. The bill was a written order from one person directing another to pay a third, the beneficiary. By the late seventeenth century, bills were circulating to third and more parties, and colonists used them to clear debts with English financiers. Thus, the West Indian planters, who exported more in sugar than they bought from London might use their surplus bills to pay a New York merchant for supplying grain and timber, who would then return the bill to London to pay for his supply of imported household goods.

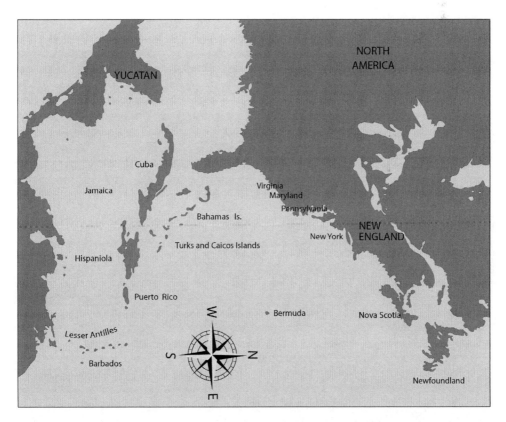

Figure 2.4 Over the course of the eighteenth century the wealth and opportunities created by British America's Atlantic Arc provided for the growing dominance of the colonies in England's foreign trade and revenues. When we reorientate our map from the usual trans-Atlantic perspective, the proximity of the Caribbean islands and the significance West Indies trade for North America is clear.

After the Caribbean, the plantation colonies of the continental south – Virginia, Maryland, and the Carolinas – were Britain's most significant colonial assets in terms of exports and revenue. In 1700, annual production of tobacco exceeded 28 million pounds in weight. By 1770, it was 80 million pounds and worth a cash value of £700,000 per annum. As much as three quarters of tobacco came from Virginia, creating downward pressure on prices and encouraging some to switch to grain and other crops with the objective of supplying the Caribbean plantations. Facing a glutted tobacco market, and too far north to grow sugar, the Carolinas benefitted from their proximity to the West Indian planters for whom they produced lumber, livestock, and pitch and tar. Relying on the horticultural knowledge of African slaves, the Carolinas also became major cultivators and exporters of rice – some £300,000 per annum by 1770 – as well as indigo, a dye produced by boiling leaves in a vat. The Carolinas also developed a profitable trade in deer skins and Indian slaves, employed locally or for sale to the Caribbean. Carolinian settlers required Indians to pay for guns, ammunition, and supplies with captives, prompting raids on vulnerable neighbours and a cycle of Native American attack and counter-attack. In 1732, a royal charter established a new colony, Georgia, south of the Savannah River to secure the colonies' southern border and provide gainful employment for English paupers transported to settle and improve their circumstances. Within 20 years local planter ambitions and the profits to be made from plantation production had encouraged a shift to slavery.

Above the plantation colonies and below New England lay a group of settlements, comprising New York, the Jerseys (later New Jersey) and Pennsylvania which historians commonly refer to as the "middle colonies." These settlements lacked the distinguishing characteristics of, say, the slave south or puritan north but nevertheless shared regional features which some argue anticipated the character of the emerging American nation: these colonies had mixed agricultural and trading economies, and relied on waterways such as the Delaware and Hudson Rivers to connect seaboard towns at New York and Philadelphia with developing hinterlands; they also employed a combination of free and enslaved workers. The enslaved comprised 15 per cent of New York City workers, a proportion that remained in evidence up to the nineteenth century. The middle colonies all came into the empire rapidly in the late seventeenth century, rather than maturing slowly from long-established early settlements; many in the middle colonies envied the seeming autonomy of earlier, chartered colonies. A diverse ethno-religious and linguistic population fueled these colonies' contentious political culture. In 1702, following decades of intermittent conflict between Quakers in the west and multi-ethnic and Dutch in the east, the crown forced the reunion of the Jersey colonies to a single New Jersey. In Pennsylvania, Quakers fell out concerning matters of doctrine and religious practice and non-Quakers resented the Friends' influence in provincial politics and the distribution of land. Another shared characteristic was the middle colonies' common interest in frontier lands on their western boundaries. This brought them into contact and increasing conflict with the French, who were expanding south from the Great Lakes region with the support of Indian allies in the west.

In the century after King Philip's War (1675–76), New England – comprising Massachusetts, Rhode Island, and Connecticut, latterly Maine and New Hampshire – recovered on the back of supply trade to southern and Caribbean plantation colonies. New England boasted no cash crop or supply of desirable resources. By the early eighteenth century, the once rich supply of furs was exhausted and the trade in decline.

New Englanders depended on family farms of between 50 and 300 acres, producing grain and livestock such as hogs and poultry. Household production sustained farm families who sold their surplus to pay debts to local shopkeepers and merchants, who exported supplies to the slave colonies in the south and Caribbean. With a seemingly endless supply of tall trees for masts and other naval stores Boston also became a centre for colonial shipbuilding, benefitting from imperial contracts to fit out expeditions launched against the French in Canada and the Caribbean. Wartime contracts introduced swings from boom to bust, creating unemployment, poverty, and public finance deficits requiring higher taxes. There were profits for some, but the attacks by combined French and Indian forces and military campaigns cost thousands of colonists their lives. Far from the plantation dynamo of colonial trade, Boston, once the colonies' busiest port, gradually slipped behind its rivals New York and Philadelphia.

By mid-century, the growing population and expanding commerce of Britain's mainland colonies on the eastern seaboard of North America demonstrated the superiority of free and loosely controlled colonising settlements over the more closely regulated French and Spanish colonies. In the north west, the tiny French population of some 15,000 was dwarfed by the hundreds of thousands inhabiting the British colonies. Given the ultimate French defeat in the Seven Years' War 1756–63 it is tempting to take British preeminence in North America for granted. This would be a mistake. Although small in population terms, New France remained a powerful presence owing to the quality of its long-standing trade and military alliances with the nearby Algonquian Indians, in particular the Hurons, Montagnais, and Micmac. The French also enjoyed the formidable support of an alliance of Indian communities known as the Anishinaabe, who oversaw a loose confederation of trade and diplomacy throughout the vast country west of modern day Montreal, known then as the Pays d'en Haut or Upper Country.

The historian Richard White coined the metaphor "middle ground" to capture the character of French-Indian interdependence and the novel attitudes and practices that mediated their reciprocal connection. The French and the Indians – the first desperate for military allies, the second coveting European trade goods and weapons – created a world that combined elements of both cultures and created a world that was new for them both. The French behaved like Indians, accepting diplomatic protocols and gift giving; the Indians behaved like the French, participating in what struck them as unwarranted conflicts and trading in captives. Indian support, particularly by the Anishinaabe, allowed the French to not only withstand the greater British presence, but also extend their influence. In 1717, they established New Orleans as the major port for the colony of Louisiana; thereafter French official settlement moved into the area of the lower Mississippi, intending to establish slave plantations and alliances with the Choctaw, the major Indian confederacy. Instead what became known as the Illinois Country filled up with the free booting fur traders and missionaries, extending French influence but not in the way imagined.

To the southwest of French Louisiana, the Spanish empire had faded from its domination in the sixteenth-century heights but endured as a significant continental power. Authorities in Spain remained committed to crown control and close regulation, but in the seventeenth century accepted a greater role for Catholic missionaries, mostly Franciscans and Dominicans. Although few in number, the missionaries seemed to enjoy impressive success in creating converts throughout New Mexico and to the north amongst Navajo and Apaches. Or did they? Rather than "converting" Indians

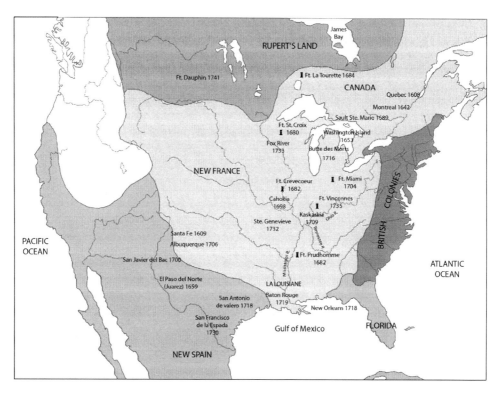

Figure 2.5 English, French, and Spanish territorial claims in 1750.

to Roman Catholicism what developed was a powerful religious syncretism or compound of missionary and Indian beliefs – a sort of spiritual "middle ground." Indians were impressed by the missionaries' dedication to their task, their abstinence from sexual relations, and their authority over other Spanish colonists, especially the military. The Indians also feared European violence and epidemics of inexplicable diseases and were ready to concede that the newcomers' deity must possess impressive supernatural powers. Thus, some Indians were prepared to abstain from religious and social practices the priests denounced as devilish and immoral, such as polygamy, as long as their expectations of security and welfare were met. However, when missionaries acted harshly or their demands for native tributes in labour and crops were considered unreasonable, the Indians looked for answers from native spiritual leaders.

In 1680, one such leader, Popé urged the Pueblo Indians to return to their own ways and led a revolt of some two dozen towns and 17,000 Indians. The Spanish crushed the rebellion but moderated their administration in the interests of joining with the Pueblos to repel a common and increasingly sophisticated enemy to the north: the Comanches. Previously hunter gatherers, by the early eighteenth century, the Comanche had developed horse-based nomadic society. Using guns acquired from the French, and combining farming and hunting with trading and raiding, they developed an empire some argue was as mighty as the Iroquois and Aztecs and which withstood the Anglo-Hispanic conquest of the west until the mid-nineteenth century.

Vast Early America

The significance of French and Spanish colonisation and their associated Native American alliances and conflicts point up the importance of ongoing historiographical revisions. Until recently there was a tendency to present early American history as a prologue to the birth of the United States, beginning with the British eastern coastal settlements and their gradual expansion westward. However, the weight of evidence and historical interpretation over the last couple of decades of concerning subjects (Native Americans, enslaved African Americans, and women) and places (Lima, California, the Arkansas River Valley, and West Central Africa) left out of this Anglo-American narrative is forcing a reconceptualisation of early American history. As scholars are uncovering the limitations and inaccuracies of a national story that omits the history Indian slavery in the west, or the significance of Mexican–Native diplomacy in the south west borderlands and innumerable other geographically disparate but interconnected experiences and histories, they are reconceiving the field as a "vast," rather than Anglo-American colonial history.

Ultimately, British strength in North American colonies depended on more than simply force of numbers and trade. Colonial loyalties also reflected their commitment to a provincial life style comprising material fortunes and political liberties that many believed were secured by membership in the empire. Colonial per capita output and standard of living outstripped English and European levels, especially in the plantation colonies. The colonists were largely free of taxation, paying less than a quarter of the amount borne by English residents. This left many with a disposable income with which to indulge their fascination for British social and cultural life which they tracked through regular contact and improved communication. Between 1700 and 1770 transatlantic sea crossings more tripled to more than 1500 per annum. In 1704, the colonies produced their first newspaper, the *Boston News Letter*; by 1762 there were 22 titles in circulation. Urban communities developed distinct identities reflecting their regional particularities: Charleston served as a trading hub and service provider for the slave economy, along the lines of the richest Atlantic towns such as Kingston, Jamaica. Northern towns such as Philadelphia, New York, and Boston resembled the English trading ports of Liverpool and Bristol.

Elite and middling colonists – civic-minded, educated, and for much of the eighteenth century, financially comfortable – also shared a fascination for metropolitan culture and aped their English peers: they built mansions, emulated the dress and deportment of the English gentry, and became renowned for their gentility and hospitality; they read novels, newspapers, and magazines; they visited theatres, joined clubs and associations, and participated in the craze for tea drinking. In many respects, the differences between, say, Charleston and Bath were outweighed by their similarities. The shortage of labour and availability of land made it possible for even relatively humble men and women to attain a comfortable living. Thus in 1757 the New York lawyer and historian, William Smith, declared that "Every man of industry and integrity has it in his power to do well, and many are the instances of persons who came here distressed by their poverty who now enjoy easy and plentiful fortunes." Setting aside the suffering and subordination of those who worked as slaves, servants, and the landless poor, and disregarding the destruction of Native American communities, colonial America appears as a land of middle-class opportunity and prosperity governed, largely without protest, by a landowning and merchant elite. But can we set aside the experience of those who were, after all, the majority of colonial inhabitants without losing sight of the determining forces and patterns that shaped colonial life?

Eighteenth-century divisions and discontents

For many colonial Americans – including but not limited to the enslaved, landless labourers, and the poor – daily life was unimaginably hard and, at best, nasty, brutish, and short. It is worth noting that three times as many migrants who came to the eighteenth-century colonies did so as slaves rather than as free men and women. Half of the 50 thousand or so English arrivals in the eighteenth century were transported convicts. Given these headline figures, it is surely insensitive and inaccurate to focus only on the prosperous and consuming classes, just because they are more apparent in the historical record. Everywhere one looks in colonial society, as in most societies, one can find evidence of discontent and resistance that shaped the experience and actions of ordinary colonists. Enslaved populations who endeavoured to construct a social and cultural life, maintaining their humanity in the face of heartless prohibitions and awful brutality. Native American peoples who compromised, made alliances, and fought back to protect their communities and lands from aggrandising European settlers. For many early America was a land of opportunity with conditions preferable to those in Europe, but we also need to consider the colonists' anxieties and struggles evident in diverse areas, from changing forms of religious worship to armed fights with landlords and speculators over rents and family farms. One important and noteworthy trend was the increasingly populist and disorderly colonial politics in which defiance often supplanted deference and the weak sometimes turned the tables on the strong.

Histories of daily life in rural and urban communities show that the opportunities and prosperity of imperial commerce did not trickle down to everyone. Social hierarchy was a long-established fact of life, but inequalities and dissatisfactions grew across the colonial period. Early migrants to late seventeenth-century western Pennsylvania had shared a broadly equitable style of frontier life in terms of property ownership and working conditions. However, the rise of the wheat trade and increasing land values allowed some to accumulate comfortable fortunes, in part and increasingly by employing landless neighbours and newcomers as labourers, servants, and tenants. In the early eighteenth century, Hudson Valley tenant farmers cleared and cultivated thousands of acres of previously unworked lands granted to elite families such as the Livingstons and Van Cortlandts as reward for supporting the crown. After a generation or more of toil, many farmers considered the land theirs by right of occupancy and improvement. These farming families resented having to hand over crop surpluses to landlords who profited from deals with Atlantic merchants supplying the slave colonies in the Caribbean. Beginning in the 1750s, and over the ensuing 40 years, tenants protested the unfairness of their leases and challenged the landlords' titles in legal battles that occasionally ended with riots.

Those who moved into towns looking for work found themselves similarly locked out of the benefits of colonial economic growth. Expanding regional and international markets and wartime booms brought good fortune for some, but instability, unemployment, and misery to others. High wages paid to colonial workers, and complained of by their employers, were soon spent keeping up with exorbitant living costs. In coastal towns enterprising women ran taverns and shops and worked at artisanal trades, and ran households that survived by providing a raft of services including food, lodging, washing, mending, and lending to those on the move in the Atlantic trade. Despite working people and their families' best efforts inequalities grew: a study of mid-century Philadelphia, by then the colonies' wealthiest northern seaport, noted that between 1750 and 1770, the top 10 per cent of taxpayers increased their share of property from just under half to more than two-thirds; the poorest 60 per cent saw their share halved to 6 per cent. It was difficult for many to accumulate the savings and investment necessary to graduate from an apprentice to a master craftsman. In the 1760s and 1770s, these already difficult urban conditions were worsened by the arrival of thousands of new migrants fleeing poverty and persecution in Europe. While the poor looked on, the wealthy dressed in the latest styles and built impressive mansions. In the 1760s, unemployment and food shortages led to mass protests and more riots.

The impact of new commercial uncertainties may also have figured in the mid-century surge in popular piety, which presented a different kind of challenge to established structures of authority. From the 1730s to the 1770s the colonies experienced a revitalisation of Christian faith, known as the Great Awakening, that drew upon a surge in religious enthusiasm sweeping Europe. Introduced to America by German and Scots-Irish immigrants, the new piety inspired itinerant preachers to minister to large and mixed or nondenominational crowds. These fervent and evangelical preachers emphasised the inherent goodness of man and preached that divine grace and everlasting life was available to all who truly repented their sins and accepted God. This message was well-received in harsh and sometimes perilous backcountry areas which were ill-served by the established churches. In 1739–41, a young English revivalist, George Whitfield, preached to huge crowds and became famous across the colonies. In New England, the itinerant pietists were initially popular with the established churches, who hoped to use their prominence to reinvigorate a religious culture diminished by commercial interests and Enlightenment secularism. Disputes broke out, however, when the "New Light" preachers denounced their established denominational peers for focusing too narrowly on questions of religious form and doctrine rather than the immediacy of emotionally charged conversion. The established churches went on the offensive, trying to ban the itinerants from preaching thereby assuring their emboldening their popularity. Overall, the Awakening challenged traditional modes of thought and deference to established institutions and, in rural areas, reinforced a sense of community and suspicions concerning the ethics of new commercial practices and unequal wealth.

The Great Awakening preachers were particularly controversial for preaching to slaves in the south. Whitfield was an advocate for slavery and campaigned for its legalisation in Georgia, but by preaching the equality of souls before God he and others also offered a measure of dignity and recognition of the humanity of the enslaved that was unpopular with their masters. Instances of outright rebellion in the plantation colonies were rare, but whites considered slave resentment and the potential for resistance a clear and present danger requiring constant vigilance and tightening of controls. In the Carolinas, masters and assemblymen were so fearful of the potential for revolt that they introduced laws prohibiting slaves from riding horses and hunting with guns, even from moving about unsupervised and gathering together without written passes giving permission.

In 1739, the same year as a Security Act required white males to carry weapons at all times, a slave conspiracy rocked South Carolina. In September, a force of 20 slave rebels succeeded in attracting 60 or so more to a muster on the Stono River to the southwest of Charleston. The rebel leader was a literate and Catholic African slave, Jemmy, recently arrived from the Kingdom of Kongo in west Central Africa. The slaves marched behind a banner proclaiming "Liberty!" and may have been inspired by the outbreak of war between Britain and Spain and the latter's offer of freedom to any who fled to Spanish-controlled Florida. A well-drilled and armed white militia met the hopelessly outgunned slaves. In fierce fighting, 20 whites and 44 blacks were killed, before surviving rebels were rounded up, executed, or sold off to the West Indies. This Stono Rebellion, and similar small-scale uprisings elsewhere, convinced legislators to condemn the most brutal masters and provide for slaves' religious instruction. However, these measures were paired with even more draconian legislation, prohibiting slaves from growing their own food or learning to read and preventing masters from freeing their slaves after a promised term or as a bequest on their enslaver's death.

Eighteenth-century Native Americans retained significant geopolitical influence, but their communities also suffered increasing pressure and often overt threat through contact with European settlers. Even as Britain, France, and Spain competed for continental predominance much if not most of North America remained under Indian control: New Yorkers referred to the vast territory to the north east bordering the British colonies and New France as "Mohawk Country" throughout the colonial period, and the Anishinaabe, Choctaw, Comanche and others controlled much of the north west, west, and south. In south-eastern frontier areas, plantation masters worried about slaves running away to join the Indians and offered native communities hefty rewards for the return fugitives. However, Indian diplomatic power masked deeper tragedies and the destabilisation of Native American society. The epidemics of European diseases such as measles and small pox that had wiped out hundreds of thousands during the early colonial era continued to afflict large numbers of Native peoples. In the south, the pervasive slave and gun trade prompted intra-Indian conflicts as war-torn communities competed for a diminishing number of slave captives.

In 1711, a combined force of South Carolina slave traders assisted by Algonquian Cherokee, Creek, Yamasee, and Catawba Indians attacked a Tuscarora village killing hundreds and seizing hundreds more to sell into slavery. The surviving Tuscarora migrated north to join with their ancestral relatives the Iroquois. Four years later the hunters became the hunted when the Yamasee faced the seizure of women and children for sale into slavery as payment of outstanding debts. In the furious fighting that followed, the Yamasee, Creeks, and Catawbas finally united against the Carolinians, killing 400 whites and driving hundreds more away from Charleston in fear for their lives. The Yamasee War (1715–17) caused shock waves throughout the colonies and only ended when northern Iroquois war parties were persuaded to journey south and join a counter assault in vengeance for the Yamasee's earlier attacks on the Tuscarora.

The Yamasee War marked the end of more than two decades of imperial wars dating back to the James II's flight from the throne in 1688. Exhausted by the conflicts, it would be 26 years before the great European powers fought another major colonial war. Throughout the years of colonial contests, the Board of Trade had tried to extend royal authority and considered proposals to unite fragmented colonial governments into larger administrative units to better enforce economic regulations, secure revenues, and ensure victory against the French. As long as Franco-Indian alliances held – cemented with "gifts" of trade goods and the activities of catholic missionaries – British efforts came to naught. Moreover, the constant and unproductive assertion of the royal and imperial prerogative generated zealous opposition in defence of colonial rights.

As early as the 1720s, and drawing on arguments from the natural rights and republican political traditions, the colonies were developing a more federal vision of their relationship to the crown and empire. The king's claim to lands in America, they argued, did not depend on inheritance or conquest but on the colonists' occupation and development of land rightfully purchased from the Native Americans. The monarch's patents, prior to and without colonial settlement and cultivation, were worthless. Given this starting point, the colonists argued it was illogical to maintain that the earliest settlers and their descendants who had improved the land had done so without guarantees of their rights. In fact, these rights and benefits were promised and secured in the original charters granted to founders such as the Virginia and Massachusetts Bay Companies and subsequent proprietors. These agreements, the colonists maintained, were quasi-contracts, guaranteeing colonial titles in exchange for loyal service to the king in enriching the empire and defending it from French and Spanish foes. Indeed, given the long distance between them this service to the empire gave colonial charters an even more solid foundation than the similar charters granted to corporations in England. Then there were practical administrative considerations, which only local governments could understand and adequately respond to thereby ensuring the imperial interest. From this perspective, denying the colonists their rights and freedoms was tantamount to undermining the empire to which all made a valuable contribution.

English imperial overseers in London took a rather different view, but unable or unprepared to commit legislative and military resources to colonial administration they left the governors to rely on provincial elites to govern the colonies. In the 1720s, a Whig coalition headed by Robert Walpole – the first parliamentarian to be designated the "prime minster" – gained control of parliament promising to end expensive military expeditions that required unpopular domestic taxes. Walpole favoured peace, as far as possible, and development of wealth produced by plantation; the colonies were increasingly left to their own devices in a period of "salutary neglect." However, the return of popular protests against taxes in the following decade, and the rise of pro-war lobbies by those who coveted access to the Spanish colonial trade, weakened Walpole leading to his eventual fall. In 1739, England and Spain again went to war over the Caribbean trade and the following year this conflict merged with the War of the Austrian Succession (1740–48) and the return of Anglo-French hostilities. This was a global war fought for great power geopolitical prizes in Europe, India and after 1744 North America, where it was known as King George's War. War's end brought the Whig royalist the Earl of Halifax and an ambitious new administrative team to the Board of Trade. Halifax was determined to reassert ministerial authority over the colonies, but his efforts were forestalled by the return of Anglo-French antagonism in the 1750s.

By mid-century, colonial expansion was running beyond the control of provincial elites and popular protests against imperial regulations and controls were blending with land riots against local landlords and settler-Indian hostilities in the west to produce a highly unstable situation. Responding to shifting and contradictory demands, the colonial gentry fractured along religious, dynastic, and self-interested lines – some favouring greater autonomy from imperial controls, others calling for greater integration. Even without the interruption of a new French war, it is not clear how Halifax's campaign would have fared. One controversy, concerning the payment of Virginian Anglican ministers' salaries in tobacco valued at the rate of two pennies to a pound of leaf, highlighted the growing tension between colonies and empire. In 1758, a bad harvest trebled the price of tobacco, inflating the minsters' salaries. The Virginia assembly – concerned about protests against the higher payments, especially among the many non-Anglican colonists – enforced payment at the lower rate. The ministers appealed to the crown, who supported their claim and struck down the colonial legislature, prompting public trials to decide the ministers' compensation. The trials featured arguments for and against the power of the royal prerogative over provincial rights, culminating with jury's award of a single penny in damages, symbolically rejecting the crown's right to strike down the local legislature.

The war for empire and after

It was in this divided and often conflicted condition that the American colonies entered the Seven Years' War (1756–1763), the largest eighteenth-century conflict between the European powers ranged in two alliance systems – Britain, Prussia, and Portugal and their allies against France, Spain, Austria and their allies – with far reaching consequences for European, American, and world history. In North America the conflict centred on the economic and political tensions arising from the asymmetrical growth of French and English interests in the Americas. French influence in the West Indies sugar colonies – on Saint Domingue (Haiti), Guadeloupe, Martinique and elsewhere – exceeded the British presence on Barbados and Jamaica. But the heavily populated and expanding 13 mainland British colonies easily outweighed the smaller French presence in New France. This geopolitical balance of power gave both sides problems. Powerful British sugar planters and the state had long tried to prevent the colonists trading with the French Caribbean, introducing the 1733 Molasses Act which set prohibitive taxes on the importation of French sugar. But colonial American merchants looking to export agricultural surpluses, slaves, and trade goods through Boston, New York, Philadelphia and elsewhere evaded the regulations and routinely smuggled their wares, denying the crown its proper customs revenue and sustaining the French islands and their crown revenues. The French, for their part, feared losing influence in the Ohio Country and being cut off from their interests in the western fur trade and the Mississippi Valley, especially New Orleans. Looking to safeguard their position in the mid-eighteenth century the French pushed southwards from Lake Erie, building Indian alliances and forts in the Ohio Country to the west of Pennsylvania and Virginia.

French incursions west of the Appalachians threatened Britain's claim and the interests of colonial speculators and farmers in new land. The two powers and their colonial and Indian forces sparred inconclusively and stories of atrocities committed by both sides circulated through mid-century colonial newspapers and journals. In Pennsylvania the image of western settlers protecting home and hearth from attacks by Indian savages became a stock character in eastern political debates between ruling Quakers and their critics concerning frontier defence. The Pennsylvania Assembly was locked

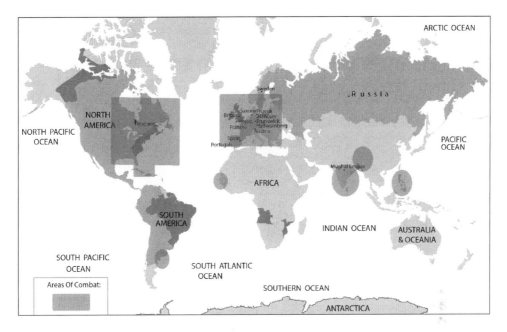

Figure 2.6 The Seven Years' War, a global conflict fought between 1756 and 1763, involved
every European great power and spanned five continents, affecting Europe, the Americas, West Africa, South Asia, and the Philippines.

in a decade-long struggle with Thomas Penn, the proprietor, over control of the provincial currency and public finance, leaving the backcountry undefended. The decisive
encounter came in Virginia, when the French retaliated to a militia attack, featuring
a young George Washington, with punitive victories over British forces, including the
death of a prominent English officer, Edward Braddock. Determined to assert Britain's
claim, William Pitt terminated London's low-key management of American affairs
and mobilised a powerful fleet and expeditionary army backed by colonial forces and
all funded with generous subsidies. In the war which followed, the British conquered
not only the French in Canada but also captured every major French island except
Saint Domingue. French defeat was so total that under the 1763 Treaty of Paris which
ended the war the British agreed to return Guadeloupe and Martinique to France. This
was largely at the insistence of the British sugar planters, who feared the increased
competition and decline in their own share of the sugar business, if the newly acquired
French plantations also supplied English domestic and foreign markets.

British victory in the Seven Years' War forever altered the balance of power in
North America, prompting colonial confidence in their future prosperity and London's determination to take a firmer hand in American affairs. For more than a century, the French threat from the north and, later, south and west had hemmed in
colonial expansion. Now it was gone. The colonists had united in a war against a
common enemy, elevating the status and fighting reputation of the colonial militias
and volunteers. Some thought that this "people's army" might be even more effective
at defending the frontier and dealing with Indian attacks than the authoritarian and

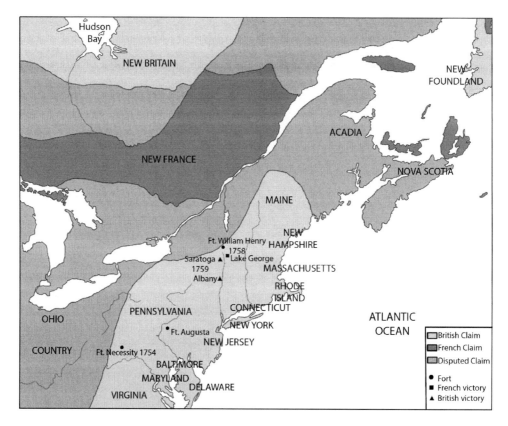

Figure 2.7 The war in North America reflected the changing priorities of Native diplomacy
and, in particular, their withdrawal of support for the French and emerging antagonism with the British colonies.

coercive British military. Above all the colonists saw the defeat of the French as an
opportunity to enlarge their already extensive commercial opportunities with new
lands to settle and farm and natural resources to exploit. Accordingly, the Americans
celebrated the end of the war and their membership in the glorious English empire
which now predominated in North America, but they did so on their own terms. As
for the Indians, especially those who had fought against the British, French defeat
meant that they could no longer rely on shrewd diplomacy, balancing evenly matched
European powers off against one another. The English, for their part, had gone heavily into debt to defeat the French and George III (1760–1820) and a new crop of ministers were loath to revert to the traditional hands-off policy. They were determined
to retain a military presence in North America, not only to govern their new French
subjects and manage restive Indian tribes, but also to rein in the colonists who they
thought should contribute more to the costs of the empire within which they prospered. However, in many respects this emerging diplomatic crisis was not as pressing
as the internal competition and disputes concerning the disposition of western lands
which threatened colonial unity.

In 1754, a conference at Albany, featuring representatives of Indian and colonial interests as well as senior imperial officials, met to try and resolve the competing land claims and problems of colonial administration and defence. The conference is often remembered for the plan for colonial union presented by the printer, politician, and polymath, Benjamin Franklin. Proposals for common colonial defence were nothing new, but Franklin's plan went further and suggested a plan of union that would create joint governance and decision-making structures that operated over the heads of local legislatures. Franklin was dismayed by the continuing divisions in Pennsylvania and the lack of effective security in the west. He was also a shrewd investor who realised that the Ohio Country offered a bonanza for well-placed speculators, but only if its acquisition and settlement could be carefully managed. However, in 1754 only 7 of the 13 mainland colonies even bothered to attend the Albany Congress, which ended without a consensus. Towards the end of the Seven Years' War, Franklin once acted to better administer and defend colonial interests in western lands, this time by travelling to London to persuade Parliament to suspend the proprietor's charter and make a Pennsylvania a royal colony. Even as Franklin tried to meet with imperial officials in London, the French defeat was producing precisely the kind of frontier conflicts and unregulated land grab he feared. Settlers sponsored by land companies spread westward and faced off with Indian inhabitants. In the summer of 1763, an alliance of Indian communities drawn from the Great Lakes region and the Illinois and Ohio Country raided the frontiers of Virginia and Pennsylvania killing more than two thousand colonists. The hostilities confirmed the need for orderly expansion westward and prompted parliament to introduce the 1763 Proclamation Act, forbidding whites from taking over Indian land until it had been formally ceded by treaties with England.

But if anything struggles over land and the relationship between frontier settlers and established and eastern seaboard governing communities worsened, threatening elite interests and internal coherence across the colonies. In December 1763, a vigilante gang of some fifty Scots-Irishmen from the town of Paxton on the Susquehanna River in western Pennsylvania attacked local Conestoga Indians whom they suspected of providing aid to French and Indian enemies. This was widely suspected as a false justification, not least because the Conestoga had lived peacefully with the settlers for decades. The gang murdered and mutilated six Indians, before the authorities placed seventeen others in protective custody in Lancaster. Two weeks later the vigilantes broke into the town jail and murdered and scalped six adults and eight children before gathering 200 or so supporters and marching on Philadelphia to demand greater representation in the assembly and a coordinated attack on Indians in the west. Further north, in the territory known as the New Hampshire Grants, lying between the Connecticut River and Lake Champlain, settlers ignored established legal land titles and set up communities along the frontier. By 1770, one group, the Green Mountain Boys, comprising several hundred men led by the brothers Ethan and Ira Allen had assumed control in what was officially a part of the province of New York. When New York authorities went to arrest those they considered squatters, their officers and supporters were beaten up and sent packing. In North Carolina, indebted farmers protested against corrupt politicians and refused to pay debts owed to wealthy merchant creditors, often recently arrived from eastern cities. In South Carolina, plantation masters and farmers established a vigilante force to tackle frontier banditry and Indian hostilities. Although they paid taxes to the government in Charleston these western residents were under represented in the provincial assembly. Receiving little or no support, they organised their own local government and even drew up a constitution addressing local concerned that were ultimately recognised by the government on the coast.

For twenty years and more following the defeat of the French in the Seven Years' War, the question of the disposition of lands and western settlement challenged imperial overseers and governing American elites' conception of order and authority. Determined to prevent what threatened to become a cycle of costly wars it could now ill-afford, Britain attempted to divide the Indians from the settlers. But a line was no sooner drawn than it was crossed, as farming families and opportunistic speculators flooded west. The Indians defended their homes and lifeways, but the European's hunger for land was insatiable. As attacks, atrocities, and bloodshed grew, large swathes of the west fell into chaos. In the absence of civil society and effective government, settlers managed as best they could, drawing on by then long-standing claims concerning occupancy, improvement, and cultivation to justify a populist and racial sovereignty. To transform these settler claims and ad hoc communities into orderly and enduring societies, westerners would require assistance in overcoming the Indians, who defended their lands, often supported by European allies. However, the collapse of the British colonial empire in the east meant that westerners would have to wait a further two decades for the support they needed. When assistance came, it was provided by a newly established American republic.

Chapter summary

This chapter considered the development of the British American colonies as provincial societies, meaning distinctive communities that nevertheless saw themselves as variations on metropolitan English practices and culture. A defining distinction of colonial society was the reliance on a slave labour force which grew dramatically in the eighteenth century, ensuring increased plantation production and colonial prosperity while heightening enslavers' fears of internal rebellion. A mid-century suspected slave conspiracy in New York raised the possibility of a coalition of discontent amongst the lower classes, free and enslaved. New World economic growth stimulated British and colonial commerce and consumption. The prosperity and connectivity fostered by the Atlantic trade and improved communications encouraged middling colonial consumers to think of themselves as Englishmen and women abroad. Prosperity also encouraged immigration and the spread of European settlement westward leading to geopolitical with Native Americans and French competitors. In the 1750s, these various regional contests coalesced in a series of colonial clashes that set the stage for the Seven Years' War – a global conflict which had enormous consequences for American and world history. In the next chapter we shall consider how in a little over a decade the American colonists were transformed from proud and loyal subjects of the British empire into its most ardent critics and rebels determined to establish a new nation, the United States of America.

Discussion questions

- Were the eighteenth-century British American colonies a land of opportunity?
- How did the Native Americans maintain and lose their power in the eighteenth century and what were the decisive factors and turning points?

- How important were notions of class and discontent concerning inequality in eighteenth-century colonial society?
- What did deference mean and how did it influence colonial political culture?
- Why were the colonists loyal to the empire in the decades up to the Seven Years' War?
- What colonial divisions and conflicts can you see that had the potential to weaken colonial loyalties following the 1763 French defeat?

Further reading

Axtell, James. *The Indians' New South: Cultural Change in the Colonial Southeast* (Baton Rouge, 1997). Classic study of encounter between Indians and Europeans in the colonial south east across three centuries.

Burnard, Trevor. "The British Atlantic World," in Jack P. Greene and Philip D. Morgan, eds., *Atlantic History: A Critical Appraisal* (New York, 2009), 111–136. Excellent survey of findings of scholars who have adopted an Atlantic perspective on colonial America.

Dowd, Gregory. *War Under Heaven: Pontiac, the Indian Nations, and the British Empire* (Baltimore, MD, 2002).

DuVal, Kathleen. *The Native Ground: Indians and Colonists in Heart of the Continent* (Philadelphia, 2006).

Griffin, Patrick. *American Leviathan: Empire, Nation, and Revolutionary Frontier* (New York, 2007). Stirring and evocative narrative describing the importance of the west in the emergence of the new nation.

Hoffer, Charles Peter. *Cry Liberty. The Great Stono River Slave Rebellion of 1739* (New York, 2010). Fascinating narrative of the colonial era's major slave revolt.

Humphrey, Thomas J. *Land and Liberty: Hudson Valley Riots in the Age of Revolution* (New York, 2004). Study of background and course of Hudson Valley land riots.

Kars, Marjoleine. *Breaking Loose Together: The Regulator Rebellion in Pre-Revolutionary North Carolina* (Chapel Hill, 2002). Study of the popular protests in North Carolina.

Lepore, Jill. *New York Burning: Liberty, Slavery, and Conspiracy in Eighteenth-Century Manhattan* (New York, 2005). Examines the background and causes for New York's 1741 slave conspiracy.

Linebaugh, Peter, and Marcus Rediker. *The Many-Headed Hydra: Sailors, Slaves, Commoners, and the Hidden History of the Revolutionary Atlantic* (Boston, 2000). Study of the lower and labouring sorts in the seventeenth- and eighteenth-century colonies.

Pearsall, Sarah M. S. *Atlantic Families: Lives and Letters in the Later Eighteenth Century* (Oxford, 2008). The culture of letter writing and family feelings in the revolutionary era.

Pettigrew, Will. *Freedom's Debt: Politics and the Escalation of Britain's Transatlantic Slave Trade, 1672–1752* (Chapel Hill, 2013). Recent study of the politics surrounding the Royal Africa Company and the expansion of Britain's role in the slave trade.

Richter, Daniel. *Facing East From Indian Country A Native History of Early America* (Cambridge, MA, 2001). Adopts the perspective of Native Americans on the history of the European arrival and encounter.

Rockman, Seth. *Scraping By: Wage Labor, Slavery, and Survival in Early Baltimore* (Baltimore, MD, 2009). Prize winning study of working-class life and labour in late eighteenth- and early nineteenth-century Baltimore.

Rushforth, Brett. *Bonds of Alliance Indigenous and Atlantic Slaveries in New France* (Chapel Hill, 2012). Important study of European and Indian relations and the enslavement of indigenous peoples.

Smith, Billy G. *"The Lower Sort": Philadelphia's Laboring People, 1750–1800* (Ithaca, 1994). Classic study of working class life in eighteenth-century Philadelphia.

White, Richard. *The Middle Ground Indians, Empires, and Republics in the Great Lakes Region, 1650–1815* (New York, 1992). Groundbreaking study of European-Indian encounter in the Great Lakes region.
Williams, Eric. *Capitalism and Slavery*. Classic study connecting slavery and abolition to the English empire and industrialization.
Yirush, Craig. *Settlers, Liberty, and Empire: The Roots of Early American Political Theory, 1675–1775* (New York, 2011). Study of the local, rather than European, origins of colonial American political theory.

3 The revolution that made a republic

Timeline

1763, February	Treaty of Paris, ending the Seven Years' War (1756–63), also known as the French and Indian War (1753–63) in North America
1763, October	Proclamation Act, prohibited all settlement west of the Appalachian Mountains without guarantees of security from local Native American nations
1764, April	the Sugar Act, the first attempt to finance the defence of the colonies by the British government
1765, March	the Stamp Act, required all legal documents, newspapers, and pamphlets required to use watermarked, or "stamped" paper on which a levy was placed
1765, October	the Stamp Act Congress, representatives from 9 of the 13 colonies declare the Stamp Act unconstitutional
1766, March	a Declaratory Act, repeals the Stamp Act, but affirms parliament's right to tax colonies
1767, June	the Townshend Revenue Act, levies duties on tea, glass, lead, paper, and paint to help pay for the administration of the colonies
1768, October	British troops arrive in Boston intent on quelling political unrest
1770, March	the Boston Massacre, following clashes between street crowds and British soldiers, kills five civilians; the Townshend Revenue Act is repealed
1773, May	the Tea Act, keeps the tax on tea leading angry Bostonians "disguised" as Mohawk Indians to ditch £9,000 of tea into the harbor
1774, May to June	the Intolerable Acts, strip Massachusetts of self-government and judicial independence as punishment for the Tea Party; the colonies responded with a general boycott of British goods
1774, September	a Continental Congress meets to organise opposition to the Intolerable Acts
1775, April	Battles of Lexington and Concord are the first engagements of the Revolutionary War between British troops and the

	Minutemen, who had been warned of the attack by a Boston silversmith, Paul Revere
1775, June	the Continental Congress appoints George Washington commander-in-chief of Continental Army and issues $2 million in bills of credit to fund the army; early engagements at Bunker Hill
1776, January	Thomas Paine's *Common Sense* is published anonymously in Philadelphia
1776, May	the French begin providing covert aid to the Americans
1776, 4 July	Continental Congress issues the Declaration of Independence
1778, February	France recognises US Independence
1781, March	Ratification of the Articles of Confederation
1781, October	Surrender of British forces under Cornwallis at Yorktown
1775–76	Virginia and Maryland farmers band together to raid the plantations of those suspected of hoarding supplies of salt
1778	Connecticut militia brigade mutiny in protest at their payment in depreciating paper currency
1780	Pennsylvania introduces gradual emancipation
1781	British under Cornwallis surrender at Yorktown
1782	Genevan Revolution
1787	Dutch Patriot movement struggles
1787–89	Belgian Revolution and French Revolution
1791–1804	Haitian Revolution
1798	Wolfe Tone Rebellion in Ireland
1800	Freetown Revolution

Topics covered

- The meaning of revolution
- English imperial reforms and patriot reactions
- Fighting the war and achieving independence
- Consequences of the Revolution
- The Revolution in its wider context

Introduction

Chapter 3 opens with a discussion of the meaning of "revolution" in the era of the American War for Independence and other, contemporary insurgencies – in particular France and Haiti. Thereafter the chapter considers the background to the breakdown in imperial relations following the 1763 Peace of Paris and London's determination to impose austerity on its American colonies. We consider the challenges facing the British after their victory over the French and their impatience with colonial resistance to the reforms and taxes necessary to defend the empire. We examine the development of colonial protests into a resistance movement during the Stamp Act Crisis, the emergence of different ideological view points, and the revolutionary process that led to the Declaration of Independence. After briefly surveying the war, noting its consequences for Indians, the enslaved, and women, we trace the development of divisions within the patriots' ranks. The chapter closes by placing the Revolution in its wider context, reflecting on the fate of the greater British empire and the spread of radical ideas around Europe and the Atlantic World. It is particularly concerned with the way in which the Haitian Revolution challenged what seems to us today the incongruous co-existence of slavery and republican liberty – a contradiction which the American patriots, in the main, easily ignored.

The meaning of revolution

The revolution which gave birth to the United States has long figured in arguments concerning American national character. An annual holiday on July 4th celebrates the Declaration of Independence and the armed struggle that established the republic. Historians continue to debate the American Revolution's radical and conservative character, and the contributions made by different individuals and groups. Some celebrate the leadership and vision of the Founding Fathers: a group of powerful and, mostly, wealthy men who signed the Declaration of Independence in 1776 and gathered in Philadelphia in 1787 to draw up the Constitution of the new United States. It is worth remembering that the Founders also bitterly disagreed on topics ranging from the structure and powers of the new government to which of them deserved to be remembered as the most important. Other commentators, at the time and since, have emphasised the role of ordinary men and women in the insurgency: the anonymous tens of thousands who resourced the struggle and fought the battles.

In the late nineteenth century the Revolution was remembered as an epic and more or less united exertion for liberty and self-determination. This was a version of the story told by gentleman scholars for whom national character was the driver rather than the product of historical change. In contrast, one of the earliest published accounts, David Ramsay's *History of the American Revolution* (1789), lauded the efforts of the "self-made and industrious" patriots, while also noting how quickly revolutionary idealism gave way to self-interest and divisions. For Ramsay the Revolution was a far from a united struggle for independence and the Americans' victory presented as many challenges as it resolved; not least how to establish a new federation of united states against a backdrop of internal disorder and external threats.

Ramsay's mixed assessment of the prevailing divisions during the struggle for independence reflected, at least in part, how he understood the meaning of revolution in his own time. Today we give revolutions singular titles – such as the Russian Revolution or the Chinese Revolution – and we think of them as root-and-branch transformations driven by historical actors; revolutions often lead to violence and chaos, but they mostly begin with understandable grievances and pursue admirable ambitions. In contrast, a century or so before Ramsay wrote, the political philosopher, John Locke, had spoken of revolutions in the plural and as uncontrolled tumult, for example when he described the disorders surrounding James II's 1688–89 flight from the English throne. This remained the conventional meaning for decades thereafter: when eighteenth-century authors discussed revolutions they associated them with words such as confusion, disruption, and upheaval. For Ramsay's generation, then, revolutions were unanticipated and feared; they were disorders that were experienced, rather than imagined and still less deliberately undertaken.

Over the 1760s and early 70s American patriots came to agree, more or less, that resistance to British administration was legitimate; they also managed to remain sufficiently united to put up significant armed struggle. However, as the divisions within the patriots' ranks soon demonstrated, this idealism and resistance was never

Engraved by J.B. Longacre from a drawing by C. Fraser after a painting by C. W. Peale.

DAVID RAMSAY, M.D.

Figure 3.1 David Ramsay, 1749–1815, was an American physician from Charleston, South Carolina, who served in the Revolutionary War and as a delegate to the Continental Congress.

Source: Courtesy of age fotostock/Alamy

sufficient to serve as a foundation upon which to establish a new nation. Equally importantly, while eighteenth-century revolutions were infrequent and unpredictable affairs, domestic and international wars were a routine and systemic feature of colonial life. Unsurprisingly, many Americans, even amongst the patriots, found it difficult to imagine the conflict of the 1770s outside their reality of these earlier and recurrent hostilities; many feared that even if they could successfully end British rule, their security and chances for prosperity outside the empire were bleak. The best that the most hoped for was that, whatever form of state did develop out of the American Revolution, it would some-day resemble the European powers which had dominated the continent's history over the preceding 200 years. Thus from early on revolutionary leaders endeavoured to establish internal and international treaties and to have the American republic recognised as a nation in its own right. Few, apart from the most idealistic, believed it would be possible or even desirable to establish a wholly new kind of society; a social and political order based on long-imagined but mostly untested principles of republican equality and democracy.

Like most upheavals, America's revolution contained radical and conservative elements. The former were most evident in the still celebrated declarations on behalf of liberty and equality, and the championing of the inalienable rights of free subjects to a government that depended on their consent. The latter was just as prominent, although less often memorialised, in the failure to extend these glittering Enlightenment principles and precious entitlements to the 250,000 enslaved African American men, women, and children who were held as property in early national America. Scholars have long puzzled over how the Revolution could produce political debates with such compelling arguments against the abstract idea slavery, while leaving the institution and those who endured its foul practices almost wholly undisturbed. The inconvenient truth is that most of America's revolutionaries compromised easily and quickly on the status of slavery in their free republic: either their racism and developing white supremacist prejudices allowed them to see little contradiction between their liberty and the conditions of the enslaved; or they believed that confronting the issue imperiled badly needed republican unity. What was compromised in North America, however, was achieved in the Caribbean: in 1800 the Haitian Revolution – inspired by the same rhetoric and politics of liberty in the face of domineering imperialism that prompted the American and French revolutions – established a republic of former slaves. The Haitian Revolution ensured that the controversy over the status and rights of those taken from African and forced to work on New World plantations could not be wholly and quietly compromised and sidelined. And so it proved to be: four score and seven years later the contradictions and antagonisms thrown up by the operation of slavery in a free republic broke the union and very nearly destroyed the nation.

Revolutionary beginnings

The story of what became known as the American Revolution developed out of the social and economic disruptions of the decade or so following the end of the French and Indian War (1754–63). There are many places one could begin to tell this story. One place is the home of Jacob Hite, a well-to-do tobacco planter, and one of the wealthiest men in Berkeley County, Virginia. Hite was the son of a successful land speculator, and had served as a sheriff and justice of the peace; his son had risen even higher and become a member of the Virginia House of Burgesses. In the late 1760s, Hite and his business partners put together a deal to settle a large tract of Cherokee land in South Carolina. In London, imperial and court officials feared that Hite's investment risked angering local Cherokee leaders, upon whom they relied for a defensive alliance against other Native American communities. London struck down the deal. In the early 1770s, the price of Virginia tobacco and thus the value of Hite's crop slumped due to over-production. Without the Cherokee land deal Hite was left unable to pay his debts to James Hunter, a Scottish merchant. Hunter was under pressure to satisfy his own creditors and so instructed the Berkeley County sheriff, Adam Stephen, to seize Hite's goods for sale. Stephen duly removed 15 of Hite's slaves and 21 horses, bringing them to the county jail for auction. Hite had to think fast. He organised a gang of family and friends who overpowered the sheriff and his men and retrieved the slaves and horses. Sheriff Stephen got up a posse to go after Hite, who persuaded his enslaved workers to join him in fighting the authorities or face having their families broken up and sold to pay his debts. Hite fled to the Cherokee land in South Carolina. No long after, the Virginian's closed their courts, in part to protest what they considered parliament's assault on their liberty, but also to prevent any other distant creditors taking out actions local, elite debtors in the manner that had befallen Jacob Hite.

Jacob Hite's story of failing economic fortunes and legal misadventures includes many of the elements that prefaced the drift to disunion and rebellion in the late 1760s and 1770s. The crippling effects of the financial crisis that followed the massive sovereign spending of the Seven Years' War (1756–63). The consequent credit crunch that drove creditors like Hunter to insist on payment from former business partners such as Hite. In circumstances replicated across the colonies, debtors from within the colonial gentry considered this insistence on payment during difficult times a breach of faith by those whom many had come to think of as personal friends. Spiraling imperial debts also intensified a long-debated parliamentary programme of colonial reforms and new taxes. One prominent measure prevented the colonists from seizing lands in the west, prompting Amerindians to look to London as allies in their struggle to retain control of their homelands. The London-imposed austerity and restrictions on land speculation were particularly galling to the colonists, who considered investment and expansion as the surest way to strengthen their own communities and the empire at large; given their recent efforts in defeating the French, the colonists also considered the western lands their rightful reward.

In previous decades, families such as the Hites were the backbone of an imperial administration overseen by a handful of English-appointed local officials. As the new taxes and reforms bit into the colonists' fortunes and stirred up protests, some came to consider London's seizure of property and seeming readiness to deny long-standing freedoms as not only ill-advised but potentially menacing. The Americans knew well how absentee English landlords maintained their subjects in subservience on their Irish lands and farms, or plantations as they were also sometimes called; the colonists were also more familiar than most with what it meant to live as a servile and abject slave. As relations between London and the colonies worsened, some feared, or at least talked up, a plot at the upper reaches of the English ministry to deprive Americans of what they had come to regard as their natural and inalienable rights. In order to defend themselves from this hellish conspiracy, the colonists were forced to countenance unpalatable choices and adopt previously unthinkable tactics to resistance imperial rule. Thus Hite's decision to arm his slaves, contrary to long-standing fears of the planter class concerning the loyalty of their enslaved workmen, offering those who lived as bondsmen and women an opportunity to radically transform their lives.

In 1760, King George III ascended to the throne, ending three decades of Whig rule and returning the Tories to power. The king and his supporters in parliament contemplated a crippling national debt, estimated at £120 million or 150 per cent of annual gross domestic product. From the English perspective the debt was the result of an imperial conflict that had raged on battlefields from Senegal to central Europe and from the Bay of Bengal in India to the Ohio Valley in North America. In 1762–63, Lord Bute, the king's choice for prime minster, was busy negotiating the end of the war and drawing up the Treaty of Paris. In America, tensions between Pontiac and the colonists threatened a renewed conflict, persuading Bute to maintain a peace-time army of 10,000 British troops.

Early in 1763 Lord Bute fell from favour and was replaced by George Grenville, a stalwart member of a group of parliamentarians and imperial bureaucrats who had long favoured greater centralisation in imperial administration. Grenville and his allies put together a package of reforms that aimed to lower the debt by cutting spending and extracting increased revenue from the colonies. To Grenville, the Americans were no different from any other British subjects and enjoyed their rights and liberties under the sovereignty of the king and parliament. The colonies had prospered in the empire and paid much lower taxes than their English peers; it was only reasonable that they should now contribute to the maintenance of empire upon which their commercial successes depended. Grenville's reforms also indicated Britain's desire to rethink their land-based territorial alliances in favour of a "blue water" strategy focused on control of the seas and imperial trade. The reforms directed at the American colonies were thus part of a wider rationalisation of the empire. If parliament allowed the Americans colonists to deny its authority, similar protests might follow in Ireland, Jamaica, or Bengal. The need to pay down the national debt, and the temptation of increased colonial revenues, made coercive American legislation legitimate and popular in Britain.

Pontiac's rebellion

Historians have long acknowledged the importance of the brutal Native American attacks on settlers intruding on Indian lands in the wake of the 1763 Peace of Paris. The war has usually been named for the prominent Odawa leader, Pontiac, who some believed masterminded the attacks. However, research indicates that he was just one figure in a much more complex and powerful alliance system led by the Anishinaabeg people from a region in the north west between Lake Huron and Lake Michigan. Combined royal and colonial forces responded with savage counter attacks: in what is perhaps one of the best remembered incidents of the war, British officers at Fort Pitt distributed blankets they suspected were infected with small pox amongst Native Americans laying siege. In many respects what we know as Pontiac's War (1763–66) would be better termed the First Anglo-Indian War, which was followed shortly thereafter by a Second Anglo-Indian War – also known as the American Revolution.

In October 1763, a Royal Proclamation laid out plans to integrate newly acquired French lands in North America, and dampen colonial tensions with Indians by forbidding unauthorised settlement west of the Appalachian Mountains. This directly obstructed access to lands the colonists believed theirs by right, following the victory over the French. The following year the Sugar, or Revenue, Act took on the widespread

Figure 3.2 The First Anglo-Indian War, 1763–66.

smuggling of molasses in New England by cutting the duty but stiffening payment enforcement; it also introduced new taxes on coffee, indigo, silks. Henceforth smugglers would be tried by vice-admiralty courts rather than local juries, who had often turned a blind eye to local breaches of the customs regulations. A new Currency Act restricted the colonial practice of producing their own paper currency, long vital to maintaining local trade. The ban on paper money intensified the credit crunch brought on by the post-war recession. In coastal towns artisan families were thrown out of work and markets for farmers' harvests collapsed, prompting widespread protest.

Colonial leaders responded coolly to the new measures: land speculators, such as George Washington, with interests in the Ohio Valley considered the Proclamation Act a temporary measure to calm Amerindian relations; some even regarded the Act as a salutary measure which prevented a chaotic land grab by ordinary settlers and squatters. The other imperial reforms had a limited effect: wily colonial merchants evaded the customs officers and relied on substitute paper instruments, such as promissory notes and bills of exchange. The Sugar Act was more disturbing: it appeared to many to move beyond the aim of the long-established Navigation Acts to regulate trade, and towards the practice of raising of revenue by taxing commodities and household goods which many middle-class Americans now coveted for their genteel status. Some worried that if they accepted the principle of internal taxation implied by the Sugar Act, without the approval of the assembly, it would set a dangerous precedent for the future.

In 1765, the first wave of English reforms culminated with the introduction of the Stamp Act, a measure designed to raise revenue by taxing all printed materials in the colonies. Henceforth anyone who bought a newspaper or pamphlet, made a will, transferred land or agreed a contract, purchased any paper document from playing cards to a liquor license, or accepted a government appointment or borrowed money using legal documents would have to pay a tax payable in specie money or coin. Those who refused, or could not pay, would be tried in English Vice Admiralty courts without juries and face stiff penalties. The Stamp Act introduced a new and directly levied tax, again raising the constitutional question that would be debated over the ensuing ten years: the colonists maintained that they contributed to the empire by paying external taxes, such as customs duties on their imports and trade; all other colonial taxes, and especially internal taxes, they argued, had to be agreed through their local representatives. This was a principle the colonists held dear, seeing it as a symbolic guarantee of their status and liberty as freeborn English subjects. The Stamp Act ran against this principle and, as James Otis Jr. of Boston declared, this "One single Act of Parliament . . . has set people a thinking in six months, more than they had done in their whole lives."

Parliament never recognised the colonists' distinction between external and internal taxes and believed the new taxes fair and proportionate given the empire's needs: as Grenville assured the House of Commons in March 1764, "we have expended much in America. Let us now avail ourselves of the fruits of that expense." Moreover, Britain's turn to austerity at home and abroad was characteristic of a general contemporary shift in European state an imperial policy in response to the widespread problem of sovereign debt. As far as parliament was concerned the protests in Boston and New York were of no more account than the disturbances by London silk workers against imported foreign silks and similar disorderly protests against economies and reforms introduced by Spanish and French governments in their colonial possessions from Quito in Ecuador to the Caribbean island of Saint Domingue, modern day Haiti.

From resistance to revolution

The colonists' resistance to the Stamp Act in the eastern coastal towns generated constitutional arguments and popular protests that fanned the flames of resistance, producing radical leaders and a heightened political consciousness of colonial rights. It was not merely a question of economic hardship. Indeed, by taxing the urban merchants and lawyers, the Stamp Act arguably hit hardest those who could most afford to pay, leaving most colonists, who lived on inland farms, alone. However, more than the level and target of the tax, the Stamp Act raised the question of parliament's authority and the colonists' status in America and the empire. Provincial assemblies debated the measures and passed resolutions affirming the Americans' right to tax themselves and protesting measures they denounced as unconstitutional.

In October 1765, nine colonies sent delegates to a Stamp Act Congress in New York City; it was the largest intercolonial gathering since the Albany Conference 11 years earlier. The congress produced a "Declaration of Rights and Grievances," offering all "all due subordination" to the King and Parliament, but maintaining the American's right to tax themselves, not least because they were unrepresented in parliament. The colonists made various constitutional arguments. Some focused on the principle of consent to taxation and trial by jury. They invoked John Locke and natural law theories in which legitimate government was founded on an implied contract between the governing and the governed. Others relied on older, more conservative arguments, declaring their allegiance to King and challenging parliament's reforms as usurpations of his majesty's sovereign authority. Some feared the reforms indicated a worrying and widespread clamp down on political liberties: in Virginia, Patrick Henry declared the Stamp Act displayed "a manifest tendency to destroy British as well as American freedom." For others discontent focused on the turn away from colonial investment and towards austerity. Overall, the Stamp Act transformed inchoate protests against what had been perceived as ill-advised reforms into a resistance movement ready to defy what looked like an increasingly threatening change in imperial leadership.

Ideological origins

Historians have long debated the ideological background to the American Revolution, meaning the intellectual and political philosophies that animated the patriots' resistance. Was it a Lockean, liberal rebellion in defence of natural and individual rights to liberty and property? Or was it a republican revolution, inspired by paranoid fears of conspiracy within the English ministry to deny Americans their rights as freeborn Englishmen? Other influential ideological strands include the colonists' zealous commitment to Protestantism, the common law, and even the monarchy – which many Americans suspected had been undermined and corrupted by the expansion of parliamentary power.

The impact of these constitutional arguments and colonial protests drew force from popular disturbances that took the American's resistance on to the streets, especially in port cities such as Boston, New York, and Philadelphia. Imperial officials in London received reports of mobs rampaging through colonial towns, confirming their already dim view of rowdy American challenges to reasonable reforms. However, this was a misperception. The street protests were mostly well-organised and led by middling merchants and artisans. These patriot leaders were supported by labouring men and women who mobilised to defend what they considered their traditional rights and liberties under the English constitution, meaning the combination of local government institutions and courts and past practices that were considered foundational to the common good. In happier times, ordinary and middling colonial subjects – farmers, carpenters, shopkeepers, housekeepers, wheelwrights, seamstresses, labourers, coopers, and the like – had deferred to elite leadership. Some middling folk were prominent in their communities as known and trusted figures who settled neighbourhood disagreements; others held minor municipal office or served as public officials or jurymen. During times of public concern and economic distress, they were able to organise and join crowds who protested unpopular measures, such as the high prices charged for bread, which threatened the general good and "common consent."

In 1765, these crowds organised to prevent the distribution of stamps and the collection of the tax, giving rise to a semi-formal association, the Sons of Liberty, who thereafter policed the streets and enforced consumer boycotts in the interest what became known as the "Common Cause" of liberty. This required merchants and

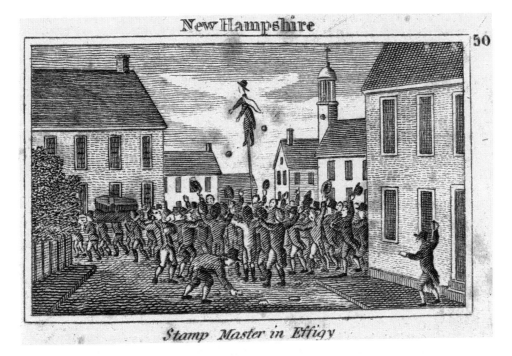

Figure 3.3 A crowd of patriots hang a stamp agent in effigy in this 1829 engraving celebrating the 1765 anti-Stamp Act protests in New Hampshire.

Source: Courtesy of Granger Historical Picture Archive/Alamy

customers to cooperate in foregoing imported household goods. In New York City, 200 merchants agreed to buy nothing from England until the Stamp Act was repealed. In Boston, protestors tore down the house of the lieutenant governor, Thomas Hutchinson, and forced the tax collector, his brother-in-law Andrew Oliver, to resign. The protests worked. In January 1766, a group of London merchants wrote to Parliament complaining they had been "reduced to the necessity of pending ruin" by the boycotts. Support for Grenville's tough stance ebbed and parliament repealed the Stamp Act.

The colonists celebrated the repeal as proof of the continued vigor and justice of English and imperial liberties. However, in London a new administration, headed by William Pitt, asserted its "full power and authority to make laws . . . to bind the colonies and people of America . . . in all cases whatsoever." Britain still needed a revenue from the colonies and introduced new duties on imported goods such as paper, paint, glass and tea. Implicitly conceding the colonists' constitutional arguments regarding internal taxes, imperial officials expected payment of what they considered straight forward duties on trade. Accordingly, they again strengthened enforcement procedures: a new American Board of Customs Commissioners supported by vice-admiralty courts, so without juries, would prosecute smugglers and fund itself from fines levied. The colonists greeted the measures with dismay. The Pennsylvanian lawyer and politician, John Dickinson, wrote that while it was reasonable for the colonists to pay general commercial duties the introduction of "special duties imposed on . . . us only, with intention to raise a revenue" were "as much taxes upon us, as those imposed by the Stamp Act."

The colonists relaunched their nonimportation and boycott campaigns. Protestors circulated lists with the names of those who had promised not to buy British goods, and pressed those who continued to do so. Female stewardship of household provisioning and domestic budgets made women particularly important to the resistance: women joined demonstrations against royal authority and high prices, and they formed spinning clubs to produce homespun cloth as an alternative to imported fabrics. Non-importation and non-consumption forged American unity and reorientated their cultural ties to Britain: whereas previously consumption of imported goods and luxuries had symbolised the benefits of empire and what the colonists shared with the mother country, their rejection of these same commodities now became markers of virtue and patriotism. The patriots formed committees of correspondence to keep each other informed of the resistance efforts elsewhere. Newspapers reprinted stories of resistance, giving the dispersed and isolated patriots a sense of their participation in a broader political movement.

In March 1770, parliament agreed a partial repeal of the Townshend Acts, but retained the three pence per pound duty on tea shipped to America via Britain. The tea tax was a symbol of parliament's right to tax its colonies; it also contributed to the costs of imperial administration. On the day news of the repeal the Townshend Duties reached Boston, a snowball fight between patriots and English redcoats outside the Customs' House turned ugly. The soldiers opened fire, killing five Bostonians. Crispus Attucks, a free man or possibly a slave of Wampanoag and African descent, was the first to fall. A published engraving of the incident showed a line of redcoats being ordered to fire upon defenceless citizens by an officer brandishing his sword. This image of the "Boston Massacre" spread in newspapers and pamphlets around the colonies. For a time tensions subsided, as economic fortunes improved and colonial merchants began to reimport tea. In 1773, however, Lord North decided to allow the East India Company to ship is tea direct to America, effectively duty-free. However, the colonists were still required to pay the tax. In Boston, a group of protesters boarded the ships and dumped 300 chests of tea valued at £10,000 into the harbor. The protestors dressed as Mohawks, possibly laying claim to the idea of Native Americans as "noble savages." Or perhaps they were countering the threat posed by the East India Company tea with a masquerade of resistance by American "Indians." Either way the destruction of the tea brought a furious response from North. In March 1774, he introduced the Coercive Acts: these measures closed the port at Boston harbor until the inhabitants paid for the tea, suspended the provincial government, and compelled Bostonians to provision the troops in their homes. Parliament followed up with Quebec Act, which reorganised the government of Canada by creating a non-representative colonial administration. It also extended toleration to the Roman Catholics who lived in the former French colony. In New England, democratic republicans and Protestants looked on in horror as the London authorities created an authoritarian government and supported the Catholic Church in North America.

North's Coercive Acts were a disastrous miscalculation: rather than intimidating and isolating Boston, they galvanised the patriot movement. Committees of correspondence extended patriot communications, across Massachusetts, then New England and then other colonies, who came to Boston's aid. Patriots assumed control of the militias and established provincial assemblies and courts, staffing them with their own appointees and bypassing the imperial administration. On 5 September 1774, a first Continental Congress met at Philadelphia attended by 55 delegates from 12 colonies. Preparing to leave for Pennsylvania, the Virginia delegate, George Washington, wrote to a friend describing the seriousness of the situation: "the crisis is arrived when we must assert our rights, or submit to every imposition that can be heaped upon us [making] us as tame and abject slaves, as the blacks we rule over with such arbitrary sway." The delegates rejected a plan for union overseen by parliament, along the lines of the 1754 Albany Plan. They heard radical resolutions from Massachusetts calling for economic sanctions and, if necessary, armed defence against the British. They adopted a Declaration of American Rights, which summarised arguments made over the preceding ten years and asserted the colonists' rights as English subjects to be taxed by their own elected representatives.

The delegates called for a "Continental Association" and blamed parliament for "the present unhappy situation of our affairs." They accused London of having plans "evidently calculated for enslaving these Colonies, and, with them, the British Empire." Once formed the Association called for boycotts and protests and recommended "that a committee be chosen in every county, city, and town . . . whose business it shall be attentively to observe the conduct of all persons touching this association." In London, the king declared the "New England colonies [to be] in a state of rebellion" and that "blows must decide whether they are to be subject to this country or independent." On 18 April 1775, a force of 700 British soldiers attempted to seize patriot weapons and supplies at Concord, Massachusetts. They were met and engaged by the local patriot militia on Lexington Green, leading to sporadic clashes throughout the day as the British made their way back to Boston. The revolutionary war had begun.

Achieving independence

A wider conflict was now inevitable, although most of the colonists were not active patriots and many remained loyal to the king. Allegiances are notoriously difficult to pin down during wartime: thousands shifted their loyalties depending on changing circumstances. In Queens County New York, admittedly a loyalist stronghold, estimates suggest that fewer than 12 per cent of the population were active patriots (27 per cent were firmly loyal, and 60 per cent neutral). Loyalists came from every colony and were estimated at one-third of the population throughout the Revolution. Predictably, many came from the ranks of imperial officials and wealthy merchants and landowners. These were conservative men of property who feared disorder amongst the lower classes if the established government was destroyed. They considered themselves no less supporters of American interests than the patriots. Many reasoned that it was foolhardy to turn away from the largest empire in the world a few short years after Americans had celebrated their membership and looked forward to a bright future. When patriots complained of British attacks on their rights and liberties, loyalists pointed to the self-appointed committees of vigilantes who roamed the streets, preventing trade, and stirring up mobs with outlandish ideas of a future society based on equality and democracy. In June 1775, the New York lawyer and loyalist, William Smith Jr., urged his patriot friends to reconsider their resistance and "ponder well upon the strange look of this tremendous roar." Even the future founding father, John Jay, described the street protests negatively as "unnatural convulsions."

Loyalism

For many years, the loyalists were largely disregarded in celebratory and nationalistic histories of the American Revolution: their presence was minimised or they were caricatured as upper class reactionaries and monarchists out of touch with liberal republicanism. In fact, the majority of loyalists were far from all propertied conservatives: they came from all walks life and their chosen affiliation depended on regional, racial, religious, and economic contexts and considerations. In North Carolina, back country poor and middling farmers chose loyalism in part because their wealthy planter neighbours and longtime antagonists were patriots. Many Native Americans chose the British side to challenge the rapacious spread of American settlement westward. The West Indies remained loyal to Britain, the planters relying on imperial military muscle for security and protection from external and internal threats: on the eve of the Revolution, Jamaica's white population of 12,000 or so kept more than 200,000 workers enslaved whom planters unsurprisingly feared would revolt. Recovering the loyalists' story emphasises the extent to which the war for political ideals was also a bitter, bloody, and often cruel civil conflict between family members and former neighbours and communities. At the war's end some 60,000 loyalists – whites, blacks, and Native Americans – and 15,000 enslaved people settled in Nova Scotia and New Brunswick, Quebec, the British Isles, and the Bahamas, East Florida, to Jamaica or to Central America, and Sierra Leone. This significant loyalist diaspora emboldened, and sometimes challenged, the greater British empire around the globe and was particularly significant in its influence over the future social and political character of Canada during a period of tremendous fluidity and change.

The outbreak of hostilities in Massachusetts prompted calls for a second Continental Congress in Philadelphia which thereafter assumed responsibility for the patriot cause. The delegates appointed George Washington, famous for his service under the British in the Seven Years' War, as head of the continental army. They also authorised the printing of colonial and continental paper money to provision the army and cover administrative costs. By the spring of 1775, thousands of patriots had established committees across the colonies: in Massachusetts patriots controlled, 160 towns, in Virginia they held 51 of 61 counties. New England militias pinned down the British in Boston. Patriot insurgents attacked supply lines and monitored loyalist movements and activities. Supported by a force from modern day Vermont, known as the Green Mountain Boys, the Americans seized Fort Ticonderoga in northern New York. Next they launched an ill-fated expedition to Canada, hoping to persuade French settlers to join the fight against the British. In Virginia, the royal governor, Lord Dunmore, raised a force of loyalists and issued a proclamation offering to free slaves who ran from patriot masters: by 1 December 1775 more than 300 runaways had joined Dunmore's Ethiopian Regiment and took to the field wearing tunics with "Liberty to Slaves" emblazoned on their chests; by the following summer, there were 800 more. As fighting spread across the colonies, congress assumed greater responsibilities, negotiating defensive treaties with Native Americans.

Even as royal authority collapsed, the Continental Congress petitioned the king, asking that he step in and rethink parliament's ill-considered reforms. George III refused to read the petition. Instead he recruited thousands of German mercenaries to send against his colonial subjects. In January 1776, an obscure English radical, Thomas Paine, who had come to Philadelphia a year or so earlier, published a hugely influential pamphlet, *Common Sense*. While many, maybe most, feared breaking with Britain and still hoped for a compromise, Paine made an impassioned and persuasive case for independence. He wrote in a plain and irreverent style that proved a smash hit. He denounced the institution of monarchy and advocated a radically republican and democratic government based on the representation of equal and consenting citizens. He was optimistic about the opportunities for American prosperity in the future. His pamphlet sold tens of thousands of copies and was read and reread out loud at town meeting and tavern gatherings across the colonies.

As all prospects of a reconciliation faded, it became imperative that the Continental Congress establish its formal independence. On 4 July 1776, a Declaration of Independence proclaimed the 13 colonies sovereign states to be part a new nation, the United States of America. The Declaration was brief at just over 1,300 words, but it has been the source of considerable interpretation and debate. It is perhaps best known for its ringing appeals to the Enlightenment principles of equality, representation, and government by consent: "we hold these truths to be self-evident, that all men are created equal," declared the preamble, and that they possess "unalienable Rights" to "Life, Liberty and the pursuit of Happiness" and a form of government "most likely to effect their Safety and Happiness." This statement of foundational principles was followed by a long list of the king's "abuses and usurpations" which reviewed events over the preceding decade. In a noteworthy reference to English favouring of Native Americans in the west and Dunmore's appeal to enslaved African Americans, the text also accused the king of encouraging attacks by "merciless Indian Savages" and of stirring "domestic insurrections."

The Declaration also looked to the future, advocating an interventionist state that would develop the American economy in the same way as provincial assemblies had earlier nurtured individual colonies. This had been the ambition of Franklin and others for the colonies within a greater British empire; now it became the patriots' vision for an independent American republic. Finally, the Declaration asserted the presence of a new power in the international system of states. The Americans knew they would need alliances if they were to have any prospect of defeating the British. They also needed to borrow money and have their own currency recognised against future revenues from taxes and the sale of lands. The Continental Congress had to be recognised as more than a possible transitory leadership of a short-lived colonial protest. The Declaration announced the establishment of this new American nation.

The war for independence lasted five years and was fought in two phases. National myths like to remember the British military as a vast and powerful force. In fact, owing to the scale of public debt and long-standing fears of standing armies, the army headquartered at New York under General Howe required the arrival of thousands of recently arrived German mercenaries to make up the impressive total of 32,000 men. Washington's continental troops, numbering roughly 19,000, suffered several early defeats, but made a daring escape to Pennsylvania and kept the Revolution alive. In 1777, the British planned to divide the rebellious New Englanders from the southern colonies by marching south from Canada and north from New York up the Hudson

River Valley. But Howe changed his mind and set out to take the patriot capital at Philadelphia, believing he had strong loyalist support and seeking a symbolic victory. However, the force in upstate New York blundered to defeat. This convinced the French, who were already covertly supplying the patriots with gunpowder and supplies, to enter the war on the American side. Franco-American trade and defensive treaties recognised the American state. This brought in the Spanish and Dutch, both of whom hoped for strategic gains from British defeat.

In an international order governed by alliances, Britain was now more alone than at any other time in her history. Realising they were losing the war, the British offered to agree American demands prior to 1776. The patriots refused to negotiate until Britain recognised American independence. Britain switched its strategy to the south, focusing on the commercially significant southern plantation colonies, which it also believed

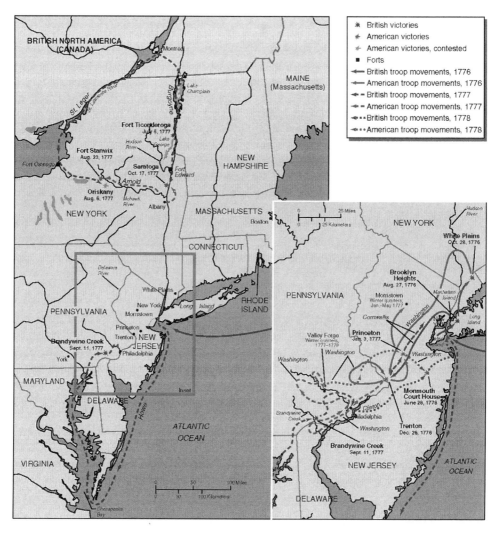

Figure 3.4 The Revolutionary War in the North, 1776–77.

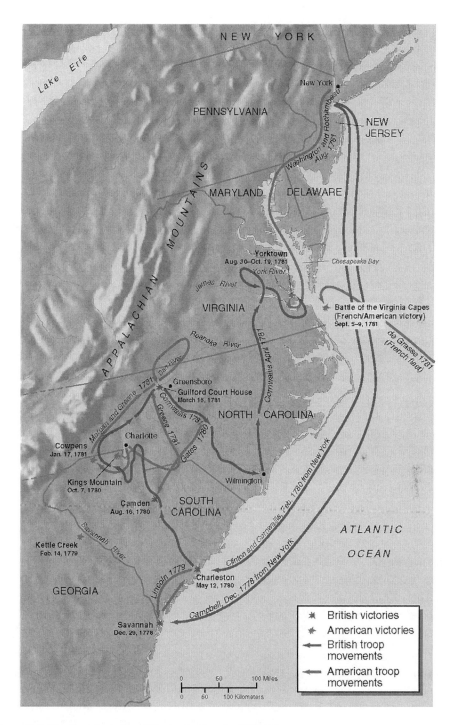

Figure 3.5 The Revolutionary War in the South, 1778–81.

were more loyal. Campaigns in Virginia, South Carolina, and Georgia captured major cities, but the redcoats lacked the manpower to retain control over large distances. When they withdrew, the patriots returned and punished loyalist neighbours. The contest in the south descended into a bloody and unwinnable civil war. In 1781, the British under Cornwallis at Yorktown, Virginia, faced Washington's much smaller continental army. However, when the French navy won control of the Chesapeake Bay they landed thousands of reinforcements: outnumbered and surrounded, with no prospect of relief, Cornwallis surrendered.

Revolutionary consequences

For Amerindians the British surrender meant a new and threatening continental balance of power. For decades regional Native American powers had played off contesting European adversaries against each other, providing friendship and support to those who promised the best terms. This had been the case, for example, in the long history of negotiations between the Iroquois, French, and English colonists in the northeast. At the outbreak of hostilities in 1776 there were approximately 200,000 Amerindians east of the Mississippi River living in as many as 85 nations, most of whom were happy to remain outside the revolutionary conflict. If forced to choose a side, only those living close to patriot neighbours generally chose to support the Americans; the majority favoured the British as the most likely continued source of trade goods and best hope for protection from the land-hungry settlers spreading westward.

The British benefitted greatly from having Amerindian allies: the Iroquois attacked patriots in New York and the Ohio Country, and Cherokee war parties harried rebellious colonists on the southern frontier. The patriots needed to win crucial victories, in the west at Cahokia (St Louis), where a force of American and French settlers led by George Rogers Clark took on local Tories and Indian allies; and in western Pennsylvania, where 4,000 continental soldiers defeated the Mohawk leader, Joseph Brant, and went on to destroy major Seneca and Cayuga villages, breaking the last vestiges of the power of the Iroquois Confederacy. When the British surrendered, however, they betrayed their Native allies. In the west Amerindian communities who considered themselves self-determining sovereign peoples, fought on against American settlers intent on taking their lands. In Paris, European political intrigues dominated the peace treaty negotiations and few regarded Amerindian rights. The British were eager to end the expensive global conflict and prevent the French from taking advantage of continued Anglo-American tensions. Although disgusted by his American subjects' ingratitude, George III agreed a quick and easy peace, ceding all the lands east of the Mississippi River and north of the Ohio River in what became known as the Northwest Territory. The American Congress wasted no time taking up its treaty rights: that autumn it sent out commissioners to inform Amerindians that by virtue of Britain's surrender, their lands now belonged to the new United States.

For some enslaved African Americans the Revolution brought opportunities, for others its consequences were distinctly mixed. The few hundred runaways who served in Lord Dunmore's Ethiopian Regiment were a handful of the estimated 30,000 to 100,000 slaves who took the chance to join whichever side offered the best chance of freedom. Many were drawn to the loyalist side, serving as soldiers as well as sailors and pilots in the British navy. When the fighting ended those who were able to convince the British authorities of their faithful service were allowed to settle as free men and women in Nova Scotia and London. Some travelled in the company of loyalists who left America with their slave property intact. Once settled these black loyalists in Canada and London became the target of discrimination and a campaign to establish a colony in Africa. Many more slaves ran away to join the patriot side, or were offered as substitutes for their masters to fill enlistment quotas. Militias in New Jersey and New Hampshire recruited slaves. The Connecticut, Rhode Island, and Massachusetts militias formed all-black regiments, including one led by Samuel Middleton, reputedly the only black commissioned officer in the continental army. The southern colonies were more reticent about arming their slaves. However, when Virginia was unable to meet its recruitment quota with freemen, despite offering volunteers bonuses and bounties, there was no choice but to send free blacks and slaves as substitutes serving in their masters' stead. This created an opportunity for slaves to run to patriot lines and declare themselves as free black volunteers; hard pressed recruiters, eager to fill muster rolls, could be relied upon not to question new arrivals too closely. Military necessity made the patriot army an integrated force. As many as 9,000 black soldiers served in the continental forces, side-by-side with whites and at every engagement from Bunker Hill to Valley Forge to the surrender at Yorktown.

Britain lost the war because it overestimated the loyalist presence in the colonies and underestimated the support for the patriot cause. At first sight, both seem like understandable mistakes. The 60,000 or so loyalists who quit the new American republic, indicate that British assumptions about the promise of loyalist support was not unrealistic. However, even in these kinds of numbers, loyalists comprised just 2 to 3 per cent of the colonial population, scattered across different communities and easily outnumbered by patriots. English forces far from home made themselves and their American supporters unpopular, when they requisitioned food and shelter from local communities. Across the war years the British army averaged 34,000 men, more than the population of most colonial towns, and, along with the 4,000 horses, requiring more than 70 tonnes of food supplies every day. The British also had to provide for the loyalist refugees, runaway slaves, and their wives and children who were drawn to their ranks. The patriot militias, in contrast, relied on local support and could melt away during lulls in the fighting.

It was not just loyalist weakness and British unpopularity that provided for American victory. The British also misjudged the potential for patriot unity, based on decades of experience of dealing with distinct and frequently competing colonial administrations. Throughout much of the eighteenth century it had been an article of British imperial faith that such was the competition between colonists over land and trade that no matter how strong an individual colony grew it was unlikely to ever join forces with its neighbours. Moreover, with the French and Spanish to the north and the south and the Amerindians at their backs, the colonies could be easily policed by a British naval force. In the political struggles of the 1760s and 70s, however, many patriots were inspired by sincere idealism and the future promised in the Declaration of Independence. Moreover, because of the long-standing experience of self-government, the transition from royal rule was surprisingly smooth. For decades colonial administrations had provided more or less representative institutions, for free white and male property holders, many of whom considered British reforms as part of a conspiracy to establish an authoritarian government in America.

There was no monolithic revolutionary ideology to which all subscribed. Patriot republicanism ranged from calls for radical and egalitarian democracy to the more conservative views of the propertied class who favoured elite and oligarchic government. However, the political language of rights and liberty – and key concepts relating to representation, virtue, equality and consent – was sufficiently malleable to allow for the coexistence of different views, at least in the early years of resistance. Patriots from diverse social classes offered their own version of sacrifice and republican integrity: the middling and poor could boycott English imports or sign on to serve in the militia; the wealthy could forego their profits as merchants and planters and contribute to the Continental Congress's coffers. Inspired by Thomas Paine's rallying cry to make the world anew, all could forego their immediate needs and desires and each give according to their means and abilities.

Part of the Revolution's radicalism lay in the opportunities it provided for previously constrained and subordinated groups to play a greater part in public life, although there were limits. As we have seen, women played a key role in the front line of consumer boycotts and street protests; a handful disguised themselves as men and joined the continental army. Others, such as the writer, Mercy Otis Warren, were instrumental in establishing early committees of correspondence and became notable as political commentators and propagandists. As ever, we know more about the lives of elite women, than we do about ordinary working women, still less African American and Amerindian women. Once the war began women took over the running of farms and businesses and continued political activities in support of the patriot cause. It is clear that women on all sides suffered cruel treatment at the hands of soldiers and militiamen, including the home invasions and sexual violence that so often accompany the brutality of war. These terror tactics were sufficiently common as to become disturbingly matter-of-fact. As one British officer in New York jovially recalled: "A girl cannot step into the bushes to pluck a rose without running the most imminent risk of being ravished . . . and of consequence we have the most entertaining courts-martial every day." During and after the war republican idealism celebrated women's familial and domestic roles. The notion of republican motherhood encouraged the education of women and invested domestic work with a dignity and public. This broke with older notions of sexual hierarchy and acknowledged women as rational subjects with a role to play in educating sons as future republican citizens, appearing to move towards the idea of the equality of the sexes. However, at the same time it reinforced the idea of a distinctive and domestic women's realm, away from the public world of men, preparing the way for nineteenth-century idealized male and female separate spheres.

The most hypocritical compromises of the Revolution's radicalism came in relation to race and slavery. Colonial abolitionist sentiment dated back to the seventeenth-century New England colonies and had enjoyed increasing currency amongst the Quakers in Pennsylvania. Even before the publication of the Declaration of Independence there were patriot radicals who acknowledged the common humanity of the free and enslaved: "The Colonists are by the law of nature born free," opined James Otis, "as indeed all men are, white or black." Similar sentiments can be found elsewhere in the literature of resistance to British rule. Not least in the writings of African American authors such as the poet Phillis Wheatley who wrote, "Remember, Christians, Negroes, black as Cain/May be refin'd, and join th' angelic train." A few enslavers, struck by the incongruity of the struggle for liberty to hold human chattel, freed their slaves. Enslaved people inspired by revolutionary rhetoric also took action themselves, bringing "freedom suits" to court seeking release from their enslavers. However, mainstream opinion acknowledged the South's reliance on slavery and considered abolition unrealistic.

Figure 3.6 In an era when women's voices were largely excluded from public debates, Mercy
Otis Warren was a leading political propagandist who published poems and plays
urging colonial resistance to Britain's arbitrary rule.

Source: Courtesy of ART Collection/Alamy

Despite the Declaration's general celebration of natural and unalienable rights to liberty, Vermont was the only state to prohibit slavery in its founding constitution. Even
in the north, most of those opposed to slavery favoured only an end to continued
importation, easing of restrictions on manumission, and some kind of colonisation
scheme for the freed people. By 1780, Pennsylvania had provided for gradual emancipation, but in states such as New York and New Jersey similar laws did not come

until 1799 and 1804. For many whites, the liberty promised by the Declaration was limited to free subjects and unthinkable outside societies ordered by what they still considered natural, social and racial hierarchies. In Virginia some planters returned to bondage their slaves who had fought in the war, and been promised their freedom. This prompted even that state's proslavery assembly to censure the enslavers' actions as "contrary to principles of justice and to their own solemn promise." The south had been ravaged by the war and could or would not contemplate its recovery and future prosperity without slavery. This recovery was driven, in part, by a shift from tobacco to wheat production in Virginia and Maryland, and the sale of their now surplus slaves to settlers heading south and west. Between 1783 and 1807 an estimated 100,000 more Africans were imported into the southern states, and Georgia's pre-Revolutionary slave population of 15,000 more than doubled.

Struggles within the ranks of patriots drawn from different social classes, in large part owing to wartime conditions, also tested the limits of revolutionary idealism. In the winter of 1776–77, Washington's army was reduced to 3,000 or 4,000 men, requiring new bounties and bonuses to attract new recruits. The following year – at Valley Forge, just outside Philadelphia – the army endured another winter of hunger, cold, and disease. In some states, entire counties resisted militia call-ups, and there were riots resisting compulsory drafts. Those caught up in the fighting lost homes, land, and loved ones; thousands of families lost parents and children were orphaned. Taxes were high throughout the war, but collectors often failed to enforce assessments on their struggling neighbours. This left the states and the Continental Congress relying on printed paper money which lost popular confidence and so its value. In 1778, a Connecticut militia brigade mutinied in protest at their payment in the depreciating currency. The following year angry crowds prevented the Connecticut assembly from requisitioning grain to supply the militia.

Inevitably, everyone did not suffer equally. There were some merchants and speculators who profited from wartime scarcities and soaring prices; others made tidy sums from contracts supplying the army, or buying up financial and other assets at bargain prices from those who had fallen on hard times. Labouring families, who bore the heaviest financial and military burdens, called for the distribution of household necessities and price controls, which merchants resented and evaded. In Virginia and Maryland, in 1775 and 1776 farmers banded together to raid the plantations of prominent and active patriots who were suspected of hoarding supplies of salt. As the war years progressed, there were signs of emerging class resentment, one man from Virginia declaring that "the rich wanted the poor to fight for them, to defend their property, whilst they refused to fight for themselves." Others began to wonder about the motives of wealthier citizens and even the wisdom of breaking with the empire: one man in Maryland refused to sign a patriot loyalty oath, believing the American opposition to Britain was not "for the defense of American liberty of property but for the purpose of enslaving the poor people thereof"; another declared that "it was better for the poor people to lay down their arms and pay the duties and taxes laid upon them by King and Parliament, than to be brought into slavery and to be commanded and ordered about as they were."

The America Revolution, like all revolutions, was a complicated and messy affair. There were, to be sure, examples of inspirational political oratory as well as courageous self-sacrifice and remarkable heroism. But once one looks beyond the celebrated, and occasionally fabricated, stories there is also evidence of considerable pain and suffering, of people ignoring or seeking to be left out of the conflict, of social division and

Figure 3.7 Born in the Gambia, Africa, and brought to America as a slave, Phillis Wheatley
was educated by her enslavers, who were considered progressive for their time, and
became the first African American to publish a book of poems that was celebrated
on both sides of the Atlantic.

Source: Courtesy of the Library of Congress Prints and Photographs Division Washington

of individuals setting their own interests ahead of the common cause. Away from the
well-known locations at Lexington Green, Bunker Hill, and Yorktown – the Revolution meant different things to different people. To unite the patriots, political leaders and commentators often relied on newspaper appeals to colonial prejudices and
stereotypes – of insurrectionary slaves and savage Indians – in the process creating
a racialised and exclusionary notion of American citizenship. These unifying bigot-
ries barely papered over the cracks that appeared in the patriot coalition, as wartime

scarcities took their toll and the wealthy and powerful endeavored to secure the elite and propertied government they felt was essential to good order. In Philadelphia, in January 1779, three years of shortages and rising prices for flour, wood, and grain prompted popular calls for regulations which merchants resisted. Tensions rose and a crowd led by a group of militiamen arrested four men identified as profiteers and marched them through the streets in a display of public humiliation. Next the militia stormed a house at which other merchants were hiding. The two sides exchanged fire, killing several on both sides before the army restored order. This clash, the Fort Wilson affair, was just one example of the class divisions appearing across the colonies as the patriots thoughts turned to victory.

The other Revolution

It is important to note that the image of the Revolution carried forward by minutemen and patriots and decided by eastern seaboard military campaigns led by famous generals did not define all Americans' experience of the 1770s and 80s. In the south, on the Gulf Coast, for example, a regional community comprising Chickasaws and Cherokees, and French and Spanish as well as English subjects focused more on local conditions and balances of power. For these and other subjects these later decades of the eighteenth century had less to do with distant diplomatic crises, elite ideologies of liberty, and independence, and more with the character of their future interdependence in whatever form of state transpired.

The revolution in its wider context

To fully grasp the extent and limits of the patriot's achievement we have to consider the Revolution in a wider context. From Britain's imperial perspective, the Revolution was definitely a loss, but one that many had come to consider unavoidable. Throughout its many eighteenth-century wars, British imperial power had depended more often than not on the strength of its alliances. During the Seven Years' War (1756–63), for example, the support of Fredrick the Great of Prussia and his forces against the French prompted William Pitt to quip that "America had been conquered in Germany." In its American War (1776–83) Britain's only supporters were its Native American allies, and in this sense the patriots' victory depended as much if not more on the support of France, Spain, and Holland than it did upon their military valor. On the British home front, the American War was also increasingly unpopular. An estimated one out of every eight adult British men fought in America, a higher participation percentage than in the colonial population. This mobilisation created hardships for English widows and fatherless families. The costs of the war were enormous. By the late 1770s, military costs and finance servicing government debt was claiming more than three quarters of national spending. Britain's war efforts were also frustrated by divisions within its command and control, the king having to work with competing factions in parliament and manage a highly complex strategy. By 1778/79, Britain's North

American garrisons were dispersed across 27 locations from South Carolina to New York, excluding those in Canada. Imperial planners and generals were also defending colonial possessions in the West Indies, the Mediterranean, Africa, and India. In 1776, Britain had 26 colonies around the world. At the end of the American War it retained 13, including the richest prizes of all – the West Indian sugar colonies. In many respects, it was the French rather than British who lost most from the war. When the Peace of Paris ceded western lands which had never been under British control to the Americans, it swept aside any lingering French claims to territories that they had once imagined they possessed.

The radical sentiments that animated early revolutionary idealism were also taken up in waves of protests against monarchical authority and aristocratic privilege elsewhere in late eighteenth-century Europe and the Atlantic World: the Genevan Revolution (1782), the Dutch Patriot movement (1787), the Belgian Revolution (1787–89), the French Revolution (1789), the Wolfe Tone Rebellion in Ireland (1798), the Freetown Revolution (1800), and the Haitian Revolution (1791–1804). These diverse struggles were knit together by the movement of people – political activists, displaced artisan workers, diplomats, freed slaves, and merchants – and circulation of writings – personal letters, political pamphlets, memoirs, books – that articulated radical political ideologies and carried them across borders. In each case, revolutionaries relied on community associations, corresponding societies, boycotts and strikes – learning new forms of political organisation and then using them to create and sustain powerful opposition movements. Thomas Paine was just one of many contemporary radicals who travelled overseas to join revolutions in America and then France. Rather than discrete national campaigns on behalf of self-determination, these various uprisings deserve to be remembered as interconnected parts of a transnational revolutionary movement featuring a radical politics of egalitarian republicanism as well as demands for recognition of ethnic and regional distinctions. Across these various contexts the radical sentiments and political enthusiasm that produced the Declaration of Independence and fired American patriot idealism were evident in the writings and struggles of others. Thus English, Dutch, and French women political writers and novelists explored the possibilities that a political revolution might hold for fundamental change in relations between the sexes and for women's emotional and intellectual fulfilment: in particular a rejection of the misogynistic conception of women as passionate dependents and their acceptance as fully realised and rational individuals with capacities equal to their men.

The radical potential of these Enlightenment ideologies was nowhere more in evidence than in the Haitian Revolution, a slave uprising which established a free state governed by the non-whites and the formerly enslaved. In the late eighteenth-century, Saint Domingue (now known as Haiti) was the richest slave colony in the Americas and, with Jamaica, the main supplier of the world's sugar and coffee. It was also a complex society, controlled by a wealthy planter class, with rigid racial and caste system that specified the inhabitants' rights and status, where they could and could not live, and even what clothes they could wear. There were three broad categories: the 32,000 white residents, rich and poor known as les blancs; the 28,000 free people of colour and those born to mixed race parents or the gens de couleur; and last of all, the 452,000 men and women who were enslaved and comprised almost half the one million bondsmen and women in all of the Caribbean plantations. The white enslavers alleviated their insecurities by establishing a particularly brutal and murderous regime to intimidate their enslaved workers. Many enslaved people seized opportunities to run away and live in camps numbering several hundred to a few thousand, sustained by hunting and raids on outlying plantations.

   In 1789, the French Revolution produced a Declaration of the Rights of Man, proclaiming all men free and equal. In Saint Domingue, the wealthy planters considered the collapse of the French monarchy as an opportunity for them to increase their control over the colony; the gens de couleur hoped for the full civil equality for which they had long campaigned; and the slaves heard rumours of possible emancipation which spread to plantations in Guadeloupe and Martinique, prompting minor revolts. Then, in August 1791 an uprising by 20,000 slaves took over key areas of the island and set up a camp in the mountains. The French authorities had clearly lost control, and the island's planters appealed to the British to intervene. This threatened French sovereignty in its richest Caribbean prize. In March 1792, the French authorities were desperate to bolster their local support and so recognised the equal rights of the gens de couleur and dispatched troops to put down the rebellion. A former slave and now freeman, Toussaint Louverture, emerged as the revolution's master military commander and tactician, switching between different allies to achieve his ends. By 1793, France was at war with Britain and Spain, who had kept the slave rebels supplied with arms and provisions. In August 1793 – to prevent losing the island to the rebels or some combination of the wealthy planters, Britain, and Spain – the French finally issued an emancipation proclamation freeing the slaves, the consequences of which reverberated throughout the West Indies and the Americas for decades to come.

Figure 3.8 The burning of the Plaine du Cap, Haiti, 1794.
Source: Courtesy of Niday Picture Library/Alamy

Just as in the American Revolution, these transnational revolutionary movements had to reckon with powerful forces of existing government structures and presiding oligarchies, as well as facing the realities of great power politics. Indeed, even as the American and French revolutionaries inspired other individuals and movements, their conservative leaders feared the radical forces unleashed and attempted to limit change and reform. The more established conservative elites and the borders of their new states became, the greater the tension between them and the earlier cosmopolitan republican idealism. Within 20 years it was the governments of the new states that did the most to bring the age of revolutions to an end. This was partly a product of war weariness and disillusionment with the carnage and excesses of revolutions, especially in France and Haiti; estimates reckon 50,000 people were executed in France's "reign of terror" 1793–94; a similar number of European soldiers and a further 350,000 Haitians died in Saint Domingue's 13-year slave rebellion. The United States' refusal to recognise a free black state in Saint Domingue was symptomatic of a general hardening of attitudes to gendered and racial divisions. Despite decades of revolutionary ferment, male power over women and the established patterns of authority remained largely intact. Women continued to be defined as self-sacrificing domestic caregivers, leaving public roles and higher purposes to men. Slavery continued for decades more in the United States and virulent racist attitudes considered all non-white peoples as naturally inferior and subordinate. The once feted itinerant radicals came to be despised in their adopted countries dying, in the case of Thomas Paine, a penniless and forgotten man.

Chapter summary

In this chapter, we considered, or historicised, the meaning of "revolution" in the era of the American War for Independence, and then investigated the breakdown in imperial relations following the 1763 Peace of Paris. In the wake of their victory over the French, the British were determined that the Americans should pay more for their defence and this meant tax and administrative reforms. In the west, Indians and settlers fought a bloody war for control of land the settlers considered theirs following the victory over the French. In the east, Americans viewed the change in British policy as a needless imposition of austerity and a denial of their customary and constitutional rights; some even suspected a plot to reduce the colonies to a subservient status. This led to widespread elite and popular protest and, following the Stamp Act, a growing sense of injustice and the organisation of resistance. Loyalists, numbering 70–100,000, thought resistance in the name of abstract political rights a treacherous and foolhardy venture. The patriots united in the cause of independence, but the experience of war emphasised ideological differences and differences of class interests. The limits of American revolutionary radicalism was evident in its implications for different groups: women were afforded new and public, but ultimately limited, roles; Indians faced a racist and increasingly powerful settler intrusion into the west; slaves took the opportunity to resist and escape their bondage, but the slave economy remained intact. Towards the end of the century, there was a backlash against radical revolutions across the Atlantic World. The success of the Haitian Revolution made it difficult for Americans to evade the contradiction between slavery and liberty even as they embraced their newly won status as an independent nation. In the next chapter, we consider the post-war challenges that prompted some to call for a stronger national government based on a new, written Constitution.

Discussion questions

- How did the patriots' notion of revolution differ from our own?
- What was more important to the patriots, home rule or who should rule at home?
- Why did some Americans remain loyal, and how does their choice complicated questions relating to patriot motives for revolution?
- How did the Americans win the revolutionary war?
- How was the meaning and implications of the Revolution different for wealthy merchants, poor farmers in western Massachusetts, slaves in Virginia, and Indians who continued their struggle against settlers moving west?
- Was the American Revolution a radical revolution?

Further reading

Bailyn, Bernard. *The Ideological Origins of the American Revolution* (Cambridge, MA, 1967). The classic account of the spread of fears regarding British tyranny that some argue provided the foundation for republican political ideology in the revolutionary America.

Bouton, Terry. *Taming Democracy: 'The People', the Founders, and the Troubled Ending of the American Revolution* (Oxford, 2009). A gripping account of the actions and fates of ordinary patriots during the revolution, especially concerning the inflationary devaluation of paper money.

Dun, James Alexander. *Dangerous Neighbors: Making the Haitian Revolution in Early America* (Philadelphia, 2016). Considers the importance of the Haitian and the international context in the American Revolution.

Knott, Sarah. *Sensibility and the American Revolution* (Chapel Hill, 2008). Considers the middle class culture of "sensibility" – denoting refinement, taste, sensitivity, and virtue – and its fate during and after the Revolution.

Maier, Pauline. *American Scripture: Making the Declaration of Independence* (New York, 1997). Tracks the production, significance, and changing meaning of the Declaration of Independence in the eighteenth century and after.

McDonnell, Michael A. *Masters of Empire: Great Lakes Indians and the Making of America* (New York, 2015). A re-imagining of early American geography and the peoples and processes that gave rise to the early republic, in particular the Anishinaabeg people from a region between Lake Huron and Lake Michigan and their role in colonial American diplomacy and warfare culminating with the American Revolution and Early Republic.

Morgan Edmund S., and Helen M. Morgan. *The Stamp Act Crisis: Prologue to Revolution* (Chapel Hill, 1995). Classic study of shift from protest to resistance during and after the Stamp Act Crisis.

Nash, Gary B. *The Urban Crucible: Social Change, Political Consciousness, and the Origins of the American Revolution* (Cambridge, MA, 1979). Study traces the development of popular protest and revolutionary class consciousness in the seaboard colonial cities.

Parkinson, Robert G. *The Common Cause: Creating Race and Nation in the American Revolution* (Chapel Hill, 2016). Study of how patriots used colonial prejudices and fears of insurrectionary slaves and "savage" Indians to create opposition to British tyranny.

Polasky, Janet L. author. *Revolutions Without Borders: The Call to Liberty in the Atlantic World* (New Haven, 2015). Wide ranging study which considers the late eighteenth century as an age of revolutions.

Shy, John. *A People Numerous and Armed: Reflections on the Military Struggle for American Independence* (New York, 1976). Classical study of patriot military resistance and winning of the revolutionary war.

Smith, Barbara Clark. *The Freedoms We Lost: Consent and Resistance in Revolutionary America* (New York, 2010). Sophisticated study about the changing conception and meaning of popular politics and the motives of the "people without doors."

Taylor, Alan. *American Revolutions: A Continental History, 1750–1804* (New York, 2016). The most recent and comprehensive survey of the era of the American Revolution.

Wood, Gordon S. *The Radicalism of the American Revolution* (New York, 1991). Now classic but still controversial study making the case for the American Revolution as a radical revolution, in eighteenth-century terms.

4　A union and a nation

Timeline

1776	Declaration of Independence
1778	Franco-American Alliance
1777–80	States ratify their individual constitutions
1781	Articles of Confederation agreed
1783	Congress discharges four-fifths of the Continental Army
1783	Peace of Paris ends the Revolutionary War
1784	Congress dispatches diplomats to negotiate alliances in Europe; they largely fail
1784, 1785, and 1787	Ordinances provide for the orderly laying out and incorporation of the Northwest Territories
1785	Influential group in Virginia successfully negotiate border differences with Maryland, leading to proposal for a follow-up and wider meeting on interstate commerce; the meeting is thinly attended by 12 delegates from five states
1786/87	Through the winter, Daniel Shays leads a rebellion by western Massachusetts farmers, adding urgency to debate concerning authority of the central government
1787, May through August	Constitutional Convention assembles in Philadelphia; Madison and the Virginia delegation present their plan for a stronger central government
	The New Jersey Plan urges continuity of one state, one vote model; a compromise brokered by the Connecticut delegation proposes a combination of federal and state authority
	The delegates debate government powers and sectional differences emerge over economy and slavery
	Comprise is reached; the enslaved are to be counted as three-fifths of a person for purposes of deciding representation in the House of Representatives, handing an electoral advantage to the South
1787, September	the delegates return to their states for ratification debates
1787–88	Publication of *The Federalist* featuring essays in favour of the Constitution by leading figures, including Hamilton, Jay, and Madison

1787	Delaware, Pennsylvania, New Jersey, Georgia, and Connecticut ratify the Constitution
1789	First Ten Amendments, the Bill of Rights, added to the Constitution
1789	Election of George Washington as the first president of the United States
1789	Judiciary Act establishes a Supreme Court with jurisdiction over civil actions between states and any state and the United States
1789	Revolution in France
1789–92	Alexander Hamilton publishes reports on public credit and manufacturing
1792	Washington agrees to serve a second term
1794	Whiskey Rebellion
1794	Treaty of Amity and Commerce
1794	The Battle of Fallen Timbers ends the Native American challenges in the Northwest Territory
1795	Treaty of Greenville requires Native Americans to cede lands
1796	Washington's retires and Farewell Address published; John Adams elected president
1798	Quasi-war with France
1798	Adams introduces the Alien and Sedition Acts
1798	Jefferson and Madison propose the Virginia and Kentucky Resolves
1800	Gabriel's Rebellion
1800	Election of Thomas Jefferson to the presidency

Topics covered

- Drafting of state constitutions and administration under the Articles of Confederation
- Disputes concerning character of new republic and relationship between the state and federal governments
- The problem of war debts and challenge of public finance
- Settler-Indian Wars in the Northwest Territory
- Shays Rebellion
- The Constitutional Convention and Ratification Debates
- The Federalist administration
- The Democratic Republicanism and divisions over response to the French Revolution
- The Election of 1800

Introduction

This chapter begins with the 1783 Peace of Paris and Washington's cautious optimism regarding the future of the new American republic. Then we survey the disagreements that prompted the Constitutional Convention four years later. Post-war America was troubled by huge domestic and international debts, disputes over the continuing war against Native Americans and the division of western lands, and the political relationship between the states and the central government. The key question was whether the new republic was to be a union of semi-sovereign states or a unified nation with the stature and authority to command respect on the international stage. The chapter traces the development of disputes around this central theme from the administration under the 1781 Articles of Confederation through to Shays Rebellion in 1786/87 which convinced many state leaders of the need to strengthen the authority of the federal government. We consider the Constitutional Convention, the character of the government that the Convention delegates established, and its relationship to the earlier revolutionary struggle. The chapter closes with a survey of Washington's two terms as president and the Federalist administration, ending with bitter divisions surrounding the French Revolution that brought Jefferson and the Republicans to power in the election of 1800.

A respectable nation

In June 1783 the Paris Treaty negotiations which ended the American War for Independence were winding up. George Washington took up his pen and wrote to John Hancock, president of the Continental Congress, resigning his commission and declaring his desire to "return to that domestic retirement" from which the war had taken him. The "Citizens of America," Washington wrote, are in a "most enviable condition" and possessed of a continent that offers all "the necessaries and conveniences of life." Americans had an opportunity to build their republic not in a "gloomy age of Ignorance and Superstition," but at a time when "the rights of Mankind were better understood" and liberal sentiments in government and commerce provided the "blessings of Society." Given these circumstances, Washington declared, if the citizens of the United States were not "completely free and happy . . . the fault will be entirely their own."

Washington then set out some of what he considered the essential "Pillars on which the glorious Fabrick of our Independency and National Character must be supported." First and foremost, the federal government had to be strengthened, so that it could serve effectively as the head of "an indissoluble Union of the States." Next, there must be a "sacred regard to public Justice," and in particular payment of legitimate public and private debts. The combination of a strong federal government, guarantees for property rights and the rule of law, Washington believed, would persuade individuals and groups to forego their selfish ambitions and ensure a "pacific and friendly disposition among the People of the United States." Doubtless reflecting on news of the discussions in Paris, Washington also reminded Hancock that "the eyes of the whole World are turned upon us." How the Americans behaved now would "establish or ruin their National Character." If they failed this test, it would encourage the defeated British and the scheming French and Spanish to draw the United States into "the sport of European politicks," playing "one State against another . . . to serve their own interested purposes." Washington dispatched his letter and retired to his Mount Vernon plantation, from where he made plans for a trip to visit the frontier and inspect his lands in western Pennsylvania.

Just four years later, in the spring of 1787, Washington was once again drawn out of retirement. This time it was to preside over a special convention in Philadelphia to revise the constitutional settlement of the Articles of Confederation. The Articles had only been agreed in 1781, but now powerful lobbies claimed that these terms and conditions were fundamentally flawed. The complaints had begun even before the end of the war and continued through the early 1780s. Leading patriots such as James Madison and George Mason from Virginia, Benjamin Franklin from Pennsylvania, and John Jay from New York declared that the federal government was "incompetent to its objects." The visiting Spanish ambassador agreed, believing America to be

Figure 4.1 George Washington (1732–99), landowner, planter, enslaver, soldier, and the first
president of the United States of America.

Source: Courtesy of Ian Dagnall/Alamy

"almost without government . . . and torn between hope and fear of whether or not
their confederation can be consolidated." In a later essay, the lawyer, politician and
ardent nationalist, Alexander Hamilton, identified the core of the problem with what
he called the "Insufficiency of the Present Confederation to Preserve the Union." In
particular, and pointing to the economic and diplomatic turmoil within and between
the states, Hamilton complained that the federal government was weak because it
lacked the authority and sanctions necessary to enforce its will. Consequently, there
was "scarcely anything" that "can wound the pride or degrade the character of an
independent nation which we do not experience": citizens and state governments disregarded contracts with impunity; private, public, and foreign debts went unpaid,
America's ambassadors overseas were considered "mere pageants of mimic sovereignty," and the republic was brought to the "last stage of national humiliation."
These were the failings that led to the Philadelphia convention, but even there the
delegates could not agree. In July, Washington wrote to Hamilton complaining of the
"Men who oppose a strong & energetic government" and dominated debate, leading

him to fear that there was "little ground on which the hope of a good establishment, can be formed."

Notwithstanding Washington's misgivings, by that September the delegates had produced the Constitution of the United States. Before considering the Philadelphia convention and its outcome, however, we need to get to grips with what had gone so badly wrong? Even as the patriots achieved their goal of independence from Britain, they faced challenges relating to internal, domestic government and external foreign relations. The domestic problems grew out of the trials and tribulations of the war years. In particular, the transformation of a system of revolutionary committees into local and state governments, and then the working out of the relationship of these state governments to the Continental Congress charged with fighting the war and leading the new nation. In order to pay for the war, the individual states and the national congress had printed their own currencies and run up massive debts. By the early 1780s, the people had lost confidence in these paper currencies. The individual states, their lands and commerce ravaged by war, were in debt and required large investments for reconstruction.

The Articles of Confederation empowered congress to request financial support from the states. However, when that support failed to materialise, congress had no way to compel payment. Any change to the Articles required the unanimous agreement of all the states, allowing a single dissenter to hold up reforms. The financial situation was particularly embarrassing for America's relations with European powers such as France and Spain, who had backed the revolutionary war with large loans and now expected repayment. Congress was also unable to deal with the many and various disputes between the states, for example concerning boundaries and the allocation of western lands, which remained as contentious as it had been during the colonial era. In the late 1770s, New Englanders and New Yorkers fought running battles over rival claims in Vermont, and settlers and speculators from Connecticut and Pennsylvania clashed over lands in the Susquehanna Valley. Congress's inability to pay its debts or command obedience of the states undermined its claim as a new sovereign authority entitled to be included in the international family of states. But if congress was not sovereign in the new American republic, then who was?

These various challenges all revolved around the same core question: was the new republic a union of semi-sovereign autonomous states or was it a unified nation claiming the stature and authority of the European states from whom the Americans sought recognition? The patriots had drawn up the Articles under pressure of war, and established a confederation that was strong enough to make alliances and fight for independence. However, they had pointedly declined to authorise the central government to interfere in the internal politics and ambitions of the individual states. The men who represented those states as delegates to the Continental Congresses carried themselves more as if they were envoys attending an international meeting, than representatives of localities and regions from within a single nation. They considered questions relating to trade, boundaries, Indian and other diplomatic relations from the perspective of their state, or at best region, rather than the still largely abstract United States of America. In this sense the financial challenges facing the union of states and the American nation were about more than very large debts which somebody had to pay. The financial difficulties could only be resolved by addressing fundamental constitutional question about who had the authority to tax and control the creation and supply of money. Of course, this was the same question upon which the patriots had recently challenged the British empire and fought the war for independence. Now they had to identify the location of this authority within their own republic. Nationalists, later known as federalists, such as Washington, Madison, and Hamilton, believed the problem was an "excess of democracy," meaning that too much power lay with the state governments. These governments, they argued, were too responsive to local elections and the popular will which was too unpredictable and occasionally chaotic and corrupt and in no way suited to the task of making a nation.

For a long-time most historians tended to agree with this view, portraying the federalists as earnest reformers and the constitutional convention as a meeting of visionaries who saved the Revolution from populist excesses. However, other scholars have argued that the new constitution also muted the Revolution's earlier radicalism and launched a political and economic project that favoured the interests of wealth and property over commitments to egalitarianism and democracy. Still others insist on the need to look beyond these essentially domestic troubles, arguing that the Constitutional Convention was as much if not more concerned with the republic's ability to survive in a competitive and turbulent system of international states who viewed America's sovereignty claims with rising scepticism. How Americans behaved towards each other at home and dealt with their Indian neighbours, mattered for their claim for recognition abroad as a respectable state. As Washington had it, Americans were "Actors on a most conspicuous Theatre."

Whatever their differences, historians agree that the federal government which emerged from the Constitutional Convention and subsequent ratification debates possessed the power to address political and economic challenges at the national and international level. Under the two-term presidency of George Washington the Federalists introduced policies on public credit, economic development, and Indian affairs which addressed the crisis conditions. However, divisions within the Constitutional Convention persisted. An opposition lobby, including some former nationalists, argued that the new government went beyond the principles agreed in the new Constitution and threatened to eclipse the democratic and republican character of the Revolution in favour of aristocratic and even monarchical society. If the Constitution saved the republic from an "excess of democracy," it also embedded struggles over political and economic principles and interests and the balance of state and federal power that echoed down the generations into the nineteenth and twentieth centuries and continue even today.

Forming an American government

As we saw in the last chapter, the challenge of uniting 13 semi-independent republics to take on the British began the moment the patriots declared their independence and the Continental Congress urged the states to adopt "Articles of Confederation and perpetual union." However, before the states could ratify these Articles, they first had to settle their own governments and resist the British invasion. Most states quickly agreed new constitutions, outlining the powers and limits of their new administrations. Rhode Island and Connecticut adapted their existing colonial charters; Massachusetts did not agree a constitution until 1780. These state constitutions reflected long-standing commitments to local representation and a determination to secure citizens' liberty and property from the kind of interventions attempted by English imperial reforms in the 1760s and 1770s.

The constitutions were written down, so there could be no arguments over interpretation of principles and laws; most included a bill of rights giving express guarantees of essential freedoms of speech, religion, and trial by jury. In Pennsylvania, a radical patriot administration drawn from the middling social rank agreed a constitution that was opposed to the rule of "great and overgrown rich men" who were too often concerned with "distinctions in society." Any white male citizen who paid taxes could vote annually for representatives who sat in a single chamber constitution, allowing voters to scrutinise legislation as it was produced. Elsewhere existing elites managed the conventions and produced more socially conservative and restrictive constitutions. In South Carolina and Maryland, property qualifications limited the numbers who could vote and restricted office holding to the richest men in the state. From the outset there were clear divisions of opinion. John Adams, a future Federalist and president, considered Pennsylvania's constitution "so democratical that it must produce confusion and every evil work." In Massachusetts, Adams co-wrote a more detailed document, comprising distinct chapters, sections, and articles which outlined a separation of powers between a two-chamber (bicameral) legislature, an executive office and an independent judiciary. In this way, each branch of the government was supposed to check the power of the others. This arrangement insulated lawmakers from the majority power of popular elections and ordinary voters, which Adams considered "as unjust, tyrannical, brutal, barbarous, and cruel, as any king or Senate."

It was not until March 1781 that the American states finally united under a new Congress empowered by the Articles of Confederation. Regardless of size and population, all 13 states had one vote on congressional legislation, and a majority of nine was required to authorise use of its major powers; any amendments to foundational terms and powers required unanimous consent. On paper, those powers were formidable: Congress could declare war, assemble military and naval forces, make treaties with foreign and Native American nations, and settle controversies between American member states. In reality, Congress remained subordinate to the states. The key problem was that it lacked the sanctions necessary to enforce its will. Congress could recruit, but not provision the army; it could settle disputes and make treaties, but not force the citizens to adhere to these agreements.

Even before the Articles were ratified, there were complaints regarding their inadequacies. In 1780, the political writer and editor Noah Webster lamented, as "long as any individual state has power to defeat the measures of the other twelve . . . our pretended union is but a name, and our confederation a cobweb." The Virginian lawyer Edmund Randolph similarly denounced the Articles for their "turbulence and follies," noting that the "chief danger arises from the Democratic parts of our constitutions" and their insufficient "checks against the democracy." Public finance was a particular cause for concern. With no independent income or power to compel the states to contribute to congressional coffers, the lawyer and jurist James Duane wrote, the government lacked the "confidence and dignity necessary to enforce its counsels" and was "surrounded by clamorous creditors and insidious speculators" and rendered "odious." At the end of its first year of operations under the Articles of Confederation, Congress lacked the funds even to publish its own proceedings. In the Spring of 1787, the Articles' "excessive democracy" and the union's financial woes were cited as key justifications for the calling of the Philadelphia convention and the drafting of a new constitution.

It is important to bear in mind the differences of opinion regarding the populist and democratic versus elite and deferential forms of republican government, and to note that the loudest complaints about the Articles came from those of the latter persuasion. Viewed more positively, the assertion of local democracy in the state constitutions reflected the understandable and even admirable political ambition of patriots inspired by pamphlets such as Thomas Paine's *Common Sense*. These middling men and women, sometimes known as the "people out of doors," staffed the committees, marched in the militias and army, and did most of the fighting for independence. Unsurprisingly, they were committed to making good on the Revolution's egalitarian ideals. Thus a suggested amendment to the Pennsylvania bill of rights declared that "an enormous proportion of property vested in a few individuals is dangerous

THOMAS PAINE.

Figure 4.2 Thomas Paine (1737–1809), staymaker, excise officer, political activist, and philosopher. His pamphlets *Common Sense* and *The American Crisis* focused rebellious protests on the demand for independence.

Source: Courtesy of the Library of Congress Prints and Photographs Division Washington

to the rights, and destructive of the common happiness, of mankind" and so argued that states should "hath a right . . . to discourage the possession of such property." The early republican governments also showed themselves to be forward looking and circumspect, breaking with colonial localism and granting the free inhabitants of any state "all the privileges and immunities of free citizens in the several states." There were notable successes under the Confederation Congress. It established departments of Foreign Affairs, War, Marine, and Treasury. It raised an army, negotiated the 1778 Franco-American Alliance, won the war against the English, and agreed the 1783 Peace of Paris. Under Jefferson's direction, the Confederation introduced Ordinances in 1784 and 1787 which organised the vast territory beyond the Appalachian Mountains, providing its orderly surveying, sale, settlement, banning slavery and enabling the assimilation of new states in the future. Looked at more positively, one could argue that the difficulties and disputes of the Confederation era reflected the experience of fighting a long, complicated, and hugely expensive war – rather than simply "excessive democracy."

Whatever the successes or failures of the Confederation era, most historians agree that the crucial problem came down to the money needed to fight the British and the debts left at the end of the war. This problem of public finance could only be resolved by the infant American state finding a way to raise the money it needed to pay its way. Ironically, the solution depended on the example of the British state's response to a similar set of circumstances a century or so earlier, when William and Mary took over the English throne and needed to borrow money to pay for the war against France. In the 1690s London merchants and financiers were not at all confident that William and Mary would defeat Louis XIV and his Stuart cousin, James II. In 1694, and in order to convince these private investors to back their claim, William and Mary gave up their sovereign authority over the production and management of money to a new and merchant-managed Bank of England. The Bank took in deposits from wealthy private investors which it lent to William and Mary to cover their expenses; the crown agreed to pay back the principal over time and annual interest using tax revenues collected from the public. In return for their deposits the merchant financiers received paper notes, and these and other Bank notes and loans circulated to third parties. This expansion of secure credit improved financial liquidity – or the circulation and spending of money – which increased commerce and consumption and generated higher tax revenues which bankrolled the expansion of the British state. The way in which the British made and managed their money after 1694 proved critical to their subsequent domestic and imperial success. In the 1780s, there were some on the nationalist side who favoured a similar strategy for the new American republic.

In the mid-1770s, however, America had no comparable financial system, required massive investment to pay for the war, and had to cobble together support while repelling the British invasion. Lacking the authority to compel the states to pay taxes, Congress and the republic relied on a patchwork of measures. As we saw in a previous chapter, colonial governments had long printed their own paper money to pay public expenses, backing the currency with either taxes or loans to borrowers who offered land and personal possessions as collateral. After 1776 the new states continued to issue notes to pay for their war supplies and soldiers wages; citizens could use the notes to pay their taxes, ensuring the bills circulated in private exchanges. Between 1776 and 1779 the 13 states together issued some $2 million. Congress also borrowed large sums from European allies, especially the French. But most of its revenue came from the sale of its own interest bearing, fixed term bonds: patriots eager to support the war bought the bonds using gold and silver coin, which the government used to pay for expenses and supplies. The bondholders received interest until the end of the specified term, when the bonds could be redeemed, or sold back to the government. After 1778 Congress also printed some $60 million in "specie certificates" which it used to pay the interest on bonds; it also printed a further $160 million of its own paper currency, the "continental," which it expected the states to back with contributions of silver and gold.

At least in the early years of the war, the various forms of patriot paper money and bonds were a notable success: 86 per cent of government funding came from paper currency and by 1781 state and continental currencies were still meeting two-thirds of public costs. However, uncertainty about the future of the republic and the increasing volume of notes issued prompted a crisis of confidence. Merchants and traders started declining payment in the paper currencies; in some cases the issuing authorities used the notes to pay their soldiers and then refused to receive them back as taxes. In May 1781, frustrated nationalists rallied around Robert Morris, a Philadelphia merchant who had made a fortune from war contracts, and whose term as Superintendent of Finance was noteworthy for its failed attempt to coerce the states into contributing to the central government. During the first six months of 1782 only New Jersey paid anything to Congress and even then it only amounted to 1 per cent of its assessment. In June 1783, Congress discharged four fifths of the continental army, paying them off with paper certificates. When the soldiers arrived home, they found their farms and businesses heavily in debt; credit was scarce, and interest rates and taxes higher than before the war. Many were forced to sell their land and possessions, and the war bonds bought a few years earlier, often at a fraction of their face value.

The bonds and other state war debts became concentrated in the hands of speculators, who then lobbied local legislatures for their interest payments and repayment of the paper debts at the original, face value. By 1786, almost all the interest paid on Pennsylvania's war debt went to just 67 people; in Rhode Island, nearly half of the taxes levied to cover interest charges on the state's war debt went to just 16 people, mostly residents of the state capital at Providence. Unsurprisingly, these circumstances prompted public dissatisfaction and conflict between debtor and creditor interests and lobbies. As one Massachusetts farmer complained "it cost them much to maintain the great men under George III, but vastly more under the Commonwealth and Congress." Working families petitioned the legislatures for debt relief, and the struggle for democratic control of local politics and against inequality became fused together. As one New York writer had it, "the security of American liberty requires a more equal distribution of property than at present."

In several states the debtor-creditor division pit western farmers and communities against eastern political elites and financial interests. The early republic experienced dramatic population growth and internal migration after the war: a 1783 census counted 12,000 whites and blacks living west of the Appalachian Mountains and south of the Ohio River; seven years later there were more than 100,000 residents settling down in the future states of Kentucky and Tennessee. The settlers who travelled west encroached upon and squatted Native American lands, leading to violent confrontations and sporadic settler-Indian wars. The central and state

Figure 4.3 Continental currencies.

Source: Courtesy of Godot13 (reproduced under CC BY-SA 3.0)

governments tried to limit unorganised settlement by distributing land in large parcels to wealthy investors, but ordinary farmers denounced the policy as corrupt favouritism.

The infant republic's disputes and government weakness undermined its reputation abroad. Notwithstanding the Americans' success at the Paris peace conference, the Europeans little regarded their claims to sovereignty. The French commander, and erstwhile ally, Charles Gravier, Count of Vergennes, considered the Confederation's territorial claims a "foolishness not meriting serious refutation." The English peer, Lord Sheffield, concurred, declaring "we might as reasonably dread the effects of combinations among the German as among the American states." Challenging the

Confederation's claim as a sovereign power, Spain closed the port at New Orleans to American vessels, denying settlers in Kentucky and Tennessee access to markets for their crops; Britain maintained their forts in the Ohio Valley, in defiance of the 1783 Treaty, and aided Native American attacks on settlers. In the Mediterranean, American ships were seized and crews imprisoned. Bypassing the Confederation, foreign powers negotiated diplomatic agreements with individual states, encouraging some to consider quitting the novel American union in preference for a more established and credible European ally.

In 1784, Congress dispatched a stellar team of diplomats, including Thomas Jefferson, John Adams, and Benjamin Franklin, to negotiate commercial treaties in Europe. They returned with two, paltry agreements: one with Prussia, which lacked a navy and was thus a more minor player in an age of maritime diplomacy; and another with Morocco, which many Europeans did not even consider a fully independent nation. The mission's failure underscored the challenge facing the national government: if the Confederation lacked the authority to control its member states and manage their interrelations, to enforce contracts and ensure the payment of public and private debts, to manage its western lands and settlements then how could it expected to be taken seriously as a sovereign power by the European nations? In 1785, a group of influential Virginians, including George Washington, James Madison, and Edmund Randolph, successfully negotiated a border agreement with Maryland. This meeting prompted a proposal for a larger gathering to consider interstate commerce, this time including Pennsylvania and Delaware. In February 1786, this growing lobby invited all the states to send delegates to a general, commercial convention to be held in Annapolis. When the convention assembled, however, only 12 representatives – from New York, New Jersey Pennsylvania, Delaware, and Virginia – attended. Styling themselves the "commissioners to remedy the defects of the federal government," and favouring a stronger, national authority, the delegates proposed a national convention. Congress rejected their recommendation, but trouble brewing in Massachusetts soon persuaded the nay sayers of the need for such a meeting.

In August 1786, a large company of angry farmers from western Massachusetts shut down the court proceedings at Northampton to prevent any more indebted families from losing their land and possessions. The protest followed the decision of the Massachusetts state assembly to adjourn their session without even considering the farmers' petitions for debt relief submitted the preceding months. Among the protestors that day was a man called Daniel Shays. Born to Irish immigrant parents, Shays was an agricultural labourer and small farmer who had fought in the continental army at several famous battles and rose to the rank of captain. When he returned from the war, injured and unpaid, he found himself in debt and, like others, facing high taxes to pay off the state and national war debts. In 1785, a wealthy Boston merchant, James Bowdoin, won the election for governor and promised to increase pressure on those who owed back taxes needed to continue paying the state's debt.

This was too much for the western farmers and they organised to resist the tax collectors. The Northampton protest was followed by similar actions against courts and debt proceedings at Concord, Worcester, and Great Barrington. Bowdoin denounced the protestors as a mob, but sympathetic militias refused to turn out against their farmer neighbours. When the Massachusetts Supreme Court at Springfield indicted 11 rebel leaders, hundreds protested and tried to shut down the hearing. By late November 1786, the state had organised its forces and sent out a company of 300 to arrest key rebel protestors. Several thousand farmers formed themselves into well-organised and democratically led units aiming to put down the "tyrannical government of Massachusetts." The farmers marched on the federal armoury at Springfield, but the attack fell apart and the protestors fled or were picked up by large and well-armed state forces early in 1787. What became known as Shays Rebellion added a sense of urgency to debate concerning the need for constitutional reform. When a new convention to consider revisions of the Articles to be held in Philadelphia was announced, all the states sent delegates.

The Constitutional Convention

The convention assembled on 29 May in the Pennsylvanian statehouse, known today as Independence Hall. John Adams later described the 55 who assembled as men of "ability, weight, and experience." He might have added authority, wealth, and education given their status as prominent merchants, landowners, enslavers, and lawyers. Most were agreed on the problems facing the union, and on the need to enhance the authority of the national government. The Virginia delegation arrived early and worked up a plan which set the terms of initial debates. James Madison – an enslaver, legislator, and leading light of the Virginian group – had studied the histories of colonial government and of republics from around the world. His inquiries convinced him that the difficulties facing the republic – whether concerning tax collection, debt payment, international diplomacy, or the allocation of new lands – all stemmed from the deeper problem of the union's organisational structure which left the national government dependent on the states.

Madison proposed that the federal government draw its authority directly from individual citizens and act independently of the states. Madison and his co-delegate Edmund Randolph proposed a federal government with three branches – legislative, executive, and judicial – with power to act on any issues of national concern. The single chamber Confederation Congress would be replaced with a new, two chamber legislature: a lower house elected by the people, with the number of representatives proportionate to the population of each state, and an upper chamber selected by the lower and thereby shielded from the direct influence of the popular vote. The new government would retain the sovereign powers of the Confederation, but also have the authority to review and veto state laws, if they were considered contrary to the principles of union. In effect, this Virginia plan reversed the relationship between the states and the national government, putting the latter firmly in control.

The other delegates agreed that the Articles of Confederation needed reform, but some worried that Madison's proposals went too far – certainly beyond the convention's official remit – and introduced dangerous innovations. Moreover, the Virginians' proposals said nothing directly about taxes and war debts, which many considered the most pressing issues. Madison's plan also advocated a large and centrally directed republican government of the sort that classical and contemporary political theorists, and the Americans' recent experience, warned against. Rather than remote leaders detached from local circumstances, many felt it was better to keep government close to the citizens where tyrannical tendencies could be monitored and checked. Delegates from states such as New Jersey and Delaware feared that the Virginians' plan for proportional representation would allow larger states to overpower smaller ones. Similar concerns were evident in the debates about the form of the executive, with some proposing a committee and others a single person elected every four years. Some delegates feared that the latter approach risked reintroducing a form of monarchy.

Intellectual influences on constitutional thinking

Historians continue to debate the intellectual influences on early constitutional thinking, put simply the political ideas the colonists drew upon to justify their rebellion and then establish a new government. Some emphasise ancient and classical republican authors, such as Cicero and Plutarch, others more recent authorities such as Harrington and Locke. Others point to the importance of religious justifications, drawing upon Calvinism, and English law as described by William Blackstone. In truth, all were influential, often via contemporary writings which brought these authors and concerns together in ways that appealed to mid-eighteenth-century readers. One such text was Charles Louis de Secondat, Baron Montesquieu's comparative study of political systems and law. Published in 1748, *De l'Esprit des Loix* (*The Spirit of Laws*) was widely read by the colonial American gentry. Montesquieu reviewed republican, monarchical, and despotic forms of government and championed the cause of liberty which depended on the connection between virtuous and politically engaged citizens and a representative and just government. These conditions, Montesquieu argued, were only likely to be achieved in small rather than large republics wherein the "interest of the public is easier perceived, better understood, and more within the reach of every citizen."

On 15 June, an alternate, New Jersey Plan, recommended retaining the single chamber in which states were equally represented. Congress was to have the authority to raise funds using tariffs on trade and poll taxes based on population numbers, including the enslaved rated at three-fifths of a full citizen. Thereafter the plan added weight to federal government sanctions, but retained the one-state, one-vote model, leaving the national authority dependent on the states. The delegates debated the two sets of proposals and voted to rejected the New Jersey plan, prompting some from the smaller states to talk of quitting the convention. The breakthrough came at the end of June, when the Connecticut delegation proposed that the new government be considered neither wholly national nor wholly federated but a mixture of the two. Congress would have a lower house, the House of Representatives, in which members were assigned according to each state's population, and an upper house, which became the Senate, in which each state would have one vote, regardless of size. In addition to establishing both types of representation, this compromise also counted the enslaved as three-fifths of a person for tax and representation purposes.

Having debated the principle of representation and the structure of the government, the convention moved on to consider its powers, in particular the authority to regulate and tax commerce. Despite their ambitions for a strong and unified nation, delegates favoured state and regional interests in these discussions, giving an indication of the emerging sectional divisions – especially between the north and south – that would dominate politics for decades to come. Southern delegates represented states that relied on enslaved workers to produce and export staples, especially tobacco and cotton. It was to their advantage to keep trade free and shipping cheap. The northern delegates, by contrast, represented states with growing interests in manufacturing, for example textiles and shoes, as well as long-standing and extensive interests in shipping. They wanted protective tariffs, along the lines of the old British Navigation Acts, to shut out competing European manufacturers and shippers, thereby driving up costs for American consumers, especially southern exporters. Another crucial division concerned slavery. In 1787, the enslaved comprised fewer than 4 per cent of northern population compared to 40 per cent in the South. Southerners worried that a strong, northern dominated government might act against slavery, levying duties on imports of new enslaved people, pushing for an end to the Atlantic trade in human cargoes, or worse ending slavery altogether – as some radicals were already openly discussing. These differences fed into debates that would continue long after the convention, concerning the scope of national government and how far it could legitimately act in the affairs of the states and the economy at large.

In the summer of 1787, it was necessary to compromise, if the delegates were to achieve their ambition of a revised and strengthened national government. On trade, the convention rejected the north's import duties, but accepted the principle that the government be able to introduce commercial legislation to defend American trade from foreign competition and regulation. The government would also be able to legislate on the slave trade, but only after a 20-year delay; duties on imported slaves thereafter could not exceed ten dollars per person. Concessions to the north were balanced by confirmation of the accounting of the enslaved as three-fifths of a person for the purposes of representation, granting the southern states 30 per cent more members in the congressional lower house than they would have otherwise possessed. In so doing the three-fifths compromise ensured the slave states greater influence over the selection of the presidency and supreme court justices and the government at large down until the time of the Civil War, 1861–65. Once the delegates had compromised on trade and slavery, they still faced long and detailed debates on the appointment and powers of the presidency and a host of other topics. It was not until early September that there was a draft constitution to sign, after which the remaining delegates made plans to return home.

Historians continue to debate the implications of the debates at the Constitutional Convention and their relation to the revolutionary idealism of the Declaration of Independence. One of the reasons there has been so much scholarly disagreement is because of the lack of a comprehensive record of the proceedings. The delegates realised the controversial nature of their reforms and, wanting to stifle rumours and opposition ahead of their eventual announcement, they agreed to keep their discussions secret. The official journal has survived, but it is a mostly dull record of procedural motions and voting tallies. Several delegates made notes concerning particular days and speeches, especially James Madison who provided the fullest account we have of the twists and turns of the debates. Years later Madison's notes were published, ensuring that his observations became a major historical source on the proceedings. However, at the time and subsequently Madison drafted and redrafted his comments. We now know that what once looked like a real-time, objective record of daily events was a more partial and deliberative account.

In the absence of such a record, historians have had to be satisfied with conjecture concerning the delegates' motives. Some take the delegates at their word, portraying them as great statesmen and "founding fathers" intent on saving the chaos and excesses of the Revolution. Others have detected more selfish concerns, seeing the conventioneers as men of property deeply disturbed by the Revolution's radical potential and intent on preserving their class positions and wealth and power. At the very least the founders' desire for a powerful and active federal government presiding over a prosperous nation republic made them less concerned with civil liberties and more with making the republic attractive to domestic and foreign investors.

In the autumn of 1787, as the delegates returned home to their states from Philadelphia, they were likely less troubled by the judgement of history than with securing acceptance of the new constitution. Presuming that the state legislatures were unlikely to vote for a plan that weakened their own authority, the delegates called for state conventions to ratify the proposed reforms. There were voting restrictions, but the majority of white adult males of each state were able to vote for the delegates to attend and either support or oppose the new constitution. The calling and convening of the ratifying conventions launched months of debate and politicking, providing support for the claim that the Constitution was adopted by "the people." Within weeks of the end of the Philadelphia convention, 61 of the republic's 80 newspapers had printed copies of the Constitution, which also circulated as a pamphlet and broadside.

Supporters, identified as Federalists, had clear head start: they came out of the Philadelphia convention prepared for the campaign and their advocates, such as Benjamin Franklin and George Washington, were the most well-known Americans of the day. Over the next ten months Alexander Hamilton, John Jay, and James Madison wrote 85 essays under the pseudonym of "Publius," making the case for the new government. The opening essay posed the question as whether or not Americans could show "by their conduct and example . . . whether societies of men are really capable or not, of establishing good government" based on "reflection and choice." Subsequent contributions considered topics such as the inadequacies of the current system and the need for a strong and active central government to preserve the union and citizen's liberty and prosperity. Other essays focused on particular challenges. For example, the tenth essay, in which Madison described how a large republic with many competing interests would prevent domination of a particular faction or tyrant. Gathered together the articles became known as the *Federalist* (later the *Federalist Papers*) and in time were hailed as a major contribution to the political theory of democratic states.

In *Federalist No. 10*, Madison addressed the concerns of those who feared that the Constitution provided for a too large republic that would be disconnected from the popular will and dominated by self-interested factions. Madison was concerned with differences between merchant and landed interests, but also the propertied and propertyless whom, he argued, "have ever formed distinct interests in society." He worried that the propertyless would form a majority faction and force a redistribution. However, he acknowledged that universal agreement was implausible and it was impossible to eliminate different interests without destroying political liberty. If one could never eliminate factions, then the best approach was to mitigate their effects. This, Madison argued, was easier to achieve in a larger republic which provided access to a greater pool of virtuous citizens, and in which many different factions would prevent the domination of a narrow interest.

The opposition to the new constitution began even as the final draft was drawn up in Philadelphia, and delegates from Virginia and Massachusetts proposed the addition a bill of rights modelled on the state constitutions. When the proposal was rejected, the delegates concerned refused to sign the draft constitution. Once the ratification debates began others joined the opposition: some believed the centralisation of government under the Articles of Confederation was sufficient; others distrusted the convention delegates, mostly wealthy merchants and landowners, and prioritised direct citizen participation in democracy. There were many who agreed that the Articles were too weak, but feared that the new government would be too strong. This large and diverse opposition became known as the Anti-Federalists. They rejected this characterisation arguing, with some justification, that as the defenders of decentralised government they were the truer federalists; but the name stuck. In general, the Anti-Federalists defended the localist tradition and state sovereignty, championing communal and consensual democratic governance. There is also some evidence that the Constitution was favoured more in populated areas linked to the commercial economy, and less so in more remote, hinterland communities. How far the opposition arguments were countered by the Federalists' published essays is debatable, given that these commentaries mostly appeared in New York and were not widely reprinted elsewhere. Even in New York voters sent 46 Anti-Federalists delegates and only 19 Federalists to the state's ratifying convention. Moreover, by the time the publication of the *Federalist* essays gathered momentum, most states had already ratified the Constitution which was declared as passed by 2 July 1788.

The Federalists were better organised and secured ratification mostly quickly and easily. Between 7 December 1787 and 9 January 1788, five states – Delaware, Pennsylvania, New Jersey, Georgia and Connecticut – ratified the Constitution. The smaller states were pleased with the representation they had won and considered the new constitution as protection from larger neighbours. There was more controversy in Pennsylvania where anti-federalists boycotted the state legislature to prevent the calling of a Constitutional Convention. In a dramatic turn of events, several Anti-Federalists delegates were dragged from the lodgings and into the state house to ensure the proceedings were quorate. Once locked in the meeting room, the Anti-Federalists were easily out-voted by the Federalist majority, and had to content themselves with issuing a minority dissenting statement. In Massachusetts, the ratification debate ended up in fist fight between Federalist Francis Dana and Anti-Federalists Elbridge Gerry. The two sides were only reconciled, and the Constitution ratified, when a compromise agreeing the addition of amendments concerning specific individual and states' rights. The Massachusetts compromise set a pattern for the future in big but divided states, such as Virginia, where Federalist minorities secured ratification by agreeing to the addition of amendments guaranteeing individual rights. On June 18, New Hampshire ratified as the ninth state, passing the required boundary, followed by Virginia by 89 votes to 79 on 25 June. New York's convention was contentious to the end, but the Constitution passed by three votes on 26 July. By then, on 2 July, Congress had already announced that a majority of states having ratified the proposals, the new Constitution was now in effect. In September 1789, the first ten amendments provided the sought-after bill of rights, guaranteeing fundamental liberties and freedoms. In the end, the Federalist won because of a combination of effective management of the ratification process and appeals to powerful interests, such as those holding bonds and debt obligations, that the new government was their best chance to get paid off.

In 1788–89, then, the Constitution became the documentary foundation of American government and the judiciary. Although subject to a further seventeen ratified amendments down to the present day, the core text remains unchanged: its famous preamble – "we the people of these United States" – is regularly intoned by rote by school children; its articles and clauses poured over by Supreme Court Justices in contentious searches for the eighteenth-century founders' "original intentions." Across the decades the Constitution has been by turns celebrated and condemned: for the nineteenth-century British Prime Minister, William Gladstone, it was the "most wonderful work ever struck off . . . by the brain and purpose of man"; for the abolitionist, William Lloyd Garrison, the compromises on slavery made it a "covenant with death and an agreement with hell." In 1788–89, the Constitution's greatest impact was to revise the organisation and election of the federal government and, more importantly, give it the authority necessary to respond to internal challenges and external threats.

The revolutionary patriot movement had always been a marriage of convenience, aimed first and foremost at defeating the British. By war's end, and in some cases before, propertied patriots unsurprisingly rejected what they considered unpredictable popular radicalism in favour of an elite social alliance that aimed to put the republic and the interests of the wealthy and powerful on a firmer footing. Whether this qualifies as a "republican remedy for the diseases most incident to republican government," as Madison described it, will likely remain forever under debate. For most citizens, living under patriarchal authority in male-headed households and on racialised plantation regimes, the Constitution had little or no effect their immediate experience of authority and government. Indeed in many respects it even left the original and central question of the national government's authority over semi-autonomous state republics largely unresolved, condemning the American union to a terrible civil war just 70 or so years later.

The Federalist administration

The election of George Washington in the spring of 1789 provided a moment of national unity and affirmation of republican ideals. Washington was the unanimous choice of the state electors for the presidency; John Adams polled second and so became the first vice president. In April, the president-elect left his Mount Vernon plantation and journeyed north through modern-day Washington DC, Baltimore, Philadelphia, and Trenton, arriving for inaugural ceremony at Federal Hall, New York City, the temporary capital of the United States. Washington was a reluctant president and, in keeping with his dutiful conception of public service, he refused the salary that came with the office. For the inaugural he shunned sartorial pomp and dressed in an American-made dark brown suit, a red overcoat with white silk stockings, and silver shoe buckles. His brief address was short on policy recommendations, other than to call on Congress to add the bill of rights to the Constitution. In a drafted but undelivered section of his inaugural, he advocated an interventionist government that was committed to clearing the war debt and supporting the expansion of trade and manufacturing in the interests of the general welfare. Washington's behaviour in office pleased some and disturbed others. Dressed in a formal black coat and powdered hair, he held weekly audiences or levees at which he greeted visitors with a bow rather than the increasingly fashionable but less genteel hand shake. Lady Henriette Liston, wife of the British ambassador to the United States, noted admiringly that Washington possessed "perfect breeding and a correct knowledge of even the etiquette of court." Others worried that the president's levees created a "distinction between the public servant and his visitors . . . [which was] incompatible with a republican constitution."

Washington proved to be an able administrator and adept at managing a cabinet of fiery characters and disagreements, most notably between Alexander Hamilton, Secretary to the Treasury, and Thomas Jefferson, Secretary of State. In 1789, the administration introduced the Judiciary Act, establishing a Supreme Court with a Chief Justice and five Associate Justices endowed with jurisdiction over civil actions between states and any state and the United States. The Supreme Court also heard appeals from lower courts and ensured the consistency of state legislation with the Constitution and related laws and treaties. In 1792, Washington reluctantly agreed to serve a second term but refused to run for a third, handing the presidency over to Adams and returning, finally, to retirement in Virginia.

In his farewell address, drafted in 1792 but not finished and published until 1796, Washington reflected on his life in public service and the challenges facing the nation. He emphasised the importance of national union and warned of the dangers of foreign influences and of America's meddling in European matters. He called for the United States to remain free of "foreign attachments," or selective alliances, and to instead seek friendship and trade with all nations. He also decried the drift towards political partisanship and spoke of his distrust of organised political parties which he believed allowed unprincipled men to gain power and influence. He did so knowing that the divisions evident in his first administration had already fostered the creation of two opposing political parties with distinct visions of the role of the government: the Hamiltonian Federalists favouring an interventionist government that promoted American trade and manufacturing; and the Jeffersonian Democratic Republicans, who were committed to restraining the creep of federal power into new areas and over the states, and preserving an economy based on land ownership and agriculture.

Alexander Hamilton's colourful life story has inspired multiple biographies and even a smash-hit Broadway musical. Born on Nevis in the West Indies' Leeward Islands, he was the illegitimate son of a French Huguenot mother and minor Scottish aristocrat and plantation owner. When his father abandoned the family and his mother died,

Alexander and his brother had to rely on the charity of extended family contacts. Starting out as a clerk, Hamilton so impressed his patron that in 1772 he sent the boy, aged 17, to New York to complete his education. He arrived just as the dispute with Britain took a turn for the worst. Hamilton supported the patriots, joined Washington's staff as an aide, distinguished himself in combat, and rose to prominence as a supporter of the nationalist cause in the constitutional convention and ratification debates. Although he fought for American independence, Hamilton was a student and admirer of British society and government, especially its active role in building the empire. He was suspicious of popular and democratic politics and, notwithstanding his own humble origins, embraced social hierarchy and inequality as "the great & fundamental distinction in Society."

In office, Hamilton aimed to bind the rich and powerful to the republic by making the federal government "a Repository of the Rights of the wealthy." To this end he published a series of controversial reports on public credit (1789–92), proposing that the federal government assume the remaining debts owed by the states and pay off war bonds at face value to the current, rather then the original, holders. Next he proposed a national bank along the lines of the Bank of England. The bank would be capitalised at $10,000,000, four-fifths of which came from private investors, 25 of whom comprised its board of governors. Not surprisingly, heavily indebted states, such as Massachusetts, Connecticut, and South Carolina supported the plan, as did wealthy speculators who looked forward to a handsome premium on their investments in state and war debt. Hamilton's plan handed control of the bank, and so effectively the money supply, to private investors. He hoped thereby to replicate England's earlier success – following the establishment of a well-managed and liquid credit-based paper currency – which he hoped would promote market activity and reward the state and federal government with rising tax revenues.

To cover the cost of assuming the states' debts and clearing the federal domestic and foreign obligations, the government needed to increase its revenue. It did this by introducing new taxes, including one on the production and consumption of whiskey which Hamilton reckoned would raise $3 million. Pennsylvania legislators opposed the tax, realising that western farmers relied on their earnings from distilling whiskey which also served as a form of commodity currency in cash strapped areas. Hamilton's concern for government revenues also featured in his second set of reports, relating to manufacturing and trade. Once again drawing on his studies of European political economy, Hamilton advocated manufacturing and the development of foreign and domestic markets over relying only on agricultural productivity as the surest route to economic prosperity. Without the development of manufacturing, Hamilton worried that America would be left to import manufactures from Europe and elsewhere. To discourage imports and stimulate domestic manufacturing, he favoured duties on goods that Americans could make for themselves. The government would use the money earned from duties to make raw materials cheaper, encourage immigration, and promote the general welfare. To encourage enterprise Hamilton teamed up with entrepreneurs from New York and Philadelphia to form the Society for the Establishment of Useful Manufactures, a public-private industrial corporation intended to promote the construction of watermills along the Passaic River in New Jersey. Hamilton's reports and recommendations interpreted the Constitution loosely and increased the power and reach of the federal government. For some these were positive moves and addressed the challenges facing the republic. However, not everyone agreed.

From early in Washington's first administration, a group of prominent, mainly southern representatives, including James Madison and Thomas Jefferson, became increasingly concerned about the increasing power of the federal government which seemed to them to be wielded on behalf of the commercial interests of northern states. This anti-administration faction opposed the measures to restore public credit which favoured heavily-indebted states, such as Massachusetts, over Virginian, which had paid off its war debts. Critics also argued that the plans for the National Bank lacked clear constitutional foundations and would, once again, again benefit northern merchants and manufacturers seeking credit to develop infrastructure and factories. Meanwhile the south – a cash rich, agricultural and exporting economy – would have to pay higher prices because of duties on imported European household goods. During Washington's second term, the anti-administration faction grew to 32 out of 72 representatives in the House of Representatives. In order to get his financial reforms through Congress, Hamilton and his allies agreed to the southerner's proposal for Washington DC as the site for the nation's capital. To secure passage of the National Bank legislation it was necessary to invoke the emergency, "necessary and proper" clause within the Constitution.

While Washington was still in office, Jefferson warned that Hamilton's policies aimed to "prepare the way for a change from the present republican form of government to that the monarchy" along English lines. Washington disagreed and rejected Jefferson's criticism. In western Pennsylvania, Hamilton's whiskey tax was met by armed resistance not seen since the Shaysites' disturbances of the mid 1780s. Western farmers chased tax collectors out of their communities, put up liberty poles, and petitioned for redress just as the patriots had in the American Revolution. In 1794, the farmers attacked federal marshals and tax collectors and a force of 7,000 gathered a few miles east of Pittsburgh. Washington assembled an army of 13,000 which moved west from Carlisle, Pennsylvania, scattering the farmers and arresting their leaders. The Whiskey Rebellion demonstrated the continued strength of local and popular resistance to remote legislators and tax demands deemed arbitrary and unjust. Washington's response showed the federal government now had the force to back its orders and would use it when required.

In the Northwest, the federalist administrations faced an effective guerrilla war by a powerful Indian Confederacy determined to defend their land and hunting rights. The 1783 Peace of Paris had granted the Americans large swathes of territory in the trans-Appalachian West. However, these lands were home to as many as 100,000 Native Americans representing dozens of different communities, many of whom were covertly supported by the British and Spanish who maintained a presence in the west and southwest. The 1784 and 1785 ordinances aimed to impose an organised white settlement, keeping out squatters and minimising conflict with the Indians. However, settlers moved west in massive and unregulated numbers, provoking conflict with Indian inhabitants. Washington adopted a two-handed approach, attempting to buy off Native Americans who agreed to integrate to American society and launching offensives against those determined to fight. The Americans lost major battles to powerful Indian forces comprising warriors drawn from the Shawnees, Delawares, Ottawas, and Wyandot. However, the American victory at the 1794 Battle of Fallen Timbers ended the Native American challenge and the 1795 Treaty of Greenville required them to cede most of modern-day Ohio and a slice of Indiana and recognise the United States as the ruling power in the Northwest Territory.

Figure 4.4 George Washington reviews the Western army at Fort Cumberland on the 18th of October 1794 before marching to suppress the Whiskey Rebellion in western Pennsylvania.

Source: Courtesy of Science History Images/Alamy

The Democratic Republicans

In the end, it was not the Constitution, popular rebellions, or problems in the west but the French Revolution and foreign affairs that intensified the antagonism between the two factions leading to the formation of formal political parties. In 1789, most Americans greeted the news of the collapse of the monarchy in France as a welcome indication that the liberty recently won in the United States was spreading across Europe. There were parades and speeches celebrating the Jacobin cause, and men and women pinned revolutionary tricolour cockades (rosettes) to their hats. However, it soon became clear that the French fight for liberty was a very different proposition than the struggle in America. French revolutionaries had to contend with a complex and entrenched socio-political ancien régime which the American colonies had largely lacked. When a radical faction of French revolutionaries gained control, they began a murderous purge of the aristocracy and their political enemies. This "reign of terror" led many Americans to reconsider their view of the Revolution. In particular, the Federalists saw in French chaos and violence the threat of "democratic excesses" they had staved off following the American Revolution and which had made threatening returns during the Shaysite and Whiskey Rebellions.

When Britain and France went to war, American conservatives sided with their old colonial masters against the upstart French republic. The faction gathered around

Figure 4.5 This image shows an execution at the Place de la Revolution, where Louis XVI and some 1,200 others met their end during the "terror" of 1793–94.

Source: Courtesy of The Print Collector/Alamy

Madison and Jefferson, on other hand, worried less about the violence against aristocrats in France, and more about the Federalists undermining revolutionary principles in America. In 1791–92, they established an anti-administration newspaper presented themselves at elections as "republican" critics of Adams and supporters of France. Following the election, attention turned to the Britain's naval war against France which also threatened American shipping. In particular, the British policy of forcibly impressing, recruiting, American sailors into the king's navy. Tacitly acknowledging America's weakness, Washington declared the United States neutral and dispatched John Jay to negotiate with the British. The resulting 1794 Treaty of Amity and Commerce was a success, of sorts. It enabled the Americans to stay out of the war and secured Britain's withdrawal from its forts in the Northwest Territory and the promise of compensation for those damaged by the naval conflict. However, the deal dismayed American republicans, who mistrusted Britain and favoured the new French state as a long-term European ally. In effect the federalists had sided with a monarchy against a republic, submitting to British influence without even ending impressment.

The debate over Jay's Treaty transformed the congressional factions into two, loosely organised political parties, the Federalists and the Democratic Republicans. Those who thought the terror of the French Revolution was a sign of its descent into disorder and anarchy sided with the federalists. Those inspired by the French revolutionary principles of *liberté, égalité, fraternité*, and suspicious of the administration's polices, supported the Republicans. In 1796, John Adams became president of an increasingly divided country. After Jay's Treaty the French considered the United States an enemy and authorised attacks on American shipping. Adams sent envoys to France to protest and negotiate but they were ignored and insulted. Americans received reports that officials in the French revolutionary government had intimated that the American envoys would need to pay a bribe before they would even be heard. When the news got out, angry American citizens and even whole towns wrote to Adams urging him to stand firm against French insults and threats.

The XYZ affair

The XYZ affair was a controversy surrounding a 1797–98 American mission to France to ease tensions between the two nations. Three French diplomats insisted the Americans provide a loan to the French government and a £50,000 bribe to the foreign minister, Talleyrand, before he would begin negotiations. Fearing news of the insulting French behaviour would fuel calls for war from within his own Federalist Party, Adams tried to keep it secret but was eventually forced to release the papers – with the names of the diplomats redacted as X, Y, and Z – provoking public outrage and the crisis that led to the Quasi-War, 1708–1800.

By 1798, the United States was fighting a quasi-naval war with France. At home many worried that the ships that had so recently assisted the Americans in their victory over the British might now be used to launch an invasion of the republic, perhaps using newly freed enslaved people as troops from Haiti and aiming at pressing similar disruption and emancipation in the American south. There were rumours that French agents were abroad in American towns, stirring up dissent and discontent. As American ships engaged the French on the high seas, more radical republicans, this time from Ireland, arrived in the United States. These radicals were fleeing the 1798 rising by the United Irishmen who, with French support, had challenged Britain's colonial rule, leading to massacres and atrocities costing an estimated 10,000 to 20,000 lives. Once in America, the Irish swelled Republican ranks and added to Federalist concerns regarding the disorder of political populism.

In response, Adams passed an Alien Act, which extended the residency term to 14 years for immigrants wanting to be naturalised as citizens of the United States and allowed the government to deport foreign nationals it deemed a threat to national security. The Republicans and their newspapers denounced the Act as proof positive of the Federalist's disregard for republican liberties and crypto-aristocratic pretensions. These protests prompted Adams to pass a Sedition Act to stamp out "false, scandalous, and malicious writing," effectively subverting free speech and criminalising criticism of the government. Late in 1798 the Kentucky and Virginia legislatures debated resolutions written, in secret, by Madison and Jefferson, declaring the Alien and Sedition Acts unconstitutional. In effect, Madison and Jefferson argued that the Constitution was a "compact" or agreement between the states and the federal government could not assume powers that were not expressly granted in the original document, a clear challenge to the legality of National Bank and Alien and Sedition Acts. The resolutions were a minor protest at the time, roundly rejected by the states, and condemned by Washington as likely to "dissolve the union or produce coercion." However, they articulated a political doctrine regarding rights retained by the states, implicitly challenging the authority of the Constitution and lay down a significant precedent for future debates.

Long before the election of 1800, Adams had become an isolated and even derided president. Fifteen years earlier the Federalists had formed as a political force to defend established social hierarchies and to protect, in their eyes, the Revolution from its democratic excesses. Federalist political economy, especially advocacy of government intervention to support domestic commerce, was forward-looking and vindicated by economic development. However, their elitist social vision and commitment to the politics of deference were increasingly out of touch in an age of democratic radicalism, mass immigration and western settlement, and populist politics. Sensitive to criticism, Adams was frequently at odds with even his supposed cabinet allies, especially Hamilton. In the election, Jefferson led the Republican Party which campaigned against the Alien and Sedition Acts. Republicans also opposed the levying of unpopular taxes that were used to build up the army and navy engaged in the quasi-war with France. Both sides used the press to engage in fiercely partisan campaigning and mud slinging. Republicans declared Adams a "hideous hermaphroditical character" with neither the "force and firmness of a man, nor the gentleness and sensibility of a woman." The Federalists countered by describing Jefferson as "the son of a half-breed Indian squaw, sired by a Virginia mulatto father," and claiming he had a sexual relationship with Sally Hemings, an enslaved woman. This latter charge – steadfastly denied at the time and afterwards, despite considerable circumstantial evidence to the contrary – was substantiated in 1998 by DNA. testing which established a link between descendants of the two branches of the family.

Both sides predicted disastrous consequences if the other won the election. The Republicans declared their campaign nothing less than a "second revolution" and a fight to save the country from an aristocratic coup d'état and preserve the principles and freedoms won during the War for Independence. Then, in August 1800, Virginia enslavers heard news of an uprising by hundreds of enslaved led by a 24-year-old blacksmith called Gabriel who planned to march on Richmond with hundreds of armed supporters. This was more than a slave revolt. Gabriel and his associates aimed to recruit poor whites to their ranks in support of a radical republican revolution against the wealthy and powerful. If the whites would not join, the rebels declared, then they would kill them except for "Quakers, Methodists, and French people" who were deemed "friendly to liberty." The Federalists seized upon the rebellion as yet more evidence of the dangers stirred up by the Republican's talk of "liberty and equality." Already anxious about the republic established by ex-slaves in Haiti and the possibility of the return of French aggression, enslavers in the south introduced new and vigorous laws restricting slave daily life and movement, shutting down the few small moves towards liberalisation in the preceding two decades.

In the end Jefferson's party, benefitting from the south's three-fifths advantage, won easily over the divided Federalists. The Republicans took control of both houses in Congress and the presidency and effected the republic's first peaceful passage of power from one party to another. The victory resulted in an important realignment, marking the end of the Federalists and the beginnings of an era of Democratic Republican predominance. Jefferson demonstrated his public dislike of formal etiquette: he arrived in the capital dressed plainly and on horseback, without an escort; after dismounting, he retired his own horse to a nearby stable. His inaugural struck a conciliatory tone, claiming that Republicans and Federalists were all as one as Americans. Once in office, he sold off the presidential coaches and silver harnesses, eschewed ceremonial rituals, and continued to dress in the plain style of the owner of a country estate. Much of this was for political show: Jefferson remained a wealthy enslaver, with a taste for the finer things in life, and committed to the political interests of the slaveholding states. In other respects, he was true to the republicans' political campaign: he reduced the wait for immigrants to become naturalised as citizens to five years, repealed the Sedition Acts, and pardoned those convicted under their auspices. Most importantly, Jeffersonian republicans stalled the Federalist drive for a powerful and interventionist central government, reducing the administration in Washington to a focus on foreign affairs and customs collection, and cutting the military to a defensive. Spending cuts allowed republicans to cut unpopular excise and land taxes. The taxes had been justified as necessary to repay the government's debt which had, in fact, increased by 10 per cent during the Federalists' 12 years in government. Over his two terms as President, Jefferson reduced the debt by almost a third.

In contrast to Hamilton's vision of paper credit and a national bank managed by a wealthy elite who drove investment in urbanisation and manufacturing, Jefferson imagined a republic comprised of small farmers or "husbandmen" and independent property owners. This social and economic foundation was essential to Jefferson's vision for the longer term survival of a self-governing republic. The "cultivators of the earth are the most valuable citizens" he wrote to John Jay in 1785, "They are the most vigorous, the most independent, the most virtuous, and they are tied to their country and wedded to its liberty and interests by the most lasting bonds." As long as citizens could find "employment in this line," Jefferson argued "I would not convert them into mariners, artisans, or anything else." Some have argued that Jefferson's political philosophy favoured rural and agricultural life over the seemingly more transient, corruptible, and socially disruptive commercial wealth: "Let our workshops remain in Europe" he wrote "The mobs of the great cities add just so much to the support of pure government as sores do to the human body." However, even as he settled into the presidency, Jefferson faced domestic and international challenges that would require him to compromise and in some respects abandon these ideals.

Chapter summary

This chapter opened with the 1783 Peace of Paris and then considered the challenges and disputes that prompted the Constitutional Convention four years later. Post-war America was troubled by huge domestic and international debts, disputes over the continuing war against Native Americans and the division of western lands, and the relationship between the states and the central government. The chapter identified the central question as whether the new republic was to be a union of semi-sovereign states or a unified nation with the stature and authority to common respect on the international stage. The chapter considered various the administration under the 1781 Articles of Confederation and various dissatisfactions leading up to Shays Rebellion in 1787, which convinced many state leaders of the need to strengthen the authority of the federal government. We considered the debates during the Constitutional

Convention and the character of the government proposed by the new Constitution. The chapter closed with a survey of Washington's two terms as president and the Federalist administration, ending with bitter divisions surrounding the French Revolution that brought Jefferson and the Republicans to power in the election of 1800.

Discussion questions

- Why did Americans have reasons to be optimistic and anxious in 1781?
- How did the position of Native Americans in the west change after 1781?
- How should we judge the administration of central government under the Articles of Confederation?
- How did the European powers regard the new American republic?
- How much of a threat was Shays' Rebellion to the new republic?
- How did the Founding Father's regard democracy?
- Why was the war debt problem also a constitutional challenge for state and federal governments?
- Did the Constitution secure or undermine the radicalism of the Revolution?
- Why were the Founding Fathers and Americans so readily prepared to compromise on the enslaving of African Americans in their republic of liberty?
- Why did the French Revolution provoke such severe divisions?

Further reading

Beard, Charles A. *An Economic Interpretation of the Constitution of the United States* (New York, 1913). A classic study which scandalized contemporaries by claiming to prove that the Founding Fathers designed the Constitution in ways that protected their individual interests.

Berkin, Carol. *A Brilliant Solution: Inventing the American Constitution* (New York, 2002). A pacey narrative history of the founding era and the men who wrote the Constitution.

Bilder, Mary Sarah. *Madison's Hand: Revising the Constitutional Convention* (Cambridge, 2015). Another, and it were needed surely the final, nail in the coffin of "original intent." This book minutely examines Madison's famous notes on the Constitutional Convention (long considered the best record we have) and finds them to be intensely personal and much revised, sometimes decades after the fact.

Edling, Max M. *A Revolution in Favour of Government: Origins of the American Constitution and the Making of the American State* (Oxford, 2003).

The *Federalist* and anti-Federalist papers are available online at www.congress.gov/resources/ display/content/The+Federalist+Papers and www.constitution.org/afp.htm with many more suggestions for additional reading.

Holton, Woody. *Unruly Americans and the Origins of the Constitution* (New York, 2007). A book in the neo-progressive tradition which traces popular action in writing of a Constitution designed to protect the republic for private investment by limiting rather than merely securing democracy.

Maier, Pauline. *Ratification: The People Debate the Constitution, 1787–1788* (New York, 2010). Examines the ratification debates following the proposing of the Constitution and captures the politicking and rough and tumble that ushered the finished document into place.

McDonald, Forrest. *Novus Ordo Seclorum: The Intellectual Origins of the Constitution* (Lawrence, 1985). An intellectual history of the Constitution which traces the Founding Fathers philosophy to key thinkers, such as John Locke, and English constitutional and economic ideas.

Morgan, Edmund S. *The Birth of the Republic, 1763–89* (Chicago, 1992). A narrative tracing the origins of the American Republic.

Morgan, Edmund S. *Inventing the People: The Rise of Popular Sovereignty in England and America* (New York, 1988). A book considering the origins of the idea of "the people" and thus the foundations for democratic political culture in the seventeenth and eighteenth centuries.

Rakove, Jack N. *Original Meanings: Politics and Ideas in the Making of the Constitution* (New York, 1996). Examines the Founders and what they thought they were doing in light of modern and conservative debates concerning the Constitution's "original intent" – a position Rakove challenges.

Wood, Gordon S. *Creation of the American Republic 1776–1787* (Chapel Hill, 1969). A study of the influence of classical republican political theory over the writing of the American Constitution.

Zuckert, Michael P. *Natural Rights and the New Republicanism* (Princeton, NJ, 1994). Study which reconsiders the development of American rights-based philosophy in a combination of republican politics and the work of seventeenth-century Dutch jurist Hugo Grotius, which later became synthesised in mid-eighteenth-century readings of John Locke.

5 The growth of the white republic

Timeline

1791	Slave rebellion begins in French colony of Saint Domingue
1793	Invention of the cotton gin
1800	Washington DC becomes the capital city
	Louisiana ceded by Spain to France
1801	Thomas Jefferson becomes president
	John Marshall becomes chief justice
1803	Louisiana Purchase
	Ohio becomes the 17th state
1804	Lewis and Clark expedition leaves St Louis
	Haiti established as an independent nation
1807	Embargo Act
1808	Closure of the international slave trade to the United States
1812	War of 1812 begins
	Louisiana becomes the 18th state
1813–14	Creek, or Red Stick, War
1814	Hartford Convention
	British soldiers burn the White House
	Treaty of Ghent
1815	Battle of New Orleans
1816	James Monroe becomes president
	Henry Clay's American System
	Second Bank of the United States chartered
	Indiana becomes the 19th state
1817	Andrew Jackson invades Florida
	Mississippi becomes the 20th state
1818	Erie Canal construction begins
	National Road completed
	Illinois becomes the 21st state
1819	US purchases Florida from Spain
	Alabama becomes the 22nd state
1823	The Monroe Doctrine
1825	John Quincy Adams becomes president
	Completion of the Erie Canal
1829	Andrew Jackson becomes president
1830	Indian Removal Act

| 1835 | Treaty of New Echota |
| 1838 | Forced removal of the Cherokee (Trail of Tears) |

Topics covered

- Louisiana Purchase
- Expansion of slavery
- The War of 1812
- Industrialisation and the American system
- The Market Revolution?
- Building a national infrastructure
- Men, women, and separate spheres
- Free blacks
- Indian removal

Introduction

The Appalachian Mountains constituted an imposing barrier to expansion in the colonial era that was quickly forgotten as settlers poured westward from the seaboard states. It is remarkable how quickly the United States grew in size and population during the nineteenth century. The Louisiana Purchase of 1803 more than doubled the original territory of the country. It helped the US consolidate as a nation and, in time, Americans envisioned a natural right to spread across the whole of North America. The confidence of the young republic was growing and figures such as George Washington, who died in 1799, were mythologised as national heroes. Nonetheless, in many respects the US remained a loose collection of states rather than a unified country. It was also a country buffeted by European wars and continued foreign imperial plans for North America. The US eventually became embroiled in a second conflict with the leading power of the age, Great Britain, but emerged unscathed and stronger from the War of 1812.

The US economy grew rapidly with far-reaching consequences for the lives of blacks, whites, and Native Americans. First, slavery was reinvigorated as cotton production soared in the Lower South and sugar plantations in Louisiana also thrived. Cotton was essential to the development of the national economy and encouraged the growth of manufacturing in New England. Plantation slavery entailed misery for African Americans. Hundreds of thousands of enslaved people migrated with their owners

Historical periodisation

Historical periodisation, found in the study of all times and places in some form, is particularly important in dividing eras of US history. Antebellum, for instance, literally means "before war" – in this instance before the American Civil War that began in 1861. Most scholars use "antebellum" to refer to the period between 1800 and 1861, although it is sometimes used to refer to 1830–60, while "early national" denotes the period 1790–1830. Periodisation is a useful tool for delineating distinctive eras, although students should be wary that these conventions can overemphasise disjunctures and minimise continuities.

or, more commonly, were sold to the emerging "Cotton Kingdom" as contemporaries called it. Second, a transportation boom connected the vast territorial expanses of the expanding United States which enabled products to be sold far from their point of origin. This encouraged commercial production as farmers specialised in cash crops rather than practice self-sufficiency. The most devastating event discussed in this chapter, though, is the forced expulsion of native peoples west of the Mississippi River. Indian removal, in conjunction with the entrenchment of slavery and the repression of free black communities, served to disseminate and popularise scientific doctrines of the natural racial hierarchy in which whites stood superior to other races.

Louisiana Purchase

The United States was built on westward expansion as tens of thousands, both immigrants and native-born, took advantage of unparalleled opportunities for land ownership. This movement was fostered by government initiative, but more forcefully by pioneers who pushed ever further into the American interior caring little for the land

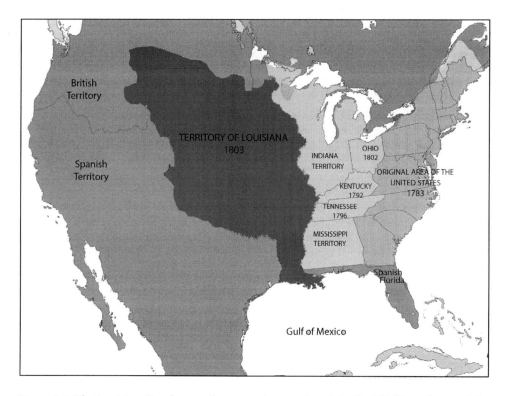

Figure 5.1 The Louisiana Purchase and westward expansion. John L. O'Sullivan first used the term "manifest destiny" in the *Democratic Review* in 1845. He called for the annexation of Texas as part of "the fulfillment of our manifest destiny to overspread the continent allotted by Providence for the free development of our yearly multiplying millions." The phrase was new but the idea that the US was divinely foreordained to occupy the whole of the North American continent was much older and underpinned the drive westward during the nineteenth century.

rights of Indians. As described in the chapter 3, the 1783 Treaty of Paris granted the United States a vast expanse of territory between the Appalachian Mountains and the Mississippi River, opening the way west from the original 13 states on the Atlantic seaboard. Settlers poured into this region during the first half of the nineteenth century. The United States offered unparalleled opportunities for ordinary people in comparison to Europe: between 1796 and 1820 the price of buying an acre of government land fell from $2 to $1.25 and the minimum allowable purchase from 640 acres to just 80. Moreover, the 1787 Northwest Ordinance permitted territories to apply to become states on equal terms. This important piece of legislation ensured that new states became full members of the US regardless of size or population.

Westward expansion was far from straightforward however. Britain, France, and Spain had their own plans for the Mississippi, Missouri, and Ohio valleys, and wanted to strengthen their position on the North American continent in various ways. This potentially compromised American expansion, as did the powerful Native American tribes who had occupied the land for centuries and stood directly in the way of the path west. As the US established itself as a fully fledged nation, though, and grew in confidence as the uncertainties of its founding diminished with the passage of time, the allure of the West became compelling. The American gaze even at this early stage extended to the Pacific side of the continent, although it was control of the Mississippi River that needed to be secured first and the key to that resided with the port of New Orleans.

The 1795 Spanish-American Treaty of San Lorenzo (known as the Pinckney treaty in the US after its negotiator Thomas Pinckney) granted American ships the right to sail the Mississippi River and send goods through Spanish-controlled New Orleans without paying duty. This agreement benefitted US trade enormously (although was not always adhered to by the Spanish) but also bolstered Spanish control of Louisiana, which was highly unsatisfactory to the Americans for several reasons. Spanish territory included present-day Florida until 1819, a popular destination for fugitive, or self-emancipated, slaves, who formed what were known as maroon colonies in swamps and other inaccessible areas. These groups allied with local Indians in many cases and were very capable of defending themselves. Any disruption of plantation security was a major irritant to the southern states. Moreover, whoever possessed New Orleans effectively controlled the Mississippi River that, because of its series of major tributaries that included the Arkansas, Illinois, Missouri, Ohio, and Red Rivers, was the major transportation route within the North American heartland. Possession of the Crescent City (New Orleans) was much prized as a result.

In October 1800, under pressure from Napoleon, the Spanish secretly ceded Louisiana back to France. The subsequent turn of events emphasised how US affairs were closely intertwined with Europe. President Thomas Jefferson understood the strategic importance of New Orleans, as had many before him. Frightened at the prospect of a French revival in North America, the US ambassador in France, Robert R. Livingston, was sent to negotiate the purchase of New Orleans. Joined by James Monroe in January 1803, the Americans were eventually offered far more than they had hoped or planned for. French plans for North America changed after failure to retake Saint Domingue and they offered to sell the whole of the vast Louisiana territory, not just New Orleans, to the United States. Napoleon wanted the proceeds to finance his ongoing war with Great Britain. This deal had not been authorised by Congress but American negotiators seized the opportunity. Louisiana was purchased in April 1803 and cost the United States $15 million in return for 828,000 square miles (roughly four cents an acre). Toussaint Loverture's successful rebellion in Saint Domingue did much to influence Napoleon's decision to sell Louisiana. Given the immense significance of this sale, it is ironic that the US refused to recognise the legitimacy of the independent country of Haiti, as Saint Domingue was renamed, until 1862.

There was considerable domestic opposition to the Louisiana Purchase. Federalists in New England saw their fortunes bound up with Great Britain and did not want closer ties with Napoleon or to risk war with Spain. Did the Constitution allow such an unprecedented measure? What was to be done with the existing settlers, of different backgrounds, who would come under American jurisdiction? The fact that this territory was already inhabited by numerous Indian tribes was not even raised during negotiations. The Louisiana Purchase was approved in the House by just two votes (59–57). At the stroke of a pen, the United States more than doubled in size. Its borders stretched from the Atlantic Ocean to the Rocky Mountains and from the Canadian border to the Gulf of Mexico. While some Americans were greatly perturbed, southerners, especially enslavers, were delighted. Slavery could not expand north of the Ohio River under the terms of the 1787 Northwest Ordinance, so the Louisiana Purchase opened a vast expanse of fresh land. Jefferson considered this the making of an "empire for liberty" but the states carved out of the massive Louisiana territory became an empire for slavery. Hundreds of thousands of slaves in the tobacco-producing states would have bitter cause to regret this acquisition.

Lewis and Clark expedition to the Pacific coast

Meriwether Lewis and William Clark were commissioned by President Thomas Jefferson in 1803 to explore the American northwest. They departed from St Louis in May 1804 and headed up the Missouri River reaching North Dakota. A wise decision was taken to spend the winter there, where cordial relations were established with local Mandan Indians who shared knowledge and advice about their next steps. The party continued along the Missouri River, crossed the Rocky Mountains and then followed the Columbia River to reach the Pacific Ocean by late 1805. The expedition was greatly helped by the linguistic skills of a Shoshone woman, Sacagawea, married to a French trapper. Lewis and Clark returned in 1806 with detailed information about the peoples and the environment of a region that was hitherto entirely unknown.

The first third of the nineteenth century proved to be a critical period in US-Indian relations as the Louisiana Purchase intensified pressure on tribes residing between the Appalachians and the Mississippi River. After lengthy speculation over Indian "character" and capacity to integrate into white society, the federal government looked to clarify its relationship with the indigenous people who had without consultation been placed under their jurisdiction. As we have seen, Indian tribes conducted a delicate diplomacy throughout the colonial period playing European rivals against one another to their advantage. The withdrawal of the French from North America in 1763, and Great Britain's defeat in the Revolutionary War, meant this was no longer possible. The Treaty of Paris took no account of Indian land rights, despite relations built up

Figure 5.2 Meriwether Lewis and William Clark.
Source: Courtesy of Ian Dagnall Computing/Alamy

with the British over many years. Creek leader Alexander McGillivray reflected rue-fully that "to find ourselves and Country betrayed to our enemies & divided between the Spaniards & the Americans is cruel & ungenerous." Spain retained control of Florida, but this northern outpost of the Spanish empire was poorly defended and not a strategic priority. While Britain abandoned many of its indigenous allies after the American Revolution, it had no intention of giving Canada up and worked with Indian tribes to check US expansion northward.

Leading American politicians and intellectuals generally held a positive view of the Indian capacity to assimilate. Reinvigorated by Enlightenment thought that presented Indians in noble terms, the late eighteenth and early nineteenth centuries witnessed an upsurge in sympathy for the plight of the indigenous peoples, particularly in New England. This sentiment was often tinged with a hint of jealousy at the supposedly harmonious relationship Indians enjoyed with the land. Jefferson suggested in 1785 that "I believe the Indian then to be in body and mind equal to the white man." This view contrasted starkly with his observations of "the black man," who, "in his pre-sent state, might not be so" according to Jefferson. Many Americans shared his view that Indians were capable of taking their place in American society. Capability, how-ever, was very different from suitability. Jefferson was crystal clear that Native Ameri-cans should be treated justly, but that they must change traditional ways. That meant abandoning hunting for sedentary agriculture, speaking English, living in settled fam-ily units, becoming educated, adopting a democratic political system, and embracing Christianity. As Indians assimilated, land-hungry Americans would be the beneficiar-ies as hunting grounds became homesteads.

The Northwest Ordinance required the US government to negotiate with Native Americans in "utmost good faith" and probably prevented crass abuse of Indian land rights. A series of Trade and Intercourse Acts were negotiated with tribes which attempted to maintain peaceful relations as the frontier pushed westward rapidly, with Kentucky, Tennessee, and Ohio achieving statehood by 1803. Powerful southern tribes resisted expansion more easily than the smaller tribes of the Old Northwest in the Great Lakes and Ohio Valley. Had the states and territories west of the Appalachians unilaterally taken charge, the outcome would have led to greater bloodshed. However, the federal government could not possibly supervise the whole of the fast moving frontier. Atrocities and reprisals between Indians and white settlers were common. In wake of the Louisiana Purchase, Henry Knox's ethnocentric view that Native Americans would grasp the opportunities available to them to become "civilised" was put to the test. The expectation was that Indians must adopt white ways. Knox, Secretary of War in George Washington's administration, had little to say about thousands of whites who broke treaties and other prior agreements as they stole, swindled, or took Native American land by force.

Expansion of slavery

Hand in hand with westward expansion came the entrenchment and extension of slavery in the post-Revolutionary era. The principal causal factor was cotton, or more precisely the fabulous returns to be made from selling cotton on European markets. Southerners had experimented with cotton in the colonial era, but chose to focus on rice and tobacco because cotton proved far too labour-intensive. It took an entire day's labour to separate sticky seeds from cotton fibres to produce one pound of raw cotton. This problem was solved by the invention of the cotton gin, usually attributed to the northerner Eli Whitney in 1793 although others claim the credit for this. The cotton gin revolutionised cotton production, enabling a single slave to process 50 pounds of cotton in one day. Cotton slavery began in the South Carolina and Georgia upcountry and higher grades of cotton flourished in the Sea Islands off the Atlantic coast. In 1790, there were 29,000 slaves in the South Carolina upcountry in the interior; by 1810, 85,000.

But it was in the Deep South that cotton's impact was greatest, leading to the formation of what contemporaries, and later scholars, called the Cotton Kingdom. Cotton was ideally suited to the environmental conditions found in a large expanse of territory stretching across Georgia, Alabama, Mississippi, and Louisiana, known as the black belt due to its dark, fertile soil. The efficiencies gained by the cotton gin and slavery's expansion into the southwest occurred just as cotton was becoming the essential raw material of the British industrial revolution. Cotton was the single most valuable export from the United States before the Civil War, worth somewhere between one-half and two-thirds of all exports up to 1861. Approximately two million pounds of cotton sold in 1791 shot up to a billion pounds of cotton by 1860.

None of this would have been possible without a huge labour force. The scale of the domestic slave trade removing enslaved people from the Upper South to Alabama, Mississippi, Louisiana, and later Texas was vast. Recent historians have overturned erroneous views that concealed the magnitude of the internal slave trade and denied its connection to "respectable" southerners. The domestic slave trade was a central feature of southern society that was also essential to the growth of the national economy. Black families and communities were uprooted and split apart for the pursuit of profit. Calculating total numbers is difficult, but approximately 1.1 million enslaved people were taken between 1790 and 1860. Between 60 and 70 per cent were sold

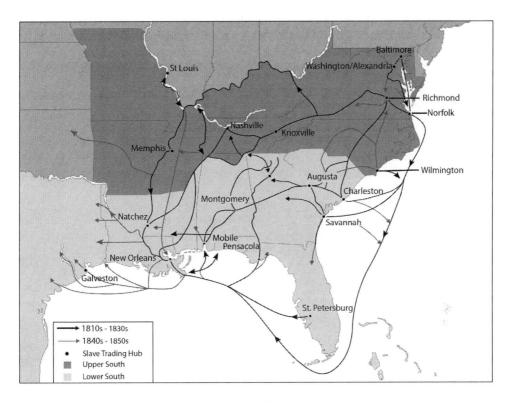

Figure 5.3 The domestic slave trade in the antebellum era.

via the internal slave trade by professional slave trading firms, the rest migrated with their enslavers or were sent to the Deep South to new plantations accompanied by an overseer. The vast majority of enslavers sold enslaved property at some point, to settle debts but also for speculative purposes when the price was high. Enslaved people dreaded being sold but moving from the Upper to the Lower South was particularly frightening.

Plantation agriculture in the Lower, or Deep, South thrived. It was spearheaded by an influx of native French speakers from Acadia (present-day Nova Scotia, Canada) as well as enslavers fleeing the chaos of Saint Domingue to reach Louisiana. The latter group contributed greatly to the growth of the sugar industry west of New Orleans. Between 1796 and 1800 at least 60 plantations switched from tobacco and indigo to sugar production. The rich alluvial soil on the banks of the Mississippi River was much coveted and sustained the most profitable cotton plantations. Short-staple cotton flourished in these conditions and the cotton gin was refined, improved, and the latest models were in high demand in New Orleans. Cotton and sugar was sold within the United States but mainly exported to European markets, predominately Britain and France. The vast profits that were to be made encouraged Upper South enslavers to relocate and they left in great numbers after 1815. The new life injected into American slavery had profound effects on the historical trajectory of the United States.

The official closure of the international slave trade to the US in 1808 did not, then, cause a decline in total numbers of slaves that had been envisaged at the Constitutional

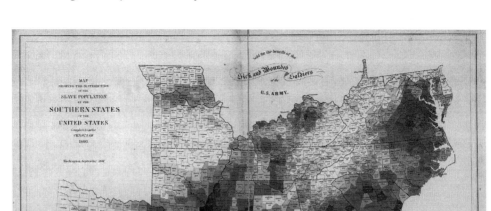

Figure 5.4 The expansion of slavery and growth of the black belt by 1860. The forced labour
of African Americans generated huge riches for enslavers. There were more mil-
lionaires per capita on the banks of the Mississippi River (which is the vertical line
of counties shaded black slightly left of centre) than anywhere else in the world by
mid-century.

Source: Courtesy of the Library of Congress, Geography and Map Division

Convention. In spite of a ban on slave imports to American shores, numbers increased
exponentially during the nineteenth century. Since the mid-eighteenth century, numbers of North American captives naturally increased, unlike in the Caribbean and
South America where low life expectancy and high infant mortality was the norm.
The enslaved population grew at the rate of approximately 25 per cent per decade
during the antebellum era. The decline of tobacco planting in the Chesapeake stimulated the growth of grain farming that was not as labour-intensive and left a surplus
of enslaved workers. One hundred and thirty-seven thousand enslaved people from
Virginia, Maryland, and North Carolina were sold west of the Appalachians between
1810 and 1820. Tobacco cultivation in the Chesapeake diminished across the antebellum decades (it was buoyant in the piedmont counties, but soil exhaustion took hold
in the tidewater region that contained the oldest tobacco plantations) providing the
backbreaking labour that was essential for the growth of cotton slavery.

This structural transformation of American slavery had appalling consequences for
the enslaved. Described by historian Allan Kulikoff as "uprooted peoples," and by

Ira Berlin as the "migration generation," enslaved people were torn from friends and family, as well as settled routines on Upper South plantations, and forced to endure an exhausting trek to an uncertain future. The journey south was arduous and conditions were comparable to the physical and mental torment endured by those on the middle passage from Africa. Some captives were transported by boat, down the Mississippi, or by sea from ports such as Norfolk (Virginia) to New Orleans and they were later transported by rail. However, the majority walked in organised groups known as coffles. Enslaved men were chained together and carefully supervised by slave traders which increased travel time and exacerbated physical exertion as progress was made at a rate of approximately 20 miles a day. Traders would meander rather than go direct, picking up further captives and supplies from farms and towns along the way. Trading was seasonal and the young and the healthy were most sought after. The majority were sold in the autumn and winter months so bad weather added to the hardship of a journey that proved fatal to many.

Conditions did not get much better on reaching the Lower South. Already weakened by the journey, the first arrivals had to clear the land and literally provide for themselves while new plantations took shape. Disease was common, exacerbated by the fact that prime land was often situated near to rivers infested with mosquitoes. A complex process of renegotiation ensued as work patterns hammered out over many years in the Upper South were redrawn. Enslavers held the upper hand however and brute force was their stock in trade. Toussaint L'Overture's successful rebellion in Haiti served as a powerful reminder of the danger of relaxing their guard. It was many years before the rights that tobacco slaves had forced, such as garden plots, were won again. The gruelling labour needed to build new plantations in the Lower South ensured that enslaved people were pushed to absolute maximum, sometimes working seven days a week. Whatever their previous occupation or circumstances, enslaved men and women joined the rank and file in the Lower South. Enslavers and overseers imposed a furious pace in order to get their operations up and running. Where possible, the enslaved chose to escape to the woods and the swamps or sought refuge with Native American tribes.

1811 Louisiana Slave Rebellion

On 9 January 1811 perhaps as many as 500 captives marched towards New Orleans, armed with cane knives, hoes, clubs, and guns, chanting "freedom or death." They were led by Charles Deslondes, a slave driver of Haitian descent, and inspired by the momentous Saint Domingue rebellion that ended in French defeat. The revolt began 8 January in St Landry Parish, 36 miles from New Orleans, and numbers grew as the enslaved burnt plantations along the River Road on the way to New Orleans. The rebellion was defeated by a combined force of regular soldiers and militia. In the aftermath, authorities claimed that the perpetrators were brigands and pirates, not that they were engaged in a desperate struggle to win their liberty. This wishful thinking was intended to dissuade other enslaved people from rebelling. The Louisiana Slave Rebellion reminded enslavers that they must remain vigilant at all times.

The War of 1812

Territorial acquisition, trade disputes, settler-Indian friction, and delicate relations between the US and the major European powers were all contributory causes of the War of 1812. While hardly conflict on the grand scale of the Napoleonic wars fought on European soil, the War of 1812 is referred to by some as a second war of independence and demonstrated that the young nation was willing to flex its muscle. Tensions mounted as the United States was caught between the two leading powers of the age, Britain and France, who officially declared war in 1803 but had been fighting one another since 1793. Each sought to disrupt their rival's economy, which hit trade with the US. Britain's maritime domination of the seas enabled its ships to blockade key ports while the French seized control of major European ports from Brest to the Elbe River.

Washington and Adams worked diligently to prevent the problem from escalating in the 1790s but Napoleon's rise saw the Anglo-Franco conflict escalate. In 1806, Napoleon's continental system (enforced by the Berlin and Milan decrees) instructed French warships and privateers to seize all vessels leaving British ports regardless of national origin as part of his attempt to prevent European countries from trading with Britain. British Orders in Council retaliated in 1807 by formalising a stricter policy that promised to stop and search neutral vessels. The disruption to American trade was bad enough, but impressment of thousands of American sailors into service for the British Navy greatly irritated the US. Britain refused to recognise the right of its subjects to become American citizens and Anglo sailors on American ships were classed as deserters and forced into the British Navy. In May 1807, the British frigate *Leopard* fired on the American ship *Chesapeake* for refusing permission to search its decks. As many as 6,000 Americans had been impressed by the end of 1807.

The Democratic-Republican administrations of Jefferson and, from 1809, James Madison responded aggressively. Frustrated by the continued disruption of the Anglo-French confrontation, Jefferson passed the 1807 Embargo Act which prohibited the export of American goods and harmed imports because European ships were not guaranteed to leave the US with a full cargo. The policy was a disaster. American trade had been boosted by European wars that increased demand for a diverse range of goods. The US embargo was irritating to the British and the French, but was not going to change their policy. American merchants simply refused to comply because the bottom line was that their livelihoods were made by Atlantic trade. Recognising that his policy was floundering, one of Jefferson's final acts as president was to pass the Non-Intercourse Act in March 1809 that prohibited trade with Britain and France. This unsatisfactory situation threatened to become farcical when Macon's Bill No. 2 (May 1810) reopened trade but promised that business with one of the belligerents would cease, dependent upon whether Britain or France first restored free trade. The intention was that both countries would be forced to respect the rights of US shipping. Napoleon promised to do so officially, but in practice continued to harass American shipping.

Violation of American sovereignty loomed larger than trade disruption in President James Madison's declaration of war against Great Britain in June 1812. Madison cited the problem of impressment as an affront to the rights of US citizens. He also accused the British of inciting Native Americans against the interests of the United

States, an accusation with some substance. William Henry Harrison, governor of the Indiana Territory, was convinced that the Shawnee were in league with the British in 1809 when they refused to sign the Treaty of Fort Wayne that ceded large parts of their territory for the miserly figure of $10,000. Far-sighted Shawnee leader Tecumseh attempted to unite Indians in the Old Northwest and elsewhere in a bold pan-Indian movement to prevent further encroachment. He inspired widespread support but the Battle of Tippecanoe (7 November 1811) demonstrated the ruthless determination of white settlers when Harrison's combined force of militia and regular troops burnt Tecumseh's Prophetstown, in the Indiana Territory, having repelled an earlier Indian attack. Tecumseh's alliance with the British enraged Democratic Republicans in the South and the West. These so-called war hawks were belligerent, aggressive, and demanded a second war against Britain in which they hoped to overpower Indian tribes and expedite plans to invade Canada, Florida, and Texas.

Andrew Jackson epitomised the war hawk mentality. Born on the Carolina frontier and raised in Tennessee, he spoke for the growing numbers living beyond the Appalachian Mountains and demonstrated their rising political influence. Jackson's Tennessee militia engaged in a bitter war against the Red Stick faction of the Creeks (1813–14), enemies he described as "savage bloodhounds" and "blood thirsty barbarians." Jackson acted savagely himself at Horseshoe Bend, Alabama, in retaliation for an earlier attack by the Red Sticks at Fort Mims. He urged his men to show no mercy but to "teach the cannibals . . . that the thunder of our arms is more terrible than the Earthquakes of their Prophets." (From December 1811 to March 1812, a series of powerful earthquakes struck the Mississippi Valley, something Tecumseh had predicted in his stirring speech protesting white hostility designed to rally tribal support.) In March 1814, Jackson's combined force of white militia, Creek, and Cherokee killed 800 warriors in the bloodiest confrontation between Indians and Euro-Americans to that point. Despite fighting alongside Indian allies, Jackson subsequently demanded 2.2 million acres of tribal land at the conclusion of the fighting. These actions paved the way for more settlers, made Jackson a hero in the Old Southwest, and established his reputation as an Indian fighter that would later help to take him into the White House.

The War of 1812 was fought on land and sea. It began with surprising success for the Americans who defeated the most powerful navy in the world off the Atlantic coast. However, by 1813 the superior British naval power, unrivalled on the open seas, blockaded the Chesapeake Bay. The most strategically important and protracted fighting on land took place around the Great Lakes as American forces invaded Canada. Between July 1812 and 1814, the British and their Indian allies repelled the US incursion at the battles of Fort Dearborn (near present-day Chicago), Thames River and Fort Niagara. However, Tecumseh was mortally wounded at the Battle of the Thames (5 October 1813) when his Indian warriors stood firm as the British fled from the Americans. The pre-war boundaries remained intact when the British retreated back to Canada after they were defeated in the naval confrontation of Plattsburg Bay, fought on Lake Champlain, 11 September 1814.

In August 1814, British soldiers entered the Chesapeake Bay. They attacked Washington DC and burnt the White House and other state buildings which forced Madison to retreat from his capital. An attack on Baltimore was repelled by American troops, however, and the British retreated back to their ships. The final battle of the war took place outside New Orleans on 8 January 1815. It was actually fought after

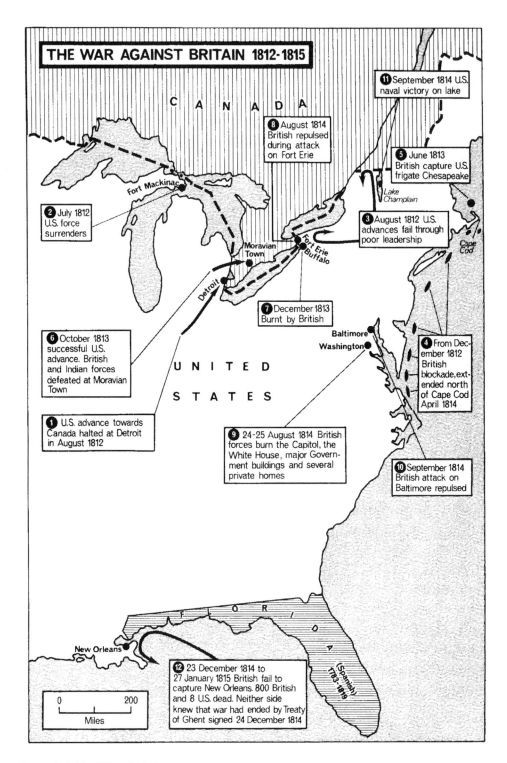

Figure 5.5 The War of 1812.

Source: Reproduced from *The Routledge Atlas of American History* 6e, published by Routledge. © Martin Gilbert, 2009. Reproduced by arrangement with Taylor & Francis Books UK. See also www.martingilbert.com

Figure 5.6 The burning of the White House by British soldiers. In spite of flash points such as this, the US consistently compared itself to Great Britain in the first half of the nineteenth century as its own culture and national identity emerged gradually.

Source: Courtesy of the Library of Congress Prints and Photographs Division Washington

the Treaty of Ghent had ended hostilities between the two nations on 24 December 1814. Fortunately, for the benefit of Andrew Jackson's reputation, the news did not reach him in time. Jackson marshalled a ragtag combination of regular militia, Choctaw Indians, French brigands and freed slaves to defend New Orleans and defeat a far superior enemy that outnumbered him at least two to one. Federal judge Wilson McCandless recalled that news of the victory "came upon the country like a clap of thunder . . . and travelled with electromagnetic velocity."

Native Americans were the clear losers in the War of 1812, as neither Britain nor the US made territorial gains. Indian tribes, that had overwhelmingly supported the British, were left in an even more vulnerable position as settlers continued to pour into the trans-Appalachian West. This was probably the last time that Canada might have been taken by the US. Canadians became more hostile towards the US subsequently and the British strengthened relations with their North American colony that had increased in strategic importance because of American expansion. National confidence was boosted, by Jackson's victory at New Orleans in particular, because the country successfully held off the British. The Federalist Party, regarded as disloyal in the so-called Era of Good Feelings in the decade after 1815, was finished. Federalist support had been galvanised by the war's prolonged economic disruption which encouraged a group of disgruntled New England merchants to seek closer relations with Great

Britain. The possibility of secession from the United States was seriously discussed at the Federalist convention in Hartford (15 December 1814–5 January 1815) although the proposal was not adopted. The War of 1812 did much to bind the original states and those in the interior closer together, even if it would be an exaggeration to describe the US as a truly united country by this point.

Economic fortunes quickly turned around and the post-war mood was one of unity and patriotism. This was enhanced when Jackson led an expedition into Spanish Florida in 1818 to pursue, Jackson claimed, Indian rebels. US forces invaded foreign territory without permission but demonstrated the vulnerability of this poorly defended outpost of the Spanish empire. Spain subsequently decided to cut its losses and the Adams-Onís Treaty of 1819 ceded Florida to the United States in return for $5 million.

Growing confidence was also demonstrated in the "Monroe Doctrine" as President James Monroe's annual message to Congress on 2 December 1823 eventually became known. Monroe's speech was an important, bold declaration that addressed concerns that Russia had designs upon the Pacific Northwest and the French and the Spanish were about to reinforce their position in Central and South America. The Monroe Doctrine established three principles: first, the US would stay out of European affairs; second, the US would not interfere with existing European colonies in the Western Hemisphere; third, attempts to establish new colonies in the Western Hemisphere would not be tolerated but regarded as hostile acts by the US. Although the US did not have the resources to enforce the Monroe Doctrine for decades, it actually rejected a British offer of help to implement the policy. This underlined American self-assurance and determination to keep European powers at bay.

Industrialisation and the American system

It would be difficult to overstress the importance of cotton and its effects were significant north of the Mason-Dixon Line if not so immediately visible on the landscape as in the plantation south. Just as the international slave trade underpinned the growth of British financial markets in the early modern era, cotton exports underpinned the US shipping, insurance, banking, and investment sectors in the antebellum period. The huge fiscal injection of the new cotton economy – which attracted investment from around the world as much as from North America – boosted the US economy. Given the significance of sectionalism as the major cause of the American Civil War – the "North" and the "South" gradually developed economic and cultural peculiarities that marked them out as contrasting regions – it is interesting to note that in 1810 northern and southern states were roughly comparable in terms of manufacturing output. The growth of southern plantation agriculture founded on enslaved labour actually worked well with the growth of northern manufacturing founded on free labour but sent the regions along divergent trajectories.

In the decades following the War of 1812, the northern and midwestern economies began the shift from predominantly farming and agriculture to industry and wage labour although this transition was protracted. As the South concentrated on cash crops – cotton, rice, sugar, tobacco – plantations that had been self-sufficient diverted resources to production of these crops primarily. The rhythms of the agricultural season allowed plantations to feed themselves as potatoes, corn, and other food crops continued to be grown, but basic manufactured goods such as shoes and even clothes were increasingly bought from outside. Increased demand for commodities stimulated the growth of factories. In turn, the greater availability of cotton spurred New England businessmen to build textile mills that processed raw cotton, encouraged by the success of British textiles. Southern farmers supplied the cotton, northern factories spun it into cloth, and the finished product was sold on the domestic market at home or shipped abroad.

The growth of American manufacturing was promoted by government policy following the War of 1812. With the Federalists finished as a major political force, and national patriotism on a high, the federal government took aggressive actions to boost the growth of American industry that ignored long-standing objections against economic intervention. Napoleon's blockade of European ports had encouraged British manufacturers to flood American markets with their products, sold at cheaper prices than domestic companies could match. Appropriating some of the Federalist's policies, Henry Clay was architect of what was called the "American System" designed to reduce reliance on overseas imports.

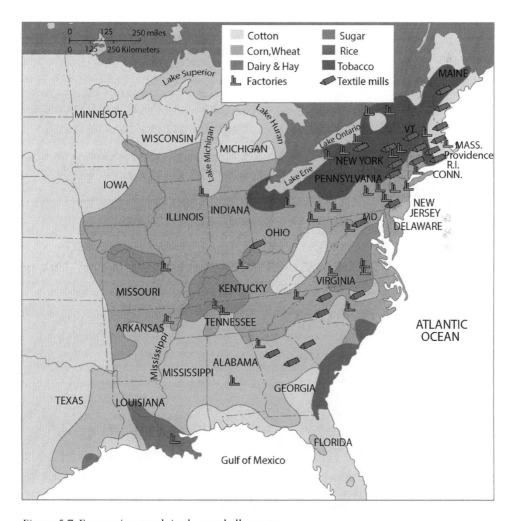

Figure 5.7 Economic growth in the antebellum era.

The American System was announced in James Madison's seventh annual message of 5 December 1815 and consisted of a three pronged economic stimulus. First, a protective tariff was placed on foreign imports, encouraging consumers to buy cheaper American products. Successive administrations imposed a variety of tariffs on foreign products at rates between 20 and 25 per cent. Second, the creation of a national bank and a single currency made trading between the states easier and more reliable. The Second Bank of the United States was chartered in 1816 for a period of 20 years. Finally, federal money was made available for improvements to the US's infrastructure. This last objective was only partially realised, however, because Madison refused to authorise federal funds for local projects, although the building of the National Road running from Baltimore to Illinois was approved. Towns, cities, and states, nonetheless, carried out substantial projects to improve the infrastructure utilising private and public funds.

The first large factory, with the capacity to integrate spinning and weaving, was built by the Boston Manufacturing Company in 1814 in Waltham, Massachusetts. This marked a new departure from the small-scale spinning mills built in southeastern Massachusetts and Rhode Island in the 1790s, notable for their "family system" that employed men, women, and children who lived in factory villages. Francis Cabot Lowell's design for the Waltham factory closely replicated mills in Lancashire and Scotland. Lowell died in 1817, but a town named in his honour was established on the Merrimack River, 27 miles from Boston, in the 1820s. As in Great Britain, water was harnessed to achieve the circular motion that drove the power looms, although the "Boston associates" (merchants investing in the textile industry) who built numerous factories in Lowell sought to avoid the oppressive working conditions endured by British textile operatives. Waltham was the model for similar ventures in Manchester (New Hampshire) and Lewiston (Maine). Later, coal-fuelled, steam powered factories were built in Providence, New Bedford, Fall River, and other towns on the New England coast.

The factory system at Lowell was internationally renowned as a model of paternal industrial organisation; it was carefully managed, large scale, and integrated all aspects of the production process. The workforce was primarily composed of young women from the surrounding area. They lived in on-site boarding houses and were encouraged to pursue avenues of improvement in their spare time, while earning comparatively high wages. From a high point in the late 1820s, labour relations deteriorated as economic slumps reduced wages and led to strikes in 1834 and 1836. The Lowell Factory Girls Association was founded in wake of the strikes and became the Lowell Female Labour Reform Association in 1845. It sought to protect worker interests and gain a reduction in the working day to ten hours. Despite this collective organisation, factory managers demanded faster work and longer hours, creating more unrest and wider agitation. Overproduction of textiles saturated the market, unfortunately, and the increased use of Irish immigrant labour in the 1840s could not save the Lowell system that was eventually abandoned in the 1850s.

The market revolution?

The eagerness which young women sought new opportunities suggested that employment patterns and traditional gender relations were in flux. Women flocked to the textile mills partly out of family necessity because New England farmers

CONSTITUTION OF THE
Lowell Factory Girls Association.

PREAMBLE.

Whereas we, the undersigned, residents of Lowell, moved by a love of honest industry and the expectation of a fair and liberal recompence, have left our homes, our relatives and youthful associates, and come hither, and subjected ourselves to all the danger and inconvenience, which necessarily attend young and unprotected females, when among strangers, and in a strange land; and however humble the condition of Factory Girls, (as we are termed,) may seem, we firmly and fearlessly (though we trust with a modesty becoming our sex,) claim for ourselves, that love of moral and intellectual culture, that admiration of, and desire to attain and preserve pure, elevated and refined characters, a true reverence for the divine principle which bids us render to every one his due; a due appreciation of those great and cardinal principles of our government, of justice and humanity, which enjoins on us " to live and let live "—that chivalrous and honorable feeling, which with equal force, forbids us to invade others rights, or suffer others, upon any consideration, to invade ours; and at the same time, that utter abhorence and detestation of whatever is mean, sordid, dishonorable or unjust—all of which, can alone, in our estimation, entitle us to be called the daughters of freemen, or of Republican America.

And, whereas, we believe that those who have preceded us have been, we know that ourselves are, and that our successors are liable to be, assailed in various ways by the wicked and unprincipled, and cheated out of just, legal and constitutional dues, by ungenerous, illiberal and avaricious capitalists,—and convinced that "union is power," and that as the unprincipled consult and advise, that they may the more easily decoy and seduce—and the capitalists that they may the more effectually defraud—we (being the weaker,) claim it to be our undeniable right, to associate and concentrate our power, that we may the more successfully repel their equally base and iniquitous aggressions.

And, whereas, impressed with this belief, and conscious that our cause is a common one, and our conditions similar, we feel it our imperative duty to stand by each other through weal and woe; to administer to each others wants, to prevent each others back-sliding—to comfort each other in sickness, and advise each other in health, to incite each other to the love and attainment of those excellences, which can alone constitute the perfection of female character—unsullied virtue, refined tastes and cultivated intellects—and in a word, do all that in us lies, to make each other worthy ourselves, our country and Creator.

Therefore, for the better attainment of those objects, we associate ourselves together, and mutually pledge to each other, a females irrefragable vow, to stand by, abide by, and be governed by the following

PROVISIONS.

Article 1st. It shall be denominated the LOWELL FACTORY GIRLS' ASSOCIATION.

Art. 2d. Any female of good moral character, and who works in any one of the Mills in this city, may become a member of this Association, by subscribing to this Constitution.

Art. 3d. The officers of the Association shall be, a President, Vice President, a Recording Secretary, a Corresponding Secretary, a Treasurer, a Collector, and a Prudential Committee, two of whom shall be selected from each Corporation in this city.

Art. 4th. The officers shall be chosen by the vote of the Association; that is, by the vote of a majority of the members present.

Art. 5th. The duties of the President, Vice President, Secretaries, Treasurer, and Collector, shall be the same as usually appertain to such offices. The duties of the Prudential Committee shall be to watch over the interests of the Association generally; to recommend to the Association, for their consideration and adoption, such By-Laws and measures as in their opinion the well-being of the Association may require: and also to ascertain the necessities of any of its members, and report the same, as soon as may be, to the Association. And whenever, in the opinion of the Committee, there are necessities so urgent as to require immediate relief, they shall forthwith report the same to the President, who shall immediately draw upon the Treasurer for the sum recommended, and which sum the Committee shall forthwith apply to the relief of the necessitous.

Art. 6th. The Treasurer and Collector shall be subject to the supervision of the Prudential Committee, to whom they shall be accountable, and to whom they shall give such security for the faithful discharge of their duties, as the Committee shall require.

Art. 7th. All moneys shall be raised by vote of a majority of the Association, or of the members present, and shall be assessed equally on all the members.

Art. 8th. All the officers shall hold their office for the term of one year, with the privilege of resigning, and subject to be removed by vote of the Association, for good cause.

Art. 9th. The Association shall meet once in three months, and may be convened oftener, if occasion require, by the President, upon a petition of twenty of the members first petitioning her for that purpose.

Art. 10th. It shall forever be the policy of the members of this Association, to bestow their patronage, so far as is practicable, upon such persons as befriend, but never upon such as oppose our cause.

Art. 11th. The Association shall have power to make all necessary By-Laws, which shall be consistent with these Provisions, and such By-Laws, when made, shall be binding upon all the members.

Art. 12th. Any member may dissolve her connection with the Association, by giving two weeks notice to the Recording Secretary; and any member shall be expelled from the Association by a vote of a majority of the members present, for any immoral conduct or behavior unbecoming respectable and virtuous females.

Art. 13th. This Constitution may be altered or amended at any time, by a vote of two thirds of the members present.

Figure 5.8 The 1836 Constitution of the Lowell Factory Girls Association

in the early nineteenth century faced a land shortage. The American population expanded at a rate of approximately 30 per cent every decade from 1790 to the Civil War. The concomitant shortage of good arable land was particularly acute for young adults looking to establish their own farms, especially as the tradition of partitioning land among heirs had continuously subdivided family plots during the colonial era. Moreover, just as tobacco overproduction drained the Chesapeake soil of its fertility, farmers in southern New England and in Pennsylvania were forced to turn to corn, rye, and other grain crops as soil exhaustion and the problem of the "Hessian fly" that devoured wheat crops altered long-standing habits of wheat specialisation. The overriding goal remained the accumulation of land, on which homes and farms could be built, but in order to achieve this, farmers were forced to take new directions.

Three principal paths were open to those seeking to get ahead: migrating westward, moving to towns and cities, or intensifying and diversifying existing landholdings on a commercial basis. To develop commercial agriculture, it was essential for farmers to mechanise their operation, especially on large plots (that were most common in the Midwest, which did not suffer from land scarcity like New England). Inventions revolutionised American agricultural production. The mechanical mower-reaper, for which Cyrus McCormick is usually given the credit although, like the cotton gin, others claim the distinction, quintupled the efficiency of wheat farming. John Deere's horse-pulled steel plough, commercially available from 1838, replaced oxen-driven wooden ploughs that had used for centuries. It enabled cheap, fast tilling of the soil without having to stop to make repeated repairs. Mechanisation and technological breakthroughs helped to produce greater surpluses than ever before. Farmers therefore had an opportunity to sell their goods beyond the local population, to distant towns and cities. The fruits of agricultural production fed a growing urban population and profits were reinvested in more land and machinery.

The dynamic evolution of antebellum American agriculture raises the important historiographical debate of the market revolution. The social and economic values of American farmers in the first half of the nineteenth century, and their relationships to commercial production ("the market"), have been of great interest to contemporary scholars. Historians such as James Henretta and Michael Merrill once emphasised that the pre-industrial New England farm family was motivated predominantly by the need to achieve family security on a cooperative basis. A "moral economy" rooted in mutuality and a network of face to face relationships with kin and neighbours was at the centre of farm family values. This interpretation stressed a considerable degree of community self-sufficiency rooted in a complex exchange network of goods, labour, and credit. It has also been suggested that southern farmers, or yeomen as they were called, similarly practised "habits of mutuality" in tight-knit communities that resented outside interference.

This view has been challenged, however, by a revisionist position depicting American farmers as more aggressively market-orientated as the nineteenth century progressed. For example, Bradley Bond asserts that farmers in the Mississippi piney-woods, away from plantation districts, were rarely self-sufficient in grain, but eager to produce and sell surplus meat. The ultimate aim of what Bond calls their "strategy of accumulation," that he juxtaposes against the practice of self-sufficiency, was to be in a position to produce cotton, the classic market crop. Household needs were not entirely neglected, but were a secondary priority. Historians of rural New England have also identified a greater concern with profit and enterprise than was recognised by earlier scholars. From their founding, New England towns were home to money-making entrepreneurs, land speculators, and fur traders. The hundreds of farm and store account books examined by Winifred Rothenberg, for example, demonstrate that in Massachusetts there was a complex market for farm products with prices fluctuating in regular cycles in both Boston and its hinterlands.

Recently, a middle ground between the opposites of self-sufficiency or commerciality, and individual or community, has emerged. A market "revolution" is probably too strong a description of antebellum economic developments that had continuities with the colonial and revolutionary periods. Historian John Majewski prefers the term "market development." Farmers had never been entirely self-sufficient and some had always planned for a surplus that was not only sold locally but might be exported to the West Indies and elsewhere. Surpluses were easier to achieve in places suited to commercial farming like the Connecticut River valley and southern Rhode Island, but most farms had some crops for sale from time to time. Towns in rural Massachusetts such as Dudley and Oxford might best be described as semi-commercial with an advancing market economy contained by traditional, community norms. People bought some clothing in stores, for example, but the bulk of their dress was homemade by family members or provided by itinerant traders. A growing variety of spices, sweets, liquors, as well as imported flour and meat, was widely available but the bulk of a family's diet was met by home, or locally, grown produce. Cash transactions increased, but old traditions of mutuality, barter, and the exchange of goods and services persisted. This was a pattern replicated beyond New England. In this way commercial capitalism grew gradually across the nineteenth century, but at varying rates in different parts of the nation. The process was uneven and piecemeal rather than wholesale and decisive.

Building a national infrastructure

The growth of the market was made possible by sustained investment and the expansion of the US infrastructure in conjunction with rapid advancements in transportation. The federal government (at times), state governments, municipal authorities, and private companies spearheaded this development. The lifestyles of all rural Americans were intimately connected to the land and the physical environment as mobility was constrained by hills, mountains, marshes, forests, and rivers. The quest to become better connected became a central concern of most communities during the antebellum era, whether in long established regions or in fresh territory. Physical barriers which had been in the way of progress previously were removed or overcome as the pressure mounted to access wider markets for trade.

The state of American roads, little more than well-worn paths in the colonial era, steadily improved after the turn-of-the-century as more than 900 companies constructed purpose-built roads in New England and the mid-Atlantic. The steamboat, invented by Pennsylvanian Robert Fulton in 1807, permitted swift, two-way, traffic on the nation's expanding waterways and within a couple of decades steamboats were in use on all of the major rivers, canals, and even on the high seas. The steamboat revolutionised shipping: mariners did not have to rely on winds and currents, so they could travel when they wanted. Enslavers could ship cotton and sugar up the Mississippi rather than send it through New Orleans, around Florida, and up the eastern seaboard if they preferred. Canals supplemented river systems that had for centuries been the most convenient way of transporting people and produce. Railroads would eventually provide an even faster and cheaper alternative. Slow starting, as technology struggled to meet requirements, the Baltimore and Ohio Railroad became the first US railway chartered for commercial transportation of freight and passengers, opening 28 February 1827. As late as 1852, however, canals carried twice the freight of railroads, although rail track increased significantly from the 1830s onward.

The Erie Canal, completed in 1825, was the technological and economic marvel of its time. DeWitt Clinton, Governor of New York, secured $7 million worth of public money for the project, despite the objections of numerous detractors. He confidently predicted that New York City would become "the granary of the world, the Emporium of commerce, the seat of manufactures, the focus of great moneyed operations," a boast largely borne out. The Erie Canal stretched 364 miles from upstate Buffalo on Lake Erie to Albany, New York, and provided a navigable waterway to the Atlantic Ocean. Buffalo, on the Canadian border, grew from a tiny settlement of 200 people in 1820 to a large town of more than 18,000 residents by 1840. The Erie Canal was a major factor in the expansion and commercial development of New York City but there were numerous beneficiaries of its construction. Widely regarded as a technological triumph, the success of this venture inspired many other construction projects. Major canals followed shortly after in Indiana, Ohio, and Pennsylvania and by 1837 more than 3,000 miles of canals had been built.

Towns vied with one another to improve lines of communication, as they strategically, and in some cases rather desperately, hoped to share in the general sense of prosperity that characterised the growth of the market in the nineteenth century. For example, the port of Mobile (Alabama) attempted to build a railroad north to Illinois in the late 1840s in order to arrest its perceived decline in comparison with New Orleans. The businessmen of Portland (Maine) the largest seaport in the state, were not enthused over the city's railroad connection with Boston and believed that business was drawn away rather than attracted. What they wanted was a railroad that opened up the interior of northern New England and gave them access to Canada, a route finally opened in 1853. A strong feeling of civic identity and competition drove these efforts.

Rapid communication improvements and the rise of commercial production had far-reaching effects. Many prospered, but others were left behind, and fears of rural poverty and isolation became more prominent. Distinct sub-regions emerged, such as the supposedly "backward" Appalachian Mountain communities. Later social commentators, such as Protestant clergyman Josiah Strong, compared impoverished farmers in the remote hill country of New England (an extension of Appalachia) with poor southern mountain whites. Towns distant from the confluence of river or road systems struggled. However, it should not be supposed that relocating west was an easy solution to economic problems. Acquiring individual and family plots was much easier than in Europe, but not necessarily straightforward, especially in the most desirable areas. Land companies and individual speculators bought vast acreages purely for profit and evicted squatters who had not legally purchased the land on which they resided. The fertile Bluegrass region around Lexington (Kentucky) was a prime example of this phenomenon as squatters were pushed out by wealthier farmers and planters. Class hierarchies that existed in older areas might be recreated west of the Appalachians.

Men, women, and separate spheres

The effects of economic changes within the social realm were demonstrated by changing gender relations. For generations, women had taken charge of the household as they prepared and cooked food, cleaned, cultivated the garden, and raised children. Like the vast majority of women in world history, they had primary responsibility in the domestic sphere. The concept of republican motherhood glorified the female role as nurturers and carers. But American women also contributed significantly to farm labour when required, made clothes and other goods, and with the onset of industrialisation took paid work in cottage industries such as textiles, shoemaking, and straw hat manufacturing. Farming homesteads were simultaneously a family domain and the site of economic production. Children made a vital contribution, with boys, and less frequently girls, working with their father in the fields. The vast majority of farm women continued to perform essential agricultural tasks in the early nineteenth century, especially at busy times of the year. The binary of masculine and feminine responsibilities and spheres of influence was clear, although roles overlapped.

During the market revolution, however, the household transformed from a site of production to one of consumption as new ideas sanctioned the separation of public (work) and private (home) spaces. The divide between masculinity and femininity widened. The cult of domesticity or true womanhood glorified the restructuring of the home as a private, feminine sphere and work as a public, masculine sphere. "True womanhood" reflected core virtues of piety, purity, submissiveness, and above all domesticity. In public discourse, the family was presented as essential to successful communities and the backbone of a civilised society. Novels, magazines, advice books, religious journals, and newspapers celebrated this conception of femininity. Some wives enjoyed physical improvements in their homes although new standards of middle-class respectability narrowed the boundaries of appropriate female behaviour. Work supposedly became a masculine pursuit, in which the male head provided the family wage, but the cult of domesticity ignored the long hours of toil that remained crucial in running a household. Technology provided tools to speed up the process, but women continued to raise children, cook, clean, and make clothes. The church and its network of auxiliary societies, such as the temperance movement that sought to limit alcohol consumption, provided some opportunities for travel but the appropriate sphere of female activity was confined to the home.

These changes took greatest effect in middle-class households. Massachusetts-born academic and Congregationalist minister Timothy Dwight inveighed against the uncivilised custom of women undertaking field work that he identified with enslaved labour or European peasants. Yet vast numbers of rural and working-class women had no choice but to work. Not much changed for poor women or those in remote localities with limited connections to the market. Their homes had no modern conveniences and their sons and daughters, if they could be spared from the fields, had to seek employment as labourers or servants. Southern yeomen farmers depended on the labour of wives and children in the fields with far fewer opportunities for casual work than in other regions. Across the antebellum era, domestic service was the most typical way for a woman to earn money.

Daughters from prosperous farming households, particularly in New England, might turn their back on work in the fields because they preferred the freedom of short-term employment in textile mills, in other urban occupations, or as school teachers. This took them beyond the confines of the domestic sphere, and sometimes of their state, and greatly impacted their sense of identity. Harriet Hanson Robinson explained the autonomy she felt in the Lowell Mills. Women "could earn money, and spend it as they pleased. . . . For the first time in this country a woman's labor had a money value." Even so, family was rarely far from their thoughts. Letters and visits kept kin networks together across New England, the Midwest, and further afield.

Commercial agriculture, industrialisation, and urbanisation had differing consequences for American men and women. The ideology of true womanhood was, in reality, beyond the reach of the vast majority not least because of the precarious nature of market production that risked the perils of debt and bankruptcy. The market revolution made it difficult to continue habits of self-sufficiency as American households were forced to engage with the market. The "putting out" system (subcontracting the production of goods to individual households) of the clothing, hat making, and shoe-making industries enabled housewives to supplement family income and their contribution might be vital. New England and the Middle Atlantic states rapidly became a hive of factories, schools, colleges, hospitals, and welfare institutions. While these were generally regarded as positive developments, there was also concern at rapid urbanisation, increased ethnic diversity, and sharper divisions between rich and poor. Nostalgic myths, such as that of "Old New England," looked back to a past, largely invented, that entailed virtuous simplicity, rural independence, and class harmony.

Free blacks

Politics in the early republic reflected a changed expectation that government was no longer the preserve of the elite. While in some ways a natural consequence of revolutionary ideology, this was a radical development in a world dominated by monarchs and emperors. It also focused attention upon the question of who was "fit" for citizenship. The answer was unequivocal: white men benefitted as evolving configurations of gender and race not only affirmed the authority and centrality of the white male in American society, but elevated his status further.

Free blacks were not so fortunate and found their position becoming increasingly precarious as their numbers rose significantly. In 20 years after 1790, the free black population increased from approximately 60,000 (7.9 per cent of the total African American population) to 186,000 (13.5 per cent). In Virginia, numbers of free blacks increased from 12,766 in 1790 (4.2 per cent of Virginian African Americans) to 30,570 in 1810 (7.2 per cent). Just under a quarter of blacks in Maryland were free by 1810 (nearly 34,000 in total, the highest number of any state). More than half the free black population of the United States was located in the Upper South by 1810, where one in ten African American was free. Even in the Lower South, the free black population tripled between 1790 and 1810. Numbers were minimal in comparison, however – just 6,000 free blacks by 1810, comprising only 2 per cent of the total black population. The rest of the free black population was predominantly located in northern states that had implemented gradual emancipation acts during the revolutionary era. Their number was steadily supplemented by fugitives escaping from the South who joined free black communities in the North.

The parameters of free black life were shaped in large part by location. In the Upper and Lower South, whites were highly suspicious of free blacks and their influence on the enslaved population. They constituted an anomalous group in southern states where to be white was to be free and to be black was to be enslaved. Manumission, which had been a feature of the post-Revolutionary era, was discouraged. Consequently, southern free blacks were subject to extremely close scrutiny. They were required to pay taxes and petition the legislature if they wanted to remain in their home states. This was not the case in the North where free blacks were largely left to their own devices, although the vast majority could only afford to live in poor urban areas, with concentrated numbers in Philadelphia, New York, and Cincinnati. Comparatively there was more room for manoeuvre in the northern states but it was clear that discrimination and racism became worse everywhere as the decades moved on. New laws restricted black civil rights, which included the right to vote in many northern states.

Northern free blacks constituted an important part of the labour force in the first quarter of the nineteenth century, but found themselves squeezed out by immigrants and by employer discrimination thereafter. Black artisans were forced to seek less skilled, less well paid work, and faced stiff competition for menial jobs. A state census of New York City in 1855, found 808 African Americans listed as servants, 122 as barbers but just six doctors and one lawyer. The growth of scientific racial doctrines legitimated powerful notions of hereditary biological differences between whites and blacks that justified racism. Northern free blacks did not passively accept these developments but challenged discrimination where they could. They were also crucial to the antislavery movement in the early nineteenth century and played a leading role in the organisation of abolitionist societies in the 1830s discussed in the next chapter.

David Walker's *Appeal to the Coloured Citizens of the World*

David Walker's *Appeal* (1829) presented a radical message of African American defiance in its call for enslaved people to rebel. Walker was a free black born in Wilmington, North Carolina, but settled in Boston in 1825. His remarkable tract emphasised black racial pride, the injustice of slavery, and attacked the popular idea of colonisation. "America is more our country than it is the whites," Walker insisted, "we have enriched it with our *blood and tears*." Walker unfortunately died of tuberculosis in 1830 but left an uncompromising critique of US racism that urged blacks to stand up for their rights.

Despite these stirring efforts, the antislavery sentiment of the American Revolution gradually became channelled into colonisation as natural rights were increasingly restricted to white men only. Virginian St George Tucker's 1796 *Dissertation on Slavery* called for a gradual end to slavery with subsequent colonisation of African Americans. Tucker cited Jefferson as his authority: "If it be true, as Mr Jefferson seems to suppose that the Africans are really an inferior race of mankind" then they must be deported. The American Colonization Society (ACS), founded in 1816, attempted to do this but was remarkably unsuccessful in transporting large numbers of blacks from US borders. Only 12,000 African Americans were taken to Liberia in total. Colonisation was simply not practical on logistical grounds, let alone because the majority of African Americans detested it. Nonetheless, colonisation remained

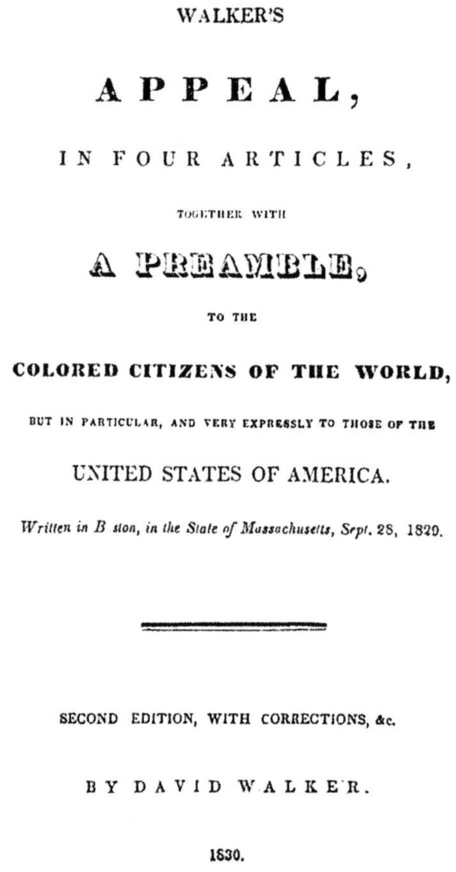

WALKER'S

APPEAL,

IN FOUR ARTICLES,

TOGETHER WITH

A PREAMBLE,

TO THE

COLORED CITIZENS OF THE WORLD,

BUT IN PARTICULAR, AND VERY EXPRESSLY TO THOSE OF THE

UNITED STATES OF AMERICA.

Written in B ston, in the State of Massachusetts, Sept. 28, 1829.

———————————

SECOND EDITION, WITH CORRECTIONS, &c.

BY DAVID WALKER.

1830.

Figure 5.9 David Walker's *Appeal to the Coloured Citizens of the World* (1829).
Source: Courtesy of Granger Historical Picture Archive/Alamy

popular throughout the antebellum era. Many critics of the ACS resented the organisational and financial failings of the society, or did not like ACS leaders, but supported the principle of colonisation. It was claimed that colonisation was in the best interests of African Americans and the best solution to the so-called American race problem. In truth, the ACS's main contribution was to foreground racial issues and further legitimise perceptions of white superiority and black inferiority.

Thomas Jefferson encapsulated the problem, or perhaps better put paradox, of race and slavery in the early republic. He owed his livelihood to the institution of slavery yet, like many others, noted the incongruity of slavery in a free nation and questioned the morality of slavery as an institution. Loyalty to his native state of Virginia, however, and the fact that its economic prosperity rested on slavery – as did all southern states – ensured that nagging doubts never developed into an active antislavery advocate. Slavery was also an institution that he claimed necessarily controlled and contained African Americans. In Jefferson's view, the problem of race relations was acute: "Deep rooted prejudices entertained by the whites; ten thousand recollections, by the blacks, of the injuries they have sustained; new provocations; the real distinctions which nature has made; and many other circumstances, will divide us into parties, and produce convulsions which will probably never end but in the extermination of the one or the other race." It is difficult in the twenty-first century to appreciate how an educated and influential man could hold such views. Jefferson was a leading proponent of scientific theories of white superiority. Nonetheless, this did not prevent him from engaging in a long-term relationship with Sally Hemings, an enslaved woman with whom he had six children after the death of his wife.

Indian removal

Growing discrimination towards free blacks did not bode well for the fate of Native Americans in the United States. By the 1820s, federal policy that respected land rights and proceeded by negotiation had reached breaking point. A rising tide of popular feeling regarded Indians as an obstacle and pointed to their demise in one way or another. Powerful ideas of white cultural and biological superiority, positing the natural inferiority of both blacks and Indians as separate races, justified the displacement of indigenous peoples. Decade by decade, belief in the superiority of the republic and future greatness of the nation became stronger. A providential strain of thinking could not understand why others might refuse the chance to become part of American civilisation. This was God's chosen country. The plight of Native Americans became more urgent in this context. The idea of the "vanishing" Indian was popular. Partly based on the scientific theory of a hierarchy of races, but also on empirical observations of the declining indigenous population since first contact, it was asserted that the Indian was actually in danger of dying out altogether, necessitating urgent action.

The racialisation of Indians as irrevocably different in the 1810s and 1820s had particular appeal west of the Appalachian Mountains and contrasted with generally positive views found along the eastern seaboard. Most settlers in the trans-Appalachian West held a far less charitable attitude towards Native Americans than was the case elsewhere. They had few nostalgic ideas about Indian character or the US's moral commitment to dealing with tribes fairly but advocated a policy of separation and removal. This position reflected the geographical proximity of whites and Indians as more and more settlers headed west and encroached on Indian lands – the 1820 census showed approximately a quarter of the nation's population living on the other side of the Appalachians. As Georgia senator John Forsyth bluntly stated, Indians "were a race not admitted to be equal to the rest of the community."

Native Americans, especially the so-called five civilised tribes, as contemporaries referred to the Creek, Cherokee, Choctaw, Chickasaw, and Seminole, were far from passive observers. They defended their land from encroachment and sometimes sold it to whites, although these transactions were often fraudulent. By 1810, for example, the Cherokee had ceded approximately half of their territory. Southern tribes, above all others, had also made fundamental changes to their traditional ways. Their economies quickly adapted to Euro-American needs, which contributed to joint collaboration with whites in the lucrative fur trade and other economic pursuits. White cultural influences had a massive impact on traditional ways. Contrary to contemporary mythology, tribes had actually lived in settled communities for centuries. By the 1820s, many had adopted a system of writing, practised mixed farming, sent children to school, were subject to a hierarchical political system, wore American clothes, and converted to Christianity. The Cherokee had an English language newspaper, the *Cherokee Phoenix*. Plantation slavery was practised in various forms, although differed tribe by tribe. Proximity to whites in the early 1800s also appears to have been the catalyst for the emergence of more prejudiced attitudes towards African Americans. As bifurcated racial lines in the United States hardened, however, Indians probably had little choice in adopting views of black inferiority or else risk being categorised as black themselves.

Whether "civilised" or not, the southern tribes were in possession of hundreds of thousands of valuable acres in the heart of the black belt. The cotton boom depended on fresh territory for new plantations. When Mississippi and Alabama gained statehood, in 1817 and 1819 respectively, the pressure on southern tribes increased further. Federal policy in the 1820s became more coercive, decisively so following Andrew Jackson's victory in the presidential election of 1828. Georgia, Alabama, and Mississippi declared that Native Americans within their borders were subject to state laws and that they would no longer respect tribal law or government. Indian land was to be opened to white settlement. Jackson ignored the Indians' historical and legal attachment to the land to support these coercive measures. After a series of heated debates in Congress, the Indian Removal Act was narrowly approved on 28 May 1830. It

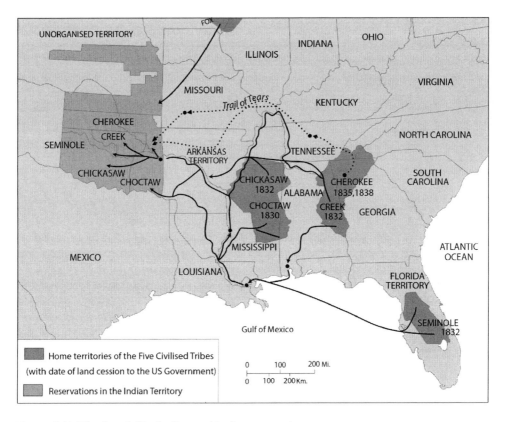

Figure 5.10 The five civilised tribes and Indian removal.

provided funds for the relocation of Native Americans west of the Mississippi to reside in perpetuity in the so-called Indian Territory (present-day Oklahoma). Indians who refused to move would be subject to state laws and would not be entitled to federal protection. The policy of assimilation was abandoned and replaced by exclusion.

In a last ditch effort to defend their sovereignty, the Cherokee took their opposition to the Supreme Court in two landmark cases (ironically demonstrating their familiarity, if not mastery, of "white" ways by skilful use of the legal process). In *Cherokee Nation v. Georgia* (1831), John Ross argued that Georgia had no jurisdiction over Indians who had occupied the land for time immemorial. Chief Justice John Marshall's response was ambiguous, seeming to agree with the Cherokee leader's reasoning, but denying the right of a "domestic dependent nation" whose relationship with the United States was "that of a ward to his guardian" to bring the case to the Supreme Court. In *Worcester v. Georgia* a year later, Marshall unequivocally supported the Cherokee, interpreting tribes as "distinct, independent political communities," entitled to federal protection and not subject to state law. Georgia's actions were "repugnant to the constitution, treaties, and laws of the United States and ought, therefore, to be reversed and annulled." Andrew Jackson's response was reportedly to say "John Marshall has made his decision; now let him enforce it," exposing any pretence of justice as a sham. This emphasised the power of the president to enforce, or not, legislative and judicial decrees.

During the 1830s, the federal government worked hand in hand with state governments in a policy of forced removal against the wishes of indigenous people and many white Americans, particularly northern evangelical women. Famous opponents of removal included Ralph Waldo Emerson, Catherine Beecher, and the renowned frontiersman Davy Crockett. Despite his reputation as an Indian fighter, Crockett wrote in his autobiography that the Removal Bill "was a wicked, unjust measure" that he could not support despite his long friendship with Jackson. Criticism did not change Jackson's mind as he argued that removal was in the best interests of Native Americans, a stance satirised in image 5.11 with Native Americans surrounding Jackson's feet and a picture of liberty trampling a tyrant in the background.

The removal policy was received by the civilised tribes with a strong sense of injustice but also of resignation. Tribal connection to the land had endured over the centuries but the pressure on native tribes and their leaders had become unbearable. This was the major reason why a small, breakaway, group of Cherokee agreed to the Treaty of New Echota on 29 December 1835, which ceded remaining Cherokee lands to the US government for the paltry sum of $5.6 million and accepted relocation to the Indian Territory. Cherokee petitions were presented to the Senate to denounce this fraudulent compact, but it was ratified as legitimate by just one vote on 23 May 1836. Although not authorised by tribal leaders or a majority, the Treaty of New Echota gave white authorities the pretext they needed to carry out forced relocation.

The Cherokee aptly called their 800-mile journey to the Indian Territory the "Trail of Tears." On 26 May 1838, 7,000 US soldiers rounded up all those who had not voluntarily left. North Carolina, Tennessee, and Alabama followed suit shortly afterwards. Of the 16,000 people who left Georgia in 1838, 4,000 lost their lives due to inadequate protection, a lack of provisions, and appalling winter conditions. Agents contracted to oversee removal made their money by undercutting promises to supply adequate food and clothing, and in some cases provided nothing at all. The Seminoles violently resisted removal in a brutal guerrilla war (1835–42) costing around

Figure 5.11 Andrew Jackson as the Great Father (1835).

Source: Courtesy of Alpha Stock/Alamy

$20 million. Others resisted in more subtle ways and some survived the transition to American rule to become farmers and enslavers in Mississippi, Alabama, and else-where. However, most Native Americans, no matter their tribal heritage, resigned themselves to their fate and set out for the Indian Territory. This was perhaps the most shameful episode in American history to that point, something recognised by thousands of contemporaries appalled by their government's policy. It constituted a brutal statement of white supremacy and determination to move westward at all costs.

Chapter summary

The Louisiana Purchase was an extremely significant milestone in US history, although Thomas Jefferson was deeply worried about its destabilising effects. In the end, white settlement proceeded relatively smoothly. The incorporation of existing communities in the American heartland – of French, British, and Spanish backgrounds, many of whom were already engaged in plantation slavery – was facilitated by the fortuitous match of cotton to the soil and environment of the black belt. In combination with the impressive efficiency gains provided by the cotton gin, profits soared. The colonisation (invasion would be the more accurate term) of the trans-Appalachian West in the first few decades of the nineteenth century, quickly became a story of triumph and national success. For hundreds of thousands of African Americans and Native Americans, by contrast, it was calamitous. What could have been a disastrous second war with Great Britain actually became an important demonstration of national unity, a point when the 13 colonies that came together in 1783 began to unify and realise a common purpose: the united States (with united an adjective) was becoming the United States (a noun). The war's aftermath saw the young republic take significant steps towards Alexander Hamilton's vision of an industrial and commercial future, overseen by a strong central government. Manufacturing and agriculture developed symbiotically as the transportation revolution and market expansion established the foundations of what would become one of the world's strongest economies.

Discussion questions

- How did westward expansion influence the development of the United States in the first half of the nineteenth century?
- What caused slavery's expansion and what were the most significant consequences?
- What were the causes and the consequences of the War of 1812?
- What were the social effects of the market revolution?
- Why were Indians removed west of the Mississippi River?

Further reading

Appleby, Joyce. *Inheriting the Revolution: The First Generation of Americans* (Cambridge, MA, 2000). Fascinating study of the first generation of American citizens.

Berlin, Ira. *Generations of Captivity: A History of African-American Slaves* (Cambridge, 2003). Detailed account of the migration of slaves in the nineteenth century in Chapter 4.

Berlin, Ira. *Slaves Without Masters: The Free Negro in the Antebellum South* (New York, 1974). Remains the most detailed account of the free black community in the nineteenth century.

Bond, Bradley G. "Herders, Farmers and Markets on the Inner Frontier: The Mississippi Piney Woods, 1850–1860," in Samuel C. Hyde, ed., *Plain Folk of the South Revisited* (Baton Rouge, 1997), 73–99. Argues for the commercial proclivities of southern farmers.

Boydston, Jeanne. *Home and Work: Housework, Wages, and the Ideology of Labor in the Early Republic* (New York, 1990). Surveys gender relations and economic development.

Castor, Peter J. *The Nation's Crucible: The Louisiana Purchase and the Creation of America* (New Haven, 2004). Examines the impact of the Louisiana Purchase.

Clark, Christopher. *The Roots of Rural Capitalism: Western Massachusetts, 1780–1860* (Ithaca, NY, 1990). Classic, and still influential, account of the market revolution in one location.

Cott, Nancy F. *The Bonds of Womanhood: Women's Sphere in New England, 1780–1835* (New Haven, 1978). Classic study of the emergence of gender roles.

Deyle, Steven. *Carry Me Back: The Domestic Slave Trade in American Life* (New York, 2005). Comprehensive analysis of the scope and significance of the domestic slave trade.

Dowd, Gregory E. *Spirited Resistance: The North American Indian Struggle for Unity, 1745–1815* (Baltimore, 1992). Discusses Native American resistance to European encroachment.

DuVal, Kathleen. *The Native Ground: Indians and Colonists in the Heart of the Continent* (Philadelphia, 2006). Fascinating study of the development of the Arkansas River Valley.

Hahn, Steven. *The Roots of Southern Populism: Yeoman Farmers and the Transformation of the Georgia Upcountry, 1850–1880* (New York, 1983). Describes the "habits of mutuality" of southern farmers.

Hammond, John Craig. *Slavery, Freedom, and Expansion in the Early American West* (Charlottesville, 2005). Important revisionist account of the settlement of the trans-Appalachian West.

Henretta, James A. "Families and Farms: *Mentalité* in Pre-Industrial America," *William and Mary Quarterly*, Vol. 35, January 1978, 3–32. Pioneering article of the community versus self-sufficiency debate.

Hietala, Thomas R. *Manifest Design: American Exceptionalism and Empire* (Ithaca, 2003 [1985]). Revised edition of a classic text probing westward expansion as the site of American empire.

Howe, Daniel Walker. *What Hath God Wrought: The Transformation of America, 1815–1848* (New York, 2007). Sweeping account of the period between the War of 1812 and the Mexican-American War that emphasises the influence of transportation and communication developments.

Johnson, Walter. *River of Dark Dreams: Slavery and Empire in the Cotton Kingdom* (Cambridge, MA, 2013). Compelling account of the rise of plantation slavery in the Mississippi valley and its global ramifications.

Majewski, John. *A House Dividing: Economic Development in Pennsylvania and Virginia Before the Civil War* (Cambridge, 2000). Argues that the market revolution is better understood as market development.

Perdue, Theda, and Michael D. Green. *The Cherokee Nation and the Trail of Tears* (New York, 2007). Recent authoritative account of the Cherokee in the era of removal.

Prude, Jonathan. *The Coming of Industrial Order: Town and Factory Life in Rural Massachusetts, 1810–1860* (Cambridge, 1983). Influential examination of the rural towns of Dudley and Oxford in Massachusetts.

Rothenberg, Winifred B. *From Market-Places to a Market Economy: The Transformation of Rural Massachusetts, 1750–1850* (Chicago, 1992). Detailed economic analysis of changing commercial practices.

Rothman, Adam. *Slave Country: American Expansion and the Origins of the Deep South* (Cambridge, 2005). Charts the emergence of the cotton kingdom.

Saunt, Claudio. *A New Order of Things: Property, Power, and the Transformation of Creek Indians, 1733–1816* (Cambridge, 2003). One of the best studies of Indian tribes and their encounter with European influences.

Sellers, Charles G. *The Market Revolution: Jacksonian America, 1815–1846* (1991). Important synthesis, examining the market in relation to other spheres.

Taylor, Alan. *The Civil War of 1812: American Citizens, British Subjects, Irish Rebels, and Indian Allies* (New York, 2010). Superb, recent analysis of the War of 1812 from noted colonial historian.

Wallace, Anthony F. C. *The Long, Bitter Trail: Andrew Jackson and the Indians* (New York, 1993). Detailed discussion of Indian removal.

6 Problems of slavery, freedom, and sectionalism in the antebellum US

Timeline

1800–1801	Great Kentucky religious revivals
1820, March 3	Missouri Compromise
1825, January 3	Robert Owen establishes the first secular utopian community
1826	American Temperance Society founded
1828, May 19	Tariff of Abominations
1828, December	Andrew Jackson wins the 1828 presidential election
1830	Charles G. Finney's revival begins in New York
1831, August 21	Nat Turner's rebellion begins
1831, November 11	Nat Turner executed
1832	Re-charter of the Bank of the United States vetoed
1832, November 24	South Carolina declares the federal tariff null and void
1832, December	Jackson re-elected president
1833, March 2	Compromise Tariff
1833, December 4	American Anti-Slavery Society founded
1835, March 2	Texas declares its independence from Mexico
1840	American and Foreign Antislavery Society founded
1842, May	Dorr War in Rhode Island
1844–45	Methodist and Baptist churches split into northern and southern sections
1845, December 29	Texas annexed by the United States
1845, July	John L. O'Sullivan coins the phrase "manifest destiny"
1846, May 13	Congress declares war on Mexico
1846, August	Wilmot Proviso
1848, January 24	Gold discovered in California
1848, February 2	Treaty of Guadalupe Hidalgo
1848, July 19–20	Woman's Rights Convention at Seneca Falls
1850, August	Compromise of 1850
1853, December 30	Gadsden Purchase
1854, March 20	Republican Party formed
1854, May 23	Kansas-Nebraska Act approved by Congress
1855, March 30	Proslavery territorial government established in Kansas
1855, December 15	Free soil territorial government established in Topeka, Kansas
1856, May 22	Preston Brooks assaults Charles Sumner
1856, November 4	James Buchanan elected president

1857, March 6	*Dred Scott v. Sanford*
1858, 21 August–15 October	Lincoln-Douglas debates in Illinois
1858, October 25	William Seward "irrepressible conflict" speech
1859, October 16	Harpers Ferry
1859, December 2	John Brown hanged
1860, April 23	Southern delegates walk out of the Democratic National Convention
1860, May 16–18	Abraham Lincoln gains Republican nomination
1860, June 18–23	Stephen A. Douglas gains Democratic nomination
1860, June 28	Southern Democrats nominate John C. Breckinridge as presidential candidate
1860, November 6	Abraham Lincoln elected president
1860, December 20	South Carolina secedes
1861, February 4	Confederacy established
1861, April 12	Confederate guns fire on Fort Sumter
1861, April 15	Lincoln calls for 75,000 volunteers to put down the rebellion
1861, April 19	Lincoln orders the blockade of Confederate ports

Topics covered

- Jacksonian democracy
- The second party system
- The contours of American slavery
- Enslaved life and culture
- Evangelicalism, capitalism, and free labour
- The reform movement
- The white South
- The politics of territorial expansion
- The road to war
- The 1860 presidential election and secession

Introduction

John Adams and Thomas Jefferson both died on 4 July 1826, the 50th anniversary of the Declaration of Independence. They shared much in common as privileged, educated white men, but viewed the institution of slavery very differently. Jefferson was a Virginian enslaver while New Englander Adams came from an antislavery background (although was not as vocal a critic as his son, John Quincy Adams). But both agreed that slavery was a thorn in the young republic's side. Jefferson's private misgivings over the American paradox – of slavery flourishing in a country devoted to liberty – was illustrated most poignantly in his reaction to the furore over Missouri's entry to the Union. "This momentous question," Jefferson told his friend John Holmes, "like a fire bell in the night, awakened and filled me with terror."

The Missouri crisis of 1820–21 was eventually resolved, but the fundamental problem of slavery remained and forms the central focus of this chapter. As Jefferson put it, "we have the wolf [slavery] by the ear, and we can neither hold him, nor safely let him go. Justice is in one scale, and self-preservation in the other." Politicians struggled to contain this problem as the nation moved westward. Slavery drove a wedge between the slave and the free states as sectional, regional identities became stronger.

This chapter discusses slave life and culture and the ways in which the North and the South diverged from one another. Slavery clearly delineated those who enjoyed the rewards of free status – white men – from those who did not – the enslaved – but free blacks and women were further marginalised in different ways as well. The expansion of political democracy, for white males only, was fundamental to the antebellum second party system although northern pressure groups that included great numbers of middle-class women pushed for reform in a variety of areas. As the United States acquired substantial territory following the Mexican–American War (1846–48), however, the fatal flaw of plantation slavery could no longer be contained. Abraham Lincoln's 1858 "house divided" speech insisted that slavery and free labour could not coexist and the final section discusses the realisation of Jefferson's nightmare as the nation split in two following the 1860 presidential election.

Jacksonian democracy?

It was a familiar story. The presidential incumbent, that is the candidate holding office and seeking re-election, rubbished his opponent and listed his violent deeds in an election pamphlet, the "Coffin Handbill." The rival was accused of being an adulterer and a bigamist. In turn, the incumbent was accused of being elected by a "corrupt bargain" and was charged with the introduction of gambling to the White House in the form of a billiard table and a chess set. The sitting president was further accused of impropriety in providing an American woman to the Russian Czar as a young diplomat in St Petersburg. Such tactics are familiar in twenty-first-century politics, but the incumbent in question here is John Quincy Adams, who won the presidency in 1824, and the opponent is Andrew Jackson. None of the accusations were without foundation, although charges of gambling and procuring women were far-fetched. Jackson had killed Charles Dickinson in a duel in May 1806, was a vicious Indian fighter and, without knowing it, had married his wife Rachel in 1794 before she had divorced her first husband. This mistake did not prevent the pro-Adams press making the accusation that Jackson had "torn from a husband the wife of his bosom" to live with her in "open and notorious lewdness."

It is an understatement to suggest Andrew Jackson was a controversial figure. He is one of few individuals to be so significant as to symbolise an entire age. One of the most potent myths in American history is that his election in 1828 ushered in the era of the "common man," as politics evolved from its eighteenth-century deferential form that privileged elites to a democratic system of white male equality. This transition had begun long before 1828. Jackson, or "Old Hickory" because of his tough, aggressive demeanour, was widely believed to be anti-elitist. He was the first president from west of the Appalachian Mountains, and a self-made man, but shared little in common with ordinary Americans. The notorious "spoils system" expanded during Jackson's administration, for instance, as political offices were handed out as rewards to elite friends and party members regardless of ability. Jackson's self-styled reputation as a "man of the people" played out very well in appealing to the electorate, however, in an era when parties and electioneering created a vibrant political culture.

The Jacksonian era, lasting roughly two decades after 1828, did not realise a sudden extension of the franchise, nor was it a high point of voter turnout in elections. This had been in motion since the turn of the nineteenth century. Greater numbers of white men had been steadily enfranchised and voted enthusiastically in local, state, and national elections. The highly competitive gubernatorial elections of 1812, for instance, had a turnout of 75 per cent in New Hampshire and 80 per cent in Vermont. New states, carved out of the Louisiana Purchase, rarely imposed restrictions on political participation for white men. By contrast, the older states had a longer, uneven process of eradicating suffrage restrictions. New state constitutions gradually emerged on a more equitable basis, although often not without a fight. Most notoriously, Rhode Island maintained a suffrage requirement of $134 in property, which prompted determined reformers to hold their own convention in 1841. Lawyer Thomas Dorr was elected as unofficial governor and federal troops were required to quell popular unrest in the so-called Dorr War (1841–42). Passions were aroused elsewhere as well, as the right to vote became an intrinsic part of American citizenship, although Virginia, North Carolina, and Georgia retained tax and property suffrage qualifications. Politics in the older eastern seaboard states were more hierarchical than the rough and ready frontier environment of states founded after the Revolution.

Jackson, and his successor Martin Van Buren, led the Democratic Party in a fight against entrenched interests and aristocratic enemies that was more imagined than real. Most notably, he attacked the Second Bank of the United States (BUS). This private corporation, founded in 1816 in Philadelphia, housed federal funds, issued reliable bank notes, and was a key component of Henry Clay's American system. It served well as a means to counter inflation because its paper currency was widely accepted in a chaotic financial system. With hundreds of banks in existence, notes elicited varying levels of trust as a means of exchange. Rivals envied the BUS's close relationship with the government and attacked the corporation for its monopolistic control over federal funds. In an era of economic instability and growing friction between classes there was plenty of anger towards an institution that Jackson portrayed as dangerous and arrogant. Workingmen regarded the bank as a tool of business interests, while western settlers accused it of denying them much needed financial liquidity. On 10 July 1832, Jackson vetoed a congressional bill extending the Bank's charter, citing the "great evils to our country and its institutions that might flow from such a concentration of power in the hands of a few men irresponsible to the people." Drawing on the language of Revolutionary-era republicanism, he withdrew all federal deposits and placed the funds in several state chartered banks which effectively closed the BUS. This decision contributed greatly to the onset of economic depression in 1837.

Jackson invoked the rhetoric of the common man but extended the power of the federal government, most notably in the winter of 1832–33. South Carolina's wealth was generated by exports of cotton and rice to Great Britain. Enslaver politicians objected to an 1828 federal tariff that protected northern manufacturing – the "tariff of abominations" – and forced South Carolinians to pay higher prices for many products. A revised tariff proposed in 1832 – from 40 per cent to 35 per cent on certain manufactured goods – did not appease concerns. In November 1832, the South Carolina legislature voted to "nullify" the tariff and ordered federal officials to suspend collection of duties within the state. It further declared South Carolina's right to secede from the Union. In a position articulated by the influential politician John Calhoun, South Carolina asserted the right of nullification: that states could invalidate, or "nullify," federal law they deemed to be unconstitutional. To make matters more complicated, Calhoun was Jackson's vice president. Jackson's response was swift and decisive: nullification was illegal and secession constituted treason. In January 1833, Jackson instructed Congress to send federal troops to collect custom duty by force if necessary. South Carolina rescinded its nullification ordinance after Henry Clay drew

An 1833 lithograph by Edward W. Clay, published by H. R. Robinson, N.Y.

Figure 6.1 Andrew Jackson and the Second Bank of the United States. Satirical cartoons like this were a key component of American political discourse. Rival parties and politicians used them to attack their opponents.

up a new tariff in 1833 but did not accept that Jackson had the right to use force as part of his presidential powers. This early clash over the proper jurisdiction of the federal government and the states was a problem that would be revisited in the 1850s and beyond.

The second party system

This direct assertion of federal power was out of character for Andrew Jackson, as he generally defended states' rights and limited government. In the decades following the nullification crisis, the Democrats pursued laissez-faire policies and government intervention was toned down. The key outcome of Jackson's presidency was to catalyse the emergence of party opposition at both the national and state levels. Powerful conservative Senators such as Henry Clay of Kentucky and Daniel Webster of Massachusetts denounced Jackson as a tyrant – "King Andrew" – and formed the Whig Party. They were joined by John Calhoun, who hated Jackson, even though he held little in common with Clay and Webster. States' rights supporters joined the anti-Jackson coalition whose main purpose was to oppose the man they regarded as a despot. This uneasy alliance typified the loose nature of the second party system that pitted Democrats against Whigs down to the mid-1850s. Matters of style often took precedence over substance although broad differences can be identified between the two parties. Whigs tended to reside in areas of greatest market penetration, welcomed government intervention and wanted more canals and railroads built. Democrats glorified "producers," rather than bankers or merchants, tended to live in areas more distant from the market, and exhibited distrust of business and of government. The tension between positive and negative visions of government was a defining characteristic of the second party system and has continued to be contentious ever since.

Politics in the Jacksonian era revolved around personalities and paraphernalia and both parties were highly effective at getting their supporters to the polls on election days. Candidates routinely claimed humble origins to appeal to voters – a familiar tactic in the present-day – as the principle of political representation superseded previous notions that the "best" men should exercise independent judgement wisely. Other democratic reforms, such as written ballots, were implemented. These radical measures allowed ordinary men a political voice in an era when the British and European working classes were struggling to secure basic political rights.

Two spheres of civic engagement grew rapidly alongside the expansion of the electorate. First, each state had its own institutions of government, that included a House and Senate, and appointed state-level legislative, executive, and judicial officials, usually by election as the nineteenth century progressed, as well having oversight of participation in federal (national) elections. Second, government was subdivided within states between counties (called parishes in some states) that varied widely in size and population. The central unit of local government was the county court located in the county seat. The county seat was the town, either existing or in some cases newly built, chosen as the administrative hub that held jurisdiction over all substantive local issues. Judges, coroners, treasurers, tax collectors, the sheriff, and many other local government officials were appointed and competition for these positions was fierce. County politics was of far more importance than national elections. The redrawing of county boundaries or the relocation of county seats were matters of controversy, crucial to political, legal, and economic relationships, as well to an individual sense of local and personal identity.

The 1840 presidential election as the first "modern" campaign

William Henry Harrison was the first candidate to actively campaign for the presidency, under the slogan "Tippecanoe and Tyler too." Tippecanoe referenced Harrison's defeat of Shawnee Indians at Prophetstown on the Tippecanoe River in Indiana in 1811 while John Tyler was his vice presidential running mate. Harrison used Democratic Party taunts that he was so old he would be happy to spend "the remainder of his days in his log cabin" with "a barrel of hard cider" to his advantage. Harrison was presented as the common man, "the log cabin and hard cider candidate." In fact, he came from an aristocratic background and his opponent, incumbent Martin Van Buren, originated from humble origins. Harrison died of pneumonia just one month after taking office on 4 April 1841.

Political participation provided white men with a sense of civic equality that foreigners identified as uniquely American. Indeed, the political experience – of party conventions, meetings, parades, toasts, and above all of taking part in election days – was intoxicating. Issues were important, but they frequently changed. What remained constant was the sense of togetherness – of democracy and of masculine ritual – that gave tangible evidence of American freedom. In New England, democracy was mythologised, with local officials fulfilling a sacred duty by walking the town boundaries every few years. All counties contained distinct neighbourhoods and competing interest groups, so the appointment of a clergyman, the location of a polling booth, or provision for the poor was rarely straightforward. Europeans were fascinated and appalled, in roughly equal measures, by the American experiment in democracy. The more astute visitors, like Frenchman Alexis de Tocqueville, believed that American politics, by which he meant not only political parties but civic clubs and other organised groups, constituted a powerful unifying thread binding the US together. In a nation with a bewildering plurality of interests, politics provided a measure of stability and encouraged nationalism in spite of numerous differences between the states.

There was a downside to this democratic narrative however. As barriers were eliminated for white men during the antebellum era, the gender and racial boundaries of civic life became more rigid. Politics became exclusively a masculine domain – property-holding women had voted in New Jersey between 1776 and 1807 – and the preserve of whites only. Virginia, South Carolina, and Georgia had been the only states that excluded African Americans from voting in the Revolutionary era. Revised antebellum state constitutions denied free blacks suffrage. Most states simply

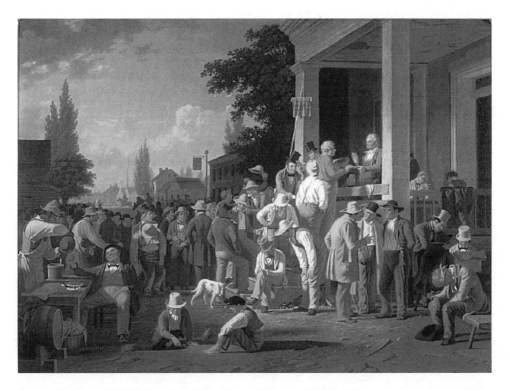

Figure 6.2 George Caleb Bingham, *The County Election* (1852). This evocative painting documents the rowdy revelry of election day as the exclusive domain of the white male.

Source: Courtesy of ART Collection/Alamy

restricted voting to "whites." Where they did not, other methods were used. New York, for instance, raised the property qualifications for free black voters to $250 in 1821 but eliminated property requirements for whites. On the eve of the Civil War, just five New England states retained free black suffrage – Maine, Massachusetts, New Hampshire, Rhode Island, and Vermont – but only in Massachusetts were there significant numbers of African Americans. There was much debate as to whether immigrants should be allowed to vote, especially when large numbers of Irish arrived in the 1840s and 1850s. The Naturalization Act of 1798 had extended the period of residency required for citizenship from 5 to 14 years but some questioned whether this was long enough. Fortunately for immigrants, as long as they were male, white, and fulfilled residency requirements, they were entitled to vote.

The contours of American slavery

Overseas visitors to the United States were drawn to American slavery. The English novelist Charles Dickens complained that he could not avoid giving his views of slavery when he crossed the Atlantic: "They *will* ask you what you think of it; and *will* expatiate on slavery as if it were one of the greatest blessings of mankind." The intense focus on the South's "peculiar institution" was unsurprising in a changing world driven by global capitalism in which slavery appeared to be a relic from an earlier age. From the perspective of Manchester, Lisbon, London or, indeed, New York or Philadelphia, bondage in the southern states was an anachronism, although a profitable one that had fundamentally contributed to the development of each city.

The romantic, rural character of the "Old South" (a term coined after the Civil War by the southern elite nostalgically looking back to the past) depicted in films such as *Gone With the Wind* (1939) exerted a powerful influence on the popular imagination long into the twentieth century. For decades, historians also emphasised southern distinctiveness. This rural, agrarian shibboleth fails to do justice to the reality of southern diversity. Indeed, most recent scholarly interpretations present a very different picture of the South connected to global markets. There were many different "Souths," not just one monolithic society. Major differences existed between the Upper and the Lower South, the urban and rural South, and between plantation districts (with a high proportion of enslaved people) and the upcountry (with an overwhelmingly white population).

The vast majority of enslaved people in 1850 worked on cotton plantations – 1,815,000 out of a total of 3,204,313 – while approximately 350,000 cultivated tobacco, 150,000 sugar, 125,000 rice, and 60,000 hemp. The geographical dispersal of the enslaved population was determined by the differing soils and environmental conditions that suited particular crops. Cotton production dominated the black belt which stretched from Georgia through Alabama and Mississippi to Louisiana and, by the 1850s, as far as Texas. Rice plantations continued to be profitable in the swampy, coastal areas of South Carolina and Georgia, while sugar thrived in southern Louisiana. Despite soil depletion, tobacco plantations remained in Virginia, North Carolina, and Kentucky (where hemp was also grown in large quantities). Foodstuffs such as corn, maize, and wheat were staples on farms and plantations, the latter becoming the most important cash crop in parts of Virginia and North Carolina. There were perhaps 200,000 enslaved captives in the industrial sector by the 1850s, predominately located in Upper South factories.

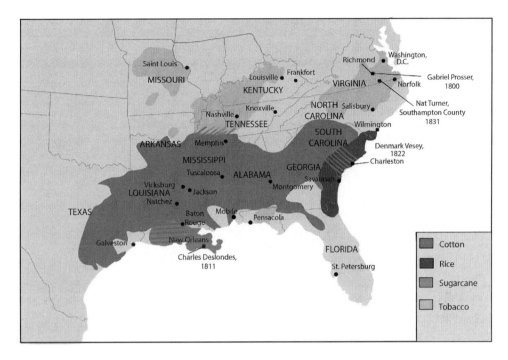

Figure 6.3 Slavery in the South. The enslaved population in US grew from 687,681 in 1790 to
2,009,043 in 1830 to 3,953,731 by 1860.

Enslaved people worked in a wide variety of settings during the antebellum era,
more so than at any time in the long history of bondage in North America, and there
was no single, definitive experience. The parameters of their lives were determined
by production of the great antebellum plantation staples – cotton, sugar, tobacco,
and rice – which each had unique agricultural cycles. The rhythm of the seasons dictated daily demands with distinct phases of production depicted in image 6.4. Plantations aimed to be self-sufficient, providing basic necessities such as food, clothing,
and housing, and thus coerced labour was varied, although approximately three
quarters of enslaved people routinely toiled in the fields. However, people held in
bondage were also blacksmiths, carpenters, carriage drivers, factory workers, boat
hands, musicians, nurses, cooks, seamstresses, and house servants. In parts of the
Upper South, such as Delaware and Maryland, slavery was in decline. Large numbers of free blacks in the Upper South created a more fluid society than that found
in the Deep South, where with the exception of New Orleans most blacks were
enslaved. In the South Carolina and Georgia Lowcountry, in the black belt, and on
the lower banks of the Mississippi River, for example, the enslaved outnumbered
whites by as much as two-thirds.

Work was diverse but always pushed the enslaved to the limits of their capacity.
Solomon Northup, born free but kidnapped into bondage in 1841, provides a vivid
description of cotton production. Cotton requires moderate rainfall, a long growing
season and becomes labour intensive at harvest time. From sowing seeds in April, to

Figure 6.4 Scenes on a cotton plantation, Alfred R. Waud, *Harper's Weekly* (1867).
Source: Courtesy of the Library of Congress Prints and Photographs Division Washington

hoeing and thinning in the summer, to picking in late August, each stage of cultivation required careful attention, especially as particular "grades" of cotton sold for different prices at market. The working day lasted from first light to dusk, although could be extended by moonlight. The gang system was the norm on cotton plantations. Small groups were supervised by drivers (enslaved men chosen for their physical prowess or experience) and by the overseer (a professional supervisor, usually white but some-times free black, hired by the owner to take care of all aspects of plantation work). Northup tells us that "the overseer or driver follows the slaves on horseback with a whip." Anyone who failed to keep up with the fastest hoer was punished. "When a new hand . . . is sent for the first time into the field, he is whipped up smartly, and made for the day to pick as fast as he possibly can." Having set a standard – the amount of cotton picked by each slave was weighed every night – anyone falling "short" would receive a whipping. The "slave never approaches the gin-house with his basket of cot-ton but with fear." The enslaved exploited the owner's reliance on their labour as far as they could, by working slowly, poorly, breaking tools, or deliberately sabotaging the crop, but the grim reality was that failure to work hard resulted in punishment or sale.

Enslaved life and culture

If colonial slavery was akin to a state of war, antebellum slavery took a different form. Some scholars interpret a paternalistic system of accommodation and resistance, oth-ers see a distinctive variant of modern capitalism, based on rewards and punishments, but both interpretations stress a level of mutual dependence and cooperation, even if forced on enslaved people and conceded grudgingly by owners. Material conditions improved on the whole. This was partly because enslavers liked to give the appearance of looking after their captives but also because healthier labourers were better able to toil in the hot sun. American slaves were portrayed by historian Stanley Elkins in the mid-twentieth century as psychically damaged – much like veterans suffering from shellshock – but this interpretation was overturned by a series of studies stressing the resilience of slave culture. Enslaved men, women, and children made the most of free time outside of work hours that usually included Saturday afternoons and Sundays. Their lives revolved around the overlapping, conflicting, settings of the work environment and the slave quarters.

Slave "agency"

To what extent American enslaved men and women exerted control over their lives has been a guiding question in the buoyant field of slavery studies. Scholars have exhibited a fascination with slave "agency" although there is little consensus. On one extreme, the enslaved are depicted as ruthlessly exploited by merciless owners who used physical punishment and withheld food to extract maximum effort from their property. Troublesome slaves were sold away from their community and loved ones and the possibility of sale was terrifying. On the other, the enslaved built a powerful, protective, and nurturing culture. Community pressure was exerted to gain concessions from owners, who were forced to accommodate if they wanted to ensure the successful cultivation of plantation crops.

Enslaved families were usually allocated one cabin each. The family was a convenient unit for distributing food supplies and provided sustenance for hungry labourers. The birth of children, who automatically became the property of the enslaver, was expected and increased the size of the workforce and the wealth of the enslaver. For enslaved women, then, US slavery was both a system of production and reproduction. The family was also a tool of control for the captor and those in bondage lived with the constant fear of being sold. Family was incredibly important none the less. Unlike Caribbean plantations where life expectancy was extremely short, and successful conception and birth very difficult, children were raised. Being husbands and wives and mothers and fathers reminded individuals of their humanity. While family relationships were welcome, they were not straightforward or secure. Most dreadfully, enslaved women were the victims of sexual assault by the enslaver in brutal acts that underlined the unfettered power of elite white males on the plantation.

A variety of enslaved family structures existed and children usually had extended kin who were not blood-related, which helped to cope with the threat of forced separation that haunted the community. The nuclear family was the most common structure, although fathers were not always present. Perhaps a third of slave marriages in antebellum South Carolina, for example, were "abroad" and involved partners from different plantations, with fathers visiting when they could. This arrangement was common in the Upper South, where large numbers were sold to the Deep South states with more men than women taken. Enslaved women exerted greater influence in

Upper South communities than was typical in the Lower South, therefore, in matrifo-
cal (female headed) families.

Parents provided a crucial emotional buffer for their children and taught survival
skills. Important lessons included the necessity of remaining silent when provoked,
of respect, especially for elders, and of hope for a better future. Given that one-
third of the American slave population was under ten years old between 1820 and
1860, this was crucial, although enslavers often interfered in the raising of children,
typically sending them to work in the fields between the ages of 10 and 12. There were
no schools on plantations and literacy was forbidden so the enslaved family was the
conduit of cultural knowledge. African heritage was handed down orally through the
generations and, as late as the mid-nineteenth century in places like the Lowcountry,
first-hand knowledge might be provided by elderly captives imported before the 1808
international slave trade ban. The captive family tried to provide essential emotional
support for all its members, although owners ruthlessly manipulated bonds between
husband and wife and between parent and child. At least one in three marriages ended
by sale. It was probably less frequent to separate mother from child although this happened regularly, with traumatic emotional and psychological consequences.

Families were the essential building blocks of a wider community. The notion that
a strong, resourceful and united "community" was built on American plantations is
controversial however. Simply because men and women were forced to live together
does not necessarily mean that communality and consensus was generated. Unlike
the Caribbean where plantation owners were often absent, southern enslavers sought
to control all aspects of their bond people's lives – and some claimed to be head of
an extended family, white and black. Paternalism was thus a double-edged sword,
as better conditions came with the price of intrusion into social lives of the enslaved.
Moreover, southern plantations were significantly smaller than elsewhere, whether
compared with slavery in the Caribbean or serfdom in Russia. In 1860, approximately
one-quarter of southern slaves lived on small farms of just one to nine slaves. Half
lived on medium holdings of 10–49, while the remaining quarter lived on large plantations of 50 or more, although figures vary between the Upper and the Lower South
(where plantations were much larger generally).

The enslaved forged links with adjacent plantations in the neighbourhood in both
formal and informal ways. Gatherings took place at Christmas and Easter, at other
ceremonies like funerals and weddings, and at communal events such as corn shuck-
ings. Captives sang songs, told stories, played games, and exchanged their news.
Covert meetings were also held away from the plantation house, subject to avoiding
random inspections by the overseer. After dark, slaves stole away to the cover of the
trees, or "brush arbors," and these meetings could be cross-plantation gatherings. The
wider slave neighbourhood also aided enslaved fugitives who took the brave decision
to abscond. While some escaped to permanent freedom across the Mason-Dixon Line,
and some fled to Canada or Britain for fear of recapture, the vast majority ran away
for a few days at most before returning.

A rich culture nurtured communality. Religion was probably the most important
component of slave culture, but folk stories (the most famous being the Brer Rabbit
tales), songs, dance, ghosts and spirits, herbal remedies, and conjuring were all vital
elements. Conjuring, the art of charms and spells that was strongest on the plantations
of the Lowcountry and the Deep South, was considered by Frederick Douglass to be
superstitious ritual incompatible with Christianity. To others, however, it provided

comfort and a means of resistance. As with most aspects of slave culture, the practice was built on a fluid mixture of African, European, and American elements. Conjuring provided a means of loosening the depressingly tight reins of bondage and however unreliable made enslaved people feel that they were not powerless. Enslavers worried that slave culture promoted independence and they coerced slaves to accept their values. Simultaneously, however, they benefitted from the way slave culture stabilised daily life and encouraged captives to make the best of their situation.

Enslavers hoped that Christianity would make their captives more compliant. The enslaved attended organised services on Sundays but the appeal of Christianity lay in its synthesis with African cultural traditions in the quarters. The formal white church service bore little resemblance to the informal gatherings in the quarters that were sometimes sanctioned legitimately and sometimes held covertly. Black preachers stressed the freeing of the Israelites from bondage and other stories of retribution, justice and deliverance. They employed a call and response style inviting audience participation. Dance and music were central features of the ceremony, releasing the pent-up frustration that slavery generated. If only for a moment, those held in bondage entered a different realm, transcending geographical constrictions that allowed little opportunity for physical movement, let alone free expression. Christianity provided a moral set of values from a higher power, giving the enslaved a way of judging their captors. Virginian Louis Hughes, who endured bondage for three decades before escaping to Union lines during the Civil War, recalled that no matter "what their troubles had been during the week – how much they had been lashed, the prayer meeting on Saturday evening never failed to be held" and was "the joy and comfort of the slaves."

Evangelicalism, capitalism, and free labour

Andrew Jackson's farewell address in 1837 confidently declared that no other populace "enjoyed so much freedom and happiness as the people of these United States." The complicated discourse of American freedom was shaped by slavery and by profound changes in the first half of the nineteenth century: economic growth, territorial expansion, and the glorification of the individual. Slavery encouraged a heightened appreciation of liberty and newspapers and other print literature brought the freedom narrative to the forefront of public life. As in the political arena, not all social groups enjoyed the full fruits of freedom but reform movements sought to change that. The huge popularity of evangelical religion spread far and wide during the Second Great Awakening and underpinned the reform impulse. Alexis de Tocqueville perceptively noted the interconnections between religion and freedom in the United States: "In France I had almost always seen the spirit of religion and the spirit of freedom pursuing courses diametrically opposed to each other; but in America I found that they were intimately united, and that they reigned in common over the same country."

The Second Great Awakening, a religious movement that gripped different parts of the United States at different times from the early nineteenth century, stimulated passion and forced a profound reconsideration of concepts such as freedom and individuality. Rejecting the Calvinist notion of predestination, that fate was determined from birth, Baptists and Methodists re-conceptualised an individual relationship with God. Charles Grandison Finney, formerly a lawyer, became an itinerant preacher who insisted people were "moral free agents" able to shape their own destinies, although time was running out. Finney's celebrated gatherings in what became known as

New York state's "burned-over district" – central and western counties that were so effectively converted to evangelicalism that there was no people (fuel) left to convert (burn) – increased church membership by 100,000 in 1831. What gained widespread acceptance was a redefinition of the individual as sovereign in religious as well as secular terms. Evangelical fervour celebrated God's love for all but on a personal basis.

Evangelicalism was wildly popular in the South, the mid-Atlantic, and the Midwest, although New England generally retained its adherence to traditional forms of Congregationalism. Women, blacks, and poor whites intermingled at huge religious gatherings. Kentuckian Methodist minister Peter Cartwright regularly attended camp meetings of thousands, traveling from miles around. They were emotive events, releasing the frustration many felt as they lost control of their working lives, that lasted for days. On one occasion, Cartwright witnessed "more than 100 sinners fall like dead men under one powerful sermon" and "five hundred Christians all shouting aloud the high praises of God at once." Evangelical circuit riders covered vast distances administering to their rapidly growing flock. Preachers pioneered modern-day evangelical techniques that encourage conversion, such as the "anxious bench" for those struggling with their conscience as well as testimony meetings for the converted. Camp meetings were huge social occasions that rural Americans travelled from far and wide to attend and the lack of formal class, race, and gender hierarchies at these occasions was striking.

Over time, the evangelical movement became more formal and hierarchical, although never to the same extent as traditional denominations. Organised religion struggled with the thorny problem of slavery. Southern brethren who owned slaves resented the criticism of northerners who insisted slavery was a sin and, in the mid-1840s, both the Methodists and Baptists split into separate northern and southern conferences. The Presbyterians had done so in 1838. While critical of the excesses of rapid economic and social changes, the evangelical message served the needs of capitalism by preaching self-restraint, temperance, and, above all, frugality and industry as the keys to success. The powerful idea that heaven might be achieved on earth – the opposite of the Calvinist notion of predestination – inspired individuals to work hard within the capitalist system, rather than to challenge it, and those on the margins pushed for full inclusion. Large numbers of middle-class women, for instance, empowered by traditional family roles as carers and nurturers, sought to carry out these duties in the public sphere. Reformers took inspiration from religious values to promote temperance and sabbatarianism. Secular concerns were also targeted such as charity and welfare, education, and other philanthropic endeavours. The five million immigrants coming to the United States between 1830 and 1860, a number larger than the entire US population in 1790, was the cause of much concern. The never-ending stream of immigrants provoked heated debate about citizenship and the need for new arrivals to acculturate to American ways.

A radical critique of capitalism's harmful effects was made by feminist and labour leaders. Gender demarcations defined and constrained women's lives and female critics bemoaned the "slavery of sex." Margaret Fuller, whose 1845 *Women in the Nineteenth Century* is considered the first major American feminist text, insisted that American women should have the right "to live freely and unimpeded" and championed female education. A famous meeting at Seneca Falls (New York) in July 1848 lamented the voting, employment, educational, and property rights routinely denied American women. The Declaration of Sentiments, drawn up by Elizabeth Cady Stanton and modelled on the Declaration of Independence, was signed by the participants and articulated feminist concerns that inspired sustained activism through the nine-teenth century and beyond.

Labour leaders responded to the working man's loss of independence as technology and mechanisation reduced the need for skilled artisans. New manufacturing jobs tended to be semi-skilled or required no skills at all. Low wages were compounded by hated factory rules and regulations that created "wage slavery" some claimed. The upturn in immigration provided a willing, and convenient, proletariat with no prior investment in the labour struggle. Wage labourers constituted more than two-thirds of the total workforce in New York and Boston by 1850. Their numbers exceeded the total number of slaves in the United States by mid-century. Although not as visible or as commented upon, the growth of wage labour was arguably as significant a develop-ment as the expansion of the Cotton Kingdom.

Empowered by Jacksonian glorifications of the virtuous small producer entitled to the fruits of hard toil, ideas that dated back to Adam Smith and John Locke, the decline of the workshop and general denigration of artisanal labour was not accepted uncriti-cally. The cities of Boston, New York, and Philadelphia had been prime locations for journeyman organisations and clubs in the late eighteenth and early nineteenth century. These clubs represented skilled artisans, stressed republican values, and were rarely long-lasting but flourished and then closed unpredictably. During the second party system, journeymen's clubs formed trade unions to defend collective interests such as wages, safety, and the length of the working day. Unions were organised by occupation although the General Trades Union, formed in New York in 1833, invited all workers to join. Even so, the legal system provided little protection and overwhelmingly favoured employers which helped to facilitate the switch from artisanship to wage labour.

The axiom that hard work was virtuous and essential for progress gained growing acceptance and also helped to legitimate changing working practices. Problems associ-ated with *wage* labour gradually dissipated, or were diverted, by the glorification of *free* labour in the northern states in the later antebellum decades. This discourse demarcated the North as a distinct section in which industry and commerce were not only highly desirable but actually critical to continued progress, casting free and slave labour systems as polar opposites. Idealisation of free labour was also heavily inflected with notions of the superiority of whiteness. Historians such as David R. Roediger argue that the north-ern worker's psychological investment in "whiteness" and rising prejudice toward free blacks was strongly influenced by a loss of economic independence. The rapidly expand-ing white working class faced an uncertain, insecure future and their alienation was subliminally projected upon African Americans in the form of racial hostility.

The reform movement

The growth of capitalism in the antebellum decades caused anxiety and much com-ment. Some Americans concluded that the logical solution to capitalism's problems was to reform the system. Others wanted to dismantle it or remove themselves from it. A number of ephemeral groups and sects devoted themselves to the communitar-ian ideal, the antithesis of the idea that freedom lay with the individual. Some were inspired by religious values, others by secular, or a combination of the two. The Shak-ers, or the United Society of Believers in Christ's Second Appearing, claimed 6,000 members in the 1830s in various communities in New England and New York. Coop-erative groups, following the teachings of Englishman Robert Owen and Frenchman

Albert Fourier, insisted that genuine freedom entailed the end of distinctions based on race, class, and gender, and even advocated the abolition of private property. In 1841, Unitarian minister George Ripley founded Brook Farm, nine miles from Boston, because he was appalled at rampant individualism of the American people and "the burning zeal with which they run the race of selfish competition with no thought for the elevation of their brethren."

The visionary, idealistic impulse behind such ventures was clear, harking back to the founding of colonial New England as an opportunity to build utopian societies. Robert Owen's short lived (1825–29) colony in Indiana was appropriately named New Harmony. Many communitarian experiments failed to match their ideals, and some were little more than vehicles to serve the needs of charismatic leaders. Nonetheless, they represented important alternative visions of American freedom and demonstrate the disillusionment, and for some deep discontent, with rampant capitalist values.

The abolitionists were the most important reform group of the antebellum era and their leading spokesman, William Lloyd Garrison, rivalled Andrew Jackson in terms of notoriety. The first editorial of his *Liberator* newspaper, published in Boston in 1831, set an uncompromising tone: "I am in earnest – I will not equivocate – I will not excuse – I will not retreat a single inch – AND I WILL BE HEARD." Garrison, supported by free blacks, women, philanthropists, and merchants, formed the American Anti-Slavery Society in 1833. Abolitionism reflected complex religious, economic, and humanitarian changes and was a transatlantic initiative. The 1840 World Anti-Slavery Convention in London brought leading British and American abolitionists together. Garrison opposed slavery on moral and religious grounds and attacked anyone or anything that supported slavery be that the government or the organised church. He famously burnt the Constitution – "a covenant with death, an agreement with hell" – on 4 July 1854. Garrison championed racial equality, believing that God had "made of one blood all nations of men to dwell on all faces of the earth." In an era when the intellectual, scientific assertion of a fixed racial hierarchy superseded the environmentalist explanation of human difference, this was a brave and radical stance.

Abolitionists bluntly charged that slaveholding was a sin and demanded immediate emancipation. They rejected gradualism that was popular at the turn-of-the-century and colonisation that had been very well received during the 1820s. Membership grew steadily during the 1830s and 1840s, even though violent mobs routinely broke up abolitionist meetings (in 1837 abolitionist Elijah Lovejoy was murdered in Alton, Illinois). Women were at the forefront of the movement. The inter-racial Philadelphia Female Anti-Slavery Society, founded in December 1833 and affiliated with Garrison's organisation, was the longest lasting of many women's abolition societies. Famous members included Lucretia Mott, Grace Douglass, Hetty Reckless, Charlotte, Harriet, Sarah and Margaretta Horton, and Angelina Grimké. Arguments split the movement into different factions. Arthur and Lewis Tappan led a break-away group to form the American and Foreign Anti-Slavery Society in 1840. Garrison had written in the *Liberator* in 1837 that he believed in "the rights of women to the utmost extent," whereas the Tappans argued that the movement should focus on slavery alone. Others objected to Garrison's tactic of "moral suasion" that placed the onus on individuals to repent rather than work to change the system from within to force abolition. Gerrit Smith and Salmon P. Chase formed the Liberty Party in 1840 to seek abolition by political means.

African Americans played an important but contentious role in the abolitionist movement, none more so than Frederick Douglass. Douglass escaped from slavery when just 20 years old by pretending to be a free black sailor. He became a spokesman for the

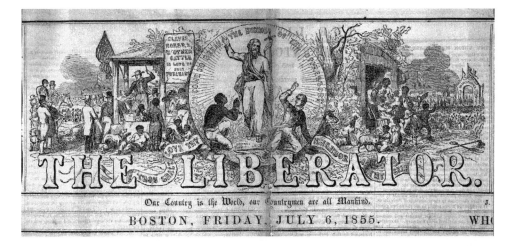

Figure 6.5 Masthead of *The Liberator*. A strong transatlantic Anglo-American abolitionist partnership evolved, epitomised by the slogan "Our country is the World." Images such as these tugged at the moral heartstrings of a middle-class readership, depicting the horror of the auction block and the violence of slavery that destroyed family. The autobiographies of self-emancipated slaves also stressed these themes.

Source: Courtesy of Granger Historical Picture Archive/Alamy

American Anti-Slavery Society, on the national and international stage, and intelligently used his first-hand experience of slavery in lectures that gave him an authenticity white speakers could not match. His autobiographical *Narrative of the Life of Frederick Douglass* (1845), published in a number of editions, was highly influential and one of the key texts of the burgeoning slave autobiographical genre that appealed to a northern middle-class readership. Even so, Douglass complained he was sometimes treated in a patronising fashion by white abolitionists rather than an equal. Nonetheless, abolitionists generally advocated equality and campaigned to remove "white" restrictions from state constitutions. They were an extremely successful pressure group that organised thousands of meetings and distributed millions of pamphlets.

Free soil

William Lloyd Garrison's insistence that slavery must be immediately abolished attracted devoted followers but was generally regarded as excessive. However, the message that slavery was immoral and economically harmful gradually gained acceptance outside the South. The short-lived Free Soil Party was made up of discontented antislavery Whigs and Democrats and fought the 1848 and 1852 presidential elections on a simple platform that opposed slavery's extension into western territory. It was eclipsed by the Republican Party in the mid-1850s that put free soil at the centre of its political manifesto. Radical abolitionism remained controversial but most Americans in the free states approved the exclusion of slavery from the West.

The white South

A proslavery argument articulated by a cross-section of southern politicians, lawyers, physicians, scientists, writers, editors, and clergymen defended slavery from abolitionist attacks. Drawing from history, religion, science, economics, and politics, they presented a comprehensive justification of the peculiar institution. Doubts over slavery had lingered down to the 1820s – the American Colonization Society was strong in the upper South – but slavery was presented as a positive good by the eve of the Civil War. The turning point is often dated to August 1831 when enslaved preacher Nat Turner shattered the myth of the contented slave. Turner and his followers killed as many as 60 whites in Southampton County, Virginia. They were eventually overpowered and Turner captured and executed but the rebellion sent shock waves across the South. In 1832, the Virginia legislature conducted a lengthy debate over slavery's future. Emancipation was an option favoured by the non-slaveholding districts in western Virginia that argued taxes were better spent on internal improvements than the costs of policing slavery. The interests of enslavers prevailed. From that point, a "siege" mentality developed in southern states. Outsiders were looked on with suspicion and the small number of southern antislavery activists, usually opposed to slavery on religious grounds, were ostracised or violently removed.

What kind of society was the Old South? Slaveholding held the key to economic and social success. The South's total white population in 1860 was just over eight million. Of the one and a half million heads of household in southern states, 385,000 (24 per cent) owned captives, although a crucial contrast must be stressed: 37 per cent of families in the Lower South were slaveholding, compared to just 20 per cent in the Upper South. Half of all enslavers owned less than five slaves. Those with more than five slaves but fewer than 20 were middling. Only 12 per cent of whites held 20 or more enslaved people and thus qualified as "planters." Less than one per cent of slaveholding families – or 2,300 families in total – owned 100 or more enslaved people. The majority of southern whites were property-owning farmers, or *yeomen*, although at least a third of whites did not own land in 1860. Some rented land, some were hunters, fishermen, squatters, and herders, but a sizeable number were labourers (about 20 per cent of the working population) working for cash or for food and shelter. Non-slaveholding, non-property owning southerners on the margins were stigmatised as "poor whites."

The proportion of whites that owned slaves is surprisingly small but planters exerted a disproportionate influence or *hegemony*. They held important political positions, in State Legislatures for instance, and typically backed the occupants of county offices lower down in the system. White southerners without captives aspired to become enslavers in time and as many as 50 per cent of non-slaveholding whites had an investment in slavery through family ties or connections to the plantation economy. Planters displayed a paternalistic concern for yeomen in the processing, transportation, and sale of crops such as cotton and routinely hired out captives to their neighbours. They shared common forms of worship and gathered together on occasions such as the fourth of July in a relationship built on common mastery of patriarchal households and control of dependents, be they women, children, or the enslaved. Poor whites, on the other hand, were not part of this white male alliance as they traded and socialised with the enslaved in a shadowy underworld outside the mainstream.

As the sectional contest over slavery heated up, the unity of white men was stressed repeatedly in southern political meetings and church sermons. In 1857, South

Carolinian Senator James Henry Hammond proclaimed "there must be a class to perform the menial duties . . . It constitutes the very mud-sill of society." He argued that the South had just two classes, black and white. We should be wary of taking this rhetoric at face value, even if it contains some truth. Yeomen in plantation districts, especially in the booming slave society of the Deep South, were most receptive to the proslavery message. The contrast between slave and free status was acute in the black belt and the Lowcountry where whites were reminded daily of the liberty they enjoyed. Outside of plantation districts, attitudes towards slavery were more ambivalent. Upcountry southerners prized their independence in rural, tight-knit, farming communities that cared little for slaves or for planters. There were murmurings of discontent that state governments favoured planter interests, but upcountry settlements were generally left alone to manage their own affairs. Artisans also complained about the competition of enslaved labourers but most southerners were farmers and their economic and political interests broadly aligned with those of wealthy enslavers.

In the urban South, however, it was a different story. Race relations in Richmond, Baltimore, St Louis, Louisville, and New Orleans, and to a lesser extent Charleston and Savannah, were fluid. Lower-class districts housed a diverse population of enslaved people, free blacks, immigrants (especially Irish and German), northerners as well as poor southern whites. The contrast between white and black that was so sharp in the countryside was far less rigid and the judicial system struggled to cope. Many African Americans had such a light skin tone that they might easily pass as white. The contrast between the urban and rural South was immense by the late antebellum period. Towns and cities housed a nascent middle class. They worked outside the plantation economy, as shop keepers, clerks, bankers, doctors, artisans, publishers, and editors, and pursued a reform agenda much like their northern counterparts.

While the equality of southern white men was held to be sacrosanct, some proslavery intellectuals rejected the Declaration of Independence's insistence that "all men were created equal." There is "not a word of truth in it" John C. Calhoun countered in 1848, because freedom and liberty were not granted as birthrights. Men were not accorded "the same right to liberty and equality" Calhoun asserted, but enjoyed particularistic rights according to their social position. A doctrine of "slavery in the abstract" was discussed in elite circles where it was even suggested by Virginian intellectual George Fitzhugh that capitalism's inequities might be solved by enslaving white people. Fitzhugh's suggestion was ignored, but potent questions were asked of capitalism by southern political economists in a critique that shared much in common with the arguments of northern labour radicals about the injustice of wage slavery. "Free" labour, southern critics argued, was a fiction that masked gross exploitation.

Ironically, parts of the South rapidly followed in the North's economic footsteps in the 1850s. The South portrayed itself as a conservative, hierarchical society and large sections reflected these characteristics. But industry grew rapidly in the Upper South. In global terms, the southern economy ranked fourth in per capita income, sixth in cotton textile production, and eighth in pig iron production by the eve of the Civil War. That the southern economy suffers in comparison to Great Britain and the American North is only to be expected because they were the industrial giants of the age. Moreover, agricultural production was buoyant and highly profitable – why would southerners diversify their economy any faster when cotton was so lucrative? Sugar production in Louisiana demonstrated that slavery was not incompatible with capitalism. Sugar plantations rapidly mechanised in the mid-nineteenth century, harnessing the benefits

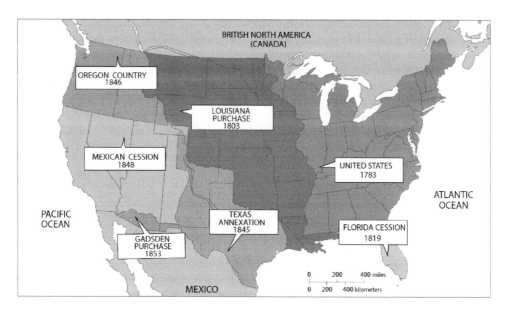

Figure 6.6 Territorial expansion in the nineteenth century. The US stretched from the Atlantic to the Pacific by the 1850s. This was an outcome of warfare and of negotiation as borders with Canada and Mexico were finally settled. The US also paid $10 million to Mexico in the 1853 Gadsden Purchase. This land was bought to facilitate plans to build a southern transcontinental railroad.

of steam power and the latest capitalist innovations. Planters provided extra rations at peak periods and paid the enslaved wages for overwork outside of normal hours. Determining what kind of society existed below the Mason-Dixon Line, then, depends very much on which particular part of the South one examines.

The politics of territorial expansion

Westward expansion, something essential to the growth of the United States and its consolidation of power, caused misery for the native population that it displaced. It was also the major cause of tension between the slave and the free states. Under the terms of the 1787 Northwest Ordinance, territories could apply for statehood when they reached the relatively low threshold of 60,000 inhabitants – to provide some sense of scale, New York City's population was over 500,000 by 1850. Congress hoped to maintain political equilibrium between the sections, especially with the growing demographic superiority of the North. A rapidly expanding population gave the northern states more seats in Congress, an imbalance that threatened to become overwhelming with millions of immigrants settling in the antebellum US (nine out of ten residing above the Mason-Dixon Line).

Southerners wanted fresh territory in which slavery might continue to grow because many believed they had reached the natural limits of the plantation system. Expansion into the West was discussed in state legislatures and elite circles in the South, as was the acquisition of Cuba by force or by sale. In the free states, by contrast, labour leaders and newspaper editors, such as the influential Horace Greeley who founded the *New York Tribune*, believed that western land were perfect for building homesteads that provided the best future for the working man and offered an alternative to wage slavery. Northern determination to keep slavery out of the West for ideological and for racist reasons grew during the antebellum era. African Americans were discouraged from heading west and Indiana, Illinois, Iowa, and Oregon prohibited them from entering altogether.

The Missouri Compromise of 1820–21 provided an early solution to the problem of expansion. In 1819, the Missouri territory applied for statehood. Congress, after considerable disagreement, eventually decided that Missouri would join as a slave state alongside Maine (that was carved out of northern Massachusetts) as a free state. The Missouri Compromise line of 36°30' delineated the future boundary between slave and free territory even though Missouri lay north of that latitude (see Fig. 6.8). This maintained a delicate sectional balance – of 12 free states and 12 slave states – and established the principle that slavery might push into the southwest but not the northwest. The Whigs and the Democrats subsequently tried to keep slavery off the political agenda. The adoption of the Gag Rule in Congress in 1836 ensured that antislavery petitions were ignored even though this measure was strongly opposed by John Quincy Adams and most northern Whigs. Repealed in 1844 on the grounds of free speech, the gag rule demonstrated the willingness of politicians to work together to maintain sectional accord. Both major parties were composed of northern and southern coalitions under the second party system that helped greatly to navigate sectional problems.

However, the Mexican–American War (1846–48), or more precisely the one million square miles of territory acquired as a consequence, upset the political equilibrium. The United States entered into a second war against a foreign country through a combination of Mexico's internal weakness, the migration of large numbers of American nationals into Texas, the threat that Mexico might cede California to the British, and rampant expansionism underpinned by manifest destiny. Mexico had been enraged by Texan independence in 1836 and hoped to regain its former province. Hesitation over whether to allow Texas to join the Union, which was much desired by the Anglo settlers who were the majority there by the 1840s, was ended when the US annexed Texas in 1845. Mexico broke off diplomatic relations as a consequence. President Polk, an aggressive expansionist, sent John Slidell to Mexico City in December 1845 with instructions to purchase New Mexico and California. Polk expected the offer would be refused, however, and sent troops into disputed territory early in 1846 as a show of force. The subsequent clash between Mexican and American forces at the Rio Grande River was used by Polk to silence public and political opposition to military conflict and Congress passed a declaration of war on May 13.

American forces captured key towns on the Pacific coast and defeated the Mexicans on the battlefield despite often being outnumbered, due to better organisation and superior fire power (see fig. 6.7). The enlistment of 50,000 volunteers was authorised. General Winfield Scott marched towards Mexico City in early 1847 and eventually entered in September, despite Mexican General Santa Anna's best efforts. The subsequent 1848 Treaty of Guadalupe Hidalgo increased the size of the United States by 20 per cent in return for a payment of $15 million, as Mexico ceded a vast expanse that included Arizona, California, New Mexico, Texas, and parts of Colorado, Nevada, and Utah. The Rio Grande River became the boundary between the two nations. The Mexican–American War was the first covered extensively by newspapers that generally adopted a jingoistic stance. Their tone popularised notions of biological and cultural white supremacy and of the nation's manifest destiny to rule the entire continent.

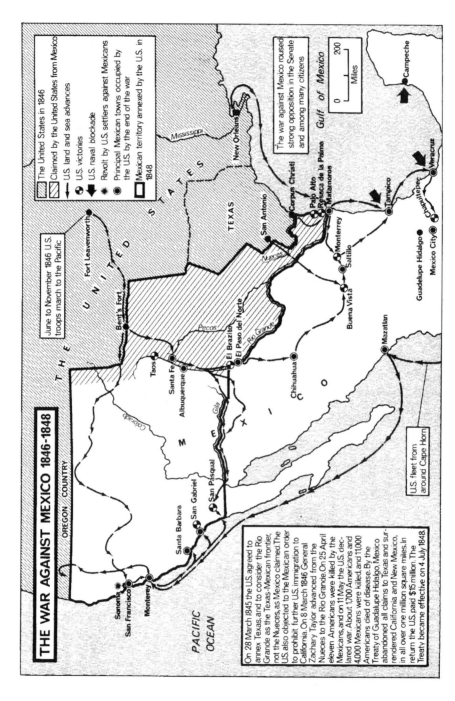

Figure 6.7 The Mexican–American War, 1846–48.

Source: Reproduced from *The Routledge Atlas of American History* 6e, published by Routledge. © Martin Gilbert, 2009. Reproduced by arrangement with Taylor & Francis Books UK. See also www.martingilbert.com

The conflict also promoted the idea of racial "Anglo-Saxonism" in which Mexicans were stigmatised as a "mongrel" race inferior to "caucasians." James Buchanan, Secretary of State and future president, insulted the Mexicans as "Spaniards, Indians, and Negroes, blended together in every way" incapable of subduing "Anglo-Saxon blood." This was very much like the rhetoric used by European imperial powers to justify their colonial conquests.

The strategic advantage of acquiring California and its Pacific ports was enhanced when gold was discovered at Sutter's Mill in northern California in January 1848. An extraordinary multi-ethnic population joined the ensuing California gold rush that decimated the indigenous population. Attempts were made by federal authorities to respect Indian rights and place tribes on reservations but the land offered was of poor quality. A rapid influx of whites, who paid no attention to the law, spread disease and encouraged alcoholism within the indigenous population. The estimated pre-Columbian native population in California of 350,000 was reduced to 120,000 by 1850. Thirty years later, it was just 20,000. George Crook, a lieutenant stationed in northern California, recalled how it was common "for an Indian to be shot down in cold blood, or a squaw to be raped by some brute." There were no repercussions as "a white man being punished for outraging an Indian was unheard of."

The Chinese were also victimised in the aftermath of the gold rush. In April 1852, the California State Assembly called on Governor John Bigler to discourage Chinese immigration as "unfair" competition. A foreign miners' license tax was set, as well as a "commutation tax" that required shipmasters to post a $500 bond for each foreign passenger landing in Californian ports. Although the Chinese were not named specifically, they were the intended target of a tax that asserted the prerogatives of whiteness, even though the bond was usually commuted by payment of a $5 fee.

How to organise new territory gained from the war, an area greater than the Louisiana Purchase, was the critical question in 1848. Pennsylvania Congressmen David Wilmot proposed a bill to keep slavery out of the southwest in 1846 and in 1847. He did so at the behest of northern Democrats who wanted to check what they perceived as the growing southern influence within the party and also, Wilmot put it, for "the rights of white freemen" so they might be spared "the disgrace which association with Negro slavery brings upon free labor." Only a unanimous rejection by southern senators prevented passage of the Wilmot Proviso. Southerners were incensed. The South Carolinian elder statesman, John C. Calhoun, argued in February 1847 that Congress did not have the constitutional authority to prevent citizens from migrating with their slaves. The sectional balance was already in danger because the free states held more seats in the House of Representatives (in which membership was based on population). In the Senate, however, each state had two members, regardless of population. Since the Senate could veto House bills, and there were 15 free states and 15 slave states in 1848, southern Senators could effectively block undesirable legislation, a position threatened by the addition of new states.

In a highly charged atmosphere on 29 January 1850, the influential Kentucky Whig Senator Henry Clay drew from decades of political experience to propose what became the 1850 Compromise. Clay had successfully placated sectional animosity during the Missouri crisis and again when South Carolina nullified the tariff in 1833. The support of the equally experienced Senator Daniel Webster, who spoke "not as a Massachusetts man, nor as Northern man, but as an American . . . for the preservation of the Union" was also crucial. After lengthy debate an agreement was brokered. California would be admitted as a free state, with Utah and New Mexico made territories where the issue of slavery was to be decided by settlers when they applied to join the Union (a measure known as popular sovereignty, proposed by Lewis Cass). Whether new states would be slave or free was therefore taken out of Congress's hands. The boundaries of the state of Texas were fixed and the slave trade in the District of Columbia was banned although slavery remained legal there. A new Fugitive Slave Act granted enslavers greater powers to pursue runaways than those provided by the original 1793 law. Not only were rewards offered for recapture but the failure of officials or the public to aid recovery could result in a fine or imprisonment. Bounty hunters merely had to present an enslaver's affidavit to prove fugitive status and captives had no legal recourse to challenge the process (nullifying the right of habeas corpus).

The Compromise of 1850 was approved in September. This package of five separate bills satisfied very few but when President Zachary Taylor died of gastroenteritis on 9 July 1850, his successor Millard Fillmore (who was the last Whig President) threw his weight behind the proposal. The Whig and Democratic parties struggled to maintain cross-sectional coalitions during the crisis. Ominously, New York Whig Senator William Henry Seward's "higher law" speech (11 March 1850) claimed that the law of "the Creator of the universe" superseded the Constitution's protection of slavery. In a famous assessment, historian David M. Potter questioned whether a compromise was achieved: "a truce perhaps, an armistice, certainly a settlement, but not a true compromise." With the deaths of Webster, Clay, and Calhoun by 1852, the political equilibrium was further endangered. It is simplistic to think that these giants of antebellum politics – Clay of the West, Calhoun of the South, and Webster of the North – could have solved the deep political problems of the age, but their absence made the search for solutions considerably more difficult. Ralph Waldo Emerson's prediction that the spoils of the Mexican–American War "will be as the man who swallows arsenic" and "poison us" had been averted, but for how long?

The road to war

A rapid turn of events marked the road to Civil War in the 1850s. A hostile northern reaction to the Compromise of 1850 strengthened popular support for free soil. Open defiance of the Fugitive Slave Law was mooted and northern states passed personal liberty laws in the 1850s that hampered the recovery of escaped slaves. This infuriated the South. Rising sectional animosity was inflamed by the proposal to organise the vast Nebraska Territory introduced by Democrat Senator Stephen A. Douglas (Illinois) on 4 January 1854. Southerners were wary because the territory was north of the line of 36°30' and therefore out of bounds to slavery according to the Missouri Compromise. Douglas was forced to propose two separate territories as a consequence, Kansas (where enslavers hoped slavery might be permitted, in spite of the 36°30' boundary line) and Nebraska, with the question of slavery to be decided by popular sovereignty at a later date. Democratic President Franklin Pierce, victor of the 1852 Presidential election, hoped to unite both wings of his party in supporting the Kansas-Nebraska Act, a terrible miscalculation as northern opposition hardened. Douglas was criticised then, and subsequently by historians, for furthering his own presidential ambitions and those of his state above the nation, because he wanted to facilitate rail construction into the West through Illinois. By breaking the Missouri Compromise, the Kansas-Nebraska Act released the slavery problem from the bottle in which it had been contained for over three decades. This polarised party politics and public opinion on a sectional basis.

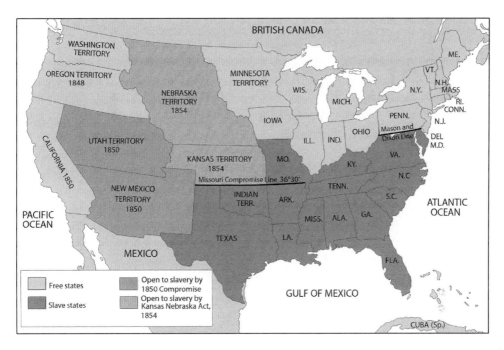

Figure 6.8 The Compromise of 1850 and the Kansas-Nebraska Act 1854.

Kansas was the subject of heated Congressional debate in the mid-1850s while a protracted struggle ensued in the territory itself. "Bleeding Kansas" is the term given to brutal fighting between antislavery and proslavery forces with each determined to push their own agenda. Attempts to organise a territorial legislature descended into farce as partisans with no intention of becoming residents voted in elections. "Missouri ruffians" simply crossed the border into Kansas, sometimes with their captives, while abolitionists and free soilers travelled further. Eli Thayer, a Republican from Massachusetts, founded the Massachusetts (later New England) Emigrant Aid Society to help slavery's opponents reach Kansas. The proslavery faction held the first meeting of its Kansas "legislature" at Lecompton in August 1855 that predictably passed a series of tough proslavery laws. Free-soil advocates responded by declaring the Lecompton legislature illegal. They set up their own government at Topeka which approved measures to ban slavery. Violence escalated when the town of Lawrence was sacked by a proslavery mob on 21 May 1856. Abolitionists led by John Brown hacked five southern men to death in retaliation at Pottawatomie Creek a few days later.

In an extraordinary few days, the violence that blighted Kansas shifted to the heart of the nation's capital. On 22 May 1856, South Carolinian Congressman Preston Brooks assaulted Charles Sumner while he sat at his desk in an almost empty Senate chamber, beating him senseless with his cane. Brooks justified his actions on the grounds that his cousin, Andrew P. Butler, had been personally insulted by Sumner's "Crime against Kansas" speech two days before. Sumner, a highly educated Bostonian, had been one of the founders of the Free Soil Party in 1848 and was noted for his hatred of slavery. This attack shocked the American public but was viewed very differently on each side of the Mason-Dixon Line. Intense outrage and sympathy for

Sumner, who took three and a half years to recover, was the typical northern reaction. In the South, however, Brooks was a hero who was sent replacement canes.

The situation in Kansas was an almighty mess. Order was restored by late 1856 but neither President Pierce, nor his successor in the White House James Buchanan, could satisfactorily resolve the situation. It was obvious that free soil was the majority position in the territory but the September 1857 Constitutional Convention at Lecompton organised by the proslavery faction (with most free soilers refusing to vote in its election) approved slavery. Deep South politicians and many southern newspapers saw an unexpected opportunity and rallied around the slogan of "Lecompton or disunion." A more objective view cautioned that the Democratic administration should reject admission on a proslavery basis because free Kansas would become a loyal Democratic-voting state. However, Buchanan decided that he could not risk alienating the southern wing of his party and attempted to persuade northern Democrats to support the proslavery Lecompton Constitution. This was a fatal error that sundered the party along sectional lines. Douglas led the opposition to a measure that made a mockery of popular sovereignty and was deeply unpopular in the free states. The Senate voted to admit Kansas under the Lecompton Constitution in March 1858 but the House eventually decided to send the issue back to the voters. In August 1858, Kansas rejected the Lecompton Constitution by a margin of 11,812 to 1,926. Deadlock was not resolved until January 1861, shortly before Lincoln's inauguration, when Kansas was admitted as a free state.

The unprecedented political crisis, as well as problems caused by mass immigration, proved too divisive for the Whig Party that imploded in the mid-1850s. Three million immigrants settled in the US between 1845 and 1855. Some Americans were particularly animated that most came from Ireland. Prior to 1845, most immigrants fitted existing ethnic patterns, leaving Northern and Western Europe – Germany, Britain, and Scandinavian countries. The 1845–49 Irish potato famine was the catalyst for an influx of generally poor, unskilled migrants to urban areas. By 1860, American cities housed a large Irish population that crowded into the poorest areas such as Five Points in New York and Boston's North End. This demographic shifted the landscape of municipal politics as corrupt city wards became controlled by party machines; by 1860 Boston contained 70,000 Irish, Philadelphia 95,000, and New York 200,000.

Nativists espoused anti-immigrant hostility towards Catholics who they claimed unsuitable for republican democracy. The short-lived Know Nothing movement capitalised on this phenomenon and by 1855 claimed one million members, each of whom was supposedly "a native born citizen, a Protestant, born of Protestant parents, reared under Protestant influence, not united in marriage with a Roman Catholic." The Know Nothing, or American, Party contested the 1856 presidential election – won by James Buchanan – with Millard Fillmore, the former Whig, gaining a very creditable 21 per cent of the popular vote. This was the high point for the Know Nothings, who faded away afterwards. Their legacy was to contribute significantly to the demise of the second party system. Without a cross-regional, national, political framework, militants and agitators were at liberty to attack one another without restraint and moderates became increasingly marginalised.

The Republican Party also contested the 1856 election from which they emerged as the main rival to the Democrats. Founded 30 March 1854 by disaffected Whigs and Free Soilers, the Republicans were the first major political party to represent a single section. The Supreme Court's *Dred Scott* decision (1857) inadvertently did much to increase their appeal across the free states. Dred Scott was an enslaved man who sued for his freedom on the grounds that he had lived in free territories for decades. Chief

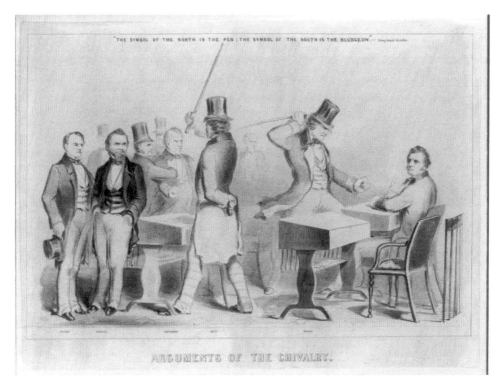

Figure 6.9 "Arguments of the Chivalry" (1856). This northern-centric depiction of the Brooks-Sumner caning shows Georgia senator Robert Toombs and Stephen A. Douglas looking on emotionless while South Carolinian Lawrence M. Keitt stands ready to prevent interference. This shocking attack underlined the growing problem of sectional hostility over the issue of slavery.

Source: Courtesy of the Library of Congress Prints and Photographs Division Washington

Justice Roger B. Taney's ruling denied Scott his freedom. It also stipulated that African Americans could not become US citizens and that property, which included slaves, could not legally be prevented from entering the territories by Congress. Taney's verdict was something that the proslavery lobby had wanted to hear for years but those in the free states were incredulous and horrified– even though few cared much for black rights. Abolitionists had warned of the Slave Power conspiracy for a number of years and this decision substantiated their case because Taney came from a family of tobacco planters in Maryland. It is an understatement to state that the *Dred Scott* case was highly controversial.

The "Slave Power" and "Black Republicans"

By the 1850s, growing numbers of northerners were persuaded that an aggressive "Slave Power" had seized control of the federal government and wished to extend slavery not only into the territories but into the free states. This

conspiracy threatened the very fabric of republican government and it galvanised support for the Republican Party. The idea of the "Slave Power" gained
much credibility when it emerged that the US ambassadors to Britain, France,
and Spain had been instructed to meet in Belgium by Secretary of State William
Marcy in 1854. They advised that the US seize Cuba militarily if Spain refused
to sell (a proposal known as the Ostend Manifesto). In turn, southerners warned
that antislavery radicals dominated northern politics. "Black Republicans," as
they called them, were supposedly obsessed with abolition at all costs followed
by the imposition of racial equality.

The high point of aggressive abolitionism happened at Harpers Ferry, Virginia,
on 16 October 1859. John Brown's mission was to arm enslaved people with weapons from a federal arsenal and begin a mass insurrection. His attempt failed after a
36-hour siege and Brown was subsequently tried in a Virginian court, found guilty,
and hung on 2 December 1859. The South reacted hysterically, especially as leading
abolitionists were implicated in the affair, including Frederick Douglass who fled to
Canada. Brown became a martyr to many northerners. His trial was followed avidly
in newspapers and even southerners conceded Brown's courage as he bravely accepted
his fate. (The injuries he suffered at Harpers Ferry forced him to lie on a bed for most
of the trial). Brown appealed to a higher law than that of the Virginian court – to God:
"Now, if it is deemed necessary that I should forfeit my life for the furtherance of the
ends of justice, and mingle my blood further with the blood of my children and with
the blood of millions in this slave country whose rights are disregarded by wicked,
cruel, and unjust enactments, I submit; so let it be done!" Harpers Ferry was a fitting
end to a decade in which US politics had been torn apart.

The 1860 presidential election and secession

The major parties met in the spring of 1860 to select their nominees. The Democratic
Convention met in Charleston in April where Stephen A. Douglas, despite his many
detractors, was favourite. His nomination was thwarted when 50 Lower South delegates, led by Alabaman William L. Yancey, walked out after a proposal to protect
slaveholding in the territories was rejected. Following 57 ballots, Douglas did not have
the required two-thirds majority to win the nomination and the decision was made to
reconvene in Baltimore in June. However, those who had walked out at Charleston
were not allowed to retake their seats in Baltimore and they promptly organised a
rival convention that nominated John C. Breckinridge on a proslavery agenda. Douglas was therefore selected by northern Democrats while Breckinridge was the choice
of southern Democrats. Breckinridge was also supported by President Buchanan and
a majority of high-ranking Democrats who disliked Douglas because he campaigned
against the Lecompton Constitution. The Democratic Party fielded two presidential
candidates in the 1860 election.

The Republicans met in Chicago on 18 May 1860. William H. Seward, the premier
Republican of the 1850s, was favourite. However, Seward's chances were undermined
by his association with extremism established in his "higher law" and later "irrepressible conflict" speeches. On 25 October 1858, Seward suggested "an irrepressible

conflict between opposing and enduring forces" that would make the US "entirely a slave-holding nation or entirely a free-labor nation." This stance was too closely connected to abolition for the liking of many Republicans. Abraham Lincoln was relatively unknown, although his unsuccessful 1858 attempt to oust Stephen A. Douglas from his Illinois Senate seat had enhanced his reputation considerably. Lincoln famously held seven debates with Douglas in Illinois between 21 August and 15 October 1858. His low profile worked to his advantage in winning the nomination as the impeccable character of "Honest Abe" was emphasised by supporters. This starkly contrasted with the notoriously corrupt Buchanan administration and Lincoln's moderate stance was considered more appealing to the voters than Seward's radicalism.

The fourth presidential candidate in 1860 was Tennessee's John Bell, representing the Constitutional Union Party. Formed by former Upper South Whigs, the Constitutional Unionists adhered to principles of moderation, economic stability, and nation. They were appalled by the prospect of secession and stood to save the Union – and their success in winning Kentucky, Tennessee, and Virginia suggested that many felt the same way in the Upper South.

The Republicans fought an excellent campaign in 1860. They did not waste time in the South where Lincoln's name was absent from ten state ballots. American Party votes from the 1856 election, particularly in Indiana, Illinois, Pennsylvania, and New Jersey, were targeted by a Republican agenda that stressed free labour, industry, and free soil on economic, not moral, grounds. The Republicans won every free state, with the exception of New Jersey that was split with Douglas. Lincoln was the clear winner with 1,766,452 votes, nearly 40 per cent of the popular vote. Douglas was next with 1,376,957 votes, with 849,781 for Breckinridge and 588,879 for Bell. Lincoln gained a comfortable majority in the Electoral College (180–123). Even if the Democratic Party had not split its vote, Lincoln would have been elected.

What happened next has been the subject of considerable debate. Lincoln stood on a free soil platform that left slavery alone where it existed but proslavery politicians responded immediately to Republican victory. Led by the South Carolinian elite of William Porcher Miles, Robert Barnwell Rhett, and Lawrence M. Keitt, with allies across the Lower South states, this group had agitated for southern independence for years. They realised that secession was far from inevitable, however. No southerner was happy with the election result, but whether there was enough support for the drastic step of secession was unknown. In fact, there was a wide spectrum of opinion on the next move. Those against immediate secession were dubbed "cooperationists," although some merely wanted to wait until the entire South was ready to leave. "Ultimationists" wished to present Lincoln with a list of demands guaranteeing slavery's protection and "conditional Unionists" would only secede in wake of an overt act of aggression on Lincoln's part.

Drawing from fear, a sense of compromised honour, and years of ill-feeling, a powerful proslavery lobby campaigned for secession in the winter of 1860–61. The unpalatable prospect of racial amalgamation was used as their trump card. Opponents were labelled as un-southern, while vigilance committees suppressed dissent. Cooperationists mobilised with varying degrees of effectiveness but to no avail as secession was pushed through on a state by state basis. South Carolina, Mississippi, and Georgia produced nearly half the total cotton yield in 1860 and possessed one-third of the total number of enslaved people and the movement gathered huge momentum as they were the first (20 December), second (9 January), and fifth (19 January) states to secede. In Georgia, though, the results of the popular vote that sent representatives to the secession convention were withheld and Governor Brown released dubious figures that recorded a secessionist majority after the state left the Union. "Declarations of Imme-diate Causes" provided by some secession conventions justified withdrawal on the grounds that the free states violated constitutional rights, encouraged abolitionism, ignored the Fugitive Slave Act, and incited the enslaved to rebel. Delegates from seven Lower South states formed the Confederacy at a meeting in Montgomery (Alabama) on 4 February, just a month before Lincoln assumed office on 4 March 1861.

Would the Upper South join them? Unionism was much stronger there than in the Deep South although some, like Virginian Edmund Ruffin, were eager to join the Confederacy. Lincoln's election was unwelcome but not necessarily a grave, immediate threat. Public opinion was generally polarised between non-enslavers who opposed immediate secession and pro-secession enslavers – although there was a wide vari-ety of views. The Crittenden Compromise, proposed by Kentucky Senator John J. Crittenden in the spring of 1861, desperately sought to hold the Union together. It called for restoration of the Missouri Compromise line of 36°30' and a constitutional amendment guaranteeing slavery where it already existed. Despite considerable sup-port for compromise of some kind to avert war, support that crossed the Mason-Dixon Line, Lincoln rejected these overtures.

The spark that ignited the Civil War – and delivered four more states critical to the Confederacy's hopes – occurred, appropriately, in South Carolina. Fort Sumter was

Figure 6.10 Secession in the South.

a man-made island occupied by Union troops in Charleston Bay that constituted an alien presence following secession. A tense stand-off came to a head in the early morning of 12 April 1861. Confederate authorities were informed that Lincoln intended to reprovision the federal garrison at Sumter, but not reinforce it with soldiers, guns, or ammunition. Confederate President Jefferson Davis ordered the fort to be taken before this happened. Major Robert Anderson refused requests to surrender and was met by a fierce bombardment from batteries on the shore. Commencing at 4:30am on 12 April, they were the opening shots of the American Civil War and 36 hours later Anderson raised the white flag. Three days afterwards, Lincoln denounced secession and called for 75,000 volunteers to suppress what he called a rebellion.

A wave of secessionist feeling was unleashed in the deadlocked Upper South. It had been anticipated that any coercive measures might be counter-productive but few predicted such a strong reaction. Tennessee lawyer and Unionist Oliver R. Temple was aghast at the way "secession had swept over . . . like a cyclone, prostrating every object before its resistless force." Unionists could not prevent a popular surge towards the Confederacy. Virginia passed a secession ordinance on 17 April; North Carolina and Arkansas followed in May, while Tennessee was the last state to join the Confederacy in June. In the summer of 1861, 11 southern states stood side by side, prepared to fight to establish their independent, slave-holding nation.

Chapter summary

In 1913, James Ford Rhodes, the first major US historian, wrote that "it may safely be asserted that there was a single cause" of the war – slavery. Rhodes grossly exaggerated in his depiction of the war as a righteous crusade to rid the nation of the peculiar institution, but no professional historian would disagree that slavery was the root cause that underpinned the succession of problems which confronted the antebellum United States. The rich history of the antebellum era is a story of political and economic change, of the consolidation of American slavery and the ways in which that institution shaped conceptions of freedom, of sharpening race, class, and gender divisions, and the growth of antagonistic sections with differing characteristics. Antebellum history is not only about the coming of the Civil War, but that is how it is most often told and there is an inexhaustible fascination with this topic. Slavery is the starting point for any serious consideration of why two sides opposed each other in April 1861, but the problem is best approached by asking three separate questions. First, why did the northern and the southern states find it so difficult to compromise over slavery in western territory? Second, why did the southern states secede in 1860–61? Third, why did the North not let them go? Answers to these questions will always be contested and agreement is unlikely but undoubtedly historians will continue to ponder them.

 ## Discussion questions

- Why did Andrew Jackson polarise opinion?
- What were the most important reform movements in the antebellum United States?
- To what extent did slavery differentiate the South from the rest of the nation?
- What were the major causes of sectional division?
- Why did southern states secede following the 1860 presidential election?

Further reading

Blassingame, John W. *The Slave Community: Plantation Life in the Antebellum South*, revised and enlarged edition (New York, 1979 [1972]). The first major discussion of slave community in the antebellum era that remains extremely valuable.

Blackett, R.J.M. *The Captive's Quest for Freedom: Fugitive Slaves, the 1850 Fugitive Slave Law, and the Politics of Slavery* (New York, 2018). Magisterial examination of the politics of slave resistance.

Blight, David. *Frederick Douglass: Prophet of Freedom* (New York, 2018). Pulitzer-Prize winning biography of arguably the most important American of the nineteenth century.

Brands, H. W. *Andrew Jackson: His Life and Times* (New York, 2005). Recent, detailed biography of this controversial figure.

Cheathem, Mark R. *Andrew Jackson and the Rise of the Democratic Party* (Knoxville, 2018). A useful introductory text that ably synthesises the large literature on Jacksonian politics.

Clinton, Catherine. *The Other Civil War: American Women in the Nineteenth Century* (New York, 1999). Comprehensive survey of the diverse female experience across the nineteenth century.

Douglas, Ann. *The Feminization of American Culture* (New York, 1977). Analyses the role of middle-class women in reform culture.

Dusinberre, William. *Them Dark Days: Slavery in the American Rice Swamps* (New York, 1996). Brutal account of rice slavery in the Lowcountry.

Foner, Eric. *Free Soil, Free Labor, Free Men: The Ideology of the Republican Party Before the Civil War* (New York, 1970). Remains the definitive account of the rise of free soil in the North.

Genovese, Eugene D. *Roll, Jordan, Roll: The World the Slaves Made* (New York, 1974). Highly influential, but controversial, account of slavery.

Greenberg, Amy S. *A Wicked War: Polk, Clay, Lincoln, and the 1846 Invasion of Mexico* (New York, 2012). The most up-to-date account of the Mexican–American War.

Glymph, Thavolia. *Out of the House of Bondage: The Transformation of the Plantation Household* (New York, 2008). Cogent analysis of the dynamics of gendered power relations within the plantation household.

Johnson, Susan Lee. *Roaring Camp: The Social World of the California Gold Rush* (New York, 2000). An intimate view of the struggles between different ethnic groups in the gold fields.

McDaniel, Caleb. *The Problem of Democracy in the Age of Slavery: Garrisonian Abolitionists and Transatlantic Reform* (Baton Rouge, 2013). Superb account of abolition and its transatlantic connections.

Pasley, Jeffrey L., Andrew W. Robertson, and David Waldstreicher, eds. *Beyond the Founders: New Approaches to the Political History of the Early American Republic* (Chapel Hill, 2004). Revisionist interpretation of the development of American politics.

Potter, David M. *The Impending Crisis, 1848–1861* (New York, 1976). Remains the best interpretation of political events leading to Civil War.

Roediger, David R. *The Wages of Whiteness: Race and the Making of the American Working Class* (New York, 2007 [1991]). The third edition of this influential study of antebellum racism contains a useful reflection on the field of "whiteness studies" that it helped to establish.

Shelden, Rachel A. *Washington Brotherhood: Politics, Social Life, and the Coming of the Civil War* (Chapel Hill, 2013). Fascinating study of social politics outside of Congress in late antebellum Washington DC that provides an intimate view of US politicians and sectional tensions.

Sinha, Manisha. *The Slave's Cause: A History of Abolition* (New Haven, 2016). Comprehensive and insightful history of abolitionism.

Varon, Elizabth R. *Disunion!: The Coming of the American Civil War, 1789-1859* (Chapel Hill, 2008). Authoritative examination of the growing antebellum sectional divergence.

Walters, Ronald G. *American Reformers, 1815–1860* (revised edition, New York, 1997). Best account of the antebellum reform movement as a whole.

Wilentz, Sean. *Chants Democratic: New York City and the Rise of the American Working Class, 1788–1850* (New York, 1983). Classic account of class relations in New York, synthesising aspects of economic, social, and political history.

7   Civil War and the wars of Reconstruction

Timeline

1861, April 12	Confederates fire on Fort Sumter and the Civil War begins
1861, April 15	Lincoln calls for 75,000 volunteers
1861, July 21	First Battle of Bull Run
1862, 6–7 April	Battle of Shiloh
1862, April 16	Confederate Conscription Act
1862, April 29	New Orleans falls
1862, May 31	Battle of Seven Pines
1862, June 25–July 1	Seven Days Battles
1862, August 28–30	Second Battle of Bull Run
1862, September 17	Battle of Antietam
1862, September 22	Preliminary Emancipation Proclamation
1862, December 11–15	Battle of Fredericksburg
1863, January 1	Emancipation Proclamation
1863, March 3	Enrollment Act
1863, April 30–May 6	Battle of Chancellorsville
1863, July 1–3	Battle of Gettysburg
1863, July 4	Vicksburg surrenders
1863, July 11–16	New York City draft riots
1863, November 19	The Gettysburg Address
1864, May 4–June 24	Overland Campaign
1864, May 5–7	Battle of the Wilderness
1864, May 8–21	Battle of Spotsylvania courthouse
1864, May 31–June 12	Battle of Cold Harbor
1865, June 15–April 2	Siege of Petersburg
1865, September 2	Atlanta falls
1865, November 8	Lincoln re-elected president
1865, November 15– December 21	March to the Sea
1865, April 9	Lee surrenders at Appomattox courthouse
1865, April 14	Lincoln shot and dies the following day
1865, May 26	Final surrender of the Confederate Army at Galveston, Texas
1865, December 6	Thirteenth Amendment
1865–66	Southern states pass Black Codes
1866, April 9	Civil Rights Act
1867, March 3	Reconstruction Act

1868, July 9	Fourteenth Amendment
1868, November 3	Ulysses S. Grant elected president
1870, February 3	Fifteenth Amendment
1870, February 25	Hiram R. Revels (Mississippi) is the first African American to serve in the US Senate; Joseph H. Rainey (South Carolina) becomes the first black Representative
1873, September 18	Panic of 1873 begins
1875, March 1	Civil Rights Act
1876, November 7	Disputed presidential election; Republican Rutherford B. Hayes eventually declared victorious
1877, April 10	Hayes orders the withdrawal of remaining federal troops from the South

Topics covered

- The Blue and the Gray: setting the scene
- Mobilisation in the Union and the Confederacy
- Fighting to Save the Union, 1861–62
- Emancipation
- Fighting to abolish slavery, 1863–65
- Presidential Reconstruction
- A political power struggle in Washington DC
- Radical Reconstruction
- Negotiating freedom: Reconstruction at ground level
- Southern politics and the Democratic Party backlash

Introduction

The American Civil War and its messy aftermath was a defining moment in the history of the United States. It was decisive because the country survived intact reestablishing the authority of the federal government. But this came at a dreadful cost. Around 750,000 people died and countless others were injured during four long and bloody years between 1861 and 1865. This chapter analyses the two competing sides, the Union and the Confederacy, and surveys the course of the war in two chronological periods: 1861–62 and 1863–65. The Union initially fought to keep the United States together but the chapter examines Abraham Lincoln's controversial change of policy to implement emancipation which had such momentous consequences for African Americans and fundamentally changed the course of the war.

The focus then turns towards the Republican Party's attempt to repair the immense political, economic and social damage caused by America's most divisive conflict in the post-war period known as Reconstruction (1865–77). Their efforts were undermined by President Andrew Johnson and the acrimonious power struggle to determine whether the legislative or the executive took charge of Reconstruction policy. Johnson's authority was effectively curtailed by the so-called Radical Republicans by 1867 and a linear transition from war to peace and from slavery to freedom was once commonly depicted in US history textbooks. This trajectory is far too simplistic. Formal hostilities concluded in 1865 but the war between the sections continued by other means as white violence and intimidation in the southern states, orchestrated by the

Democratic Party, not only hampered the implementation of reforms but tested the capacity of the federal government to enforce law and order. Slavery was abolished but what kind of freedom African Americans were granted and how long that freedom lasted is highly contentious.

The blue and the gray: setting the scene

The Union enjoyed overwhelming superiority in terms of manpower, industry, and financial resources but took considerable time to harness them effectively. Confederate President Jefferson Davis confided to his wife that "we are without machinery, without means, and threatened by a powerful opposition" but neither side was at all prepared for war. There were 22 million people in the Union states compared to nine million in the Confederacy, of whom more than a third were slaves. Southern manufacturing capacity in 1860 was just one-twelfth that of its opponents and its infrastructure far inferior. While cotton was lucrative, land and slaves were of limited value to a wartime economy. It was widely believed that the fighting would be over quickly and young men on both sides worried that they might miss out. This proved a tragic underestimation of the duration and brutality of the American Civil War which became a contest of industrial might and civilian morale as much as one fought on the battlefield.

Despite a grossly inferior starting point, all was not lost for the Confederacy. It defended hearth and home, its men prided themselves on a strong martial tradition, and its women offered their support (at first). Recruits rallied to the cause from a sense of honour, duty, and masculine pride and were eager for the chance to whip the Yankees. Their enemy did not need to be conquered but simply made to give up the struggle. The Confederacy measured 750,000 square miles in total and its "offensive-defensive" strategy, protecting ports and key locations while engaging the enemy in morale-boosting, but selected, offensive battles, seemed promising. The Union strategy, developed by Mexican–American War veteran General Winfield Scott, arguably played into Confederate hands. Scott's "Anaconda Plan" sought to prevent imports and exports entering or leaving rebel states and divide the Confederacy in two by naval blockade of the Atlantic seaboard to the East and gunboats along the Mississippi River to the West. The Confederacy, therefore, only needed to hold out.

Foreign intervention was also anticipated. "King Cotton" diplomacy withheld southern raw cotton to force Great Britain and France to recognise the legitimacy of the Confederacy. The *Charleston Mercury* crowed that the South held "the cards" to be deployed until "the bankruptcy of every cotton factory in Great Britain and France or the acknowledgement of our independence." The Union blockade of southern ports announced on 19 April 1861 enabled Confederate agents abroad to blame Lincoln for curtailing the supply of cotton that was widely expected to plunge the British economy into depression. There were moments that threatened international involvement in the war. A major diplomatic incident ensued when an American warship stopped the British mail steamer *Trent* on 8 November 1861 and arrested two Confederate envoys bound for London, while the Union was furious about covert shipbuilding for the Confederates in Britain. The *CSS Alabama*, which left Liverpool in July 1862, sank 65 Union vessels.

Joint Anglo-French mediation was discussed in late 1862, on humanitarian and economic grounds, even though William Seward, Union Secretary of State, threatened war with any country that recognised the Confederacy. He did not need to. There were more considerations to foreign policy than economics alone. Neither Britain nor France could easily recognise a nation founded on slavery. Existing stocks of cotton in British warehouses delayed the impact of the shortage and the war boosted production in shipbuilding, armaments, clothing, medical supplies, and other sectors of the economy. Public and private relief, that included donations from around the world, mitigated the worst effects of the Lancashire cotton famine.

The war was fought primarily in two theaters. In the East, the key battle ground was the 100 miles or so separating Washington DC from the Confederate capital in Richmond, Virginia. In the western theater, from the Atlantic seaboard to the Mississippi River, Tennessee was the focus as each side sought control of the Tennessee and Cumberland Rivers and the ultimate prize of securing the Mississippi River. Regular warfare orchestrated by generals and fought by soldiers was not the only form of conflict however. Vicious guerrilla fighting in Missouri, eastern Kentucky and Tennessee, western North Carolina, and northern Georgia, Alabama, and Arkansas pitted southerner against southerner in many neighbourhoods. Renegade groups, either pro- or anti-Confederate that varied greatly in size and strength, fought with one another and with official forces of both sides as authorities struggled to enforce law and order. Irregular combat is often overlooked but constituted a major problem on the Confederate home front.

A third theater was the trans-Mississippi West, which included states and territories west of the Mississippi River except those bordering the Pacific. Fighting here involved fewer men and was of less strategic importance but reignited old tensions between tribes in the Indian Territory. Confederate authorities solicited Indian support early

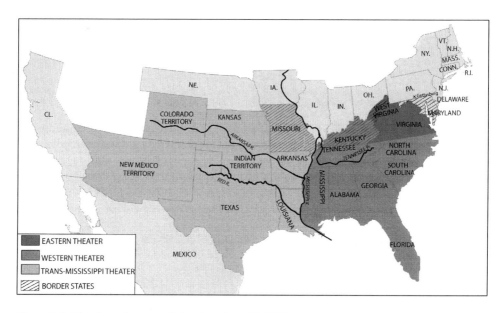

Figure 7.1 The three theaters of the American Civil War.

in the war, sending Arkansan Albert Pike to negotiate agreements. Braves from the Five Civilised Tribes, known by then as the Five Civilised Nations, fought for both sides during the American Civil War but a majority – most of whom owned slaves – sided with the Confederacy. They formed four regiments in gray. Brutal fighting in the Indian Territory between pro-Confederate Indians and those who either wanted to be left alone or were pro-Union resulted in casualty rates of around 25 per cent within the Five Nations. Families fled, leaving homes, property, and farms behind, with those sympathetic to the Union heading north and those sympathetic to the Confederacy heading south.

Mobilisation in the Union and the Confederacy

Both sides required vast numbers of troops in the field. Estimates vary widely as to how many soldiers served due to incomplete records, desertion, and bounty jumpers. However, the Union outnumbered the Confederacy at least 2–1 in overall numbers, with a total enrolment of 2,500,000 that probably delivered around 1,500,000 soldiers in the field. The Confederates recorded between 850,000 and 900,000 enrolments, approximately 80 per cent of available men of fighting age. Mobilisation was a local phenomenon as family and community pressure to enlist was intense. Towns enthusiastically waved goodbye to their menfolk, presenting them with gifts and closely following their progress for the duration of the war. On both sides, army units were organised by place and sometimes by ethnicity. Approximately 25 per cent of federal soldiers were foreign-born, with large numbers of Irish and Germans. As the war progressed, however, volunteers were not sufficient to meet military needs. Inducements, in the form of cash bounties, were offered but eventually compulsory service was required.

The Confederacy acted first, because the Union's advantage (greater than three to one in military-age males) made it imperative to get every able-bodied man into Confederate service. The Confederate Conscription Act (April 1862) decreed all men between 18 and 35 (later raised to 45 and then 50) eligible for service. This was unprecedented in US history and highly controversial. Ambivalent southerners, who had avoided fighting for a variety of reasons such as family responsibilities or Union loyalty, now risked arrest if they refused. Conscription was unpopular, particularly because of exemptions for certain professions and the loophole that drafted men could pay for a substitute to take their place. Most notoriously, the Twenty Negro Law codified in the Second Conscription Act (October 1862) exempted one white man for every 20 slaves. This led to the cry "a rich man's war and a poor man's fight." Abraham Lincoln was also criticised when he announced the Enrollment Act in March 1863. However, Lincoln drew from a much larger population and the draft did not need to be implemented as rigidly in the Union. The threat of conscription was sufficient for the free states to meet their quotas through volunteers but they faced the problem of bounty jumpers who signed for service, absconded with the bounty, and then enlisted again elsewhere.

War affected the home front in ways that no one could have anticipated, although only in the Confederacy was daily life transformed. The Union Treasury Secretary, Salmon P. Chase, successfully raised revenue from public and private sources that funded the gigantic war effort. Chase introduced the first national income tax in 1861 (3 per cent on incomes above $800), raised $6.2 billion by issuing government bonds sold by the private company Jay Cooke and Co., and authorised the use of paper currency (greenbacks). Paper money was issued sparingly and the National Bank Act (1863) helped to control inflation, whereas inflation spiralled out of control in the Confederacy. In July 1862, the federal Internal Revenue Act taxed a wide variety of goods including liquor and tobacco and other taxes were levied. Lincoln's administration did not intervene in the economy to any great extent but worked in partnership with businessmen and financiers, becoming a much larger customer of products and supplies. Women stepped into the workplace as men enlisted but rationing was not required and daily life in the North was relatively stable.

The war's effects were far more traumatic in the Confederacy. Initially, Treasury Secretary Christopher Memminger was reluctant to impose direct taxation and lacked a means to collect revenue. But the Confederate Congress eventually had no option but to tax its citizens and the March 1863 Impressment Act authorised seizure of civilian goods in return for rapidly depreciating promissory notes. This tax was extremely unpopular but not as hated as the April 1863 Tax-in-Kind which required families to hand over 10 per cent of their crops. Tariffs were levied on incoming goods from 1861 onwards and Confederates enjoyed some success in selling shares and bonds tied to cotton on European markets. However, revenue generation was a problem that became worse over time, exacerbated by a fiscal policy that never clarified the balance of public and private funding. The Confederacy invested heavily in industry but from a position so far behind its opponent that was impossible to match production levels. Attempts to switch from cotton production to foodstuffs were hampered by planters who in many cases refused to cooperate. Chronic inflation blighted the Confederacy and sapped the will of its citizens. The price of coffee, tea, sugar, paper, soap, cloth, and salt (used to preserve meat) rose 10 per cent on average every month from late 1861 to early 1864. By the final year of the war, basic commodities were in very short supply at astronomical prices.

Confederate economic failures had disastrous consequences and made the task of white women who assumed responsibility for running the plantation or farm intolerable. Used to strong antebellum gender roles in which men took charge, females left at home were placed in an unfamiliar and increasingly unwelcome position. Mostly enthusiastic at first, Confederate women struggled to cope as economic circumstances deteriorated. With no training in managerial duties or in agriculture their commitment was sorely tested and some eventually wrote to loved ones asking them to return home. Women publicly protested against the lack of basic provisions in "bread riots" that occurred in a number of Confederate towns in 1863 (including Richmond on 2 April). The antebellum patriarchal status quo, in which females were subservient in return for male protection, was broken by the war. Confederate state Governors received numerous letters from mothers and wives who emerged from the household to assert their political voice. Nancy Mangum, for instance, wrote to Governor Zebulon Vance of North Carolina in April 1863 threatening that "if you dont take thes yankys a way from greenesborough [Greensboro] we wemen will write for our husbans to come . . . home and help us."

Fighting to save the Union, 1861–62

The rebels had the better of the contest in the first two years of the war in the East as their generals outmanoeuvred the cautious Union command, but were less successful in the West. The contest began 25 miles west of Washington DC on 21 July 1861 in the First Battle of Bull Run/Manassas. (Civil War battles were named after towns or transport links by the Confederacy – Manassas Junction in this case – but by natural landmarks, usually bodies of water – Bull Run Creek – by the Union.) Both sides fielded around 18,000 disorganised and unprepared troops and the Confederates prevailed. Union General George McClellan replaced General Irvin McDowell subsequently and set about moulding the newly formed Federal Army of the Potomac into a fighting unit. He was an excellent administrator and successfully transformed the diverse array of recruits, from many different backgrounds, into soldiers. McClellan was a Democrat who constantly derided Lincoln, however. He was reluctant to engage in battle and hoped that bloodless victories might persuade the rebels to give up. In the winter of 1861–62, the Confederates dug in behind the Rappahannock River in defence of Richmond, while far greater numbers of Federal troops were stationed in and around Washington DC. McClellan refused to take advantage of his numerical superiority.

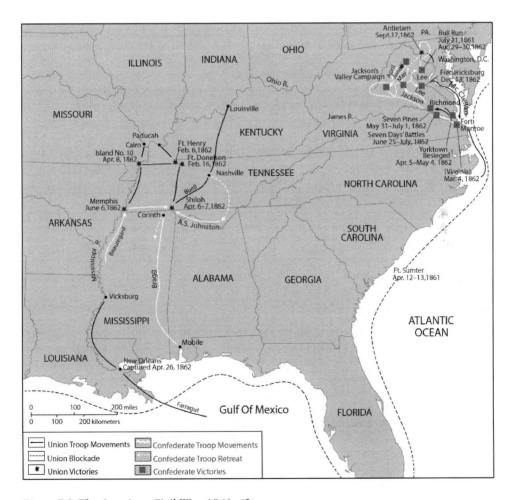

Figure 7.2 The American Civil War, 1861–62.

It was a different story in the western theater. The Union's first priority was to establish control of Kentucky and Missouri. Both of these Border States might have joined the rebellion and their loss would have been disastrous. The Federals then advanced through Tennessee in the spring of 1862 where inviting river systems flowed southward and the terrain was not impeded by physical barriers as it was in the eastern theater. The Battle of Shiloh (6–7 April 1862) in southwestern Tennessee provided an important strategic victory that facilitated the later acquisition of Corinth in northern Mississippi and led to the extended siege of Vicksburg on the upper Mississippi River. Shiloh dramatically brought home the human cost of the war as casualties mounted to more than 23,000, higher than the casualties in all previous American wars and a total that shocked the nation and indeed the world. A poorly defended New Orleans was captured in a combined attack by land and sea led by General Benjamin Butler and Admiral David G. Farragut in late April 1862. The loss of this crucial port city was a major setback for the Confederacy, exacerbated when Memphis fell in June, leaving the Union in control of the Mississippi River save for a 200-mile stretch between Vicksburg (Mississippi) and Port Hudson (Louisiana).

Border States

The Border States, in which slavery was legal (Delaware, Maryland, Kentucky, and Missouri) fought on the Union side even though they were slave states. Slavery was also retained in West Virginia when it broke away from the Confederacy to join the Union on 20 June 1863. Support for the Confederacy was considerable, particularly in Kentucky and Missouri where vicious internal fighting got worse as the war progressed, but Lincoln acted swiftly to dispatch military units to counter pro-secession forces. Supposedly Lincoln said "I hope God is on my side, but I must have Kentucky." The Border States would have increased the Confederacy's white population by 45 per cent and added 80 per cent to its manufacturing capacity.

Lincoln ordered McClellan to advance in the spring of 1862. The Union's Peninsular Campaign in Virginia began well as Federal troops sailed down the Chesapeake Bay to avoid the enemy defensive line and approach Richmond by land from the rear. All that stood between the 100,000 strong Army of the Potomac and Richmond was a small force of 11,000 Confederates at Yorktown. Instead of engaging, McClellan halted, overestimating the strength of his opponents. He commenced a one-month siege of Yorktown while waiting for further reinforcements. This enabled the Confederacy's Army of Northern Virginia, under General Joseph E. Johnston, to re-group. When Johnston was wounded at the Battle of Seven Pines on 31 May, the Civil War's most celebrated military figure, Virginian Robert E. Lee, replaced him. In stark contrast to McClellan's dithering, Lee attacked in a series of confrontations known as the Seven Days Battles (25 June–1 July 1862). The Confederates lost twice as many men as the Federals but forced McClellan to retreat ignominiously with Lincoln worried that Washington DC was vulnerable.

The Army of Northern Virginia followed the retreating Federals, sensing an opportunity to deliver a knockout blow, and was victorious at the Second Battle of Bull Run in August 1862. Lee's forces marched on into Maryland but the Confederate advance was halted at the Battle of Antietam (17 September). Antietam was the single bloodiest day of the entire war with a total of 24,000 soldiers on both sides killed, wounded, or missing. While technically a draw, it is regarded as a strategic victory for the Union because it stopped Lee's invasion of the North and boosted northern public morale. McClellan failed to make the most of the fortuitous discovery of enemy orders detailing Confederate troop movements, however, moving too slowly to take advantage of the information. Nonetheless, Antietam enabled Lincoln to announce the preliminary Emancipation Proclamation five days afterward (discussed in the next section). Any momentum gained quickly dissipated as the overcautious McClellan refused to pursue Confederate forces into Virginia. Lincoln replaced him as commander of the Army of the Potomac with General Ambrose Burnside.

In November 1862, Burnside ordered an advance on Richmond through the town of Fredericksburg that stood directly between Washington DC and the Confederate capital. His forces camped on the north bank of the Rappahannock River opposite Fredericksburg awaiting pontoon bridges. The Confederates had plenty of time to fortify their position on the south bank and around 73,000 troops dug in on high ground known as Marye's Heights. Having waited two weeks to cross the river, Federals, numbering 120,000, fought their way through the town to approach the elevated and entrenched Confederate line. The Battle of Fredericksburg (11–15 December) was a Confederate rout that involved the largest number of troops of any Civil War encounter. An exasperated New York infantryman commented "we might as well have tried to take Hell." Burnside's reputation was damaged and he was eventually replaced as commander of the Army of the Potomac by General Joseph Hooker following another failed attempt to cross the Rappahannock in January known as the "Mud March." As

Figure 7.3 Dead Confederate troops in front of a Dunker Church at Antietam. The total number of soldiers killed during the war was accepted as 620,000 for many years. In 2011, however, historian J. David Hacker's analysis of US census data moved that figure upwards significantly to 752,000. This revised estimate included a 20 per cent margin of error, so perhaps as many as 850,000 soldiers lost their lives in total.

Source: Courtesy of the Missouri Historical Society

both sides camped for the winter of 1862–63, when rain and mud effectively curtailed mass transportation, neither held the advantage in the eastern theater.

Was the American Civil War the first "modern" war?

The orthodox view, proposed by James M. McPherson among others, suggests that the US Civil War was distinct from European wars that preceded it. It incorporated new forms of transportation, armoured steamships, improved weaponry, and modern tactics of trench warfare and artillery moving in step with infantry. Previous tactics of soldiers facing one another and trading musket volleys were redundant. Technological advances ensured that rifles were accurate from 500–600 metres, far superior to the previous limit of 100–150 metres. Claude Minié's 1848 invention of a small, conical shaped bullet that expanded to fit the rifle barrel enabled two or three rounds to be fired per minute. Huge armies of citizen-soldiers, high casualty rates, and disruption to civilian populations also distinguished the US War. On the other hand, Mark E. Neely Jr. has suggested continuity of tactics in a war that avoided some of the uglier features of later conflicts, such as wide scale atrocities and abuse of women. He questions the usefulness of "modern" as an analytical category. Military historian Paddy Griffith argues that the majority of skirmishes were at close range – at around 140 metres. The debate continues, but it seems that the American Civil War was "modern" or "Napoleonic" depending on which aspects one selects.

Emancipation

From the outset, free blacks and abolitionists tried to force the issue of emancipation onto the Civil War agenda. Frederick Douglass urged Lincoln to utilise African Americans and challenged the nation to live up to the promise that all men were equal, as did Harriet Tubman. Tubman was the most famous "conductor" of the antebellum Underground Railroad which consisted of a series of clandestine safe houses on escape routes from the slave states. She claimed her freedom by taking flight from her Maryland enslaver in 1849 to reach Philadelphia, bravely returning to help other family members escape. Tubman suggested both a divine and practical purpose for emancipation. It would save the lives of countless young white men if blacks enlisted. Emancipation would also transform a dispute about nationhood into a righteous moral crusade. "God won't let [Lincoln] beat de South till he do the right thing" abolitionist Lydia Maria Child reported her saying in late 1861.

The enslaved did not wait for politicians to deliberate but left plantations in their tens of thousands in acts of self-emancipation. As early as March 1861, eight slaves entered Fort Pickens off the Florida coast, only to be returned to their owners under the terms of the Fugitive Slave Act. This anti-climax did not prevent a subsequent mass exodus. By arriving in huge numbers, the problem of what to do with escaped people went up the chain of command from the soldier to the captain to the general to the war department and ultimately to the president. General Benjamin F. Butler did not return runaways at Fort Monroe Virginia in late May 1861 and called them "contraband of war." Subsequent instructions from Secretary of War Simon Cameron ordered the protection of fugitives whether they were claimed by loyal or disloyal owners. In August 1861, the First Confiscation Act legitimated Butler's position, declaring that property used "for insurrectionary purposes" could be confiscated, although the status of those who escaped was unresolved. In two separate episodes, General John C. Frémont in Missouri in August 1861 and General David Hunter in South Carolina, Georgia, and Florida in May 1862 interpreted these measures as granting freedom to blacks under their jurisdiction. However, Lincoln countermanded both orders. This confusing situation was eventually resolved by passage of the Second Confiscation Act (17 July 1862) which clarified that self-emancipated blacks were "captives of war" henceforth to be "forever free."

Mass defection caused serious problems for the Confederacy which lacked manpower and utilised enslaved labour to compensate. State authorities hired or more often impressed (compulsorily appropriated) the service of enslaved people as the war progressed. Each enslaved person who crossed into Union lines not only reduced Confederate capacity but was a potential asset to the Federal army. About one in five slaves escaped during the war, between 500,000 and 700,000 out of a total Confederate slave population of three and a half million. The more resourceful enslavers "refugeed" their captives to what they hoped were safe locations within the southern interior such as Texas. Even where there was no prospect of escape, the enslaved became more assertive and less compliant than in normal circumstances. This caused anxiety on the Confederate home front where females, in conjunction with wounded, young, or elderly males – and perhaps an overseer if lucky – took charge.

The Federal army hired blacks to carry out many different tasks in contraband camps that were haphazardly constructed as the Union advanced, a practice codified by the July 1862 Militia Act. They dug ditches, built forts, loaded and unloaded ships, and used their skills as carpenters, blacksmiths, coopers and so forth. Some volunteered for dangerous work as scouts and spies, roving inside Confederate lines and risking recapture. The intelligence provided by African Americans proved invaluable during the Peninsular Campaign, and vital elsewhere, and was praised by military commanders who reported back to Lincoln. Black women and children washed, cleaned, carried, cooked, and worked in makeshift hospitals. Disease – malaria, measles, smallpox, and other fevers – was rife in contraband camps, however, spread by the co-mingling of people. The failure to stem epidemics reflected the primitive state of medical knowledge at the time but also the Federal army's general indifference to plight of black people.

In the Lower Mississippi Valley, where early inroads were made by the capture of New Orleans, African Americans were contracted back to Louisiana planters who renounced the Confederacy. The primary aim was to restore economic prosperity and enable both blacks and whites to provide for themselves. Unfortunately, black labourers endured low wages, harsh discipline, close supervision, and contracts that tied them to specific plantations. The arrangement constituted an early test of the parameters of black freedom in which there was widespread confusion over the status of liberated enslaved people. This situation was uncomfortably reminiscent of the unsuccessful apprenticeship system in the West Indies after British emancipation in 1833, abandoned after four years. Benjamin Butler and Nathaniel Banks, Union Commanders in Louisiana, unthinkingly associated blacks with plantation labour, as did many whites.

To what extent enslaved people influenced Lincoln to make abolition a war aim is fiercely debated. Lincoln was heavily criticised, at home and abroad, for avoiding emancipation in the first eighteenth months of the war. He worried that the Constitution did not permit executive action against slavery. He was also wary of a hostile reaction to emancipation in the strategically important Border States and more widely. Emancipation was certainly a high risk strategy given racial tensions in the North, demonstrated most terribly by the New York City draft riot (11–16 July 1863) seven months after the policy's approval. A mob destroyed the New York recruiting station and attacked government buildings following the announcement of the first draftees. Their fury turned towards African Americans whose homes and business were targeted. Hundreds of black men were beaten and lynched with 119 fatalities officially recorded but the death toll was probably far higher. Thousands were injured and millions of dollars' worth of property destroyed in the largest US civil disturbance to that point. The riot was triggered by conscription laws but reflected white working class fears, stoked by the Democratic Party, that emancipated slaves would take their jobs. Irish American dockworkers were prominent in this deadly reminder of deep class and racial problems in the North.

Lincoln informed his cabinet on 22 July 1862 that he intended to issue the preliminary Emancipation Proclamation. There were mixed responses, and concern it would be unpopular, but only Postmaster Montgomery Blair opposed the measure. On 22 September, following the Battle of Antietam – William Seward wisely advised Lincoln not to introduce the policy from a position that might appear weak militarily – the announcement was made. Unless the Confederates ceased hostilities, enslaved people in rebel states "shall be then, thenceforward, and forever free" from 1 January 1863. What would have happened if the Confederates had conceded is unclear but there was no chance of that.

The Emancipation Proclamation took effect in the New Year. Controversially, slavery in the Border States and parts of the Confederacy under Federal control was unaffected, although efforts to encourage emancipation in these areas continued. The official recruitment of black soldiers was also authorised. Lincoln's motivation has been probed extensively, as have the limitations of a bill that did not technically free any more slaves than the Second Confiscation Act. A variety of factors explain his momentous decision. Lincoln stated that "decisive and extensive measures" were required and emancipation was "a military necessity." He also wanted to "set an example and strike at the heart of the rebellion." Pleas to fight for a cause greater than the Union influenced him, although Lincoln undoubtedly acted strategically to deliver new supplies of troops at a crucial time. He also calculated that the Emancipation Proclamation ended the prospect of British or French intervention on the Confederacy's behalf.

The Bureau of Colored Troops was established 22 May 1863 to coordinate recruitment that was already well underway. Black troops led by white officers in segregated regiments made their way into combat during the summer of 1863. Placing black men in uniform was controversial, as critics pointed out in no uncertain terms, but hugely significant. African American men joined up to win permanent freedom, to prove their valour, and take revenge on enslavers. Their contribution was vital. Approximately 180,000 African Americans were mustered into service (10 per cent of the entire Union army), 10,000 served in the navy and tens of thousands more served as labourers. The majority of recruits, approximately 134,000, were black southerners. However, so-called coloured regiments were under resourced and initially suffered

Figure 7.4 Assault of the Second Louisiana Colored Regiment at Port Hudson. Black troops
made a timely and decisive contribution to the Union's victory.

Source: Courtesy of the Library of Congress Prints and Photographs Division Washington

discriminatory pay: $10 a month, compared to $13 for regular soldiers. Some Federal
commanders were reluctant to put them in the field and allocated fatigue duties. Black
troops fought a war on two fronts, against the Confederates and against institutionalised racism.

African American units fought with distinction. On 27 May 1863, 200 members of
the Louisiana Native Guards were killed or wounded in a heroic charge on a heavily
fortified Confederate fortress protected by ditches, parapets, and heavy artillery at
Port Hudson (Louisiana). In July, the 54th Massachusetts Infantry Regiment similarly
led a doomed assault on Fort Wagner that protected Charleston, depicted in the film
Glory (1989). Confederates promised to execute captured black troops as well as their
white officers. Notoriously, they carried out this threat at Fort Pillow near Memphis,
14 April 1864, when black and white soldiers, alongside women and children, were
slaughtered after surrendering. African American bravery captured the popular imagination and sent a powerful message. Relations with white troops, many of whom
had never encountered African Americans before, improved as they witnessed black
heroism. Those acts were described in soldiers' letters that disseminated the news back
home. Not all changed racist opinions and some were pleased that blacks were now
killed as well as whites. Undeniably, though, African American soldiers shattered racist stereotypes and advanced claims for full citizenship to an extent unimaginable in
wake of the 1857 Dred Scott decision.

Fighting to abolish slavery, 1863–65

Two years into the conflict the military tide turned towards the Union in the summer
of 1863. The logistics of replacing fallen troops was becoming increasingly pressing
for the Confederates while Union ranks were swelled by African American recruits.
The Confederacy was far from beaten though. At Chancellorsville in Virginia in the
first week of May 1863, the Federals suffered a resounding defeat in what is considered Robert E. Lee's finest moment, albeit tempered by the death of Stonewall Jackson

Figure 7.5 The American Civil War, 1863–65.

who was mistakenly shot by his own men. Jackson taught at the Virginia Military Institute and was a graduate of West Point. He was a brilliant military strategist, with a reputation for fearlessness, and an inspirational figure to the Confederate nation.

The Union recovered to complete two devastating blows almost simultaneously at Vicksburg and Gettysburg. The town of Vicksburg surrendered following a prolonged siege (18 May–4 July) which handed control of the Mississippi River to the Federals and split the Confederacy in two. Lee had ignored advice to relieve Vicksburg or to mount an offensive in Tennessee because he was convinced that only victory on northern soil would deliver Confederate success. The Battle of Gettysburg (1 July–3 July) in Pennsylvania was the largest, bloodiest, and most famous engagement of the war in which 90,000 Federal troops faced 75,000 Confederates with 50,000 combined casualties. To break the stalemate, Lee ordered what became known as Pickett's charge on the afternoon of the third day, a frontal assault against Union lines dug in on high ground at Cemetery Ridge. Nearly half of General George E. Pickett's 13,000 men were killed, wounded, or captured, and the Confederates withdrew the following day because they could not risk further casualties. The invasion of the North was repelled and Lee was now forced onto the defensive with depleting numbers in the field due to death, injury, and desertion.

Gettysburg Address

Four months after Gettysburg, Lincoln gave a short speech at the dedication of a national cemetery to commemorate the terrible events. The 272-word Gettysburg Address took less than three minutes to deliver on 19 November 1863 – Edward Everett was the main speaker not Lincoln – but became the single most celebrated speech of the entire war. "Fourscore and seven years ago our fathers brought forth, on this continent, a new nation, conceived in liberty, and dedicated to the proposition that all men are created equal" it began. "Now we are engaged in a great civil war, testing whether that nation, or any nation so conceived, and so dedicated, can long endure." Lincoln's eloquent words aligned the Civil War with the Declaration of Independence rather than the Constitution that implicitly supported slavery. He emphasised nation above Union, and pointed towards the global significance of the US as a bastion of liberty. The speech redefined the moral righteousness of the struggle. Lincoln's simple but inspirational message contrasted with the "Declarations of Immediate Causes" of seceding states that prioritised the defence of slavery.

These twin victories greatly strengthened the Union's position and when Ulysses S. Grant became General in Chief in March 1864 at last Lincoln seemed to have found someone to deliver victory. Grant, who came from the western theater, assumed command of the Army of the Potomac and had a much better understanding of the conflict than his predecessors. The pace of the war accelerated as a series of bloody encounters – including the battles of the Wilderness, Spotsylvania, and Cold Harbor among others – were fought in Virginia in May and June 1864 in the Overland (or Wilderness) Campaign. Grant's strategy focused on the destruction of Lee's Army of Northern Virginia rather than taking Richmond, while Sherman advanced in the west. The Union lost 60,000 men, compared to just 20,000 Confederates, in fighting at close quarters as Federals repeatedly attacked entrenched positions, a forerunner of the horrific trench warfare of World War I. Proportionally, though, the damage took a greater toll on the Confederates and Lee's resources were stretched further by the ensuing Siege of Petersburg (24 miles south of Richmond, Petersburg was a crucial supply link to the Confederate capital).

The American Civil War was not decided on the battlefield alone however. By mid-1863, the North was war-weary, opposition to emancipation had hardened, and Lincoln's administration was in the firing line. Northern Democrats supported the war at first but joined northern and midwestern Confederate sympathisers in raising concerns over Lincoln's presidential authoritarianism. Criticism centred upon the suspension of habeas corpus, the expansion of federal bureaucracy, the threat to private property, and the favouring of banks. Copperheads, as they were derisively known, were particularly prominent in the southern portions of Illinois, Indiana, and Ohio, home to large numbers of migrant southerners, as well as in big cities. The arrest of Lincoln's fiercest critic in May 1863, Ohio Democrat Clement L. Vallandigham, might have become a focal point of this discontent. Vallandigham was found guilty of treason in a military court but Lincoln cleverly commuted his life sentence to banishment to the Confederacy.

Lincoln's leadership continued to be scrutinised during 1864, particularly in light of the heavy casualties of the Overland Campaign. He was not certain to gain the Republican nomination in the pending presidential election and expected to lose to the Democratic candidate George McClellan, whom he had previously relieved of command, anyway. The Democratic Party's slogan was "The Constitution as it is; the Union as it was; the Negroes where they are" and they were prepared to negotiate peace. However, civilian morale reflected events on the battlefield and when Sherman took Atlanta in early September, Lincoln's popularity rebounded. Lincoln gained 55 per cent of the popular vote in the November 1864 presidential election to win a resounding victory (212–21 in the Electoral College). Soldiers voted for him by a majority of 4 to 1. The Confederacy somehow continued to find troops, by now exhausted, hungry, and lacking basic supplies, to stave off the Union for another five months but Lincoln's victory effectively ended their last realistic hope of avoiding defeat.

The beginning of the end was heralded by William Tecumseh Sherman's March to the Sea (15 November–21 December 1864). Sherman and Grant developed a policy of hard war, concluding that the Confederacy would only be defeated by making war as brutal for civilians as it was for soldiers. "We cannot change the hearts of those people of the South but we can make war so terrible," Sherman wrote in 1864, "that generations would pass away before they would again appeal to it." In late 1864, he led 60,000 soldiers through Georgia, capturing Atlanta and Savannah, taking food, burning barns, and destroying infrastructure in a campaign of psychological intimidation (which continued into the Carolinas in early 1865). Sherman marched through the heart of the Confederacy. He encountered dispirited Confederate soldiers suffering from inadequate food, clothing, and medical supplies. Tens of thousands deserted and between a third to a half were absent without leave by the latter stages of the war. The major decision facing the Confederate high command was whether to engage in guerrilla warfare. Lee chose not to do so and surrendered at Appomattox courthouse, Virginia, on 9 April 1865. Fighting continued in the West until Lt. General E. Kirby Smith's Army of the Trans-Mississippi surrendered at Galveston, Texas, on 26 May.

Why did the Union prevail? Historians suggest a variety of reasons, not least the substantial disparity in resources and manpower, but have also stressed the problem of Confederate unity. Jefferson Davis, Confederate figurehead and focal point of nascent southern nationalism, struggled to instil a strong sense of loyalty to himself or with the Confederate nation. His performance pales in comparison to Abraham Lincoln's decisive leadership and ability to delegate. The relationship between ordinary southerners and the Confederate government was strained and policies of conscription, taxation, and impressment of goods were deeply unpopular. Confederate state governors, such as Joseph E. Brown of Georgia and Zebulon Vance of North Carolina, made things worse by accusing Davis of acting despotically. But in order to take on a superior foe, Davis had no choice but to act autocratically, which enabled the Confederacy to survive for four years in worsening circumstances. In accounting for the Confederacy's defeat, a *loss* of will to continue the fight must be distinguished from a *lack* of will to fight in the first place. A majority of white southerners demonstrated enthusiasm for the war and many maintained their commitment despite the unsustainable sacrifices demanded.

The war was disastrous for tribes in the Indian Territory. James Harlan, Secretary of the Interior, reported in 1865 that "the Indian territory has been laid waste, vast amounts of property destroyed, and the inhabitants reduced from a prosperous condition to such extreme destitution that thousands of them must inevitably perish during the present winter." This predicament elicited little sympathy as Congress decided Indians made "treaties with the enemies of the United States" that invalidated previous agreements. At Fort Smith Arkansas in September 1865, tribes were required – no matter their wartime allegiance – to sign treaties that endorsed abolition, worked towards inter-tribal peace and peace with the United States, and agreed to right-of-way for railroad construction through their territory. More land concessions were also demanded, set aside as new reservations for tribes further west.

Presidential Reconstruction

The politics of readmitting southern states to the Union was highly contentious. They began during the middle of the war, when Abraham Lincoln announced his Proclamation of Amnesty and Reconstruction 8 December 1863, popularly known as the ten per cent plan. This was partly a matter of necessity: local governments had to be reformed in captured territory, first in Louisiana and later in Tennessee and Arkansas. But Lincoln also had a strategic purpose. His plan required voters for delegates to new southern state conventions to swear only an oath to "the Constitution of the United States and the Union of the States." The process of readmission would begin when just 10 per cent of the 1860 electorate had done so, provided slavery's abolition was accepted. In offering such lenient terms of readmission, Lincoln surely was testing the loyalty of all wavering Confederates.

The 10 per cent plan received a mixed response that became mostly negative, even though it was not necessarily Lincoln's final word. Emancipation proposals were popular within the Republican Party. But an oath that ignored Confederate service was considered far too favourable towards southern "traitors" not only by Republicans but by the public as well. The mood became worse in April 1864. The Louisiana Convention, organised by Union General Nathaniel Banks, accepted abolition but asked for compensation for enslavers and prevented African Americans, who constituted 47 per cent of Louisiana's population, from voting. This prompted a counter measure, sponsored by Radical Republicans Benjamin Wade and Henry Winter Davis, which demanded more stringent terms of readmission: a majority of "white male citizens" must swear an "ironclad" oath that they had not voluntarily participated in the rebellion. All holding Confederate office or willingly supporting the Confederacy were excluded. The Wade-Davis Bill passed on 2 July 1864 but Lincoln pocket-vetoed it (he did not sign the bill which subsequently expired), leading to stalemate. Attention then turned to the 1864 presidential election.

This political spat exposed contentious constitutional issues. Which branch of the government had the authority to decide terms of readmission? Could southern states simply return? The Lincoln administration had insisted that rebellion was constitutionally impossible in a union of the people. Treasonous secessionists were blamed which left the door open for a swift return. This position became less tenable as the war dragged on and the casualties mounted. But on what grounds could states be excluded? The Constitution granted the president war powers, did they enable him to dictate terms of re-entry? Some Republicans argued that Confederate states had forfeited their political rights in a form of state "suicide" and that they should therefore be treated as territories. These were difficult, divisive issues.

These questions came to the fore during presidential Reconstruction, May 1865–December 1866. It is one of the great ironies of American history that Lincoln's assassination by John Wilkes Booth on 14 April 1865 brought Andrew Johnson to the White House. Johnson had been chosen as vice president to underline Lincoln's desire to reunite the nation during the 1864 presidential election. Johnson, wartime governor of Tennessee, was a Democrat and the only southern Senator to remain loyal to the Union. He came from yeomen roots and made his reputation as a caustic critic of planters. He was expected to take a hard-line approach; Jefferson Davis described his elevation as "disastrous for our people." In fact, Johnson's racism and commitment to states' rights proved greater than his antipathy towards enslavers. Johnson issued two proclamations in May 1865 that mandated the federal government should not interfere in economic, social, or suffrage issues and offered lenient terms of readmission.

Booth's coordinated assassination conspiracy, that simultaneously targeted Secretary of State William Seward and Johnson, was intended to inspire continued Confederate military resistance after Appomattox. It failed to do so but Lincoln's death and Johnson's subsequent elevation provided a window of opportunity in which southern enslavers were able to play a major role in immediate post-war developments. It is fruitless to speculate what Lincoln would have done during Reconstruction but at the same time undeniable that Johnson missed an opportunity to force far-reaching change in the beaten Confederacy straightaway.

In the summer of 1865, Johnson recognised southern state governments that had already reformed and appointed provisional Governors to oversee elections on the basis of pre-war suffrage in states yet to do so. His candidates for Governor were at least opponents of secession but all white southerners that swore an oath of future allegiance to the United States were entitled to vote, with the exception of high-ranking Confederate officials or those owning $20,000 in taxable property. Even where they were excluded, however, planters exerted influence by indirect means. Numerous former Confederates were elected to state legislatures as Johnson liberally granted presidential pardons – there were 15,000 applications and 6,000 pardons issued by 1866. There were no mass arrests or punishments, as happened in the aftermath of major conflicts such as the world wars. Jefferson Davis was held in prison for two years but never put on trial. Johnson also ordered the Federal Freedman's Bureau, discussed later, to return confiscated land to enslavers by evicting African Americans.

A political power struggle in Washington DC

The Republican Party watched, horrified and powerless, during the summer of 1865 because Congress did not reconvene until December. Reconstituted southern state legislatures made the situation worse. For Republicans, they were illegitimate because they did not meet the terms of the ironclad oath and African Americans were excluded from their proceedings. New southern constitutions repudiated secession and abolished slavery, grudgingly in the case of the Deep South, but failed to grant suffrage to freedmen. Worst of all, black codes restricted the basic civil rights of African

Americans. Beginning in late 1865, Mississippi and South Carolina passed a series of laws (known as black codes) that controlled freedom of movement, limited land ownership, forced acceptance of labour contracts with low wages, and authorised compulsory apprenticeships for black children. Other southern states followed their lead. Any freed person who did not agree to work on a plantation could be charged with the crime of vagrancy (being without permanent home or paid employment). South Carolina even required African Americans to pay an annual tax of between $10 and $100 for any job other than servant or labourer.

This was anathema to the Republican Party. From December 1865 when the 39th session of Congress opened, it acted decisively. In a direct challenge to Johnson, the House refused to recognise state governments formed in 1865 or admit their representatives (which included former Confederate Vice President Alexander Stephens and four Confederate generals). A Joint Committee on Reconstruction, chaired by William Pitt Fessenden and Thaddeus Stevens, was formed to draw up alternative terms of readmission. A series of bold legislative actions were proposed that invalidated the black codes and supported African American civil rights. On 4 December 1865, the Second Freedmen's Bureau Bill extended and expanded the Bureau's work. Vetoed by Johnson in February 1866, the bill eventually passed over the president's objection on 16 July 1866. Most significantly, the Civil Rights Bill of April 1866, again passed over Johnson's veto, became the first law to define American citizenship (to include all those born in the US regardless of race) and enabled the federal government to intervene wherever civil rights were threatened.

The power struggle between president and party constituted a disastrous breakdown of the relationship between the executive and the legislative. How did this happen? It is important to realise that the Republican Party was not monolithic, but divided into factions. Radical Republicans were predominantly from a New England, antislavery background in some form or another, such as Charles Sumner from Massachusetts. But the radicals were never homogeneous: Thaddeus Stevens, the other leading Radical Republican, was from Pennsylvania. While never speaking with one voice, radicals insisted on civil rights for freed people, including suffrage, and they wanted to establish free labour in the former Confederate states.

The moderate wing of the party, led by James G. Blaine and Lyman Trumbull, prioritised restoration of pre-war prosperity in which cotton was king. It was ambivalent towards black suffrage and worried that the issue of civil rights was a political liability. Just five northern states allowed black men to vote. Referendums held in New York, Ohio, Wisconsin, Kansas, and Connecticut in the 1850s and 1860s had rejected black suffrage. Iowa and Minnesota narrowly voted in favour in 1868. All Republicans, no matter their affiliation, understood that re-admitting the South greatly strengthened the Democratic Party. African American enfranchisement would likely deliver thousands more Republican voters but any gain was counterbalanced by the prospect of millions of returning southern Democrats.

The battle line between president and party was drawn in April 1866 by the proposed Fourteenth Amendment. Building on the Civil Rights Bill, the Fourteenth Amendment contained three major provisions. First, "all persons born or naturalized in the United States" became citizens and "no state could abridge their rights." Second, if states denied the vote, their political representation in Congress would be reduced accordingly (a clear warning to southern conventions which had denied black suffrage). Third, southerners who had sworn loyalty to the Confederacy, which included all officials and officers, were excluded. The Fourteenth Amendment was subject to fierce debate within the Republican Party and represented a compromise between the moderate and radical wings. Most controversially, it sanctioned black male suffrage, although radicals complained it did not go far enough in doing so. The Republicans asserted their authority to dictate policy and enforce legislation, normally the responsibility of the president. Southern states were required to adopt the Fourteenth Amendment before their politicians could return to Congress.

Women's rights and the Fourteenth Amendment

The women's rights movement confronted a dilemma over the Fourteenth Amendment that wrote the gender specific "male inhabitants" into the Constitution (who, if US citizens and 21 years old, should not be denied the vote). Lucy Stone supported the amendment and believed women would be enfranchised shortly afterwards. Elizabeth Cady Stanton was far less sanguine; "it will take us a century at least to get it [male] out." Hitherto, only state laws restricted suffrage on a gendered basis. The issue split the Equal Suffrage Association formed in 1866 to campaign for black and female enfranchisement and two rival organisations emerged. The New York-based National Woman Suffrage Association, established in May 1869, was led by Stanton and Susan B. Anthony and focused on female suffrage exclusively. Stone and Julia Ward Howe led the American Women Suffrage Association, formed in November 1869, which regarded black suffrage as a positive development and continued to work with male allies on a range of issues.

Johnson's response to what he regarded as a congressional coup became increasingly ill-tempered. In the months before the regular mid-term elections to the House and Senate in November 1866, Johnson sought to galvanise the support of conservatives and reach out to Democrats. He toured the country in his "swing around the circle." There was widespread opposition among northern conservatives to the Fourteenth Amendment. While the public had been impressed with black loyalty during the war, racism and an underlying belief in white supremacy had not gone away. However, Johnson's campaign was a dismal failure in which he came across as a self-pitying megalomaniac being persecuted by tyrants. Horrific race riots in Memphis in May and in New Orleans in June provided further evidence that his leniency towards the South was misplaced. It hardly helped that his predecessor in the White House had been accorded mythical status, which he did not enjoy in his lifetime, in wake of his assassination. Johnson's failings were put in sharp relief even though there is no reason to assume that Lincoln could have solved the intractable problems of Reconstruction.

The Republicans gained a landslide victory in the November 1866 mid-term elections, giving them a 2:1 majority in Congress and a 4:1 majority in the Senate. The American electorate was not prepared to allow Johnson to surrender the fruits of military victory that had cost so many lives. Johnson continued his tirade but was effectively a lame duck. He was later impeached "for high crimes and misdemeanours" when attempting to dismiss War Secretary Edwin M. Stanton, the only member

Figure 7.6 Political cartoon ridiculing Andrew Johnson's swing around the circle.

of the cabinet who supported the radical agenda. An unprecedented trial took place in the Senate (4 March–16 May 1868) and Johnson narrowly escaped impeachment. The required two-thirds majority for conviction was just a single vote short: 35–19 (7 Republicans and 12 Democrats voted against impeachment). While a side show to the main events, Johnson's trial emphasises the turbulent nature of Reconstruction politics and the high stakes involved. It also reflected the emotionally charged aftermath of a savage conflict that made reunion an exceptionally difficult task.

Radical Reconstruction

The opening of the second session of the 39th Congress on 3 December 1866 marked the beginning of Radical (or Congressional) Reconstruction (which began to unravel after ratification of the Fifteenth Amendment on 30 March 1870). The Republican Party, riled by events of the previous 18 months, sought to rebuild the Confederacy as they saw fit. The 2 March 1867 Reconstruction Act, passed over Johnson's veto, was one of the most radical bills in the history of American politics. It invalidated all southern state governments formed under Lincoln and Johnson with the exception of Tennessee and divided the South into five military districts occupied by federal troops. It set out stringent terms of readmission: the election of new state conventions on the basis of universal male suffrage; acceptance of the Fourteenth Amendment; and disqualification of ex-Confederate office holders from the political process. Ironically, the

Reconstruction Act was implemented just as southern states, encouraged by Andrew Johnson, confirmed their rejection of the Fourteenth Amendment.

From June 1868 onwards, legitimate southern legislatures, voted in by a biracial electorate with former Confederates excluded, began to return their elected representatives to Washington. These newly formed southern state governments were Republican coalitions which included northerners who crossed the Mason-Dixon line for a variety of reasons (unkindly known as carpetbaggers), white southerners, many of whom were wartime Unionists (unkindly called scalawags) and black men, most prominently those who had been free before the war or held important community roles (preachers, for example). Two hundred and sixty-five African Americans sat in southern Constitutional Conventions, while around 800 served subsequently in southern state legislatures.

In the decades after Reconstruction, these governments would be criticised if not demonised for being corrupt and wasteful. The reality was that the former Confederate states faced unprecedented problems. Important reforms of the welfare, education, and tax systems were achieved, as well as the rebuilding of a devastated infrastructure. Corruption was a problem, although was hardly the preserve of southern Republican governments but endemic throughout the entire political system. Later myths of African American political dominance over white southerners, popularised by the notorious film *The Birth of a Nation* (1915) and presented as fact by white historians in the early twentieth century, were highly exaggerated: there were just two black southern senators, sixteen black congressmen, and not one black governor during Reconstruction.

On 26 February 1869, Congress approved the Fifteenth Amendment, forbidding federal or state governments from depriving the right to vote "on account of race,

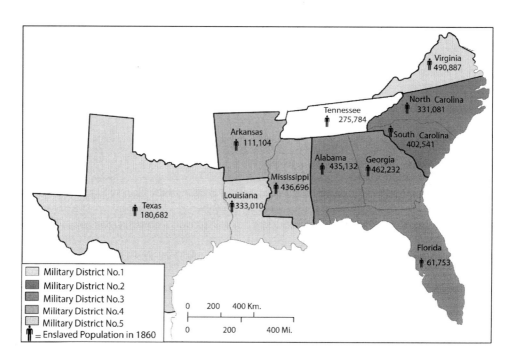

Figure 7.7 Military Reconstruction.

color, or previous condition of servitude." Republicans feared that black suffrage was not secure, despite all they had accomplished, were dismayed that states outside the South continued to prevent blacks voting, and worried that their ability to secure further legislation was diminishing. In large part this was because of a narrow victory in the 1868 presidential election for Ulysses S. Grant. This was the first election in which black southerners voted and their support was important to the outcome. The close popular vote (Grant gained 56 per cent) surprised everybody and indicated that public sympathy for the radical agenda was declining. Nonetheless, the Fifteenth Amendment was ratified on 30 March 1870 in spite of fierce opposition from Democrats. Three constitutional amendments in the space of five years was unprecedented; the next was not until 1913. For good reason has this tumultuous period of political history been described as a second American Revolution.

Republicans continued to seek legislation that supported a radical agenda, such as three Enforcement Acts (1870–71) that effectively shut down the Ku Klux Klan in the early 1870s. Political violence was redefined as a federal, rather than a state, offence, and Federal marshals in conjunction with the army were mobilised to tackle the problem. Hundreds were prosecuted in an operation generating extensive case files and the immediate problem of Klan intimidation was dealt with. Unfortunately, the Enforcement Acts were costly to implement fully and consistently. In reality, intimidation was suppressed only for as long, and as far, as Federal troops were stationed. As discussed in the final section, violent white supremacy took a variety of guises during Reconstruction. Racist attitudes were persistent, especially when it came to politics where blacks were considered unfit to participate by many whites regardless of section.

Grant was re-elected president in 1872 but the Republican Party was faltering. The "Liberal Republicans," a splinter group, accused Grant of corruption and supported Horace Greeley on a platform of sectional reconciliation and southern home rule. Although defeated, Greeley's campaign contributed to a resurgence of northern racism. The Democrats did very well in the 1874 mid-term elections and regained control of the House of Representatives. Voters had grown tired of the southern problem by this point and other issues such as labour relations and an economic depression beginning in 1873 took priority. Radical Republicanism lost its momentum, not least due to the death of its foremost proponents such as Thaddeus Stevens in August 1868. The 1875 Civil Rights Act, in honour of deceased Charles Sumner, sought to tackle discrimination, but was a diluted bill, not applicable in schools, that was more symbolic than effective. It was declared unconstitutional by the Supreme Court in 1883, on the grounds that individual prejudice was not outlawed by the Fourteenth Amendment, only state-level discrimination. It would be another 82 years before civil rights legislation was passed again in 1957.

Negotiating freedom: Reconstruction at ground level

As a series of dramatic acts polarised national politics, an equally frenetic narrative played out in the southern states. Reconstruction at the ground level was as complicated as that which unfolded in Washington DC, perhaps even more so. As pointed out in the previous chapter, the South was not monolithic and Reconstruction worked differently in different places. There were subtle and more profound variations at the local and the state level, often reflecting the relative strength of the Republican Party's and the Federal army's presence. In a few locations with large black majorities, such as low country South Carolina, African Americans could exert their freedom more vigorously than where they were in the minority.

Large parts of the South lay in ruins in April 1865. The desolate image of the burned-out Confederate capital (Fig. 7.8) was replicated across the southern states in which countless towns and communities had been razed to the ground and houses, farms, barns, factories, and mills demolished. The southern infrastructure had been destroyed and roads, bridges, and rail track blown apart or ripped up. Businesses were closed and plantations at a standstill. There was no capital for rebuilding and the South lacked basic necessities. The threat of starvation was a serious concern. Most citizens would turn to politicians at times like this, but who governed the southern states? State and local governments had to be reconstituted in order to begin a return to normality but this took years.

Equally troublesome, what constituted normality in the post-slavery era? Social turmoil was as profound as the political and economic chaos. The human trauma of the war, costing at least 250,000 Confederate lives and innumerably more injured, physically and psychologically, left no family untouched. The humiliation of defeat was deeply felt and the hatred of Yankees undiminished with the war's conclusion, in fact hatred became stronger for some white southerners over the course of Reconstruction. Gertrude Thomas, an elite white woman from Augusta Georgia, described

Figure 7.8 Richmond in ruins, April 1865.

Source: Courtesy of the US National Archives and Records Administration

how her "faith in God's Holy Book was terribly shaken. For a time I doubted God." Slavery was abolished but African American freedom was consistently challenged and restricted wherever possible. The southern social order had been conditioned by centuries of slavery and racism was deeply ingrained. Legal measures were passed to implement equality, but their successful application proved difficult. White supremacy constituted a massive barrier to progress and became the primary weapon of the Democratic Party as it reorganised.

For black southerners emancipation was an entirely different story. Union victory constituted the biblical day of Jubilee. As the news filtered from plantation to plantation, some enslaved people broke down in an instantaneous, emotional reaction while others felt a sense of bewilderment. Most immediately, African Americans sought to reunite families broken under slavery and couples legalised their marriages as quickly as possible. Army chaplains and Freedmen's Bureau officials were kept busy conducting official ceremonies. Others were not so fortunate in finding loved ones, who were scattered far and wide, and southern newspapers contained heart-breaking notices from those who refused to give up the search. Black southerners asserted their autonomy in many ways but none was more important than the stabilisation of black family life. Some former masters continued to try to interfere after emancipation, while others unceremoniously evicted "their" people as the paternalistic facade shattered. Regardless of their former owner's reaction, though, African Americans established a new sense of order in their family life.

Freedmen and Southern Society Project

The Freedmen and Southern Society Project (www.freedmen.umd.edu/) has published tens of thousands of documents detailing the end of slavery and the course of Reconstruction. This series mines the voluminous documentation generated by the federal government and its various organisations and departments, housed at the National Archives and Record Administration (NARA). It seeks to capture "the drama of emancipation in the words of the participants: liberated slaves and defeated enslavers, soldiers and civilians, common folk and the elite, Northerners and Southerners" and has transformed study of the topic.

Freedom fundamentally reshaped gender relations in black households. Idealised gender roles had been denied to African Americans under slavery and reserved for whites only. Black men now bore with pride the opportunity to become the sole economic provider. Working hours were reduced and wives and children withdrew from the fields. Whites scorned black women who left the fields and accused them of "playing the lady." What they perceived as a sign of indolence was actually an affirmation of black independence. Politics also became a shared endeavour between black men and women. While black women could not vote, political issues were deliberated between husbands and wives as were other important decisions. Black women attended political rallies and made speeches. Once black males were enfranchised, they accompanied their husbands to the ballot box, something which became increasingly hazardous as the Democratic backlash gathered pace. Gender roles were a key battleground as whites and blacks sought to redefine the social terrain of the post-war South.

Concern for the future of their families also led freed people to prioritise educational opportunities. Most blacks had been denied the opportunity to read and write under slavery. Education offered them the hope that they could better themselves. More than 600,000 black children attended schools built by the Freedmen's Bureau and state authorities. Educational initiatives were spearheaded by local communities. African Americans pooled their meagre collective resources to purchase land, construct schoolhouses, and pay the salaries of teachers. By 1870, more than $1 million been raised. The results were impressive. When slavery was abolished, 90 per cent of African Americans could not read or write; by 1880, the black illiteracy rate had decreased to 70 per cent and would fall to just 50 per cent by 1900. A 200 per cent increase in black literacy during Reconstruction was a major step forwards that laid foundations for future progress.

Progress was also made by establishing black colleges and universities. The first generation of African American institutions of higher education in the South included Fisk University in Nashville (Tennessee), Hampton Institute (Virginia), Tougaloo College in Jackson (Mississippi), and Howard University (Washington DC). Howard was named after Oliver Otis Howard, former Union General and Commissioner of the Freedmen's Bureau. These institutions were emblematic of the profound desire to build an autonomous African American community free from white interference. At the core was the black church. The most popular denominations were the African Methodist Episcopal Church, the African Methodist Episcopal Zion Church, and the Baptists. Churches were not only a source of spiritual inspiration but also crucial in nurturing secular growth. They provided the space for schools, meetings of mutual aid and fraternal societies, political assemblies, and social gatherings. Religion had been an essential foundation of the slave community and the local church was the focal point of community activity in the post-war era.

If building the black household was the most satisfying element of freedom, the essential foundation of future prosperity lay in land ownership. As independent farmers, African Americans hoped to establish not only economic autonomy but a sense of personal empowerment. Former slaves felt a strong sense of attachment and entitlement to land they worked, particularly where their family had resided for generations. As Virginian freedmen Bayley Wyatt insisted in 1866 "we has a right to the land where we are located" precisely because "our wives, our children, our husbands, has been sold over and over again to purchase the land."

Early signs had been encouraging. African Americans worked under demeaning contracts on plantations in Louisiana during the war, but they successfully occupied abandoned plantations in the South Carolina Sea Islands from late 1861. Hundreds of northern missionaries, mostly young female abolitionists, set up schools and taught Christianity. African Americans were tutored in the ways of free labour in what is known as the Port Royal experiment in South Carolina. Ownership of land was contested by both the federal government and northern speculators but some freed men eventually purchased the land on which they laboured. Hopes were raised further by General Sherman's Special Field Order No. 15 (16 January 1865) which set aside some 400,000 acres of captured coastal territory for freed people stretching from Charleston to Florida. This was not a grand philanthropic gesture but a practical measure, following a meeting in Savannah between Sherman, Secretary of War Stanton, and 20 black preachers, to address the issue of contrabands. By June 1865, approximately 40,000 black families occupied farms of 40 acres.

African American hopes were dashed when President Johnson returned property to white southerners. Despite lengthy and heated debates subsequently, a minority of Radical Republicans including George W. Julian and Thaddeus Stevens could not persuade Congress to authorise land redistribution and an opportunity was lost. South Carolina was a partial exception, as the Republican administration empowered a land commission to purchase land and resell it on extended terms of credit to African Americans. By 1876, about 14,000 families had acquired their own homesteads under this scheme. The Southern Homestead Act (21 June 1866) also facilitated the sale of public land to blacks and loyal whites. Unfortunately, most of the land made available was of poor quality and white officials did their best to obstruct the bill's implementation. Moreover, no financial assistance was provided for the purchase of tools, seeds, and fertiliser. The failure to provide economic tools to former slaves, without which freedom was precarious, was Reconstruction's greatest flaw.

Why did the Republican Party not facilitate acquisition of land? Despite the efforts of some Radical Republicans, most party members held misgivings over land redistribution and opponents vehemently opposed it. Land confiscation conflicted with the inviolable right of the individual to own private property, enshrined by the Constitution. (Ironically, of course, these reservations were never raised when it came to taking Native American territory). The vast majority of whites believed that giving land to African Americans undermined their ability to become self-reliant. This position ignored the ways in which racist structural barriers created formidable impediments to progress. Unable to fulfil their ambition of becoming independent farmers, African Americans had little choice but to work for white landowners. The failure of land reform demarcated the limits of successful federal intervention during Reconstruction.

The Bureau of Refugees, Freedmen, and Abandoned Lands also exposed flaws in Republican good intentions. The Freedmen's Bureau, established in March 1865, was the major federal agency on the ground in the former Confederate states and the subject of much criticism. It provided vital services for freed people, without which a perilous situation would have become much worse. The Bureau's responsibilities included providing food and medical supplies, supporting educational initiatives, implementing free labour arrangements, advising on employment contracts, and ensuring fair court hearings. Bureau officials acted in what they considered to be the best interests of black southerners. However, their core agenda was to stabilise the economy and restore credit, which necessitated returning to cotton production as quickly as possible, and promoting industrialisation. In this endeavour, the Bureau's major allies were bankers, landholders, merchants, and mill owners, not African Americans.

This problem was underlined in the fraught transition from slave to "free" labour. Without land, African Americans returned to work as labourers and tried to resist restoration of the gang system – they much preferred to work independently. They wanted freedom of movement to force white landowners to compete for their service by offering improved working conditions. Yet Bureau officials regularly sided with white landowners in contract negotiations that restricted free movement and legitimated close supervision, thereby recreating the bonds of dependency that had existed under slavery. Bureau agents wanted to instil a free labour ideology based on working for wages that avoided contractual disputes and squabbles over land ownership as far as possible. Unfortunately, this one-sided view benefitted landowners and contributed

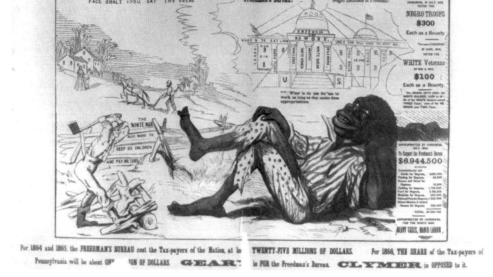

Figure 7.9 Political cartoon lampooning the Freedmen's Bureau. Racist propaganda like this was common in American politics.

to the emergence of sharecropping which caused misery for decades. The disastrous impact of this system is discussed in next chapter.

The Medical Division of the Freedmen's Bureau, which assumed primary responsibility for the welfare of men, women, and children from former owners, also had a mixed record. Tens of thousands of freed African Americans died during and after the war, as the effects of disease were exacerbated by food shortages and primitive or nonexistent medical treatment. In the Carolinas in 1865, to take one example, 30,000 African Americans died in a smallpox epidemic. With only 1,000 agents at most in the field at any one time, across the southern states, inadequate resources were also to blame as senior officials failed to perceive the scale of the problem. Individual and institutional racism blighted the Bureau's response. The high death toll was blamed on the victims for their lack of cleanliness and seemingly confirmed the erroneous but pervasive belief in the innate frailty of the black body. Thirty thousand black troops were killed in action, but many more African Americans died from disease in the war's aftermath.

Southern politics and the Democratic Party backlash

Black politics thrived in the post-war period, but was short lived. Under slavery, African Americans were denied a political voice but nonetheless eagerly followed political

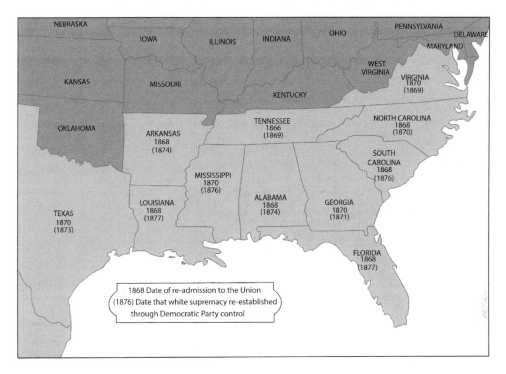

NEBRASKA
IOWA
ILLINOIS
INDIANA
OHIO
PENNSYLVANIA
DELAWARE
MARYLAND
WEST VIRGINIA
KANSAS
MISSOURI
KENTUCKY
VIRGINIA
1870
(1869)
OKLAHOMA
ARKANSAS
1868
(1874)
TENNESSEE
1866
(1869)
NORTH CAROLINA
1868
(1870)
SOUTH CAROLINA
1868
(1876)
MISSISSIPPI
1870
(1876)
TEXAS
1870
(1873)
LOUISIANA
1868
(1877)
ALABAMA
1868
(1874)
GEORGIA
1870
(1871)
FLORIDA
1868
(1877)

1868 Date of re-admission to the Union
(1876) Date that white supremacy re-established
through Democratic Party control

Figure 7.10 The Restoration of white supremacy in the South.

developments – news of Lincoln's presidential victory, for example, spread from one plantation to another. This political tradition came to the fore during Reconstruction. In the summer of 1865, long before enfranchisement, former slaves and free blacks held regular political meetings. In some cases, they met at the same time as white state conventions sanctioned by President Johnson, specifically to register their protest at his pro-planter agenda. Political mobilisation was coordinated by the Union League, an organisation formed in the North during the war to support Lincoln. After 1865, the Union League acted as an auxiliary of the Republican Party to organise white southerners and African Americans. The message was clear: black southerners opposed presidential Reconstruction and demanded political rights.

The Republican Party had a tiny foothold in Maryland, Delaware, Kentucky, and Missouri before 1861, but established organisational structures in all southern states post-war. African Americans seized the opportunity to participate in electoral politics and for a limited period southern state governments were bi-racial coalitions. In no other time or place had abolition been followed by immediate political inclusion – from emancipation in the British Caribbean to the emancipation of Russian serfs. The Republicans gained white support in locations that were not dominated by former planters, like the North Carolina piedmont. The record of Republican state administrations – which reformed taxes and the judiciary system, built schools and hospitals, promoted women's rights, and sought to prevent discrimination, as well as embarking on a process of economic redevelopment – was certainly no worse than their counterparts in the North. Their actions benefitted poor whites as well as African Americans, particularly by the creation of a public education system. However, the coalition was always fragile. Black Republicans might suffer the condescension of their white colleagues who did not always recognise them as equals.

Republican administrations were challenged at every step by Democratic opponents. The reconstitution of southern state governments in late 1865 on a white basis gave the upper hand to those wishing to restore the antebellum status quo, even if those governments were only temporary. It was not just that the Democratic Party was given vital impetus county by county and state by state. The fatal flaw of presidential Reconstruction was that long-established mechanisms of white violence and intimidation used to control African Americans, at once personal, political, and extra-legal, were reinvigorated. The mobilisation of white militia, sometimes former Confederate soldiers picking up their rifles, was justified on the basis of the "threat" that African Americans posed to white property or to white women. For instance, authorities in Alabama and Mississippi used rumours of black insurrection in late 1865 to justify establishing militia units. Bureau agents warned President Johnson that the threat was exaggerated and militias were being used to police African Americans to no avail. Paramilitary units enforced Black Codes but the reality was that freed people were being brutalised before the laws were written.

Levels of violence during Reconstruction were appalling. Most notorious was the Ku Klux Klan founded in Pulaski, Tennessee, in December 1865, a secret order of former officers and rank-and-file Confederates sworn to the restoration of white supremacy. The Klan rapidly built a powerful network in southern states that included local and state officials. It ruthlessly harassed black leaders and their white allies, targeting Union League and Republican officers – including members of state legislatures. African American Benjamin Randolph, for instance, who founded the *Charleston Advocate* newspaper and was elected to the South Carolina senate where he played a major role in establishing free public education, was murdered on 16 October 1868. The Democrat leader D. Wyatt Aiken had publicly called for his assassination and was subsequently arrested but released. Randolph was shot in broad daylight, in front of witnesses, and charges were brought against white suspects but the case never went to trial. Randolph was one of 19 Republicans murdered during the 1868 campaign in South Carolina's third district alone. Federal intervention via the Enforcement Acts brought some relief but rifle clubs, Red Shirts, and White Leagues followed in the footsteps of the KKK in the 1870s. The only difference between these groups and the Klan was that they did not wear hoods to hide their identity.

The Democratic Party deployed violence and intimidation to create an atmosphere of political terror and overthrow Republican administrations. Black and white Republicans were not passive and responded in kind by mobilising their own units, which included black war veterans. But in most places they were confronted by superior numbers. On 13 April 1873, the White League massacred more than 100 African Americans in Colfax, Louisiana. This preceded a counter-revolutionary coup carried out in Louisiana in 1874 to oust the Republican Governor and legislature that was only thwarted by the last-minute intervention of Federal troops. A year later, Mississippi Democrats waged a campaign of ruthless violence to regain control of the state, known as the Shotgun Policy or the Mississippi Plan. This time the federal government did not intervene. On 4 July 1876, black militia were killed in cold blood by

Figure 7.11 Colfax Riot historical marker. Erected in 1950, this "historical marker" presents a
   white supremacist memory of Reconstruction that was typical in the modern South.

Source: Courtesy of Billy Hathorn (reproduced under CC BY-SA 3.0)

Red Shirts in Hamburg, South Carolina, after surrendering. White elites blamed this
incident on rowdy elements and no one was charged, when in fact it was they who had
orchestrated the mob. The overthrow of Republican state governments in the South
was called "redemption," but "redeemers" were effectively white mobs, led by elites,
attacking African Americans and their allies in the name of white supremacy.

   The formal end of Reconstruction is usually demarcated by the disputed presidential election of 1876. Contested votes from three southern states, Florida, Louisiana,
and South Carolina, were eventually given to Republican Rutherford B. Hayes in
March 1877 in return for the removal of remaining Federal troops from the region.
This "corrupt bargain," as it became known, signalled the final Republican retreat
from civil rights. Recently, however, dating Reconstruction's end to 1877 has been
challenged. The Republican focus turned away from the South in the early 1870s
to problems of western expansion, Native Americans, labour unrest, and a faltering
economy, discussed in the next chapter. By 1877, there were very few troops left on
the ground and the reality was that white supremacy through Democratic rule had
already been restored in most places. Black southern politics also endured after 1877
where African Americans resided in large numbers. African Americans held political
office in South Carolina, for instance, until the 1890s.

Chapter summary

Two key issues were resolved by the Civil War. First, the fragile political basis of the American nation was secured. With rapid territorial expansion, unprecedented immigration, clear ethnic and religious differences, not to mention sectional divisions, many Europeans had not expected the United States to survive. Confederate defeat confirmed the North and South under one flag, even though hostilities continued between the sections to such an extent as to question whether the fighting ended in 1865. Second, slavery was abolished and, unexpectedly, four million African Americans became US citizens. The shortcomings of the post-emancipation settlement are obvious and constitute an important corrective to triumphal narratives of American freedom. A minority of Radical Republicans believed in integration but the majority of white Americans, North and South, accepted racist doctrines and southern elites used this to their advantage to win the peace. Violence during Reconstruction was endemic and was deployed strategically by the Democratic Party to reassert white supremacy.

At the same time, it is important not to lose sight of emancipation's significance. The Crittenden Constitutional amendment in early 1861 guaranteeing slavery in perpetuity attracted cross-party, cross-sectional support; had it been successful, the implications are mind-boggling. Although Reconstruction was a trial, if not an ordeal, with an entirely unsatisfactory ending, African Americans never doubted the importance of the Thirteenth Amendment (ratified 7 December 1865) that abolished slavery, a momentous act which they have commemorated ever since. The great African American leader and intellectual W. E. B. Du Bois later wrote of Reconstruction that "the slave went free; stood a brief moment in the sun; then moved back again toward slavery" but he never underestimated the significance of that brief moment.

Discussion questions

- Why did it take so long for emancipation to become a war objective?
- What factors explain the Union's victory?
- How far do you agree with historian Eric Foner that Reconstruction was "an unfinished revolution"?
- What were the most important consequences of emancipation for black southerners?
- How was violence deployed to restore white supremacy during Reconstruction?

Further reading

Berlin, Ira, et al., eds. *Free at Last: A Documentary History of Slavery, Freedom, and the Civil War* (New York, 1992). An important collection of primary source materials published as part of the *Freedmen and Southern Society Project*.

Boritt, Gabor S., ed. *Why the Confederacy Lost* (New York, 1992). Comprehensive discussion of the reasons for Confederate defeat.

Downs, Gregory P. *After Appomattox: Military Occupation and the Ends of War* (Cambridge, MA, 2015). A revisionist account that questions whether the Civil War ended in 1865 as the fighting continued by other means.

Downs, Jim. *Sick from Freedom: African-American Illness and Suffering During the Civil War and Reconstruction* (New York, 2012). A harrowing examination of the fate of African Americans under the medical wing of the Freedmen's Bureau.

Du Bois, W E B. *Black Reconstruction in America 1860–1880* (New York, 1935). Pioneering study of Reconstruction that challenged the racist historiography of its era and is still extremely influential in the present.

Edwards, Laura. *Gendered Strife and Confusion: The Political Culture of Reconstruction* (Urbana, 1997). A brilliant cultural history of gender and Reconstruction.

Farmer-Kaiser, Mary. *Freedwomen and the Freedmen's Bureau: Race, Gender, and Public Policy in the Age of Emancipation* (New York, 2010). Considers African American women, gender, and the Freedmen's Bureau.

Foner, Eric. *Reconstruction: America's Unfinished Revolution* (New York, 1988). Remains the most widely read and authoritative one volume account of Reconstruction.

Gallagher, Gary W. *The Confederate War* (Cambridge, MA, 1997). An important revisionist book challenging the view that the Confederacy was internally disunited.

Glymph, Thaviola. *The Women's Fight: The Civil War's Battles for Home, Freedom, and Nation* (Chapel Hill, 2019). A magnificent study placing women at the centre of the war.

Hahn, Steven. *A Nation Under Our Feet: Black Political Struggles in the Rural South From Slavery to the Great Migration* (Cambridge, MA, 2003). A brilliant account of African American politics from the plantation to the State Legislature.

Manning, Chandra. *Troubled Refuge: Struggling for Freedom in the Civil War* (New York, 2016). A favourable account of the Union's treatment of escaped slaves in Federal camps.

McPherson, James M. *Battle Cry of Freedom: The Civil War Era* (New York, 1988). The classic one volume account of the American Civil War, despite the publication of many similar books subsequently.

McPherson, James M. *Abraham Lincoln and the Second American Revolution* (New York, 1991). A probing examination of the long-lasting consequences of the Civil War.

Neely, Mark E. Jr. *The Civil War and the Limits of Destruction* (Cambridge, MA, 2007). Revisionist challenge to the idea that the American Civil War was the first modern war.

Ransom, Roger L., and Richard Sutch. *One Kind of Freedom: The Economic Consequences of Emancipation* (Cambridge, 1977). Provides a sweeping economic analysis of the southern economy after the war.

Rosen, Hannah. *Terror in the Heart of Freedom: Citizenship, Sexual Violence, and the Meaning of Race in the Postemancipation South* (Chapel Hill, 2009). A poignant and harrowing examination of the violence inflicted on African Americans during Reconstruction.

Schwalm, Leslie A. *A Hard Fight for We: Women's Transition from Slavery to Freedom in South Carolina* (Urbana, 1997). An important discussion of black women from slavery to freedom.

Sheehan-Dean, Aaron. *The Calculus of Violence: How Americans Fought the Civil War* (Cambridge, MA, 2018). A sobering examination of the levels of violence used by each side in the war and the justifications for so doing.

Summers, Mark Wahlgren. *The Ordeal of the Reunion: A New History of Reconstruction* (Chapel Hill, 2014). A new, comprehensive one volume history of Reconstruction that takes a wide view of events from a northern, southern, and western perspective.

Trelease, Allen W. *White Terror: The Ku Klux Klan Conspiracy and Southern Reconstruction* (Baton Rouge, 1971). A classic but still valuable analysis of the most powerful white supremacist group.

Varon, Elizabeth R. *Armies of Deliverance: A New History of the Civil War* (New York, 2019). The most recent survey of the war which connects home front and battlefield while deftly synthesising social, cultural, political, and military history.

Williams, Heather Andrea. *Help Me to Find My People: The African American Search for Family Lost in Slavery* (Chapel Hill, 2012). Considers the often heartbreaking attempts of freed people to find members of their families.

8 Western conquest, white supremacy, and the rise of a superpower

Timeline

1862, July 1	Pacific Railroad Act
1863, January 1	Homestead Act
1867, March 30	US purchases Alaska from Russia
1869, May 10	First transcontinental railroad completed
1871, March 3	Indian Appropriations Act
1872	Montgomery Ward begins the delivery of mail order goods
1873, September 18	Panic of 1873 begins
1876, June 25	Battle of the Little Big Horn
1877, July 16	Great Railroad Strikes begins
1878, January 10	Female suffrage amendment in the Senate defeated
1881, July 2	President James A. Garfield shot by Charles Guiteau and dies on September 19
1882, May 6	Chinese Exclusion Act
1883, October 15	Supreme Court invalidates the Civil Rights Act of 1875
1883, November 18	The US and Canada adopt standard time
1884, May 1	Construction of the first skyscraper in Chicago (William Jenney's ten-story Home Insurance Company)
1886, May 1	300,000 workers demonstrate for an eight-hour work day
1886, May 4	Haymarket Square affair
1886, October 28	President Grover Cleveland unveils the Statue of Liberty
1886, Dec. 8	American Federation of Labor founded
1887, February 4	The Interstate Commerce Act
1887, February 8	The Dawes Severalty Act
1888	Edward Bellamy publishes *Looking Backward*
1889, April 22	Oklahoma opened to settlers
1890, February 18	National American Women Suffrage Association founded; Elizabeth Cady Stanton is the first president
1890, July 2	Sherman Anti-Trust Act
1890, November 1	New Mississippi State Constitution
1890, December 15	Sitting Bull killed
1890, December 29	Wounded Knee Massacre
1891, May 19	Populist Party founded
1892, January 1	Ellis Island opens

1892, June 26– November 20	Homestead Strike
1894, May 10–July 20	Pullman Strike
1896, May 18	Supreme Court *Plessy v. Ferguson* decision
1896, July 7	William Jennings Bryan "Cross of Gold" speech

Topics covered

- Native Americans and the western trails
- The Wild West
- The final resolution of the Indian question
- The subjugation of Plains Indians
- Railroads and industrial growth
- The robber barons
- Life and labour in the Gilded Age
- A New South?
- Jim Crow
- Rural problems in industrial America
- The Populist insurgency

Introduction

The two decades following Reconstruction are commonly known as the Gilded Age, a term first used by Mark Twain and Charles Dudley Warner. Their satirical novel, *The Gilded Age* (1873), caricatured the corruption and chicanery of politics in the age of big business. The final stage of western expansion, and the advance of the American economy to become a world leader, dominated the last third of the nineteenth century. This chapter explains how, within a generation, powerful Native American tribes were forced onto reservations that opened up millions of acres of land for white settlement. It then discusses transcontinental railroad construction, heavily subsidised by the federal government, that heralded the rise of corporate capitalism and violent conflict between workers and employers. In the South, the pre-war planter class re-established control of southern labour as black and white sharecroppers and tenant farmers became mired in a cycle of debt. A system of racial segregation was established that institutionalised white supremacy across the southern states. Agriculture expanded during the Gilded Age but farmers felt increasingly marginalised as formidable tycoons such as Andrew Carnegie and J. P. Morgan were the era's dominant figures. The Populist movement responded to the changing landscape to attack politicians, industrialists, bankers, and southern landed elites in a powerful articulation of discontent but was defeated in the critical 1896 election. By the turn of the century, American society was divided along lines of race and class to a greater extent than ever before.

Native Americans and the western trails

Settlers pushed the frontier beyond the Mississippi River by the mid-nineteenth century to a line of outposts that stretched from Saint Paul in Minnesota down to Fort Worth in Texas which constituted the demarcation of civilisation from the great unknown. Beyond that stretched a huge expanse, some 1.25 billion acres, which contained

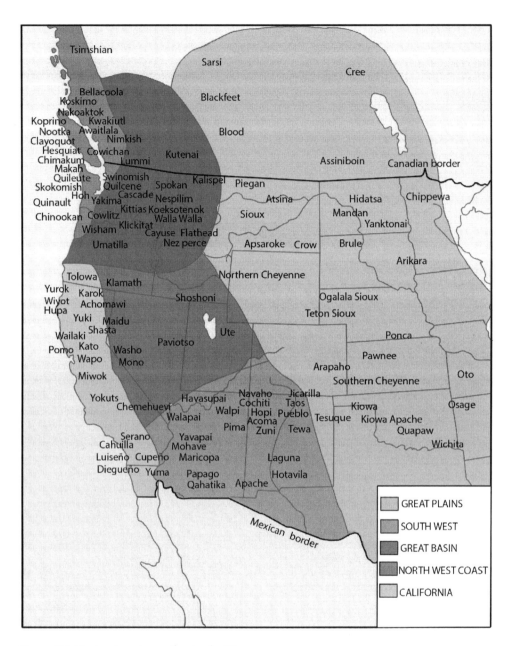

Figure 8.1 Native American tribes in the West.

distinctive sub-regions including: the Great Plains immediately west of the frontier line; the Rocky Mountains, the Sierra Nevada mountains, and California (which became a state as early as 1850) towards the far west; the Great Basin, a mixture of desert and high grassy plateaux; and finally the sweltering, arid wilderness of the southwest (see Fig. 8.1). Each area posed different but challenging problems for settlers. Western mountain ranges were more than double the altitude of the highest point east of the Mississippi. Rainfall was only about half as much on average in comparison with eastern states. The West was depicted as the Great American Desert on maps in the mid-nineteenth century, an inhospitable wasteland. In fact, it was home to a diverse array of indigenous peoples who would be devastated by expansion in the post-war period.

Perhaps 75,000 Indians lived on the Great Plains, a vast expanse of grassland and shrub. Tribal life revolved around hunting herds of bison that provided food, shelter, and clothing. But bison were not just an economic asset to Indians, but the basis of spiritual inspiration as well in tribal folklore and foundational myths. Indians on the high western plains, distinct from those in the Missouri Valley, developed a highly mobile, warlike lifestyle revolutionised by the horse and the gun. Women played a central role in tribal life, cultivating corn, making clothes, and taking charge of family politics. The concept of private property and landownership was unfamiliar within tribal culture, as was the notion of an internal hierarchy with one designated leader.

American goods and ideas changed traditional ways, however, exemplified by the transition from bow and arrow to rifle. As Plains tribes encountered whites more frequently, Indian "leaders" emerged to speak on behalf of others, although they never did so absolutely, something which whites failed to understand. Tribal power was decentralised and rested with different constituent bands or clans. The Sioux, Cheyenne, Yankton, and Crow on the northern plains, and the Arapahoe, Kiowa, (southern) Cheyenne, and Comanche to the south, were fearsome, proud warriors with a long history of rivalries. They were highly experienced in defending their hunting grounds and waging war as vast networks of trade and subjugation were built on the plains that extended into the borderlands of Canada and Mexico. Along the Missouri River in the Dakotas, the Mandan and Pawnee cultivated corn and other crops in sedentary communities in contrast to nomadic cultures.

The Southwest was dry, hot, and desolate. The Navajo, Apache, and Ute were the most powerful tribes in the region and like their counterparts on the Plains lived a nomadic lifestyle. The Hopi, Anasazi, and other Pueblo Indians lived in small, settled communities and inhabited dwellings made of stone or adobe. They built ingenious irrigation systems that were essential for crop farming. Present-day northern New Mexico was once the site of a powerful confederation of 12 villages, centred around Chaco Canyon, with connections to satellite communities 65 miles away. A series of severe droughts, a perennial problem, dispersed the community into scattered groups by the thirteenth century. Like all western tribes, Pueblo Indians enjoyed a rich spiritual life connected to the environment. The histories and cultures of indigenous peoples in the West are varied and defy generalisation and numbers are also elusive – perhaps 300,000 in total by the mid-nineteenth century including California.

What historian Gregory H. Nobles calls "an epidemic of gold fever" underpinned US incursion westward. A combination of quick riches, manifest destiny, and adventure proved intoxicating. Some 350,000 Americans made the arduous overland journey to California and Oregon between 1840 and 1870. They travelled in wagon trains along the California, Oregon, and Santa Fe trails that crisscrossed the hazardous topography. It took at least three weeks to make the journey and often much longer. For a short period of 19 months from April 1860, they were joined by the famous Pony Express riders who provided swift mail delivery until the invention of the telegraph.

The earliest white settlers in the far West built the Church of Jesus Christ of Latter-day Saints, having been hounded out of Illinois in 1844. Under the leadership of Brigham Young, the Mormons established a settlement in the Salt Lake valley, Utah, in July 1847. By 1860, they numbered around 40,000.

The scale of movement through Indian tribal lands forced a federal response. In 1848, Indian Commissioner William Medill suggested the creation of two huge Indian colonies on the southern and northern plains. Luke Lea, Medill's successor, advocated a policy of concentration. "There should be assigned to each tribe, for a permanent home, a country adapted to agriculture, of limited extent and well-defined boundaries" until "general improvement" was achieved. The Indian Appropriation Act (1851) provided $100,000 to fund this policy of concentration. Later that year at Fort Laramie, the Arapahos, Arikaras, Assiniboines, Cheyennes, Crows, Hidatsas, Mandans, and Lakota Sioux signed treaties with the federal government. In 1853, at Fort Atkinson, the Comanches, Kiowas, and Kiowa Apaches signed. The treaties delineated tribal territory (in perpetuity), guaranteed safe passage for settlers, and provided annuities of $50,000 a year to tribes in compensation for the destruction of bison and grassland and loss of precious water supplies. Fifty treaties were signed with western tribes by 1856 that covered approximately 174 million acres of western land.

The Wild West

Relations between migrants, soldiers, and Indians were relatively cordial in the mid-nineteenth century and it is easy to exaggerate the threat of Indian attack which has been sensationalised in cowboy movies. The reality was that harsh weather, incompetence, and disease (cholera in particular) accounted for the majority of white fatalities. Historian John D. Unruh estimates that Indians were responsible for just 400 deaths on the trails between 1840 and 1860. Relations deteriorated following gold and silver strikes that brought prospectors to uncharted areas. Gold and silver "rushes" were a regular occurrence in the second half of the nineteenth century. Prospectors, predominantly men who travelled from around the world, rushed to the epicentre, fearful not to miss their opportunity. In time, they faced competition from corporate operations that sought to monopolise fresh strikes. Virginia City, built on top of the US's richest silver deposit – the 1859 Comstock Lode in Nevada – was an archetypal boom and bust town. Its population shot up from 4,000 in 1862 to 25,000 in 1874. At its peak, there were 110 saloons, several opium dens, and 20 music halls. By 1930, just 500 inhabitants remained.

Samuel Clemens took the pseudonym Mark Twain as a young newspaper reporter in Virginia City and provided a vivid description of the rowdy, lawless frontier town in *Roughing It* (1872). As Twain emphasised, the life of the prospector was arduous, not least because of the difficult process of extraction and refinement. Approximately 15 million pounds of poisonous mercury was needed to process gold and silver from the Comstock Lode which resulted in substantial mercury contamination. In the post-war era, ramshackle towns sprang up to service rail construction crews and trappers, miners, and buffalo hunters as encroachment on Indian land became an invasion. Some communities closed as soon as the railroad moved on. Others, by railheads or close to natural resources, were long-lasting. These hotbeds of drinking, gambling, prostitution, and violence created the enduring mythology of the "Wild West."

The heyday of the cowboy came in the 20 years after the Civil War. More than five million cattle were driven northward annually from Texas bound for St Louis, Kansas City, and Chicago. Cattle drivers took huge herds of longhorns from Texas to

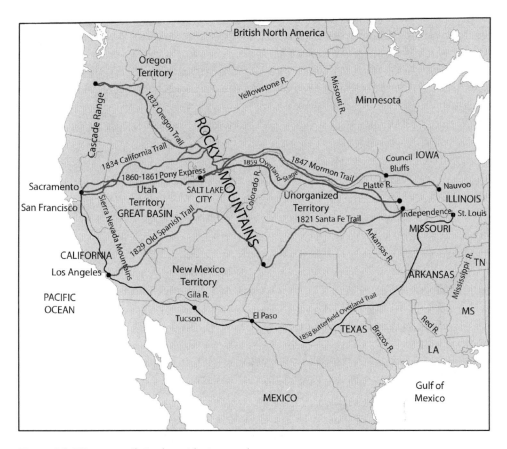

Figure 8.2 Western trails in the mid-nineteenth century.

markets in Dodge City and Abilene (both in Kansas). Cowboys, of whom perhaps one in four was African American, were romanticised as men of integrity and self-reliance. Dodge City was the iconic cowboy town. Established in 1872, it catered to soldiers from nearby Fort Dodge, crews of the Santa Fe Railroad, and was a centre of trade in buffalo hides. Residents included an illustrious list of lawmen and gunfighters between 1875 and 1885 that included Doc Holliday, Clay Allison, the Thompson brothers, and Wyatt Earp. Dodge City stood then and now as an enduring symbol, populated by confidence men, whiskey peddlers, card sharks, horse thieves, saloon proprietors, and unruly women. It was never as wild as presented in contemporary dime novels although violence was substantial and it took years for the rule of law to be established.

The West and American history

Historian Frederick Jackson Turner's "The Significance of the Frontier in American History" (1893) presented the frontier as the incubator of American character. Traits of resilience, resourcefulness, adaptability, and manliness were forged on the frontier. Turner's thesis revolutionised American historiography and was later reinvigorated by Henry Nash Smith's *Virgin Land* (1950) in a foundational American Studies text. This romanticised concept underpinned notions of American exceptionalism, even though US territorial expansion was similar to "settler colonialism" in South Africa, Australia, and elsewhere. The New Western Historians, including Patricia Nelson Limerick, Richard White, Donald Worster, and William Cronon, challenged Turner's thesis in the 1980s. They portrayed the West as a diverse multicultural region and rejected its conceptualisation as a frontier. Turner's positive spin of taming the wilderness was replaced with a story of exploitation and environmental destruction, sponsored by the federal government, that devastated Native American societies.

The Civil War served to accelerate westward expansion. The Republican Party took advantage of the absence of southern opposition in Congress to pass two landmark pieces of legislation. The Homestead Act (1862) granted 160 acres to individuals who promised to cultivate the land for five years for a $10 fee. The Pacific Railroad Act of 1862, that was refined and extended in 1863, 1864, 1865, and 1866, implemented rail construction from the Atlantic to the Pacific. New territories were organised in Colorado, Nevada and Dakota (1861), Idaho and Arizona (1863), and Montana (1864). Following the acquisition of territorial status, rapid settlement was championed by "rings" of businessmen, lawyers, and politicians – in conjunction with railroads, ranchers, and mining companies – whose primary motivation was profit. Western colonisation was a Republican Party policy but increasingly became the nation's most important priority. Antebellum political opposition caused by the problem of slavery no longer impeded the congressional drive towards incorporation of the West.

The Colorado Territory ring was responsible for the infamous slaughter of Native Americans in 1864, one of the worst atrocities of the Civil War. Relations in Colorado were tense after gold was found in the Rocky Mountains in the late 1850s. The Cheyenne and Arapahoe conceded substantial territory in the Treaty of Fort Wise (1861) that enabled safe passage to the gold fields. However, chiefs later claimed they had not intended to give up so much land, while Indian bands refused to recognise the treaty and confrontations escalated in 1863 and 1864. Colorado Governor John Evans had an eye on gaining a US Senate seat and was also anxious that the Union Pacific Railroad (with which he had close connections) not be deterred from coming through his territory. Evans broke promises made during peace negotiations to pursue a more hostile policy. Colonel John Chivington led 700 militiamen southeast of Denver at Sand Creek where 750 Cheyenne and Arapaho were peacefully assembled in their winter camp. An unprovoked, ruthless attack began at dawn on 29 November 1864. The total number killed is disputed but was perhaps as many as 230. What is not in doubt is that at least half of the victims were women and children. The flimsy pretext was that the Indians were hostile towards the Union, even though Cheyenne Chief Black Kettle flew the Stars and Stripes on his tepee. Historian Mardell Plainfeather appropriately describes Sand Creek as "the saddest, most devastating event in the history of white and Indian clashes."

The final resolution of the Indian question

The Indian question was as contentious and divisive in the post-war era as Reconstruction. For many years scholars treated these two issues separately but more recently the parallels between western conquest and Reconstruction – such as federal intervention, racial conflict, and indiscriminate violence – have been recognised. Sand Creek, and many other episodes like it, were widely condemned and Bureau of Indian Affairs officials were charged with incompetency. Reformers insisted they wished to act with respect, inspired by evangelical fervour and a renewed sense of moral purpose following restoration of the Union. Even so, public opinion cared little for the fate of indigenous peoples but held great stock in the nation's destiny to rule the continent. A committee headed by Senator James R. Doolittle was formed in March 1865 to investigate the situation. Its 1867 *Report on the Condition of the Indian Tribes* blamed "the aggression of lawless whites" for prior violence, expressed regret over atrocities, but also emphasised the extent of Indian decline. Without suitable measures, it was claimed, tribes faced extinction. Relocation to reservations, by agreement if possible but force if necessary, was recommended.

In October 1867, the Indian Peace Commission (established 20 June 1867) signed treaties with tribes from the southern Plains. The Treaty of Medicine Lodge was in fact three separate agreements: with the Kiowa and Comanche; with the Kiowa-Apache; and with the Arapaho and Cheyenne. The Kiowa, Kiowa-Apache, and Comanche gave up traditional hunting grounds for considerably less land in the southwest corner of the Indian Territory. The Cheyenne and Arapaho exchanged their territory for relocation south of the Kansas state line. To secure the agreement of the Dog Soldiers – a fierce band of Cheyenne warriors – the continued hunting of bison north of the Arkansas River was conceded. Whether Indians fully accepted these terms is debatable and the required ratification by three-quarters of tribal members was never secured. Kiowa chief Satanta signed with hesitation: "I love the land and the buffalo and I will not part with any." He did not understand why federal negotiators insisted that the government build schools and homes on reservations and train Indians to be farmers rather than hunters. "I love to roam over the wide prairie, and when I do, I feel free and happy, but when we settle down we grow pale and die."

Red Cloud's War raged on the northern plains as the Treaty of Medicine Lodge was negotiated. The discovery of gold in Montana in 1862 prompted a mob of prospectors to invade hunting grounds. Between 1866 and 1868 bands of Lakota Sioux, (northern) Cheyenne, and Arapaho fought with the invaders. The US Army protected whites and, in contravention of prior agreements, began to construct new forts along the Bozeman Trail from Nebraska's Platte River to the goldfields. Indians laid siege to the forts. In December 1866, 79 soldiers led by Captain William J. Letterman were killed and mutilated on the Powder River.

This was the context in which the Indian Peace Commission opened negotiations with northern plains tribes in Wyoming in 1868. The subsequent Treaty of Fort Laramie (1868) conceded much to the Indians: the US Army evacuated forts along the Bozeman Trail and the "Great Sioux Reservation" was established in South and North Dakota that preserved traditional hunting grounds. "We want to live as we have been raised, hunting the animals of the prairie," insisted Crow chief Blackfoot. "Do not speak of shutting us up on reservations and making us cultivate the land." Red Cloud did not sign the agreement until the forts had been abandoned. He had shown that resistance could be effective but it proved only a temporary respite.

President Ulysses S. Grant's Peace Policy provided the final resolution of the long-standing problem of US-indigenous relations. Grant, who assumed office in 1869, lamented how "the management of the original inhabitants of this continent – the Indians – has been a subject of embarrassment and expense." He reformed the Indian Bureau and removed corrupt agents. He proposed a system of educational and agricultural training, carried out by missionaries (the majority female) to transform Indians into Christian citizens. Tribal annuities were abolished, because they encouraged dependence Grant argued. An equitable solution was sought, but from a white perspective only. Significantly, the Indian Appropriations Act (1871) ended federal recognition of tribes as separate entities but considered them "wards of the nation." Even though previous treaties had often not been worth the paper on which they were written, they had provided some legal protection of Native American territory, so this was a major departure. Since independence, the federal government had recognised tribal land rights but it now insisted reservations were the only solution.

Figure 8.3 General William T. Sherman in negotiations with Indian chiefs at Fort Laramie, Wyoming (c.1868).

Source: Courtesy of the US National Archives and Records Administration

The Peace Policy divided opinion at the time and subsequently. The president was under enormous pressure. Americans craved western land and most did not care about the fate of Indian tribes. Grant resisted pressure to transfer Indian policy from the Department of the Interior to the US Army that might have brought an even more belligerent approach. In April 1869, he established a new Board of Indian Commissioners composed of "men eminent for their intelligence and philanthropy, to serve without pecuniary compensation." Ely S. Parker, Grant's aide during the Civil War and a Seneca Indian, was made the first native Commissioner of Indian Affairs. Indians should be "located, where practicable upon reservations; assisted in agricultural pursuits and the arts of civilized life," Parker asserted. Should that offer be rejected, however, they were "subject wholly to the control and supervision of military authorities."

Parker's statement exposed the fundamental tension between negotiation and force in the federal position. A humanitarian policy was proposed but unilateral relocation was mandated. Grant's view of the "Indian problem" was as culturally one-sided as previous policies. As the Cherokee found in the 1830s, no matter how "white"

Figure 8.4 John Gast's painting *American Progress* (1872) vividly captured American notions of manifest destiny and the movement west. Columbia represents the US republic, dressed in a Roman toga, and is flanked by white settlers, railways, and the telegraph. Native Americans and bison retreat from the relentless American expansion that illuminates the "darkened" West.

Source: Courtesy of Granger Historical Picture Archive/Alamy

they became, Indians remained racial others. There could be no compromise. Grant insisted natives must accept American ways – stable households, horticulture, Christianity, democratic politics. Some critics of the policy recognised how destructive it might be. Former abolitionist Wendell Phillips was ridiculed for his suggestion that the US should "abandon the railroad and give the Great Plains back to the Indians" but it was probably the only way to protect native lifestyles. Most problematically, government officials and reservation missionaries who professed their deep concern for Native American welfare were convinced that "Americanising" the Indian was the ultimate solution. This stance constituted a US variant of the western world's subjugation of indigenous populations, in the name of civilisation, that characterised the age of colonialism.

The subjugation of the Plains Indians

Millions of acres of western land was further promised by the federal government in the General Mining Act (1872), the Timber Culture Act (1873), and the Desert Lands Act (1877). A ruthless military campaign confronted tribes that refused to sign treaties and Indian bands who remained beyond the reservation. Generals Philip H. Sheridan and William T. Sherman were well trained in total war and the Civil War had taught that violence was acceptable to achieve desirable outcomes. They had no hesitation in pursuing so-called "progress" and eliminating "barbarism." Sherman advocated "vindictive earnestness against the Sioux, even to their extermination . . . the soldiers cannot pause to distinguish between male and female" in an 1867 letter to Grant. Sheridan is remembered for the aphorism "the only good Indian is a dead Indian." This cold statement of white supremacy was a logical corollary of manifest destiny. Sheridan followed orders and did not sentimentalise his task: "We took away their country and their means of support, broke up their mode of living, their habits of life, introduced disease and decay among them, and it was for this and against this that they made war. Could anyone expect less?"

Bands of warriors fought against superior numbers, guns, and supplies. Sitting Bull and Crazy Horse defeated the Seventh Cavalry at the Battle of Little Big Horn on 25 June 1876. George Armstrong Custer's foolish attack on a huge Lakota Sioux encampment, with 225 soldiers killed, came in the wake of gold strikes in the sacred Black Hills in 1874. A ruthless military backlash punished those involved in the attack. Four months after Crazy Horse surrendered with his band of Oglala Sioux, either a soldier's bayonet or an Indian knife took his life on 6 May 1877 in a guardhouse scuffle. Sitting Bull and his starving followers eventually surrendered at Fort Buford in the Dakota Territory on 20 July 1881. Continued resistance was seemingly futile and in 1885, Sitting Bull joined Buffalo Bill's travelling dramatisation of the mythical Wild West (as did Apache chief Geronimo), an internationally popular show in the late nineteenth century.

Nonetheless, Chief Joseph, Gall, Geronimo, Cochise, and others, clung precariously to traditional ways in the 1870s and 1880s. The Modoc War in California, the Red River War in Texas, and the Nez Perce conflict in Oregon were the most well-known of numerous confrontations with American forces. They were not wars of resistance, because in most cases treaties had been signed, but wars of rebellion as Indian bands refused to be confined to reservations. The US Army, helped by Indian trackers, pursued intransigent groups, burnt hunting grounds and winter camps, and stole or

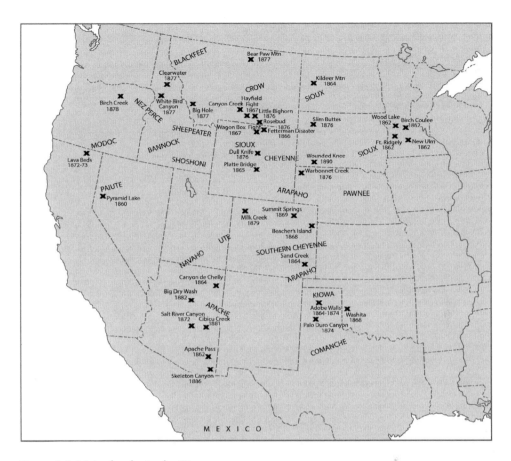

Figure 8.5 Major battles in the West.

destroyed Indian property. Geronimo led the last defiant group who were protected by the remoteness of the border lands in which they roamed. He surrendered at Skeleton Canyon (Arizona) on 4 September 1886. The destruction of the once huge herds of bison that numbered in the millions made surrender virtually inevitable. A deliberate policy of slaughtering buffalo struck at the heart of the indigenous economy and devastated the nomadic lifestyle. Deadly bacteria transmitted by close contact between whites and Indians spread diseases such as smallpox and measles that also weakened native resistance. White pollution, consumption of water supplies, and deforestation caused environmental chaos. These were all critical factors in the conquest of indigenous peoples in the West.

The Dawes Severalty Act (8 February 1887) divided Indian reservations into 160-acre family allotments and established a cultural programme of de-tribalisation. It assumed the only way to "civilize" the Native American was to eradicate tribal identities. As Indian Commissioner Thomas J. Morgan underlined in 1889, traditional ways "should be broken up, socialism destroyed and the family and autonomy of the individual substituted." A House Indian Committee minority report of 1880 had earlier admitted that the true purpose of the allotment policy was to "get at the Indian lands and open them up to settlement." To force Indians to abandon their culture and live in family units, the report argued, "in the name of greed, it would be bad enough; but to do it in the name of humanity and under the cloak of an ardent desire to promote the Indian's welfare by making him like ourselves, whether he will or not, is infinitely worse." This objection did not prevent passage of the Dawes Act but accurately summed up the callousness of de-tribalisation policy.

The symbolic end of Indian resistance came at Wounded Knee in South Dakota. Reservation authorities were alarmed by the cult of the Ghost Dance, a religious revival that envisioned whites gone and the return of dead Indians and buffalo. Tensions escalated when Sitting Bull was killed 15 December 1890 by reservation police sent to arrest him on the false grounds that he planned an uprising. Two weeks later, the US cavalry intercepted around 350 Lakota Sioux. Having camped overnight at Wounded Knee Creek, a shot was fired when soldiers attempted to disarm Indians on the morning of 29 December 1890. A horrific massacre ensued, killing between 150 and 300 Native Americans. The history of US-Indian relations had been punctuated by many shameful episodes, suffering that was described in detail in New England author and activist Helen Hunt Jackson's scathing *A Century of Dishonor* (1881), but the late nineteenth century was surely the nadir as men, women, and children were herded on to reservations. The Indian population was not fully included in the decennial census counts until 1890, and there were differences in the counting of "full" and "mixed-bloods," but numbers dropped to a low point of 237,196 in 1900.

Railroads and industrial growth

"The old nations of the earth creep on at a snail's pace," wrote the powerful steel magnate Andrew Carnegie, "while the republic thunders past with the rush of the express." This was the opening line to *Triumphant Democracy* (1886) in which Carnegie argued the US had "reached the foremost rank among nations, and is destined soon to out-distance all others." It was not an exaggeration. Britain's gross national product was nearly three times greater than the 13 American colonies in the 1770s. By 1840, it fell to one and a half times greater than the US. On the eve of World War I, Britain's GDP was not even half that of the United States (41 per cent). The industrial growth of the US in the last third of the century was staggering. The American economy was in deficit ($354 million of total imports compared to $316 million of total exports) in 1860. By 1897, a huge surplus was recorded as exports tripled to $1.03 billion that far exceeded the $765 million in imports. The US share of world trade increased from 6 per cent in 1868 to 11 per cent by the eve of World War I. This economic performance not only surpassed Britain, but France and Germany as well, as the American economy grew tenfold between 1870 and 1921.

Railroads led the way during the last third of the nineteenth century. They reduced the time, danger, and expense of intercontinental travel (the average cost of travel from east to west fell from approximately $1,000 to $150) and stimulated economic growth. The 1862 Pacific Railway Act provided generous terms for the Central Pacific Railroad and Union Pacific Railroad to push eastward from Sacramento California and westward from Omaha Nebraska across the trans-Mississippi West (although the transcontinental lines did not literally span the whole continent). The Central Pacific, led by Leland Stanford, the Crocker brothers, and Collis P. Huntington, was a

Californian company while the Union Pacific was the first corporation formed by the federal government since the Bank of the United States in 1816. Each had the incentive of as much as $48,000 in government bonds and 6,400 acres of land (ten square miles) in return for each mile of track they built. Indian land titles were extinguished, 400 metres right of way was granted (later reduced to 200 metres), and further land was set aside for depots, sidings, and other buildings. In 1864, even more generous terms were offered by the federal government: it doubled land per track mile to 12,800 acres, granted mineral rights on company land, and allowed railroads to sell their own bonds.

Around 15,000 Chinese workers were recruited to construct the transcontinental railroads. Some had previously worked on rail construction projects, others came directly from China. The Central Pacific Railroad was particularly keen to use Chinese workers who they considered dependable and less likely to strike (this turned out not to be the case) and could be paid less than Irish labourers. The work was arduous and dangerous, particularly the months spent blasting through the Sierra Nevada Mountains to create tunnels such as the 1,659-foot long Summit Tunnel. Overcoming these considerable challenges, as well as Native American attack, the transcontinental line was completed on 10 May 1869. At Promontory Point in Utah, officials from both rail companies attended a ceremony where a symbolic Golden Spike was driven into the ground. This momentous occasion was widely reported domestically and internationally. It made a lasting impression in the national consciousness despite the fact that Stanford (president of the Central Pacific) missed the golden spike with his first swing of the hammer.

Railroads facilitated colonisation of the West long before western territories became states. Railroad companies received 171 million acres of land grants to build 19,000 miles of track between 1850 and 1871. They could then sell this public land for profit. Companies also received financial incentives as well, amounting to tens of millions of dollars, usually in the form of government bonds. The only payment required for this enormous investment was reduced rates for federal freight. Track in the US increased from 35,000 miles in 1865 to 93,000 miles by 1880. In the 1880s, 70,000 miles of track were laid down. The 1893 panic slowed the frantic pace of growth but by then five transcontinental lines had been built. They were supplemented by new local and regional lines along existing routes, the majority built east of the Mississippi. In the South, railway lines destroyed during the war were rebuilt. By 1890, 164,000 miles of rail infrastructure across the continental United States formed the world's largest system.

Four hundred thousand men worked on the railroads in 1880, 2.5 per cent of the nation's total workforce The Pennsylvania Railroad alone covered more than 6,000 miles – only Britain and France possessed greater total track. Finance was the key. This scale and pace of construction was possible because the federal government subsidised four of the five transcontinental railroads. Unlike canals and turnpikes, financed in conjunction with state and municipal governments, transcontinental railroads were major federal undertakings as the government flexed its power in the West. Without this financial assistance, it is doubtful that so much would have been built so quickly and not all of the construction was needed. Companies built railway lines to claim government subsidies, and to outdo their rivals, but sometimes extended into remote areas with little prospect of commercial development. Private investment, from Americans and overseas (especially Great Britain), was also important and underpinned the growing company securities market in New York City. The 1873 crash began when panicked investors dumped their recklessly inflated railroad portfolios that were valued at far more than they were worth.

The advantage of branch lines in distance places was that they reached the abundant natural resources of the North American continent. Minnesota, Idaho, Colorado, Montana, New Mexico, and Arizona added substantially to existing riches that included coal in Pennsylvania and West Virginia, iron ore from the upper reaches of the Great Lakes, and oil from Texas and the Gulf Coast. The West provided "an extraordinary storehouse," as historian Elliott West puts it, vital to an industrial economy. Western timber was the basic raw material of construction but precious metals – silver from Nevada and gold from California, Colorado, and Alaska – proved even more valuable. Gold mined from the Black Hills in the 1870s yielded approximately 10 per cent of the world's supply over the next century. Lead, manganese, and copper from the West was mined in vast quantities. Copper served a variety of purposes in an industrial economy and Arizona and Montana contained some of the world's richest deposits. Alaska was purchased by the US from Russia on 18 October 1867 for $7.2 million to provide access to the far north and end the interests of a rival in the region. For decades, this was known as "Seward's Folly" – an extravagant purchase by Secretary of State William Seward. Critics fell silent when gold was discovered in the Yukon in 1896 and Alaska became the gateway to the Klondike gold fields. These precious minerals provided the raw materials of American economic success.

The enormous expenditure of railroads had substantial knock-on effects in other sectors of the economy. Rail companies devoured timber, iron, steel, and coal. Bridge construction was boosted and the 1057 foot suspension bridge across the Ohio River at Cincinnati (1867), as well as bridges over the Missouri River at Kansas City (1869), Omaha (1871), and Bismarck (1882), were major feats of engineering. Technological

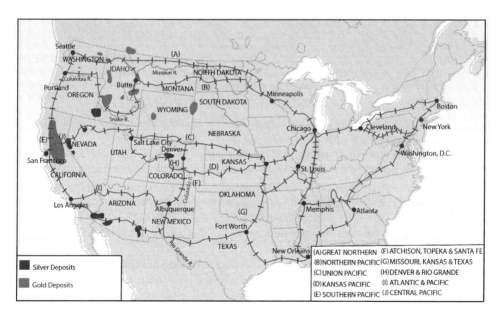

Figure 8.6 Transcontinental railroads and natural resources in the American West.

breakthroughs such as the implementation of air brakes (patented in 1869) and standard gauge track size of 4 feet 8½ inches (by the mid-1880s) improved safety, enabled trains to carry greater loads, and increased average speeds. Railroad companies developed complicated business structures – that included finance, accounts, management, operations, construction, and repairs. It was also the railroads that solved the problem of temporal variations across the US even though standard time was not officially sanctioned by Congress until 1918. On 18 November 1883, the American Railway Association introduced four separate time zones, with one hour difference in-between, that replaced a myriad of different local practices. A uniform time-keeping system was essential not only to the smooth running of rail timetables but to the successful functioning of an economy and was quickly accepted by the public.

The robber barons

The term "robber baron" was first used in 1859 by the *New York Times* to describe Cornelius Vanderbilt, the shipping and railroad magnate. Rail tycoons returned spectacular profits by dubious means. The Associates of the Central Pacific turned an investment of around $275,000 in 1862 into a corporation valued at more than $135 million by 1873. Historian Richard White argues that railways were not successful corporations, however, because they relied on borrowed money which was inherently unstable. The example of Jay Cooke provides a case in point. Having made a fortune selling Union bonds during the Civil War, Cooke's bank bought a controlling interest in the Northern Pacific Railroad in 1870. When investors panicked over a new route through Indian land in the Yellowstone River Valley in eastern Montana, the company was bankrupted. This was an extreme case, but railroad debt exceeded assets and operating profits. Sham companies, the most famous of which was Crédit Mobilier, offloaded railroad stocks far in excess of their worth and bribed politicians to keep quiet. Railroad executives ensured newspapers provided favourable coverage and published false accounts that demonstrated economic robustness.

Crédit Mobilier of America

Crédit Mobilier of America was a bogus construction company formed by the Union Pacific Railroad in 1864. Union Pacific exchanged contracts with Crédit Mobilier for construction work as if it were an independent company, but the price agreed far exceeded actual costs and the difference was pocketed by officials. Congressman Oakes Ames became president of Crédit Mobilier in 1867 and sold shares to members of Congress at discount, perhaps to ward off suspicion of financial impropriety. The *New York Sun* uncovered the story in 1872. The subsequent congressional investigation implicated outgoing Vice President Schuyler Colfax, incoming Vice President Henry Wilson and future President James A. Garfield, among others, in a scandal that demonstrated how far Gilded Age corruption extended.

Scottish-born immigrant Andrew Carnegie was the pre-eminent robber baron. Carnegie's huge multinational business dominated the steel industry. He took advantage of contacts in the Pennsylvania Railroad and made shrewd appointments in hard-nosed businessman Henry Clay Frick, chairman of Carnegie Steel, and Charles M. Schwab, company president by 1897, who smoothed fractious workforce relations. The company replaced skilled labour with machinery, driving costs down, and cutting wages. Carnegie exploited the latest technological breakthroughs such as the Bessemer and open-hearth processes that enabled production of greater quantities and better quality steel. He had the vision and drive to control all stages of the productive process, something known as vertical integration. As well as factories and heavy machinery, Carnegie Steel owned coalfields, iron mines, coke ovens, limestone deposits, and ships and railroads to transport raw materials. It took control from the moment iron ore was mined to the point it reached customers. Carnegie sold his company in 1901 for $400 million (worth around $10 billion today).

Carnegie Steel, and Standard Oil, Eastman Kodak, Singer Sewing Machine, McCormick Harvester, American Tobacco, the Du Pont chemical firm, and many others, were at the forefront of the structural evolution of business in the Gilded Age. Their size and capacity provided economies of scale and other efficiencies. Corporations were complicated structures, spread across multiple sites in the United States and abroad, with huge workforces. Oversight shifted from individual entrepreneurs to boards of directors who appointed managers to oversee day-to-day activity. As companies grew ever larger, different types of activity required functional specificity. Legal, finance, purchasing, sales, and personnel departments were entirely separate from the production process. Modern businesses sent thousands of communications that created huge paper trails and required secretaries, clerks, and typists. In 1870, there were approximately 11,000 women in secretarial and sales work but two million by 1920. A complicated division of labour advanced the production process, overseen by supervisors, foremen, and plant managers trained in the latest principles of scientific management.

Businesses took steps to eliminate risk and competition. The invention of the corporation as a legal entity facilitated the accumulation of enormous amounts of capital at limited risk to shareholders. Boards of directors were relieved of personal legal and financial obligations as global investors provided corporations with massive investment. Oil tycoon John D. Rockefeller organised the first business trust. Rockefeller's early career followed in Carnegie's footsteps as he signed freight deals to price out rivals and work towards vertical integration from the pipeline to the pump. However, Rockefeller realised it made better sense to *minimise* competition by seeking agreements with rivals. Standard Oil Company of Ohio, established in 1882, was the world's first trust as 77 different oil companies transferred their stock, ownership, and control to nine trustees (an economic arrangement known as horizontal integration). This huge oil conglomeration effectively eliminated competition by controlling 90 per cent of the market. It enjoyed an unrivalled position to regulate costs, manage its workforce and dictate terms to suppliers and customers. In 1913, Rockefeller's total wealth was nearly $1 billion, or 2 per cent of the US's gross national product. In comparative terms, he was three times as wealthy as Bill Gates today.

Life and labour in the Gilded Age

The final ingredient of American economic growth in the late nineteenth century was an abundant supply of labour. Sixty per cent of the US workforce was employed in agriculture in 1860 but 50 years later it was just 30 per cent, as manufacturing boomed. Twelve million immigrants arrived in the US between 1870 and 1900. They joined a multi-ethnic urban population that experienced new forms of transportation, construction, mass produced consumer goods, advertising campaigns, and a bewildering variety of new inventions. Immigrants and native-born Americans alike confronted a rapidly changing labour market. Small firms and artisans struggled on in the age of big business but the trend was towards large-scale mechanised mass production in factories. By the 1890s, consumer goods such as shoes, hats, clothes, and boots – which were not monopolised by big business – were dwarfed in value by the products of heavy industry – rubber, petroleum, iron and steel, chemicals, and heavy machinery – dominated by corporations.

As the gap between skilled and unskilled work became much larger, white collar managerial work built on specialist knowledge became increasingly important. The middle class flourished not because they owned property or established businesses but because of the knowledge and services they provided, particularly if they benefitted from a university education. Conditions for salaried professionals were completely different from blue collar manual labour as holidays, wage increases, and promotions became integral to career expectations. The divide between urban and rural America also widened, although it is important not to underestimate the extent of change in the countryside. A potato farmer in Idaho could transport his goods anywhere in the country and get the latest consumer product from Sears Roebuck delivered to his door. Everywhere, the pace of change was rapid. Inventions of many different kinds were transformative. Alexander Graham Bell made the first phone call in 1876 and by 1900 some 800,000 telephones were fitted in American homes. *The Adventures of Tom Sawyer* (1876) was the first novel written on a typewriter. Perhaps the most important invention of all time was the light bulb, patented in November 1879 by Thomas Edison, as electric lighting replaced gas lights and candles. The key was mass production – one million lightbulbs were being manufactured per year by 1890 – widespread availability, and a quick turnaround from factory to consumer.

Trade unions attempted to protect the interests of working people but confronted even more powerful employers than before the Civil War. The earliest American unions represented skilled workers predominantly, organised by profession. A more holistic approach was taken by the Knights of Labor, formed in Philadelphia in 1869, that crossed lines of gender, ethnicity, skill, and race (although the Knights supported the Chinese Exclusion Act of 1882). Membership grew to 700,000 (approximately 10 per cent female) by 1886 under the leadership of Grandmaster Workman Terence P. Powderly. This was just a fraction of the total workforce, however, and Powderly's non-confrontational stance – he opposed strikes in favour of arbitration – was largely ineffective. A rally in Chicago's Haymarket Square on 4 May 1886 turned into a bloody riot after a bomb was thrown at police and blame was unfairly laid on the Knights. Eight people died, including seven policemen, and hundreds more were injured. Eight anarchists were subsequently convicted of murder, despite a lack of evidence, and a renewed nationwide crackdown on labour activism followed.

Chinese Exclusion Act of 1882

The Chinese Exclusion Act prevented Chinese skilled and unskilled workers from coming to the US and was the first federal legislation to specifically target an ethnic group. The ban was initially for a period of ten years but was renewed subsequently in 1892 and made permanent in 1902. The act also denied the right of Chinese people to become American citizens. It was signed by President Chester A. Arthur on 6 May 1882 and its origins lay in friction between white settlers and Chinese labourers on the West Coast. Proponents claimed to protect white racial "purity" and that the Chinese were unassimilable. The act heralded a major change in immigration policy and there were subsequent calls for restrictions on other "undesirable" or "alien" ethnic groups.

The Federation of Trades and Labor Unions (later the American Federation of Labor) became the largest union following the demise of the Knights of Labor. Founded in 1881 and led by cigar maker Samuel Gompers, the AFL modelled itself on the British Trades Union Congress. However, Gompers took an even more conservative position than Powderly that favoured skilled workers and excluded African Americans, immigrants, and women. Gompers wanted "to work out our problems in the spirit of true Americanism, a spirit that embodies our broadest and our highest ideals." The AFL brought together more than a hundred separate craft unions – carpenters, printers, brick makers, and so forth – but each retained their individual autonomy which diluted the strength of the movement as a whole. The AFL worked within the system rather than confront the inequities of capitalism and sought the right to bargain collectively over wages, benefits, hours, and working conditions.

Violent strikes were common during the Gilded Age, indeed no period of American history experienced greater turmoil between workers and employers. The business cycle in the late nineteenth century was particularly severe: an 1873–1877 downturn was followed by a partial recovery in the late 1870s. A further depression 1882–85 caused more misery, made worse during a severe recession 1893–97. Prices consistently declined: making the 1873 price index 100, by 1890 it had fallen to 71. Employers responded by cutting costs and wages. There were around 500 strikes a year in the early 1880s that had increased to 1500 by 1886. It was not only the frequency of strikes but the scale. The great railroad strike of 1877 began in West Virginia when the Baltimore and Ohio Railroad announced a pay cut. Protests spread to Baltimore, Pittsburgh, Chicago, and St Louis, and thousands of workers unconnected to the railroad joined the strike. The railway system was paralysed for months. The size and ferocity of the disturbances – more than 100,000 workers participated, 100 were killed, and 1,000 jailed – created a sense of panic. *Harper's Weekly* reported that the US was "fighting for its own existence just as truly as in suppressing the great rebellion." Employers reacted with brutal force, backed by Governors across ten states who mobilised 60,000 state militia.

The most savage confrontation took place at Andrew Carnegie's steel plant in Homestead, Pennsylvania, in 1892. Pitched battles were fought between Pinkerton Guards and strikers. (Formed in 1850 by a Scottish immigrant, the Pinkerton Nationwide Detective Agency was a private police force that was hired by industrialists to fight their battles). Eventually 8,000 state troops were required to protect the strikebreakers Carnegie hired to resume production. Two years later, federal government intervention broke the 1894 Pullman Palace Car Company strike that began after one-third of the workforce were fired and wages were cut by 30 per cent with no reduction in rent and food costs paid by employees in the company town of Pullman in south Chicago. The strike spread far and wide as 250,000 workers in 27 states refused to handle trains with Pullman carriages. Federal Attorney General Richard Olney, who served on several railroad boards, sought a legal injunction to crush what he described as "a reign of terror." President Grover Cleveland sent in the army against the wishes of the Illinois governor who was sympathetic to the strikers. This was a first use of a federal injunction to break a strike. Eugene V. Debs, president of the American Railway Union, was jailed for six months because he defied the injunction and became so disillusioned that he converted to socialism.

These portentous developments were not uncontested. Henry George in *Progress and Poverty* (1879) and Henry Demerest Lloyd in *Wealth and Commonwealth* (1894) attacked corporate business. State legislation attempted to regulate railroads, as did the federal 1887 Interstate Commerce Act which sought "reasonable" rail freight rates and outlawed preferential deals for customers. The 1890 Sherman Antitrust Act was designed to curb trusts such as Standard Oil. However, business found a way to get around regulations. The Sherman Antitrust Act was ambiguously worded and failed to define "trust" or "restraint of trade" precisely and consequently it was difficult to make a sound legal case against collusion. Moreover, Congress did not enforce legislation rigorously because politicians mostly supported big business.

In the mid-twentieth century, historian Richard Hofstadter criticised corrupt Democrat and Republican politicians who squabbled over "patronage, not principle" and "spoils, not issues" during the Gilded Age. This interpretation has been refined subsequently but unquestionably politics championed big business and politicians held substantial stocks and shares in companies or were on the payroll. Tariffs protected and promoted American industry as did the post-war return to the gold standard

Figure 8.7 The bosses of the Senate (1889). Corporate tycoons tower over the members of the most distinguished chamber in the US political system.

Source: Courtesy of Granger Historical Picture Archive/Alamy

(confirmed in the Coinage Act of 1873). Supreme Court decisions were conservative and strengthened the employer's hand, while the US tax structure was far less punitive towards the wealthy in comparison to other countries. Unregulated economic forces generated much concern before the Civil War but by the 1890s corporations were essentially unfettered and considered the engine of American economic power.

A new South?

"The New South" slogan captured the post-1877 southern drive for economic reform and national reconciliation. Henry Grady, editor of the *Atlanta Constitution*, was the foremost proponent although Francis Warrington Dawson (*Charleston News and Courier*), Henry Watterson (*Louisville Courier-Journal*), and Walter Hines Page (*Atlantic Monthly*) were also important boosters. Grady captured the nation's attention in New York City in 1886. He was the first southerner invited to the New England Society in Manhattan and his speech followed that of William Sherman who had overseen the burning of Atlanta during the Civil War. Grady made light of this however and insisted that divisions were forgotten and the Old South was a relic of the past. "There was a South of slavery and secession – that South is dead," Grady asserted. "There is now a South of union and freedom – that South, thank God, is living, breathing, growing every hour."

This rhetoric encouraged economic diversification and southern states offered tax incentives to businesses. Southern rail track doubled in the 1880s bringing rural communities within reach of commercial markets. Employers paid for the use of cheap prison labour, overwhelmingly African American, via the convict-lease system. Chattanooga and Knoxville, both in Tennessee, built furnaces, foundries, and machine shops. Birmingham (Alabama) exploited local iron ore, coal, and limestone deposits as the roar of blast furnaces was loud in the so-called Pittsburgh of the South. Iron ore production increased from 397,000 tonnes in 1880 to nearly two million tonnes by 1900. The turpentine, petroleum, sulphur, and lumber industries became bigger and better organised. Between 1880 and 1900, southern textile mills grew substantially as the workforce expanded from 17,000 to 98,000. In North Carolina, James Buchanan Duke invested in the latest technology, kept costs and wages low, and squeezed his tobacco rivals. Duke's sales techniques included the use of cards and photos in cigarette packaging. His multinational American Tobacco Company accounted for three quarters of all US tobacco production by 1904.

Progress was made but by 1900 the South had only 10 per cent of the nation's factories, a smaller percentage than in 1860. A decade later, just 15 per cent of the southern workforce was employed in manufacturing. Urban growth, crucial to the development of a commercial economy, lagged behind elsewhere and the South depended on the North and Midwest for basic household products. Historian C. Vann Woodward famously argued that a new southern business-merchant class challenged the power of former planters in the post-war South. He probably exaggerated the extent of their challenge as the southern landed elite emerged from the Civil War relatively unscathed and sought to restore the economic status quo. President Franklin D. Roosevelt described the South as the nation's number one economic problem in the 1930s and the root of the problem lay in the return to cotton.

The majority of post-war southerners, black and white, were cotton farmers trapped in a cycle of debt as cotton output returned to the record level achieved in 1860 as early as 1879. The cotton harvest of 1894 was twice the size of 1860 and by 1914 nearly doubled again. However, competition from India, Egypt, Brazil, and elsewhere caused a global cotton glut. The price per bale fell from approximately 30 cents in the 1860s to 10 cents in the 1880s to less than five cents by the mid-1890s. Cotton producers – families whose livelihoods depended on a successful harvest – found themselves mired in debt. The failure of land redistribution ensured that freedmen had no choice but to rent land as their former owners became landlords. Poor whites, particularly in rural areas with limited employment opportunities, struggled to avoid the cotton nexus. Even yeomen farmers found it difficult to remain solvent. Many planted cotton, erroneously hoping it would solve their cash flow problems. By the mid-1870s, whites grew 40 per cent of the South's cotton crop, whereas in 1860 it had been just one-tenth.

How to pay for rented land, raw materials, and other supplies haunted thousands of southern families. Two arrangements were common, although subject to variation from place to place: sharecropping and tenant farming. Sharecroppers paid for land, accommodation, and supplies by promising a share of their crop, usually at least half. At harvest time, in theory, the debtor settled with the landlord and local store owner. This unstable arrangement left sharecroppers in a vulnerable situation with cotton prices in permanent decline. Moreover, landlords took charge of account books and regularly cheated their clients out of a fair share of the return no matter how well they had done. Year after year, sharecroppers failed to pay off what they owed, becoming permanently indebted and unable to leave for better plots or different jobs without breaking the law. Local authorities enforced payment of debt and generally colluded with landlords and merchants. This miserable situation was known as peonage.

Tenant farmers paid a fixed sum for annual rent of their land. They usually owned their own tools and maybe a mule. But most tenant farmers mortgaged their profits to obtain supplies from the local store (an arrangement known as the crop lien). Southern states passed crop lien laws that strengthened the merchants' hold and provided them with the first claim to sale of the crop. If the debt could not be repaid, outstanding payments carried over to the following year. Like sharecropping, this built a relationship of economic dependence and exploitation. Merchants could insist that cotton was cultivated to the exclusion of other crops which prevented farmers from growing edible crops and forced the purchase of basic family provisions on credit. This problem was so acute that the South imported basic necessities like wheat and corn, something unthinkable before the Civil War. By the 1880s, a huge rural proletariat of black and white sharecroppers and tenants was exploited by landlords and merchants. The nostalgic myth of the Lost Cause gained considerable traction in the 1880s and 1890s and symbolised a region which struggled to break from its agrarian past. From the 1890s onwards, increasing numbers of African Americans, and many lower-class whites, left the South in hope of better lives in northern and western cities.

The Lost Cause

The Lost Cause – a term first used in Edward A. Pollard's *The Lost Cause: A New Southern History of the War of the Confederates* (1866) – was a movement that grew stronger decade by decade after 1865. It denied that slavery was the cause of the war, portrayed the Confederacy's intentions as noble and its leaders as heroic, and asserted that defeat was the result of northern aggression and superior resources. Women played a prominent role in the movement. The United Daughters of the Confederacy, formed in 1894, dedicated numerous monuments to Confederate heroes and ensured that textbooks presented states' rights as the primary cause of secession. The Lost Cause became a civic religion that perpetuated an enduring, yet erroneous if not malicious, white southern historical memory of the war.

Jim Crow

Having successfully re-established a dependent labour force, the southern elite turned its attention to the matter of race relations that had been in flux during Reconstruction. Political demagogues, such as South Carolina's Ben Tillman, resented black enfranchisement. They also wanted to prevent third parties from constructing biracial political coalitions, as the Readjuster Party in Virginia had done to control state government between 1879 and 1883 and the Populists, discussed in the final section, attempted in the 1890s. Some New South boosters realised that racism hampered the development of a commercial economy. The novelist George Washington Cable wrote in *The Silent South* (1885) that African Americans should be entitled to equality before the law. Even though he did not advocate full equality, Cable was hounded out of the South for his suggestion. From the 1880s, the rights of African Americans were eroded and the Democratic Party built a racist institutional structure that enforced white supremacy. Southern segregation or Jim Crow – named after a famous character from minstrel shows – was built on five key foundations: political restrictions, legal apartheid, racial violence, the indifference of the federal government, and virulent, nationwide racism.

Mississippi rewrote its state Constitution in 1890 to impose a $2 poll tax which also limited suffrage to those who could "understand" the Constitution. The language of this, and other state Constitutions that followed, made no overt reference to race, but the target was clear. Some 123,000 blacks, as well as 11,000 whites, were disfranchised in Mississippi subsequently. Ben Tillman was so keen that South Carolina follow Mississippi's lead that he returned from the Senate to serve as Chairman of the South Carolina Committee on the Rights of Suffrage in 1895. The 1898 Louisiana Constitution contained the most blatant example of discrimination as the "grandfather clause" restricted suffrage to males whose fathers or grandfathers had been qualified to vote on 1 January 1867, a date when blacks were not registered. By 1910, African Americans had been disfranchised in Alabama, Georgia, North Carolina, Virginia, and Oklahoma. The Democratic Party's white primary system (by which the party selected its candidates) effectively decided who held political office in uncontested southern elections.

As new state Constitutions disfranchised tens of thousands, a steady stream of laws enforced the separation of the races in public spaces. Segregation had origins in Reconstruction legislation such as the black codes and the separation of black and white children in public schools. However, it was on trains and streetcars that southerners mingled most frequently. Tennessee passed the first Jim Crow law that segregated first class rail facilities in 1881. With the exception of Virginia and the Carolinas, other states followed between 1887 and 1894 as restrictions extended into a variety of public spaces. Jim Crow legislation covered transport, schools, hospitals, parks,

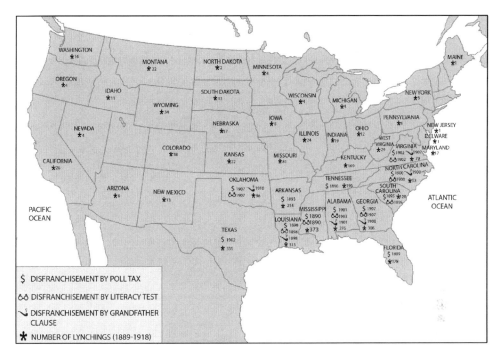

Figure 8.8 Disfranchisement and Lynchings. This map shows that while lynchings were nation-wide they mostly took place in the South, where voting laws were discriminatory as well. The statistics per state are taken from the NAACP's *Thirty Years of Lynching in the United States* (1919) which recorded 3,224 victims between 1889 and 1918, a total that most likely undercounts the true number.

restaurants, courts, hotels, cemeteries, barbers, cinemas, and washrooms. The precise implementation differed across the South but by 1915 the region had established racial segregation in every aspect of public life.

De jure segregation would not have been possible without what historian Harvard Sitkoff calls a "legal counter-revolution." Laws that protected civil rights were weakened by the Supreme Court and the federal government relinquished its oversight of constitutional protections in the Gilded Age. The 1873 *Slaughterhouse Cases* ruled that the Fourteenth Amendment had not intended to "transfer the security and protection" of civil rights "from the states to the federal government" and was approved by the slimmest possible margin of five votes to four. On 15 October 1883, the 1875 Civil Rights Act that integrated public transport and accommodation was ruled unconstitutional. The Republican Party also failed to pass a bill that mandated federal supervision of elections proposed by Henry Cabot Lodge (Massachusetts) in 1890 and 1891. The "Force Bill," as opponents called it, attempted to protect suffrage rights and demonstrated that black southerners still had northern allies uncomfortable with the retreat from Reconstruction. An overwhelming majority of white Americans shared racist views however and were comfortable with sectional reconciliation that left southern blacks to their fate.

The *Plessy v. Ferguson* Supreme Court decision (18 May 1896) provided the ultimate federal sanction of Jim Crow. Homer Adolph Plessy, a New Orleans salesman who was one-eighth black, challenged a Louisiana law that segregated rail carriages on the basis of "equal but separate accommodations for the white and coloured races." Plessy's lawsuit rested on violation of the Thirteenth and Fourteenth Amendments and progressed through the Louisiana judicial system after his arrest in 1892. It reached the Supreme Court in May 1896 where the constitutionality of the Louisiana law was upheld by a majority of seven to one. The lone dissenter, Chief Justice John Marshall Harlan, maintained that the Constitution was "colour-blind" but his fellow justices established the doctrine of "separate but equal": segregation was legal as long as equal facilities were provided for whites and blacks. Harlan described the decision "as pernicious as the decision made by this tribunal in the Dred Scott Case." Injustice was compounded because facilities for African Americans were rarely equal and regularly not provided at all. Blacks endured decades of grossly inferior schools, housing, and medical care.

The imposition of legal segregation was underpinned by appalling racial violence. Regular attacks on black and white Republicans during Reconstruction served a political purpose. In the Jim Crow era, these assaults continued and white violence manifested itself most brutally in lynching. Lynchings only began to be documented in the 1880s and calculating the precise number of victims is impossible due to incomplete information. The 1880s, and especially the 1890s, were probably the peak decades, however, of a practice that continued into the twentieth century. There were more than 100 lynching fatalities every year between 1891 and 1901 – it is no coincidence that the economic downturn was severe in this decade. African Americans were the primary targets although Mexican Americans and other groups were also victims. The National Association for the Advancement of Colored People estimated that 3,224 people were lynched between 1889 and 1918 although the total is probably much higher. These assaults were a savage enforcement of white supremacy.

Lynching was a ritualised form of terror, most likely to occur in rural communities in times of depression. Numerous victims were nameless, murdered by white men cheered on by crowds that included women and children. Up to 2,000 white southerners were present at the torture of black labourer Sam Hose in Newnan, Georgia, on 23 April 1899. These assaults were justified as a defence of white women. Georgian Rebecca Latimer Felton, the first woman to serve in the US Senate in 1922, told the Georgia State Agricultural Society in 1897 "if it takes lynching to protect woman's dearest possession from drunken, ravening human beasts, then I say lynch a thousand a week if it becomes necessary." Whites stereotyped blacks as childlike and docile in the antebellum era but it was the pernicious myth of the black male as rapist that vindicated protection of "vulnerable" white women in the Jim Crow South. Historian Joel Williamson calls this relentless violence and masculine rage towards black men "radical racism." The rituals of deference that African Americans had to endure included entering white homes from the rear, giving up seats on buses, and addressing whites as "sir" and "madam" while black men were called "boy" or "uncle."

The black southern response was severely constrained in this repressive climate. Ida B. Wells-Barnett (1862–1931), co-owner of the Memphis *Free Speech*, was the most brave and outspoken critic. She accused the South of "shielding itself behind the plausible screen of defending the honour of its women" and detailed the scale and terror of lynchings in *Southern Horrors* (1892) and other writings. Wells was forced to leave the South but tirelessly campaigned against lynching on the international stage. Booker T. Washington (1856–1915) – like Wells born enslaved – was the

Figure 8.9 Jesse Washington, an 18-year-old African American, lynched in Waco, Texas (15 May 1916). Tragically, images like this were all too common in the Jim Crow era.

Source: Courtesy of the Library of Congress Prints and Photographs Division Washington

most powerful black southern leader by the turn of the century and pursued a policy of accommodation. Washington's famous 1895 Atlanta Compromise address urged African Americans to slowly work their way up in economic partnership with whites. He told his white audience "in all things that are purely social we can be as separate as the fingers, yet one as the hand in all things essential to mutual progress." Washington's public appeasement of Jim Crow was bitterly resented by African American critics as betraying his race. In private, however, he spoke of justice, funded legal challenges to segregation, and wrote unsigned newspaper editorials protesting segregation. Washington's educational and industrial initiatives depended upon finance from white benefactors attracted by a conciliatory message.

African Americans had little room for maneuver because racism was not a southern affliction alone as prejudice and discrimination were nationwide. President Theodore Roosevelt believed blacks to be "wholly unfit for the suffrage" and Indians "savages" as he exalted the virtues of the Anglo-Saxon race. President Woodrow Wilson segregated the federal bureaucracy in Washington DC and fired black employees. US consumer culture advertised soda pop and ice cream with "coon" iconography – racial caricatures of black faces with bulging eyeballs, thick lips, and wide grins. Novels, music halls, and minstrelsy shows popularised malicious stereotypes in which Anglo-Saxons lorded over Native Americans and African Americans. The bestselling fiction of Thomas Dixon depicted the heroic Ku Klux Klan defending the South from black rapists during Reconstruction in *The Leopard's Spots* (1902) and *The Clansman* (1905).

Rural problems in industrialising America

When manufactured goods surpassed the value of farming goods for the first time in 1890 it would be easy to assume that the agricultural sector was in a period of contraction. In fact, more fresh land was cultivated between 1870 and 1890 than the whole of the previous 250 years as farms tripled in number between 1870 and 1910. The population of the prairie states of Minnesota, the Dakotas, Nebraska, Iowa, and Kansas, rose from one million in 1860 to seven million by 1900. Joseph F. Glidden's refinement of barbed wire in 1874 solved the problem of fencing boundaries on the plains and enormous cattle ranches were built. The refrigerated railroad car, patented by J.B. Sutherland in 1867 and improved by Andrew Chase in 1878, enabled the transportation of beef to Chicago and New York. The rail network made the entire US one gigantic market and American farmers fed the fastest growing population in the world. Between 1870 and 1900 wheat production more than doubled to 600 million bushels and numbers of cattle tripled to 68 million.

Homesteading was precarious however. Rain was scarce on the western plains and a ranch of 160 acres too small to be economical. Capital was needed to buy seed, stock, and tools. Mechanisation also became increasingly important to successful farming on the prairies as across the rest of the nation. About a third of farming homesteads failed. But the biggest problem was the emergence of a world market in grains. Global production of wheat doubled in the second half of the nineteenth century and US agriculture competed with the Canadian prairies, the Australian outback, the Argentinian Pampas, and the Russian and the Austro-Hungarian steppes. The greatest expansion of acreage in American history coincided with a global agricultural explosion that created unprecedented overabundance. The average price of corn in the US fell from 41 cents a bushel in 1874 to 30 cents by 1897 as supply far exceeded demand. New England farmers switched to dairy production for big city markets on the eastern seaboard but on the plains it was large producers and corporations that coped best. Ordinary farmers found capital in very short supply.

In depressed circumstances emerged a quite extraordinary social, economic, and political movement of tens of thousands of grass roots agricultural producers that took on the establishment. It is easy to forget that the Civil War was fought over the issue of free soil, free labour, and free men in which the Jeffersonian farmer constituted the quintessential building block of American republicanism. Jefferson's heirs rejoiced that the Homestead Act might finally realise a nation of propertied, independent citizens. Post-war economic development proceeded in a totally different direction, however, and American farmers confronted the resulting challenges head on.

The National Grange of the Patrons of Husbandry was founded by Oliver Kelley in 1867. Grangers were farmers from the Midwest with particular strength in Minnesota (Kelley's home state), Iowa, Wisconsin, and Nebraska. Embattled farming communities attempted to assert economic control by forming cooperatives that pooled capital and purchased machinery, supplies, and financial services. The movement quickly spread from the Dakotas to Texas and claimed 20,000 branches and 700,000 members by the mid-1870s. Grangers opened stores, warehouses, and grain elevators as they fought back against agribusiness. They cooperated with the Knights of Labor in a joint attack on Wall Street financiers and shared demands for railroad regulation. So-called Granger laws attempted to curb the excesses of big business in several midwestern states as the movement elected their own candidates and influenced state politics. The Supreme Court upheld the right of a state legislature to regulate railroad rates in *Munn v. Illinois* (1877) but later reversed the decision in *Wabash Railroad v. Illinois* (1886). The Granger movement nonetheless represented a determined effort by farmers to push their own agenda.

Debt was a perennial problem and farmers frequently complained at the high cost of credit. In the 1870s, Grangers gravitated to the Greenback Party (1876–84) that urged the government to print paper notes (greenbacks) to increase the money supply, as had been done during the war. Rural Americans consistently advocated new fiscal policies as the panacea for their economic woes. Three regional organisations succeeded the Grange. The Farmers and Laborers' Union of America was formed in Texas in 1876 (also known as the Southern Alliance) and by 1890 had three million members across the Southwest. The National Farmers' Alliance, or Northwestern Alliance, was formed in Illinois in 1880 and had two million members by 1890. The Colored Farmers National Alliance, led by R.M. Humphrey and J.J. Shuffer with as many as 250,000 members, was formed in Texas in 1886 because blacks were excluded from the Southern Alliance. These umbrella organisations built on Granger principles of self-help and mutual cooperation and attracted thousands of female activists as

The Situation; The Result of Interest Bearing Bonds and Sherman

Figure 8.10 "Here Lies Prosperity." Rural America consistently complained about the problem of debt and obtaining credit, arguing that the US banking system favoured urbanites.

women took important leadership roles. A radical agenda to solve rural stagnation emerged: tax reform, loans at low interest rates, huge government-built warehouses that would store crops until demand picked up, currency reform, nationalised railroads, and unlimited coinage of silver.

By the end of the 1880s, Alliance enterprises were struggling. The continued decline of commodity values forced farmers to grow more crops to sustain basic income that caused prices to further spiral downward. Tens of thousands faced the threat of foreclosure. Alliance-backed political candidates were elected in Nebraska, Kansas, and the Dakotas and the subtreasury plan was introduced in Congress in February 1890. This ingenious idea of Charles Macune, of the Texas Alliance, proposed that the government provide credit to farmers secured against surplus crops stored in federal warehouses until market conditions improved. The subtreasury plan was met with indifference and became buried in congressional committees. Worse, the Tariff Act of 1890 (or McKinley Tariff, after its Republican sponsor William McKinley) increased import duties from 38 per cent to 49.5 per cent which raised consumer prices. Kansas populist Mary Elizabeth Lease told audiences in 1890 that the "Parties lie to us and the political speakers mislead us." The indifference of the Democrats and Republicans to the farmer's plight required a more radical solution. "Wall Street owns the country. It is no longer a government of the people, by the people, and for the people, but a government of Wall Street, by Wall Street, and for Wall Street," Lease charged. "Common people" were "slaves" while "West and South are bound and prostrate before the manufacturing East."

The Populist insurgency

The People's Party, widely known as the Populists, emerged as the political response to agricultural crisis following meetings in Cincinnati (May 1891) and St Louis (February 1892). Alliance members, and others radicals, met in Omaha Nebraska in July 1892 at the first Populist national convention. Ignatius Donnelly, Minnesota writer and former Radical Republican, wrote the party manifesto which called for the "union of the labor forces of the United States . . . to restore the government of the Republic to the hands of the *plain people*, with which class it originated." The People's Party proposed measures to combat monopolies and revive grass roots prosperity: nationalisation of railroads, telegraphs and other monopolies; a graduated income tax; the subtreasury system; direct election of senators; greenbacks; coinage of silver dollars at the ratio of 16 ounces to one gold dollar coin; public ownership of railroads; and public land restored to federal control. It was an extraordinary programme designed for the masses – although immigrants were excluded as the party opposed mass immigration – that also endorsed trade unions and calls for a shorter working day.

In the South, Populists stressed the common plight of black and white farmers. "The colored tenant is in the same boat as the white tenant, the colored laborer with the white laborer" argued Georgia Populist Tom Watson. Attempts to unite black and white farmers attempted to bridge deep divisions at a time of severe depression. The People's Party advocated social justice, but steered clear of the issue of racial equality to form a fragile biracial alliance. Nonetheless, southern Populists and Republicans agreed electoral pacts in which they supported one another and shared political power. The "fusion" strategy was successful in North Carolina in 1894, which strengthened the resolve of southern Democrats to disfranchise blacks.

The Populists did very well in the 1892 presidential election despite being organised just months previously. Presidential candidate James Weaver of Iowa gained a million votes and People's Party candidates also won five Senate and ten Congressional seats, as well as three state governorships and 1,500 state and county positions. Third parties in American politics traditionally found it difficult to sustain their impact but Populists hoped to build on this success. They faced formidable obstacles. The powerful Democrat and Republican Party machines were entrenched. Populist strength was confined to rural states. Moreover, the appeal to African Americans, large numbers of whom were still enfranchised in the early 1890s, was a brave but risky move. Racism was endemic and although the dire economic straits of the 1890s cried out for a new departure, this was a step too far for many whites.

The People's Party was torn between remaining independent ahead of the 1896 presidential election or joining forces with the Democrats (who had promised to take up Populist demands). This was a difficult decision. Many Populists were Democrats previously and "fusionists" argued that a regionally based third party could never successfully contest national power. The best strategy was to influence from within and merge with the Democrats. "Mid-roaders" wanted to remain in-between the two established parties. They suspected that the Democrats were planning to take advantage of Populism to boost their chances and absorb the third-party threat. Both positions had merit. Without urban appeal and votes from outside the South and the West, victory was impossible. However, merging with a national party undoubtedly threatened to dilute Populism's radicalism.

Charismatic William Jennings Bryan, leading candidate for the Democratic nomination, assuaged many Populist doubters. He appeared to line up Tom Watson as his vice presidential running mate and delivered one of the great American political orations to the Democratic convention in Chicago on 9 July 1896. His electric "Cross of Gold" speech harked back to Jeffersonian idealism of the farmer and advocated the minting of silver coinage at the ratio of 16 to 1. Bryan attacked proponents of the gold standard, who included Republican nominee William McKinley: "you shall not press down upon the brow of labor this crown of thorns. You shall not crucify mankind on a cross of gold." Rather than split the vote, the People's Party chose to endorse Bryan, although not without reservation. Their unease grew when the Democrats announced a conservative industrialist from Maine, Arthur Sewall, as vice presidential nominee, not Watson.

The 1896 presidential election was one of the most important in the nation's history and the most crucial since 1860. The money question overshadowed other issues as the Democrats venerated farmers and labourers as the true producers of wealth and reviled parasitic tycoons. Big business rallied behind the Republican campaign. Industrialists and financiers were alarmed at Bryan's castigation of corporate America. Contributions flooded into the Republican coffers, estimated to be at least three and a half million dollars and possibly much more. In comparative terms, the 1896 election was one of the most expensive in US history, although there was a gross disparity on each side as the Democrats had a budget of just $600,000. McKinley's team, led by Republican National Committee chairman Mark Hanna, targeted key states and undecided voters. The American flag was used as the symbol of the Republican Party that associated McKinley with patriotism, while a media campaign tarnished "Bryanism" with revolution and anarchy.

The popular vote was close (7,102,246 to 6,492,559) but McKinley won a decisive victory in the Electoral College (271–176) having swept the populous northeastern states. Bryan covered 18,000 miles on the campaign trail but failed to appeal to urban Americans and immigrants. This signalled the defeat of the People's Party that won a few seats in western states subsequently but disbanded by 1908. The 1896 election was a turning point, or critical realignment, in US politics. The stark differentiation between voters in the urban economic heartland of the Northeast and voters in the "periphery" of the South and West swept the Republicans to power where they remained until 1932 with the exception of Woodrow Wilson's administration (1913–1921). An economic recovery had begun by the time McKinley took office in 1897 and, in the longer term, both the Democrats and Republicans implemented Populist policies such as a federal income tax, direct election of senators, and banking reform. It is easy to dismiss the Populists as radical dreamers or rural reactionaries who harked back to an agrarian past. This is a mistake: the Populists sought an alternative road to modernity and practical solutions to the problems of industrialisation but were confronted by the formidable opposition of corporate capitalism.

Chapter summary

Mary Elizabeth Lease supposedly told farmers to "raise less corn and more Hell" as she spoke tirelessly to thousands of rural audiences. Her call to agitate reverberated across Gilded-Age America. Violence and racial conflict were widespread. The consequences for Native Americans and African Americans were dire and whiteness reigned supreme by the beginning of the twentieth century. Eighteen million acres of land claimed by homesteaders constituted just a fraction of the 521 million acres given to railroads, states, and land speculators. Western conquest underpinned momentous changes in the American economy. Urban and rural life was transformed. Farmers, sharecroppers, and factory workers struggled to make ends meet. Billionaires practiced philanthropy and spent vast sums to build libraries and parks but regularly undercut their employees. The fiction remained that American greatness was rooted in competition but the US economy was characterised by oligopoly in markets dominated by a handful of firms. Most major sectors – banking, steel, manufacturing, meat packing, oil refining, and railroads – were controlled by giant corporations. Just 318 companies possessed 40 per cent of all manufacturing assets in the US in 1904. The federal government was a crucial ally of big business. When the Supreme Court interpreted the Fourteenth Amendment in such a way as to enable the abrogation of black civil rights but protect corporations, it was clear where priorities rested.

Discussion questions

- What factors account for the defeat of Native American tribes in the West?
- What were the most important effects of railroad construction in the second half of the nineteenth century?
- How successful was the labour movement in the era of industrialisation?
- Were Robber Barons a help or a hindrance to American development in the Gilded Age?
- Was the New South characterised by change or continuity? Why was segregation imposed in the southern states in the late nineteenth century?
- Why did the Populist movement not have mass appeal?

Further reading

Bensel, Richard Franklin. *The Political Economy of American Industrialization, 1877–1900* (New York, 2000). A powerful examination of the connection between politics and economics during the Gilded Age.

Edwards, Rebecca. *New Spirits: Americans in the Gilded Age, 1865–1905* (New York, 2006). Excellent, thematic survey of Gilded Age society.

Gates, Henry Louis. *Stony the Road. Reconstruction, White Supremacy, and the Rise of Jim Crow* (New York, 2009). Sobering and succinct account of the post-war white supremacist backlash and the African American response.

Gilmore, Glenda Elizabeth. *Gender and Jim Crow: Women and the Politics of White Supremacy in North Carolina, 1896–1920* (Chapel Hill, 1996). Superb analysis of the politics of gender and white supremacy.

Green, Julie. *Pure and Simple Politics: The American Federation of Labor and Political Activism, 1881–1914* (New York, 1998). Authoritative, recent history of the AFL.

Hahn, Stephen. *A Nation Without Borders: The United States and its World in an Age of Civil Wars* (New York, 2016). Impressive, transnational history of the US rise as a global power.

Krause, Paul. *The Battle for Homestead, 1880–1892: Politics, Culture, and Steel* (Pittsburgh, 1992). Explosive study of Andrew Carnegie and industrial conflict.

Lears, Jackson. *Rebirth of a Nation: The Making of Modern America, 1877–1920* (New York, 2009). Comprehensive synthesis of this period.

Limerick, Patricia Nelson. *The Legacy of Conquest: The Unbroken Past of the American West* (New York, 1987). Classic statement from the foremost New Western historian.

Litwack, Leon F. *Trouble in Mind: Black Southerners in the Age of Jim Crow* (New York, 1998). Harrowing examination of African American life in the Jim Crow era.

Nobles, Gregory H. *American Frontiers: Cultural Encounters and Continental Conquest* (New York, 1998). Useful survey of US-Native American relations.

Postel, Charles. *The Populist Vision* (Oxford, 2007). Bold reinterpretation which argues that the populists were modern revolutionaries.

Richardson, Heather Cox. *West from Appomattox: The Reconstruction of America After the Civil War* (New Haven, 2007). Revisionist history of the last third of the nineteenth century.

Unruh, John D. *The Plains Across: The Overland Emigrants on the Trans-Mississippi West, 1840–60* (Urbana, IL, 1979). Excellent study of Western trails.

West, Elliott. *The Contested Plains: Indians, Goldseekers, and the Rush to Colorado* (Lawrence, 1998). Engaging history of the Great Plains, delineating the clash of Indian tribes with white pioneers and prospectors.

White, Richard. *Railroaded: The Transcontinentals and the Making of Modern America* (New York, 2011). Revisionist account of railroads and their impact.

Williamson, Joel. *The Crucible of Race: Black-White Relations in the South Since Emancipation* (Chapel Hill, 1984). Superb analysis of race and racial ideology in the South.

Woodward, C. Vann. *Origins of the New South, 1877–1913* (New York, 1951). Classic account of the post-Reconstruction South.

Wrobel, David M. et al. "Forum: The American West Enters the Twenty-First Century," *The Historian*, Vol. 66, no. 3, 2004, 437–564 special issue dissecting New Western History.

Wood, Amy Louise. *Lynching and Spectacle: Witnessing Racial Violence in America, 1890–1940* (Chapel Hill, 2010). Unflinching examination of mob violence and the ways in which lynching underpinned a culture of white supremacy.

9   The rise of imperial America

Timeline

Allied blockade of German ports
US military invasion of Veracruz, Mexico
1915   US military intervention in Haiti
German torpedo attack on *Lusitania*
1916   US invasion of Dominican Republic
German torpedo attack on *Sussex*
Pancho Villa's raid on Columbus, New Mexico
1917   Zimmerman telegram
Russian Revolutions and withdrawal from the war
US enters World War I
1918   Battle of Château-Thierry
The Allied Meuse-Argonne Campaign
World War I Armistice
1919   Treaty of Versailles
Ratification debates in US Senate
1921   Washington Naval conference #1
Treaty of Berlin
1922   Washington Naval conference #2
World War Foreign Debt Commission set up
Naval disarmament treaties
1923   French and Belgian troops invade the Ruhr
Departure of American Forces in Germany (AFG)
US recognition of Mexican government
1924   Dawes Plan
1925   Locarno Treaty
1927   Geneva Naval Disarmament conference
Kellogg-Briand Pact
1928   "Red Line" oil agreement in the Middle East
1930   Young Plan

Topics covered

- "Remember the Maine, To hell with Spain"
- War in Cuba
- Taking control of the Philippines
- Domestic conflicts over imperialism
- Chasing China's markets
- Transnational communities and border controls
- Defending the Western Hemisphere
- War in Europe 1914–18
- The American expeditionary force in Europe
- Post-war European entanglements
- Isolationism, unilateralism, and America first

Introduction

This chapter begins with the explosion of the USS *Maine* in Havana harbour in February 1898 which hastened American military intervention in Cuba. In early 1898, Cuba was still one of Spain's imperial "New World" possessions, but this small Caribbean island, just 1290 kilometers long and 84 kilometers wide, became the crucial springboard for the US imperial surge of the late nineteenth and early twentieth centuries. In 1860, the US did not a have a single overseas colony or dependency; in 1902 it had eight. This chapter focuses first on US conquest of Cuba and the annexation of the Philippines, the increasing importance of China's economic potential to US international relations, expanding US military, political and economic power in the Caribbean and Central America, and construction of the Panama Canal. America became the dominant power in the Western Hemisphere during this transformative period of empire building and nation building at home but was pulled back into Europe's entangled imperial alliances during the First World War. The US joined the Allies as an associate power on 6 April 1917. The last sections of the chapter examine how US involvement in the Great War, President Woodrow Wilson's efforts to shape European geopolitics, and 1920s foreign policy issues helped elevate the United States from bit player to key player on the world stage.

Imperialism in 1890s

Broadly defined, imperialism is the domination and control of a formerly sovereign people, their government and territory by a stronger foreign power, usually by military force. This would include the domination and control of formerly self-governing Indian/Native American tribal nations by the United States government and the Office of Indian Affairs in the Department of the Interior, as well as military campaigns and economic warfare against indigenous peoples on the Plains in the 1860s and 1870s, and the seizure of Native American land for non-Indian sale and settlement in the Dakotas, Oklahoma and Wyoming the 1870s and 1880s [discussed in Chapter 8]. Colonialism, the subjugation of a people by transplanted members of a different but dominant racial or ethnic people is a form of imperialism and would include the dominance of Cuba by Spain. Domination of a nation's economy or religious and cultural institutions by an outside power is also imperialism and characterises US policy towards Hawaii and Samoa in the late nineteenth and early twentieth centuries. Those who advocated US territorial and economic enlargement were also called "expansionists" or "jingoists."

"Remember the Maine, To hell with Spain"

By January 1898, Cuban civilians, rebel forces, and Spanish troops had endured three years of civil war, malnutrition, and disease. Local rioting, mutiny by Spanish troops, and attacks on newspapers sympathetic to the recently established Cuban home-rule government, led the American Consul in Cuba to cable Washington DC for the urgent dispatch of a US warship to protect American interests. The USS *Maine* anchored in Havana harbour on 25 January. At 9:40pm on 15 February 1898, the forward part of the ship exploded and what remained of the twisted wreckage quickly sank. Of the 350 personnel on board, more than 260 were killed.

Newspaper headlines in the United States immediately proclaimed the "Destruction of the War Ship Maine Was the Work of an Enemy!" and denounced "Spanish Treachery!" The New York *Journal* offered a reward of $50,000 for exposure of the "Perpetrator of the Maine Outrage." In late March 1898, a US Naval Court of Inquiry determined that a submarine mine had triggered the explosion of two or more forward magazines that obliterated the front part of the ship. Neither the exact cause of the explosion nor who was responsible has ever been fully established, but historians believe the vessel's boiler blew up. Many contemporary Americans remained convinced this was a deliberate act of Spanish aggression. It became the catalyst for US invasion of Cuba. "Remember the Maine, To hell with Spain" became an emotive rallying cry during the Spanish-Cuban-American War that followed.

Cubans were caught between two metropoles: they remained under Spanish political control yet were increasingly economically dependent on the United States. The island's capital, Havana, had been founded as an imperial trading port for the export of sugar, rum, and tobacco. It was a vibrant multiracial city and commercial hub with approximately 236,000 residents in 1895. American companies supplied Havana with gas lighting, had built bridges and railroads across the island, and laid international cable lines linking the Cuban capital to New York and New Orleans. Sugar plantations in Cuba's western provinces had been built by generations of African and Afro-Cuban slaves, until slavery was abolished in October 1886, after which black freed-people were employed alongside Chinese and Indian servile labour. Large numbers of American investors, including Edwin F. Atkins, had acquired Cuban sugar companies and plantations, with investments worth $50 million. By the early 1890s, more than 90 per cent of Cuban sugar was exported to the United States. When the US Congress passed a new tariff which privileged Hawaiian sugar imports over Cuban ones when a major economic recession began in 1893, this had a profound effect on Cuban wages and exports.

There had been growing islander opposition to the corruption and inefficiency of Spanish rule and empty promises of reform from the 1860s, but resistance to economic oppression, racial injustice, and Spanish colonialism reignited in the 1880s and 1890s. Poet and journalist José Martí embodied the political consciousness of the *Cuba Libré* (Free Cuba) movement and provided crucial leadership in exile, while Juan Gualberto Gómez, José María Aguirre, and others coordinated opposition in Cuba. Martí established the Cuban Revolutionary Party at Key West in 1892, to raise money for the growing Cuban Liberation Army's (CLA) military preparations on the island. In Spring 1895, the revolutionary leaders in exile declared war on Spain and demanded an independent democratic Cuba. *Cuba Libré* drew wide public and political support from many Americans, including US Congressmen, such as Ferdinand Brucker, of Michigan, and thousands of Cuban immigrants in Ybor City in Tampa, Florida. Local women such as Paulina Pedroso, an African Cuban who had moved with cigar production from Cuba to Key West to Ybor City, organised fiestas, parades, and raffles to raise funds and consciousness, while Ruperto Pedroso and others established revolutionary clubs and labour unions.

Rebel CLA forces of around 50,000 were reorganised into guerrilla units to fight a Spanish army of over 100,000 troops and Martí returned to Cuba in April 1895 to lead the insurgency. He was unfortunately shot and killed by Spanish troops five weeks later but his perceived martyrdom energised CLA guerrilla tactics to destroy transport links, blockade Spanish-controlled towns, and disrupt telegraph communications and food convoys. As they moved west from Oriente to Matanzas, Havana, and Pinar del Río in early 1896, CLA forces set fire to cane fields, sugar refineries, and tobacco plantations to render Cuba unprofitable for its Spanish masters. Thousands of civilians fled to protected towns as the brutal civil war continued.

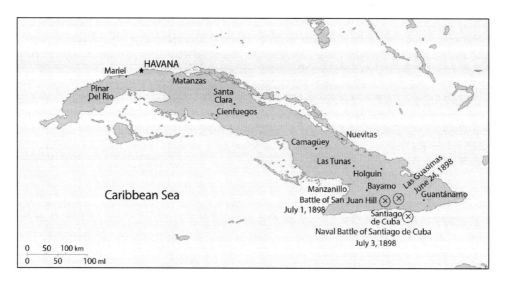

Figure 9.1 War in Cuba, 1898.

American landowners and investors looked to the Cleveland and McKinley presidential administrations to restore economic and racial order but both resisted direct intervention. The McKinley administration sought to block émigré-led filibustering missions to Cuba although dozens successfully evaded US navy and coast guard patrols. There were powerful domestic restraints on US intervention. Plantation owners in the sugar parishes of Southern Louisiana feared war and annexation would extend American tariff protection to Cuban sugar, at their expense. Many anti-imperialists worried that a free Cuba would generate political disorder and social upheaval throughout the circum-Caribbean as other colonial entities demanded self-determination and home rule, and the resulting racial conflict would spread to American shores. Spanish officials, such as ambassador to the US, Enrique Dupuy de Lomé, blamed the uprising on "negroes" and "mulattoes," and claimed that the end of the Spanish rule would lead to black republican leadership of the island, thus tapping into hostile southern US memories of Reconstruction.

Increasingly vocal calls for US intervention followed Captain General Valeriano Weyler's prohibitions on tobacco exports, closure of the sugar industry, and his controversial *reconcentrado* policy in September 1896. To thwart assistance to the insurgents, Spanish troops forcibly relocated around half a million rural civilians to squalid overcrowded barracks, or concentration camps, in fortified towns such as Matangas and Cientvegos. The numbers are disputed but more than 150,000 *reconcentrados* died (including disproportionate numbers of women and children), from either starvation or during recurring epidemics of smallpox, typhoid, and dysentery. Reports of camp conditions and of Spanish brutality towards ordinary Cubans regularly appeared in US tabloids such as the New York *World*, owned by media magnate Joseph Pulitzer, and its rival, the New York *Journal*, owned by another media giant, William Randolph Hearst. Weyler was recalled to Madrid and *reconcentrado* had officially ended in November 1897, but neither the Cuban patriots nor their US sympathisers were satisfied by these changes.

Yellow journalism

The term *yellow journalism* originated with a popular cartoon strip, "Hogan's Alley," drawn by Richard F. Outcault, and its character the "Yellow Kid." It appeared first in the New York *World*, until the New York *Journal* outbid its rival for the strip in 1896. Nevertheless, *yellow journalism* soon referred to a style of newspaper reporting that was light on facts but heavy on sensationalism. Stories of crime, political corruption, immorality, and urban decline were staples of the tabloid press, but events in Cuba and the contest between brutal Spanish rule and noble Cuban republican defiance made great copy. These reports were also carried by major dailies in Atlanta, Chicago, New Orleans and San Francisco, and by local newspapers. The peak of *yellow journalism's* patriotic intensity and popular influence was the sinking of the *Maine* and the four-month war with Spain. Tabloid jingoism did not cause the Spanish-Cuban-American War but it did stoke public and political support for military action.

THE BIG TYPE WAR OF THE YELLOW KIDS.

Figure 9.2 Newspapers at war. Media magnates Joseph Pulitzer and William Randolph Hearst are dressed as Yellow Kid characters as they fight a circulation war and for profits to be made from their coverage of the Spanish-Cuban-American War in 1898. The jingoistic cartoon also mocks Pulitzer's ethnic heritage.

Source: Courtesy of Pictorial Press Ltd/Alamy

McKinley's cautious policy of neutrality and attempts to persuade the imperial government in Madrid to adopt a conciliatory line towards the Cuban insurrectionists were heavily criticised by his Assistant Secretary of the Navy, Theodore Roosevelt, hawkish senators and congressional representatives, Republicans fearful of a victorious Democratic "Free Cuba and Free Silver" campaign in 1900, and many in the US business community. The USS *Maine* incident led to a more robust US response. McKinley presented Spanish ministers with an ultimatum in March 1898: an armistice until 1 October; immediate cessation of the *reconcentrado* policy; authorisation to distribute US relief supplies to the Cuban people; and acceptance of McKinley as arbiter if the conflict continued after 1 October. The Madrid government still refused to promise eventual independence to Cuba, but popular momentum was growing and the exclusion of Cubans from US–Spanish discussions over the island's future was increasingly untenable. This was the context for the private letter written by Ambassador de Lôme, in which he attacked the integrity of President McKinley, and which was published in the New York *Journal* a week before the Maine exploded.

War in Cuba

Prospects for peaceful settlement sank with the *Maine* and the Cuban War of Independence transitioned into the Spanish-Cuban-American War. On 11 April, McKinley asked Congress for a formal declaration of war. In the Teller Amendment, on 20 April, Congress decried the "abhorrent conditions" on the island that were "a disgrace to Christian civilization" and had "shocked the moral sense" of Americans. The right of the Cuban people to be free and independent of Spain was recognised: Spain was to cede control of the island and withdraw "land and naval forces," and McKinley was empowered to use the military might of the US to ensure this occurred. Congress further asserted that the US had no "disposition or intention to exercise sovereignty, jurisdiction, or control over" Cuba, and US forces would "leave the government and control of the Island to its people" once it had been pacified. The Spanish government rejected these terms and severed diplomatic relations with the United States; America and Spain were officially at war by 25 April.

McKinley ordered a US naval blockade of Cuban ports on 22 April. A Volunteer Bill passed by Congress on 23 April and called for 125,000 men between the ages of 18 and 45 years. There were to be three cavalry regiments of frontiersmen. Secretary of War Roger Alger offered command of the First US Volunteer Cavalry, often referred to as the "Rough Riders," to Theodore Roosevelt. Roosevelt initially deferred leadership to Major Leonard Wood, but resigned from his government position on 15 May and joined Wood's men. The war in Cuba gave many American men of Roosevelt's generation, who were too young to have fought in the Civil War, an opportunity to show off their physical prowess and militarism which were important markers of manly virtue in this period.

Moving the nation onto a war footing could not be achieved overnight, and journalists referred to the period from April to June 1898 as the "rocking-chair period of the war." Tampa was the main port of embarkation for US troops – Cuba was a mere 145 kilometres from south Florida – and was soon swamped with 25,000 soldiers and war department officials. They were joined by journalists and illustrators, from Manchester, London, and Toronto, and across the United States, working for tabloid and broadsheet dailies as well as literary-political magazines such as *Harpers Weekly*,

Figure 9.3 Preparing for the Spanish-Cuban-American War. Soldiers and weapons, including cannons and field guns, were loaded onto transport ships at Tampa. Florida, which was the main embarkation port for US troops heading to Santiago, Cuba.

Source: State Archives of Florida/Florida Memory/Alamy

Outlook, and *McClure's* (which were all part of an Anglo-American publishing revolution). More than 4,000 black soldiers accompanied the army of invasion, and when billeted in Tampa they endured racial abuse and harassment from locals and other soldiers. Tensions escalated and the city was rocked by a race riot on the eve of the army's departure. Armed black men in uniform challenged powerful southern and national beliefs about white supremacy and racial hierarchy, but these citizen-soldiers were also potent symbols of freedom, equality, and loyalty in a period when racial segregation, discrimination, and disfranchisement were part and parcel of southern progressive reform.

On June 30, US marines landed at Guantanamo Bay and another expeditionary force landed to the east of Santiago. On 1 July, Roosevelt led a cavalry charge up Kettle Hill, and the "Rough Riders" assisted the African American Tenth Cavalry in taking San Juan Heights north of Santiago in the decisive battle of the conflict. Press reports glorified the fearlessness and heroic masculinity of white troops at Las Guasimas, San Juan Heights, and El Caney. Further evidence of American superiority came when US battleships forced Spain's Caribbean fleet out of Santiago harbour then took less than five hours to destroy it. Cubans served as scouts, guides, and interpreters for the American invasion and fought alongside US troops in critical military operations. The city of Santiago formally surrendered on 17 July and an armistice was concluded on 12 August. Meanwhile, in late July, American troops led by Major General Nelson A. Miles had taken control of the island of Puerto Rico and a key Caribbean naval station at the island's capital city of San Juan. The short war, superior American military prowess, and decisive American–Cuban victory was celebrated by Secretary of State John Hay as a "splendid little war."

Nevertheless, the Spanish-Cuban-American War had exposed the poor state of US military preparedness. The US Army had around 28,000 regular troops but the addition of 200,000 volunteers overwhelmed the quartermaster department. Soldiers wore woollen winter uniforms unsuited to tropical conditions and were fed "embalmed" or canned beef that was unfit for consumption. There were shortages of modern rifles, field guns and other equipment. Medical supplies were inadequate while soldiers quickly fell victim to typhoid, yellow fever, and malaria. (Spanish troops were similarly under-equipped and afflicted by disease and malnutrition.) The US Surgeon-General later reported there had been 968 deaths on the battlefield between 1 May 1898 and 30 April 1899, but 5,438 from disease. The parallel Philippine-American War also claimed the lives of over 4,000 US troops (and approximately 50,000 Filipino fighters), and three-quarters died from non-combat causes. The resulting national scandal ensured the dismissal of the Secretary of War. America's new colonial responsibilities spurred military modernisation and professionalisation that would be put to the test during World War I.

Formal peace negotiations were concluded in Paris in December 1898, with Spain relinquishing its title to Cuba, and ceding Puerto Rico, the Pacific island of Guam, and the Philippines to the United States. No Filipino or Cuban representatives had been invited to the formal peace negotiations. The island of Cuba was annexed by the US on New Year's Day 1899 and it remained under US military occupation until 1902. Cubans were permitted to draft their own constitution and the Cuban Constitutional Convention met in 1900. However, US Congressmen demanded that Cuban delegates accept the Platt Amendment, which gave the US the right to land troops in Cuba to maintain law and order, limited the amount of debt the island could accumulate, and later established a US naval base at Guantanamo. Cuban delegates initially refuted these demands. Consequently, several Cuban leaders were summoned to Washington and courted with favourable economic concessions, particularly over access to the American sugar market. Convention delegates subsequently accepted the amendment by a narrow vote in June 1901. The Roosevelt administration had also made clear to Cuban officials that the terms of the Platt Amendment would be put into effect by force if no agreement could be reached. In May 1902, Tomás Estrada Palma finally became leader of the independent republic of Cuba, but it remained part of a growing constellation of US client states.

Taking control of the Philippines

The 1898 war with Spain had two main "fronts": the Spanish-Cuban-American confrontation in the Caribbean and the Spanish-Filipino-American conflict in the Pacific. The Philippines, an archipelago of more than one thousand islands, was Spain's largest Asian colony. Filipinos had been in direct revolt against Spanish rule during the 1890s, and an insurrection in Manila in 1896 quickly spread under the direction of Emilio Aguinaldo, now leader of the powerful Katipunan society. This secretive revolutionary organisation of labourers, clerks, peasants, and petty merchants sought separation from Spain as well as moral and religious reform.

Prior to 1898, a handful of US merchants operated out of the Philippines. Britain, rather than Spain, was the dominant colonial power in these islands, which were within close naval, telegraph, and commercial proximity to Britain's important Asian possessions. However, American expansionists believed US control of the magnificent harbour at Manila Bay would provide a crucial strategic stepping-stone to China, a justification for building up US naval strength, and confirm America as the dominant power in the Western Hemisphere. Theodore Roosevelt greatly admired naval officer and historian Alfred Thayer Mahan and his argument that the US needed a modern navy to protect its growing economic and strategic interests around the world. As Assistant Navy Secretary, Roosevelt had developed contacts with Mahan and other naval strategists who anticipated war with Spain and appointed political ally George Dewey to command the US Asiatic squadron. In early 1898, Dewey was ordered from San Francisco to Hong Kong to prepare for a possible attack on the Philippines.

On 1 May, US cruisers easily blockaded then defeated a decrepit and ill-equipped Spanish squadron at Manila Bay, killing or wounding over 380 but sustaining minimal American casualties. Such a decisive victory transformed Dewey into a national hero. Dewey's men occupied Manila until the arrival of 11,000 US soldiers in July and August. US occupation also eased the return to the Philippines of exiled revolutionary leaders, notably Aguinaldo. They quickly mobilised local forces to resume the revolutionary insurgency and issued a proclamation of independence on June 12. Initially sympathetic, the attitudes of US officials towards the Filipino people and their plans for republican self-government changed with the arrival of US troops. Filipinos were increasingly excluded from military and political decisions, and local forces had been prevented from entering Manila after its capture by US troops on 12 August. General Wesley Merritt became military governor two days later. This confirmed American possession and protection over the island but stoked further hostilities.

Eleven days later after the Paris peace treaty, on 21 December, McKinley's "Benevolent Assimilation" proclamation claimed US sovereignty over the entire Philippine

Figure 9.4 The Philippine Islands, 1899.

archipelago, established a military government to ensure property rights, taxation and tariffs, and effectively defined US–Filipino relations as that of metropole-colony. Meanwhile, a Philippine Constitutional Convention had met, and Aguinaldo had been proclaimed president of the Philippine Republic on 1 January 1899; the McKinley administration did not recognise the legitimacy of either. Local Filipinos resented the American forces of occupation while Americans viewed Filipinos as the ungrateful recipients of benevolent US liberation and governance. Months of simmering

Figure 9.5 American occupation of the Philippines. There was considerable suspicion, mistrust, and hostility between Filipino civilians and US troops. Local Filipinos were often racially abused by occupying Americans, and Filipino women threatened with sexual violence. This photograph of three Filipino women surrounded by white American men highlights the vulnerability of these women.

Source: Courtesy of Granger Historical Picture Archive/Alamy

resentments and violent skirmishes between US and Filipino troops erupted into open warfare when US sentries fired on Filipino soldiers outside Manila on February 4. Thus, the 1896–98 Filipino war of national liberation against Spanish imperialism became the Philippine-American War of 1899–1902.

US victories during 1899 confirmed that American forces had the upper hand during the first period of the war. American officials further cultivated the support of Filipino commercial, political, and legal elites, and established local Filipino army units that were deliberately segregated by tribe, to bolster US control and undermine colonial resistance. Even Filipino allies were often racially abused by US troops. And, as in Cuba, Filipino insurgents were frequently lower-class and non-white, and many US troops and policymakers railed against indigenous brown and black guerrilla fighters who employed "savage" methods rather than the "civilised" conventional tactics equated with white-Spanish-metropole forces. Class, racial, and religious divisions between Christian, Spanish and lighter-skinned English-speaking Filipino elites, and the indigenous darker-skinned "Negroes," "Orientals" and "Malays" were emphasised in US journalism, military reports and policymaking, and were part of the process of legitimising US conquest of the islands.

In November 1899, General Arthur MacArthur declared the war was over and the revolutionaries had been dispersed, but the conflict was merely evolving into an anti-colonial guerrilla struggle. The Aguinaldo leadership had divided the country into military zones, each with a military commander overseeing smaller campaigns that utilised local geographic knowledge and crucial material support from rural communities. This demanded changes to the command structure, organisation, and tactics of US forces and increased their reliance on local guides, translators, and food suppliers. By early 1900, ongoing hostilities in a war that was supposed to be over, also rankled at home.

Domestic conflicts over imperialism

American imperialism meant the acquisition of new territories, markets, and peoples, as well as extension of American laws, ideologies, and governance, often driven by faith in racial, religious (mainly Protestant), republican, and national superiority. To some, the annexation of the Philippines and the extension of American moral and political influence throughout the Pacific was Divine Providence, and a special mission for which only the United States was truly qualified, so was closely allied to Protestantism. Anglo-Saxonism – belief in the racial superiority of white Northern Europeans and their descendants – with its vigorous masculine language of order, force, and power was used to justify the military conquest of decadent and feminised (and Catholic) Latin or indigenous populations. It celebrated the US's racial destiny to transform and redeem other nations, especially through the example of its superior republican institutions. It justified self-sacrificing missions of political education, religion, and instruction in democratic governance among "backward peoples." At the same time, extensive immigration of Irish- and German-Americans throughout the nineteenth century and their political influence in an already multi-ethnic America, meant the ideology was losing some of its "Saxonism." However, trade, commerce, and the search for overseas markets for American-produced goods were equally important drivers of overseas expansion.

The Philippine-American War precipitated bitter congressional, press, and public debates over national exceptionalism, imperialism, and the racial and political implications of colonial occupation. Few Americans wanted a large, expensive, and unmanageable colonial empire on the British or French model, but many statesmen and policymakers believed that their nation's engagement with overseas territories and peoples would advance universalistic goals of social justice, individual liberty, and democracy, and safeguard important economic and trading markets. Yet, there were deep popular and political divisions over whether the US should even acquire an empire. The December 1898 peace treaty with Spain had to be ratified by a two-thirds majority vote in the US Senate, and the ratification debates took place in Washington DC in January and February 1899. The most controversial section in the document was the article providing for the cession of the whole Philippine archipelago to the United States. At that time, there were 46 Republicans and 34 Democrats in the US Senate, and ten senators representing minor parties.

The burdens of empire

In February 1899, British poet Rudyard Kipling addressed American colonial ventures in "The White Man's Burden: The United States and the Philippine Islands," which was published in *McClure's* magazine. The poem began:

> Take up the White Man's burden –
> Send forth the best ye breed –
> Go bind your sons to exile
> To serve your captives' need;
> To wait in heavy harness
> On fluttered folk and wild –
> Your new-caught sullen peoples,
> Half devil and half child.

Kipling's ode to racial imperialism generated many anti-imperialism poems, including Anna Manning Comfort's "Home Burdens of Uncle Sam" published in *The Public* in May 1899, and which highlighted the domestic oppressions felt by African Americans, Native Americans, and women:

> Take up the white man's burden,–
> Yes, Uncle Sam, oh do!
> But why seek other countries
> Your burdens to renew?
> Great questions here confront you.
> Then, too, we have a past –
> Don't pose as a reformer!
> Why, nations look aghast!

From 1898 a powerful Anti-Imperialist League (AIL) mobilised to oppose US annexation of the Philippines. Former Treasury Secretary and Massachusetts Senator, George S. Boutwell, served as AIL president until 1905. Progressive reformer Jane Addams was one of the League's vice presidents, while Josephine Shaw Lowell became the first female vice president of the New York Anti-Imperialist League in 1901. The

AIL was linked to the Democratic Party but attracted support from all political parties. Its 30,000 members included literary figures such as Samuel Clements (Mark Twain), steel baron Andrew Carnegie, black leader and educator Booker T. Washington, and American Federation of Labor (AFL) leader Samuel Gompers. Rank and file support came from working-class whites, rural populists, and progressives, as well as the Colored National Anti-Imperialistic League and the black women's club movement, and white female auxiliary AIL organisations in the Northeast and Midwest.

Such a wide-ranging movement offered many reasons for opposing annexation. Many AIL supporters believed imperialism was incompatible with US democracy and worried that colonisation would undermine the moral foundation of the US constitution. Others feared that the nation's racial integrity would be compromised by the arrival of new groups of undesirable "aliens." Several labour leaders argued that migration of Filipino and other colonial workers would lead to the incorporation of "coolie" labour standards that would undercut the hard-won freedoms of white workers. By contrast, anti-imperialist black critiques emphasised domestic prejudices towards Native Americans, African Americans, and Chinese, and the export of domestic disfranchisement and violent racial-political exclusion to US territories overseas. In his 1900 address to the Pan-African Congress in London, and 1903 book *The Souls of Black Folk*, W.E.B. DuBois observed, "The problem of the twentieth century is the problem of the color line – the relation of the darker races to the lighter races in Asia and Africa, in America and the islands of the sea." During the Aguinaldo-led republican period, Filipinos had already begun to establish an orderly governing infrastructure, but the most radical anti-imperialist view was that Filipinos – generally characterised by US policymakers, military officials and journalists as racially inferior and hopelessly fragmented into "warring tribes" – had the right to govern themselves.

The peace treaty with Spain was ratified but a proposal to grant eventual Philippine independence was defeated by one vote in the US Senate in February 1899. The AIL endorsed Democrat William Jennings Bryan who was also roundly defeated by the Republican McKinley-Roosevelt ticket in the 1900 presidential election. However, AIL campaigns continued amid domestic and international outrage over the conduct of US troops. The contradictions between the perceived civilising mission of the US and the violence and brutalities of the Philippine-American War became clearer following Brigadier General MacArthur's December 1900 order to destroy the rural economy. To isolate and starve out the guerrillas, US troops obliterated Filipino villages, burned rice stores, and slaughtered livestock. As in Cuba, the "reconcentration" of rural civilian populations into overcrowded village centres, as undertaken for example by General James Franklin Bell's troops at Batangas in November 1901, aggravated malnutrition and disease. An estimated 250,000 Filipinos died during US reconcentration.

Despite rigorous censorship of news correspondents by the US Army, specific instances of torture and killing of prisoners and collaborators were recorded by US soldiers. A military wife also helped break the story of the Army's controversial use of the "water cure" where a captured Filipino was interrogated as buckets of filthy water were poured into his mouth to create sensations of drowning. Evidence of atrocities was sometimes linked to the degenerating impact of guerrilla warfare on US troops, for example in "Fighting Life in the Philippines" by US Army surgeon, Dr Henry C. Rowland, and published in *McClure's Magazine* in June 1902. Black anti-imperialists also drew parallels between white troops torturing brown guerrillas and widespread racialisation of violence in the Philippines and lynching and racial violence in the metropole. A largely ineffective Senate investigation followed.

Aguinaldo was captured by American forces in March 1901 and swore an oath of allegiance to the US a month later. A public ceremony in Manila on 4 July 1901 marked the formal military to civil transfer of all executive governmental functions. The islands were ruled by US-appointed Governor, William Howard Taft, and a civil government under the Philippine Commission which was largely made up of collaborating Filipino elites. The final and formal end of the Philippine-American War was announced in President Roosevelt's proclamation of 4 July 1902. In November, the Philippine Commission passed the Brigandage Act which established an insular police force under its control that would continue the "pacification" process and allow the demobilisation of US troops. Even so, Filipino resistance continued in several provinces including the Moro region until 1913. And, political revolution and economic instability continued to plague many countries under US protection in the 1910s and 1920s.

Chasing China's markets

By the beginning of the twentieth century, the US was involved in nation-building in Cuba, colonial state building in the Philippines, and economic penetration of overseas markets for export. Many contemporaries and later historians contended that the post-1890 empire was different to that of European models, which sought to deliberately acquire new colonial territories to formally control and populate, because in the decades after the Civil War, America sought new areas primarily for trade, and therefore allowed native inhabitants to rule themselves under informal US protection. The reality was more complicated and there was no one-size-fits-all model of American administrative colonialism, plus economic motivations were as powerful as military prowess.

Many nineteenth-century Americans firmly believed that China offered unlimited commercial possibilities and profits: huge new markets for American goods would absorb domestic overproduction, stabilise employment at home, and enhance private business and investment overseas. There was already a vibrant Pacific trade in luxuries like tortoise shells, silks, ambergris, and sandalwood, as well as opium and tea. By 1890, companies such as Standard Oil and British American Tobacco benefitted from a series of trade agreements and low tariffs which privileged the importation of foreign goods at the expense of native Chinese industries. However, Japan's defeat of China in the 1894–95 Sino-Japanese war, and the establishment of French, German, Russian, and British "spheres of influence" along the Chinese coast seriously compromised US trade aspirations.

Preservation of China's territorial and administrative integrity, equal access to Chinese ports, and equal trading privileges for all nations remained central planks of McKinley-Roosevelt foreign policy. Two reasons for formal US annexation of the Hawaiian Islands in early 1898 were the importance of Pearl Harbor as a US naval base and Hawaii's strategic position in relation to trade with China and Japan. The "Open Door" notes issued by US Secretary of State John Hay in 1899 and 1900 called on European and Asian imperial powers to maintain equal trading access to China and for Chinese sovereignty to be preserved in each region of its empire, but US ambitions were frequently challenged. A secret society of anti-Christian Chinese nationalists, known as "Boxers," opposed to the spread of western and Japanese political, economic, and cultural influences led an uprising in northern China 1899–1901. When Peking's (Beijing) foreign district was besieged by Boxers during the summer months of 1900, US Marines were part of the international force that defeated the rebellion.

How important was China to imperial America?

Historians continue to debate the importance of the China market to American interests. In 1910, less than 1 per cent of American exports went to China (2 per cent by 1930) and Americans held around 3 per cent of foreign investments there (6 per cent by 1930), which still accounted for an impressive $49 million. One school contends that the open-door rhetoric of American policymakers was more important that the actual scale of exports and investments, while others underline American policymaker and business convictions that the China market was crucial to absorb US domestic overproduction, and to ensure long-term political and economic stability at home.

Several studies confirm that China was an extremely difficult market for US firms to conquer, particularly during periods of prolonged Chinese political instability. The most successful American companies in China accommodated themselves to local business customs and practices and offered an attractive product to Chinese consumers. They could withstand threats from Chinese nationalist officials determined to limit imports by imposing heavy taxes on foreign firms or company buy-outs, as had occurred in the mining sector. Standard Oil had a strong network of well-trained and well-paid local agents and merchants operating in port cities such as Shanghai and Hong Kong and with contacts in the interior, and an elaborate marketing network that could successfully compete with Russian and Dutch rivals. The company also developed a cheaper type of Kerosene for Chinese consumers, in the same period that gas and electricity increasingly powered American homes and factories. American textile firms were less successful in maintaining a foothold in Chinese markets and competing with the native textile industry.

In the early twentieth century, following incursions into northern China, Russia became the chief threat to Anglo-European and US Open Door policies, but the "Slavic menace" was neutralised with Japanese victory in the Russo-Japanese war of 1904–05. President Roosevelt mediated peace negotiations in Portsmouth, New Hampshire, and consequently became the first American recipient of a Nobel Peace Prize. Ironically, Japan's military and political ascendancy, and its growing presence in south Manchuria and Korea, stoked US-Japanese tensions over their Pacific territories and commercial competition in South Asia. Then, in October 1911, revolutionaries in southern China led a successful rebellion against the Qing dynasty, which further threatened foreign investments and treaty privileges. The end of imperial rule and the establishment of a new Republic of China drew crucial US support, and the US established diplomatic relations with the new government in 1913.

Transnational communities and border controls

The incorporation of overseas territories and their populations into a rapidly expanding US orbit created new Caribbean and Pacific diasporas and transnational communities. For example, Puerto Rican labourers were recruited by American sugar estates in Cuba, the Dominican Republic, and Hawaii. Cuban sugar fields were worked by thousands of Haitians and Jamaicans. Barbadians helped build the Panama Canal. Emigrants included skilled workers, professionals, and entrepreneurs, but North American corporations operating overseas, such as the United Fruit Company, and industrial employers at home particularly encouraged the movement of unskilled labourers. Between 1901 and 1910, slightly over 100,000 Caribbean migrants arrived in the US, and a further 135,000 during the 1910s. Puerto Rican migration increased after passage of the Jones Act (1917) which conferred US citizenship on islanders. Cubans benefitted from easy travel to the US, by ferry from Havana to Key West, and train from Key West to New York City. Unlike Asian residents in the United States, Cuban émigrés could maintain dual households in the US and Cuba.

Overseas expansion and American colonisation of Hawaii and the Philippines generated stronger border enforcement policies and new immigration restrictions, long demanded by the Asian Exclusion League and similar groups. Despite angry local protests in China, in 1902 Congress extended the Chinese Exclusion Act to cover entry to the new territories. Chinese immigrants already in Hawaii and the Philippines were further prohibited from entering the mainland United States amid growing nativism and xenophobia in the West in particular. The Canadian government willingly assisted with the enforcement of US Chinese exclusion laws, when it permitted US inspectors to examine all Asian and European steamship arrivals to Canada from 1894, then extended this to the Canadian Pacific Railway Company's transcontinental rail routes and cargo ships at Pacific ports such as Vancouver in 1903. The Vancouver-Puget Sound border region included major smuggling routes for people, drugs, and other contraband goods in a period of growing international concern over the flourishing opium trade. The US government banned opium imports from the Philippines in 1905.

Mexican policymakers generally viewed immigration as essential to the modernisation of the country's infrastructure so passed fewer restrictions on Chinese immigrants. Many Americans considered Mexican and European immigrants to be more desirable than Asians while southwestern farmers and industrialists found a cheap labour force in unskilled Mexican migrants. Nevertheless, vocal politicians, business interests, labour leaders and voters expressed increasing concerns over the insecurity of America's continental borders. By 1908, inland border inspection points had been established across the US-Canadian boundary, the same year that a special Chinese Division was established in the US Bureau of Immigration and a diplomatic agreement between American and Japan curbed Japanese immigration. By 1909, around 300 US immigration officers were committed to protecting both the Canadian and Mexican borders. Even so, an estimated 17,000 undocumented Chinese immigrants arrived in the US through the "backdoors" of Canada and Mexico between 1882 and 1920. The US Army patrolled the southern border while American customs officials and police conducted raids and engaged in formal and informal surveillance of so-called illegals. Many hundreds of people of different nationalities were deported.

Defending the Western Hemisphere

American officials were vexed over renewed European meddling in the Western Hemisphere that threatened to undermine US economic and political power in the Caribbean and Central America. In his fourth annual message to Congress, on 6 December 1904, President Roosevelt declared, "It is not true that the United States feels any land hunger or entertains any projects as regards the other nations of the western hemisphere save such as are for their welfare." If a neighbouring country could show "that it knows how to act with reasonable efficiency and decency in social and political matters, if it keeps order and pays its obligations, it need fear no interference from the United States." However, swift reassertion of the Monroe Doctrine and US intervention under the guise of "international police power" would follow "flagrant cases of [chronic] wrongdoing or impotence." A series of US military outposts and naval stations were positioned at strategic points in the Caribbean and Pacific to support Roosevelt's Corollary to the Monroe Doctrine. These included Guantanamo Bay (Cuba), as well as Pago Page Bay in Western Samoa, Midway Island, and Pearl Harbor (Hawaii). In addition, a new trans-isthmian canal was needed to accommodate an expanding Navy with modern Dreadnought battleships and destroyers.

The successful French-built Suez Canal in Egypt had facilitated cheaper and more direct trans-continental routes between Europe, Africa and East Asia from 1869, but French efforts to construct a canal across the Panamanian isthmus in the 1880s were crippled by bankruptcy and disease. President Roosevelt quickly revived plans to build a canal connecting the Pacific and Atlantic Oceans, a project of major economic, geo-political, and strategic importance to United States' expansionism, not least because it would link the different American naval fleets. When the "Great White" US fleet of 16 battleships circumnavigated the globe in 1907–09, it had to sail around South America, and through the Straits of Magellan.

Under the Hay-Pauncefote Treaty of 1901, the United States secured the rights to build and manage a canal, which the US Senate decided in 1902 should be in Panama, then part of Columbia. The US Secretary of State and the Columbian Foreign Minister agreed terms, but when the Columbian Congress rejected the financial settlement, Roosevelt ordered US warships to Colón and Panama City. The US encouraged a nationalist uprising then recognised the new independent Republic of Panama in November 1903. A treaty concluded between US Secretary of State John Hay and Panama's Envoy Philippe Bunau-Varilla that same month created a US-controlled Canal Zone, around 16 kilometres wide and 80 kilometres long, in return for a one-off payment of $10 million and an annual annuity of $250,000 to the Panama government.

Nine years of construction commenced in May 1904, on a railroad to service the site, then on blasting and excavating to create the dams and locks of one of the most challenging engineering projects of the period. The multinational workforce, of 40,000 at its peak, was recruited from North America, the Caribbean and Europe. Jim Crow colonialism framed the experiences of West Indian workers who were subject to racial segregation and discriminatory labour practices. Work conditions were brutal, and nearly 6,000 workers died from accidents and disease. Yet, the Panama Canal embodied Progressive-era optimism and unshakable faith in human ability to control nature. It also transformed Roosevelt's Corollary from a declaration of principle into a statement of American power and hegemony. The passage in August 1914 of the first French boat through the canal, and the first US trading ship travelling from

San Francisco to New York without having to sail around South America, were truly momentous events.

The Panama Canal project also promoted important scientific and medical advances, particularly in epidemiology, that resulted in life-changing public health reforms. With a US government investment of $20 million in sanitation, medical care, burial services, and other public health improvements, Chief Medical Officer, Dr. William Crawford Gorgas, waged war on the mosquitoes transmitting yellow fever and malaria. Drawing on methods pioneered in post-war Havana, sanitation workers in the Canal Zone drained, or covered with kerosene, all sources of standing water to eradicate mosquito eggs and fumigated areas infested with adult mosquitoes. Proper screening of buildings and the use of netting were other simple but effective measures. In major urban centres, new domestic water systems provided running water to residents, thereby eliminating the collection of rainwater in barrels which offered perfect breeding sites for the insects. Dispensaries were set up along the canal route and trains carried hospital cars. In the work camps, patients afflicted with yellow fever or malaria were quarantined in special medical areas and treated with quinine. Yellow fever had abated from the Canal Zone by 1906 and malaria was largely contained. Several doctors and public health officials who had worked in the Philippines, Cuba and the Canal Zone

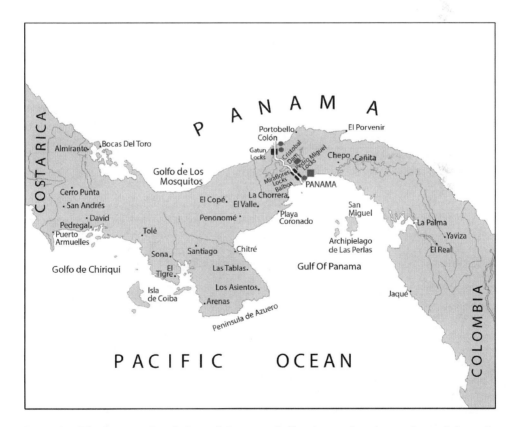

Figure 9.6 The Panama Canal. One of the most challenging engineering projects of the early twentieth century was completed with a multinational workforce and officially opened in 1914.

went on to direct domestic initiatives to eradicate hookworm, malaria, and pellagra in the southern US states in the 1910s and 1920s.

American claims of exclusivity in the Caribbean and Central America, and a policy of "preventive intervention," which enabled US armed forces to restore order where local military forces had failed, provided an important ideological platform for continued invasions in the early twentieth century. In 1905, US forces arrived in the Dominican Republic, and customs houses were seized and placed under American control. The island remained a protectorate until 1907, but US Marines returned in 1916 to quell a domestic rebellion and occupied the island for eight more years. Both the Platt Amendment and the Roosevelt Corollary were invoked for US intervention in Cuba 1906–1909, and again in 1912, following an Afro-Cuban uprising in the Eastern provinces. Additional US interventions in Nicaragua, Haiti, and Mexico further demonstrated that Roosevelt's successors, presidents William Howard Taft (1909–1913) and Woodrow Wilson (1913–1920), remained committed to maintaining and extending US hegemony in the Western Hemisphere.

Taft's foreign policy is often characterised as "Dollar Diplomacy." American control of the national economic affairs of financially unstable or politically turbulent neighbouring countries and safeguarding US financial interests, including that of private corporations and investors, were central to decisions about US military and political intervention. Economic stability was necessary to increase US investment in Latin and Central America and the Caribbean and to displace European financial influence and foreign creditors. American economic intervention could have malign impacts on local populations: the Foraker Act (1900) changed local landownership rules and quickly transformed Puerto Rico into a sugar monoculture economy that privileged US sugar companies and undercut local plantation owners.

The United Fruit Company became the archetypical US corporation: through its ownership of large swathes of land, reliance on subservient political elites in Honduras, Nicaragua and elsewhere to deliver a compliant labour force, monopoly of transportation networks, and dominance of fruit importation to the US. The company came to embody a new era of corporate empire that promised modernisation and civilisation. The profitability of banana, sugar and coffee crops did increase after World War I and there were tangible improvements to the living standards of many workers, but US corporate penetration meant that crucial economic decisions affecting workers' wages and wellbeing were made by foreigners in distant boardrooms. Company jobs were also used to maintain racial and class hierarchies because they promoted white Anglo supremacy and company control over subordinate black and brown servile labourers.

Economic imperialism did not fully replace military action. American marines landed in Haiti in July 1915 to restore order and protect property after the brutal murder of President Vilbrun Guillaume Sam. The US State Department also sought to neutralise the threatened establishment of a German submarine base on the island, which lies just 1287 km from southern Florida. In August, US-supervised elections were won by Phillippe Sudre Dartiguenave. President Wilson described the new Haitian president as a man "we can trust to handle and put an end to revolution." Wilson had vowed "to teach the South American republics to elect good men" and many policymakers and ordinary US voters agreed that their nation's legal, political, and constitutional values should be extended to their "backward," "underdeveloped," and non-white Caribbean and Central American neighbours. However, when Dartiguenave signed a

treaty which made Haiti, with a population of two million, into an American protec-
torate with limited sovereignty, there was considerable criticism from leading African
American journalists, reformers and political leaders. Articles by W. E. B. DuBois in
Crisis, the NAACP's official magazine, and Oswald Garrison Villard in the *New York
Evening Post* called for a presidential commission to investigate US conduct in Haiti
and demanded the withdrawal of US troops. There were similar protests when US
Marines occupied the Dominican Republic in 1916, but attention was increasingly
turning towards Europe.

War in Europe, 1914–18

Between 1914 and 1918, Europe's major powers divided into two main groups of
combatants: the Allied Powers, which included Great Britain, Russia and France, Ser-
bia and Belgium, and Italy after 1915, and the Central Powers, which included Germany, Austria-Hungary, Bulgaria and the Ottoman Empire. America had no alliances
with any European belligerents when the complex system of "Great Power" defensive
pacts unravelled in summer 1914. When war became official in August, President
Wilson asked that the American people be "neutral in fact as well as in name" and
"impartial in thought as well as in action." However, American policies were progres-
sively undermined by evolving and entrenched conflicts in Europe, Africa, the Middle
East, and Asia. American attitudes also evolved from a mixture of horror and indifference in 1914 to uneasy neutrality in 1915–16 to unhappy acceptance in spring 1917
that moral suasion and diplomacy could not contain German militarism and the US
had run out of alternatives to military involvement.

Americans demonstrated their support, particularly to the Allied cause, in various ways. In October 1914, following graphic reports of German atrocities, Herbert
Hoover formed the Committee for Relief in Belgium to raise millions of dollars to
provide shelter, food, and protection for Belgian civilians. Thousands of American
volunteers, including doctors, nurses, and relief workers headed to France and Belgium in 1914–15, often with the Red Cross. By 1916, approximately 6,000 Americans
had volunteered for service in British army units and thousands more were serving in
Canadian units. The Ontario-organised 135th Middlesex Battalion included the first
Native American companies to land in France in January 1917. Many were decorated
for their bravery in combat.

Americans' desire to continue to trade freely with European nations at war was
severely tested in 1914–15 by the Allied blockade of German ports, British and German mining of North Sea shipping routes, and Britain and France's growing war
debts. However, US agriculture, industry, and workers all profited from increased
export orders to war-torn Europe, including Kansas wheat and southern cotton, as
well as timber and munitions. The war necessitated a new phase of Dollar Diplomacy.
In August 1915, US bankers received government permission to lend $500 million to
the Allies, and credits were also extended to Germany. By early 1917, American bankers had provided $2.5 billion in credits or loans to the Allies, and less than $300 million to the Central Powers, a clear indication of where US government and corporate
sympathies lay.

In late April 1915, the German Embassy placed advertisements in 50 US newspapers
to warn Americans of the risks of travelling in war zones on British and Allied ships.
This followed the German launch of unrestricted submarine warfare in February, that

did not discriminate between fully weaponised naval warships, unarmed merchant ships, or civilian transports. The luxury passenger liner, *Lusitania*, departed New York for Liverpool on 1 May. Seven days later, the *New York Herald* informed a shocked nation: "The Lusitania Is Sunk; 1,000 Are Probably Lost." At 2:12pm on 7 May the ship was struck by a U-boat torpedo and sank just off the south coast of Ireland in less than 20 minutes. Of the 1,198 who perished, 128 were Americans. German claims that the liner was carrying war materiel were first denied, but later confirmed. The Wilson Administration protested the sinking in the strongest terms; the German government apologised and pledged to end submarine attacks. Theodore Roosevelt viewed the *Lusitania* attack as a crucial test of US capacity for global leadership, which he believed the nation had failed, and he denounced Wilson's weak and dishonourable response.

U-boat attacks continued but when Congress threatened to pass a resolution preventing Americans from travelling on armed belligerent ships in February 1916, Wilson refused to support a motion that restricted Americans' constitutional rights and undermined the "honor and self-respect" of the nation. The political tide began to change after the sinking of the *Sussex*, an unarmed French passenger liner, in March 1916, even though Wilson believed he had secured a German pledge not to sink any more civilian vessels. This attacked galvanised support for Preparedness at Home, where it was argued that strengthening national security and building up the pool of army reservists would preserve US isolation. In June 1916, Congress passed the National Defense Act which bolstered National Guard units in every state as a reserve force, created a Reserve Officer Training Corps, pledged money for new technology such as military aviation, and gave the US Navy $315 million for new battleships. Nevertheless, there was still a massive technological gap between US and European forces, in an age of long-range steel field artillery, poison gas, and submarine warfare.

There was growing evidence that German agents operating in the US and Canada were attacking factories, ships, and goods. Fires like that at the Roebling Steel foundry in Trenton, New Jersey, in January 1915, and the use of cigar bombs concealed in sacks of sugar to sink munition-carrying ships at sea in later 1915, were clearly designed to halt crucial shipments reaching Allied countries. A series of dramatic explosions at the massive Lehigh Valley "Black Tom" Railroad terminal in Jersey City, New Jersey, in July 1916 increased fears of sabotage. Nearly three-quarters of all overseas munitions' shipments left from this terminal. German saboteurs were later confirmed to have been responsible.

German officials also sought to exploit deteriorating US–Mexican relations, which were still fragile following a US military invasion of Veracruz in April–November 1914 (Japanese warships had also appeared near Hawaii and Mexico in late 1914). Then, in March 1916, several hundred Mexican guerrillas under the command of Francisco "Pancho" Villa, crossed from Chihuahua to attack Columbus, a small border town in New Mexico. Seventeen Americans were killed and much of the town was burned. Wilson sent General John J. Pershing and 12,000 US troops to Mexico with orders to capture Villa, which aggravated relations with the Venustiano Carranza government, and led to further clashes with Mexican troops. Villa continued to evade US capture. In January 1917, the German foreign minister, Arthur Zimmermann sent a telegram to the German ambassador in Mexico, directing him to propose a German–Mexican alliance, and to offer Mexico the return of "lost territories" Texas, Arizona, and New Mexico if this was agreed. Japanese threats to US Pacific interests were also to be encouraged. The telegram was intercepted and deciphered by British intelligence, thus revealing that the UK was actively spying on a neutral country. Zimmermann's text was released to the US press in late February 1917 to acute US political and public outrage. Meanwhile, the German government had announced the resumption of unrestricted submarine warfare in the Mediterranean and North Atlantic, just as other profound changes were occurring.

In March 1917, the Russian imperial order was overthrown, replaced by a republican government that promised the Russian people democracy, war success, and food. Domestic dissention and battlefield failures precipitated its collapse six months later, and in October, the Bolshevik wing of the Russian Social Democratic Labor Party, a forebear of the Russian Communist Party, came to power. Under the leadership of Vladimir Ilyich Lenin, the party sought to transform global war into an international civil war in which the proletariat would defeat capitalism, abolish private ownership, and establish workers' states, first in Russia. In March 1918, Russia's withdrawal from World War I was formalised with the Treaty of Brest-Litovsk, just as the German High Command launched the Ludendorff Offensive along the Western Front. It seemed as if the war would never end. As the slaughter of millions of young soldiers and civilians continued indefinitely, the destruction of European civilisation and the starvation of its peoples seemed inevitable. How long could Americans refrain from military involvement? Further, if Allied defeat in Europe led to German control of Canada and Britain's Caribbean colonies, this would directly threaten US hegemony in the Western Hemisphere and could increase the likelihood of warfare on US soil.

On 2 April 1917, at a Joint Session of the US Congress, President Wilson requested a declaration of war against Germany, citing the resumption of submarine warfare and the threat of a German–Mexican alliance. Senators voted 82–86 in favour of the declaration on 4 April, and Representatives voted 373–50 on 6 April. "I want to stand by my country, but I cannot vote for war," declared Montana's recently elected Congressional Representative Jeannette Rankin, a leading light in the Women's Peace Party, and one of the 50 members of the House who refused to support Wilson's request. The war declaration did tap into patriotic fervour, and strong anti-German and anti-radical sentiment but many ordinary Americans were dismayed when Wilson reneged on his promise to keep America out of war. Nevertheless, Americans who were convinced of the inherent superiority of US values and governance also believed intervention in the war would save Christian civilisation, safeguard democracy, and ensure a progressive post-war settlement. The US later formally declared war on the Austro-Hungarian empire, on 7 December 1917.

To cultivate wartime unity and support for military preparedness, the Committee on Public Information, under George Creel, engaged in a massive propaganda campaign, while the Wilson administration imposed harsh restrictions on anti-war expression. The American "doughboy" or solider was a key figure in the visual culture of World War I, in illustrations, advertisements, popular magazines, and posters. Wartime conscription bills were passed in May 1917 and 1918, under which 24 million men registered to fight, and three million were drafted. A further 1.8 million volunteered to fight. Cartoons, posters, and speeches designed to promote "100 per cent Americanism" were rife with nativism and xenophobia, but nearly 500,000 immigrants of 46 different nationalities (and including volunteers from territories under Central Power control) as well as thousands of second-generation immigrants, undertook military service. Several thousand had already volunteered before 1917.

Yet, conscription drew intense opposition from many quarters including peace and socialist movements and the historic peace churches (Quakers, Mennonites, and Brethren). National liberal pacifist organisations established during World War I included the Women's Peace Party, later Women's International League for Peace and Freedom (1915) and American Friends Service Committee (1917); the absolutist Fellowship of Reconciliation was established in 1915. Around 450 conscientious objectors who refused military service were court-martialled and imprisoned. They organised work protests and hunger strikes at Fort Leavenworth and other military prisons. Conscription also spurred a Green Corn Rebellion in Oklahoma in August 1917 where an interracial group of hundreds of tenant farmers angry at wealthy landowners and fearful of economic insecurity planned to march to Washington to demand an end to the war. Incidence of burned bridges and cut telegraph wires precipitated numerous arrests. Around 150 were convicted, and sentenced to up to ten years in federal prison.

The American Expeditionary Force in Europe

The American Expeditionary Force (AEF), under Pershing's command, made its way to Europe during 1917 and early 1918. Images of doughboys climbing over the top of trenches, breaching the barbed wire of no-man's-land, and throwing grenades or brandishing bayonets featured in post-war commemorations, but also embodied Pershing's commitment to offensive action and open warfare, and emphasis on personal combat skills. Female civilians in uniform accompanied the AEF. The Army Signal Corps employed 700 women, half of whom were bilingual French-speaking telephone operators, and the Army Nurse Corps had more than 12,180 medical personnel serving in 200 hospitals in Europe and worldwide by 1918.

Figure 9.7 Doughboys in the trenches. Around 2.8 million American troops served overseas during World War I and were popularly known as "doughboys." As with troops serving in European armies, American Expeditionary Force (AEF) soldiers endured trench warfare and gas attacks.

Source: Courtesy of Everett Collection Inc/Alamy 9.8 – The Western Front, World War I, 1918

American troops were divided by race and all 350,000 African Americans served in segregated units. Fewer than 700 African Americans became officers and many were consigned to manual labour, such as stevedores for the US Navy. However, black doughboys did fight in France in all-black regiments such as the 369th Harlem Infantry. There was strong African American support for military mobilisation and home-front contributions, but after the war, W. E. B. DuBois wrote passionately of the need to keep fighting a battle for equality that had not yet been won. In fact, the War Department had attempted to persuade Allies to follow racial segregation practices in Europe. Native American military service was also dogged by debates over whether recruits and volunteers should be in segregated or integrated units, and wider questions over the assimilation of Natives into "mainstream" US culture.

Many historians have documented the AEF's inexperience, poor training, and disproportionately high casualty rate. Nevertheless, American troops did have a decisive impact on the Western Front: by the time of the Armistice, US troops held over 20 per cent of Allied front lines. In June–July 1918, more than one million US troops assisted Allied forces in halting the German drive towards Paris. The Americans won a major victory at Château-Thierry and nearby Belleau Wood, but suffered almost 10,000 casualties. The AEF played a crucial role in a combined French and American counteroffensive in the Aisne-Marne region in July to push the Germans back to the Hindenburg Line. Pershing's goal of AEF forces fighting as a fully trained separate army was not realised until the autumn, but the US First and Second Armies (with over one million troops) played decisive combat roles in the last Allied offensive of the war,

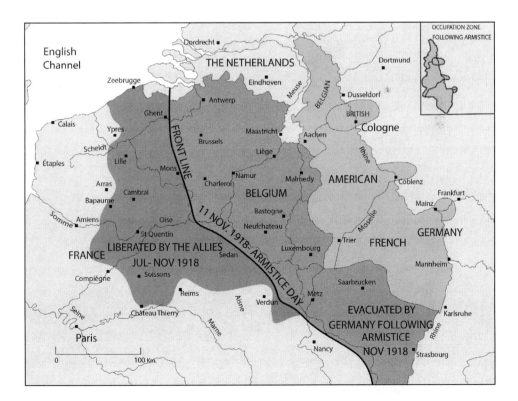

Figure 9.8 The Western Front, World War I, 1918.

the Allied Meuse-Argonne Campaign from September to November 1918. American military support took many forms. When the 142nd Infantry of the 36th Division near St Etienne, discovered that their radio lines had been compromised in October 1918, Choctaws at different communication posts used their native language to frustrate German eavesdropping. A unique unit of Native American radio talkers soon developed. Recent histories of American involvement in the Great War have re-emphasised these innovative US contributions along with the diversity of military recruits.

Figure 9.9 World War I US Marine poster. First in France – US Marines. This 1917 recruiting poster shows a marine carrying a mortar into combat. The first US Marines arrived in France in July 1917. American expeditionary forces made decisive contributions to Allied campaigns on the Western Front from spring 1918.

Source: Courtesy of Everett Collection Historical/Alamy

European entanglements

Wilson's grand strategic post-war agenda was laid out in a speech to a joint session of Congress on 8 January 1918, and his "Fourteen Points" included freedom of the seas, removal of trade barriers, armament reduction, and "open covenants of peace," as well as Restoration of Poland as an independent nation, self-determination for former imperial entities, and other European territorial adjustments. The centrepiece of Wilson's plan was the "general association of nations" in Point #14, where an international organisation to promote international peace and collective security, a League of Nations, would supersede traditional European great power alliances. In January 1919, representatives from 30 countries (not the former Central Powers or Russia) began peace negotiations at Versailles. In the following weeks, the "Big Four" former Allied Powers – France, Britain, Italy and the United States – dominated discussions over the future of post-war Germany and other key issues. Wilson quickly found that the post-war territorial designs of the leaders of Britain, France and Italy, and their expectations of economic reparations were at odds with his plans to make a world "safe for democracy" with the US at the helm.

Wilson also faced growing political opposition at home, particularly from the Republican-dominated Senate already angered that no important Republicans had been appointed to the American Peace Commission. In March 1919, Senate Republican leader, Henry Cabot Lodge, produced a petition with a long list of Treaty objections, signed by 39 Republican Senators and Senators-elect, which underlined Wilson's weakening domestic position. Returning to Paris, Wilson did press successfully for treaty amendments on tariff issues, immigration restriction, regional security pacts, and support for the Monroe Doctrine. There were no concessions on Article X of the League Covenant which Republicans were most hostile to. It asked League members to "respect and preserve . . . the territorial integrity and existing political independence of all members" in the face of external aggression.

Under the terms of the Treaty of Versailles, Germany lost around 13.5 per cent of its pre-war territory, 10 per cent of its population (or seven million citizens), and all overseas possessions. Alsace-Lorraine was returned to France, an area of East Prussia became part of Lithuania, and the Sudetenland went to Czechoslovakia. The German military was limited to a maximum of 100,000 men, and banned from using heavy artillery, gas, tanks, aircraft, and submarines. A war guilt clause identified Germany as solely responsible for the Great War. Further, the former Allied powers had all incurred huge debts to the US during the war, so there was strong support for German financial compensation to enable repayment. In 1920, the Reparations Commission determined that Germany should pay $33 billion in reparations, which was finally paid in full in October 2010. The recently established German civilian government denounced all these articles and the provision for a 15-year occupation of the Rhineland by Britain, France, and the US. American politicians also found many shortcomings in the Treaty. Nevertheless, Wilson's continued advocacy of national self-determination did produce tangible results: an independent Polish nation emerged after a century of partition, while Czechoslovakia, Yugoslavia, Austria, Estonia, Finland, Hungary, Latvia, Lithuania, and Romania all became post-war nation-states, as well as buffers between Russia and Germany. However, self-determination was waived in the Pacific when the former German-controlled Chinese province of Shantung was claimed by Japan, just as another revolution was occurring in China in May 1919.

Wilson formally presented the treaty to the US Senate on 10 July 1919; he needed to win two-thirds of the votes to ensure ratification. Most Democrats were willing to support ratification and US membership of the League of Nations. Republicans were split between those willing to support US League membership either with significant or moderate reservations, and those who rejected completely both the treaty and the League. Staunch opponents such as Lodge and Senator Albert J. Beveridge, opined that it would compromise US military power and national sovereignty, and could emasculate national honour.

To win popular support and put voter pressure on Republican "reservationists" and "irreconcilables" as well as several hostile Democrats, Wilson undertook an intense three-week speaking tour in September 1919. He travelled over 10,000 miles to deliver 32 major speeches and eight shorter addresses to educate ordinary Americans on the terms of the Versailles treaty, the purpose of the League of Nations, America's post-war role and responsibilities, and to refute Republican charges that Article X undermined Congress's constitutional powers to declare war. Already beset by health problems, the speaking tour gravely weakened the president, and had to be cut short. Back in Washington, on 2 October 1919, Wilson suffered a massive stroke and was incapacitated for several months, just when crucial national and Democratic Party leadership was needed.

The Treaty of Versailles failed to pass the Senate on 19 November 1919 and again on 19 March 1920. Warren G. Harding categorically rejected any American involvement with the League of Nations after he was elected president in November 1920. America and Germany were therefore technically still at war and American troops were still deployed to the occupied German territory west of the River Rhine, ostensibly to provide stability, preserve order, and protect German civilians. As the US did not sign the peace treaty, a civil government was not fully established in the American section of the occupation zone. The occupying US Third Army was replaced by a new 15,000-strong American Forces in Germany (AFG) partly to complete wartime demobilisation. War officially ended between the US and Germany with the 1921 Treaty of Berlin, but AFG troops stayed put.

Isolationism, unilateralism, and America First

Isolationism, protectionism, and distrust of international institutions are often used to describe US foreign policy and international relations in the 1920s. In 1921, President Harding and the Republican-dominated Congress ruled out any direct US government aid for post-war European economic recovery and political stabilisation and there was no official American participation in international conferences on European reconstruction in 1920 and 1922. Congress rejected calls from some business leaders and diplomats to cancel or reduce European war debts. All US war loans were to be fully repaid. And, new tariffs designed to protect US industries from foreign competition in the early 1920s saw import taxes increase to 40 per cent.

By contrast, two Naval Conferences took place in Washington DC in 1921 and 1922, following congressional and popular pressure for arms reduction. Lengthy negotiations generated a series of agreements on naval disarmament and the delicate political situation in the Far East. Despite considerable opposition in the US Senate, these treaties passed, often with reservations to ensure Americans would not be committed to armed or defensive actions overseas. The US also worked closely with the

League of Nations on international drugs policy to curb trafficking and disrupt global supply routes as domestic anti-narcotics enforcement increased at home. Congress established a Federal Narcotics Control Board in 1922 and outlawed the import and export of opium and heroin amid a panic over rising numbers of addicts and drug-related violence. American delegates attended most of the major League drug conferences in the 1920s.

The central principles of the Republican Party world order, aptly characterised by Warren Cohen as an "Empire without Tears," were: reduced military force and intervention, increased free trade and free currency, and promotion of economic activities by private individuals rather than governments. The sheer size of the US economy was clear: in 1920 crude steel production in the US dwarfed that of the UK, Germany, France, Russia, Japan, and Italy combined. In addition, the US overtook Britain as the pre-eminent trading nation, partly due to rapidly increasing exports from the booming radio, automobile, and aeroplane industries for example, and of Hollywood movies. America's share of world trade rose from 12.9 per cent in 1913 to 17.3 per cent in 1928. Dollar Diplomacy was reshaped in the 1920s to support a new global private business order with American banks and bankers at the centre.

Secretary of Commerce, and future president, Herbert Hoover was a key advocate of expanding the overseas economy and exploiting global opportunities. US corporations such as Standard Oil, Ford, and Eastman Kodak built overseas factories in Europe and South America. By 1926, Ford automobiles were assembled in 36 cities in the United States as well as 19 foreign countries. Several US corporations invested in roads and other construction projects to reach lucrative natural resources such as oil, and American banks extended large loans to Latin American governments. Mineral development and secure oil supplies were important drivers in commercial negotiations in Latin America and in the Middle East. American investors bitterly struggled with the British and French to control oil reserves but under the 1928 "Red Line" agreement, the giant oil companies simply used a map and a red pencil to divide a large Middle Eastern area among themselves. Several US corporations also willingly invested in the Soviet Union; portraits of Henry Ford and Vladimir Lenin appeared together in Soviet factories.

American officials tried to make Latin America the showcase of American foreign policy, for example, by finally recognising the Mexican government headed by Alvaro Obregón in 1923, although he was superseded by Plutarco Calles in 1924. Control of Mexican oil reserves, American investment in Mexican business, and increasing American loans to Mexican governments and private investors shaped US policy here. The US Commerce Department also supported private investment in Mexican highway, utilities, and communication expansion. By 1924, nearly three-quarters of the 20 Latin American nations were under some kind of military or economic US "management." American investments in Latin America more than doubled to $5.4 billion between 1924 and 1929, and consequently made military intervention more precarious if it affected US investors. Congress had fewer qualms about increasing tariffs on imported goods from Mexico thus underlining the one-sided emphasis of the "empire without tears."

The linked subjects of reparations and war debts continued to dominate international economic concerns during the 1920s. In January 1923, 60,000 French and Belgian troops invaded the Ruhr industrial areas, as the governments of these respective nations sought to collect unpaid reparations, from a Germany whose economy was beset by severe currency problems and crippling inflation. The AFG left the Rhineland in early 1923, partly to convey US disapproval of the invasion, but also in deference to domestic US concerns over the possible outbreak of another European war. Yet, Secretary of State Charles Evans Hughes convinced British and American bankers, including JP Morgan, to lend $200 million to German government and businesses and despite French objections negotiated easier reparation terms for Germany. The deal was completed at a 1924 conference headed by Chicago banker Charles G. Dawes. The following year the Locarno Treaty (1925) guaranteed Germany's western boundary. Another agreement to restructure Germany's reparations payments in 1930, brokered by another American banker Owen D. Young, attempted to offer stability at a time when domestic economies and global financial markets were collapsing.

An international campaign for disarmament and to outlaw war did draw considerable popular and political support in the US across the decade. New pacifist organisations were established in the 1920s, including the secular War Resisters League (1923). A subsequent proposal by French Foreign Minister Aristide Briand that the US and France should conclude a bilateral agreement to outlaw war transmuted into a multinational pact promoted by US Secretary of State Frank B. Kellogg. In August 1928, the Kellogg-Briand Pact was signed in Paris by the representatives of 15 states who agreed to renounce war "as an instrument of national policy" and seek to solve their disputes "by pacific means." Because Kellogg and other US leaders insisted there should be no enforcement provisions, the US was not obliged to intervene in European disputes, and this helped get Senate approval. Sixty-three nations eventually signed the Pact, and while it did not ultimately prevent the outbreak of another global conflict in 1939, it did change the international rules of war, including ending an aggressor state's right of conquest and right to retain goods, territory and people acquired by military force.

American investment in military power and new military technology continued in the 1920s, to bolster national and international security. For example, a permanent system of army chiefs of staff for planning was developed, as was an air force of approximately 10,000 men and 3,000 planes, and orders for new warships peaked in the early 1920s. Even after demobilisation in 1919, the regular US Army had around 140,000 troops. The US Navy also remained at strength: to keep sea-lanes of communication open, protect US overseas territories, and support the Marine Corps with quasi-policing duties throughout Latin America. Despite the withdrawal of troops from the Dominican Republican and Nicaragua, US military forces remained in numerous countries in the Western Hemisphere. The Coast Guard was also tasked with bolstering border security and stopping the flow of contraband liquor, cigarettes, fruit, and narcotics, and undocumented people into the United States. Failure to reach an agreement with the British government over limits on cruisers at the Geneva naval disarmament conference of 1927, spurred Congress to authorise expenditure on 15 new cruisers and an aircraft carrier. Military planners also highlighted the growing importance of naval aviation.

By the 1920s, the US has replaced Britain as the leading financial and commercial global power, and the Republican presidents of the 1920s would not countenance any return to the pre–World War I era in which European "great powers" held sway. They confidently, even arrogantly, believed that only a new order, constructed and dominated by US economic power would avert future world wars and neutralise revolutionary and political instability. American foreign policies and international relations were therefore not characterised by isolationism in the 1920s but by unilateralism. As President Hoover asserted in 1929, the "colossal power of the US overshadows scores of freedom-loving nations and thus makes concomitant American leadership in world affairs indispensable." No European country had the military capacity to threaten US continental coastlines, challenge the Monroe Doctrine, or endanger the Panama Canal, although an increasingly assertive Japan could menace American interests in the western Pacific and East Asia.

Chapter summary

This chapter explored how the US was transformed from a marginal global power to an economic, military, and political force to be reckoned with, and was intent on preserving its hegemony in the Caribbean and Pacific. It examined how the Spanish-Cuban-American War, Philippine-American War, economic intervention and military invasion in Latin American countries and China, the opening of the Panama Canal, and the growth of the US as a major creditor nation during World War I all contributed to this transformation in status. It discussed several key drivers of US imperialism and overseas intervention: securing important trade routes and domestic markets, racial and religious ideology, humanitarian concerns, and naval ambition. It showed also that the acquisition of new territories and peoples impacted on immigration to the US and brought new forms of racial categorisation and control.

Many early twentieth-century accounts presented American intervention in the Caribbean and Central America as a benign force for order and stability, but this was often far from reality. Under Dollar Diplomacy, US occupation could deliver political stability and economic investment as well as education reform, new roads and buildings, radio communications, and better public utilities, as well as a local professionally trained army, but it also undermined local commerce and local democratic-republican politics and US presidents continued to sanction the deployment of US Marines to restore "order." It was argued that this was not European imperialism but American progressivism in action, good neighbourly instruction in civil government, and racial uplift. As the next chapter shows, while Americans engaged in state building in their new colonial possessions, they sought to perfect US republicanism, democracy, and society at home.

 ## Discussion questions

- Which was the most significant reason for US intervention in the Caribbean and Pacific in the 1890s: the search for new trading markets, Anglo-Saxonism and racial concerns, naval aggrandisement, Manifest Destiny, Protestant religious ideas and a sense of Christian mission, or humanitarianism?
- In what ways might gendered ideas about power or masculinity and military prowess shape attitudes towards imperialism and anti-imperialism?
- How did Wilson's racial views shape his decisions to intervene in Latin America but initially pursue neutrality in the early stages of World War I?
- Does American rejection of the Treaty of Versailles and League of Nations signal that it was still a novice world power?
- Why did "Dollar Diplomacy" reach a highpoint in the 1920s?

Further reading

Brody, David. *Visualizing American Empire: Orientalism and Imperialism in the Philippines* (Chicago, 2010). Innovative and insightful exploration of the cultural and visual aspects of Philippine-American perceptions and relations.

Ford, Nancy G. *Americans All: Foreign-born Soldiers in World War I* (College Station, 2001). Fascinating study of the diversity of military volunteers and recruits, war department Americanisation policies, and the impact on the US military.

Gould, Lewis L. *The Presidency of Theodore Roosevelt* (Lawrence, KS, 1991). A solid, informative and thorough assessment of one of America's most enigmatic presidents.

Hannigan, Robert E. *The Great War and American Foreign Policy, 1914–24* (Philadelphia, 2017). A well-research and well-considered evaluation of Wilson's more conservative foreign policy and the continuities between Democrat and Republican administrations.

Herring, George C. *The American Century and Beyond: US Foreign Relations, 1893–2015* (New York, 2017). A detailed and thorough examination of evolving US foreign policy over the long 20th century that expertly analyses the tensions between isolationism and interventionism as the US became a world power then superpower.

Hoganson, Kristin L. *Fighting for American Manhood: How Gender Politics Provoked the Spanish-American and Philippine-American Wars* (New Haven and London, 1998). An insightful and provocative study of the importance of manhood, masculinity and honour to late 19th century US foreign policy that underscores the importance of gender to understanding US imperial interventions.

Hunt, Michael H., and Steven I. Levine. *Arc of Empire: America's Wars in Asia from the Philippines to Vietnam* (Chapel Hill, NC, 2012). Very useful study of empire building and world-then-superpower responsibilities by focusing on the Philippines, Japan, Korea and Vietnam as cognitive phases of US dominance in Asia.

Keene, Jennifer D. *Doughboys, the Great War, and the Remaking of America* (Baltimore, MD, 2001). A nuanced and insightful account of the transformative experiences of war on US soldiers (and the War Department and other branches of US government) and the challenges by US soldiers to domestic social, racial, and political issues.

Keene, Jennifer D. *The United States and the First World War* (Harlow, 2000). This is a great starting point for understanding the causes of World War I, home front and military mobilisation, and the fraught peace negotiations.

Kramer, Paul A. *The Blood of Government: Race, Empire, the United States, and the Philippines* (Chapel Hill, NC, 2006). An impressive pathbreaking transnational examination of US imperialism in action and the racial politics of empire and colonial resistance.

LaFeber, Walter F. *The New Empire: An Interpretation of American Expansion, 1860–1898* (1963; Ithaca, NY, 1998). A classic bold revisionist study of formal and informal imperial expansion that argued that economic imperatives, particularly the search for new commercial markets, drove formal and informal imperial expansion and military interventions in the Caribbean and East Asia.

Lenz, Lawrence. *Power and Policy: America's First Steps to Superpower, 1889–1922* (New York, 2008). This is a useful study which questions the importance and strategic value of military and naval power to US foreign policy objectives during the period of empire building overseas.

McCullough, David. *Path Between the Seas: The Creation of the Panama Canal 1870 to 1914* (1987; New York, 1999). A fulsome and comprehensive examination of an epic engineering and construction project, the workers, and the conditions they endured from one of the most prolific and well-known US historians.

McPherson, Alan. *US Interventions in Latin America and the Caribbean: A Short History* (Chichester, 2016). A well-organised and engaging study of 200 years of US military interventions in neighbouring countries and their responses to US hegemony and aggression that is a very useful starting point for understanding these topics.

Moore, Colin D. *American Imperialism and the State, 1893–1921* (Cambridge, 2017). Impressive examination of US state building in newly-acquired territories by colonial administrators and private enterprise and the interplay of progressive, corporate, and republican ideologies. Complements Rosenberg's study.

Mormino, Gary R., and George E. Pozzetta. *The Immigrant World of Ybor City* (Gainesville, FL, 2017). A fascinating, now classic, exploration of the vibrant Italian, Cuban, and Spanish communities linked to cigar manufacture in Tampa, Florida, and changing class, politics, and work cultures, as well as their links to *Cuba Libre*.

Perez, Louis A. *The War of 1898: The United States and Cuba in History and Historiography* (Chapel Hill, NC, 1998). This study provided an important historiographical challenge and compelling case for the need to examine the Spanish-Cuban-American War through wider perspectives and utilisation of Cuban sources and Cuban voices.

Rosenberg, Emily S. *Spreading the American Dream: American Economic and Cultural Expansion, 1890–1945* (1982; New York, 2011). An important study that demonstrates the ways in which American economic, technological, commercial, and cultural power, not just military and political interventions, were integral to US overseas imperial expansion.

Silbey, David. *A War of Frontier and Empire: The Philippine-American War, 1899–1902* (New York, 2007). A very readable military history of three inter-related (anti-colonial, nationalist, and imperial) conflicts, key Filipino and US personalities, and key issues.

Thompson, John A. *Woodrow Wilson* (London, 2013). An excellent short biography that provides a challenging yet convincing interpretation of Wilson as pragmatist.

10 State building in the United States

Timeline

1889	Hull House founded in Chicago
1890	Sherman Anti-Trust Act
	Jacob Riis, *How the Other Half Lives*
1905	Upton Sinclair, *The Jungle*
1906	Meat Inspection Act
	Pure Food and Drugs Act
1908	*Muller v. Oregon* US Supreme Court ruling
	First US policewoman appointed
	Ford Model T or "Tin Lizzy" introduced
1909	"Uprising of the 20,000" garment strike, New York City
1910	Founding of the National Association for the Advancement of Colored People
1911	Dillingham Commission on Immigration
	Neighborhood House founded, Atlanta, Georgia
	National Federation of Settlements established
	Triangle Shirtwaist Factory Fire
1912	New Nationalism vs New Freedom presidential platforms
	Woodrow Wilson elected president
1913	ASL-WCTU call for a constitutional prohibition amendment
	NWP-NAWSA call for a constitutional female suffrage amendment
	Direct election of senators approved
1914	Harrison Narcotics Act
1915	"Grandfather clause" declared unconstitutional
	Release of "The Birth of a Nation"
	Leo Frank lynching, Georgia
	Ku Klux Klan re-founded
1916	National Defense Act
1917	US enters World War I
	Increased anti-German hysteria
	Creel Committee on Public Information established
	Liberty Loan Campaigns begin
	Lever Food and Fuel Control Act
	Food riots in several US cities
	East St Louis race riot
	Immigration Act
	Eighteenth Amendment passes Congress

1918	Wartime government take-over of railways
	Wilson endorses female suffrage
	Continued NWP pickets and protests
	Influenza pandemic
1919	Wave of strikes
	Mail bombs
	Red Scare raids
	Wave of lynching
	Chicago's "Red Summer"
	Black Sox baseball scandal
	Economic recession begins
	Eighteenth Amendment is ratified by the states
	Victory Bond campaign
	Nineteenth Amendment passes Congress
	National Prohibition Enforcement Act
	Voting rights given to Native American war veterans
1920	National Prohibition begins
	Bureau of Prohibition established
	Red Scare raids
	US is officially a predominately urban nation
	Nineteenth Amendment ratified by the states
	Warren G. Harding elected president
	Food-Vending Automats open
1921	Sacco and Vanzetti murder trial
	Introduction of annual immigration quotas
	White Castle fast food chain established, Kansas
	First drive-in restaurant established, Texas
1922	Economic recession subsides
	"Herrin Massacre"
	Defeat of Dyer anti-lynching bill
	Import and export of opium and heroin is banned
1923	Rising political power of Klan
	US Supreme Court approves anti-Japanese laws
1924	National Origins Act
	Progressive Party challenge
	Klan controversy at Democratic Party convention
	Calvin Coolidge elected president
	US Board Patrol established
	Virginia's Racial Integrity Act
	Indian Citizenship Act
	Chicago "Beer Wars" break out
1925	Wilson Dam completed
	Klan March, Washington DC
	Alain Locke, "Harlem: Mecca of the New Negro"
1926	Florida real estate boom collapses
1927	Sacco and Vanzetti executions
	Release of "The Jazz Singer"
	Ford Motor Company layoffs

1928   Alfred E. Smith vs. Herbert Hoover presidential race
       Herbert Hoover elected president
       Release of "Lights of New York"
1929   St Valentine's Day Massacre, Chicago
       Permanent numerical immigration quotas confirmed
       Stock market and financial crash

Topics covered

- The Uprising of 20,000 and the Triangle Shirtwaist Fire
- Mobilising reform coalitions
- Political reforms and voter campaigns
- Mobilising the home front from 1914
- Hyper-nationalism and xenophobia
- The "brink of anarchy"
- The "return to normalcy"
- Black urban growth and self-defence
- Race, immigration, and citizenship
- National Prohibition

Introduction

This chapter focuses on the urbanising, modernising, and supposedly sober America between the dawn of the twentieth century and the Crash of 1929. It begins with the "Uprising of 20,000" garment strike in New York City in November 1909 and the deadly Triangle Shirtwaist Factory fire of March 1911 to highlight working conditions in urban-industrial America. It examines the motivations of different groups of reformers to improve public health and city life, increase participatory politics, and crackdown on corruption that are included under the broad term "Progressivism." It underlines that "progressive reform" was double-edged: democratic government extended the suffrage to mainly white women but disfranchised southern black male voters. The chapter goes onto examine wartime mobilisation that brought greater federal government economic intervention and local and state regulation of food conservation as well as racial and anti-radical violence and the suppression of civil liberties. Immigration restriction was a major demand of both mainstream political parties and rising right-wing challengers such as the Ku Klux Klan in the 1920s so there was considerable support for a series of post-war restrictive laws and a new quota system based on "national origins." These drastically reduced the numbers of arrivals to the US after 1921. The affluent Jazz Age, described by novelist F. Scott Fitzgerald, coincided with an extraordinary "experiment" in social engineering to restrict the consumption of alcohol. The final section of this chapter highlights the challenges of prohibition enforcement, and its unintended consequences such as the rise of urban crime syndicates. The chapter ends with the taut presidential election of 1928 that was dominated by Prohibition and Catholicism.

The Uprising of 20,000 and the Triangle Shirtwaist Fire

America's industrial labour force of 24 million workers in 1900 included native-born urban whites, migrants from America's embattled farm populations, African

Americans, immigrants, about 19 per cent of working age women, and 1.75 million children under 14 years of age. Male workers in full-time manufacturing jobs generally worked up to 60 hours per week, but days and weeks could be shortened without notice and without pay during the many economic downturns. In 1908, the US Supreme Court had restricted female wage earners to a ten-hour day (but not southern black agricultural workers or domestic servants) yet state protective laws increased the financial precariousness of women workers who earned 40 to 60 per cent of the equivalent male wage. Female department store employees and garment workers earned less than six dollars per week.

In November 1909, more than 20,000 immigrant and native-born shirtwaist and dress makers from over 500 New York City garment factories went on strike to demand a 52-hour working week, a 20 per cent wage increase, and additional pay for overtime. The International Ladies' Garment Workers' Union (ILGWU) and the National Women's Trade Union League (NWTUL) co-ordinated picketing and rallies. Strikers were assaulted by thugs hired by anti-union factory owners and harassed by police officers whose urban machine bosses had close political connections to factory owners. Many male and female garment workers were arrested and convicted of public order and incitement offences. Several society women and wealthy progressive reformers, such as Alva Belmont, organised fund-raising events to sustain public support for the strike and to raise funds to cover strikers' fines. The "Uprising of 20,000" was therefore part of a broader cross-class struggle for social and economic justice. In an era before universal female suffrage, labour disputes and consumer campaigns enabled many female activists such as Clara Lemlich and Margaret Dreier Robbins to hone their organising, public speaking, and lobbying skills. The garment strike finally ended with agreements on shorter hours and higher pay in February 1910 but no health and safety reforms.

Every year, hundreds of thousands of fatal accidents occurred in coal mines, textile mills, and factories because there were few health and safety regulations. Sometimes only the most tragic events could spur popular and political action. One of the last factories to resume production after the 1909–10 garment strike was the Triangle Shirtwaist Factory which had over 500 female employees and occupied the top three floors of a ten-story building in Manhattan's Garment District. Around 4:30pm on Saturday 25 March 1911, a small fire started in the cutting room on the eighth floor but quickly spread to the floors above. The city fire department had arrived within minutes, but their ladders and hoses did not reach the ninth or tenth floors. Women on the upper floors suffocated from smoke because they were trapped behind steel doors that were routinely locked by foremen to prevent "interruption of work." Twenty-four women died when the building's only fire escape twisted and collapsed. Thousands of spectators gathered in surrounding streets and watched in horror as 60 women chose to jump from the ninth floor rather than burn inside the building. United Press reporter William Shephard recalled, "Thud – dead; thud – dead; thud – dead; thud – dead. Sixty-two thud – dead." By the time the flames were under control, the factory was a mass of charred machines and the street below was lined with the bodies of girls and young women: 146 women had died within 45 minutes. More than 350,000 New Yorkers attended the funeral march a few days later. New city and state laws on employment of women and children, fire safety, factory inspections, worker protection, and sanitation were quickly passed but national reforms were needed. During the presidential campaign of 1912, Theodore Roosevelt's New Nationalism programme

Figure 10.1 Ladies' tailors or female garment workers on strike, New York City, 1910. Thousands of immigrant and native-born garment workers took part in mass protests
and strikes in New York City in 1909–10 to demand better wages and working
conditions. Similar protests occurred in garment factories across the United States
in the early twentieth century.

Source: Courtesy of Granger Historical Picture Archive/Alamy

included a standard 40-hour working week, minimum wage laws, and a federal system of social insurance, but he failed to win election.

Mobilising reform coalitions

In the late nineteenth and early twentieth centuries, many voters and reformers welcomed greater government intervention and business regulation to reduce poverty,
illness, and injustice, to improve workplace safety and public health, and to challenge corporate monopolies. "Progressivism" comprised both grass roots activism and
government-led initiatives, and a compliment of innovative measures was introduced
before and after World War I. One early success was the Sherman Anti-Trust Act
(1890) designed to curb unfair business practices. The main presidential platforms,
Theodore Roosevelt's "Square Deal" and later "New Nationalism," William Howard
Taft's pro-business agenda and anti-trust measures, and Woodrow Wilson's "New
Freedom" varied considerably but all envisaged an expanded interventionist role for

government and greater state regulation of the economy. Roosevelt also championed environmental protection and Wilson advocated banking reform.

Changing definitions of "progressivism"

In the 1950s "progressives" were portrayed as an anxiety-ridden group of status-conscious, middle-class Americans worried that traditional society was being steady eroded by big business, new political alliances, and the social mores of a growing, predominately immigrant working class. Since then numerous local and regional studies have painted a more diverse picture of reformers, campaigns, and followers. Rather than one group of reformers, there was a complex *range of movements*, made up of shifting and interlocking coalitions of working-class, immigrant, African American, and middle-class native-born leaders and supporters. Different advocates and reforming groups were influenced by diverse, even contradictory, impulses and ideologies: liberal and conservative, moralistic and permissive, agrarian and urban, nativist and pluralistic, white supremacists and advocates of racial equality, anti-intellectual populists and social and scientific experts, and militarists and pacifists.

A cluster of investigative journalists, termed "muckrakers," helped generate popular support for reform coalitions. They exposed corrupt local politicians and government officials, unsafe and unsanitary working practices and conditions, the exploitation of workers, and corporations or trusts which monopolised markets so that prices and their profits remained high. Standard Oil's unfair business practices were exposed by journalist Ida Tarbell in 1904 and the Roosevelt and Taft administrations launched trust-busting campaigns against Northern Securities, Standard Oil and the American Tobacco Company. Roosevelt promised greater "government supervision of the capitalization" of corporations in his "New Nationalism" speech in 1910. Popular magazines such as *Ladies Home Journal* and *Colliers* often carried advertisements for factory-made cosmetics and patent medicines alongside serial exposés of corrupt and unsafe practices, inaccurate weights and measures, and inflated retail prices. Journalist Samuel Hopkins Adams lambasted the pharmaceutical companies for peddling sugar-flavoured patent medicines full of narcotics and poisons that endangered rather than improved people's health. There were similar exposés of beauty products; best-selling ladies' face creams contained strychnine and arsenic.

Powerful consumer organisations, including the National Consumers League, lobbied for national safeguards as Americans were more likely to eat, drink, clean with, wear, sleep and sit on products made in factories rather than at home. They were purchased in local general stores, large urban department stores, or from the Sears or Montgomery Ward mail-order catalogues. Thanks to the growth of advertising, consumers of all classes and in all regions were very aware of the wonders of Gillette safety razors, Colgate toothpaste, and Pears soap, and the scientific promotion of canned soups, fish and meat. But were they safe? Upton Sinclair's *The Jungle* (1905) described Chicago's rat-infested meat factories and mislabelling of processed horse, goat, and offal. Home economics professionals and larger food manufacturers quickly got behind consumer campaigns for greater regulation.

A new Meat Inspection Act (1906) prohibited the sale of adulterated and mislabelled meat products and required slaughterhouses to improve conditions, although it would take time to plug the gaps between implementation and enforcement. The Pure Food and Drug Act (1906) prohibited the manufacture, sale, and shipment of impure, adulterated, and inaccurately labelled products. It also precipitated a decline in medicinal use of narcotics and paved the way for the first federal anti-drug legislation. In 1900, opium and heroin were popular painkillers and employers used cocaine to increase employees' labour productivity. Racialised and sensational news reports of Chinese opium dens and cocaine-fuelled black male criminality helped garner support for policy reform in the same period that the US was at the forefront of international campaigns to limit drug trafficking. In 1914, Congress passed the Harrison Narcotics Act (1914) which required all narcotics users to have medical or pharmacy prescriptions, established a federal registration system, and increased sales taxes to control the sale and distribution of heroin, cocaine, and opium.

The "Progressive era" was also a period of mass immigration. Around 25 million immigrants entered the US between 1880 and 1917 through federal processing centres such as San Francisco's Angel Island (1910–40), New York's Ellis Island (1892–1954), and at Galveston, Texas. Overall, 14 per cent of Americans were foreign born by 1914. Post-1896 arrivals came predominately from Southern and Eastern Europe but also from the Caribbean, Mexico and South America. They often settled in immigrant "colonies" in major cities (usually called "Little Italy" or "Little Poland" or similar) and created bustling communities with self-help societies, churches and temples, saloons, parochial schools, festivals, clubs, small businesses, and foreign-language newspapers. Immigration dramatically transformed the populations and public spaces of American cities, counties, and states; inflected habits of speech; redefined manners, cuisines, and drinking cultures; created new political alignments; and altered the so-called national character. However, these transformations were more obvious in some areas than others: in the 1910s, around three-quarters of Americans were still living in the state they had been born in but 41 per cent New York City residents were foreign-born and two-thirds of Chicago's population in 1920 were either foreign-born or the children of foreign-born parents.

Immigration restriction became a key progressive goal. Police reporter, investigative journalist, and photographer Jacob Riis exposed the squalor and misery of immigrants' lives as well as their resilience in *How the Other Half Lives: Studies among the Tenements of New York* (1890), but also characterised poorer Jews, Italians, and African Americans in derogatory terms. The 1911 Dillingham Commission highlighted the threat to American culture and society from unmanaged immigration. The "new immigrants" were often perceived to be racially, religiously, and culturally inferior to "older" groups of British, Irish and German immigrants. They helped expand America's industrial and urban infrastructure – constructing sewers, steel mills, and skyscrapers – but were accused of undercutting US workers and wages, as well as alcoholism and crime, and of selling their votes to corrupt urban political machines. Some reformers proposed Americanisation programmes which focused on public school curricula and intensive language instruction; others argued that "degraded races" of Eastern Europeans and Asians could never assimilate. An English language campaign in 1915 had backing from the president and many business leaders, including Henry Ford, whose 7,000 workers at Highland Park, Detroit, conversed in 50 languages but not all spoke English.

Other groups of reformers were more tolerant of working-class mores and old-world customs and helped ease the transition of immigrants into American ways. Located in crowded immigrant or non-white neighbourhoods of major cities, settlement houses provided education, including language, art, home economics and history classes, social services such as homeless shelters, day nurseries and kindergartens, and community spaces for trade union, civic organisations, and women's clubs. Many college-educated and socially aware native-born women and men lived cooperatively in the settlements alongside their ethnic and working-class neighbours. Hull House, established in Chicago in 1889, by Jane Addams and Ellen Gates Starr, was the most well-known of the 400 settlement houses in the US by 1910. Lugenia Burns Hope established the first African American Neighborhood House in Atlanta the following year. A National Federation of Settlements was established also in 1911 to coordinate reform efforts and support public policy initiatives, including municipal government reform, better public schooling, more public amenities such as local parks and libraries, and better public health.

Family health and welfare were central to many progressive women's social and political campaigns, including Margaret Sanger's efforts to decriminalise birth control, and the Indianapolis Woman's Improvement Club drive to help black children with tuberculosis. Many public health campaigns drew on scientific and medical research. Northern city health officials utilised germ theory studies to demonstrate that outbreaks of typhoid and diphtheria could not be confined to lower-class "slums" and to argue that investment in public sewers and water treatment plants was essential. There were mass vaccination programmes to control childhood diseases and lower child mortality, and new housing codes to reduce residential overcrowding and the spread of tuberculosis, as well as controversial slum clearance policies. Southern campaigns against malaria, yellow fever, hookworm, and pellagra borrowed medical knowledge and public health expertise from Cuba and the Philippines. States built new hospitals and sanatoria and established centralised boards of health, often with assistance from the US Public Health Service and northern philanthropies, such as the Rockefeller Foundation.

Morality concerns over vice and sexually transmitted disease often paralleled the expansion of "furnished room districts" for young single male and female factory and service workers in major north-eastern industrial cities, and in the burgeoning movie industry in Los Angeles. Many middle-class reformers criticised young low-paid women who allowed male companions to pay for meals, clothing, and dancehall visits in exchange for sexual services, but also readily campaigned for minimum wage laws, safer and more respectable urban lodging houses, temperance, and the employment of police matrons at dance halls. In 1905, the YWCA's Travelers' Aid Society asked city officials in Portland, Oregon, to confer police powers on Lola Greene Baldwin during the Lewis and Clark Centennial Exposition to protect vulnerable women and girls from "white slavers" who might drug them and sell them to brothels or pimps. Three years later, Baldwin became the first policewoman in the US, followed by Alice Stebbins Wells, who joined the Los Angeles Police Department in 1910 as an assistant pastor and social worker in the Juvenile Bureau, in the same year as a "white slavery" panic gripped the nation.

Political reforms and voter campaigns

Many of those involved in the aforementioned campaigns were frustrated by American government institutions and obstructionist politicians. Lincoln Steffens' *The Shame of the Cities* (1904) exposed the widespread corruption of municipal and city politicians and the nepotism of urban political machines. New forms of local government appeared: city commissions were adopted in Berkeley, California, 1909–23, and Denver, Colorado, 1913–17, and city managers in Dayton, Ohio, 1914–17. Voters also gravitated to alternative parties. In 1911, socialist party candidates were elected mayors in 73 municipalities and socialist ideas gained traction in labour unions and local politics.

Reformers demanded an end to the "spoils system" where urban machine bosses, and local and state politicians routinely distributed public offices to political allies or as favours to immigrant and working-class voters. This included police jobs. Successive investigations of the New York Police Department had found precinct captains soliciting protection payments from saloon keepers, brothel madams, and gaming houses, that were collected by beat officers. Exposés of police corruption in many cities stimulated calls for police professionalisation, including greater honesty and discipline among patrol officers and their commanders, a civil service examination for new recruits, and better training and educational qualifications, with mixed results. Civil Service reform where applicants took up jobs because they were qualified to do so was part of the larger compliment of good government reforms that emphasised professionalism, respectability, and public service. To reduce federal political patronage, 35,000 postmasters, 20,000 skilled shipyard workers, and diplomats were subject to Civil Service employment practices during the Taft administration. However, the withdrawal of patronage appointments and introduction of civil service rules could be used to favour white employees and dismiss "less qualified" non-whites in some instances.

In the South, the use of the poll tax, separate ballot boxes, and the adoption of the "white primary" to exclude African American men from local and state politics and government were also termed "good government" reforms. Black leaders differed on the best way to challenge their second-class status, with Booker T. Washington arguing for temporary accommodation and emphasising economic advancement through vocational education and W. E. B. DuBois's more defiant calls for full voting rights, equal job opportunities, and an end to segregation. Campaigns to restore the citizenship rights of black Americans were coordinated by the National Association for the Advancement of Colored People (NAACP) and the National Association of Colored Women. Outrage at white violence in Springfield, Illinois in 1908 had led prominent blacks and progressive whites to meet in New York in May 1909 to find solutions to the "Race Question."

The interracial NAACP emerged from these discussions and was officially created in 1910 to fight discrimination and ensure African Americans could exercise their constitutional rights. W. E. B. DuBois became NAACP Director of Research and Publicity, and editor of the organisation's influential magazine, *The Crisis*. The National Association of Colored Women, the largest federation of local black women's clubs, formed in 1896 with Mary Church Terrell as president and in response to black exclusion by white female suffrage organisations. Like the NAACP it campaigned for black education, wages, and jobs, against lynching and disfranchisement, and for an end to segregated transport. It also endorsed full female suffrage in 1912. One notable NAACP victory was the US Supreme Court ruling in June 1915 which found Oklahoma's use of a "grandfather clause" to restrict black voting rights to be unconstitutional. Even so, black voters were disfranchised in all southern and nine western states by 1920.

The NACW was part of a broader national and international woman's suffrage movement. Two rival US organisations had merged in 1890 to form the National American Woman Suffrage Association (NAWSA), a coalition of state and local associations, to push first for women's voting rights at the state level. Western states such as Wyoming, Utah, Colorado, and California all seemed much more progressive than southern and northeastern states. Early twentieth-century NAWSA recruitment had focused on college-educated and elite women but soon broadened to immigrant and working-class women, some of whom had emigrated from countries with female suffrage. In 1913, under the leadership of Carrie Chapman Catt, NAWSA launched its campaign for a constitutional amendment to guarantee voting rights to women across the nation. Catt's "Winning Plan" used print media to publicise speeches and meetings, intense political lobbying and mass parades, as well as local fund-raising activities to increase publicity and support. Women had achieved equal suffrage in 15 states by 1918, and partial suffrage in several others, but the southern region remained the most resistant.

Broader democratic participation in electoral politics was encouraged through the initiative (enabling ordinary citizens to initiate legislation), the referendum (where proposed laws were decided by popular vote), and the recall (enabling ordinary voters to remove an elected official from office). Such reforms enabled new single-issue non-partisan pressure groups such as the Anti-Saloon League (ASL) to challenge the traditional Republican and Democratic parties. The ASL and Women's Christian Temperance Union (WCTU) used public education, rallies, boycotts and pledge initiatives to mobilise church congregations and moral reformers to vote in state referenda to outlaw saloons and restrict the liquor trade, and to elect dry candidates in local and state elections. Deep animosity towards black, immigrant, and working-class drinking in saloons constituted the core unifying principle of the prohibition movement. Native-born ASL supporters equated the saloon with depravity, poverty, and domestic violence and campaigned for its eradication. Yet, there was also considerable black support for prohibition.

In the southern states the "liquor question" became entwined with removing African American voting rights and increasing white supremacy. Dry supporters claimed black drunkenness posed an acute sexual menace to white southern women and targeted black saloons for closure. Nine southern states passed state prohibition laws between 1907 and 1915, usually after African American men in that state had been disfranchised. From 1913, the ASL-WCTU focused on achieving national prohibition through a constitutional amendment by building on local and state success, using ASL lobbying power in Washington DC, and capitalising on the new popular method of electing senators in the 1914 and 1916 congressional elections to vote sympathetic supporters into national office.

Mobilising the home front

Wartime patriotism, food conservation and voluntary rationing campaigns, and increased hostility to brewers with German-American names all benefitted prohibition campaigns. The Lever Food and Fuel Control Act (1917) prohibited the use of essential foodstuffs for distilled spirits and the manufacture of beer and wine was further restricted in May 1919. To safeguard military health and discipline, alcohol and prostitution were banned in new "dry and decent zones" around military camps, alcohol use was not permitted by the Navy, and men in military uniform were forbidden from purchasing liquor. The Eighteenth Amendment, which prohibited the manufacture, sale, and transportation of alcohol across the United States and its territories, passed both houses of Congress in mid-December 1917, and had been ratified by 36 states by mid-January 1919.

Federal government authority dramatically increased during World War I as the Wilson administration took control of important sectors of the economy to coordinate production, distribution, and consumption, and increase military procurement and supply. New agencies such as the Food Administration headed by Herbert Hoover, the Fuel Administration headed by Harry Garfield, and the War Industries Board chaired by Bernard Baruch, facilitated government management and planning. In every state, wartime federal agencies worked with state and local administrators to coordinate the resources and residents for the war effort. For example, shipyards in Jacksonville and Tampa, Florida, increased the nation's seagoing tonnage and the state's forests yielded much-needed lumber and naval stores, while states with significant food crops such as Kansas, Minnesota, and Wisconsin were quickly incorporated into centralised supply and conservation efforts from 1914. Road construction and other strategic public works projects increased also. The National Defense Act (1916) authorised the federal government to use the power of the Tennessee River at Muscle Shoals, Alabama, to produce nitrates for ammunition, and later fertiliser, and to construct a dam for hydroelectric power (the Wilson Dam was eventually completed in 1925). Nevertheless, national and state mobilisation were hampered by recurring conflicts between government, business, and workers, so compulsion quickly replaced earlier voluntarism. The federal government took over management and running of the railroads on 1 January 1918.

Food became a principal weapon of the home front, with women forming the "the first line of defense" in wartime conservation and donation efforts. However, soaring food prices in early 1917, after the poor US harvest of 1916, sparked riots by thousands of predominately immigrant women in New York City, Philadelphia, and Boston. Prior to 1917, Americans were urged to save wheat, sugar, fat, and meat to feed the embattled Allied populations; from early 1918 they were urged by the US Food Administration to observe "wheatless" and "meatless" days so ample food reached American troops. County food administrators ensured the public was fully informed through local newspapers. They published recipes and conservation advice and encouraged the planting of victory gardens. The black and white women's club movements ran pledge-card drives so every household could pledge voluntary co-operation to the Food Administration, formed canning clubs, and raised money for Liberty Kitchens, or mobile field kitchens that could cater for up to 200 troops in France.

The Committee on Public Information (CPI), headed by George Creel, drummed up patriotic support and action at home and abroad. It recruited numerous journalists, artists, film directors, psychologists, and writers to create morale-boosting slogans and imagery. A raft of striking posters was produced by the Division of Pictorial Publicity. They included James Montgomery Flagg's 1917 finger-pointing Uncle Sam declaring "I want YOU for U.S. Army," and Howard Chandler Christy's young woman in

Figure 10.2 Wartime mobilisation on the home front. Food became a principal weapon of the home front, with women of every background forming the "the first line of defense" in wartime conservation and donation efforts. The Committee on Public Information's Division of Pictorial Publicity produced a raft of striking posters with morale-boosting slogans and dramatic imagery to stimulate patriotic support and action at home and abroad.

Source: Courtesy of Prisma by Dukas Presseagentur GmbH/Alamy

naval uniform proclaiming "Gee!! I wish I were a man, I'd join the Navy." The CPI's 75,000 "Four-Minute Men" (and women) speakers were employed to deliver short talks written in Washington but reliant on local community delivery and support. Famous sports and entertainment figures like actor Charlie Chaplin joined the Liberty

Loan campaigns which helped pay for the war, along with increased taxes and government borrowing.

War bonds

The US government issued five Liberty bond or Liberty loan drives during World War I to finance the nation's war effort. The first Liberty Loan Act, passed by Congress in April 1917, authorised the US Treasury Department to raise money to provide loans to the Allied powers. Further drives in October 1917, then April and September 1918 raised money for American military operations as well as civilian relief in Europe. The final bond issue in April 1919, the Victory Bond, raised funds to consolidate short-term war debts. From early 1917, the Committee on Public Information developed effective poster and newspaper and magazine campaigns which portrayed bond purchases as a patriotic duty. Bond purchase quotas were assigned to each county, city, and town, but many drives were oversubscribed. The Treasury Department raised a staggering $20 billion from the five wartime bond drives.

Social justice progressives found many positive wartime gains: recognition of collective bargaining, minimum wage laws, and efforts to eradicate child labour, such as a 10 per cent tax on products produced by workers under age 14 – although both the child labour tax and minimum wages for women workers were later declared unconstitutional by the US Supreme Court. Demands for higher wages and shorter workdays gained more traction during the war, particularly among munitions and steel workers, as employers sought to maintain a stable labour force. More than a million women entered hundreds of occupations previously closed to them, including manufacturing, construction, transport, and communications. They made munitions and gas masks, became radio electricians and streetcar drivers, as well as taking up more traditional roles as nurses and clerks. The war had challenged the pacifist principles of many woman suffragists but NAWSA leader, Carrie Chapman Catt, urged support for the war effort, through the Red Cross, and work in war industries and government bureaucracies. By early 1917, women had gained full voting rights in 12 states, and suffragists would cite female wartime service in their demands for a constitutional woman suffrage amendment.

Wartime hyper-nationalism and xenophobia

The war years exposed deep social cleavages in every region of the United States. Intense wartime nationalism and anti-radicalism meant pacifists, conscientious objectors, German-Americans, and "Bolsheviks" were subject to press and official criticism as well as verbal and physical abuse in public. Teaching German in public schools in Nebraska and other states was forbidden, and there were purges of German-authored books from local libraries and music from orchestral and popular repertoires. In November 1917, residents of Osakis, Minnesota, gave E. H. Stratemeyer, a naturalised German, a coat of tar and feathers. The lynching of another German-American, coal miner Robert Praeger, in Collinsville, Illinois, in April 1918, was condemned by President Wilson and many others, but the 11 men later prosecuted for Praeger's murder were all acquitted.

There were state and local authority crackdowns on radicals and union members, especially those affiliated to the radical International Workers' of the World (IWW). A long strike over wages and unionisation by 2,500 copper mine workers in Bisbee, Arizona, in June–July 1917, was interpreted as an outrageous demonstration of disloyalty by the town's leaders, mine owners, and journalists. More than 2,000 members of the Citizens' Protective League and the Workmens' Loyalty League took direct action. Led by the local sheriff, they marched at gunpoint nearly 1,200 residents and strikers onto trains and transported them to the New Mexico desert. The state governor objected, but did not intervene, and the federal government later initiated half-hearted prosecutions against the sheriff and others. There were similar coerced deportations at Jerome, Arizona.

Xenophobia also framed wartime immigration restrictions. The 1917 Immigration Act imposed a literacy test on everyone over age 16 years who sought to enter the US, thus privileging the better educated, and excluding many poorer, lower-class, and less cultured hopefuls. Entry to the US was denied to a long list of so-called undesirables that included "idiots, imbeciles, epileptics [and] alcoholics," as well as polygamists, anarchists, and prostitutes, and so reflected both popular eugenic ideas about regulating fertility to strengthen white families and American (Anglo-Saxon) civilisation and anti-radicalism. The Act also created an "Asiatic Barred Zone" stretching from Afghanistan and British India to the Pacific to curtail Asian immigration, but there were exemptions for Japan (which the State Department did not wish to antagonise) and the US territory of the Philippines.

Four wartime laws, the Espionage Act (1917), Trading with the Enemy Act (1917), Alien Act (1918), and Sedition Act (1918) addressed political and popular fears of German saboteurs and anti-American sentiment. More than 2,000 people were prosecuted under the Espionage Act, including Socialist Party leader Eugene Debs, former Congressman Victor Berger, and Kate Richards O'Hare. As chair of the Socialist Party's Committee on War and Militarism, O'Hare delivered speeches across the states condemning Allied and Central Power war mongering and capitalist wartime profits, and was arrested in Bowman, North Dakota, in July 1917. She was sentenced to five years' imprisonment, but this was later commuted in May 1920 by President Wilson. Debs was also arrested for supposedly disloyal speeches and sentenced to ten years' imprisonment. His conviction was subsequently affirmed by the US Supreme Court, but he too was released by presidential order, in 1921. At least 1,000 people were prosecuted under the Sedition Act. Socialists, anarchists, or IWW members were often people on the political and economic margins of society and thus convenient targets. Other groups of war critics, which included more respectable figures or advocated reforms with greater support, had different experiences.

At 10:00am on 10 January 1917, a dozen well-dressed and behatted women, wearing sashes of purple, gold and white, stood silently before the White House gates and bore banners addressed to President Woodrow Wilson: "Mr. PRESIDENT, HOW LONG MUST WOMEN WAIT FOR LIBERTY?" Groups of 12 to 15 protestors from the National Women's Party (NWP) arrived day after day to advance the fight for voting rights for all American women. Delegations from almost every US state participated in the pickets, in the frontline of a large army waging a war for liberty and full citizenship. The ironic performances of the politically silenced women drew curious but largely peaceful spectators until US war entry in early April 1917, when the NWP's gendered militancy increased and public tolerance of attacks on Wilson decreased. A provocative banner addressed to "the envoys of Russia" (Russian women gained the vote during the March 1917 revolution) declared: "We, the Women of America, tell you that America is not a democracy. Twenty million American Women are denied the right to vote."

Between June and November 1917, the Sentinels endured repeated abuses from onlookers, police, and soldiers, but the watchwomen continued to defend their posts. By November, 218 pickets had been arrested, often for "obstructing traffic," and 97 women were sent to either prison or the workhouse. NWP leader Alice Paul was sentenced to seven months in solitary confinement at the Occoquan Workhouse. When NWP inmates went on hunger strikes, they were force-fed three times a day. The pickets were released following intervention by Representative John Baer of North Dakota who had witnessed first-hand the attacks upon the Sentinels and sponsored a congressional investigation into the abuses they endured. On 9 January 1918, less than two months after the Sentinels were released from prison, President Wilson publicly endorsed woman suffrage, as did many Republicans. The next day the Susan B. Anthony amendment was passed in the House of Representatives, only to stall in the Senate. NWP pickets continued through 1918 and early 1919. They continued to target the president, symbolically burning presidential speeches in "watch fires" in Lafayette Park, across the street from the White House. In early February 1919, a column of 36 suffragists marched to the White House and burned a cardboard effigy of "Kaiser Wilson," thus recalling actions of the Sons of Liberty in 1765 and an earlier patriotic fight for liberty.

The nineteenth amendment finally garnered a two-thirds majority in the Senate in June 1919, and then went to the states for ratification, which was achieved in August 1920. Consequently, the number of eligible voters in the November elections nearly doubled to 54 million, although less than 40 per cent of eligible women actually voted. Some did not vote out of choice but legislators in the southern states quickly adapted poll taxes and other discriminatory methods to disfranchise black female voters.

Figure 10.3 The silent sentinels. Members of the National Women's Party silently picketed the White House in 1917–19 as part of their campaign for full voting rights for American women. Known as the "silent sentinels," they drew both public support and public abuse. Many were arrested and imprisoned, then engaged in hunger strikes and were force fed by prison and workhouse personnel.

Source: Courtesy of Chronicle/Alamy

The "brink of anarchy"

Wartime labour shortages in key industries accelerated the migration of black (and many white) southerners to northern and western cities with the often-unfulfilled promise of better economic opportunities and escape from prejudice and segregation. Racial hostilities and white-supremacist violence continued during the war years. In 1915, preacher-salesman William J. Simmons, inspired by *The Birth of a Nation* (1915), D. W. Griffith's deeply racist cinematic depiction of the Reconstruction period, founded a new Ku Klux Klan at Stone Mountain, Georgia. A few months earlier, Jewish factory superintendent Leo Frank was convicted of the rape and murder of a 13-year-old white female employee. After the governor commuted Frank's sentence from death to life imprisonment, he was taken from Georgia's state prison farm by the self-proclaimed "Knights of Mary Phagan" and hanged from an oak tree in Marietta. Virulent anti-Semitism had surrounded the case at every stage from accusation to lynching.

Encouraged by employers and the northern black press, as well as informal networks of families and friends, a million African Americans relocated between 1916 and 1920, and probably a further million during the 1920s. However, the toxic combination of black migration and labour tensions produced a devastating riot in East St Louis, in July 1917. Riot leaders declared "East St. Louis must remain a white man's town." Racial tensions in northern cities and white supremacist violence in the south increased again during peacetime reconversion and demobilisation. There were 25 urban race riots, including in Knoxville, Tennessee, and Washington DC. However, the Lake Michigan drowning of a black teenager, the refusal of Chicago police to arrest the white man responsible, black disgust at de facto segregation, and festering racial tensions, fuelled a week of violent confrontations in Chicago in late July 1919. At least 38 people died, hundreds were injured, and the homes of 1,000 black families were destroyed in arson attacks during the "Red Summer." In Elaine, Arkansas, a gun battle between black sharecroppers and a group of white men outside a church in which a recruitment meeting of the Progressive Farmers and Householders' Union was taking place, triggered days of violence in October 1919, and claimed more than 200 lives. Federal troops restored order but left a white vigilance organisation in control of Phillips County that proceeded to round up and arrest local African American men for prosecution over the riot.

A wave of lynching claimed the lives of 76 African Americans in 1919. There were in fact over 500 lynch victims across the US between 1917 and 1929, and 90 per cent were African American. Violent racial retribution was often directed at those who had been fighting to make the world safe for democracy as ten lynching victims were veterans in their military uniforms. Carrie Williams Clifford's poem "The Black Draftee from Georgia" (1922) refers to the lynching of Wilbur Little, who was forced to take off his uniform by a group of white men at a local Georgia train station. He was murdered for his quiet defiance of their repeated threats:

> What though the hero-warrior was black?
> His heart was white and loyal to the core;
> And when to his loved Dixie he came back,
> Maimed, in the duty done on foreign shore,
> Where from the hell of war he never flinched,
> Because he cried, "Democracy," was lynched.

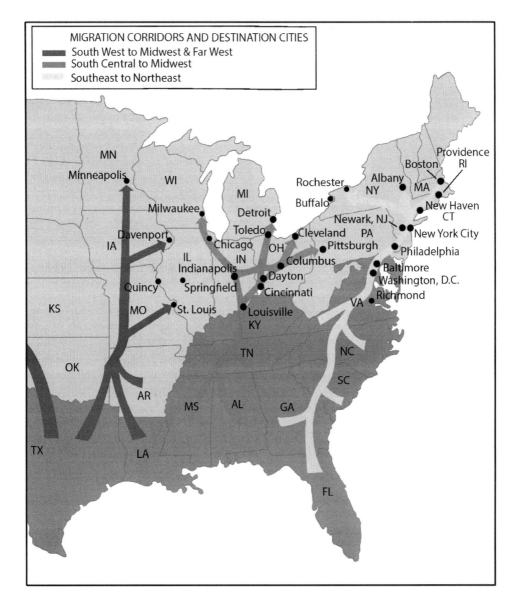

Figure 10.4 Early twentieth-century African American Great Migration routes.

The white mayor of Omaha, Nebraska, was threatened with lynching by a crowd of 6,000 angry whites in September 1919 as he sought to protect a local black packing-house worker accused of interracial rape. The crowd then stoned and set fire to the local courthouse, seized Will Brown from the jail, and murdered him anyway. Federal troops arrived the following day to protect government and judicial buildings, and patrol black neighbourhoods. Machine guns emplacements were set up on several streets and the troops remained for several weeks.

As the war in Europe was ending, many Americans were increasingly at war with themselves, over wages and prices, immigration, suffrage, and political loyalties. Many feared their country was on the brink of revolution. Two waves of mail bombs targeting prominent politicians and business leaders in different cities in April and June 1919 stoked fears that revolutionaries intended to destroy American institutions. Anti-socialist riots broke out in several cities on Mayday 1919. Thirty states passed peacetime sedition acts and at least 300 people were convicted. Attorney General A. Mitchell Palmer, whose home had been destroyed by one of the June letter-bombs (the bomber was also killed), ordered a series of raids on the offices of suspected radical organisations. These were conducted first in November 1919 by J. Edgar Hoover's General Intelligence Division, which made hundreds of arrests and seized correspondence and membership lists. There followed the much-publicised deportations of 249 persons to Russia in December, including anarchists Emma Goldman and Alexander Berkman, and many foreign-born individuals. Then, on 2 January 1920, thousands were arrested during raids in 33 cities, and another 500 persons were deported, often after legal protections and due process were ignored. The "Red Scare" was only one episode in a much larger story of violent confrontations and nativist responses.

Anarchism on trial

The July 1921 trial of anarchists Nicola Sacco and Bartolomeo Vanzetti for robbery-homicide, from a shoe company in Braintree, Massachusetts, and the killings of the paymaster and a guard took place amid intense xenophobia. A prejudiced judge and compliant jury ensured conviction and sentence of death. Both were executed in August 1927, following six long years of appeals. The case generated international interest and overseas demonstrations of support for the condemned in London, Berlin, and Buenos Aires. Sacco, Vanzetti, and their supporters continued to protest their innocence to the end. Modern forensic testing of surviving evidence suggests that Sacco was involved in the murder. The Commonwealth of Massachusetts later acknowledged that both men had been denied due process in highly prejudicial trials.

The American Federation of Labor (AFL) had three million members in 1917 and five million by 1920. Workers continued to complain that prices were rising faster than wages and there were acute fears of unemployment, which rose from a low of 1.8 per cent in 1918 to 12 per cent during the recession of 1919–1921. When 20,000 men from Omaha, Nebraska, returned from war service, they found their old jobs had been filled by lower-paid employees. In January 1919, a general strike broke out in Seattle when workers throughout the city walked out in support of shipyard workers demanding higher wages. It ended after pressure from the AFL leadership and official threats to deploy US Marines. Charges of Bolshevism, subversion and disloyalty were frequently levelled at those on strike. More than four million workers took part in 3,600 strikes in 1919 to consolidate wartime gains that employers wanted to withdraw or reduce or to demand better conditions and AFL union recognition. These included 350,000 steelworkers across the US from Pittsburgh to Seattle and 1,100 Boston police officers in September 1919. US Steel employees generally worked a daily 12-hour shift for seven days a week until the early 1920s while Boston policemen worked up to 98 hours a week for less than 25 cents per hour. The police strike ended within days after Governor Calvin Coolidge summoned the Massachusetts National Guard and the steel strike was called off in January 1920 after resources were spent.

In August 1921, federal troops were deployed to end a war between 20,000 miners affiliated to the United Mine Workers of America (UMWA) and sheriffs and company guards in Logan County, West Virginia. The "Herrin massacre" of Southern Illinois Coal Company employees during a strike in June 1922 also made national headlines. When company guards armed with machine guns killed two union men who were preventing the loading of coal, they were surrounded by a large group of UNWA supporters who rounded up another 50 mine managers, guards, and strikebreakers. Some of the hostages were killed immediately, others were killed after they fled. Six captured strikebreakers were roped together, taken to the local cemetery, the tortured and killed by a mob that included miners and their wives. Critics compared UNWA "butchery" to German wartime atrocities, and President Harding denounced the "shocking crime, barbarity, butchery, rot and madness." Those arrested were all subsequently acquitted

Figure 10.5 Armed state troopers in Pennsylvania during the 1919 steel strike. More than four million workers took part in 3,600 strikes in 1919 to consolidate wartime gains that employers wanted to curtail, or demand better pay and working conditions and labour union recognition. These included 350,000 steelworkers across the United States. Many of the strikes were put down by armed police and national guardsmen.

Source: Courtesy of Everett Collection Historical/Alamy

by local juries, underlining the social and psychological gulf between the politically powerful and those who felt increasingly powerless. During the next five years, labour, anti-immigrant, and Klan violence claimed a further 70 lives in Williamson County.

Many violent confrontations between workers, local and company police originated with disputes over wages, but were linked to deeper industrial and technological changes, particularly in mining, agriculture, and textiles that were undergoing rapid mechanisation. Agricultural employment was decreasing overall; 27 per cent of men were employed in agricultural and farm occupations in 1920 compared to 30 per cent in 1910. The introduction of the moving assembly line – in effect a large circular rubber belt – at Ford's Highland automobile plant in Detroit revolutionised production across all industrial sectors: from summer 1914 it took less than two hours to assemble a car, a process that had taken over 12 hours previously. But skilled craft workers were now displaced by lower-skilled and cheaper assemblers.

The automobile

The Ford Motor Company's Model T or "Tin Lizzy" was introduced in 1908 and quickly revolutionised both the auto industry and automobile ownership. By adopting some of the tenets of "scientific management" advocated by Frederick Winslow Taylor where individual workers produced or affixed specific components, a design with machine-produced interchangeable parts, and a continuous moving assembly line to boost efficiency and speed up production, the car cost $850 in 1909 and $490 by 1914. However, car buyers still had to purchase additional extras such as the accelerator, shock absorbers, and a fuel gauge. With a top speed of 35 miles an hour, the Model T opened up a new world of automobility albeit with significant geographic limits as there were so few paved roads. However, state highway and local road construction increased during the war years and from new federal-state funding arrangements during the Wilson administration. Chain gangs of convict road labourers were a frequent sight in the southern states. Numerous motels, camp sites, and roadside food stands appeared with the growth of motor tourism. The first drive-in restaurant franchise was created by Jessie Kirby and Reuben Jackson, whose "Kirby's Pig Stand" opened in Dallas, Texas, in 1921. There were 26 million cars on American roads by 1929.

The "Return to Normalcy"

The 1920 Republican Party platform called for an end to lynching, government-facilitated arbitration in industrial disputes, and protective legislation for women workers, as well as a retreat from foreign intervention and "abnormal" wartime spending. When Warren G. Harding promised a "Return to Normalcy" he was elected to the presidency in November with 60 per cent of the popular vote and 37 of 48 states' electoral votes. Domestic politics in the 1920s was dominated by the Republican Party, despite the Harding administration becoming mired in scandal, Harding's death in office in November 1923, and a third-party challenge from a resurgent Progressive Party led by Robert M. LaFollette in 1924. All three Republican presidents, Harding, J. Calvin Coolidge and Herbert Hoover were fiscal conservatives who believed that limited government intervention in the economy and less business regulation would promote economic prosperity at home while business and trade would advance US interests and values abroad.

Republican presidents governed a country that was undergoing significant changes. The 1920 census revealed that for the first time in its history, more than half of the 106 million Americans were urban rather than rural residents. The metropolitan population of New York City and its boroughs grew from 3.4 million in 1900 to 5.6 million in 1920, with 2.2 million occupying the island of Manhattan. (By comparison, London had a population of 7.1 million in 1910.) Chicago grew from 1.6 million residents in 1900 to 2.7 million in 1920. Even smaller southern and western cities experienced unprecedented growth. In 1920, there were 53.9 million males living in the United States and 51.8 million females. The population was predominately white. African Americans comprised nearly 9 per cent of US residents in 1900 and 10.5 per cent in 1920. The Asian American population more than doubled to 264,766 between 1900 and 1930; it had been predominately Chinese in 1890 but legal restrictions meant there were fewer than 50,000 Chinese residents by 1920. Urbanisation, vertical living in tenements and skyscrapers, and horizontal suburban sprawl, as well as new technology in the home and the workplace, changed the daily lives of many Americans.

Technology was also changing leisure pursuits. Americans were entranced by the moving image. Small, storefront movie theatres with five-cent admission – hence the name "Nickelodeon" – were popular before the war years. Screenings included Edwin S. Porter's groundbreaking 12 continuous minutes of *The Great Train Robbery* (1903) and D.W. Griffith's one-reel gangster tale, *The Musketeers of Pig Alley* (1912). Growing audiences flocked to larger and more opulent venues, such as Minneapolis's 1913 Lagoon Theatre, renamed the Uptown Theatre in 1929, and Grauman's Chinese Theatre in Hollywood, which opened in May 1927. Among the new short films of the day were Charlie Chaplin's *The Tramp* (1915), and full-length feature films such as D. W. Griffiths' *The Birth of a Nation* (1915) and *Intolerance* (1916). Actors in these silent films relied on exaggerated gestures and mime, and musicians, later replaced by phonographs, provided musical scores and additional entertainment. In the later 1920s, movie audiences were mesmerised by the first full-length "talkies" or films with spoken dialogue. In *The Jazz Singer* (1927) Al Jolson played the son of a Jewish cantor, ostracised for performing at a local saloon in blackface, who became a Broadway musical theatre star. However, *Lights of New York* (1928), a crime drama with a speakeasy raid, a murdered police officer, and a love triangle between the culprits, contained the first fully synchronised dialogue.

The "affluent" years (late 1922 to mid-1929) were certainly impressive: industrial and manufacturing output (particularly in "new" industries" such as automobiles, radio, and household appliances) increased by 70 per cent, Gross National Product increased by 60 per cent, output per worker grew by 33 per cent, and employees' wages grew by 22 per cent. Unemployment fell to 4 per cent and inflation held at 1 to 2 per cent. American factories produced 46 per cent of the world's industrial goods between 1925 and 1929 and shipped 15 per cent of the world's exports. Yet, the decade was bookended by recession and depression, and millions of American workers were far from affluent.

The Democratic Party was fracturing as its increasingly urban-ethnic-industrial labour northern section was at odds with its conservative-white supremacist-agrarian/ small town section anchored in the south and west. This geographic splintering was exacerbated by the party leadership's failure to deal decisively with the "Klan problem." Klan recruitment and membership soared after 1920 under the direction of two public relations experts and a team of salesmen. Dallas dentist Hiram Wesley Evans became self-appointed Imperial Wizard in 1922. By the mid-1920s, the Klan's anti-Catholic, anti-immigrant, anti-Semitic, and white supremacist messages had won over at least three million Americans.

At the Democratic Party nominating convention in New York in summer 1924, the Catholic, immigrant son, and anti-prohibition Governor Alfred E. Smith of New York went head to head with Klan-backed, native-stock, California lawyer William Gibbs McAdoo. As delegates argued over candidates inside a disorderly and highly polarised convention, 20,000 Klansmen gathered in New Jersey to denounce Smith. Neither Smith nor McAdoo was able to secure the nomination, even after 103 ballots, so a compromise candidate John W. Davis was proposed. A resolution at the 1924 convention to condemn the Klan by name failed by one vote, adding further to the shame of many Democrats. Davis was roundly defeated by Coolidge in November.

In contrast to its Reconstruction-era counterpart, the 1920s Klan flourished in northern cities such as Chicago and New York, and northern and western states, including New Jersey, Indiana, Colorado, and California, as well as in the Jim Crow South. It acquired formidable political power in the 1920s by attacking immigration, parochial schools, and prohibition violations, and electing governors, national and state senators, and other high officials. Further, local and state civic leagues, temperance organisations, and church groups formed the backbone of an army of concerned citizens anxious to clean up local politics and fight the "ethnic" bootleggers. The dry lobby had quickly scapegoated ethnic Americans, Catholics, Jews and African Americans for violating the Volstead Act and undermining prohibition, even though native-born citizens were just as complicit.

In August 1925 and September 1926, thousands of white-robed and hooded men, women, and children led by Evans paraded down Pennsylvania Avenue in Washington DC. Some members were drawn to the costumes and secret rituals, while others genuinely believed Klan warnings that alien groups were mongrelising "American" culture and threatening core institutions. Many others were clearly attracted to the extra-legal violence that Klan leaders sought to play down. However, several communities also resisted Klan infiltration by violent means. A gun battle between Klan supporters and opponents in Herrin, Illinois, in August 1924 resulted in six deaths, and another six men were killed in fighting during an election in April 1926. Klan support declined dramatically in the late 1920s through a combination of popular opposition, a series of corruption and immorality scandals involving several Klaverns, and a murder conviction against one of its high-profile leaders, Davis Curtis Stephenson of Indiana, but the white supremacist views of these voters did not diminish.

Black urban growth and self-defence

During the 1920s, African Americans continued to challenge racial segregation and assert their civil rights with a renewed sense of determination and militancy, from both within and outside existing power structures. Vigilance societies for self-defence were formed in black sections of larger cities by both groups and individuals, often after confrontations with white police. But there were also calls for better policing of black areas. By 1910, there were nearly 600 African American police officers in northern cities, including Chicago and Milwaukee (black police in southern forces had declined dramatically since 1890). African Americans in Chicago's Second and Fourth wards continued to secure symbolically important police appointments and promotions above the rank of patrolman precisely because they wielded political and economic power which white politicians sought to manipulate.

Black populations in northern cities had increased, by 59 per cent in Philadelphia, 115 per cent in New York City, and 148 per cent in Chicago. Restrictive housing covenants, "white flight," and white hostility to any expansion of black districts helped maintain residential racial segregation. Overcrowding was the norm, and generated acute health, sanitation, and mortality concerns. Harlem became a "profitable slum" for white landlords as residents' rent was four times that of equivalent white areas, and for poorly maintained and often dilapidated residences. Vice – gambling, prostitution, liquor, and narcotics – also thrived in black districts like Chicago's South Side, much to the consternation of respectable wage-earning families. But Harlem and other vibrant black sections were full of bustling commercial streets with storefront churches, restaurants, pawn shops and hair salons, and dynamic voluntary, club, and community groups. Black sections thus provided crucial space and patronage for new cultural and political movements.

In March 1925, under the title "Harlem: Mecca of the New Negro," the magazine *Survey Graphic* devoted a whole issue to a bold new African American literary phenomenon. The magazine's editor was Alain Locke, a professor at Howard University and the first black Rhodes Scholar. Later that year, Locke published an anthology of poetry, literary fiction, music, and art, that included contributions from Zora Neal Hurston, Countee Cullen, W. E. B. DuBois, and Jean Toomer, as well as his own highly perceptive essays on African American contributions to American art and literature, and the portrayal of African Americans in "white" fiction. There was an explosion of African American Arts throughout the decade, including musical theatre, such as the minstrel-influenced "Shuffle Along" in 1921; new magazines such as *Fire!!* in 1926; poems such as Langston Hughes's *The Weary Blues* in 1926; and novels such as Nella Larsen's *Quicksand* in 1928. Locke hoped these black cultural achievements would help change white perceptions of African Americans and foster greater racial equality. As well as promoting and celebrating black art and culture, the Renaissance movement was directly linked to black political mobilisation, civil rights protests, calls for urban reform, and efforts to increase black economic prospects.

Nevertheless, those who challenged the racial status quo could still meet violent resistance. When Ossian and Gladys Sweet sought to own their own home away from the crowded and less desirable "Black Bottom" segregated Detroit neighbourhood, hostile white residents surrounded the house, threw rocks, and threatened the occupants. Local police merely looked on. However, the Sweets and their friends were heavily armed. When they took defensive action against the crowd, and a white man was killed, all 11 African Americans were arrested and tried for murder. Bolstered by fundraising in cities across the US, NAACP support, and the engagement of celebrated defence lawyer Clarence Darrow, the defendants first went to trial in November 1925. A mistrial and an acquittal followed, suggesting that public tolerance of mob justice and police inaction had some limits.

There was significant urban black disenchantment with the two main political parties' action on civil rights and mainstream leaders such as the NAACP's James Weldon Johnson and W. E. B. DuBois and the National Urban League's Eugene K. Jones. Socialism and communism appealed to many African Americans disillusioned with the racial limitations imposed by American capitalism as did Black Nationalist ideology. The Universal Negro Improvement Association (UNIA), led by the charismatic Marcus Garvey, had over 700 branches in 38 cities by the mid-1920s, and its numerical strength clearly worried NAACP and NACW leaders. Garvey's messages of African redemption, racial pride, rejection of racial integration as a middle-class delusion, and defence of black entrepreneurship particularly appealed to working-class African Americans. UNIA members experienced first-hand the low-paying and limited range of jobs available to black men and understood that black women were especially vulnerable to sexual exploitation and often engaged in prostitution to make ends meet. Many contemporary critics, including DuBois and Robert S. Abbott, the editor of the *Chicago Defender*, viewed its working-class membership and appeal to Caribbean immigrants as evidence of the UNIA's insignificance, and dismissed it as an organisation of "Negro sharks and ignorant Negro fanatics." They also mocked the UNIA costumes, parades, and flags, but the theatricality clearly appealed to many non-elite African Americans, and its diverse membership was actually a source of strength.

Figure 10.6 Strong support for a UNIA parade, Harlem, 1920. The United Negro Improvement Association (UNIA), led by Marcus Garvey, drew enormous African American support in northern cities such as New York, particularly in Harlem, which was regarded as the capital city of Black America. This was one of several huge parades in Harlem. The sign "The New Negro Has No Fear" embodied a resurgent sense of black cultural, political, social, and economic pride in the face of white racist violence and continued racial discrimination in the 1920s.

Source: Courtesy of Everett Collection Inc./Alamy

Race, immigration, and citizenship

Racial categorisation and quantitative restrictions were key features of dramatic immigration restrictions in the 1920s. Congress passed an emergency bill in May 1921 which capped immigration at 355,000 per year and introduced annual quotas, based on 3 per cent of each foreign-born population that was resident in the US and counted in the 1910 census. This gave 55 per cent of the quotas to northern and western Europeans, and 45 per cent to southern and eastern Europeans. In addition, no more than 20 per cent of any quota could be admitted during a single month. The law was a direct response to over a million war refugees seeking US entry, but also reflected deeper cultural anxieties over the failures of assimilation in an era of 100 per cent Americanism. However, the dissolution of four European empires, emergence of new ethnically complex nations such as Czechoslovakia and Yugoslavia, and rising numbers of stateless persons posed distinct challenges for a quota system based on national origins.

A permanent National Origins law, the Johnson-Reed Act, was passed in May 1924, and its numerical quota scheme remained the cornerstone of US immigration policy until 1965. Nativists had successfully lobbied for tighter annual quotas – 2 per cent of the total number of foreign-born individuals of each nationality resident in the US as determined by the 1890 Census – ostensibly to mirror the country's white Anglo-Saxon "national origins" (deliberately overlooking four centuries of multiculturalism). The revised 2 per cent quotas were implemented using a temporary formula for the three fiscal years beginning on 1 July 1924. This ensured 85 per cent of entry quotas went to northern and western European nations. An average one million immigrants per year had arrived in the US before the war; the 1924 law imposed an annual numerical limit of 160,000 persons. After 1 July 1927, the total immigrant quota was set at 150,000 per year, to be distributed according to the population of the US in 1920. There were no numerical limits for Canadian, Mexican, or South American immigrants. The Johnson-Reed Act received strong nativist support but stirred angry opposition among Irish, German, and Scandinavian Americans in particular.

Calculating quotas was a complicated and highly technical process for statisticians at the Bureau of Census, who utilised scientific and social science methods borrowed from demography, political science, and geography. The process was coordinated by the Secretaries of State, Commerce, and Labor, and eventually completed in March 1929. Permanent quotas were announced in one of Herbert Hoover's early presidential proclamations. From 1 July 1929, the largest quotas were 65,721 for Great Britain and Northern Ireland; 17,853 for the Irish Free State; and 25,957 for Germany. By comparison, the quota limit was 2,784 for Russia, 5,802 for Italy, and 6,524 for Poland. Minimum quotas of 100 persons per year were set for nearly 40 countries including the Arabian Peninsula, Egypt, and South Africa. Quota counts, restrictions on entry and exit, and port-of-entry enforcement further necessitated other important bureaucratic changes, including more formal passports and border or port inspections. Prospective emigrants to the US now required "immigrant visas" which they had to apply for in person at overseas American consular offices.

The permanent exclusion of persons ineligible for US citizenship was another key plank of the 1924 law and specifically targeted "Asiatic" peoples. Restrictionists' rhetoric often relied on ethno-racial slurs and stereotypes, political judgements about "desirable" and "undesirable" groups, and scientific racism to calculate immigrants' potential for assimilation and positive contribution to American institutions. The Asiatic Exclusion League had long highlighted the racial characteristics and poor assimilability of Asian immigrants in their demands to curtail Japanese immigration. In addition, four rulings by the US Supreme Court in 1923 upheld state laws in California and Washington which outlawed land ownership by Japanese "aliens ineligible to citizenship." Such exclusion measures, alongside existing anti-Chinese laws, and the "barred Asiatic zone," meant entry would be denied to all "Asiatic" peoples.

During the 1920s there were new prohibitions against white and Asian intermarriage, as marriage between whites and blacks was already illegal in many states. Several states also strengthened their anti-miscegenation and segregation laws amid acute eugenic anxieties over "race-mixing." The "origins" of white Americans were shaped by centuries of intermarriage between Euro-Americans, African Americans, and Native American Indians, as well as slavery and enforced miscegenation, yet "races" in the 1920s continued to be defined by bloodlines and blood quantum. These brittle binary terms ignored mixed-race persons who did not fit into census categories of "white" or "Negro." Under Virginia's Racial Integrity Act (1924), a "colored person" had one-sixteenth or more of "negro blood" and a white person had "no trace whatsoever of any blood other than Caucasian." This had huge economic, civil, political, legal and social implications for a person of mixed racial heritage.

Nativists in the West, including on the California Joint Immigration Committee also sought to restrict Mexican immigration on the grounds of racial ineligibility to citizenship. Quota limits did not apply to most persons born in the countries of the Western Hemisphere, because a sizeable migratory and seasonal labour force was essential to large-scale commercial production of fruit and vegetables, particularly in the Southwest. Quotas would also undermine the softer Pan Americanism and "good neighbour" policies in Latin America being pursued by state department officials. More than 500,000 documented Mexicans entered the US during the war years and through the 1920s, taking up crucial agricultural, industrial, and railroad work in the Southwest and Midwest, but there was strong worker resistance to illegal/undocumented Mexican immigration, which was estimated at 100,000 a year throughout the 1920s. It was no coincidence that the US Border Patrol, formed in 1925, to enforce federal immigration laws, was assigned primarily to the US–Mexican border.

One group which did not fit neatly into nativist conceptions of 100 per cent Americanism was Native Americans. Despite crippling poverty and high mortality rates, their population numbers began to rise to around 300,000 by 1920, yet reservation out-migration was also increasing as people left in search of work. The Indian Citizenship Act (1924) conferred US citizenship on all American Indians born within US territorial limits. Some had become US citizens through the earlier nineteenth-century allotment process or following a special law passed in November 1919 extending citizenship to war veterans, but almost half of adult male Native Americans were not US citizens in 1920. American citizenship was championed by the Society of American Indians established in 1911 and was positively linked to assimilation but was very controversial: the Six Nations of the Iroquois Confederacy and many other tribal nations remained intensely hostile to the changes. The 1919 war service measure supposedly did not affect an individual's rights to tribal property, but this and the 1924 law directly undermined tribal sovereignty, in a period when significant amounts of Native land was being lost through fraudulent sales, state taxes, and other dubious measures.

As of 1924, American Indian women and men were eligible to vote in regular US elections and stand for political office. Voter turnout remained very low but there was a surge in political activity in many native communities, such as the Crow and Cheyenne in Big Horn County, Montana. Several American Indian men ran for sheriff, state senator, and US Congress in the 1920s and 1930s, including influential Crow leader Robert Yellowtail. None were elected to office at this time, and communities continued to encounter severe limits on citizenship rights in the twentieth century, because states could set voting criteria. South Dakota, Mississippi, New Mexico and other states continued to bar or limit Native American voting rights until the 1950s, just as African American voting rights remained severely limited in the southern region.

National prohibition

The Eighteenth Amendment was ratified by the states in January 1919. It gave liquor distillers, brewers, and bar keepers a year to wind up business so national prohibition officially commenced on 17 January 1920. However, previous local and state reforms meant that over two-thirds of the US population was already living in dry states; the other third was subject to wartime restrictions. Congress passed the National Prohibition Enforcement (Volstead) Act over President Wilson's veto in late October 1919. This set out the terms of the federal prohibition code, including the definition of an "intoxicating" beverage, as containing more than 0.5 per cent of alcohol, and the regulations governing the production and distribution of alcohol for industrial and scientific purposes so that manufacturers, doctors, pharmacists, and religious leaders could still legally obtain alcohol by permit. Personal consumption within a private residence was also still allowed.

There was considerable opposition to national prohibition, from immigrant communities, returning war veterans, women who rejected the home protection ethos of the WCTU, and the American Federation of Labor. "No Beer, No Work" was the slogan of protesting union workers in New York and New Jersey in Spring 1919, and many brewery employees faced financial uncertainty. Yet, WCTU membership peaked at 350,000 in the early 1920s, ASL membership was nearing the half-million mark, there was overwhelming dry support in Congress, and many Americans remained hostile to the liquor trades. Early modification campaigns to increase the 0.5 per cent threshold to the wartime limit of 2.75 per cent so as to permit the production of light beers and wines, could not win enough political support.

Every federal agency from the Coast Guard to the Postal Service, was involved in prohibition enforcement, as were state police forces, highway patrols, and local sheriffs' officers. The Justice and Treasury Departments led federal enforcement, with revenue officers and district attorneys playing key roles. A Bureau of Prohibition was set up in 1920 with 1,550 agents across its 18 administrative districts, but it was always understaffed and under-resourced even though its funding kept rising, from $5 million in 1921 to $13.4 million in 1930. In addition, patronage appointments, low salaries, and inept leadership proved a recipe for systemic corruption which stretched all the way to the attorney general Harry Daugherty, formerly Harding's presidential campaign manager. Mabel Walker Willebrandt, a Republican prosecutor originally from California, and the first female assistant attorney general, took charge in 1921 and faced an uphill battle to clean up the Bureau.

Figure 10.7 National Prohibition came into effect in January 1920. Prohibition advocates genuinely believed that the Eighteenth Amendment would create a new nation in which the problems of alcoholism, domestic violence, poverty, and unemployment would be eliminated. However, millions of ordinary Americans willingly broke the law and continued to drink, while criminal gangs aided by corrupt law enforcement profited handsomely from the flawed experiment in liquor control.

Source: Courtesy of The Granger Collection/Alamy

Economic, medical, and criminal studies suggest that alcohol consumption did fall, to around 30 per cent of pre-prohibition levels in the early 1920s, largely because of rising consumer costs, then rose to around 60 to 70 per cent of pre-Volstead levels by the mid-1920s. Household liquor production expanded as working-class families brewed beer, made home-made wine by fermenting fruit juices, and distilled whiskey in small-scale operations for personal consumption or "kitchen-table" sale to neighbours. At the same time, Americans were drinking more coffee, carbonated drinks such as *Coca-Cola* and *Dr Pepper*, fresh fruit juice, and milk, because of changing ideas about nutrition and diet as well as better refrigeration and transportation facilities. However, it was still very possible to obtain illegal alcohol.

Within minutes of national prohibition coming into effect, criminal gangs launched successful raids on government warehouses and hijacked trucks carrying medicinal and industrial liquor for conversion into bootleg whiskey. Journalists exposed physicians issuing bogus prescriptions and corrupt priests and rabbis abusing their sacramental wine exemptions. Bootleggers soon cultivated a roaring telephone-order and door-to-door delivery service in cities across the country and rural moonshine production boomed. Ordinary citizens carried alcohol in hip flasks in their pockets, corsets and socks, and in suitcases and baby carriages. "Rum running typists" secreted bottles in their handbags as they crossed the bridge connecting Windsor, Canada, with Detroit, Michigan.

Saloon closure had been at the forefront of dry campaigns, but these disappearing male-dominated drinking spaces were soon superseded by the speakeasy, and its rural and small-town equivalent, the roadhouse. Underground nightclubs and speakeasies, buffet flats, and loft parties, often with concealed entrances and admission by password, were firmly embedded in a new permissive nightlife which catered for men and women as couples. Lower-class drinkers often consumed cheaper and harmful concoctions. Several hundred deaths and many thousands of cases of paralysis were reported in the South and Southwest in 1930, from consumption of "Jake" ginger, manufactured at a plant in Brooklyn, using ingredients from hair tonics and perfumes. Even better-manufactured bootleg liquor had an unpleasant taste, which could be masked with flavourings and juices, hence the popularity of the "cocktail."

Jazz

A unique blend of ragtime and blues, as well as older African, Creole, and European music traditions, jazz emerged in New Orleans's Storyville district at the turn of the twentieth century. Ferdinand "Jelly Roll Morton" LaMothe, a pianist in one of the district's sporting clubs (brothels), claimed to have invented jazz in 1902, but jazz had many creators. Travelling musicians brought the fusion of piano, guitars, drums, and brass to black clubs and dancehalls across the South in the years before World War I, in the same period that blues musicians such as W. C. Handy, and blues vocalists such as Ma Rainey were also attracting new audiences. Early recordings of iconic pieces such as Handy's "Memphis Blues" and Morton's "King Porter Stomp" helped introduce jazz to new black and white audiences in northern and western cities. Both African American musicians and musical genres migrated northward in the 1910s and 1920s. Many jazz musicians left New Orleans when Storyville closed in 1915, others were leaving anyway during the Great Migration. They joined jazz orchestras in the post-war nightclubs of Chicago and New York. They included a young cornet player, Louis Armstrong, in King Oliver's Creole Jazz Band, which played to a full house every night at Chicago's Lincoln Gardens. Armstrong headed to New York City in the mid-1920s to spearhead hot jazz. Piano player Duke Ellington's jazz orchestra was playing at Harlem's Cotton Club. The phonograph and the radio, particularly live radio broadcasts from the 1920s, further popularised jazz in the interwar years.

Wealthy white male patrons of the most glamorous urban clubs ordered imported branded liquor displayed on collapsible shelves or stored in hidden cellars, as in New York City's 21 Club, to thwart raids. Their female companions wore the latest "flapper" fashions and hair-styles. They were entertained by African American jazz musicians such as Louis Armstrong, recently arrived from New Orleans, and floor-shows with exotic female dancers, some of whom were entwined in pythons. They were served by black male waiters and bartenders – black customers were generally not welcome at Harlem's vibrant elite nightclubs – and white female hostesses and "cigarette girls." New York City's "Queen of the Nightclubs" Mary Louise "Texas" Guinan's delighted customers at the El Fay club by shouting "Hello, sucker!" when they arrived. Conservatives were of course horrified by these changes, as well as the sight of young women wearing make-up, smoking cigarettes, kissing in automobiles, drinking alcohol, or dancing the Charleston and the Turkey Trot.

These activities were all linked to a broader set of social and sexual changes shaped by early twentieth-century urban growth, geographic mobility, and work-leisure patterns, that undoubtedly accelerated during the prohibition years. Thousands of young wage-earning women and men, living in furnished-room districts, along with middle-class college students, and bohemian artists, intellectuals and political radicals, redefined or rejected pressures to conform to conventional family roles and gendered respectable behavior. Blossoming homosexual subcultures were found in clandestine networks of underground bars, bath-houses, and "Panzy" shows in many cities, at a time when homosexuality was illegal.

Many manufacturers, including leading automobile companies, had adopted reforms collectively referred to as "worker capitalism": housing, education, medical, religious, and recreations facilities for employees, profit-sharing plans, paid vacations, and retirement plans, and new shift patterns where three eight-hour shifts replaced two 12-hour ones, although not all workers benefitted equally or at all. Nevertheless, as Americans' social lives adapted to shorter working hours, increased leisure time, and more disposable income, they flocked to flourishing "bright light" centres to eat, drink, and socialise. In Philadelphia in 1920, Joseph Horn and Frank Hardart adapted a German-style eatery to create the low-cost, uniform-menu, food vending Automat for the American market. Diners made their selections from coin-operated chrome and glass machines and ate in large ornate cafeterias. The vending machines were immediately restocked by staff on the behind-the scenes salad and pie assembly lines. White Castle, the first fast-food chain established in Wichita, Kansas, in 1921, served what would become an American staple: the hamburger.

Temperance and prohibition were international mass movements with significant support in both Mexico and Canada, yet neither country adopted national prohibition on the American model, and Canadian wartime liquor restrictions had been lifted by the early 1920s. Schooners packed with branded liquor from Europe, the Caribbean, or South America, anchored along "Rum Row" which stretched from Newfoundland, Canada, to the Bahamas, and waited for buyers in speedboats who played a game of cat and mouse with the US Coast Guard. The Coolidge Administration increased investment in naval and coast guard defence and concluded a series of anti-smuggling agreements with Cuba, Great Britain, Denmark, Panama, and the Netherlands but smuggling continued. Mexican, Canadian, and Cuban brewers and distillers all profited handsomely from prohibition-era liquor tourism and the booming smuggling industry. Burlap-wrapped liquor bottles concealed in animal carcasses, rubber tyres, or hidden compartments, flowed into the US by railroad, truck, speedboat, and aeroplane. Efforts to blockade the Detroit River, Hudson River, and cross-border overland routes had little effect and often led to gun battles between revenue agents and bootleggers.

Prohibition demanded large, centralised and integrated business organisations and a coterie of bold, savvy, and ruthless operators came to monopolise the drugs, gambling, prostitution, and highly lucrative illegal liquor trades. Detroit's Purple Gang controlled the wholesale importation and distribution of Canadian whiskey and supplied Chicago's Torrio-Capone crime syndicate. New York gang boss William "Big Bill" Dwyer owned or supplied hotels, nightclubs, breweries, casinos, and racetracks in many parts of the United States and assembled a fleet of oceangoing vessels to guarantee his liquor supply, along with payments to Customs and Coast Guard officers, police and prohibition agents. Arnold Rothstein was the millionaire-owner of gambling parlours, nightclubs, and cabarets. His notoriety stemmed from the Black Sox Scandal of 1919, in which eight players for the Chicago White Sox baseball team, accepted $80,000 to lose the World Series to the Cincinnati Reds. Rothstein bet on the Reds to win and won a fortune. He dominated the New York-centred narcotics business until his murder in 1928. Guided initially by his one-time mentor, Johnny Torrio, Alphonse "Scarface" Capone built a large, disciplined, ethnically diverse criminal organisation that dominated Greater Chicago during the Beer Wars 1924–1928. By the late 1920s, the Chicago Crime Commission estimated the Capone syndicate's profits at about $60 million dollars per year.

Gangsters relied on violent elimination of rival gangs, wide-scale intimidation, rigging local elections, and corruption but also successfully utilised the new technology of automobiles, telephones, radios, and submachine guns. Ordinary brewery and distillery owners without political contacts or unable to afford to buy protection from politicians, judges, and police simply could not compete. Willebrandt's efforts to break up alcohol supply networks netted some big fish including Cincinnati lawyer turned "King of the Bootleggers" George Remus, but she continued to encounter incompetent officials, widespread disregard for the law, and growing public indifference. However, the 1926 murder of an Assistant State Attorney in Capone's headquarters, and the infamous 1929 St Valentine's Day Massacre in which seven associates of Capone's rival Bugs Moran were gunned down in a warehouse on Chicago's North Clark Street by gunmen probably hired by the Capone organisation, became major turning points in public tolerance of organised crime.

Prohibition and Catholicism dominated the presidential election of 1928 in which Democrat Alfred E. Smith, then governor of New York, took on Republican Herbert M. Hoover, then Secretary of Commerce. Many conservative white southern Democrats refused to back a man who epitomised the northern-urban-ethnic-wet wing of the party, and for the first time since Reconstruction, the Republicans captured five southern states including Florida and Texas. However, in a nation seemingly awash in illegal liquor and lawlessness, and with an overburdened criminal justice system, Hoover also appeared as the best man to address the failures of prohibition. To begin the process, the new president established a National Commission on Law Observance and Enforcement, led by retired jurist George Wickersham, to study the system of criminal justice system and propose remedies. Meanwhile, a powerful repeal movement was mobilising in early 1929, energised by Pauline Morton Sabin and the Women's Organization for National Prohibition Reform.

Chapter summary

This chapter examined the living and working conditions of ordinary Americans and the challenges of urban-industrial life prior to World War I, and the motivations of different groups of reformers seeking to improve urban conditions, politics, and public health. Traditionally, progressivism fitted into the history of the United States between Populism and World War I, but this chapter has signalled that many reform movements and campaigns continued into the 1920s. It is clear also that the United States was a fractious and divided nation, as the numerous strikes over wages, working conditions, and union membership illustrate. The outbreak of World War I and eventual American entry exacerbated existing ethnic, nativist, and class tensions as well as fuelling anti-radical hysteria and racial animosity. Continuing debates over race, ethnicity, and citizenship, reshaped the civil rights of Native Americans but severely limited the mobility of European emigrants. The architects of national prohibition genuinely believed that the Eighteenth Amendment would create a new nation in which alcoholism, domestic violence, poverty, and unemployment would be eradicated. However, throughout the 1920s the flawed experiment in liquor control turned millions of ordinary Americans into willing lawbreakers, overwhelmed state and federal criminal justice systems, and cultivated widespread cynicism for law and order.

Discussion questions

- Did progressive-era reforms address and relieve serious social, economic, and political problems, or were they a means of increasing social control over working-class, immigrant, and non-white residents?
- Why would Americans from different regions, backgrounds, and political organisations have differing views about World War I and its impacts on their society?
- To what extent could education, the vote, economic prosperity, and the typewriter change American women's lives in the 1910s and 1920s?
- What alternatives to "national origins" or numerical quotas might have been used to check immigration in the 1920s?
- Could national prohibition have worked with better federal and state regulation of the manufacture, sale, and distribution of alcohol? What kinds of controls and restrictions could have been implemented?

Further reading

Ackerman, Kenneth. *Young J. Edgar: Hoover, the Red Scare, and the Assault on Civil Liberties* (New York, 2007). Intriguing study of the post–World War I tumultuous clash between radicals, organised labour, defenders of civil liberties and US government reform, and the formative period of one of the most controversial federal law enforcement figures of the twentieth century.

Baker, Jean H., ed. *Votes for Women: The Struggle for Suffrage Revisited* (New York, 2002). An invaluable collection of essays and commentaries that offers a very useful starting point for understanding the long history of women's rights and female suffrage in the nineteenth and early twentieth-century United States.

Boyle, Kevin. *Arc of Justice: A Saga of Race, Civil Rights, and Murder in the Jazz Age* (New York, 2004). A carefully researched and compelling examination of the self-determination of Ossian and Gladys Sweet and their landmark civil rights court case, and a detailed political, racial and social history of 1920s Detroit.

Capozzola, Christopher. *Uncle Sam Wants You: World War I and the Making of the Modern American Citizen* (New York, 2010). An insightful exploration of the obligations and rights of citizenship and the expanse and limits of federal power in wartime America.

Esch, Elizabeth. *The Color Line and the Assembly Line: Managing Race in the Ford Empire* (Oakland, CA, 2018). An innovative and impressive study that details the global reach of the Ford Motor Company, from the early twentieth century, and corporate maintenance of colour lines and racial hierarchies at home and abroad.

Flexner, Eleanor. *Century of Struggle: The Woman's Rights Movement in the United States* (1959; 3rd edition, New York, 1996). A classic study of the women's rights and suffrage movements, strategies and leaders.

Green, Venus. *Race on the Line: Gender, Labor, and Technology in the Bell System, 1880–1980* (Durham and London, 2001). A fascinating and pioneering study of telephone technology, the racial and gendered organisation of work, and the exclusion of black women from the twentieth-century labour force.

Hofstadter, Richard. *The Age of Reform* (1955; New York: Vintage, 1960). A landmark pioneering study of American political thought 1890–1940 and reformers. Later historians have challenged many aspects including the "status politics" of the Progressives and the agrarian nostalgia of the Populists but it remains a touchstone study for these periods.

King, Shannon. *Whose Harlem Is This, Anyway? Community Politics and Grassroots Activism During the New Negro Era* (New York, 2015). A vibrant and multilayered portrait of black life, labour, leisure, social movements and political cultures in early twentieth-century New York.

Krugler, David F. *1919, The Year of Racial Violence: How African Americans Fought Back* (New York, 2015). A sobering and well researched study of racial violence, black resistance, and police responses in one of the bloodiest years in early twentieth-century America.

Link, William A. *The Paradox of Southern Progressivism, 1880–1930* (Chapel Hill, 1997). Historians interested in progressive-era reform have increasingly examined key regional characteristics and differences, and this is a valuable starting point for examining social reform and the southern region and the interplay of race, ruralism, localism, and external pressure for change.

McGerr, Michael. *A Fierce Discontent: The Rise and Fall of the Progressive Movement in America, 1870–1920* (New York, 2005). Compared to the classic studies of late nineteenth- and early twentieth-century reformers and reform movements, twenty-first-century readers may find this a livelier and more digestible study of the varied reform coalitions, strategies, goals, leaders, supporters and opponents.

McGirr, Lisa. *The War on Alcohol: Prohibition and the Rise of the American State* (New York, 2015). There are many popular books on Prohibition and its infamous gangsters, but this is a carefully researched and through study of a complicated era that moves beyond traditional narratives and simplistic explanations.

Meye, G. J. *The World Remade: American in World War I* (New York, 2018). A detailed political history centred on the question of why the United States entered World War I in 1917.

Ngai, Mae M. *Impossible Subjects: Illegal Aliens and the Making of Modern America* (2003; Princeton, NJ, 2014). A groundbreaking study of federal and state government restrictions on immigration and consequences for defining and redefining racial and gendered citizenship.

Nye, David E. *America's Assembly Line* (2003; Cambridge, MA, 2015). A clever study of the inter-dependency of technology, work, business, culture and global exports in the development of the pre-World War I assembly line and its later adaptations.

Pegram, Thomas R. *One Hundred Percent American: The Rebirth and Decline of the Ku Klux Klan in the 1920s* (Chicago, 2011). A wide-ranging history of an important, national, and disturbingly popular social movement and political institution of the 1920s.

Tuttle, William M. *Race Riot: Chicago in the Red Summer of 1919* (1970; Champaign, IL, 1996). A pioneering, strongly crafted, and still relevant social history of race relations in the urban North, black urbanisation, and the myriad forces that explain why Chicago was engulfed in violence in July–August 1919.

Wiebe, Robert H. *The Search for Order, 1877–1920* (New York, 1967). A classic study of the Populist and Progressive reform movements grappling with industrial corporate capitalism and urbanisation, and of the late nineteenth- and early twentieth-century presidential responses. Early twenty-first-century readers may find it rather dated.

11 Depression and New Deal America

Timeline

1929   Wall Street Stock Market Crash
White House Conferences on voluntary price and wage controls
Revolutions break out in several Latin American nations

1930   Tougher immigration restrictions for Mexicans
Domestic tariff increases

1931   Scottsboro nine black defendants arrested, convicted, sentenced
Honolulu-Massie rape case
Breakdown of voluntary price and wage controls
One-year moratorium on reparation and loan payments is announced
Hoover retreats from Roosevelt Corollary
Alabama Sharecroppers Union established

1932   Dust Bowl storms
Great Britain and France default on war debts
Good Neighbor Policy continues in Latin America
Reconstruction Finance Corporation set up
Lindbergh kidnapping
Emergency Relief and Construction Act passed
Bonus Expeditionary Force protests in Washington DC
Farm Holiday Association protests
FDR elected as president, Democratic Party electoral victories

1933   Dust Bowl storms
Withdrawal of US troops from Nicaragua
FDR inaugurated as president
Federal Emergency Relief Administration set up
Civilian Conservation Corps set up
Agricultural Adjustment Act passed
National Industrial Recovery Act passed
Public Works Administration set up
Civilian Works Administration set up
Tennessee Valley Authority set up
Series of Dillinger bank robberies
Bonnie and Clyde crime spree
War on Crime begins
Prohibition ends

1934   Dust Bowl storms
       Omnibus Crime Bill passed
       Formation of Southern Tenant Farmers Union
       Indian Reorganization Act passed
       Hoover, "The Challenge to Liberty" speech
       Formation of American Liberty League
       Dillinger killed
       Bonnie and Clyde killed
1935   *Federal* Bureau of Investigation launched
       Rural Electrification Administration set up
       Intense Dust Bowl storms
       National Industrial Recovery Act struck down by US Supreme Court
       Resettlement Administration set up
       National Labor Industrial Relations Act passed
       Social Security Act passed
       Harlem Riot
1936   Agricultural Adjustment Act struck down by US Supreme Court
       Congress of Industrial Unions (CIO) established
       FDR wins second presidential term, defeats Alf Landon
       Crystallisation of the "Roosevelt Coalition"
1937   "Settlement" of the Scottsboro case
       Farm Security Administration set up
       Return of the recession
       FDR's unpopular Judicial Reform Act defeated
1938   Fair Labor Standards Act passed
       FDR's failed purge of Democratic Party anti-New Deal opponents

Topics covered

- 1929 economic meltdown
- Federal economic relief under the Hoover administration
- Roosevelt's New Deal for the American people
- The New Deal in action: work relief
- The New Deal in action: crime control
- The New Deal in action: conservation and Native American life
- The New Deal in action: tackling agriculture and rural poverty
- The New Deal in action: restructuring industry and labour unions
- The social insurance revolution
- New Deal political realignments

Introduction

This chapter begins with the stock market crash in October 1929 which triggered an economic meltdown in the United States and disrupted the complex global economy until World War II. It assesses the impact of the Great Depression on ordinary Americans, their strategies for survival, and demands for government action. The chapter then examines the different approaches of presidents Herbert Hoover (1929–33) and Franklin D. Roosevelt (1933–45) to stimulate recovery. Hoover continued to stress individual responsibility, voluntary cooperation, and limited government intervention, but in November 1932, Americans chose a different presidential plan for recovery and relief, and from spring 1933, the Roosevelt administration would push for huge federal investment in the economy and public works. The chapter considers the range of New Deal federal programmes and alphabet agencies created to restore economic stability and prosperity. New Deal policies and agencies helped millions but there were recurring complaints of racial and gender discrimination. We then look at the evolution of the post-1935 "second" New Deal with its more radical "social insurance" programmes and far-reaching industrial-labour reforms, and the rise of the regulatory state. The last section of the chapter demonstrates that Roosevelt was a divisive president who attracted widespread popular support as well as intense criticism from populist leaders, the radical left, and conservative Republicans.

1929 economic meltdown

The value of the US stock market had increased by more than 200 per cent since 1922 as many Americans flocked to invest. There was a dramatic surge in stock market prices and trading volume during 1928 as investors speculated on profits to be made from selling securities. To do this, they bought on the margin i.e. bought shares with a small amount of cash and large broker loans. This practice had topped $7 billion by late 1929. Some banks invested their depositors' savings on the margin without their knowledge. When the stock market peaked in early September 1929, its value was 27 per cent higher than a year previously. Then, during the last hour of trading on Thursday 23 October 1929 stock prices suddenly plummeted. When the stock market reopened the following day, unprecedented trading of 16 million shares led to losses of $9 billion. Despite an attempted bailout by three leading banks and reassuring radio messages from President Hoover, the value of the stock market dropped further after the weekend, by 13 per cent on Monday, and a further 12 per cent on "Black Tuesday" October 29. Brokers called in margins, and stockholders who couldn't pay lost their investments and life savings. All over the country panicked depositors queued outside banks to withdraw their money. Stocks continued to fall during the following weeks, finally bottoming out in mid-November, by which time over $25 billion had been lost.

"Black Thursday" and "Black Tuesday" in late October 1929 were only the beginning of a series of stock market dislocations which continued through the 1930s and helped transform a domestic recession into a global depression. Economists and historians continue to debate what went wrong in 1929. For most of the 1920s, the American economy had appeared buoyant, but the affluent years masked many flaws: a poorly regulated banking structure and banks without adequate financial reserves; underperforming industries such as mining and textiles but overproduction in others such as construction and automobiles; unequal distribution of wealth and purchasing power; and high levels of corporate and personal debt. Many families had bought consumer goods on instalment plans while farmers were often heavily mortgaged and struggling with debt because of low crop prices and high operating costs. These problems became more obvious in the second half of the 1920s after a spectacular land boom collapse in South Florida, falling car sales, plant closures and layoffs at Ford, declining steel production, and several bank failures in 1927–1928. Unstable global markets and investments placed additional strain on the post-war American economy, as European demand for American goods was declining and the complex post-war credit-debt-reparations arrangements of former belligerent powers were also beginning to unravel.

The US economy quickly spiralled from recession in 1929–30 to major depression by 1930–31, from a period of sharply declining employment and government income, which many hoped would be short-lived, to a prolonged period of diminishing wages and tax revenues, collapsing prices, declining industrial production, numerous bank failures, and high unemployment. Around 3 per cent of the labour force, or one and a half million workers, were jobless in 1929, rising to 9 per cent in 1930 and 16 per cent by mid-1931. In every US region, desperate families sold possessions to make ends meet, waited in lengthy bread and soup lines, or plundered garbage cans and waste sites for food or sellable scrap. If evicted from homes they could no longer afford, they lived in cardboard or metal shelters in shantytowns. Known as "Hoovervilles" they were populated by Filipinos, Mexicans, Native Americans, and Japanese, as well as native-born whites and second-generation European immigrants. The Great Depression was a national, multi-ethnic, and multiracial crisis that affected Americans of every class and background, but not necessarily equally. Sharecroppers evicted from failing farms, rising rural and urban unemployment, and white violence and intimidation reinvigorated black migration northward (of 400,000+) and westward. Yet, the African American unemployment rate was often twice as high as the white rate: it was nearly 50 per cent in New York City in the early 1930s.

Family survival strategies included home fruit and vegetable growing, recycling of clothing, cars, and other materials, bartering, and part-time work by different members of increasing numbers of multigenerational households. Hopefuls queued for hours at urban labour exchanges or on work-sites for a day's paid employment. In New York City numerous jobless white men became street vendors selling five-cent apples, and groups of black women of all ages waited in "slave markets" on street corners for white women to drive up and offer them a day's work, sometimes for less than ten cents an hour. Single and married women used prostitution to counter poverty and supplement family income. Marriage and birth rates both declined during the decade; single and married women of all ages and backgrounds used contraception and abortion to regulate family size. Divorce numbers decreased but rates of family abandonment rose. Before the New Deal, private charities such as the Red Cross and Salvation Army, and local government relief agencies bore much of the burden of aiding jobless, hungry, and desperate families and were completely overwhelmed by the magnitude of the economic crisis.

Economic hardship also fuelled nativism and racial resentments. White Americans demanded jobs held by black, Asian, and Chicano workers. Growing anti-Mexican sentiment in the Southwest together with domestic security and immigration concerns over the US–Mexican border led to tighter enforcement of existing US laws. American consuls in Mexico denied visas to Mexican labourers via literacy tests, by upholding a ban on contract labor, and excluding any person "likely to become a public charge." Immigration from Mexico had averaged nearly 59,000 per year during the late 1920s but dropped to just over 3,000 in 1931. From September 1930, unlawful entry into the US became a felony and deportations of "illegals" increased. More than 8,000 Mexicans were deported formally under warrant in 1930 but widespread economic pressure and intimidation led to a further one to two million "voluntary" deportations between 1929 and 1939. Federal and local relief agencies, local repatriation boards, state militias, and the Mexican government were supposed to work together to deliver a nationwide repatriation campaign. However, many Mexicans were simply rounded up by local police and sheriffs in southwestern cities and states and forcibly transported across the border.

Depression-era joblessness and transience stoked public fears over social disorder, crime, and general lawlessness. Crime fears had increased during the last years of Prohibition over gangsters and a dramatic rise in young shoplifters, car thieves, and gas station stickup artists. Many Americans believed that rising unemployment would lead to increased theft, robbery and other types of property crime. As hundreds of thousands of Americans crossed the country searching for work, community fears of outsiders and strangers also increased. By the early 1930s, more than two million men, including 250,000 teenagers, and maybe 8,000 women were "hoboes" – homeless persons or tramps. Prosecutions for vagrancy rose dramatically in these years, particularly for African Americans.

Hoboes, migratory workers, and other predominately young male transient populations used America's extensive railroad system to "ride the rails" or hop on and off freight trains without paying a fare. Many travellers hid near coal yards, engine sheds, or rail junctions then jumped onto slow-moving freight trains. Once aboard, they lay on iron rods in dangerous cramped spaces underneath the train, scrambled onto the tops of wagons or "cars," or jealously guarded spaces inside the boxcars. Railroad companies hired private police or "bulls" to forcibly remove riders from the trains and the "jungles" (hobo communities) near water sources and tracks, as at Mansfield, Ohio, where several rail lines converged. Train crews frequently messaged sheriffs further up the line so they were waiting to make arrests as the train pulled into the station. In March 1931, a series of fights between young white and black hoboes on a freight train headed for Memphis, Tennessee, resulted in the arrest of nine African American "boys" for vagrancy and disorder at Paint Rock station in Alabama. Most of the teenagers met for the first time at the Scottsboro jail but all were subsequently charged with the rape of two young white women also taken from the train.

Accusations of interracial gang rape, white supremacist attitudes, threats of lynching, and Depression-era anxieties over crime and disorder produced a toxic atmosphere in Jackson County, Alabama. Southern black defendants accused of interracial rape often faced death at the hands of a lynch mob or in the electric chair. Within three weeks of the initial incident, all but the youngest, who was 12 years old, had been convicted by local all-white-male juries at Scottsboro and sentenced to death even though doctors who had examined the female complainants testified that no rapes had occurred. The Scottsboro case was one of two interracial gang rapes that outraged the nation in 1931. Five young men of Hawaiian, Japanese and Hawaiian-Chinese descent were charged with assaulting the wife of a Navy lieutenant stationed at Pearl Harbor. In contrast to the Scottsboro case, the racially mixed jury in Honolulu could not reach a verdict and a mistrial was declared. The rape complainant's mother and husband were subsequently convicted of the manslaughter of one of the five original rape suspects, but their sentences were commuted to one hour of prison time by Hawaii's territorial governor after pressure from the US Navy and many US Congressmen.

Scottsboro and civil rights

Public and political interest in the fate of the "Scottsboro Boys" – Olen Montgomery, Clarence Norris, Haywood Patterson, Ozie Powell, Willie Roberson, Charlie Weems, Eugene Williams, Andy Wright, and Roy Wright – continued for many years because of a highly publicised wrangle between the NAACP and the Communist Party's legal arm the International Labor Defense (ILD) over who would represent the "boys" in court, the five different trials between 1931 and 1937, and because one of the female rape complainants had retracted her allegations by 1935. Charges of repeated gross miscarriages of justice from civil rights organisations and northern black and white journalists generated a major civil rights offensive in the 1930s, that was fought in the courts as well as in communities across the United States.

In the case of *Powell v. Alabama* (1932), the US Supreme Court overturned the conviction of Ozie Powell because the trial court had denied him due process (which is guaranteed under the Fourteenth Amendment) by failing to provide any reasonable opportunity to secure an effective defence lawyer in his first trial. The Court also overturned the convictions of Clarence Norris and Haywood Patterson in *Norris v. Alabama* (1935) and *Patterson v. Alabama* (1935) because African Americans had been systematically excluded from juries. Both Norris and Patterson were retried, reconvicted, and resentenced to death. Following a controversial political "settlement" of the Scottsboro case in summer 1937, four men were released, and rape charges against the other five defendants including Norris and Patterson were dropped but they remained in prison for years until they were eventually paroled.

For more information, see "Famous American Trials" by Douglas O. Linder http://law2.umkc.edu/faculty/projects/Ftrials/scottsboro/scottsb.htm

Federal economic relief under Hoover

Of the three Republican presidents of the 1920s, Hoover was undoubtedly the best qualified, most experienced, and intellectually astute. A committed public official with a long record of wartime humanitarian relief, support for voluntarism, business progressivism, civil rights concerns, and interest in conservation, he certainly seemed well-equipped for the challenges of executive office. Hoover announced in 1928: "We in America today after nearer to the final triumph over poverty than ever before in the history of any land. The poorhouse is vanishing from among us." Unfortunately, by the end of 1929, there were millions of poverty-stricken Americans.

Often portrayed as an unrelenting supporter of laissez-faire government and much criticised for his lacklustre response to the Great Depression, President Herbert Hoover reminded fellow Republicans in August 1932 that his administration had risen to the economic challenges "with proposals to private business and to Congress of the most gigantic program of economic defense and counterattack" in the nation's history. However, Hoover's vision of "associational corporatism" rested on decentralisation, individual responsibility, voluntarism, and cooperation between the functionally independent units of labour, industry, agriculture, management and government which were to work together in the public interest. Starting with a series of White House Conferences in late 1929, leading financiers and industrialists agreed with the American Federation of Labour (AFL) and farmers' leaders to stabilise industrial and agricultural production and maintain wages through voluntary controls to restrict production and manipulate prices. For example, the Federal Farm Board encouraged wheat farmers to form cooperatives, and for all members to withhold their wheat stocks from the market until prices rose.

Presidential and congressional anti-depression economic strategies also focused on revitalising export markets. To stimulate domestic production, increase foreign sales, and protect American manufacturers and farmers from foreign competition, Congress approved higher taxes on imported goods, but European nations quickly reciprocated thus making it even harder to sell US goods overseas. Increased tariffs had also hurt Caribbean and Latin American exports including Cuban sugar. Several revolutions erupted in Latin America between 1929 and 1931 against the backdrop of deepening global economic crises, and Latin American governments' inability to secure additional loans from US banks. Hoover set aside the Roosevelt Corollary and refused to sanction US military intervention when Latin American governments defaulted on debt obligations to the US in October 1931. Under the "Good Neighbor" policy, there was re-emphasis on building business investment, improving diplomatic relations, and stabilising export markets throughout the Western Hemisphere.

By 1931–32, many European investors were withdrawing gold reserves from American banks while European governments opted to abandon the gold standard and devalue their currencies. This had serious international trade implications for the US. European governments also owed American banks around $11.5 billion in war debts and their own economic problems threatened the delicate balance of reparations-war debts-US loans-to-Germany established under the Dawes Plan (1924). Hoover declared a one-year moratorium on war reparations and loan payments in June 1931 to help shore up European finances and expand overseas consumer markets for US goods. However, both Britain and France were forced to default on the inter-allied debt in 1932. Meanwhile, powerful belligerent governments often headed by strong-men, dictators, or militaristic factions in Germany, Italy and Japan were advocating territorial and colonial expansion to counter their domestic economic problems.

At first, domestic voluntary controls seemed relatively successful but broke down as the depression deepened. In September 1931, US Steel cut wages by 11 per cent, and the automobile, textile and rubber firms quickly followed; Ford Motor employees received wage cuts of 20 to 40 per cent from October. By early 1932, city governments also began to cut their employees' salaries, often by up to 25 per cent, and other industries such as construction imposed similar wage cuts. Many firms struggled to retain full-time employees or provide even 20–30 hours of paid work per week. Higher farm prices could not be sustained because of massive overproduction so a pound of cotton cost 16 cents in 1929 but dropped to 6 cents in 1932. Industrial and agricultural leaders demanded greater government action, for example, the reorganisation of trade associations into compulsory cartels to restrict production and introduce currency controls, but the Hoover Administration did not agree.

Hoover proudly highlighted the expansion of local and state public works programmes supported by federal monies – usually financed through matching grants and loans which required state contributions rather than federal handouts. Construction projects included roads, bridges, airports, and public buildings, and the Boulder,

Grand Coulee, and California Central Valley dams. Federal aid for highway construction jumped from $105 million to $260 million annually, and the numbers of workers on such projects increased from 110,000 to 280,000. However, the president was troubled by the cost of public works and the moral impact that dependency would have on workers. There was therefore little direct poor or business relief until mid-1932. The Reconstruction Finance Corporation was created by Congress in January 1932 to provide 30-day business loans to promote recovery, and $1.78 billion was extended to 7,400 banks, insurance companies, railroads, and other businesses. More federal loan money was authorised under the Emergency Relief and Construction Act in June 1932, including $300 million to the states for poor relief and public works. Yet, there was no sign of recovery.

Gearing up for change

Voters geared up for the 1932 presidential and congressional elections against a backdrop of mass unemployment and increasing unrest, including hunger marches, food riots, and armed resistance to banks foreclosing on farms, businesses, and homes. In Atlanta, more than 1,000 unemployed labourers marched on the courthouse in June 1932 to demand the resumption of relief payments that local officials had recently suspended. County commissioners agreed to provide $6,000 for relief but labour and racial tensions remained high. A violent confrontation in Washington DC between serving soldiers and war veterans who had fallen on hard times led to intense criticism of the Hoover Administration as hopelessly out of touch with the suffering of ordinary Americans. In 1924, Congress promised a cash bonus of several hundred dollars to veterans of World War I, to be paid in 1945. More than 22,000 jobless veterans led by Walter D. Waters of Oregon came to Washington to demand early payment in spring 1932. Calling themselves the "Bonus Expeditionary Force," they camped in a "Hooverville" near the Anacostia River, along with their wives and children. Despite some scuffles between veterans and local police, this was a largely peaceful camp and protest. A bill providing immediate payments was passed by the House but rejected by the Senate.

As Congress adjourned for the summer, legislators approved $100,000 in loans to enable marchers to return home, but most stayed on, and numbers swelled. Some "Bonus Army" protestors occupied abandoned federal buildings. Hoover refused to meet with a veterans' delegation or to sanction "preferential" financial treatment for any specific group of Americans. Amid rumours of communist agitation, Hoover, Secretary of War Patrick J. Hurley and the District of Columbia commissioners, directed General Douglas MacArthur to disperse the Bonus Army by force. On 28 July 1932, a machine gun squadron, mounted cavalry with sabres drawn, and infantry troops brandishing rifles with fixed bayonets and tear gas, cleared the business district of protestors, then set fire to the Anacostia encampment. Newsreel images of the violence generated national condemnation of the army's callous tactics and shamed administration officials.

By 1932, growing support for new presidential leadership and different economic policies came from many directions. After ten years of falling prices and agricultural distress, corn and dairy farmers in Iowa organised the Farmers' Holiday Association (FHA), which quickly spread to other mid-western and western breadbasket states. It drew significant support from both landowning and smaller farmers as well as a

Figure 11.1 The Bonus Expeditionary Force, Washington DC, 1932. Jobless World War I veterans came to Washington DC in spring 1932 to demand early payment of cash bonuses due in 1945. Calling themselves the "Bonus Expeditionary Force" they camped in a shanty town called "Hooverville" not far from Congress and the White House.

Source: Courtesy of Everett Collection Historical/Alamy

longer populist heritage of agrarian protest. Under the leadership of Milo Reno, of the Iowa Farmers' Union, FHA demanded that Congress enact a cost-of-production plan under which the federal government would maintain food prices to allow farmers to cover their operating costs, generate a 5 per cent return on their investment, and provide a living wage. The plan would have increased the price of a bushel of oats from 11 to 45 cents and a bushel of corn from 10 to 92 cents. A series of withholding protests commenced in August 1932 in which FHA supporters set up patrols and picket lines to prevent transportation of farm products to market. There were violent clashes between pro- and anti-FHA farmers, and with sheriff's deputies attempting to keep the roads open. Direct action was suspended in September as attention shifted to the forthcoming presidential and congressional campaigns, and to support local and state pro-farm candidates. It was significant that Hoover failed to carry a single rural county in his home state of Iowa in the November elections.

A New Deal for the American people

Franklin D. Roosevelt (FDR) succeeded Al Smith as Governor of New York in 1928. His earlier political career had been interrupted by polio, a debilitating illness which left him largely paralysed from the waist down and confined to a wheelchair, although metal leg braces and the arm of an aide enabled him to move short distances. A compliant press and political elite ensured that the American public knew little of his disabilities. As presidential contender, he built a pragmatic coalition within a Democratic Party that was still deeply divided over race, religion, and prohibition, and offered a different plan for recovery and relief to Hoover. In the summer of 1932, Governor Roosevelt accepted the Democratic party presidential nomination and pledged a "new deal for the American people." Americans' profound disillusionment with existing depression remedies was clear when voters ignored Hoover's warning that FDR's plan would increase the size, power, and cost of the federal bureaucracy, undermine local and states' rights, and destroy the nation's key institutions. Roosevelt won over 22.9 million voters compared to Hoover's 15.8 million, and the Democratic Party secured clear majorities in both Houses of Congress.

The contours of the New Deal took shape in the short period between the November election and Roosevelt's inauguration on 4 March 1933. Roosevelt's political pragmatism, willingness to listen to different proposals, and lack of fixed ideology or economic orthodoxy were viewed positively by many but dismissed as evidence of shallowness and an eagerness to please by others. However, Roosevelt's biographers and New Deal historians emphasise the extraordinary range of economic, scientific, sociological and legal expertise that the president drew on to formulate his responses to the depression. These included the "Brains Trust," a formidable team of academics such as Adolf A. Berle, Rexford G. Tugwell, and Raymond Morley from Columbia University, FDR's wife Eleanor Roosevelt who was a powerful social and political activist in her own right, and long-time Democratic Party allies such as Louis Howe and James A. Farley. Such expertise was desperately needed as the task ahead was enormous. By early 1933, the US unemployment rate had risen to 25 per cent overall, and 46 per cent in the leading manufacturing industries. Around 13 million people were without paid work, and malnutrition and homelessness were affecting both rural and urban Americans, including those still in work.

During the administration's First Hundred Days in March–June 1933 Congress passed a comprehensive programme of emergency banking and currency measures, emergency relief and work relief programmes, and longer-term agencies for industrial and agricultural recovery. Roosevelt's Cabinet contained talented administrators such as Secretary of the Interior Harold L. Ickes, Secretary of Agriculture Henry A. Wallace, and Secretary of Labor Frances C. Perkins, all with different views on appropriate forms of relief and government intervention but a willingness to experiment and innovate to deliver economic stability and general prosperity. The severity of the national crisis meant there was extraordinary cooperation from Congress, business, and labour in early 1933. The administration also cultivated significant public support through resourceful use of the media. Roosevelt was a wealthy and elite politician but in newsreels and in print he came across as an empathetic, inventive, and energetic doer who understood the problems of ordinary Americans. His famed radio-broadcast "fireside chats" began on 12 March 1933 with an explanation for the recent "banking holiday" or extended closure of banks and he thanked the American people for their forbearance. Around 40 per cent of American households had radios by 1930.

The New Deal in action: work relief

Federal work relief to provide employment and funds for needy Americans was an integral component of New Deal programmes from the outset. Hoover's Emergency Relief Administration became the Federal Emergency Relief Administration (FERA), headed by Harry Hopkins. It distributed surplus food, clothing, and other necessities directly to those in need from April 1933. Hopkins advocated direct relief, including cash payments, rather than stigmatising grocery credit. Other New Dealers such as Frances Perkins believed that performing work in exchange for necessities was less degrading and morally productive particularly if training was included. There was considerable political and popular resistance to "dole" handouts. Congress authorised

$500m for work relief, half in direct cash grants to states and half in matching grants, where the states would provide $3 for each federal dollar of aid. Despite the successes, local studies of New Deal relief efforts, in Kansas and South Carolina for example, confirmed that poor administration and discriminatory practices hampered FERA's direct relief efforts. Further, most local and federal relief programmes excluded Mexicans from their rolls or offered them benefits far below those available to whites, but many Mexican Americans accepted relief when it enabled them to refuse exploitative fruit picking and domestic labour at starvation wages.

During the winter of 1933–34, FERA was augmented by the Civil Works Administration (CWA) which paid unskilled workers up to 50 cents an hour for 30 hours of work per week. Within two months, 4.2 million CWA male recipients were building roads, improving schools and playgrounds, and laying sewer pipes. By January 1934, 300,000 women were employed in CWA sewing, canning, and clerical jobs. Following employer complaints about CWA's relatively high wages, both working hours and wages were reduced. CWA wound up in April 1934 and FERA re-emerged as main relief agency, but even FERA was envisioned as a temporary expedient in a national crisis rather than long-term government assistance. Its operations ceased in 1935 or were redistributed to other agencies, most notably to the Works Progress Administration (WPA), directed by Harry Hopkins.

As the second largest New Deal work relief programme, WPA employed more than eight and a half million Americans between April 1935 and 1943 (usually 2.1 million at any one time) at a cost of $10.7 billion. Toleration of racial and gender discrimination were problems common to all federal New Deal agencies and state equivalents. To qualify for WPA relief, women had to be heads of households, and more than half of recipients were employed in sewing rooms. A much wider range of work opportunities was available for men. Male WPA workers were recruited from local relief rolls and were paid relatively good wages to construct and renovate thousands of public buildings such as schools, libraries, post offices, water and sewerage systems, roads, airports, and recreational facilities in small towns and rural communities across the US. Big city projects included the 1.5-mile-long Lincoln Tunnel underneath the Hudson River, connecting New Jersey to Manhattan, and smaller city projects such as the municipal airports at Long Beach, California, and Houston, Texas. Many WPA building are still in use.

The WPA also created a federal writers project that enabled unemployed writers, teachers, and chroniclers to produce a series of guidebooks for every US state, and work on folklore and life history projects. These included the FWP Slave Narrative project which eventually recorded 2,300 first-person oral accounts of slavery and continues to inform historical understanding of African American life during the last decade of slavery and the decades after the Civil War. Federal relief monies supported an extraordinary array of cultural productions in the 1930s, including concerts, plays, and comedy reviews. They were performed by talented musicians, actors, directors and others who were employed by federal music and theatre projects in the 1930s. In 1936, the federal theater project employed 12,500 actors who performed before audiences of 350,000 every week. A Negro Theatre Project was set up in 23 cities between 1935 and 1939. Its "Negro Units" employed hundreds of black actors, playwrights, technicians, and directors, and brought Shakespearean productions of Macbeth and Othello, an all-black Cinderella, and jazz operettas such as *The Swing Mikado* (1938) to black audiences in Chicago, New York and other cities. A federal art project offered work to painters, sculptors, and muralists. Several hundred murals were created in the 1930s, including the *Coit Tower Murals* (1933–34) in San Francisco.

The New Deal in action: crime control

The National Youth Administration, championed by Eleanor Roosevelt, provided scholarship assistance to high-school and college students ages 16 to 25 years in exchange for work at those institutions, and later vocational training programmes. They were set up to address youth unemployment rates but could also steer disaffected jobless teenagers away from radical politics and petty crime. Both the Hoover and Roosevelt administrations expressed concerns over declining public morals and rising crime rates, thus vocational training together with work relief programmes such as the Civilian Conservation Corps (discussed in the next section) had important crime control, social control and political functions. They became part of an all-out federal war on crime waged during the early New Deal years.

In the early 1930s, Americans followed the rise of a group of professional criminals and gangs whose interstate activities exposed the weaknesses of local and state law enforcement. Kansas criminal and later Alcatraz prison resident, Alvin Karpis, noted, "My profession was robbing banks, knocking off payrolls, and kidnapping rich men. I was good at it." Expertly tutored by fellow inmates in Indiana's state prison system in the 1920s, "Handsome" John Dillinger graduated from petty teenage thief to ruthless interstate bank robber. Many ordinary Americans regarded the banks as the main purveyors of economic misery and bankers as thieves and racketeers, thus Dillinger quickly achieved "Robin Hood" status when he robbed at least ten major banks in five states between May 1933 and July 1934. Under Director J. Edgar Hoover, the Bureau of Investigation targeted a midwestern and western crime corridor stretching north from Texas to Minnesota where bank robbers plundered less secure local banks and eluded capture by fleeing across state lines, usually in stolen automobiles. Similarly, Bonnie Parker and Clyde Barrow became criminal celebrities during an 18-month deadly crime spree from 1932, that included robbery, auto theft, and car chases with law enforcers in Texas and neighbouring states.

It was however the kidnapping of Charles Lindbergh Jr. that stirred popular and political action on crime. On 1 March 1932, the 20-month-old son of aviator Charles A. Lindbergh and Anne Morrow Lindbergh, daughter of a wealthy and politically prominent New Jersey family, was taken from his bedroom in the family home near Hopewell, New Jersey. The family received several ransom notes and $50,000 was paid for Charles Jr.'s safe return. His body was discovered two miles from the Lindbergh home on 12 May; he had almost certainly been dead since the night of the abduction. Kidnapping was not a federal crime or a death penalty offence at this point, but this was later addressed by Congress and in state "little Lindbergh laws." It was not until 1935 that investigators were able to follow the ransom money trail – the serial numbers had all been recorded in 1932 – to Bruno Richard Hauptmann who was executed for Charles Jr.'s murder in April 1936.

From 1933, Bureau of Investigation Director J. Edgar Hoover and Attorney General Homer Cummings transformed the Bureau into the leading surveillance and crime-fighting force in the nation. Major crimes such as kidnapping and armed robbery were cast as "declarations of war" on respectable and law-abiding citizens. The murder of several law officers by Clyde, and possibly Bonnie, ensured they would be hunted down by local and federal crime agencies. Celebrity criminals such as Dillinger, George "Machine Gun" Kelly, and Arthur "Pretty Boy" Floyd were branded "public enemies" and were to be eradicated. Dillinger, Public Enemy No. 1, was killed by federal agents in front of a Chicago movie theatre in July 1934. When Bonnie and Clyde were killed in an ambush by Texas Rangers and Louisiana state police in May 1934, many celebrated the demise of two calculating cop-killers while others mourned the rugged individualism of doomed folk heroes.

Congress approved an Omnibus Crime bill (1934) which dramatically expanded the number of federal offences to include transportation of kidnapped persons across state lines, murder of federal officers, extortion, interstate flight, and tougher bank robbery laws. The old military prison on Alcatraz Island in San Francisco Bay was refurbished as a super-maximum federal prison for public enemies like Capone and Karpis. From 1935, the renamed *Federal* Bureau of Investigation became the national government's strike force against all "public enemies," including civil rights activists, domestic communists and dissident intellectuals. The Hollywood movie industry, with encouragement from Hoover, gave the FBI exclusive possession of the nickname "G-Men" which had previously been underworld slang for all government operatives.

The New Deal in action: conservation and Native Americans

The Emergency Conservation Work legislation of March 1933 created a military-style Civilian Conservation Corps of 250,000 physically fit, usually urban, men between the ages 18 and 25 and from families on relief. There were several parallels between CCC and European youth conservation programmes, including the *Reicharbeitsdienst* in Germany. The CCC "boys" were put to work across the US constructing roads, bridges, and camping facilities, building fire towers and animal shelters, planting trees and clearing fire lines, and installing telephone cables. They worked for up to 40 hours a week for six-month terms, and received $30 per month, of which $25 went directly to their families. The first CCC Camp Roosevelt was established in Virginia in mid-April 1933; by September 1935, there were 500,000 volunteers in more than 2,500 camps across the United States, including 17,000 men in 103 camps in Michigan alone. The US Department of Labor oversaw enrolments, the War Department used regular and reserve Army officers as well as local civilians to supervise the camps, and the Departments of Interior and Agriculture organised and directed the conservation work. The contributions of four major executive departments were coordinated by Robert Fechner, a labour leader from the South. Of the two and a half to three million total CCC recruits, around 200,000 were African American, but racial separation was the norm. Fechner complained in 1934, "There is hardly a locality in this country that looks favourably or even with indifference, on the location of a Negro CCC camp in their vicinity." Yet, CCC was an important and highly successful conservation programme 1933–42 with an enduring legacy of national forests, parks, and wildlife refuges.

Several Bureau of Indian Affairs (BIA) officials argued that the CCC emergency relief programme should be extended to Native Americans and reservation conservation. FDR did approve establishment of an Indian Division, the CCC-ID, but Indian civil rights organisations had to push to ensure Native employment and for concessions on recruitment as the continuous six-month enrolment period did not fit with traditional tribal life. The US Forest Service did modify the CCC programme for Alaska Natives, including Tlingit and Haida, so that older married men could be employed for longer periods as needed. One successful CCC project in Alaska employed Native carvers and painters to restore over 500 historic totem poles. They remain important tourist attractions.

At the same time, FDR's Secretary of the Interior Harold Ickes and John Collier, head of the Bureau of Indian Affairs (BIA), were deeply critical of federal government policies towards Native Americans. They advocated preservation of traditional cultures and tribal structures rather than continued emphasis on of assimilation. They also recognised that the allotment policy implemented in 1887 (see Chapter 8) had been an unmitigated disaster. By 1932, tribes and individuals had lost 63 million acres or almost two-thirds of the lands that had been in their possession in 1887, through disposal of "surplus" lands by public auction, tax seizures or fraud, or direct land sales to non-Indians. This, together with the poor quality of reservation lands, severely limited the ability of Native Americans (around 333,000) to be self-supporting. Many Natives faced acute economic pressures to leave reservations in search of paid work, usually as unskilled labourers, in nearby cities and other regions.

In June 1934, Congress passed the Indian Reorganization Act which repealed the earlier Dawes/General Allotment Act, supported conservation of native natural resources including forests, herds, and arable land, and encouraged tribal enterprise and tribal sovereignty. Reservation tribes could form governments under new constitutions but were still overseen by the BIA, so some critics viewed this as one form of federal control being replaced by federal paternalism. In 1937, the federal government, with little tribal consultation, designated 4.8 million acres of Indian lands as "roadless" or "wild areas" as conservation measures. These included the 125,000-acre Mission Range in Montana and desert and canyon lands on Navajo and Fort Apache reservations in Arizona. The "Indian New Deal" therefore paralleled some of the conservation, communal and cooperative strands in other New Deal programmes. Despite many patronising officials and discriminatory features, it did promote the cultural revitalisation of indigenous peoples.

The New Deal in action: regional planning

Probably the most ambitious early New Deal programme for recovery, cooperation, and long-term planning was the Tennessee Valley Authority (TVA) created in May 1933. Following a visit to Muscle Shoals in January, president-elect Roosevelt had observed "we have an opportunity of setting an example of planning, not just for ourselves but for the generations to come, tying in industry and agriculture and forestry and flood prevention, tying them all into a unified whole over a distance of a thousand miles." TVA actually covered 40,000 square miles. In 1933, it was "an innovative New Deal agency without a blueprint for action" and the administrative and organisational details took years to hammer out, but its primary purpose was to improve the navigability of the Tennessee River and create more effective flood control.

A 650-mile improved water channel was cleared from Paducah to Knoxville, an extensive system of inland waterways was developed, and five dams were upgraded. Construction of 16 additional dams, huge reservoirs, and coal-fired steam plants were constructed between 1933 and 1944 by over 28,000 workers. Re-forestation and soil improvement initiatives followed. Water power was also used in the manufacture of

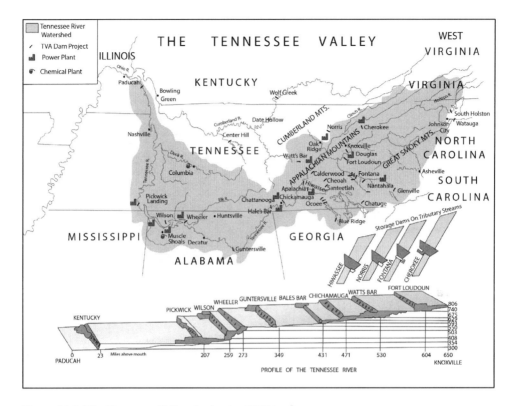

Figure 11.2 The Tennessee Valley Authority (TVA).

fertiliser nitrates, whose value would increase after war broke out in 1939. TVA was governed by a fractious three-person board of directors until 1938 and weathered a series of legal challenges from private utility companies, but it did deliver work relief, new infrastructure, new jobs, and economic recovery for many regional residents. Thousands of displaced families were resettled in homes and farms in experimental communities with organised health care and schooling, although these generally excluded African American farmers. There were also limited efforts to challenge local racial customs and racial prejudice when TVA set up demonstration projects to educate famers on new techniques and farm products and sought to revive regional industries such as pottery and weaving. Hydroelectric power did provide affordable electricity for thousands of previously neglected rural farmsteads, homes, and businesses in seven states, and thus paralleled another New Deal agency, the Rural Electrification Administration created in 1935.

Tackling agriculture and rural poverty

The main agricultural and industrial alphabet agencies sought to control production, prices, and wages. The Agricultural Adjustment Administration (AAA), headed by Henry A. Wallace, included a domestic allotment plan whereby farmers signed acreage reduction contracts, for seven main products including wheat, cotton, and milk, in return for government subsidies that were calculated by AAA. A key goal was to eliminate over-production so from May 1933 cotton farmers were paid $160 million to destroy 25 per cent of their cotton bales and pig farmers received $30 million to slaughter millions of livestock (surplus pork was distributed to needy families by FERA). By ensuring better prices and farm incomes, AAA was to enable farmers to reduce debt, pay their mortgages, and prevent foreclosure. From 1934, destruction would be replaced by limits on planting and livestock.

Nevertheless, during the 1930s US farmers continued to produce far more than consumers could afford to buy, so remained dependent on unstable international export markets. When AAA was struck down by the US Supreme Court in January 1936, it had raised gross farm income by 50 per cent, increased prices by 66 per cent, and reduced farm indebtedness by $1 billion. Like all New Deal programmes, the AAA produced winners and losers. Subsidies generally went to large commercial farming enterprises rather than smaller family farms, and by 1934, a quarter of American farm owners had lost their land. Further, for the 2.86 million tenant farmers and sharecroppers, 1.6 million of whom were African American labouring in southern cotton fields, reduced acreage and limited farm production meant increased unemployment and tenant evictions. This spurred a large wave of sharecropper and tenant farmer organising and protest in the South to challenge New Deal racial inequities.

The 1930s was a decade of dynamic working-class activism and labour organising and there were numerous left-wing challenges to white supremacy, states' rights, and black disfranchisement that was fuelled by the rise of a radical democratic movement for social transformation. The Popular Front courted support from black and white industrial and agricultural labourers, students, and professionals. It included non-communist socialists, communists, liberals, and independent left-wing groups who were united around three broad platforms: more democratic electoral politics, anti-fascism and anti-imperialism, and campaigns for civil liberties and civil rights. The pro-Roosevelt Democratic Front pushed for similar goals within the Democratic Party.

Against the backdrop of a resurgent American Communist Party (CPUSA), local Birmingham organisers such as Mack Coad and Harry Simms helped establish the Alabama Sharecroppers Union (ASU) in the summer of 1931. It had an African American leadership and 600 members by 1932, which included Ned Cobb of Tallapoosa County whose recollections of sharecropping and union activism were recounted in Theodore Rosengarten's *All God's Dangers: The Life of Nate Shaw* (1974). The ASU faced violent opposition from local landowners who rejected any demands for increased wages and improved living conditions. There were some white ASU members, but many southern landowners and white farmers opposed any interracial alliances that threatened white supremacy. The ASU and CPUSA filed a suit against AAA in 1935 to challenge landowner monopoly of subsidies and to demand direct relief payments to labourers but AAA was struck down before the case could be pursued. By 1936, ASU had 10,000 members and had branches in both Mississippi and Louisiana. Similarly, the Southern Tenant Farmers Union (STFU) formed in mid-1934 by sharecroppers and socialists in Tyronza, Arkansas, to oppose AAA policies and demand better wages for cotton-pickers, but the Roosevelt Administration would do little to jeopardise landowner support for its policies. By 1938 STFU was an interracial, multi-state, organisation of 35,000 members.

Agricultural depression in the Plains and western states including Colorado, Kansas, and Oklahoma was compounded by an ecological disaster: the Dust Bowl. Rising

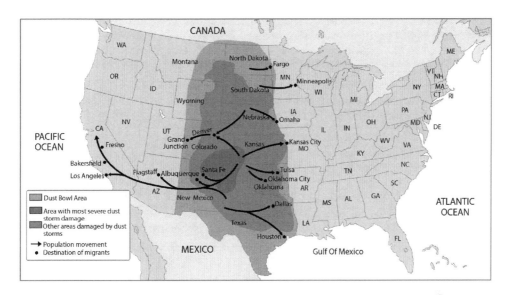

Figure 11.3 1930s ecological disaster: the Dust Bowl.

sea temperatures and several years of reduced rainfall helped create a drought while decades of poor land use and overproduction led to acute soil depletion. Drought and swarms of grasshoppers left a barren landscape which was further ravaged by massive dust storms whose choking clouds travelled for miles, buried homes, livestock and equipment, and deposited dust and debris as far as the eastern seaboard. There were 14 storms in 1932 and 38 in 1933, but the worst came in April 1935. One observer wrote, "We live with the dust, eat it, sleep with it, watch it strip us of possessions and the hope of possessions." Three million Plains residents left their farms, and at least half a million "Okies" migrated westward in search of relief. Some found work as low-wage fruit-pickers and a new start; others endured unsanitary labour camps and personal tragedy. John Steinbeck's Pulitzer Prize winning novel, *The Grapes of Wrath* (1939) chronicled the tragic Dust Bowl migration of the Joad family from Oklahoma.

The Wizard of Oz (1939)

Dorothy Gale, a lonely orphan living with her kindly aunt and uncle on their Kansas farm, is forcibly transported by a tornado to Oz, a fantasy world in conflict. When Gale's farmhouse lands on the Wicked Witch of the East, her powerful ruby slippers are magically transported to Dorothy's feet, but her evil sister, the green-faced Wicked Witch of the West, vows to kill Dorothy and repossess the slippers. Yet, in killing the evil witch, Dorothy also ended her tyrannical rule over the Land of Munchkins and the enslavement of these "little people." Glinda the Good Witch instructs Dorothy to follow the Yellow Brick Road to the Emerald City where a powerful wizard will grant her wish to return home. During this eventful journey, the anxious girl-next-door from Kansas becomes a fearless leader, organiser, and liberator of the doubters and the downtrodden: the Scarecrow, the Tin Man, and the Cowardly Lion. After reaching the Emerald City, her pet dog Toto exposes the Wizard to be a bumbling charlatan and he refuses to help until Dorothy brings him the broomstick of the Wicked Witch of the West. Dorothy ultimately triumphs when she causes the death of this second witch. All ends well and Dorothy finally returns home with the help of Glinda's instruction to click her ruby-slippered heels together three times and repeat the mantra "there's no place like home."

The Metro-Goldwyn-Mayer 1939 classic *The Wizard of Oz* was partly based on L. Frank Baum's book *The Wonderful Wizard of Oz* (1900), and its numerous sequels, which has been variously critiqued as sentimental, subversive, or feminist fairy tale, social satire, and populist parable (with, for example, the Yellow Brick Road and Dorothy's original silver slippers as a joint metaphor for late nineteenth-century bimetallism). There were several stage shows and earlier film productions, but the 1939 movie filmed in glorious technicolour enthralled audiences across America and Europe, particularly the contrast between monochromatic rural Kansas and the vibrant dream world of Oz. Motifs of ecological disaster, good versus evil, and the courage and perseverance of ordinary folk in the 1930s film version must have struck important chords with depression-weary audiences who were increasingly fearful of growing overseas conflicts. Themes of disillusionment with foreign rulers, retreat from external conflicts, and celebration of home and hearth undoubtedly resonated also. Sixty years later Oz's political corruption and internal conflicts were further exposed in Gregory Maguire's 1995 imaginative novel *Wicked*, and the musical of the same name. Thus, Elphaba, the green-skinned Wicked Witch of the West, was never really "wicked" at all but the victim of intolerance, ignorance, and prejudice. And, Dorothy did not murder her, but created an opportunity for Elphaba's self-imposed exile, all with the connivance of her loyal friend Glinda.

In July 1935, a Resettlement Administration was established to assist dispossessed farmers acquire their own land and tools. It was superseded by the Farm Security Administration (FSA) in 1937, tasked with relocating hundreds of thousands of rural families from unproductive land to productive homesteads and small farms, and to support cooperative agricultural communities in which government experts taught more efficient farming methods. Less than 12,000 families were resettled. A different initiative to provide tenants with loans and other financial assistance to purchase farms was more successful, as were New Deal mortgage relief measures for farm and home owners. However, Federal Housing Administration policies were used also to restrict non-white home ownership in major metropolitan areas and rapidly growing suburbs, particularly after World War II.

FSA was part of a wider government and sociological project to understand the realities of rural poverty. As a result, the FSA Photographic Division 1935–42 headed by Roy Stryker employed photographers such as Arthur Rothstein, Walker Evans, Dorothea Lange, and Margaret Bourke-White to document migrant labourers, field workers, and rural communities. They travelled extensively and produced many of the iconic images of Depression and New Deal America. Lange's "Migrant Mother, Nipomo, California" (1936) of Florence Owens Thompson and her starving children in a pea worker camp, and Rothstein's "Dust Storm Cimarron County, Oklahoma" (1936) are undoubtedly the most famous. The plight of the southern tenant farmer and exposure of rural injustice were also leading themes in novels such Erskine Caldwell's *Tobacco Road* (1932).

Figure 11.4 Dorothea Lange's haunting portrait of Florence Owens Thompson (1936).

Source: Courtesy of RKive/Alamy

Figure 11.5 Arthur Rothstein's dramatic image of Dust Bowl devastation (1936).
Source: Courtesy of Glasshouse Images/Alamy

Restructuring industry and labour unions

Often described as the keystone of the early New Deal, the National Recovery Administration, headed by Hugh S. Johnson, was created in June 1933 to promote partnership between private business and government and to establish national labour standards. To create jobs, stimulate spending, and reduce exploitation, Johnson asked every American business establishment to accept a temporary "blanket" code with a minimum wage of 30–40 cents an hour, a maximum workweek of 35–40 hours, and abolition of child labour. Employers who adopted these codes could proudly display the NRA Blue Eagle and slogan "We Do Our Part." Public support for NRA policies was cultivated through patriotic parades and wide publicity. Additional industry-government-labour negotiations produced a set of "codes of fair competition" for every major industry that also regulated prices, limited new plant construction, and forbade a broad range of competitive practices, all subject to presidential approval. Some of the richest and most powerful corporate leaders of the 1930s played a major role in the formulation of industry codes and were willing at first to accept NRA reforms because they promised stability and a route back to prosperity.

NRA reforms were not perfect. Small business operators complained that the codes privileged larger corporations at their expense. Every industrial code allowed

Figure 11.6 The National Recovery Administration, the Blue Eagle, and "We Do Our Part." A pen and ink cartoon by Clifford Berryman from 1933 showing "The spirit of the New Deal." It depicts the partnership between private business, the national government, and American workers under the National Recovery Administration, to establish national labour standards, provide decent wages and working conditions, and to stimulate industrial economic recovery. It had mixed results.

Source: Courtesy of Science History Images/Alamy

employers to pay women less than men. And, agricultural and domestic service workers were not covered by NRA agreements and were excluded from minimum-wage provisions. The predominately black labour force of cotton pickers still earned a lowly 30 to 60 cents per hundred pounds of cotton. Many Mexican Americans were also excluded from the codes and minimum-wage protections. A Public Works Administration (PWA) was set up under the National Industrial Recovery Act in June 1933 with $3.3 billion in funding but few projects received approval from Harold Ickes until the mid-1930s. PWA did sponsor major slum clearance and new public housing construction for tens of thousands of low-income and middle-income families. However, several controversial projects entailed the destruction of buildings occupied by African

Americans or Chicanos and their replacement with all-white housing, as in Atlanta and Los Angeles.

The parent National Industrial Recovery Act (1933) required employers to make important concessions to employees. For example, Section 7(a) prohibited employers from interfering in workers' rights to join or form unions and engage in collective bargaining but it did not create adequate enforcement machinery or require employers to bargain in good faith. Consequently, employers continued to set up non-independent company unions, of which there were 600 with two million members by 1935, with few protections for those members. Employers continued also to use private police, agent provocateurs, and spies to limit union activity, and employ strike-breakers to defeat labour disputes. There were thousands of violent confrontations and strikes in the early 1930s, involving Minneapolis truck drivers, Florida cigar makers, California agricultural workers, Kentucky miners, Alabama cotton mill workers, and many others. When San Francisco's International Longshoremen Association demanded higher wages, shorter workdays, and union control of waterfront hiring halls, there was disruption to all major ports along the Pacific coast for nearly three months. Despite the economic uncertainty and mass unemployment, more than one and a half million workers went on strike in 1934 alone.

The US Supreme Court found NRA's price and wage controls to be unconstitutional in May 1935. However, New York Senator Robert F. Wagner secured congressional and presidential approval to reinstate some NRA provisions and push for stronger labour laws. The National Labor Relations Act (1935) upheld the right of workers to join unions. It created the National Labor Relations Board (NLRB) to investigate and counter "unfair labor practices" such as blacklisting workers, refusing to reinstate strikers, and use of industrial espionage. Congress also passed the Fair Labor Standards Act (1938) which established a federally mandated minimum wage (25 cents an hour), maximum work hours per day and week (44 hours per week), provisions for overtime pay, and prohibited child labour.

Depression-era leisure

Changing work patterns impacted on Americans' leisure time and social activities. By 1938, listening to radio and going to the movies were the most popular entertainments. By 1940, around 80 per cent of American households had radios and could tune into hundreds of radio stations. In 1935, box-office revenues topped $518 million, with Americans on average making 18 movie visits per year and paying 25 cents admission each time. By the mid-1930s, the major studios like Metro-Goldwyn-Mayer, Warner Brothers and RKO Productions had to release 50 to 60 new films every year to cater to consumer demand. These included Busby Berkeley's big budget musical spectacular *42nd Street* (1933), Mervyn LeRoy's social realism film *I Am a Fugitive from a Chain Gang* (1932) and his fantasy *Wizard of Oz* (1939), musical romantic comedies such as *Top Hat* (1935) starring Fred Astaire and Ginger Rogers, Walt Disney's animated fairy-tales such as *Snow White and the Seven Dwarfs* (1937), and David O. Selznick's monster movie *King Kong* (1933) and epic Civil War-era romance *Gone With the Wind* (1939). Both commercial and community recreation increased. Local amateur athletic, baseball and basketballs leagues were also very popular, as were amateur dramatics, church-based socials, and gardening and book clubs.

These reforms were part of what has been termed the "Second New Deal" of 1935–1936. Some historians view them as evidence of a genuine federal government commitment to improve the social and economic rights of American workers. They note also that from 1935, FDR became more critical of large corporate monopolies such as the 13 utility holding companies which controlled three-quarters of US electric power, and championed legislation to reduce their power. Other studies have portrayed New Deal labour legislation as a calculated strategy to blunt worker support for radical economic and socialist reform and to capture the loyalty of the labour movement for the Democratic Party. Conservatives frequently characterised New Deal reforms as socialistic, anti-capitalist, and anti-American but many economic and historical studies have shown that big business and big landowners benefitted more than workers and farmers and that the New Deal protected rather than undermined industrial capitalism.

Yet, the Wagner Act did reinvigorate the labour movement. Union membership exploded, rising from 2.8 million in 1933 to 8.4 million by 1939. During the 1930s, John L. Lewis, charismatic leader of the United Mine Workers, and other proponents of industrial unionism gained influence, largely because the spectacular growth of mass-production industries in the 1920s meant that unskilled workers had come to dominate the industrial labour force. Industrial unionists argued that all workers in an industry should be organised into a single union to take on the dominant corporations rather than remain in smaller unions of specific craft or skilled workers, as was the AFL's long-standing practice (the AFL remained a decentralised federation). Conservative AFL leaders resisted change, but the National Labor Relations Act established the principle that the union winning a majority of votes would represent all employees in a specific industry.

Delegates at the fractious AFL convention in September 1935 rejected Lewis's proposal that industrial unions be allowed to establish their own charters for AFL membership. He walked out. Two months later, the leaders of major mine and garment worker unions, and of developing unions of automobile, rubber, and steel workers, created the Committee on Industrial Organizations which was then expelled from the AFL. A burgeoning Congress of Industrial Organizations (CIO) was established in 1936, with Lewis as president, to enable unskilled and industrial workers to take full advantage of New Deal reforms and as a rival to the AFL. The NAACP worked diligently to enhance the position of black workers within the changing labour movement and found that the CIO was much more receptive to organising non-white and female workers than the AFL. More than one and a half million African Americans joined CIO unions. They accounted for more than 20 per cent of the Steelworkers Union by the end of the decade.

Union changes coincided with wider transformations to the US labour force that created a reservoir of potential new members. Despite severe public criticism and gender discrimination, both single and married women continued to work in the 1930s out of financial necessity and despite many obstacles. From 1932 to 1937, it was illegal for more than one family member to hold a federal civil-service job, and state and local governments often introduced similar restrictions, thus leading to the dismissal of thousands of female employees. Wage-work for professional women declined as unemployed men were hired to fill teaching and social work positions, and any reductions in the domestic service sector disproportionately impacted African American women. Yet, there were 25 per cent more women working in 1940 than in 1930. Economic recovery was slower in the male-dominated heavy industry sector and male unemployment remained high overall so many wives took up wage work, often for the first time in their lives. Service sector positions and clerical work continued to increase, largely because the New Deal created expanding federal and state bureaucracies, and men were less likely to apply for jobs as sales clerks, stenographers or typists. There were small increases in clerical positions for African American women and Chicanas, particularly high school and college graduates. Segregated hospitals, schools, and black-owned businesses also continued to provide female employment in nursing, teaching, and book-keeping. By 1940, 38 per cent of black women were in wage work compared to 24 per cent of white women – black female employment rates had always been higher than white rates, but this highlights that discriminatory employment and differential wages persisted despite New Deal reforms.

The social insurance revolution

The details, shortcomings, and impacts of New Deal programmes were continuously debated by Roosevelt's Cabinet, agency administrators, and members of Congress as well as local and state politicians, journalists, and ordinary Americans. There was no shortage of both supporters and opponents. Several critics proposed alternative economic programmes. As Louisiana governor, Huey P. Long had worked to improve public education by building schools, providing free books, and introduced evening classes for adults; funded new roads, bridges, and highways; and eliminated the poll tax and property taxes on poorer residents. Unusually for a southern Democrat, Long did not court Klan or white supremacist support. Long was elected to the US Senate in 1930, but his controlling political machine continued to dominate the Louisiana state legislature in Baton Rouge. Blaming the economic crisis on monied elites, Senator Long suggested a dramatic redistribution of wealth. His "Share Our Wealth" programme called on the government to limit individual wealth to $4 million and use the excess to provide all citizens with a $5,000 homestead and a guaranteed annual income of $2,500. There were further promises of free education, a 30-hour work week, and old-age pensions to be funded by taxes on the rich. Long's critics denounced him as a demagogue and dictator. Sinclair Lewis's novel *It Can't Happen Here* (1933) centred on the establishment of a fascist regime in the US and was modelled on Long. Yet, the Louisiana senator's criticisms that the New Deal was moving too slowly resonated with many working-class Americans, and drew significant popular support in Louisiana, Arkansas, and Mississippi.

Catholic priest and radio evangelist Charles E. Coughlin called for monetary reforms to increase the amount of currency in circulation and nationalisation of public utilities as well as higher taxes on the wealthy to guarantee a living wage to ordinary families. Coughlin created the National Union for Social Justice to lobby for his economic programme in late 1934 and established the Union Party in 1936. California physician Francis Townsend's 1933 Old Age Revolving Pension plan proposed that every American over 60 years should receive $200 per month, on the condition that they retire from paid employment and spend the full amount each month, to create jobs for younger workers and increase consumer spending. The plan would be funded by national sales tax. Townsend's proposals highlighted the devastating impact of the depression on older Americans; more than 40 per cent of those aged 60 and above were unemployed and reliant on public charity. Many lost their savings which had been invested in now worthless stocks and failed banks. Only 28 of 48 states provided old-age pensions at this time.

Long, Coughlin, and Townsend were dismissed as fascists, demagogues, and power addicts interested primarily in political gain. Coughlin was a virulent anti-Semite. More sympathetic studies have signalled their earnest desire to promote major socio-economic structural reforms or characterised their conservative defence of individual autonomy amid the encroaching power of federal government. Each tapped into significant pools of popular frustration with economic inequity and the pace of recovery. For example, Share Our Wealth Clubs began forming in February 1934, quickly rising to 27,000 clubs with 4.7 million members, and Roosevelt's leadership was

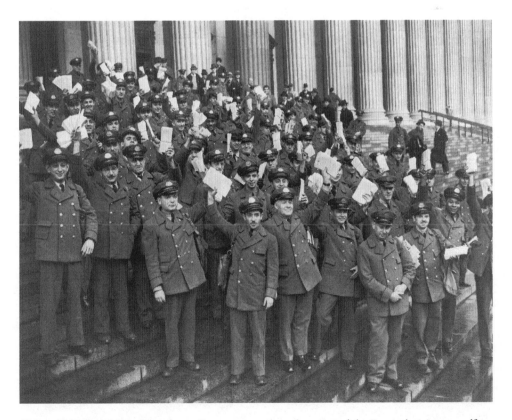

Figure 11.7 Social Security reform. Postmen posed on the steps of the Pennsylvania post office, New York City, holding the new Social Security forms that were being mailed out across the country, 1936.

Source: Courtesy of Everett Collection Inc./Alamy

under challenge. Long's presidential ambitions ended with his assassination in September 1935, yet FDR approved increased tax rates for higher earners, corporate incomes, and on inheritances that year. The Townsend movement crystallised popular support for old-age pensions and helped generate congressional and executive support for the Social Security Act (1935).

In 1935, Congress approved $50 million for what FDR considered was the cornerstone of New Deal domestic social programmes: the Social Security Act. It provided Americans with the key components of a modern welfare state, but its supporters underlined that this was an insurance system where recipients would *earn* their benefits rather than one based on dole and dependency. An old-age pension scheme administered by the federal government and funded by a 1 per cent payroll tax would give retired workers over 65 years a monthly income of $10 to $85, depending on the amount they had contributed, from 1942 (later 1940). Those already retired would receive up to $15 per month. It established a joint federal-state system of unemployment insurance based on employer contributions. The Act authorised federal aid for the care of the blind and to dependent children without parental support, and training for the physically handicapped. Secretary of Labor, Frances Perkins's goal of federally mandated universal health insurance was not included - but later implemented by the Obama administration's 2010 Affordable Care Act. The legislation was revolutionary but also contained many shortcomings. For example, the old-age insurance and unemployment provisions did not cover agricultural, domestic, self-employed or contract workers. During the 1930s, nine out of ten black women were agricultural labourers or domestic servants, thus less than 10 per cent got any direct benefit from new federal policies on minimum wages, maximum hours, unemployment compensation, or social security.

New Deal political realignments

As noted earlier, the rise of the radical left and alliances between the CPUSA, labour organisations, socialists, independent leftists, and civil rights activists provided a powerful lobby of New Deal critics and opponents who largely agreed that Roosevelt's policies were too limited. Many New Deal opponents in the business community and the Republican Party, including former President Hoover, criticised Roosevelt's "March to Moscow" and genuinely believed that Roosevelt planned to replace republican democracy with a socialist-style dictatorship.

Throughout the 1930s, Hoover remained a formidable New Deal critic. He viewed TVA's challenge to private ownership and its "socialist characteristics" as particularly problematic. He contended that AAA's acreage allotment and subsidies would destroy agrarian independence while the NRA promised regimentation rather than cooperation. In his "The Challenge to Liberty" (1934) speech, Hoover condemned FDR's decisions to abandon the gold standard and devalue the dollar as a recipe for rampant inflation and social instability. He warned against social insurance programmes which would increase the power of the executive branch of government and offered austerity as the best remedy for the Great Depression. New Deal supporters countered that New Deal banking and currency reforms of March 1933 had helped restore public confidence and stability, while additional measures in 1933–34 to increase the authority of the Federal Reserve Board and create a Securities and Exchange Commission to police the stock market signalled that the financial establishment was being properly regulated.

In August 1934, a group of wealthy Americans formed the American Liberty League to stimulate public opposition during the mid-term elections to the New Deal's "dictatorial" policies and its supposed attacks on free enterprise. The dictatorship analogy gained traction because of events in Europe. Benito Mussolini's Fascist Party had been in control of Italy since the early 1920s and the regime became increasingly nationalistic and militaristic during the global economic crisis. Hitler's National Socialist (Nazi) Party had swept into power in Germany in 1933. However, many Republican Party moderates such as the Senate Minority Leader, Oregon's Charles McNary, and western Progressives from states with large public works programmes and farmers dependent on subsidies were willing to accept key New Deal reforms. By early 1936, it was no secret that many Republicans favoured moderate Kansas governor Alf Landon's bid for the presidency as the ex-president had become a political liability.

There was little doubt that the Democratic Party would re-nominate FDR and he would run for a second presidential term. In accepting the party nomination, Roosevelt told supporters and millions of radio listeners that modern governments had "inescapable obligations to their citizens" including the protection of homes and families, promoting economic opportunity, and to provide assistance to those in need. He described the current fight against a "new industrial dictatorship" which was not interested in ordinary workers and citizens and which sought to limit the scope of the New Deal as "a war for the survival of democracy" that would move forward despite business opposition, and because the current generation of Americans had a "rendezvous with destiny." Roosevelt was defiant even though his first administration had not delivered full economic recovery. The 1936 presidential election was a clear demonstration of public approval for both the president and the New Deal. FDR received 27.5 million votes to Landon's 16.7 million, and carried every state except Vermont and Maine, and the Democratic Party maintained healthy majorities in both the Senate and the House of Representatives. Voter preferences were however increasingly divided by wealth as FDR won with 76 per cent of lower-income voters but only 42 per cent of upper-income voters.

The 1936 results also provided evidence of wider political shifts and confirmation of the emergence of the "Roosevelt coalition," an awkward inter-regional alliance of southern white and northern black voters, rural dwellers and urban immigrants, middle-class intellectuals and blue-collar workers. The increased appeal of the Democratic Party to recently enfranchised women working outside the home, African Americans who had migrated from the South seeking greater opportunities in northern cities, and immigrants disillusioned with prohibition and restrictive quotas, had been clear by the late 1920s. By 1936, black voters were firmly embedded within the "Roosevelt Coalition." Changing voter preferences and successful mobilisation of voters by northern Democratic Party and civil rights organisations as well as New Deal welfare and work policies all help explain why African Americans rejected their traditional Republican Party loyalties.

Roosevelt's conservative critics also launched a massive offensive after 1937 because of his supreme court packing plan. Frustrated by the US Supreme Court's striking down of the NIRA and AAA, and fearful that the Wagner and Social Security Acts would share the same fate, FDR proposed to appoint up to six additional justices, all of whom would most likely be more sympathetic to administration policies. Conservative critics viewed this as a blatant attack on the Constitution and evidence of FDR's dictatorial ambitions, and there was widespread popular and press censure. The reform proposal was further doomed when the existing nine Supreme Court justices began to vote 5–4 to uphold New Deal laws, including the Wagner labour protections and Social Security legislation.

The Democratic Party was still made up of uneasy regional factions: the southern and conservative wings were contracting, so that 35 per cent of Democrats in Congress came from the South in 1936 compared to 75 per cent in 1920, but conservative and white supremacist anti-New Deal Democrats still wielded considerable power. Southern Democrats were perturbed by rising black party membership and possible demands for racial equality while northern conservatives opposed the centralisation and liberalism of party policy. They sabotaged Roosevelt's second-term agenda by undermining the Fair Labor Standards Act, slashing funds for the Wagner housing programme, and joined Republicans to defeat the judicial reform bill. Roosevelt retaliated in 1938 by campaigning against Walter George of Georgia, Ellison Durant "Cotton Ed" Smith of South Carolina, and Millard Tydings of Maryland, but badly miscalculated. All retained their seats. Within 18 months, FDR was reaching out to his conservative foes for crucial foreign policy support.

During the Spring of 1937, recession returned, industrial production dropped by over 35 per cent, four million workers lost their jobs, and funding for work relief was drastically reduced. FDR had to ask Congress for emergency funding of $5 billion for relief and public works programmes in April 1938. During 1937, there were 4,720 strikes and more than 80 per cent were settled in favour of the unions. A CIO recruitment drive in the steel and auto industries in 1937 helped steel workers win a 10 per cent wage increase and guarantees from US Steel over an eight-hour workday and a 40-hour work week. Communist and social democratic activists also supported Detroit United Auto Workers' sit-down strike action (where workers sat inside the plants and refused to work or leave despite court orders to do so, thus preventing the company from utilising strike-breakers) against General Motors. The CPUSA had provided skilled experienced organisers for these disputes. It generally remained too radical for the majority of labour unionists, but the strikes showed that there was still significant radical-left, social democratic, and liberal disillusionment with government policies.

The Republican Party experienced a revival in the late 1930s. Concerned to recapture Republican voters who had switched allegiances in 1936, a new generation of moderate and pragmatic party members accepted the need for some federal government intervention in the economy and social insurance responsibilities to be balanced by greater efficiency in government and less federal spending. In other words, they wanted a milder version of the New Deal reforms. Republicans made solid gains of seven seats in the senate, 75 seats in the House of Representatives, and 12 governors in the midterm elections of 1938, and looked to be re-establishing the Republican Party as a credible electoral alternative to the Democratic Party. However, the highpoint of New Deal activism had passed. In the second half of the 1930s, both parties could no longer ignore the declining international situation as European nationalist and fascist leaders launched active campaigns of imperial and territorial expansion, and Europe again appeared to be on the brink of war. Foreign affairs, international relations, and national defence demanded as much attention as domestic policies.

Did the New Deal work?

The New Deal

It is generally accepted that the New Deal represented a watershed moment in twentieth-century US history as the federal government took on new powers and responsibilities to guarantee the social and economic well-being of its citizens. Recent studies of Roosevelt's first and second administrations and the New Deal's social programmes offer a tempered assessment of their effectiveness: reformers and planners were restricted politically and administratively from making any truly radical reforms or structural changes. They highlight the unbridgeable gap between New Dealers' highly idealistic plans and the harsh political, social, racial and economic realities that agencies operated in. The willingness of New Dealer planners and agency employees to improvise and experiment were applauded but left-wing criticisms that reforms did not go far enough are still valid. By contrast, revisionist studies have recently contended that New Deal policies and extended federal regulation of the economy restricted competition and actually increased economic instability thus prolonging recession in the 1930s.

The New Deal's large-scale programmes for unemployment relief, public works, and social security, and the policies concerning business, agriculture, conservation, and labour did bring tangible benefits to millions of Americans, but these were not shared equally. By 1939, around 15 per cent of the workforce was still unemployed, and African American incomes were generally 50 per cent less than white incomes, while 90 per cent of black families still lived in poverty. Continuing economic struggle and black frustrations over ongoing racial discrimination and police brutality provided the background to a race riot in Harlem in 1935. Voter support for the New Deal helped create a powerful coalition within the Democratic Party that dominated US politics for the next 40 years. And the New Deal's imprint on infrastructure and social and cultural life continues: the Tennessee Valley Authority remains the largest public power company in the US and major recreation hub for outdoor activities such as camping, fishing, and sailing, while WPA airports, roads, and schools remain important parts of the New Deal legacy.

Chapter summary

This chapter began with the stock market crash in October 1929 and examined the impact of economic meltdown on ordinary Americans. It considered the federal relief plans implemented by presidents Hoover and Roosevelt, contrasting pre-1932 emphasis on voluntarism and corporatism with huge post-1933 federal investment in work relief, conservation, crime control, and major industrial and agricultural reforms. It signalled that all New Deal programmes and agencies had many positive economic, cultural, and social impacts but were often discriminatory as well. The chapter then examined how ongoing recession as well as populist criticisms of New Deal policies helped shape the post-1935 second New Deal with its more radical "social insurance" programmes and far-reaching industrial-labour reforms, and the rise of the regulatory state. The last section of the chapter focused on criticism of New Deal policies and Roosevelt's presidential style and the political realignments that resulted in the late 1930s.

 ## Discussion questions

- Why do you think marriage, birth and divorce rates all decreased during the Depression decade?
- Would it have been possible to run major New Deal programmes such as NRA, AAA, CCC, and WPA as state or local initiatives and without federal government input?
- Which workers benefitted most from New Deal reforms?
- Why was conservation such a core component of so many New Deal programmes?
- How do Depression-era and New Deal photographs add to our understanding of the 1930s?

Further reading

Badger, Anthony J. *The New Deal: The Depression Years, 1933–1940* (New York, 1989). Very readable, now classic, broad-brush overview of the New Deal recovery and reform programmes, and FDR's political skills.

Burrough, Brian. *Public Enemies: America's Greatest Crime Wave and the Birth of the FBI, 1933–1934* (New York, 2005). Detailed, carefully researched, and chronologically attentive account of the rise and fall of Dillinger, Karpis, Bonnie and Clyde and the other glorified major criminals of the early depression years, and federal police responses.

Chafe, William H. *The Achievement of American Liberalism: The New Deal and Its Legacies* (New York, 2003). Highly useful wide-ranging edited collection of 11 essays by leading historians of liberalism that cover high politics, culture, and gender and race, that traces the arc of liberalism from the New Deal to the end of the twentieth century, and looks at both the impact of the New Deal and its legacies.

Cohen, Adam. *Nothing to Fear: FDR's Inner Circle and the Hundred Days That Created Modern America* (New York, 2009). Highlights the disagreements, debates, and decision-making among leading New Dealers and the president that produced innovative responses and key recovery programmes.

Domhoff G. William, and Michael J. Webber. *Class and Power in the New Deal: Corporate Moderates, Southern Democrats, and the Liberal-Labor Coalition* (Stanford, CA, 2011). Provides an interesting class dominance challenge to the historiography of the New Deal by focusing on three policy areas (agriculture, industry, social security) to argue that business elites and corporate moderates significantly influenced key New Deal agencies.

Fearon, Peter. *Kansas in the Great Depression: Work Relief, the Dole, and Rehabilitation* (Columbia, 2007). An important state study of a Republican-dominated western state during the 1920s and 1930 which examines the changing relationship between state and federal government and the ways in which New Deal aid was administered.

Gilmore, Glenda Elizabeth. *Defying Dixie: The Radical Roots of Civil Rights, 1919–1950* (New York, 2008). An impressively researched, pathbreaking, and intriguing intervention in the debate over the "long civil rights movement" which examines labour, liberal, and radical left groups and individuals fighting Jim Crow disfranchisement and discrimination.

Goodman, James E. *Stories of Scottsboro* (New York, 1995). A detailed and revealing retelling of the Alabama rape case, the key figures, and its wider context from differing perspectives.

Greenberg, Cheryl. *"Or Does It Explode?" Black Harlem in the Great Depression* (New York, 1991). African Americans were traditionally overlooked in New Deal histories and this remains an important study of the changing social, economic, cultural and political conditions facing black Americans and their responses (including the riots) in the capital city of Black America.

Hayes, Jack Irby Jr. *South Carolina and the New Deal* (Columbia, 2001). A very useful study of the impact of the New Deal recovery and reform programmes and their legacy of modernisation on an agriculture-heavy state whose population was 50 per cent African American, and where there was acute structural poverty and racial discrimination was firmly embedded.

Kasson, John. *The Little Girl Who Fought the Great Depression: Shirley Temple and 1930s America* (New York, 2014). An engaging biography of one of the most famous child stars of the twentieth century that offers a different perspective on New Deal social and cultural history.

Kennedy, David M. *Freedom from Fear: The American People in Depression and War, 1929–1945* (New York, 2001). Thorough, carefully researched, and very readable Pulitzer-prize winning social and political history of US domestic and foreign policy through the Depression and War years. Its 850 pages and a go-to study for this crucial period.

Maher, Neil. *Nature's New Deal: The Civilian Conservation Corps and the Roots of the American Environmental Movement* (New York, 2008). Individual New Deal agencies have received greater scholarly focus in recent years, and this study of one of the more popular agencies links environmental, labour and social history.

O'Sullivan, Patricia. *Days of Hope: Race and Democracy in the New Deal Era* (Chapel Hill, 1996). An important regional study of the relationship between the federal government, the Democratic Party, rising labour and civil rights organisations as well as the crisis of southern poverty and impetus for economic and political change.

Powell, Jim. *FDR's Folly: How Roosevelt and His New Deal Prolonged the Great Depression* (New York, 2004). One of the libertarian-conservative critiques of FDR's policymaking and New Deal policies that underlines their failure to ensure economic recovery and highlights the problematic New Deal legacies.

Rauchway, Eric. *The Great Depression and the New Deal: A Very Short Introduction* (New York, 2008). An excellent starting point for understanding the series of economic crises from 1929 and the responses of the Hoover and Roosevelt administrations.

Sklaroff, Lauren R. *Black Culture and the New Deal: The Quest for Civil Rights in the Roosevelt Era* (Chapel Hill, 2009). Examines the cultural representation of African Americans in New Deal cultural programmes covering theatre, art, music, literature, the importance of middle and mass cultural forms, and rising black agency and expression.

12 From neutrality to war

Timeline

FDR wins third presidential election

FDR's "Arsenal of Democracy" speech

1941   Lend-Lease approved

March on Washington Movement

Fair Employment Practices Commission established

Manhattan Project begins

US naval escorts across North Atlantic

German military successes in Eastern Europe, Mediterranean and North Africa

German invasion of Soviet Union

Japanese invasion of French Indo-China

Japanese attack on Pearl Harbor

US declares war on Japan

Japanese invasions in south and central Pacific

1942   German U-boat attacks on US merchant shipping in the Atlantic

Japanese military successes

US retreat from the Philippines

Battle of Coral Sea

Battle of Midway Island

US-led Solomon Islands offensive

Battle of Guadalcanal

Formation of Congress of Racial Equality

Nation of Islam leader Elijah Muhammad arrested

Japanese-American internment begins

US "work or fight" order

Bracero Programme set up

War Production Board set up

Office of War Information set up

Major Allied offensive in North Africa begins

Battle of Stalingrad

1943   Detroit and Harlem Riots

Zoot Suit Riots

Office of War Mobilisation set up

Axis defeated in North Africa

Allied offensive of Italian peninsula begins

Red Army turns back Axis forces

1944   D-Day Normandy landings

Battle of Philippine Sea

Battle of Leyte Gulf

Allies liberate Rome then Paris

Battle of the Bulge/Ardennes Offensive

1945   Battle of Iwo Jima

Battle of Okinawa

Allies capture Berlin

V-E Day

Potsdam Conference

US drops atomic bombs on Hiroshima and Nagasaki

Japan surrenders

Korea divided at 38th parallel

Topics covered

- A Day of Infamy at Pearl Harbor
- Growing American isolationism and neutrality
- From appeasement to war in Europe
- Pre-1941 US assistance to the Allies
- America enters the war
- Military mobilisation
- Wartime protest
- Domestic enemies
- Work or fight
- Combat in the Pacific
- Combat in Africa, Europe, the Middle East, and Russia
- Nuclear warfare

Introduction

This chapter begins with the surprise Japanese air and submarine attacks on the US Naval base at Pearl Harbor on the Hawaiian island of Oahu on 7 December 1941. It examines the evolution of American public and policymaker attitudes on international relations, isolationism, economic sanctions, and military action throughout the 1930s. The global economic crisis continued against the backdrop of Japanese militarism, Italian fascism, and German Nazism. US policy centred on neutrality and *non*-intervention, to steer clear of military involvement for as long as possible, but the Roosevelt administration did provide material aid to the Allies including second-hand destroyers and Lend-lease aid. And, American industry, manufacturing, and agriculture were fully mobilised to make the US "the arsenal of democracy."

After the attack on Pearl Harbor, mass military mobilisation and civilian defence recruitment quickly ensured US intervention in all theatres of war, but also exacerbated racial, labour, and nativist tensions at home. It also led to Japanese-American internment. This chapter underlines that World War II was much more than a war on two fronts in Europe and the Pacific; this was a truly global conflict and American troops were engaged on multiple fronts and in campaigns on different continents and fought alongside troops from many Allied nations and their colonies. The chapter ends with US deployment of atomic bombs in 1945.

When did World War II begin?

For most Americans, the Japanese attack on Pearl Harbor marks the beginning of World War II. For Europeans, this was a critical event in a war that was already two years old and had started with Nazi Germany's invasion of Poland on 1 September 1939. For many historians of Asia and the Pacific, the Battle of Beiping-Tianjin (July–August 1937) was the first major campaign of the Second Sino-Japanese War and thus the opening battle of World War II.

A day of infamy at Pearl Harbor

Figure 12.1 A haunting vintage photograph of the USS *Arizona* burning and sinking after the Japanese attack on Pearl Harbor, 7 December 1941.

Source: Courtesy of Stocktrek Images, Inc./Alamy

A large Japanese fleet including six aircraft carriers and 360 planes had reached a point 440 kilometres north of Hawaii by late November 1941 ready to attack the United States. On the quiet Sunday morning of 7 December, Admiral Yamamoto Isoroku, commander of Japan's Combined Imperial Fleet, ordered the deadly and spectacular attacks on Pearl Harbor. His plan was to immobilise the US Pacific Fleet to facilitate Japanese invasions of the Philippines and Dutch East Indies, as well as eventual Japanese dominance of the Solomons, the Coral Sea, Midway Island, Samoa, New Caledonia, the Fijis, and the Western Aleutians. The attack came in two deadly waves over two hours: some 183 fighters, bombers, and torpedo planes in the first wave and 168 in the second, along with 28 submarines and several midget subs (each with two men and two torpedoes). American ships, including eight major battleships, were lined up in the harbour and planes were bunched on nearby Naval Air Station fields to protect against sabotage. All became easy targets.

Pearl Harbor

A Joint Congressional Committee described Pearl Harbor as "the greatest military and naval disaster in our Nation's history." Japanese forces were commonly said to have "destroyed or severely damaged" up to 21 American ships and 339 aircraft; and 2,403 people were killed, including 1,177 who went down with the USS *Arizona*. A further 1,000 military personnel were injured. Japanese losses were minimal in comparison. For months afterward, rumours circulated that the entire fleet had been destroyed and many thousands of military personnel had perished. Fearing the impact on morale, FDR's radio address in February 1942 denounced "the rumor-mongers and the poison-peddlers in our midst," confirmed the numbers of deaths and that naval repairs would transform damaged ships into "more effective fighting machines."

Later historians offered more measured assessments of the damage caused and military impacts. Most of the Pacific Fleet's major ships and all three aircraft carriers were not at Hawaii on 7 December. No US submarines were destroyed. A third wave of Japanese attacks did not materialise due to fuel shortages so dry docks, ammunition dumps, and fuel storage facilities were spared. All eight battleships were damaged, but six were back in action either within three weeks or two and a half years depending on the extent of repairs. The oldest battleships in the Fleet, *Arizona* (1913) and *Oklahoma* (1914), were total losses. Three of 30 destroyers were badly damaged (the Fleet had 54 in total) but were fully repaired within three months. Naval personnel without ships were quickly redeployed. Some 151 American aircraft were damaged and 188 were destroyed but within months had been replaced with newer and more efficient craft. Admiral Chester W. Nimitz became commander in chief of the Pacific Fleet in late December 1941 and watched it expand dramatically during the war years as American industry churned out new aircraft carriers, destroyer escorts, cruisers, submarines, and landing craft. Yet, the psychological impact of the attack on Pearl Harbor was profound and long-lasting.

American isolationism and neutrality

During the 1930s, the global economic crisis impacted both domestic politics and international relations and a series hostile military actions in the Pacific, Africa, and Europe can be directly linked to the rise of Japanese militarism, Italian fascism, and German Nazism. Clearly there was a longer and more complex story leading up to Pearl Harbor that shaped popular opinion and policymaker decisions, but US isolationist sentiment and political support for stronger neutrality laws both increased significantly in the late 1930s.

Economic downturns, rising tariffs and reduced exports had slowed Japanese industrial modernisation (Japan was totally reliant on imports of energy and at least 13 key raw materials), while its economic sphere of influence in Manchuria was under threat from the Chiang Kai-Shek's Chinese nationalist government. Japanese leaders were also increasingly anxious over encroaching Soviet power in Asia. The Japanese government established a Greater East Asia Co-Prosperity Sphere to increase its regional economic control, while military leaders launched a major invasion of northern Manchuria and created a puppet state of Manchukuo in the autumn of 1931. The Hoover administration refused to cooperate with the League of Nations in imposing economic sanctions on Japan. Although the Roosevelt administration did not formally recognise Manchukuo, it maintained diplomatic relations with Japan to preserve open door trade and commercial privileges for American firms and investors in China as well as continued US exports such as petroleum and cotton. When the Japanese government signed an anti-communist pact with Nazi Germany in 1936 it seemed as if there was hesitant US-European acquiescence in its expansionist policies.

In July 1937, under pressure from the army, Japan's civilian government ordered a broader invasion of China's five northern provinces. Well-armed and highly disciplined Japanese troops took over Peking (Beijing) on 8 August, then moved against other Chinese cities, eventually reaching Nanking (Nanjing) on 13 December. There were already numerous reports of Japanese atrocities against both military targets and civilian populations, but European and American newspapers highlighted the "Rape of Nanking" or "Nanking Massacre" where Chinese soldiers were hunted down after the city fell, were murdered and left in mass graves, entire families were executed and bodies were left in the streets, and tens of thousands of Chinese women were raped by Japanese troops. At least one-third of the city was burned. In October, FDR declared that Japanese aggression posed a threat to world peace and that aggressors should be "quarantined" by the international community to prevent the contagion of war from spreading but this did not go down well with American audiences. Even after Japanese aviators deliberately bombed and sank the US gunboat *Panay* in the Yangtze River in December 1937, there was little US public support for retaliation. Nevertheless, US material assistance was provided to the Chinese Republic from mid-1937.

The 1919 Treaty of Versailles imposed severe restrictions on the German military, including an army limited to 100,000 men, and prohibitions on tanks, submarines, and planes. By the mid-1930s it was clear that Adolf Hitler's National Socialist (Nazi) government had ignored these restrictions. A clandestine German rearmament programme started in 1933 and from 1935 the results were revealed at a series of celebratory mass rallies. Images of Nazi symbolism and militarism were broadcast internationally via newsreels. Compulsory German military conscription commenced in March 1935 and armament productions rose dramatically just as the Spanish Civil War began. And, under an Anglo-German Naval Agreement (1935) Germany's surface and submarine fleets were permitted to expand. Hitler denounced the Locarno Agreement (1925), and an increasingly confident and well-equipped German army moved into the Rhineland and began to remilitarise an area under French control since 1918.

Italian fascist forces invaded Abyssinia (Ethiopia) in October 1935 and forced Emperor Haile Selassie into exile. When the League of Nations condemned the Italian invasion and voted to impose economic sanctions, Mussolini simply withdrew Italy from the League and formed an alliance with Nazi Germany which had also left the League in October 1933. Over two-thirds of Americans responding in public opinion polls opposed any US action to punish Italian fascist aggression, even after widespread condemnation of Italian use of poison gas in Abyssinia. This together with Senate rejection of American membership of the World Court underlined an important US shift away from internationalism during the 1930s.

Keen to strengthen hemispheric relations, the Roosevelt administration continued the Good Neighbor Policy in Latin America. In the late 1920s and early 1930s, US military commitments were scaled back; there was re-emphasis on building business and diplomatic relations and expanding US missionary activity to spread US values and promote political stability throughout the Western Hemisphere. But this was offset by growing reliance on local pro-US strongmen, as in Nicaragua. During Nicaragua's costly civil war, guerrilla leader Augusto Sandino mobilised peasants and workers against American occupation and US Marines from 1927. Growing protests in the US finally led Hoover to withdraw US troops in early 1933, but he left behind a new diplomatic innovation: a US-trained Nicaraguan national guard that could replace US Marines in keeping order. In 1934, the US-picked leader of the National Guard, Anastasio Somoza, arrested then murdered Sandino, and established a dictatorship.

By the mid-1930s, many Americans were persuaded by rumours, which had been circulating for some time, that Wall Street bankers, munitions makers, and other powerful business interests had tricked the US into participating in World War I. A Senate Special Committee Investigating the Munitions Industry, chaired by Senator Gerald R. Nye of North Dakota, launched a series of hearings 1934–36 that revealed exorbitant profiteering and blatant tax evasion by many wartime corporations. It was suggested that the Wilson administration had been pressured to go to war by bankers anxious to protect American loans to European nations, but this was not proven. The Nye Committee was also deeply suspicious of War Department plans for wartime industrial mobilisation and labour control formulated in the 1930s. As many Americans feared another devastating overseas war, policymakers sought stronger protective and defensive measures to ensure American *non*-involvement.

A series of legal safeguards were outlined in the Neutrality Acts of 1935–37. The first established a mandatory embargo on arms to both aggressor and victim nations in any military conflict. It gave the president powers to warn US citizens that if they travelled on ships belonging to warring nations, they did so at their own risk. During World War I, German U-boat attacks on ships carrying Americans citizens and agreements to protect neutral rights had led to fervent debates over US military engagement, and the Nye Committee proposals sought to remove this excuse for US intervention. The 1937 neutrality law established a "cash-and-carry policy" under which nations at war could only purchase non-military goods from the US, for cash i.e. no loans or credit arrangements, and they would have to ship their purchases themselves.

Domestic support for neutrality increased after the outbreak of the Spanish Civil War in summer 1936. Nationalist and neo-fascist Falangists led by General Francisco Franco, and backed by the Catholic Church hierarchy, overthrew Spain's Republican government. On 1 October 1936, Franco was declared head of the Spanish government and commander-in-chief of the armed forces which precipitated three years of Republican and Loyalist armed resistance to his dictatorship. Twenty-seven states signed an agreement not to intervene and banned the sale of weapons to both Republican-Loyalists and Nationalists. Signatories included Germany and Italy which both immediately provided massive military assistance to the Nationalists. The US did not sign but FDR approved a parallel embargo in January 1937 which made it unlawful to ship arms directly or via other countries to Spain. However, there is some evidence that FDR approved an ill-fated plan during spring 1938 to secretly send 150 US-manufactured aircraft to France, for Republican-Loyalist use in Spain. If it had been discovered that the US president was planning to break the neutrality laws, especially in the wake of the court-packing plan fiasco and increasing Republican Party attacks on the "dictatorial" Roosevelt administration, FDR's political future would have been severely damaged.

Republican-Loyalists were aided by the Soviet Union and international brigades of foreign fighters. Over 3,500 American and around 1,600 Canadian volunteers (including Mack Coad of the CPUSA and Alabama Sharecroppers Union) travelled to Spain to serve in the pro-Republican Abraham Lincoln and Mackenzie-Papineau battalions which were recruited and organised by the Communist International. Many US volunteers were linked to the CPUSA, others were involved in Depression-era union organising, unemployment politics, and civil rights protests, and there was a heavy working-class immigrant presence. American audiences read graphic details of the war in newspaper dispatches sent from journalists and writers such as Ernest Hemingway. Hemingway's play "The Fifth Column" (1938) and novel *For Whom the Bell Tolls* (1940) further illustrated the profound intellectual and literary impact of the Spanish Civil War. Many international volunteers and contemporary observers believed the Spanish crisis would have global effects. They all shared a powerful desire to fight Fascism which they believed was not matched by governments and policymakers and opposed any form of appeasement. When German forces marched into Austria and Hitler proclaimed an *Anschluss* or political union between Austria and Germany in March 1938 there was little official opposition in either the US or the rest of Europe.

From appeasement to war

During the second half of the 1930s, the US appeared to be an observer of European entanglements rather than an active strategy shaper, although Roosevelt did broker an international conference, attended by representatives from 32 countries, at Evian, Switzerland, in July 1938 to address a growing Jewish refugee crisis. German Jews had suffered economic discrimination, violence, political intimidation, and loss of civil rights since Hitler's accession to power as German Chancellor in January 1933. In March that year, the first concentration camp was established at Dachau, initially for political prisoners then other "undesirables," and as a training centre for *Schutzstaffel* [SS] guards. Hitler's views on Aryan supremacy, virulent anti-Semitism, and promises to deal with the "Jewish problem" had been outlined in his autobiographical *Mein Kampf* (1925). In 1933, there were around 600,000 German Jews, but one-quarter had already left when Germany annexed Austria in 1938. *Anschluss* brought a further 185,000 Jews under Nazi control and Jewish flight escalated. An ineffective Intergovernmental Committee on Refugees (ICR) was set up to coordinate an orderly emigration from Germany and find permanent settlements. Most representatives at Evian expressed sympathy for German and Austrian Jews but refused to accept additional refugees.

The violent Nazi attacks on Jewish persons and property during the *Kristallnacht* pogroms of November 1938 were widely reported in US newspapers. Yet, strict numerical quotas, nativism and nationalism, and widespread anti-Semitism prevented any relaxation of US immigration policy. Between 1933 and 1939, over 300,000 Germans applied for immigration visas to travel to the US, and 90 per cent of applicants were Jewish. By 1940, around 90,000 German Jews had resettled in the US and a further 40,000 arrived during the war years but this equated to 10 per cent of the quota allowed by law. The liner *St Louis* carrying nearly 1,000 escaped German Jews was turned away from Havana then Miami in September 1939 and forced to return to Europe. A bill to admit 20,000 endangered Jewish refugee children failed in the US Senate in 1939 and 1940 despite Nazi expansionism and wartime pogroms.

In September 1938, Hitler demanded that Czechoslovakia relinquish part of the Sudetenland, an area on the Austro-German border in which around three million ethnic Germans lived, to help create a German Reich to last 1,000 years. Czechoslovakia had a substantial army and alliances with France and the Soviet Union, but neither France nor its key ally Britain were willing to assist or risk another war. The Czechoslovak government was excluded from a series of international meetings on the disputed boundary areas but expected to accept the "Munich Agreement" concluded by the leaders of Germany, Britain, France, and Italy. It permitted German occupation of the entire Sudetenland. Many policymakers and commentators believed the threat of war had been defused. British Prime Minister Neville Chamberlain informed British voters that he had secured "peace with honour. I believe it is peace for our time," but the "dishonour" of appeasement was excoriated by Winston Churchill and others.

FDR's post-Munich strategy centred on aiding Britain and France with US-produced materiel. The Spanish Civil War had underlined that mechanised weapons, especially aircraft and tanks, would play decisive roles in mid-century warfare – but vast infantry battles still continued throughout World War II. In October 1938, Roosevelt outlined a plan to assemble 5,000 planes a year for France in Canadian factories in which US neutrality laws would not apply. In the end, only 200 US aircraft had reached France by September 1939. The covert aid plan illustrated FDR's wider policymaking in the late 1930s – full of promises, often indecisive, incomplete, and full of dissemblance – but he did face powerful non-interventionist opponents in Congress, in the press, and among the public. However, FDR's private assurances of US support during 1938–41 then his failure to follow through angered many. Chamberlain famously remarked that it was best to count on nothing from the Americans except words.

In March 1939, Nazi forces occupied the rest of Czechoslovakia thus unashamedly violating the Munich agreement. In April, Hitler began issuing threats against Poland, thus deliberately defying the 1934 Polish-German non-aggression pact that was supposed to maintain trade, borders, and peaceable relations for ten years. Both Britain and France had assured the Polish government of assistance in the event of German invasion. European tensions increased dramatically after 23 August 1939 when news of a non-aggression pact between Nazi Germany and the Soviet Union reached European and American governments (US spies already knew of these plans but not the launch date) because it freed Hitler's military forces from a war on two fronts to focus on its western borders with France and Belgium. It also enabled Germany and the Soviet Union to carve up Poland and other Eastern European nations. The USSR annexed the Baltic republics of Latvia, Estonia, and Lithuania, and then Finland by late November 1939. Meanwhile, Japan had signed an anti-communist pact with Germany in 1936, the Soviet Union in turn allied with China and provided military and financial aid, and a Soviet-Japanese ceasefire from September 1939 further secured the Soviet Union's Pacific borders.

On 1 September 1939, Nazi Germany launched a full-scale invasion of Poland and on 3 September, Britain and France declared war on Germany. "This nation will remain a neutral nation," declared FDR, "but I cannot ask that every American remain neutral in thought as well." Despite British, French, Low Country, and Scandinavian resistance, the German *blitzkrieg* offensive of fast-moving tanks, mobile infantry, paratroopers, and field artillery, and relentless ariel bombing smashed through Denmark, Norway, Netherlands, and Belgium in spring 1940 and attacked France in May. British, Belgian and French troops were forced to withdraw to the French coast at Dunkirk. Miraculously, under relentless bombing and shelling, nearly 340,000 were evacuated by an armada of naval and civilian vessels and transported back to Britain 26 May to 3 June. Those unable to reach Dunkirk, such as the survivors of the 51st Highland Division, became German POWs. On 22 June, German troops marched into Paris, and a collaborationist French government formed at Vichy.

Pre-1941 US assistance to the Allies

In late 1939, there was little agreement among the president, Congress, and the American public over the extent or form of US assistance to Britain and France. Aware of the ultra-productive German munitions industry, FDR believed that Allied armies should be able to procure US military materiel and armaments. Under a 1939 amendment to the Neutrality Acts, US ships were still prohibited from entering war zones, but belligerents could now purchase arms on the same cash-and-carry basis as non-military materials. From 1940, American officials were more committed to aiding Britain, particularly after the defeat of France. Winston Churchill became British prime minister in early May as the French, Danish, and Norwegian coastlines and ports were about to fall under Nazi control. He quickly appealed to FDR for assistance "as a matter of life or death" to defend Britain against invasion across the English Channel as "the only hope of averting the collapse of civilization as we define it."

Britain had lost half of its destroyers available for home defence since 1939 and the US Navy was reconditioning more than 100 old destroyers. Yet there was no guarantee they could be given to Britain because of the neutrality laws and it was feared they would ultimately fall into German hands. The US ambassador to London, Joseph P. Kennedy, was one of many Americans who believed Britain was a lost cause and would soon be defeated. Others were alarmed by the prospect of a German-dominated North Atlantic, especially as German influence in Brazil, Argentina, and Chile was increasing. This would have serious implications for US trade and national security, and so aiding Britain could help prolong US nonintervention.

Several interventionist groups lobbied the Roosevelt administration during summer 1940 to pursue a destroyer deal. The Fight for Freedom advocated all-out US military and economic intervention in Europe. The Committee to Defend America by Aiding the Allies (CDAAA) chaired by influential journalist William Allen White was the leading organisation advocating US naval support for Britain and the Commonwealth, along with financial credit and munitions exports, as the best way to keep the US out of the European war. Core support came from Catholic churches, women's groups, and organised labour. To mobilise public support for the destroyer transfer, the CDAAA and the like-minded Century Group wrote press releases and arranged a series of radio broadcasts by influential figures such as General John J. Pershing, commander of the American Expeditionary Force during World War I. The CDAAA became an intermediary between FDR and Republican presidential candidate, Wendell Willkie, who was privately supportive. Both candidates were clearly concerned about the political implications of any transfer just before the November elections. However, as early as July, more than 66 per cent of Americans believed that following the defeat of France, Germany posed a direct threat to the US and signalled they were willing to provide additional support to Britain.

On 3 September 1940, Americans were informed that the US had acquired the right to lease naval and airbases in Newfoundland, Bermuda, the Bahamas, Jamaica,

St Lucia, Trinidad, Antigua, and British Guiana and the Destroyer-Bases deal would improve US security "beyond calculation." The first two bases were gifts from Britain and the other six were in exchange for 50 overage US destroyers. The US also supplied torpedo boats, bombers, tanks, and airfields for British pilots to train on, along with 250,000 Enfield rifles and bomb sights. All were desperately needed after Dunkirk when military hardware and weapons were abandoned in France. FDR's use of an executive order and failure to send the measure for Congressional debate led Senator Nye to call the agreement a dictatorial step, while Republican Representative Hamilton Fish and many non-interventionists denounced it as "virtually an act of war."

The day after the Destroyer-Bases Deal was announced, an America First Committee was formed by Yale University students to mobilise public support for national defence, limits on aid to Britain, and binding assurances of non-intervention from the president and Congress. AFC founders included Potter Stewart, a future Supreme Court Justice, and Gerald Ford, a future US president. High-profile leaders included General Robert E. Wood, also chair, Senator Nye, Senator Burton K. Wheeler, and Charles Lindbergh who formally joined in April 1941. AFC was also backed by the Hearst newspaper corporation, and like CDAAA used radio broadcasts by military leaders and policymakers to publicise its platform. Membership grew quickly across the country but was particularly strong in the Midwest. Relations between internationalists and non-internationalists rapidly deteriorated in late 1940, with the AFC accusing CDAAA of warmongering, and CDAAA highlighting the Nazi sympathies of some AFC members. Roosevelt's orders to the FBI to investigate America First and his encouragement of pro-Nazi characterisations of Charles Lindbergh and other isolationists highlighted his limited tolerance of opponents.

In September 1940, Congress also voted to inaugurate the first peacetime draft in US history. Under the Selective Training and Service Act, all males of 21–35 years of age were eligible to serve one year of military duty. The first draft registration began in October 1940. This was framed as a measure to safeguard national security and bolster military preparedness; it supposedly did not mean that US involvement in the war was inevitable. During the November 1940 elections, neither Republican presidential contender Wendell Willkie nor FDR wanted to be portrayed as a war-monger. When Willkie suggested that FDR's policies would result in US troops fighting in Europe, Roosevelt famously told Bostonians: "Your boys are not going to be sent into any foreign wars." FDR won decisively with 55 per cent of the popular vote and 449–82 electoral votes, and embarked on an unprecedented third presidential term.

In a December 1940 radio address on national security, Roosevelt observed "never before since Jamestown and Plymouth Rock has our American civilization been in such danger as now" and noted that in the wake of the Tripartite Pact, the US would be living "at the point of a gun" if Britain fell. Arguing that "there can be no appeasement with ruthlessness" he called for the US to become "the arsenal of democracy." The US would stay out of the war but would provide whatever material aid was needed to keep Britain fighting. (A more active foreign policy was also envisaged moving into 1941 because the Tripartite Alliance required the US to refocus on its Pacific foreign policy.) Unfortunately, Britain was virtually bankrupt by late 1940 and struggling to comply with the cash-and-carry system. FDR was reluctant to overturn either the cash for munitions policy or an earlier law barring loans to nations who had defaulted on their debts to the US, so a more innovative solution was needed.

In his annual message to Congress in early January 1941, FDR endorsed continued aid to Britain and US defence of fundamental universal freedoms – freedom of speech, freedom of worship, freedom from war, and freedom from fear – which would eventually frame America's war aims. He used an analogy of lending a garden hose to a neighbour whose house was on fire to outline a new Allied loan system to be repaid with similar materials at the end of the war. Four days later, the Lend-lease bill which allowed the US government to sell, lend, or lease armaments and other vital supplies to any nation deemed "vital to the defense of the United States" was introduced to Congress and a heated political debate began. Senator Wheeler described Lend-lease as "the New Deal's Triple-A foreign policy – it will plough under every fourth American boy," which FDR denounced "as the most untruthful, as the most dastardly, unpatriotic thing that has ever been said."

Both political parties were split over Allied support. The northern wing of the Democratic Party included voters of German, Irish, and Italian heritage who had little sympathy for Britain. Former presidential candidate Alf Landon and other Republicans continued to oppose formal American participation in the war until December 1941. Many non-interventionists objected to the vast executive powers that the "war dictatorship bill" gave the president. CDAAA again led the effort to mobilise public and political opinion behind Lend-lease, but many internationalists were deeply troubled by the possibility it would hasten US entry into World War II. The American First Committee accused CDAAA of being the tool of international bankers and part of British propaganda. However, the Lend-lease bill passed both Houses of Congress by wide margins and was enacted into law in March 1941.

Lend-lease provoked a series of public and legislative debates over increasing US naval convoys in the North Atlantic during spring and summer 1941. US merchant shipping had been harried by wolfpacks of German U-boats since summer 1940. Supporters believed convoying i.e. where several merchant ships travelled together and were accompanied by military escorts of warships and planes, was essential to get Lend-lease materials to Britain when German U-boats and surface raiders were imposing huge naval and merchant shipping losses. Opponents argued convoying would lead to naval clashes between German and American warships in the Atlantic, guarantee US entry into a war that FDR had promised to keep American boys out of, and could provoke Japanese naval aggression in the Pacific (because of the Tripartite Pact). There were numerous anti-convoy rallies, parades, and petitions, anti-war speeches by Lindbergh and other celebrities over national radio hook-ups, and AFC-sponsored speaking tours. Meanwhile, the German army was crashing through Yugoslavia and Greece during April and May, there was a pro-Nazi coup in Iraq, and German General Erwin Rommel's Afrika Korps was approaching Egypt.

FDR continued to hedge his bets. He ordered US naval patrols as far as Iceland where they would seek out German submarines then radio their positions to waiting British planes and destroyers. He quietly ordered the occupation of Greenland by US forces in April. He further declared the Red Sea open to American merchant ships by pretending it was not a war zone so military supplies could reach British forces in North Africa. Only after the German invasion of the Soviet Union on 22 June 1941 did FDR act more decisively. He ordered US forces to occupy Iceland in July, met Churchill off Newfoundland in August, approved the transfer of three battleships, an aircraft carrier, and supporting vessels from the Pacific fleet to the Atlantic, and made further commitments to supply Britain, China, and Soviet Russia as proxies against the Axis powers. Naval escorts of convoys as far as Iceland were announced in early September following a U-boat attack on the destroyer USS *Greer*. FDR also persuaded Congress to extend Lend-lease privileges to the Soviet Union, now part of a Grand Alliance with Britain and the US. Naval patrols then escorts could be justified in defence of the Monroe Doctrine to keep the German fleet away from US waters – albeit at a time when Hitler was bogged down in the Russian campaign and was unlikely to attack the US directly. National polls showed growing support for convoys, rising from 41 per cent in favour in April to 60 per cent by September.

Congress was informed of these actions but not consulted, partly because FDR continued to face strong opposition to his policies from both Democrats and Republicans. A bill to extend Selective Service had been passed by Representatives by only one vote. FDR was willing to include Republicans in his wartime administration, but most were fairly outspoken internationalists such as Congressman James Wadsworth of New York, Secretary of War Henry Stimson and Secretary of the Navy Frank Knox. As late as October 1941, FDR had warned the British ambassador that he would not get a declaration of war from Congress if he asked for one, and public opinion would swing against him if he did so. The US therefore inched ahead through executive action just as events in the Pacific would completely transform World War II.

America enters the War

The German invasion of the Soviet Union crystallised Japanese decisions to call up a million reserves and to invade the French colony of Indochina (Vietnam, Laos, Cambodia) on 2 July. American intelligence had already broken Japanese codes so knew that the next target would be the Dutch East Indies which were vulnerable to attack after German defeat of the Netherlands in 1940. The Japanese planned to invade Indochina immediately following Germany's defeat of France. The Roosevelt administration froze all Japanese assets in the US to limit Japan's ability to purchase US exports and cut off its oil supplies, and deliberately sought to damage the maritime trade that was vital to Japan's imperial and regional dominance. However, the oil embargo was somewhat undermined by German military defeat of the Netherlands and resulting Axis control of the oil-rich Dutch colonies, and concessions by the French Vichy government over Japanese occupation of French colonial airfields and ports in southern Indochina.

During 1941 there were more than 40 meetings between US Secretary of State Cordell Hull and his Japanese counterparts, but relations deteriorated in the summer when the Roosevelt administration insisted that Japan withdraw from both China and Indochina. Meanwhile, the civilian government in Tokyo was increasingly under the control of a fanatical, militaristic faction. Although other political factions sought to avoid war, national pride and the threat of economic destruction from the US-imposed oil embargo increasingly dictated military solutions. Japan's leaders also believed that they were racially and spiritually superior to weak and effeminate Americans who lacked the will and stamina for a long fight in the Pacific.

In early November, the Japanese Cabinet decided to continue negotiations with the US while simultaneously preparing for war, but the military objectives were limited to the Pacific. There was no plan to invade the US mainland. Final approval for a military attack came on 1 December. Decoded Japanese messages confirmed an attack was imminent but American intelligence did not know the location. Americans quickly learned of the attacks on Pearl Harbor and that ten hours later Japanese airplanes struck US airfields at Manila in the Philippines. Three days later, Japanese forces took over Guam, Wake Island, and the British colony of Hong Kong. And, American ships had been torpedoed between San Francisco and Honolulu.

The day after Pearl Harbor, President Roosevelt used the rhetoric of America's frontier-fighting heritage to proclaim 7 December 1941 as a "date that will live in infamy." He denounced Japan's deliberate act of aggression, undertaken without any formal declaration of war: "I believe that I interpret the will of the Congress and of the people when I assert that we will not only defend ourselves to the uttermost, but will make it very certain that this form of treachery shall never again endanger us." He asked Congress to confirm the "state of war" between the two nations. He did not specifically ask Americans to go to war to protect the national interest, to stop Japan's imperial ambitions, to protect vital resources, or defy the Tripartite alliance dictators.

Senators voted unanimously for the declaration of war, and it was approved 388–1 in the House of Representatives, with only Jeannette Rankin of Montana voting against the Congressional declaration of war. Advocates of military preparedness gained significant support while isolationists, pacifists and "America Firsters" appeared naïve and defeated. Yet, outspoken critics of FDR's "internationalist" foreign policy used Pearl Harbor and US naval unpreparedness as evidence of war provocation, duplicity, and presidential abuse of power. Some continued to accuse Roosevelt of deliberately provoking the attack as a backdoor entry into World War II.

Naval preparedness was severely tested in both the Atlantic and the Pacific. British intelligence warned US naval officials that German U-boats were heading to the coastal area between Newfoundland and New York and attacks would begin on 13 January 1942. Numerous fuel tankers and cargo ships were attacked along the eastern seaboard and in the Atlantic: more than 5,000 US merchant sailors were killed during the first six months of 1942 and disruption to fuel imports from Mexico and other counties led to gasoline rationing. Convoying, mining of North American harbours, use of mobile artillery, naval attacks on submarines, civilian air patrols, and night-time coastal and marine blackouts, all helped to reduce submarine attacks from late 1942.

Military mobilisation

Regardless of political divisions, over the next three years US military and civilian production had to support key infantry, naval, air, and marine offensives in the Pacific, Africa, Europe, and the Middle East as well as civil defence at home. In 1939, the US had 200,000 men in the Army, 125,2000 in the Navy, and less than 20,000 in the Marine Corps. The Japanese army was three and a half million strong. By the end of World War II, some 15 million men, or roughly 9 per cent of the US population, and more than 500,000 women had served in the armed forces. Military mobilisation and civilian defence industry recruitment spurred a mass migration of Americans of every age, class, race, and ethnic group, and across every region.

Eastern and midwestern recruits went west to a succession of training camps such as Camp Stoneman in California or the Naval Training Station at San Diego. Even the train ride to a military camp in Indiana could be life-changing for a soldier from Rhode Island who had never been further than Washington DC. A Women's Army Corps (WAC) recruit from Rochester, New York, travelling west in 1943 remembered "my first glimpse of the prairie in Nebraska, with scattered windmills and grazing white-faced cattle." GIs became new pioneers and adventurers in every theatre of war. Journalist Tom Brokaw dubbed these citizen soldiers who endured the Great Depression, made enormous sacrifices to defeat the Axis and win the "good war," and then reformed post-war America as the "greatest generation."

Figure 12.2 Selective Service and military mobilisation. Some 15 million men and more than 500,000 women served in the armed forces during World War II. Both military mobilisation and civilian defence recruitment led to mass internal migration and overseas deployment of Americans of every region, class, race, and ethnic group. These servicemen are departing from Pennsylvania Railroad Station, New York, in 1942.

Source: Courtesy of Chronicle/Alamy

The experiences of the diverse World War II military (and civilian workforce) were often framed by race, gender, and class as well as the exigencies of war. In 1940, the US military was still racially segregated, the Navy had no black units, the Marines refused black applicants, and the Army's 4,450 African American soldiers were in six regimental sized units. Neither the Secretary of War nor Secretary of the Navy were willing to experiment with integration. During Congressional debates over Selective Service, African American labour and civil rights leaders such as Walter White and A. Philip Randolph insisted on equal treatment and the final bill prohibited racial discrimination. FDR announced in early October that African Americans would serve in the armed forces in proportion to their percentage of the general population (10 per cent) The use of quotas meant that armed services and local draft board personnel would shape racial definitions: deciding which percentage of "Negro blood" made a person "black" in the Deep South, defining Louisiana's Creole population, and confronting Puerto Rico's range of racial classifications. Whites were often called to service much quicker than non-whites while disproportionate numbers of African Americans were classified as "unfit for combat" so relegated to support duties or manual labour such as stevedore work and messmen duty in the Navy. By early 1943, an estimated 300,000 blacks had been selected for military service and were awaiting induction but there were still not enough "Jim Crow" training facilities.

The most famous black serviceman was the "Brown Bomber," heavy-weight boxing champion Joe Louis, who had triumphed over German Max Schmeling in 1938, and enlisted in the army in 1942. Louis took part in military boxing exhibitions, and appeared in recruitment films, war posters, and other government propaganda as the heroic, patriotic, and victorious black male icon. More than one million African Americans undertook military service during World War II, including some 80,000 who enlisted outside of the draft. They included the Tuskegee Airmen, the first group of black US Air Force pilots, and initially trained by Puerto Rican aviators. Pressure from black newspapers, civil rights organisations, and historical black colleges had compelled the US Army Air Corps to diversify its training programme and a designated facility was established at Tuskegee in Alabama. Nearly 1,000 black military pilots graduated in 1941–45 and at least 450 served overseas. Their duties included protecting American bombers from German fighter planes. African American women served in all-female auxiliary units for the major military branches, as nurses, and in all types of military support.

More than 500,000 Mexican Americans served in the US military. Chicanas joined the Army's WACS, the Navy's Women Accepted for Volunteer Emergency Service (WAVES), or all-female auxiliary units in the US Air Force, and many more took up wartime civilian work. The all-Latina Benito Juarez Air-WAC squadron was sworn in at San Antonio's Municipal Auditorium in March 1944 after a vigorous recruitment campaign in southern Texas. Most Puerto Ricans served in regular Army units rather than segregated black units but also experienced discrimination. They were initially confined to hemispheric defence, of the Philippines for example, because of their Spanish language skills. The 65th Infantry Regiment was in the Galapagos Islands and in the Panama Canal Zone, where some soldiers became subjects in army medical experiments on the effects of mustard gas. Puerto Rican troops were later deployed to North Africa and Italy to guard supply lines under assault from Axis forces. They took on combat roles during the D-Day landings at Normandy, France, in June 1944 and at the Battle of the Bulge or Ardennes Offensive during the winter months of 1944–45,

Figure 12.3 African American nurses in Australia, 1943. African American women served in all-female and segregated auxiliary units for the major military branches. They served as nurses and in all types of military support during World War II, as did white, Native American, and Latina women.

Source: Courtesy of Gado Images/Alamy

and throughout the Pacific hostilities. Joseph P. Martinez, the child of Hispanic immigrants and a Colorado beet harvester before the war, was posthumously awarded a Medal of Honor for leading a dangerous but strategically critical charge up a snow-covered mountain on the Aleutian Island of Attu. A number of Chicanos from New Mexico experienced the horrors of the Bataan death march.

Around 99 per cent of eligible Native Americans aged 21 to 44 years registered for the draft in 1942 although high rates of tribal enlistment also reinforced long-standing Indian "warrior" stereotypes. Several hundred American Indian women served in the WACS, WAVES, and Army Nursing Corps. Major General Clarence Tinker, an Osage and a career pilot, was the highest ranking Native in the armed forces, in charge of the Seventh Air Force in Hawaii. He was leading bombing raids on Wake Island and

Midway Island in June 1942 when he was killed. He was posthumously awarded the Distinguished Service Medal. As in World War I, the US military utilised Native American languages in military intelligence and communications. The Fourth Signal Company recruited 30 Oklahoma Comanches for a special Signal Corps Detachment in January 1941 and the US Marine Corps actively recruited Navajo to outwit Japanese listeners first on Guadalcanal in late 1942. Special Code Talker units were eventually assigned to each of the Marine Corps' six Pacific divisions, and there were over 400 Navajo Code Talkers by 1945.

By war's end, an estimated 150,000 Native Americans had directly participated in industrial, agricultural, and military mobilisation, including 44,000 in combat and support duties. Around 2,500 Navajos helped construct the Fort Wingate Ordnance Depot in New Mexico, and Pueblo Indians helped build the Naval Supply Depot in Utah, while Alaskan tribes' hunting, survival, and navigational skills were utilised in territorial defence. Thousands left reservations for work in munitions factories, aircraft plants, and shipyards, while reservation Native women joined the American Womens' Volunteer Service, Red Cross, and civil defence groups.

The US Army and Navy also recruited 10,000 white women from small towns and elite colleges to work as Washington DC-based code-breakers. More than 400,000 white women joined the armed services and served in all theatres. Women were barred from combat however. More than 1,000 Women's Airforce Service Pilots instructed

Figure 12.4 World War II Native American Navajo Code Talkers in the South Pacific, 1943.

Source: Courtesy of Alpha Historica/Alamy

male recruits, flew all types of US Army Air Forces aircraft as ferry pilots, and undertook target-towing for anti-aircraft. Female military capabilities did expand as the war continued. For example, when the British began to train army women to operate land based anti-aircraft guns (they still were not permitted to fire them), the US experimented with similar tasks towards the end of the war. Yet, women who volunteered for military service frequently encountered misogyny, gender discrimination, and charges of sexual immorality: WACS were smeared as "government-issue whores." Yet, military service and civilian work created a unique wartime feminism often defined by quiet practical demonstration rather than intellectual discussion.

Wartime protest

At least 43,000 conscientious objectors (COs) opposed military intervention; they included members of pacifist organisations and socialists opposed to capitalist wars. Religious objectors came from the historic peace churches (Quakers, Mennonites, and Brethren) and mainstream Judeo-Christian denominations, as well as Black Muslims, Hopi Indians, and Jehovah's Witnesses. The 1940 Selective Service Act permitted COs to undertake "non-combatant service" for military branches or "work of national importance under civilian direction." More than 25,000 men worked in army and naval communications and as clerks and medical personnel, or transported food, medical supplies, and munitions to combat zones. After January 1943, most non-combatants were limited to Medical Corps service and could be deployed to front-line positions as in Guadalcanal. The Civilian Public Service (CPS) directed 12,000 COs to 151 public works camps across the US from 1941 to 1947 to labour with other civilian defence workers in reforestation, dam construction, agriculture, and soil conservation, and on public health projects. CPS camp workers in Mulberry, Florida, built 2,500 portable toilets for local residents to help combat hookworm. Other COs volunteered as nurses and care-workers in mental hospitals or took part in medical experiments for malaria and hepatitis.

Another 6,000 COs served prison terms because they were radical pacifists, refused to register for the draft or CPS, or had been denied CO status by their draft boards. One of every six men in federal prison during the war years was a conscientious objector. They included Bayard Rustin and Jim Peck who led work and hunger strikes to end racial segregation in federal correctional institutions. CPS camps and federal prison cells therefore became laboratories of wartime social activism and complemented other battles for civil rights. For example, the Congress of Racial Equality (CORE) formed in 1942 and organised interracial sit-ins, boycotts, civil disobedience, and other non-violent direct action to challenge racial segregation and discrimination in housing, restaurants, skating rinks, barbershops, movie theatres and interstate bus transportation. There were many anti-poll tax and voter registration campaigns during the 1940s: the Virginia Voter's League launched a sustained black voter registration campaign in May 1941 and US Senator Claude Pepper sought to outlaw the poll tax that had been used to "pollute, contaminate, and prostitute" federal elections in southern states.

Wartime industrial conversion created new job opportunities in cities on the West Coast, Northeast, and Midwest. However, most skilled or semi-skilled defence jobs were reserved for white workers, and non-whites were consistently relegated to menial labourer positions or worked as cooks and waiters in company cafeterias. Many labour unions continued to segregate or ban African American members. A. Philip Randolph, president of the African American Brotherhood of Sleeping Car Porters and Maids, argued that employment should be non-discriminatory because defence industries were using American taxpayer dollars and serving the national interest. He called for a mass march on Washington DC in June 1941 to demand an end to racial discrimination in defence employment and the armed forces. March on Washington committees sprang up across the US and black newspapers such as the *Chicago Defender* gave prominent coverage.

Labour union and civil rights pressure paid off when FDR issued Executive Order 8802 in June 1941 forbidding racial, religious, and nativist discrimination in defence industries and government agencies. The Fair Employment Practices Commission (FEPC) was established to investigate allegations of racial bias and make recommendations to redress grievances but did not have any enforcement powers – in deference to uncooperative congressmen, often Southern Democrats, and stubborn industrialists. Nevertheless, wartime labour shortages and an increasingly assertive black workforce did force change. African Americans comprised 3 per cent of workers in national defence industries in 1942 and 8 per cent in 1945. The number of black federal employees also tripled to 200,000 during those years.

Unfortunately, neither the March on Washington Movement nor the FEPC could eradicate racial hostilities or end discrimination completely, particularly as mass migrations of black and white southerners intensified divisions in many northern and western communities. Northern cities such as Detroit now had huge African American populations. Important western centres of war production and military institutions such as Los Angeles and San Diego were similarly transformed by black and Hispanic newcomers, as well as white Americans from the South, Midwest and Northeast, and US service personnel. Vibrant intra-racial and interracial communities developed but wartime shifts also exacerbated nativist, racial, and class tensions.

Local Mexican American and Chicano teenagers and *pachuco* street gangs (and some Filipino and African Americans) had adopted a distinctive style of dress of broad-shouldered drape jackets and balloon-leg trousers known as a "zoot suit" and accessorised with dapper hats and two-tone shoes. *Pachucas* often wore tight V-neck sweaters, balloon-leg trousers or pleated skirts, fishnet stockings, and platform heels, complimented by bright lipstick and bouffant hair styles. Often manufactured by bootleg tailors, zoot suits appeared to directly undermine wool and cloth rationing. Conservatives linked pachuco/a fashion to racial and juvenile delinquency. Local media were particularly critical of zoot suiters after José Díaz was murdered during a fight near the Sleepy Lagoon reservoir in August 1942. The California governor sanctioned a roundup of 600 Mexican Americans by the Los Angeles Police Department, and a high-profile murder trial in January 1943 resulted in 20 pachucos being convicted of murder on dubious evidence and in a prejudicial atmosphere. The convictions were reversed in October 1944.

From 3–10 June 1943, white servicemen, many from nearby US Naval bases, attacked local pachucos and other young Mexican Americans with clubs and rifles. Many pachucos were violently beaten and stripped in what came to be known as the "Zoot Suit Riots." This was more than an outbreak of anti-Mexican hysteria; it was rooted in Los Angeles' wartime demographic and geographic changes, resentments over the construction of a Naval Reserve Armoury next to the Mexican American residential area, and major cultural clashes between white interpretations of patriotism and Mexican American challenges to white privilege and defiance of racial discrimination. Zoot suit violence spread to other cities such as San Diego, Baltimore and New York in summer 1943.

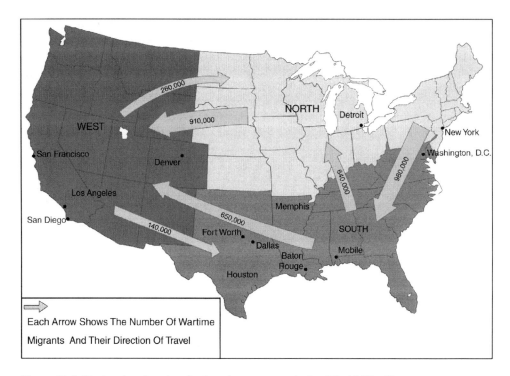

Figure 12.5 National and regional migration patterns during World War II.

Northern cities with large numbers of wartime black workers also experienced acute racial violence. Black workers in Detroit's automobile factories faced vocal white opposition throughout the war and there were numerous hate strikes. The city had both an active Klan membership and was a civil rights stronghold with over 20,000 NAACP members alone. A major race riot in the city in summer 1943 left more than 30 people dead, hundreds injured, and millions of dollars of damage to homes and property. The city was "pacified" by 6,000 soldiers in tanks and carrying automatic weapons. The shooting of a black serviceman by a white police officer precipitated serious racial violence in Harlem in 1943 also.

Domestic enemies

Internment

Internment usually involves the forcible removal of individual civilians or groups of people who are deemed to pose risks to national security during wartime, their confinement in guarded camps, and the seizure of their property. There are similarities to imprisonment except internees usually have not been formally charged with any crimes or been tried in a court of law. Wartime internees are often "enemy aliens" i.e. natives, citizens or subjects of a foreign country that is at war with the country they are currently living in, or supporters of specific political ideologies, organisations or parties which are characterised as being sympathetic to enemy war objectives or unsympathetic to domestic war aims. Prisoners of War might also be confined in internment camps as well as in separate POW camps.

All belligerent powers in the First and Second World Wars established internment camps. Some were mixed sex while in others, men, women and children were held separately. Conditions ranged from basic and uncomfortable to brutal and deadly. Generally, World War II civilian internment camps were not the same as Axis-power concentration camps and extermination camps which were part of systematic programmes of deliberate starvation, forced or slave labour, and death.

The most famous World War II examples are of Japanese-American and Japanese-Canadian internment in North America. However, thousands of British citizens originally from Germany, Italy, and Austria (including Jewish refugees), were interned on the Isle of Man. And, around 2,800 mainly British internees were held in the Stanley internment camps in Hong Kong after the Japanese invasion of the colony.

Naturalisation proceedings for Italian, German, and Japanese immigrants were suspended on 8 December 1941. In 1940, there were around 600,000 Italian "aliens" living in the US; as many as 1,600 Italian citizens were interned during the war years and about 10,000 Italian-Americans were forcibly relocated from their homes in California coastal communities to locations inland. There were 264,000 German aliens also. During the war, 10,905 Germans and German-Americans as well as Bulgarians, Czechs, Hungarians, and Romanians were placed in internment camps. Aliens from Axis nations were generally required to register with local police and the State Department, their mobility was restricted, and they were prohibited from owning items such as cameras and shortwave radios that could be used for sabotage or espionage. Most were subject to curfews which were gradually lifted from late 1942. Of the 378,000 Germans POWs held in 45 of the 48 US states, about 10,000 were held in 27 prison camps in Florida and were put to work in the lumber and naval stores industries, as fruit pickers, or serviced military bases.

As in World War I, there were major federal and state crackdowns on individuals and groups that were considered disloyal or liable to undermine the war effort. Members of the Ethiopian-Pacific Movement, Brotherhood of Liberty for Black People, and the Temple of Islam were arrested in Chicago in September 1942 on charges of sedition and "conspiracy to promote the success of the enemy, making false statements, to those about to be inducted into the armed forces, disrupting morale and causing mutiny." Nation of Islam leader, Elijah Muhammad was among those arrested. He was convicted of three counts of draft evasion and given a five-year prison term.

Within hours of the attacks on Pearl Harbor, the FBI had begun to round up hundreds of Japanese-Americans allegedly involved in "subversive activities" and nearly 6,000 were quickly interned on Terminal Island near Long Beach, California. Fears of Japanese espionage and sabotage as well as virulent xenophobia framed FDR's Executive Order 9066 in February 1942 to compulsorily relocate and intern 120,000 Japanese Americans. Most internees were US citizens; they included Japanese-born parents (Issei), their American-born children (Nisei), and third-generation Japanese-Americans (Sansei). They were moved by the War Relocation Authority (WRA) from their homes, businesses, and communities on the West Coast to ten concentration camps in desolate or semi-desert areas of the West, such as Heart Mountain, Wyoming, Minidoka, Idaho, and Topaz, Utah. Several socialist and pacifist organisations campaigned against the internment policy, including the Women's International League for Peace and Freedom and the American Civil Liberties Union.

Each camp was organised as a model city and administered through a series of departments, such as agriculture, education, and medical care, headed by Anglo administrators. All able-bodied internees were expected to undertake low-paid wage work at the camps. Doctors, teachers, and other professionals earned $19 per month; skilled and unskilled workers received $12 to $16 per month. Most internees reacted to the trauma of removal and implied disloyalty with acute anger, shame, and confusion, many suffered deep financial losses. Family unity was severely tested in the cramped barracks with communal facilities. In late 1942, the WRA permitted day and temporary releases of internees so they could undertake voluntary farm work such as fruit picking or slaughtering poultry. This was followed by the departure of younger Nisei women for college education and war industry employment in the Midwest and

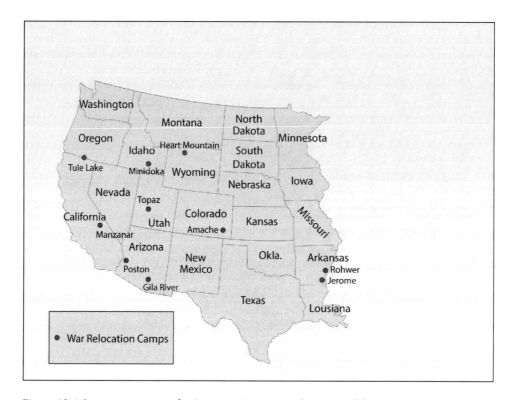

Figure 12.6 Internment camps for Japanese Americans during World War II.

East, often with help from religious organisations such as the Young Women's Christian Association and the Society of Friends.

Internees responded to internment in various ways. Some renounced their US citizenship. Nisei men determined to prove their loyalty to the US chose to enlist and were encouraged to do so by Mike Masoka, head of the Japanese American Citizens League. They served in the 100th Infantry Battalion formed in June 1942 or the 442nd Regimental Combat Team formed in February 1943. Both units were composed of Nisei and native Hawaiians but led by white officers. US officials argued that Nisei service would counter Japanese charges that the "war was a racial conflict" and bolster US global propaganda efforts that emphasised victory over fascism, racism, and imperialism. Nisei and Hawaiian troops participated in major European battles in 1945, including the Seventh Army's push into Germany in April 1945 and liberation of Dachau concentration camp. Only in 1990 did the US government attempt to make amends with a formal apology and financial compensation for internment survivors.

Work or fight

In 1940–41, German advances across Europe and the attack on the Soviet Union demanded full-scale economic and military mobilisation; after Pearl Harbor the US had to support both Lend-lease and its own military "Victory Plan" so legions of engineers, steel workers, electricians, and welders swung into action. A "Work or Fight" order from the Selective Service System in October 1942 directed local draft boards to review the deferments of men younger than 38 years who worked in jobs deemed unessential to the war effort. These men were given the choice of enlisting or working in war industries on the home front. American industry, manufacturing, and agriculture successfully rose to the challenges of simultaneously supporting millions of men and women in the US armed forces engaged in combat around the globe for nearly four years (1942–1945) and millions of Americans on the home front. This inevitably strengthened the relationship between the federal government and big business.

From cars to bombers

In 1940, the US automobile industry employed more than 500,000 workers in 1,375 cities in 44 states, and another seven million were indirectly employed in glass, rubber, lead, and other industries. Civilian automobile production stopped by mid-1942. For the next two years, automobile workers produced aircraft engines, machine guns, tanks, jeeps, army trucks, amphibious vehicles, and airplanes. The Ford Motor Company's 40 domestic plants all switched to wartime production. The massive River Rouge plant near Dearborn, Michigan, had 120,000 employees at its peak. Workers at a new government-funded plant at Willow Run, Michigan, produced 10,000 B-24 Liberator bombers under the management of the Ford Company and using their assembly line techniques.

War production peaked in 1943. Seventeen million new jobs were created during the war years. Overall, the civilian workforce rose from 46.5 million to more than

53 million by 1945; the additional seven million came from those previously unemployed as well as groups of teenage and older workers, and several million women. Numbers of older and married female workers rose dramatically, and of women with young children. They were often doing industrial and manufacturing jobs that were previously designated as "male." A War Production Board study in 1943 found that 40 per cent of 150,000 war workers in Detroit were mothers while a similar study of automobile workers found that 68 per cent were married and 40 per cent had children. Before 1940, the typical waged female worker was younger and single.

Figure 12.7 Petrina Moore the welder. This photograph of Petrina Moore, a Native American female welder at the Todd Hoboken dry dock in New Jersey, 1943, highlights the entry of several million women of all ages, backgrounds, and racial and ethnic groups into the wartime labour force. The wartime emergency led to significant female gains, but many women were summarily dismissed even before the war had ended, ostensibly to provide jobs for returning male veterans.

Source: Courtesy of Granger Historical Picture Archive/Alamy

A series of agreements between the US and Mexican governments led to the creation of the Bracero or Mexican Farm Labor Program in August 1942. Hundreds of thousands of Mexican workers, mainly men, were permitted to take up agricultural jobs in the Southwest and California or worked on the railroads in the Pacific Northwest. Both US and Mexican officials used militarised rhetoric to promote the programme, casting agricultural workers as "soldiers in the fields." To many, earlier Depression-era deportations and the wartime emigration programme confirmed that Mexican Americans were a disposable workforce. Low wages, long hours, discriminatory employment and housing, and separation from their families spurred both national debates and a nascent Chicano civil rights movement.

Drawing on lessons from World War I and the New Deal, wartime mobilisation was organised through a series of central agencies such as the National Labor Relations Board, Office of Civilian Defense, War Food Administration, and War Manpower Commission, overseen by the Office of Emergency Management, headed by William H. McReynolds. In January 1942, FDR created the War Production Board (WPB) under the direction of former Sears Roebuck executive Donald Nelson and with a bureaucracy of 20,000 employees. It was to supply vital raw materials, such as copper, steel, rubber, and wood, for war and essential civilian production; provide plants and equipment in factories to manufacture war materiel; and staff the plants with enough people with the right skills. It therefore oversaw much of the conversion of civilian to military production. An Office of War mobilisation took over from WPB in May 1943 to balance civilian and military production, and later oversee reconversion. The Office of War Information (OWI), the best known and most influential wartime propaganda agency, was created by executive order in June 1942.

As early as 1941, the economic problems of unemployment, deflation, agricultural overproduction, and industrial sluggishness were disappearing. Incomes and savings rose dramatically, as did prices. The federal government spent $321 billion between 1941 and 1945, and the national debt rose from $49 billion to $259 billion. Around $100 billion of federal bonds were sold to raise money to pay for the war, and millions of Americans patriotically bought the bonds and dutifully held fund-raising events. A Revenue Act (1942) levied new taxes on all earners, including 94 per cent on the highest incomes. Partly to control inflation and in response to public complaints over profiteering, Congress also grudgingly passed the Anti-Inflation Act in October 1942 which enabled the Office of Price Administration to freeze agricultural prices, wages, salaries, and rents throughout the country. However, "black marketing" and over-charging continued, particularly of rationed consumer goods such as coffee, sugar, meat, and gasoline.

Labour union membership rose from 10.5 million in 1941 to over 13 million in 1945. The National War Labor Board secured a wartime "no-strike" pledge, a 40-hour week with overtime pay, and a 15 per cent limit on wage increases from CIO-AFL union leaders. In return, the thousands of new workers pouring into defence plants would be automatically enrolled in labour unions that had previously established bargaining rights. However, many workers resented strike and wage restrictions and there were nearly 15,000 work stoppages during the war.

One of the more unusual strikes was organised by prostitutes – a diverse workforce of white, Hawaiian, Japanese, Puerto Rican, and Chinese women – in Honolulu's vice district in June 1942. Prostitution was illegal in Hawaii but was open and regulated by the police department, government officials, and the military. Business boomed with the arrival of thousands of servicemen and war workers. Each brothel made around $10 million during the war years. Brothel madams earned up to $40,000 per year, but the average prostitute earned less than $2,000 per year for 100 customers per day for 20 days a month. The women raised their prices to $5 for three minutes in early 1942 and sought to resist police crackdowns on their freedom of movement and businesses, and their strike was successful. But an anti-vice crackdown by influential local citizens and the Admiralty led to the closure of the vice district in 1944.

Other employers looked to Congress to limit worker action. Following a huge United Mine Workers strike in May 1943, Congress passed (over FDR's veto), the War Labor Disputes Act which required unions to wait 30 days before striking and empowered the president to seize a war plant affected by strike action. Many states also imposed laws designed to limit labour union power.

Combat in the Pacific

Popular unity and political confidence were severely tested during the first half of 1942 as Allied strongholds in the Pacific fell under Japanese control: the British imperial fortress of Singapore surrendered in February 1942 and over 60,000 Commonwealth troops became POWs, the Japanese navy defeated British-Dutch-US-Australian forces in the Battle of the Java Sea and occupied the Dutch East Indies in March, then Japanese air raids and the capture of Rangoon precipitated the fall of Burma in April, raising the spectre of a Japanese invasion of India. Exhausted Filipino and US troops under the command of General Douglas MacArthur finally retreated from the Philippines on 6 May. The Pacific war was primarily a clash between imperial powers over trade, colonies, and naval superiority, but also racial superiority. Throughout the conflict, American and Allied media consistently characterised Japanese troops and civilians as subhuman or as vermin, apes, and insects that need to be destroyed. Themes of extermination, revenge, and retribution dominated discussion of the Pacific War for its duration, in both Japan and the US, leading to its designation as primarily a racial war.

American military strategists planned two broad offensives against the Japanese: one under the command of General MacArthur would move north from Australia through New Guinea and eventually back to the Philippines; the other under Admiral Chester Nimitz would move west from Hawaii towards major Japanese island outposts in the central and south Pacific. Also, because the US Navy had broken Japanese codes, strategists could use information on enemy locations, troops numbers, and materiel to strategic effect. The two offensives would ultimately come together to enable Allied forces to invade Japan itself.

A major battle between US-Australian and Japanese aircraft carriers and aerial warfare in the Coral Sea 4–8 May 1942 resulted in an important military and psychological Allied victory. US codebreakers identified a diversionary Japanese attack on the Aleutian Islands on 3 June 1942 and the main target of Midway Atoll. A huge naval battle raged for four days, 3–6 June 1942, at Midway Island. There were major losses on both sides but US destruction of four Japanese aircraft carriers and the loss of 250 aircraft seriously impaired Japanese naval and air power. Victory enabled US-Allied forces to eventually regain control of the central Pacific. Military historians often describe Midway as one of the most decisive naval battles and a key turning point in the Pacific war.

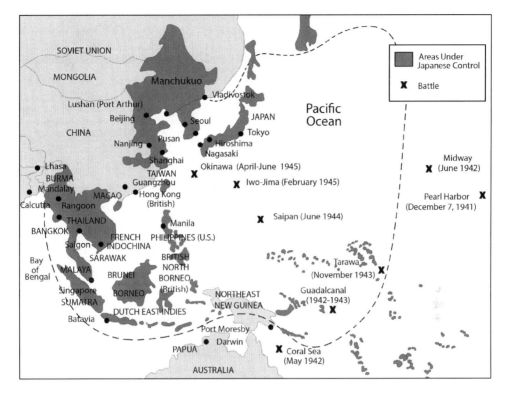

Figure 12.8 World War II: the war in the Pacific.

During the summer of 1942, a major US-Australian-New Zealand offensive to recapture the Solomon Islands commenced to reclaim a Japanese base used for air raids against US and Australian forces, and to disrupt Allied supply lines and communications. In August 1942, US forces assaulted three of the islands: Gavutu, Tulagi, and Guadalcanal and there followed six months of ferocious flighting at Guadalcanal in particular. Both sides sustained heavy losses of troops – 30,000 Japanese and 7,500 US (and thousands of locals) – warships and aircraft. The remaining 10,000 Japanese troops were evacuated in early February 1943. This effectively ended Japanese military ability to launch an offensive in the South Pacific, thus by mid-1943, the war in the southern and central Pacific was beginning to move in the Allies' favour. As planned, US forces alongside Australians and New Zealanders began the slow arduous process of moving towards the Philippines and Japan itself. First Lady Eleanor Roosevelt made a gruelling five-week 17-stop tour to the South Pacific in August and September 1943 during which she met many veterans of the Guadalcanal battle.

US and Commonwealth troops were involved in a series of hard-fought Pacific battles during 1944, in the Philippine Sea and at Saipan in June–July, and the Battle of Leyte Gulf in October. With 270 warships, Leyte Gulf was the largest naval battle of the war. It ended in disaster for the Japanese Imperial fleet which lost numerous craft and 12,000 men (there were at least 2,500 US casualties). Five of the six US battleships that helped inflict this significant naval defeat on Japan had been damaged at Pearl Harbor in December 1941.

Associated Press photographer Joe Rosenthal's iconic image of US Marines raising the American flag over Mount Suribachi on Iwo Jima, on the Volcano Islands, 1,200 kilometres southeast of Japan in February 1945 came to symbolise the Pacific war. US forces had superior numbers of troops and military hardware, but Japanese troops tenaciously defended their cave positions during weeks of preliminary naval and air bombardment and for a month after US Marine landings. Of the 22,000 Japanese defenders, 21,000 were killed, while 20,000 US troops were wounded and another 6,800 killed. US forces needed this strategically important island base so that their fighter planes could accompany heavy bombers flying from Saipan to Japan. Equally bloody and important was the Battle of Okinawa fought from 1 April to 22 June 1945. Again, US forces met fierce resistance from Japanese troops and islanders, but Okinawa was strategically important for firebomb air raids on Tokyo and other major cities, and for the planned invasion of the main island of Honshu. US forces suffered nearly 50,000 casualties including 12,000 deaths, but the Japanese lost around 100,000 men, and an estimated 100,000 civilians also perished.

Combat in Africa, Europe, Middle East, and Russia

In the campaigns in Africa, Europe, and the Middle East, US forces were allied with British, "Free French" and other European exiles from countries under Nazi control, and the Soviets. Early in 1942, Allied plans for an invasion across the English Channel were formulated for April 1943 and had the support of US Army Chief of Staff, George C. Marshall. The relatively unknown General Dwight D. Eisenhower planned the operation. However, Winston Churchill and Josef Stalin had differing views on military priorities. The Soviets wanted the invasion to commence in late 1942 but the British wanted to strike German forces first in north Africa and southern Europe (the collaborationist Vichy government controlled the southern half of France and the French north African colonies) prior to any major invasion of northern France.

By spring 1942, the German Afrika Korps had reached El Alamain, 75 miles west of Alexandria, Egypt, thus threatening the Suez Canal and British-controlled Middle East. German forces were also heading to the Caucasus. FDR agreed to support Churchill's aims, so US-British forces successfully attacked Algiers and Casablanca October–November 1942, and Germans and Italian forces were effectively driven out of North Africa by May 1943. However, the British postponed cross-channel invasion plans much to the anger of the Soviets who had spent the winter desperately repelling Nazi forces at enormous human cost. The 200-day Battle of Stalingrad began with German air and bombing raids, followed by tanks, shells, and infantry invasions and Red Army and civilian responses, then hand-to hand, building-to-building fighting, all of which would claim more than 1.7 million casualties. But the Red Army prevailed in February 1943. After beating back the German offensive on Europe's Eastern Front, Stalin persuaded FDR to agree to Churchill's plans for an Allied invasion of Sicily. The plan crystallised at a meeting in Casablanca in January 1943. American troops played key roles in the July invasion of Sicily which precipitated the collapse of Mussolini's government, and the Allied offensive on the Italian peninsula from September 1943. Rome was liberated on 4 June 1944, although German forces in Italy would not surrender until May 1945. The Italian campaign claimed 114,000 US casualties.

Churchill and FDR had also agreed at Casablanca to demand unconditional surrender from the Axis powers.

In early June 1944, millions of troops, with millions of tonnes of hardware and weapons, assembled along Britain's southern coast in preparation for the amphibious British-US-Canadian D-Day landings on 90 kilometers of Normandy beaches. The slow Allied drive eastward commenced with one million troops capturing Caen and St Lo by late August with the US First and Third Armies playing leading roles. The Third Army under General Patton took on German troops in Brittany and secured crucial Breton ports. British, US forces from the Twelfth Army, and other Allied troops pushed east towards the Ardennes Forest in Belgium, and headed for Germany's industrial centre in the Ruhr, while the Third Army headed across the Seine. News of Allied advances encouraged French patriots to rebel against German troops stationed in Paris, and to support this uprising, a column of US and Free French troops entered Paris on 25 August 1944. The US First Army reinforced British and other US troops heading towards Aachen and Antwerp, while the Third army continued to the south of Ardennes. By 11 September 1944, France, Belgium, and Luxembourg had been liberated. Meanwhile, Soviet troops pushed westward, reclaiming the Baltic Republics that had been under German control since late 1941, East Prussia, the Balkans, and Hungary.

With hindsight, it is clear that by the end of 1944, the Axis was heading towards total defeat. For example, Eisenhower, now Supreme Commander of the Allied Expeditionary

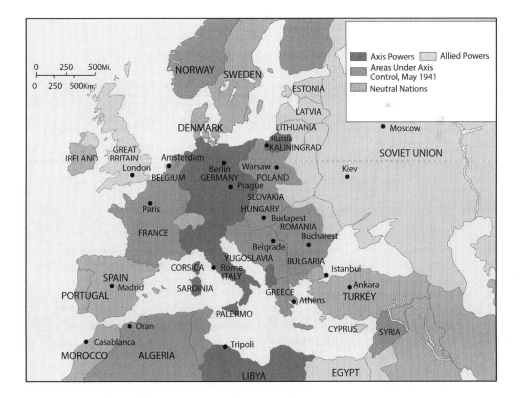

Figure 12.9 World War II: the European-North African war.

Force, oversaw 48 troop divisions stretched along a 1,000-kilometre front between Switzerland and the Dutch-German border. Yet, German forces launched a massive counteroffensive in Belgium on 16 December. Panzer divisions progressed through the Ardennes Forest, encircling the US 101st Airborne Division at Bastogne, and forced an Allied retreat of 75 kilometres. The Germans sustained 120,000 casualties and lost valuable materiel, and the Allies suffered 75,000 casualties. Ultimately, the month-long Battle of the Bulge or Ardennes Offensive December 1944–January 1945 disrupted rather than halted the Allied push towards Germany itself. Patton's forces reached the German border at the end of January, and the Third Army captured Trier on 1 March. They pushed on through the Moselle River region and joined the Seventh Army to capture the Saarland and Palatinate. Patton was all set to continue to Berlin but liberating the German capital was to be a Soviet honour under the terms of the Yalta agreement. The Red Army reached Berlin in late April 1945, Italian partisans killed Mussolini on 28 April as he attempted to flee to Switzerland, Hitler committed suicide on 30 April, and German resistance had ended by early May. Victory-Europe Day was declared on 8 May 1945.

With German defeat and Allied arrival at Nazi concentration camps, the full horror of the Holocaust was revealed. During World War II, the Nazis and their allies operated six death camps in Eastern Europe between December 1941 and the end of 1944: Chelmno, Belzek, Majdanek, Treblinka, Sobibor, and Auschwitz, and systematically exterminated 11 million people, including Roma Gypsies, Slavic peoples, homosexuals, Polish Catholics, Soviet POWs, and six million Jews; no more than 450,000 to 500,000 Jews survived World War II in German-occupied Europe. At Auschwitz in Poland, gas chambers and crematorium ovens killed 20,000 victims a day. Early in the war, high officials in Washington DC and London had received irrefutable evidence that European Jews were being rounded up, transported, and murdered but their response was limited. For example, Allied bombers were not ordered to bomb either the death camps or the railway lines carrying cattle trucks of prisoners to their deaths.

From late July to early August 1945, Prime Minister Churchill then Clement Atlee, Communist Party General Secretary Josef Stalin, and President Harry Truman (FDR had died on 12 April) met at Potsdam in Germany to discuss key issues such as reparations and the future of Germany and its borders. Under the Potsdam Agreement, Germany and Austria were each divided into four zones of occupation for Britain, France, the Soviet Union, and the US. German-speaking people in Czechoslovakia, Hungary, and Poland were forcibly relocated to Germany thus adding to wartime migration, refugee, and housing crises. Truman also took the momentous decision to approve the use of a new weapon of mass destruction on Japan to hasten the end of the war in the Pacific.

Nuclear warfare

Truman's decision to use nuclear weapons against Japan remains controversial and the subject of considerable historiographical debate: did it bring the war to an earlier end? how many casualties would have resulted from a US invasion of the main Japanese islands? was the Japanese government ready to surrender? However, several factors converged in August 1945. The US government had spent nearly $2 billion since late 1941 on a secret research and development project on atomic technology. Under director J. Robert Oppenheimer, the Manhattan Project had over 120,000 employees working at nuclear facilities in Tennessee, Washington, and New Mexico, and in several elite US universities. Only a few inner scientists including physicist Enrico Fermi, a refugee from Italian fascism, and select government officials knew that the goal was to create atomic bombs. It was later revealed that a Soviet spy Klaus Fuchs had infiltrated the inner circle, but the Axis powers had no knowledge of the Los Alamos, New Mexico, laboratories or the wider project. The first bomb was successfully tested in mid-July 1945, and there were two more bombs ready for use.

The gruelling battles at Iwo Jima and Okinawa had underlined that any US invasion of Japan – initially planned for November 1945–March 1946 – would result in huge casualties on both sides, perhaps 50,000 US casualties during the first phase alone. A prolonged and bloody Pacific war would attract severe public and political criticism at home. And, freed from the war in Europe, the Soviet Union might turn its attention back to China, threaten what was left of the open door and US hegemony in the Pacific, then turn its sights on the Western Hemisphere. The Allies demanded Japan's unconditional surrender on 2 August, but Japanese leaders failed to respond to the US threat of "utter devastation" if they refused. The first atomic bomb dropped on Hiroshima on 6 August destroyed the city and left 160,000 casualties. The second bomb was dropped on Nagasaki on 9 August with similarly horrific results, including up to 80,000 dead.

The Japanese government did surrender on 11 August thus bringing World War II to an end. However, on 10 August, US policymakers divided the Korean peninsula at the 38th parallel without consulting the wartime Korean Provisional government and essentially replaced Japanese colonial occupation with US occupation. On 16 August, in the Dutch East Indies, the Viet Mihn Committee called for a Vietnamese insurrection, thus signalling that World War II was just one phase in a much longer struggle against Japanese, French, and US colonialism and militarism that would continue long after 1945. Even before the defeat of the Axis in May 1945 and the use of nuclear warfare in the Pacific three months later, it was clear that the US was now a major diplomatic force and at the centre of global international relations. Like the USSR, the US was no longer a great power but had become a *superpower*, which would demand new duties, responsibilities, and expectations, particularly as a new conflict, the cold war, was emerging.

Sixty million people were killed during World War II, including 38 million civilians. Millions more would carry the physical and psychological scars of warfare for the rest of their lives. Landscapes and cities were seared by warfare and littered with body parts, graves and abandoned military hardware. Civilians on every war-torn continent lost family members, communities, farms, businesses, cities, industries, and homes. Many survived Allied and Axis bombing raids, interment, concentration camps, years as prisoners of war, physical and sexual violence, poverty, hunger, and disease. By contrast, 400,000 American military personnel died in World War II along with 11,000 civilians, but most of the states had not suffered physical or economic destruction so wartime recovery and rebuilding would be very different to other former Allied and Axis powers. Nevertheless, just as the American Civil War had dramatically transformed the US in the mid-nineteenth century, World War II would dramatically transform America in the mid-twentieth century, as outlined in the following chapters.

Chapter summary

This chapter has shown that during the 1930s, US politicians and ordinary Americans wanted to believe that neutrality and isolationism could be pursued indefinitely, thus aid to Allied belligerents such as the Destroyer-Base deal, naval convoys, and Lend-lease ensured the US could support Britain, the free French, and (after 1941) the Soviet Union in the war in Europe without direct military involvement. In December 1941, the Japanese gambled that their surprise attack would neutralise the American Pacific fleet for enough time to allow Japan to consolidate its victories in Asia, but this proved to be a major miscalculation. The attack on Pearl Harbor irrevocably changed the course of World War II, and US service personnel waged brutal, costly, and decisive campaigns in every theatre of war between 1942 and 1945. The industrial, manufacturing, and agricultural might of the US enabled America to be the "arsenal of democracy" before 1941 and to successfully support both civilians at home and crucial military campaigns around the globe for four long years after 1941.

Discussion questions

- Looking at American foreign policy in the late 1930s, why do you think Roosevelt wanted to be pushed into World War II rather than actively shape international relations?
- How important was US civilian and military mobilisation to Allied successes?
- What might have been the implications for the US of a German victory in Europe and Japanese victory in the Pacific?
- How useful or problematic are the terms "good war" and "greatest generation" in defining Americans' experiences during World War II?

Further reading

Baime, A. J. *The Arsenal of Democracy: FDR, Ford Motor Company, and Their Epic Quest to Arm America at War* (Boston, 2014). Provides a detailed account of the impact of wartime mobilisation on Detroit and its key industries and the rise of Willow Run, although the focus is on the Ford men.

Bernstein, Alison R. *American Indians and World War II: Toward a New Era in Indian Affairs* (Norman, OK, 1999). A useful exploration of the changing social, economic and political tribal landscapes from the 1930s to the 1950s.

Brandt, Nathan. *Harlem at War: The Black Experience in WWII* (New York, 1996). Includes many eyewitness accounts and reminiscences to provide a sobering yet fascinating exploration of wartime conditions and racial hostilities in black communities across the US as well as the background to the 1943 Harlem riot.

Dahl, Erik J. *Intelligence and Surprise Attack: Failure and Success from Pearl Harbor to 9/11 and Beyond* (Washington, DC, 2013). Very informative for those interested in the military intelligence questions surrounding Pearl Harbor, and the longer story of surprise attacks and preventive actions throughout the twentieth century to the 9/11 terrorist attacks.

Dower, John W. *War Without Mercy: Race and Power in the Pacific War* (New York, 1986). A path-breaking revisionist study of racial stereotyping and demonisation in Japanese and American wartime propaganda that underscored the racial animosity that defined the military and home fronts in the War in the Pacific.

Hagan, Claudia. *American Women During World War II* (CreateSpace Independent Publishing Platform, 2015). Readable and informative account of women's home front and military contributions and experiences, that is a very useful starting point for these topics.

Honey, Maureen, ed. *Bitter Fruit: African American Women in World War II* (Columbia, MO, 1999). Fascinating and important anthology of literary accomplishments, work, economic and political contributions of African American women in wartime America and overseas, and as pioneers in the fight for racial and gender equality.

Howard, John. *Concentration Camps on the Home Front: Japanese Americans in the House of Jim Crow* (Chicago, 2008). An innovative and revealing exploration of gender, race, and sexualised power relations in two wartime detention camps for Japanese Americans in "Jim Crow" Arkansas. Read alongside Reeves' study.

Johnstone, Andrew E. *Against Immediate Evil: American Internationalists and the Four Freedoms on the Eve of World War II* (Ithaca, 2014). Focuses on three major internationalist organisations to examine the relationships between government institutions, special interest groups, the FDR administration, the president, and public opinion that shaped elite decision-making on intervention 1938–1941.

Kennedy, David M. *Freedom from Fear: The American People in Depression and War, 1929–1945* (New York, 2001). Thorough, carefully researched, and very readable Pulitzer Prize–winning social and political history of US domestic and foreign policy through the Depression and war years. It's 850 pages and a go-to study for this crucial period.

Mitchell, Don. *They Saved the Crops: Labor, Landscape, and the Struggle Over Industrial Farming in Bracero-Era California* (Athens, 2012). A bold analysis of the Bracero programme in California, that began in 1942 as a state-sponsored contract labour scheme to funnel Mexican workers into wartime agriculture but whose exploitative, racist and violent impacts continued for decades.

Pagan, Eduardo Obregon. *Murder at the Sleepy Lagoon: Zoot Suits, Race, and Riot in Wartime L.A.* (Chapel Hill, 2002). A fascinating study of masculinities, youth cultures, and race relations in 1940s California that provides important contextual understanding of episodes of violence and disorder.

Reeves, Richard. *Infamy: The Shocking Story of the Japanese American Internment in World War II* (London, 2016). Draws on oral histories and a range of private correspondence for a very accessible but often harrowing account of the round-up and forced relocation of 120,000 Japanese Americans.

Rosenberg, Emily S. *A Date Which Will Life: Pearl Harbor in American Memory* (Durham, NC, 2003). An innovative and compelling study of Pearl Harbor as cultural icon and cultural battleground from 1941 through to the 50th anniversary commemorations, weaving history and memory into new cultural approaches to diplomatic history.

Takaki, Ronald. *Double Victory: A Multicultural History of America in World War II* (Bay Books, 2001). This is a great starting point for understanding the contributions of different communities to the war effort, at home and abroad, as well as the racial and nativist realities of the 1940s.

Townsend, Kenneth William. *World War II and the American Indian* (revised edition, Albuquerque, NM, 2002). Carefully researched and comprehensive examination of the impacts of the war on different tribal nations as well as individual and collective responses during a critical juncture in Native American-US relations.

Yellin, Emily. *Our Mother's War: American Women at Home and at the Front During World War II* (New York, 2005). A wide-ranging broad-brush exploration of women's changing responsibilities and challenges at home and their roles overseas that was inspired by the author's own family story.

13 Cold war America, 1945–1954

Timeline

1945   Yalta Conference
          Potsdam Conference
          Atomic Bombing of Hiroshima and Nagasaki
1946   Kennan's Long Telegram
          Employment Act
          Congress of Industrial Organizations launches Operation Dixie
          Republicans win control of Congress
1947   Communist seizure of power in Czechoslovakia
          Truman announces containment doctrine
          Marshall Plan announced
          Taft-Hartley Labour Act of 1947
1948   Truman's Loyalty-Security Program initiated
          Berlin Airlift
          Truman elected president
1949   Truman announces Fair Deal
          Formation of North Atlantic Treaty Organization
          Soviets test their first atomic bomb
          Establishment of the People's Republic of China
1950   North Korean invasion of South Korea
          NSC-68 adopted
1951   Korean War stalemates
1953   End of Korean War
1954   Joseph McCarthy receives Senate censure

Topics Covered

* From wartime co-operation to the Potsdam Conference
* Containment
* The Marshall Plan and the division of Europe
* China and Korea
* Impact of the Korean War
* The Red Scare
* Domestic politics and the waning of social reform

Introduction

Chapter 13 opens with a meeting of American and Soviet troops in Germany in April 1945, when soldiers celebrated their joint victory over Nazi Germany. It fast-forwards to a tense US–Soviet standoff over Berlin in 1948 that precipitated fears of World War III. The next section develops explanations for the deterioration of American-Soviet relations that led to the cold war. The Democratic administration of Harry Truman (1945–53) was horrified by Stalin's Europe policy, raising Western fears that large parts the war-torn continent would fall under communist control. In response, the USA adopted the containment doctrine that sought to restrain Soviet expansionism and remained the cornerstone of American foreign policy throughout the cold war. Containment took the form of American military aid to Greece and Turkey in 1947, followed by the Marshall Plan that provided American economic assistance to Western Europe, hastened the continent's division, and led to the Berlin Crisis of 1948. The formation of the North Atlantic Treaty Organization in 1949 and the establishment of West Germany "froze" the East-West divide in Europe, but the cold war spread into Asia as a result of the Chinese communist revolution and communist North Korea's invasion of South Korea in 1950 that led to US military intervention. The Korean War facilitated massive American rearmament, the US-sponsored resurrection of Japan, and West Germany's integration into NATO. At home, the cold war led to an anti-communist crusade with major consequences for domestic politics and foreign policy.

Cold war

The phrase "cold war" denoted a hostile US-Soviet relationship that did not feature outright combat ("hot war") between its main protagonists but could not be described as "peace" either. The phrase was introduced by the British journalist and intellectual George Orwell in a prescient essay entitled "You and the Atomic Bomb" published in October 1945. Orwell warned that "monstrous super-states" capable of developing atomic bombs (the USA, the Soviet Union, and China) would divide the world among them. "Unable to conquer one another" for fear that nuclear warfare would destroy both victor and vanquished, each of the three would find itself in "a permanent state of 'cold war' with its neighbors," he predicted. The atomic bomb would "put an end to large-scale wars at the cost of prolonging indefinitely a 'peace that is no peace.'"

In the USA, the phrase was popularised by journalist Walter Lippmann in his book *The Cold War: A Study in U.S. Foreign Policy* that was sharply critical of President Harry Truman's confrontational diplomacy *vis-à-vis* the Soviet Union.

The cold war evolved from a series of diplomatic confrontations in the late 1940s into an arms race between the USA and the Soviet Union in the 1950s and thereafter. Though the two powers did not engage in direct combat with one another, military conflict became a salient feature of the cold war when the two powers fought so-called proxy wars in which each sponsored one of the combatants, for example communist North Vietnam (supported by the Soviet Union) and pro-Western South Vietnam (USA) in the 1960s and 1970s.

The phrase "cold war" has also been used to describe hostile relationships short of direct military confrontation between India and Pakistan, Saudi Arabia and Iran, and – most recently – the USA and the People's Republic of China (sometimes labelled "cold war II" or "cold war 2.0").

Torgau, Germany

On 25 April 1945, American combat forces invading from the west and Red Army troops arriving from the east met in Torgau on banks of the River Elbe, the great waterway that bisects Germany. Celebrating their victory over Nazi Germany with handshakes and toasts, the soldiers remembered their fallen comrades who had died on the battlefields of the Second World War. Senior commanders soon joined in. General Dwight D. Eisenhower, the architect of the landing at Normandy, shared a drink of Coca-Cola with General Georgy Zhukov, commander of the Soviet invasion of Germany from the east, and together they toasted the performance of their troops.

Interpreting the cold war

Explanations of the cold war have changed considerably. The earliest Western interpretation placed the blame squarely on Stalin, whose attempts to expand Soviet power imperilled Western Europe, prompting Truman to commit America's vast resources to the containment of communism. Called the "orthodox" school of thought that shared the assumptions of US foreign policymakers, this interpretation was challenged in the 1960s by so-called revisionist historians of the New Left who attributed growing tensions in US-Soviet relations to America's determination to gain access to overseas markets through open door policies that would sustain the capitalist order. According to revisionist William A. Williams, Truman tendency to "react, think, and act as an almost classic personification of the entire Open Door policy. A more balanced "post-revisionist" school of thought blames the cold war equally on the USA and the Union of Soviet Socialist Republics (USSR, also known as the Soviet Union), positing that America's vision of a democratic and capitalist Europe collided with Stalin's attempts to safeguard Soviet security by establishing communist regimes in Eastern Europe. Post-revisionist historian John Lewis Gaddis argues, "Leaders of both superpowers sought peace, but in doing so yielded to considerations which, while they did not precipitate war, made a resolution of differences impossible."

Three years later, the USA and the Soviet Union faced each other in a tense standoff when the Red Army blocked access to Berlin and threatened to starve the western parts of the city that were controlled by the Western powers. This prompted fears that American attempts to reach Berlin via roads from the west through communist eastern Germany would result in armed conflict and unleash World War III.

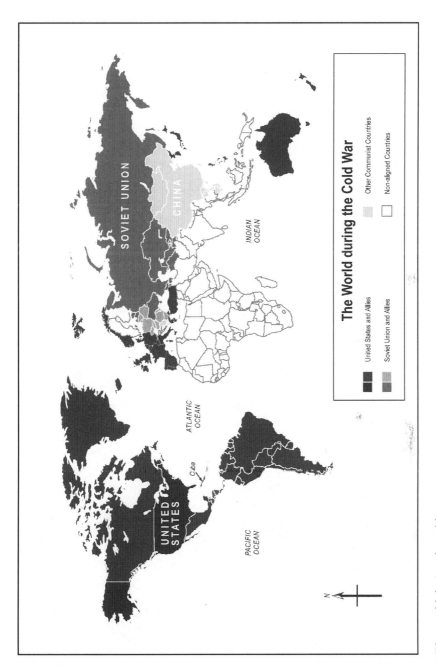

Figure 13.1 The world during the cold war.

From wartime cooperation to the Potsdam Conference

The "Grand Alliance" between the USA, Britain, and the Soviet Union began auspiciously in 1941 after Japan attacked the American Pacific Fleet in Pearl Harbor in December 1941 (see Chapter 12). Making American military supplies available to Stalin, President Franklin Roosevelt extended Lend-lease aid to the Soviet Union in order to support the Red Army's desperate fight against the Germans with American-made lorries, radio, and other military equipment. In 1943, Roosevelt and British Prime Minister Winston Churchill met Stalin face-to-face at the Tehran Conference, where Roosevelt announced that the USA, Britain, and the Soviet Union would cooperate closely for generations.

Major disagreements were already evident behind closed doors because Stalin was increasingly frustrated with Anglo-American failure to invade German-occupied Western Europe. For three years he urged the USA and Britain to open a Second Front in France in order to force Hitler to withdraw some of his troops from the USSR and relieve the Red Army of some of the enormous pressure it endured at German hands in the East. Soviet foreign secretary Vyacheslav Molotov used four English words in his negotiations with Americans: "Yes," "No," and "Second Front." Roosevelt told him in 1942 that the USA would open the Second Front that year, but logistical problems and British objections made a successful invasion of France across the English Channel impossible until June 1944. Stalin detected far more sinister motives behind the Anglo-American delay of the Second Front, worrying that the Western powers were not planning to invade France at all but instead wanted to sign a separate peace with Germany at the USSR's expense – a gross misinterpretation of Western intentions that fuelled his suspicions that the USA and Britain would sooner or later turn on their wartime ally.

In February 1945, Roosevelt, Stalin, and Churchill met in the Soviet resort town of Yalta to map out the post-war order. At the time, senior American officials warned Roosevelt that Stalin was determined to impose communist regimes on Eastern European countries recently liberated from the Germans by the Red Army. Averell Harriman, the US Ambassador to Moscow, wrote as early as September 1944, "Unless we take issue with the present policy, there is every indication the Soviet Union will become a world bully." At the Yalta Conference, the post-war fate of Eastern Europe worried Roosevelt, who pressured Stalin for a commitment to democratic elections in liberated Europe. The Yalta Agreement indeed included a pledge to "form interim governmental authorities broadly representative of all democratic elements in the population and pledged to the earliest possible establishment through free elections of governments responsible to the will of the people." The Soviets broke that commitment in Poland, where they installed a communist-dominated government that discriminated against non-communist political parties and turned the country into a Soviet satellite. Stalin explained that Poland could never again become a "corridor for attack on Russia," as it had been for Napoleon (1812), Imperial Germany (1914), and Nazi Germany (1941). Any future aggressor nation, he argued, should have to fight its way through a pro-Soviet Poland before invading the Soviet Union itself. Western leaders doubted the veracity of Soviet national security concerns and instead interpreted the establishment of a communist regime in Poland as the first step towards Soviet control of Europe.

When Truman succeeded Roosevelt in April 1945, the new president was unaware of key aspects of his predecessor's foreign policy because he had not been a member of FDR's inner circle. He relied on advisors who reinforced his determination to get tough with the Soviets, notably ambassador Harriman, who warned Truman in a crucial meeting on 23 April 1945 that the USA confronted a "barbarian invasion" of

Europe (their meeting took place two days before American and Soviet troops shook hands in Torgau, Germany). By contrast, Secretary of War Henry Stimson warned Truman that an uncompromising American stance on Eastern Europe risked an irreparable diplomatic breakdown, but Truman sided with the hardliners. In a meeting with Soviet foreign minister Molotov later that day, Truman told him that attempts to install communist governments in Eastern Europe violated the Yalta Agreement and would have serious consequences for US-Soviet relations. A dumbfounded Molotov responded, "I have never been talked to like that in my life," prompting Truman to bark, "Carry out your agreement, and you won't get talked to like that."

The episode reinforced Stalin's impression that Truman was hostile to the Soviet Union even before he met the president in person at the Potsdam Conference in July 1945 to negotiate key issues, including Eastern Europe and the future of Germany. Stalin's demand for extensive reparations from Germany to repair some of the damage the USSR had suffered during the war was bound to be disputed by the Americans and the British, who worried that large payments would cripple Germany to such an extent that it would unable to contribute to Europe's post-war economic recovery. Moreover, Truman and Churchill remained opposed to a communist-dominated government in Poland, which Stalin regarded as essential to Soviet national security.

In the middle of the contentious negotiations in Potsdam, Truman received information that American scientists had successfully tested the world's first atomic bomb near to Alamogordo, New Mexico. Churchill noticed that Truman returned to the meeting with Stalin a changed man and "generally bossed the whole meeting." America's possession of the bomb cast a long shadow over the Potsdam Conference when Truman told Stalin casually that the USA possessed a "powerful new weapon" of unusual destructiveness. The Soviet leader was unsurprised because he knew of the Manhattan Project long before Truman due to Soviet spying in the United States, but he understood that the president was trying to use his new leverage to extract Soviet concessions on reparations and Eastern Europe. Despite Truman's pressure tactics, Stalin kept his nerve and the Potsdam Conference ended with compromises: Germany would be divided into four occupational zones, each administered by the USA, Britain, the Soviet Union, and France; Berlin would also be divided into four occupation zones; the USSR received permission to collect reparations from its occupational zone in Eastern Germany, though not from the Western zones; and the USA and Britain recognised the communist-dominated government of Poland, but not that of Bulgaria, Hungary, and Romania.

A furious Stalin returned to Moscow determined to create a nuclear bomb development project of his own, suspecting that the Americans would use their atomic monopoly to exert continued pressure on the Soviet Union to "accept their plans on questions affecting Europe and the world," he told his confidants. "Well, that's not going to happen." Ordering nuclear physicists to accelerate their atomic bomb programme, which was tellingly code named "Problem Number One," he appointed Lavrentiy Beria, the brutal chief of Soviet secret police, as administrative head of the project and instructed him to spare no expense to ensure the swift development of a functioning bomb. Stalin understood that resource mobilisation for the project would require enormous sacrifices from the Soviet people who had suffered through famine and mass killings under his regime during the 1930s, followed by the most destructive war in their country's history that killed 22 million people and left large parts of the USSR physically devastated at a time when America's gross national product was six times larger than that of the Soviet Union. In February 1946, Stalin told Communist Party faithful in the Bolshoi Theatre that the country must undertake a major industrial and scientific effort to prepare for "any eventuality," a phrase that was interpreted in the West to mean that he seriously considered another world war.

Containment

When an alarmed US State Department asked the American embassy in Moscow to analyse Stalin's speech of February 1946, diplomat George Kennan responded with the so-called Long Telegram, one of the most important documents of the cold war. Kennan traced Soviet belligerency all the way back to the Russian czars, who like the communists felt a deep sense of inferiority *vis-à-vis* the politically and economically advanced West and hence developed a paranoid worldview in which Russia was surrounded by enemies hell-bent on its destruction. Supercharged by Marxist ideology, Kennan argued, these beliefs prompted the Soviet regime to deny the possibility of peaceful coexistence with non-communist countries and see itself in a perpetual state of war with the Western world. Despite his bleak assessment, Kennan stressed that the Soviet problem could be solved without military conflict or expensive rearmament. Emphasising that communism is like a "malignant parasite which feeds only on diseased tissue," he proposed social and economic policies "to solve internal problems of our own society, to improve self-confidence, discipline, morale and community spirit of our own people." Positing that Soviet rulers were averse to unnecessary risks and susceptible to a "logic of force," he urged the consistent application of economic, political, and military pressure to prevent the further spread of communism and ultimately to bring about the downfall of communism in Eastern Europe and the USSR itself. America's tasks in this life-and-death struggle were obvious to Kennan: To harness its formidable resources at home, create a sense of unity and purpose abroad, and demonstrate the superiority of Western-style capitalism and democracy through a systematic reconstruction of war-torn Europe.

The harsh reality of post-war Europe was a world removed from Kennan's vision. Millions of refugees displaced by armed conflict and ethnic cleansing searched for shelter, food, and lost relatives in Eastern and Central Europe. Large German urban industrial areas that had long constituted a vital core of the European economy lay in ruins, making recovery a distant dream. France, another powerhouse of the pre-war European economy, was bled white by years of German occupation and torn by deep political divisions. Britain, exhausted from a world war that exceeded its economic resources, was struggling to provide for the basic needs of its people at home, fend off national independence movements in its colonies, prop up client states, and maintain its occupational zone in Western Germany. To make things worse, the extraordinarily harsh winter of 1946–47 left tens of millions of hungry Europeans huddling in the cold amidst burned-out ruins.

The political implications of complete social collapse were deeply worrisome to Kennan and other American policymakers who feared that abject poverty created a fertile ground for the rise of communism and the growth of Soviet influence in Europe. Amidst the post-war devastation and chaos, communist parties in France and Italy attracted support with promises that government management of the economy along the lines of the Soviet model would produce an increased standard of living for the great majority. Once in power, Kennan feared, communist governments would align their foreign policies with those of the Soviet Union and effectively deliver their countries to Stalin on a silver platter. As a result, the USA would find itself economically and strategically isolated in an increasingly hostile world with dire consequences for its domestic economic and political order.

This bleak scenario paved the way for the containment doctrine against the backdrop of a foreign policy drama that unfolded in the Eastern Mediterranean. Since the end of World War II, a Greek communist guerrilla organisation had waged a brutal civil war against a right-wing government in Athens that received financial and military support from Britain, which sought to maintain a pro-Western government in order to safeguard the approaches to the British-held Sues Canal. In early 1947, however, Britain drastically curtailed its presence in the Eastern Mediterranean as well as globally in response to a deepening financial crisis that led to food and fuel shortages at home, leaving Britons hungry and cold amidst raging blissards. In February, the British informed the Americans that they would terminate their support for Athens' struggle with the Greek communists. Was America prepared to take on the burden of financial and military assistance to the right-wing Greek government, and, by implication, assume the mantle of global leadership of the Western world as a superpower (see concept box)?

Superpower

The term "superpower" connotes a nation whose vast military, economic, and political resources enabled it to project its influence on a global scale. The concept's earliest proponents included William Fox, an American professor of foreign policy and author of the book *The Super-Powers: The United States, Britain, and the Soviet Union* (1944) which argued that the three nations named in the title could shape the fortunes of the entire world, in contrast to the more regional influence exercised by traditional "great powers" like France, Imperial Germany, and Austria-Hungary in the nineteenth century.

Later definitions of the term gradually excluded Britain from the ranks of superpowers as its global influence waned with the dissolution of the Empire after World War II, reserving the term exclusively for the USA and the Soviet Union. Paul Dukes, a British professor of history, argued that a superpower had to be capable of enunciating a universal ideology, for example, Soviet communism. Other proponents of the term define superpowers as combining immense land masses, large populations, enormous economic resources, strategic capability, and the ability to project both "hard power" (military) and "soft power" (political and cultural influence) around the world.

The question received attention at a senior-level meeting between Truman, the US State Department, and Congressmen who controlled the funds necessary for any major departure in American foreign policy. Leaders of the Republican Party, which had recently taken control of both houses of Congress in the midterm elections of 1946, were initially in no mood to appropriate money for an initiative that would be exceedingly costly for the American taxpayer and was proposed by Truman, a Democrat. Moreover, many Republicans were committed isolationists who worried that Truman's plan to assist Athens would propel American foreign policy down a path of Wilsonian internationalism that had produced disastrous results after World War I.

The domestic sense of unity and purpose Kennan had urged in the Long Telegram seemed beyond reach during the leadership meeting until Assistant Secretary of State Dean Acheson intervened. The civil war waged by the Greek communist guerrillas, he claimed, was part of Stalin's strategy to gain strongholds in the Eastern Mediterranean, the Middle East, and North Africa that threatened Western interests on all three continents. "The Soviet Union [plays] one of the greatest gambles in history at minimal cost," Acheson insisted, implying that America must raise the stakes or fold. This line of reasoning convinced key Republicans to support US aid to countries that faced the communist threat, fostering the sense of domestic political unity Kennan deemed vital for the success of containment.

Capitalising on the growing sense of cold-war bipartisanship, Truman unveiled the containment doctrine in a speech to Congress in March 1947. Explaining his request for $400 million in military aid for Greece and Turkey, he urged Americans to assist "free peoples who are resisting attempted subjugation by armed minorities or by outside pressures." Congress shortly appropriated funds to supply the Greek military with weapons and ammunition, and the US military provided training, air support, and logistics.

In addition to adopting the containment doctrine, the Truman administration established a national security apparatus that played a key role during the cold war and beyond. First, the National Security Act of 1947 merged the old departments of war and the navy into the newly formed Department of Defense, which also included the US Air Force as an independent service. Headquartered in a five-sided building near to Washington DC called the Pentagon, the Department of Defense sought to improve civilian control of the armed services and coordinate their activities. Second, the act created the National Security Council (NSC) in the White House to help the president formulate foreign and military policies independent of the Department of State, which was considered too narrowly focused on diplomacy and too averse to more aggressive policies. Truman initially took only passing interest in the NSC but gave it greater prominence after the outbreak of the Korean War (see next section), when he made it the principal advisory body in the executive branch of government on national security. Third, the National Security Act of 1947 created the Central Intelligence Agency (CIA), a civilian organisation that was tasked with the collection and analysis of secret intelligence collected overseas to assist the president. Initially a small-scale operation that assumed intelligence-gathering functions the Office of Strategic Services had performed in World War II, the CIA vastly expanded its scope and scale during the Korean War to include covert operations, guerrilla training, and the overthrow of foreign governments.

The Marshall Plan and the division of Europe

In addition to requesting military aid to contain communism in the Eastern Mediterranean, Truman's speech of March 1947 laid the groundwork for the Marshall Plan, also known as the European Recovery Program (ERP) of US economic assistance for post-war reconstruction. Echoing Kennan's assessment that communists exploited the wretched economic and social conditions in post-war Europe to further their own agenda, Truman noted "The seeds of totalitarian regimes are nurtured by misery and want. They spread and grow in the evil soil of poverty and strife." Europe's post-war squalor accordingly called for an American aid package to stabilise the stricken continent and provide European governments with the tools necessary for economic recovery, argued Britain's Foreign Secretary Ernest Bevin, the project's senior European promoter. A proposal to this effect, drafted by Kennan and others, was introduced by US Secretary of State George Marshall in a speech at Harvard University in June 1947 inviting European governments to develop economic recovery plans that could be financed by the USA. Though phrased in less combative terms than Truman's containment speech, Marshall's proposal included a warning that American economic aid would not be available to governments that blocked the recovery of other countries – a thinly disguised jab at the Soviet Union, whose insistence that Germany pay war reparations could easily be construed as sabotage of German economic reconstruction efforts. Though Moscow was theoretically eligible for American aid, "The Marshall Plan was offered to the Soviet Union with the intention that it would be turned down," Kennan later acknowledged.

The Marshall Plan marked a watershed in US-Soviet relations and a point of no return in the escalation of the cold war. As expected, the Soviets rejected the aid offer when they learned that the Americans insisted on certain conditions before making Marshall Plan funds available to potential applicants. First, only countries that did not extract war reparations from Germany would be eligible because reparations drained the German economy of resources that were regarded as critical for European economic recovery by US policymakers. The Soviet Union would not be eligible for Marshall Plan aid unless it dropped its demands for German war reparations. Second, the aid programme would be centrally managed by American administrators in collaboration with the British, raising the spectre of Anglo-American officials reviewing Soviet economic statistics and demanding changes in government policy before disbursing recovery funds. Stalin regarded the proposed procedure as an unacceptable infringement on Soviet state sovereignty and ordered foreign minister Molotov to reject it outright on behalf of the Soviet Union in July 1947. Moreover, Stalin was determined to prevent Eastern European countries under Soviet control from participating in the Marshall Plan because he feared that Truman would use American aid to penetrate Eastern Europe economically and erode Soviet influence. Poland, Romania, Yugoslavia, Bulgaria, Albania, Hungary, and Finland ultimately rejected American aid. In Czechoslovakia, the communists crushed the last vestiges of democracy during a *coup d'état* in February 1948, followed shortly by the death under suspicious circumstances of foreign minister Jan Masaryk, the last non-communist member of an Eastern European government. The countries of Eastern Europe turned from a Soviet sphere of influence into subservient satellite states where communists ruled with an iron fist for the next four decades. Important exceptions included Finland, which maintained strict neutrality in the cold war but developed a democratic-capitalist order domestically, and Yugoslavia, a communist-ruled country in southeastern Europe that maintained friendly relations with the West.

In Western Europe, the CIA sabotaged democratic elections to stop the spread of communism and grease the skids for the Marshall Plan. One covert operation targeted Italy, where the communists assembled a coalition of left-wing parties that was widely expected to win parliamentary elections in April 1948. Kennan told US diplomats in Europe, "If the communists win elections there, our whole position in [the] Mediterranean, possibly in Europe as well, would probably be undermined." To forestall that possibility, CIA operatives arrived in Italy with "bags of money that we delivered to selected politicians, to defray their political expenses, their campaign expenses, for posters, for pamphlets," one agent later recalled. Soviet agents distributed modest amounts to the communists but could not compete with the CIA, which supplied $10 million (mostly laundered funds taken from seized Nazi accounts) to the right-wing Christian Democrats who won the elections, formed Italy's first post-war government, and promptly applied for Marshall Plan aid.

In the USA, Congressional debate of $13 billion economic aid package under the European Recovery Program hastened the transformation of American foreign policy that had begun with the passage of military aid to Greece and Turkey in 1947. During the initial debates in early 1948, the ERP came under heavy political fire from isolationists mainly in the Republican Party who objected to the idea of the USA taking a leadership role in world affairs on an unprecedented scale; conservative fiscal hawks worried that Marshall Plan aid would contribute to American budget deficits; some leftists saw the programme as a manifestation of American economic imperialism designed to benefit big business; conservative economists objected to the use of government funds instead of private savings and capital accumulation for European reconstruction. ERP proponents responded that Congressional failure to pass the programme would lead to the complete collapse of the European economy and a possible communist takeover of major countries in the region, with dire consequences for American national security; some argued that the Marshall Plan would benefit the US export economy by stimulating Western European demand for American goods; others noted that the Marshall Plan built on a tradition of generous American aid to people in need, notably the American Relief Administration that provided food for starving Europeans and Soviets after World War I. Champions of the initiative were encouraged by growing support for the ERP in the American public as opinion polls indicated that a clear majority favoured its passage. The communist *coup d'etat* in Czechoslovakia meanwhile convinced influential Republicans to endorse the ERP. In March 1948, a broad bipartisan coalition in Congress passed the Marshall Plan with comfortable margins, consolidating a cold-war consensus among many Republicans and Democrats who agreed that the USA should take an active leadership role in world affairs. Congressional approval of the Marshall Plan also dealt a major blow to isolationist sentiments that had pervaded American politics for more than a century.

The Marshall Plan had a mixed impact on the American and Western European economies, but on balance the results were positive. Staggering food and fuel shortages among the 17 nations that received aid compelled plan administrators to divert significant amounts of American agricultural and coal production from the domestic market to Western Europe, contributing to a higher US inflation rate, but on the whole the US economy proved quite capable of meeting the increased demand. Indeed, the Marshall Plan served as a stimulus package for major American industries because Congress mandated that ERP participants had to spend more than two-thirds of their assistance in the USA. Equipped with American-made locomotives, harbour cranes, and machine tools, Western Europe achieved the fastest growth rate in its history for the duration of the Marshall Plan from 1948 to 1951 as industrial production increased by one-third, unemployment fell rapidly, the standard of living increased, and American technical advisors taught European managers to adopt advanced production practises that had been pioneered in the USA. Though most recipients of Marshall Plan aid were grateful (a Dutch poll taken in 1948 revealed that 85 per cent of the population liked the programme), some felt "humiliated and indignant at the thought that they may now be reduced to accepting American charity," one observer noted. Importantly, the ERP

Figure 13.2 Marshall Plan aid arriving in Hamburg, Germany, 1948.

Source: Courtesy of INTERFOTO/Alamy

contributed to the integration of Germany's western regions into the wider European economy through the Organization for European Economic Cooperation (OEEC), founded in April 1948 to coordinate the distribution of Marshall Plan aid, develop intra-European trade, and promote a division of labour among the 16 member states. Within this framework, Western Germany was to become a hub of the European capital goods sector that would supply other ERP recipients with machine tools and other engineering products. In Germany's western regions, American, British, and French occupation authorities introduced a new currency, the Deutschmark, to curb inflation, encourage industrial production, and pave the way for an eventual merger of the three occupational zones into West Germany to create a viable democratic state with a capitalist economy that could fulfil its designated economic function in Western Europe.

The currency reform triggered the Berlin Blockade of 1948–49 that brought the USA and the USSR close to military conflict in the first major confrontation of the cold war. In June 1948, the Western powers announced plans to introduce the Deutschmark in the three Western occupation zones of Berlin controlled by the USA, Britain, and France, respectively, which were located deep inside the Soviet occupation zone in Eastern Germany. Stalin deemed the introduction of the Deutschmark in Berlin unacceptable because he saw it as a first step towards the creation of a West German state to which he objected fiercely. In June 1948, the Soviets blocked access by land and water to the Western part of Berlin and conducted military exercises, precipitating fears of their takeover of the city by force. Since Western attempts to break through the land blockade would have likely resulted in armed conflict with Soviet forces, the USA responded to Stalin's attempt to starve the Western occupation zones in Berlin into submission with an airlift in which American transport planes loaded everything from food and coal to pharmaceuticals and powdered milk in Western Germany, flew across the Soviet occupation zone in the east, and landed in Western Berlin for unloading. Though some worried that Soviet attempts to disrupt the airlift would result in World War III, the Soviets contented themselves with diplomatic protests and finally reopened the land and water routes from the Western occupation zones in Germany and Berlin in 1949. By then, Stalin's attempt to bend the West to his will had created enormous resentment against the Soviet Union throughout Western Europe and hastened the formation of West Germany, which was officially founded in May 1949 only weeks after the blockade had ended. The Soviet Union responded a few months later with the formation of communist East Germany.

The Berlin Blockade also contributed to the formation of the North Atlantic Treaty Organization (NATO), an alliance between the USA, Canada, and ten Western European states. In the minds of many Americans and Europeans, Stalin's conduct during the Berlin crisis raised the spectre of future Soviet attempts to threaten vital Western interests that could end in armed conflict. American and Canadian participation, forcefully promoted by Britain's Foreign Secretary Ernest Bevin, was considered vital because Western Europe was militarily too weak to resist the Soviet military threat, but membership in a full-fledged military alliance was far from uncontroversial in the USA. Isolationists in Congress objected to the idea of collective defence that was central to the concept of NATO, whose proponents regarded an attack on one member nation as an attack on all. Senator Robert Taft, former President Herbert Hoover, and other isolationists argued that collective defence would mean that the USA could find itself at war in order to fulfil its treaty obligations without a formal declaration of war by Congress (similar arguments had contributed to the defeat of the League of Nations Treaty in the US Senate in 1920; see Chapter 9). Moreover, the establishment of a Western alliance would force the USA to spend significant amounts of money on arms to assist allies that were too poor to pay for their own defence, leaving the American taxpayer to shoulder most of the financial burden. Lastly, American NATO membership ran counter to a long tradition in US foreign policy that avoided alliances with foreign countries (the USA had only once entered into military alliance in order to obtain French support for the American Revolution; see Chapter 3). Though isolationist arguments were endorsed by significant portions of the American public, Taft, Hoover, and their political allies found little support in Congress, where a bipartisan coalition had gathered strength ever since Republicans and Democrats had appropriated military aid for Greece and Turkey in 1947. The US Senate ratified the

NATO treaty by a comfortable margins in July 1949. The collective defence clause was invoked only once throughout the history of NATO in response to the terrorist attacks on the USA on 11 September 2001, providing a justification for NATO participation in the war in Afghanistan and other military operations.

China and Korea

The late 1940s and early 1950s witnessed an intensification of the cold war as the USA confronted a communist revolution in China, the development of a Soviet atomic bomb, and the Korean War. These events, in addition to dragging Asia into the vortex of superpower competition, had a profound effect on Europe, where the USA significantly increased its military presence and pulled a rearmed West Germany into NATO.

In China, a long-simmering conflict between Nationalist forces led by Chiang Kai-shek and the communists under Mao Zedong climaxed in the late 1940s. Having agreed on a temporary truce to fight the Japanese occupation of China during World War II, the two sides resumed their civil war in 1946. While the Nationalists received $2 billion in US aid because Truman worried about a possible communist seizure of power, Soviet assistance to the Chinese communists was miniscule because Stalin had territorial ambitions in Asia that did not coincide with theirs. Mao nevertheless managed to equip his troops with captured Japanese weapons, enabling them to inflict a crushing defeat on the Nationalists at the battle of Liaoshen. In 1949, Chiang withdrew to the island of Taiwan off China's east coast to establish the Republic of China and Mao proclaimed the People's Republic of China (PRC) on the mainland, turning the world's most populous nation into a communist country. Though some American policymakers had considered this outcome likely, the "loss of China" rankled the Truman administration, which was confronted with Republican charges that it had done too little, too late to prevent Chiang's defeat. Extremist Republicans went so far as to claim that Communist sympathisers in the US State Department had deliberately sabotaged the Nationalists in order to facilitate Mao's victory. In truth, the Truman administration went to great lengths to isolate the Chinese communists internationally, refused to extend diplomatic recognition to the new regime, and engineered the PRC's exclusion from the United Nations. These policies were reversed only in the early 1970s by Republican President Richard Nixon (see Chapter 16).

The communist seizure of power in mainland China coincided with a successful Soviet test of an atomic bomb that ended the American monopoly on nuclear weapons, fuelling suspicions of communist subversion in the USA. Soviet agents indeed recruited scientists who worked in the Los Alamos National Laboratory in New Mexico who supplied the USSR with information that enabled Soviet researchers to develop a bomb that was tested successfully in the Kazakh desert in August 1949, years earlier than Western analysts had expected. Though the Soviet Union was as yet unable threaten the USA with a nuclear attack because it did not possess the prerequisite long-range bombers, many observers warned that mere possession of nuclear technology would embolden Stalin. National Security Council memorandum NSC-68 urged the administration to respond to Soviet atomic bomb making potential with vast increases in American defence spending and the development of a hydrogen bomb that was hundreds of times more destructive than an atomic weapon, but Truman shelved the proposal in April 1950.

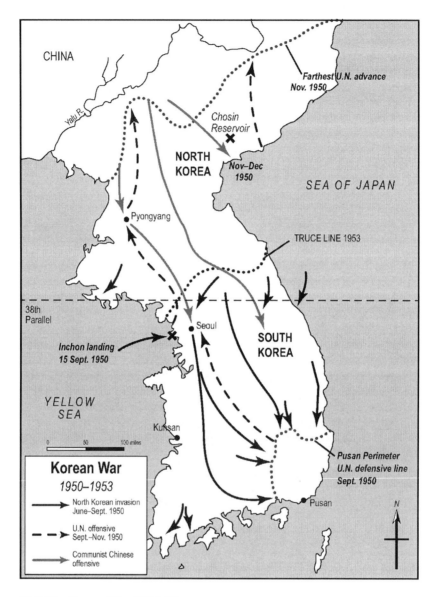

Figure 13.3 The Korean War, 1950–53.

Doomsayers who predicted a fresh round of communist aggression felt vindicated when North Korea invaded South Korea in June 1950, less than a year after the Soviets had broken the American nuclear monopoly. After World War II, the USA and the USSR had divided the Korean peninsula along the 38th parallel into a communist North under dictator Kim Il-Sung and a pro-American South ruled by President Syngman Rhee. Seeking to exploit popular dissatisfaction with the partition among the Korean people, Kim planned to invade the South and informed Stalin in April 1950 that he wanted to reunify the country under communist auspices. The

Soviet dictator liked the idea but worried that American forces could intervene before the North Koreans could complete their conquest, warning Kim, "If you should get kicked in the teeth [by the Americans], I shall not lift a finger. You have to ask Mao for all the help." Having obtained Mao's reluctant approval, Kim ordered his troops to cross the 38th parallel on 25 June 1950. The South Korean army suffered a series of defeats during the subsequent engagements and withdrew southwards.

North Korean aggression prompted swift US intervention, much as Stalin had feared. Truman, who was under the false impression that the invasion had been instigated by Stalin, worried that American inaction would encourage Soviet-engineered aggression in other parts of the world. Immediately after the North Korean invasion had begun, the United Nations Security Council condemned the attack and authorised United Nations military action to force North Korea to withdraw from the South (the Soviet Union as a permanent member of the Security Council with veto powers was unable to derail these resolutions because it boycotted the Security Council at the time to protest communist China's exclusion from the United Nations). Truman ordered American forces under the United Nations flag to land on the peninsula in order to support the retreating South Korean army. In August 1950, Congress appropriated $12 billion – almost as much as for the entire Marshall Plan – for the Korean War, indicating American determination to beat back the North Korean offensive.

The Korean War became a see-saw struggle for control of the peninsular that eventually provoked Chinese military intervention. The situation initially looked bleak for United Nations and South Korean forces, which were driven all the way to the southeast, barely hanging on to a perimeter around the port city of Pusan. The tide turned in September 1950, when US Marines under the command of General Douglas MacArthur landed at Inchon on the east coast of the peninsular near to the 38th parallel, threatening to cut off North Korean troops that besieged Pusan. To avoid capture, the North Koreans pulled back to the 38th parallel under a hail of American bombs that destroyed most of their equipment. Having restored South Korean government control, MacArthur then crossed the 38th parallel into North Korea with the blessing of US Defense Secretary George Marshall, captured the North Korean capital Pyongyang, and pursued the enemy all the way up north to the Sino-Korean border along the River Yalu. These developments rattled the nerves of Chinese communist leaders who worried that continued American victories could imperil their own regime at home. With limited Soviet support, the Chinese Army attacked along the River Yalu and drove American and other United Nations forces back south of the 38th parallel. Here the fighting stalemated and continued for another two years before a ceasefire was signed, re-establishing the status quo that had existed before the war.

Impact of the Korean War

The war had profound consequences for American foreign and defence policies. Most important, Truman approved the national security policy laid out in the NSC-68 memorandum he had tabled when the National Security Council had originally submitted it shortly before the outbreak of the Korean War. NSC-68, written primarily by State Department official Paul Nitze, claimed that the Soviet Union sought global dominion and was in the process of developing "military capacity to support its design for world domination." Seen from this perspective, the North Korean invasion appeared as the USSR's first attempt to erode American power by military means. According to NSC-68, the situation warranted a massive increase in US defence spending over the long haul in order to develop sufficient military capabilities "to check and to roll back the Kremlin's drive for world domination" through a "policy of calculated and gradual coercion" and by creating "situations of strength," which denoted US military interventions in regions faced with Soviet aggression. Though the authors of NSC-68 carefully avoided mentioning of specific amounts to be spent on military rearmament, their recommendations implied a tripling of the US defence budget to $50 billion annually. As a result of such lavish military spending, the size of the US Army doubled to three and a half million men, the US Navy received new aircraft carriers unequalled in size and fighting power, and the US Air Force procured new types of intercontinental bombers that could lay waste on the Soviet Union with hydrogen bombs. Moreover, the armed forces established a network of military bases across the globe that provided the USA with control of the air and the sea.

Some American policymakers worried at the time that NSC-68 exaggerated the Soviet threat, underestimated extant US strength, and damaged the civilian economy. George Kennan, the author of the containment doctrine, doubted that the Soviets planned to achieve world domination by military means. Others insisted that the Soviet Union would be unable to achieve victory in a global conflict; in a Third World War, the USA would mobilise its industrial might just as it had in the Second World War and turn the conflict into a war of attrition in which the Soviet economy would eventually collapse. From this point of view, the massive peacetime military build-up advocated by NSC-68 was largely unnecessary. Lastly, the enormous size of American defence budgets fostered the rise of a military-industrial complex of companies dependent on military spending that diverted valuable economic and technological resources from the civilian sector, a development that deeply worried Dwight D. Eisenhower, Truman's Republican successor in the presidency (see Chapter 14). Hindsight largely confirms the validity of these objections, but the fact remains that NSC-68 became the blueprint for America's heavily militarised cold war strategy.

In Asia, the Korean War set in motion Japan's recovery as the US armed forces ordered vast amounts of materiel for the war effort from Japanese companies, with momentous consequences for economic development in the twentieth century. Japanese industrial production had plunged from 1945 to 1950, partly because American occupation authorities imposed tight restrictions on industrial conglomerates called *zaibatsu* that had produced military hardware for Japanese forces in World War II. These constraints fell away at the start of the Korean War, when the USA began to order massive amounts of supplies for its forces in Korea, injecting $3.5 billion into the Japanese economy (twice the amount West Germany received under the Marshall Plan). Industrial production doubled from 1949 to 1953. Major beneficiaries included companies such as Toshiba, Nikon, and Mitsubishi that later became household names in consumer markets. Toyota was saved from bankruptcy when the US Army ordered 1,500 lorries a month from the company, which used the profits to branch out into civilian production and later became the world's largest carmaker. Moreover, the Korean War prompted a large-scale recalibration of US economic policy in the Pacific Rim as the Truman administration encouraged Malaysia, Indonesia, and the Philippines to supply Japanese manufacturers with raw materials. This was a stunning reversal because the USA had fought the Pacific War in part to prevent Japan from gaining control of Southeast Asia, precisely the region that was now pulled into Japan's economic orbit to provide a bulwark against communism.

Third World

The phrase "Third World" was first introduced by the French social scientist Alfred Sauvy in 1952 to designate developing countries that were not aligned with the "First World" (NATO countries) or the "Second World" (communist bloc countries). Sauvy's definition referenced eighteenth-century France, where the "Third Estate" comprised of common people rebelled against the "First Estate" of noblemen and the "Second Estate." He hoped that the First World would sympathise with the Third World's "slow and irresistible thrust, humble and ferocious, to life. Because that Third World, ignored, exploited, despised like the Third Estate also wants to be something."

Representatives of African and Asian countries, mostly former colonies that gained independence after World War II, met in 1955 at the Bandung Conference in Indonesia, where they castigated Western and Soviet attempts to interfere in Third World affairs, condemning "colonialism in all of its manifestation." The Bandung Conference was a step towards the formation of the Non-Aligned Movement (NAM) in 1961 comprised of India, Indonesia, and other developing countries that pledged respect for territorial integrity, resistance to imperialism, adherence to non-violent conflict resolution, and mutual cooperation. The NAM frequently criticised American and Soviet foreign policy, notably the USA's quasi-colonial control of Puerto Rico.

Events in Korea had a profound impact in the Third World, where the USA began to support anti-Communist regimes (see dialogue box). After World War II, anti-colonialist movements forced European powers to abandon their holdings, notably India which gained independence from Britain in 1947 and the former Dutch colony of Indonesia in 1949. In light of the fact that the USA itself traced its roots to an anti-colonial struggle during the American Revolution, some nationalist leaders expected to win US support for their attempts to drive the Europeans out and establish independent states. These hopes were often dashed because US foreign policy makers who perceived events in the Third World through the lens of the cold war feared that the Soviet Union would fill the power vacuum that resulted from the decline of European imperialism with communist regimes. After the outbreak of the Korean War, the USA supported a variety of European attempts to cling to their colonial claims and installed pro-Western regimes. In Vietnam, for example, a nationalist movement headed by communist Ho Chi Minh declared independence from France in 1945 citing the American Declaration of Independence of 1776. A year later, when the French tried to regain control of their former colony, Ho begged Truman "to interfere urgently in support of our independence" but received no reply because the USA did not want to alienate France, its ally in Europe. A day after the North Korean invasion of South Korea, however, the USA provided $15 million in military aid for France's fight to against Ho's independence movement, which Secretary of State Acheson portrayed as an integral element of Soviet aggression against the West. Over the next four years, the USA financed 80 per cent of the French war effort, and after France had been defeated militarily by the nationalists in 1954, the anti-Communist Ngo Dinh Diem won rigged elections in South Vietnam and established an autocratic regime with the support of the CIA. Thus the Korean War, combined with containment in the Third World, paved the way America's deepening involvement in Vietnam, which escalated further with the deployment of US ground forces in the 1960s (see Chapter 15).

The Korean War also resulted in seismic shifts in Western Europe, where the USA called for the rearmament of West Germany. Fearful that the North Korean invasion was merely a prelude to communist aggression in Europe, the USA requested that the NATO allies raise their military spending, but their $8 billion in defence expenditures for 1951 were deemed insufficient to deter the Soviet threat. Seeking to capitalise on West Germany's economic prowess, Secretary of State Dean Acheson demanded that country's remilitarisation and its integration into NATO. Though many Western European NATO members initially balked because they had suffered at German hands in World War II, they grudgingly acquiesced to Acheson's plan and West Germany joined NATO in 1955. Further bolstering its commitment to the defence of Western Europe against possible Soviet aggression, the USA stationed four army combat divisions in West Germany and eventually deployed thousands of nuclear weapons on its territory.

The Red Scare

In addition to transforming American foreign policy in Europe and Asia, the cold war had a deep impact on domestic affairs due to fears of communist spying and subversion. Concerns about Soviet intelligence activity on American soil were far from unfounded as some US government officials passed considerable amounts of top-secret information to Soviet intelligence officers. The notion of subversion also implied active sabotage of American foreign policy on behalf of the USSR and pro-Soviet propaganda in the American media, but little evidence exists that this was actually the case. Most historians agree that proponents of such beliefs, notably Senator Joseph McCarthy, vastly inflated the threat to further their own political ambitions and besmirch the reputation of their political opponents.

Soviet intelligence enlisted important figures in the American political establishment who began their careers in the 1930s as informants. Working in collaboration with the Communist Party of the USA, intelligence officers in the Soviet embassy in Washington recruited individuals who were sympathetic to the idea of a "popular front" of liberals and communists against fascism during the New Deal. Enlistees who worked in high-level government positions, including Assistant Secretary of the Treasury Harry Dexter White and Alger Hiss of State Department, passed sensitive documents to their Soviet handlers. The Soviet spy Klaus Fuchs, a communist refugee from Germany who researched uranium enrichment at the Los Alamos laboratory in New Mexico, supplied the USSR with technical information on American atomic bomb design. Most of this activity ceased after World War II, either because the recruits changed their minds about the wisdom of spying for the USSR, changed careers, or were arrested. Soviet archival material released after the end of the cold war documents that the USSR's spy networks ceased to function by the late 1940s, much to the frustration of intelligence officials.

In 1947, Truman instituted the Loyalty-Security Program, the first initiative of its kind in American history that led to investigations of three million government employees. His motives were entirely political. During Congressional elections the previous fall, Republicans had successfully used the charge that Democrats were soft on communism to gain electoral advantage with their slogan "Communism vs.

Republicanism." Only weeks after the election, Truman established a commission to develop loyalty standards, even though he was privately convinced that "the country is perfectly safe so far as Communism is concerned." Launched with much fanfare in March 1947 shortly after Truman had announced the containment doctrine, the Loyalty-Security Program empowered the Federal Bureau of Investigations (FBI) to investigate all current and prospective federal employees; activities as trivial as having participated in a communist-organised rally decades before sufficed as grounds for dismissal from federal service. More than 300 government workers were fired, and another 5,000 resigned voluntarily.

The anti-Communist crusade of the early cold war years also involved the US House of Representatives' Un-American Activities Committee (HUAC), which expanded the scope of investigations from government employees to the entertainment industry. It gained notoriety in 1947, when it cited ten Hollywood screenwriters and directors for contempt of Congress because they refused to testify about their links to the Communist Party, despite the fact that the party was a legal political organisation and their refusal to testify was legal under the Fifth Amendment to the US Constitution, which protected witnesses from self-incrimination. The Hollywood Ten were blacklisted in the entertainment industry and were denied employment by major studios. In 1948, HUAC investigated Alger Hiss, a former State Department official who had become president of the Carnegie Endowment for International Peace after the war. In his testimony before HUAC, he falsely denied accusations that he had passed sensitive documents to a Soviet spy early in his career. The investigation created much visibility for California Congressman Richard Nixon, a leading member of HUAC who began his meteoric rise on the right wing of the Republican Party. Hiss's eventual conviction and imprisonment for perjury also enhanced the credibility of HUAC and those who shared its proclivities.

The Red Scare intersected with a "Lavender scare" that targeted gay and lesbian officials. Led by Republican Senator H. Styles Bridges, it exploited widespread homophobia whose protagonists claimed that homosexuals were vulnerable to blackmail because Soviet intelligence could threaten to "out" them unless they betrayed US government secrets, even though there was virtually no evidence for such blackmail attempts by foreign powers. Hundreds of gays and lesbians lost their State Department jobs, often as a result of bizarre accusations (a secretary claimed her supervisor was lesbian because she had "peculiar lips, not large but odd-shaped"). Army astronomer Frank Kameny, who lost his US Army job after he refused to answer questions about his sexual orientation, later became a leading gay rights activist and the first openly gay candidate for Congress in 1971.

The FBI under its director J. Edgar Hoover who had spearheaded the First Red Scare after World War I (see Chapter 10) played a key role in the anti-communist witch hunt of the post-war era. Hoover illegally made confidential information collected during the Loyalty-Security Program available to HUAC and harassed the left-leaning National Lawyers Guild, whose members were among the few solicitors willing to provide legal representation to victims of McCarthyism. FBI agents conducted more than a dozen burglaries of the organisation's office to steal files and handed their loot to prosecutors who used them to tailor their trial strategies.

The US Senate took centre stage in the Red Scare during the early 1950s, when anti-Communist rhetoric reached grotesque proportions. The preamble to the Subversive Activities Control Act of 1950, which prevented communists from obtaining passports and permitted the forced deportation of radical foreigners, stated scurri-lously "World Communism has as its sole purpose the establishment of a totalitar-ian dictatorship in America, to be brought about by treachery, infiltration, sabotage, and terrorism." Named the McCarran Act in honour of Democratic Senator Patrick McCarran of Nevada, the legislation established the Senate Internal Security Subcom-mittee headed by McCarran himself that spent most of its time investigating the Insti-tute of Pacific Relations, whose members included experts in Asian affairs. During the late 1940s, these so-called China Hands had predicted the communist victory in the Chinese civil war and recommended that the State Department establish contact with the Chinese communists in order to exploit their differences with the Soviets. The McCarran committee accused Owen Lattimore, the leading China Hand, of being "a conscious and articulate instrument of the Soviet conspiracy" and claimed that the group was responsible for the "loss of China."

These claims were echoed by Republican Senator Joseph McCarthy of Wisconsin, who announced during a speech in Wheeling, West Virginia, "I have here in my hand a list of 205. . . a list of names that were made known to the Secretary of State as being members of the Communist Party and who nevertheless are still working and shaping policy in the State Department" (McCarthy later changed that number to 57 but then raised it to 81). As chair of the Senate Permanent Subcommittee on Investigations, he alleged that communist sympathisers in the State Department, the Department of Defense, and the Democratic Party systematically sabotaged American foreign policy to benefit of the Soviet Union. His most prominent targets included former Secre-tary of State George Marshall, whom he charged with responsibility for the "loss of China." Among McCarthy's strongest supporters were the Roman Catholic Church hierarchy and members of the prominent Kennedy family of Boston, whose patriarch Joseph Kennedy, Sr., was one of McCarthy's closest friends (his son Robert F. Ken-nedy served as legal counsel for McCarthy's Senate subcommittee). Some Republi-cans privately expressed unease with McCarthy's methods but backed him publicly to capitalise on his good relations with Roman Catholics as well as many Italian and Irish Americans, all key constituencies that had historically supported the Democratic Party but looked favourably on McCarthy's endeavours. His downfall came in 1954, when he conducted hearings on subversives in the US Army that were televised, giv-ing Americans a first-hand look at his peculiar methods and his support declined. In December 1954, the US Senate censured him for conduct unbecoming a member of Congress. The measure that ended his career was engineered by Democratic Senator Lyndon B. Johnson of Texas; Senator John F. Kennedy, Democrat of Massachusetts, contrived to miss the vote.

Though some protagonists of the Red Scare exited the scene, the episode left a bitter legacy. Hundreds of directors, screen writers, and actors dragged before HUAC had their careers ruined. Fears that the same fate would befall others who explored contro-versial issues like racial segregation turned Hollywood film making into a bland affair for much of the 1950s. The McCarran and McCarthy investigations' claims that criti-cal thinkers like the China Hands were responsible for the "loss of China" instilled fears among foreign policy analysts who did not dare to point out obvious problems in US foreign policy, notably American support for autocrats like Ngo Dinh Diem in South Vietnam. The anti-Communist witch hunt also tarnished America's image in the West: Britain's *New Statesman* magazine called McCarthy "a grotesque and unpleas-ant feature of American public life" who epitomised "a deep social malaise" in the

USA. Important facets of the anti-communist crusade remained in place for decades. When the US Supreme Court limited the government's ability to prosecute communists and other "subversives," the FBI in 1956 instituted the Counter Intelligence Program (COINTELPRO) that targeted radical political groups with surveillance, illegal wire-taps, and tax audits to sabotage their organisations. CONITELPRO quickly expanded the scope of its activities to include the civil rights movement of the 1950s and 1960s, focusing on activists like Martin Luther King, Jr., who were suspected of communist sympathies (see Chapter 15).

Domestic politics and the waning of social reform

The cold war cast a long shadow over liberal aspirations to extend the reform impulse of the 1930s into the post-war period. Time and again, ambitious proposals for government-sponsored universal health care, full employment, federal aid to education, and similar initiatives met defeat at the hands of conservatives who argued successfully that liberal reforms amounted to state socialism – the very menace America sought to defeat worldwide in its confrontation with the Soviet Union. As a result, liberal reform efforts produced only meagre results by the end of Truman's tenure in January 1953.

Truman initially embraced an ambitious social reform agenda initially formulated by Franklin Roosevelt in 1944 called the "Second Bill of Rights." Key items, notably the right to employment, income, housing, healthcare, and education, required substantial government involvement in post-war economic and social affairs that provoked strong opposition. A liberal bill that obligated the federal government to achieve full employment by means of extensive economic planning and public works programmes, for example, was denounced by Republicans, conservative Democrats, and business lobbies as a tool to strangulate free enterprise. After much debate, a watered-down version of the legislation resulted in the Employment Act of 1946 that eliminated the original bill's declaration of a "right to employment," aimed at "maximum employment" rather than "full employment," and stressed the role of private business rather than government in achieving these goals.

The left-leaning trade union movement of the Congress of Industrial Organizations (CIO), which had strongly supported the Employment Act's original version, suffered a series of other setbacks. Having agreed to wage controls in World War II, it demanded significant increases after the war, launching massive strikes in the steel, railway, and coal industries that met with a hostile response from Truman, whose worries about inflation prompted him to ask Congress to for legislation that would allow him to draft the strikers into the army and thus terminate their job action. Contempt for organised labour by a Democratic president was followed by "Operation Dixie," an ambitious CIO attempt to unionise Southern workers that failed due to racism and anti-Communist sentiments among many whites. The 1946 Congressional elections meanwhile resulted in Republican majorities in the House of Representatives and the Senate that passed the stridently anti-union Taft-Hartley Act of 1947. Rolling back rights the labour movement had gained during the New Deal, Taft-Hartley permitted states to outlaw mandatory union membership, banned financial contributions by unions to federal elections, and empowered the president to intervene into strikes during national emergencies. Importantly, the Taft-Hartley Act required union officials to swear anti-Communist affidavits, in effect forcing the unions to expel radical leftists who had played a significant role in the rise of the CIO.

The New Deal coalition that had been instrumental in achieving Democratic victories during the 1930s splintered during the 1948 presidential elections. While the Democratic Party nominated Truman, leftists who were dissatisfied with his anti-Communist foreign policy and his anti-union stance during the strike wave of 1946 formed the Progressive Party that supported former cabinet member Henry Wallace, whose pursuit of friendly relationships with the Soviet Union caused him to oppose the containment doctrine and the Marshall Plan. Southern conservative Democrats, dismayed Truman's executive order to desegregate the armed forces, formed the so-called States Rights Party known as the Dixiecrats ("Dixie" is a designation for the Southern states) who favoured white supremacy. Though pollsters predicted confidently that the three-way split of the Democrats would ensure the election of Republican nominee Thomas Dewey, Truman eked out a victory with a campaign that lambasted his right-wing opponents as enemies of the New Deal and the left-leaning Progressives as communist sympathisers.

In his state of the union address of January 1949, Truman announced a fresh catalogue of reform proposals that included universal health care, civil rights legislation, expanded social security, public housing, and other progressive measures, only few of which were eventually enacted. His plan for a single-payer compulsory health care system was designed to provide comprehensive coverage for the vast majority of American who lacked health insurance. Lobbying groups that had defeated similar proposals in the past mobilised a massive campaign that labelled Truman's plan "socialised medicine." The powerful American Medical Association, a professional organisation of physicians, claimed that "Truman's health insurance plan would make doctors slaves" and that the president's aides were "followers of the Moscow party line." Opposed by Republicans and conservative Democrats, the Truman proposal suffered a crushing defeat in Congress. Most other Fair Deal proposals shared the same fate, except an expansion of Social Security and a public housing programme enacted in 1949. The following year, rising defence expenditures for the Korean War left preciously little money for new initiatives, repeating a failure of domestic reforms due to war that was a common feature of American history, journalist Walter Lippmann commented later: "in every war this century, the internal movement of reform and development has been stopped by war. The First World War did that to Theodore Roosevelt's Progressivism and Wilson's New Freedom. The Second World War did it to the New Deal. The Korean War did it to Truman's Fair Deal." And at the time of Lippmann's writing in 1966, the Vietnam War "is now doing that to Johnson's Great Society," a reference to President Lyndon Johnson's ambitious social reform programme called Great Society that foundered on the shoals of American military involvement in Southeast Asia (see Chapter 15).

A comparison of post-war domestic reforms in the USA and Britain sheds light on important characteristics of the American political scene. Truman's inability to pass most of his Fair Deal stood in stark contrast to the successful passage of the British Labour Party's socialist reform programme, which was in some respects considerably more radical than its American counterpart. In addition to enacting a welfare scheme that provided state pensions, unemployment benefits, and sickness insurance, Labour nationalised the railways, coalmines, and the steel industry. American liberals looked on with envy when the government of Prime Minister Clement Attlee established universal medical coverage under the National Health Act of 1948 in a single-payer system, a socialist policy that was initially supported by some members of the Truman administration. Labours' success under Attlee was largely attributable to the fact that the party was unified in its determination to enact its reforms, in contrast to the Democratic Party, which was badly divided between a liberal and a conservative Southern wing that often sided with Republicans. Moreover, Labour possessed huge majorities in the House of Commons, unlike the Democrats, who constituted a minority in Congress for most of Truman's presidency. Lastly, Labour's aggressive embrace of the label "socialist" did not alienate a large portion of Britain's public whereas most Americans did not distinguish between socialism and communism, opening the door wide for right-wing propaganda that discredited many Fair Deal reform proposals with cold war rhetoric.

Chapter summary

This chapter chronicled growing tensions between the USA and the Soviet Union that led to the cold war in Europe and Asia with profound consequences for global affairs and America's domestic political order. Strains in their relationship were already evident in World War II, when the delay of the Second Front raised Soviet suspicions about American intentions and proliferated in disagreements over the post-war European order, particularly the fate of defeated Germany and the future of Eastern Europe at the Potsdam Conference in 1945. Soviet domination of Eastern Europe caused Kennan and other American policymakers to worry that the USSR planned to control the western half of the continent as well, giving rise to the containment doctrine and the Marshall Plan that led to the division of Europe, which solidified with the establishment of West Germany and the NATO alliance in 1949. American confidence that Soviet expansionism had been successfully curbed was shattered by the Chinese Revolution and the Korean War, both of which were incorrectly viewed as Soviet-engineered attempts to bring Asia under the complete control of the USSR. In response, the USA involved itself deeply in Asian affairs, intervened militarily in the Korean War, resurrected Japan, and buttressed France's efforts to maintain its control of Vietnam. Adopting a policy of massive military rearmament, the USA also encouraged West Germany's integration into NATO in 1955. In addition to transforming American foreign policy, the cold war had a deep impact on domestic affairs as anti-Communist hysteria became a lever to gain political advantage and defeat liberal reforms.

Discussion questions

- Why is the post-war confrontation between the USA and the Soviet Union called the "cold war"? What other phrases would be appropriate?
- How did Truman contribute to the cold war? What was Stalin's role?
- Was America's adoption of the containment doctrine justified?
- Why was the Berlin crisis so dangerous?
- How did the USA profit from the Marshall Plan?
- What was the impact of the Korean War?
- What were the domestic ramifications of the cold war and specifically the Korean War?

Further reading

Alperovitz, Gar. *The Decision to the Use the Atomic Bomb* (New York, 1996). A classic and controversial study by a leading revisionist historian who argues that the atomic bombing of

Hiroshima and Nagasaki was intended by the Truman administration to render the Soviets more amenable to American post-war plans for Europe.

Cumings, Bruce. *The Korean War: A History* (New York, 2010). Written by a leading authority of the Korean War, this study examines the conflict in the global context of the cold war.

Gaddis, John Lewis. *We Now Know: Rethinking Cold War History* (Oxford, 1997). Using recently declassified American and Soviet sources, this magisterial study argues that American foreign policy makers pursued a largely prudent and realistic strategy *vis-à-vis* the Soviet Union and built an "empire of invitation" in Western Europe.

Harbutt, Frazer. *The Cold War Era* (Malden, MA, 2002). A well-written introductory overview of the cold war from the Truman presidency to the end of the Soviet Union in 1991.

Johnson, David K. *The Lavender Scare: The Cold War Persecution of Gays and Lesbians in the Federal Government* (Chicago, IL, 2004). This groundbreaking study documents the long-neglected history of post-war LGBT persecution in the context of the Red Scare.

La Feber, Walter. *America, Russia, and the Cold War, 1945–2006* (New York, 2006). This classic account of superpower relations demonstrates how domestic politics shaped American containment strategies.

Leffler, Melvyn. *A Preponderance of Power: National Security, the Truman Administration, and the Cold War* (New York, 1993). This massive and detailed study of the early cold war argues that the USA exploited its vast economic and strategic superiority over the Soviet Union and dominated Western Europe.

Takaki, Ronald. *Hiroshima: Why America Dropped the Atomic Bomb* (San Francisco, 1996). A short and highly readable survey of one of the twentieth century's most controversial decisions.

Williams, William Appleman. *The Tragedy of American Diplomacy – 50th Anniversary Edition* (New York, 2009). Originally published in 1959, this controversial revisionist interpretation of American foreign policy argues that an aggressive US foreign policy in Europe and elsewhere triggered the cold war.

Zubok, Vladislav, and Constantine Pleshakov. *Inside the Kremlin's Cold War: From Stalin to Khrushchev.* (Cambridge, 1996). A critical examination of Soviet cold war policy from 1945 to the Cuban Missile Crisis of 1962.

14 Prosperity and crisis in the 1950s

Timeline

1951	First transcontinental television broadcast
1952	Republican Dwight Eisenhower elected president
	Republicans control US Senate and House of Representatives
1953	Korean War armistice
	Department of Health, Education, and Welfare formed
1954	US Supreme Court decision in *Brown v. Board of Education* mandates desegregation of public schools
	Secretary of State John Foster Dulles announces massive retaliation strategy
	Geneva Accords separate North and South Vietnam
	Democrats win control of US Senate and House of Representatives
1955	Montgomery Bus Boycott
	American Federation of Labor merges with Congress of Industrial Organizations
1956	Elvis Presley appears in the Ed Sullivan television show
	Suez Crisis
	Congress passes National Interstate and Defense Highways Act
1957	Launch of Soviet Sputnik satellite
	High school desegregation in Little Rock, Arkansas
1958	Congress passes National Defense Education Act
	Sit-in protests in Wichita, Kansas
1959	Steel strike idles major portions of US economy
1960	Greensboro, North Carolina, sit-ins
	John F. Kennedy elected president

Topics covered

- The economic boom
- America's economic empire
- Consumer society
- Youth culture
- The Americanisation of Western culture
- The liberal consensus and the politics of the 1950s
- Eisenhower and the cold war
- The civil rights movement

Introduction

Chapter 13 opens with Elvis Presley appearing on the Ed Sullivan Show in 1956 and the frenzied public reaction, both positive and negative, to his socially and culturally transgressive performance. The incident epitomises three of the chapter's principal themes: domestic tensions, youth culture, and consumerism in 1950s America. Upon examination of the post-war economic boom that transformed middle-class life in America and the Western world, the chapter introduces the concept of the "liberal consensus" to analyse mainstream politics. The era witnessed escalating international tensions. Republican President Dwight D. Eisenhower (1953–1961) distanced himself from the dramatic expansion of defence budgets under Truman and ushered in the New Look in US foreign policy. His administration emphasised nuclear diplomacy and covert intervention that saw US intervention in Iran and elsewhere as the cold war spread into the Middle East. The chapter places particular emphasis on the civil rights movement, which shook the country out of its complacency by exposing the disparities between the principles and practises of American democracy.

Elvis Presley: symbol of age

When rock star Elvis Presley burst onto the American music scene in 1956, he was instantly engulfed in controversy because many people felt offended by his sexually suggestive performances. *Look* magazine complained that he "wiggles like a peep show dancer," *Life* magazine indicted his "bump and grind routine," and other commentators were appalled by "the fans' unbridled obscenity, their gleeful wallowing in smut." Many parents echoed these sentiments after Presley's first appearance in the popular Ed Sullivan television show in 1956, when a record-breaking 60 million viewers watched his hip gyrations as he performed "Love Me Tender." After the show, the CBS television network was flooded with letters that called Presley's performance lewd, vulgar, and woefully inappropriate for a family show. The show's producers, worried that Presley's follow-up performance in January 1957 would create another firestorm, told their cameramen to film his torso only from the hip up to keep the offending hips out of the picture. Host Ed Sullivan introduced Presley as "a real decent, fine boy" and a "nice person" as the star walked on stage with his distinctive hairstyle and eye makeup that sent teenagers into a screaming frenzy when he performed his hit song "Don't Be Cruel," later followed by the gospel song "Peace in the Valley."

The episode highlights the emergence of a rebellious youth culture that proved difficult to contain by parents and teachers who preached conformity with conservative values during the 1950s. Presley's unconventional performance style challenged notions of chastity, modesty, and proper self-control middle-class parents sought to instil in their progeny. In addition to his suggestive body language, Presley offended many because his performance was inspired by African American gospel, rhythm and blues, and jazz (people who listened to him on the radio in fact often assumed he was black). This was bound to be controversial in a society where racial segregation remained the norm and crossing the "colour line" was considered subversive. Conservative radio hosts who feared "race mixing" refused to play Presley's songs, and many Southern towns denied him permission to hold concerts. None of this prevented

Figure 14.1 Elvis Presley's controversial performance during *The Ed Sullivan Show*, 1956.
Source: Courtesy of PictureLux/The Hollywood Archive/Alamy

committed Elvis fans from buying his records by the millions, making him one of the most successful American artists of the twentieth century.

At the same time, rock 'n' roll culture was deeply embedded in a mainstream consumer culture that was a hallmark of the 1950s. In addition to spending money on concert tickets, albums, and transistor radios, fans expended sizable amounts on fashionably slim trousers, hair products, and leather jackets. Presley and other rock 'n' roll stars owed much of their fame and notoriety to television, a new technology found in middle-class homes that served as the main conduit of mass consumerism. In more ways than one, rock 'n' roll culture encapsulated both rebelliousness against and conformity to American bourgeois values.

Interpreting the 1950s: "Age of Complacency" or "The Best of Times"?

Historians, social critics, and political commentators have developed sharply divergent interpretations of the fifties. Those who perceive an "Age of Complacency" include Derek Bo of Harvard University, who notes "in the 1950s lots of very legitimate problems in the United States were simply ignored: poverty, the environment, women's rights, and civil rights. Nostalgia for the 1950s is an emotional feeling, but it doesn't stand up under analysis." Conservative political activist Paul Weyrich disagrees, charging that "the elite media convinced the country that the 1950s were a terrible time. As a matter of fact it was the best time that we had in my lifetime. The family was in good shape. It was a great time to be an entrepreneur. You didn't have any revolutionary activity."

The way people view the decade depends on their time horizon and analytical perspectives. In the short run, post-war business strategies contributed to an economic boom that produced wealth and prosperity for millions of Americans. From the point of view of most middle- and working-class whites, the fifties had much to offer, notably stable employment, rising wages, affordable housing, and access to consumer goods. Only the benefit of hindsight reveals that business strategies that appeared safe and sound at the time actually contributed to long-term problems that left the American economy poorly prepared for an onslaught of foreign competition in later decades. Moreover, those who see the fifties as an "Age of Complacency" detect social deficiencies from the perspective of minorities, women, and urban dwellers. The post-war boom produced only limited benefits for African Americans and women eager to join the professions because both groups encountered employment discrimination in the vibrant core of the US economy. The outmigration of the white working class from cities into suburbs drained cities of financial resources and left behind an increasingly impoverished urban population with little access to decent housing. Egregious deficiencies were visible from the perspective of African Americans who suffered as a result of legal segregation and their exclusion from Southern ballot boxes.

The economic boom

The period from the late 1940s to the mid-1960s was characterised by a preponderance of US corporations in world markets that was sustained by American-dominated economic institutions. Moreover, many companies commercialised a range of technological innovations from television sets to microchips and adopted a variety of advanced business strategies such as product diversification that broadened their scope and scale. Escalating military spending during the cold war meanwhile gave rise to a burgeoning defence sector called the military-industrial complex. As a result, growing segments of the white middle and working classes enjoyed stable employment and rising wages that enabled them to buy their own homes in suburban developments.

American exports benefitted from government efforts to develop global trade, which had suffered before World War II as a result of currency depreciation and protectionism. At the United Nations Monetary and Financial Conference in Bretton Woods, New Hampshire, delegates from 45 countries met in 1944 to negotiate a system of fixed international exchange rates in which the currencies of participating countries were pegged to the U.S. dollar, which in turn was convertible into gold (one British pound sterling, for example, bought $2.80 during the 1950s; $35 bought one ounce of gold). Member governments committed themselves to complementary monetary policies by controlling inflation and ensuring price stability within their respective national economies. To compensate for a temporary imbalance of payments, a member country could apply for loans to the International Monetary Fund, which was founded at the Bretton Woods Conference and primarily financed by the USA. Fixed exchange rates benefitted mostly American businesses that could export to and invest in Western Europe and elsewhere without having to worry about losing money as a result of currency fluctuations. The General Agreement on Tariffs and Trade facilitated global commerce by lowering tariffs and trade barriers, enabling US companies to export more freely (see concept box). American exports almost doubled during the fifties, contributing to a major trade surplus.

General Agreement on Tariffs and Trade (GATT)

Established at Geneva, Switzerland, in 1947 under US leadership, GATT sought large-scale reductions of trade barriers. It was a policy response to the unprecedented breakdown of global trade during the Great Depression as a result of protectionism, notably the USA's Smoot-Hawley tariff of 1930 and Britain's system of Imperial Preferences of 1932 that privileged trade within the Commonwealth and hurt US exports. Initially joined by 23 countries, GATT gradually expanded to include 123 nations, by the 1980s, that agreed to cut tariffs, reduce subsidies, and protect intellectual property rights in order to foster global economic integration. GATT was succeeded by the World Trade Organisation in 1995 that provided mechanisms to settle conflicts between member nations, often in collaboration with the International Monetary Fund (IMF).

US business also benefitted from a "scientific-technological revolution" as companies commercialised existing inventions and their research departments developed new ones. The sale of television sets, whose base technology predated World War II, skyrocketed as declining per-unit costs made them more affordable; the share of homes equipped with a television set grew from 9 per cent in 1950 to 87 per cent in 1960. A key factor in this success story was the introduction of microwave transmitters that made it possible to broadcast shows live across the USA. Leading consumer electronics companies that controlled most of the market for television sets included RCA, General Electric, and Zenith (the latter pioneered the hand-held remote control). Closely related developments included the invention of the electronic transistor in 1947 by William Shockley of Bell Laboratories, whose research built on work for the military in World War II. The transistor, a microchip that amplified electrical signals, replaced heat-intensive vacuum tubes in mainframe computers, whose size and energy consumption fell dramatically during the 1950s as manufacturers mass produced the new devices. The mechanical engineering industries meanwhile commercialised the jet engine, a revolutionary propulsion system first introduced in World War II that permitted jet planes to travel at twice the speed of comparable propeller aircraft. Jet engines gained popularity in civilian passenger liners with the introduction of Boeing's 707 on long-distance routes, notably those across the Atlantic, where carriers like Pan American Airlines offered luxurious nonstop service from New York to Paris in nine hours, about the same time it takes today.

Technology development was usually embedded in broader corporate diversification strategies as firms expanded their product lines to insulate themselves from boom-and-bust cycles. Diversification enabled companies to avoid excessive dependence on a single product line; the profitability of products that faced growing demand could offset losses in market segments where demand slowed. For example, an engineering company that produced turbines for electric power plants branched out into jet engines, based on the expectation that when demand for electric power equipment was down, demand for jets would be up and vice versa. As a result, product diversification could smoothen out a company's financial performance and prevent excessive losses. Companies that embarked on this strategy in the 1950s diversified into sectors that were closely related to their existing core business. The Philadelphia-based Philco Corporation, for example, a specialty manufacturer of radios and batteries, gradually expanded into other product lines that required expertise in electrical engineering, including air conditioners, refrigerators, television sets, and transistorised computers for military and scientific applications. In 1960, it received a government contract to build and operate tracking systems for the National Air and Space Administration's manned spaceflight programme.

Major segments of the American economy were dominated by only a handful of firms, creating a market form called oligopoly. This was particularly evident in industries that required large investments into physical plants, making it difficult for small start-up companies to gain a foothold. Lack of competition often contributed to complacent business strategies in oligopolies that resulted in slowdowns of technological innovation. In the steel industry, which was dominated by U.S. Steel, Bethlehem, Jones & Laughlin, and Republic Steel, the "Big Four" churned out one-quarter of world steel output with tried-and-proven production methods but neglected investments into new technologies. Their profits remained healthy during the 1950s because the oligopoly followed U.S. Steel, which served as a price leader, but the strategy left the industry poorly prepared for the onslaught of foreign competition in the 1960s, when Japanese steel makers elbowed their way into the American market with lower prices and high-quality steel usually produced in modern electric furnaces. Similar dynamics were evident in the post-war car market, which was controlled by an oligopoly comprised of General Motors, Ford, and Chrysler after smaller companies like Studebaker and Packard declined. Partly due to reduced competition, the "Big Three" car makers significantly increased their profitability during the 1950s and 1960s, but like the steel makers, they were ill-prepared for the entry of foreign car companies into the American market. Their failure to develop fuel-efficient engines came back to haunt American automobile companies as skyrocketing gasoline prices caused budget-conscious consumers to look for small cars imported from West Germany and Japan in the 1970s (see Chapter 16). Oligopolistic market forms, in short, served American companies well during the 1950s and early 1960s, but they contributed to difficulties later on.

Defence contractors profited from heavy peacetime spending that created the military-industrial complex. Military spending remained at high levels even after the fighting in Korea ended in 1953, never falling below 10 per cent of Gross National Product (GNP) for the remainder of the decade. This marked a sharp break with defence spending prior to World War II, when the USA had rarely devoted more than 1 per cent of GNP to defence during peacetime. The high level of defence spending attracted companies that were prepared to produce the high-performance military hardware demanded by the armed services, including Boeing (bombers and land-based missiles), General Dynamics (submarines), and Lockheed (submarine-launched missiles). In some instances, highly specialised firms enjoyed a quasi-monopoly in their respective fields, for example Newport News Shipbuilding, a builder of nuclear-powered aircraft carriers. On the downside, defence contractors accustomed to building expensive high-performance systems for the military faced enormous difficulties in civilian markets, where customers paid close attention to prices. Lockheed, for example, maker of sophisticated spy satellites, proved unable to meet civilian demand for standard communication satellites because its products were overdesigned and too expensive. Companies that derived a large share of their overall profits from military contracting had a manifest interest in high levels of defence spending. To ensure that defence dollars kept rolling their way, they lavished campaign donations on Congressmen and Senators who voted for large defence appropriations, most notoriously Senator Henry Jackson from Washington state, home to Boeing Company in Seattle. Jackson's highly successful efforts to keep the company supplied with a steady flow of contracts for B-52 bombers and Minuteman intercontinental ballistic missiles earned him the nickname "Senator from Boeing." Jackson and others like him could brag to their constituencies that they helped to create well-paying jobs in their home districts. Congress also facilitated arms exports to America's Western European allies that peaked at $15 billion in 1953.

Economic growth created millions of stable, remunerative jobs in core sectors of the US economy, raising the standard of living for large segments of the working class as the unemployment rate rarely exceeded 6 per cent even during the mild recessions that occasionally punctuated post-war prosperity. The unionisation of semiskilled labour during the New Deal enabled these workers to gain high wages that had traditionally been reserved for skilled mechanics. The United Automobile Workers (UAW), one of the nation's largest unions with a membership of one and a half million of mostly semiskilled workers, wrested major concessions from employers under the leadership of Walter Reuther. Reuther sought higher wages and better benefits in a series of confrontations with the Big Three automakers. Instead of threatening all three with strikes at the same time, he used "divide and conquer" tactics by concentrating his efforts on the one company that was most likely to grant concessions. In 1949, Ford agreed to establish a fully funded pension plan to avoid a labour conflict. When Chrysler refused to adopt the same policy, the UAW conducted a 104-day strike that ended with concessions from management. Contract negotiations with General Motors, which was anxious to avoid a strike, yielded not only a fully funded pension plan along the lines of the Ford and Chrysler contracts, but also health coverage for General Motors' employees and their families that was eventually adopted by Ford and Chrysler. George Meany, the president of the American Federation of Labor and

Congress of Industrial Organizations told the organisation during its merger in 1955, "American labor has never had it so good." Trade unions paid a hefty political price for these material achievements: Prodded by the Taft-Hartley Act of 1947, which required organisers to reject communism, labour leaders purged unions of Communist Party members who had been prominent in establishing industrial organisations during the New Deal (see Chapter 11).

United Automobile Workers (UAW)

Founded in 1935 during the New Deal, the UAW was one of America's largest and influential industrial unions that organised workers regardless of their skill, in contrast to traditional craft unions whose membership consisted of skilled workers. It rose to prominence in a series of sit-down strikes that forced the General Motors Corporation and other major car makers to recognise the UAW as a collective bargaining agent. Having gained hundreds of thousands of new members during World War II, the UAW abandoned its long-standing demand for shorter work hours during the post-war era to focus on higher wages and improved benefits like health insurance. Its membership and influence declined in the 1970s, when the American automobile industry lost major market shares to Western European and Japanese car makers.

Confrontations between management and labour occasionally assumed massive proportions and produced stunning gains for unionised workers. The United Steelworkers (USW), which gained large concessions on wages and benefits during fifties, demanded union control of workplace regulations in 1959. When management balked, the union launched a 116-day strike that crippled not only the industry itself but also sectors that depended on steel deliveries, idling 300,000 automobile and railroad workers. (To compensate for the lack of domestic supplies, automakers imported steel from Japan and Western Europe, whose market share in the USA doubled during the strike and continued to grow afterwards.) In the middle of the conflict, Eisenhower invoked the Taft-Hartley Labor Act of 1947 that authorised him to force labourers back to work and imposed an 80-day cooling-off period to give labour and management an opportunity to negotiate under government supervision. The resulting contract included some management concession on work rules and boosted hourly wages, enabling American steelworkers to earn five times as much as their West German counterparts.

Wages also grew because the American workforce well educated. The Servicemen's Readjustment Act of 1944 (popularly known as the GI Bill of Rights) funded the education of returning veterans, enabling three and a half million to attend vocational and technical schools, in addition to 2.2 million who went to college. Government funding of tuition expenses helped educate hundreds of thousands of tradesmen and engineers, as well as doctors, scientists, and teachers whose earning power increased dramatically. In 1960, the number of white-collar employees exceeded that of blue-collar workers for the first time in American history, inaugurating a trend that continued into the twenty-first century.

America's economic empire

US businesses dominated the global economy on an unprecedented scale, producing a staggering 60 per cent of world manufacturing output in 1950. Partly attributable to the crippled condition of other leading industrial economies after World War II, America's share in global industrial production began to shrink during the 1950s as the Western European and Japanese economies recovered, but a considerable share of industrial development overseas was directly or indirectly related to American initiatives.

Most important, many US corporations resumed a course of multinational expansion by establishing manufacturing facilities in foreign countries, continuing a trend that dated to the 1920s. In the two decades after World War II, American firms were responsible for more than 80 per cent of Foreign Direct Investments (FDI) worldwide by acquiring foreign subsidiaries or building up operations from scratch. The lion's share of American FDI initially went to Britain, where the absence of language barriers enabled US multinationals to accustom themselves to foreign markets, communicate easily with fellow managers and customers, and deploy marketing and advertising methods similar to those prevalent in the US domestic market. For example, Pfizer Corporation, a leading American drug maker, built a pharmaceutical factory in Folkstone, Kent, and acquired the London-based chemical manufacturer Kemball Bishop & Company as well as the Exning Biological Institute that specialised in the development of animal health products. As a result of similar initiatives, American FDI soon accounted for more than 10 per cent of Britain's total investments into research and development. Having acclimatised themselves to foreign cultural and regulatory environments via their British operations, many American multinationals set their eyes on continental Europe. After 1957, when the establishment of the European Economic Community (EEC) hastened the development of a common market, American FDI usually targeted sectors with significant growth potential, notably pharmaceuticals and chemicals, plastics, computers, and aluminium. Over the next half-decade, more than 3,000 US multinationals acquired companies or established subsidiaries in EEC countries, cementing America's dominance in key sectors. In Rotterdam's Europoort, the new shipping gateway into Western European markets, Dow Chemical, Esso, and Gulf Oil built major port facilities. These trends worried critics who charged US multinationals with economic imperialism. The French journalist Jean-Jacques Servan-Schreiber wrote in 1967, "Fifteen years from now it is quite possible that the world's third greatest industrial power, just after the USA and Russia, will not be Europe, but American industry in Europe. [Today, the] European market is basically American in organization."

During the 1950s, American economic dominance extended beyond exports, direct control of major industries, and technology transfers. Prodded by American reformers who were determined to encourage oligopolistic competition, most Western European governments began to restrict the cartels that had long dominated continental markets and the European Economic Council outlawed them in cross-border trade. Faced with the American challenge, moreover, many Western European businesses selectively adopted management systems and production techniques that had been pioneered by US firms earlier in the twentieth century. Some introduced decentralised corporate structures pioneered by the DuPont Chemical Corporation and General Motors, where product divisions enjoyed operational autonomy from headquarters in managing factory operations and marketing. Others embraced Henry Ford's emphasis on parts standardisation and high volume production. West Germany's Volkswagen Corporation, perhaps Europe's most Americanised automobile manufacturer, mass-produced a small, simple, and fuel-efficient passenger car called the Beetle in assembly line formats that closely resembled Ford's production techniques for the Model T decades earlier in Detroit. Sold by the hundreds of thousands to economy-minded car buyers, the Beetle faced little competition largely because General Motors and Ford neglected the development of economy-sized automobiles, leaving the market segment to Volkswagen. American failure to offer an alternative to the Beetle proved a costly mistake in the US domestic market, where Volkswagen became the first foreign car-maker to make serious inroads during the early 1960s.

Consumer society

In the USA, the economic boom created enormous amounts of purchasing power that fuelled the growth of consumer society as real incomes grew by more than 20 per cent over the course of the decade. The percentage of American families owning their homes increased from 55 per cent (1950) to 62 per cent (1960) and spending on advertising doubled. Americans bought consumer durables (defined as household items that lasted for more than two years) like refrigerators, vacuum cleaners, washing machines, and above all automobiles. The number of cars on American roads grew from 43 million (1950) to 68 million (1960), mostly chrome-encrusted petrol guzzlers sporting tailfins and V-8 engines. Clever marketers introduced the concept of dynamic obsolescence into the automobile market, where annual model changes encouraged consumers to buy new cars every few years so they could "drive in style."

The automobile was also a key factor in the rapid development of suburbs. Suburban neighbourhoods had been a central feature of metropolitan growth since the late nineteenth century, when streetcar suburbs had emerged on the outskirts of major cities to house white-collar employees and their families. Unlike streetcar suburbs, post-war suburban developments rarely featured public transport systems and instead required automobiles to get to and from work, go shopping, or visit entertainment venues. The new concept found its earliest expression in Levittown, New York, in 1947, when the real estate developer William Levitt applied mass-production techniques he had learned as a government contractor in World War II to residential home construction. Located 25 miles east of Manhattan on Long Island, the site originally featured potato farms and trees that were bulldozed and replaced with concrete slabs spaced 60 feet apart. Each foundation accommodated a box-shaped, single-family home in the Cape Cod style with two bedrooms, a kitchen, one bathroom, and an unfinished attic but no garage or cellar, making the Levittown house far less spacious than a traditional home located in a streetcar suburb. The average monthly mortgage payment of $60 for a Cape Cod was 40 per cent less than the rent for a small flat in New York City, luring thousands of working-class people to the sales office to take advantage of the opportunity to own a Levittown home. Each home came equipped with a washing machine and an eight-inch television set, and the town included playgrounds, swimming pools, supermarkets, and a Roman Catholic Church. Like other suburban real estate developers, Levitt sold homes only to Caucasians who had to pledge not to resell to members of other races, a policy that was endorsed by the Federal Housing Administration, which did not insure mortgages in racially mixed neighbourhoods.

Figure 14.2 Mass-produced homes in Levittown, Long Island, where Levitt's company sold 17,400 units, making Levittown the largest suburban development ever constructed by a single American builder.

Source: Courtesy of Ewing Galloway/Alamy

The federal government played other roles in suburban development in addition to sponsoring racial segregation. The GI Bill of Rights enabled veterans to obtain home loans with no money down by providing free mortgage insurance through the Veterans' Administration, which also loaned money directly to former servicemen. Equally important, the federal tax code included a mortgage interest deduction clause that enabled home owners to subtract the interest they paid on their mortgages from their taxes. Lastly, the Eisenhower administration initiated the construction of the 40,000-mile Interstate Highway System that connected many suburbs to urban centres and rural areas (when the initiative was launched in 1956, there were only few four-lane motorways outside of New York, Chicago, and Los Angeles).

The vast majority of suburban residents, who comprised one-third of the nation's population by the end of the 1950s, consisted of families with three or more children. This reflected an unusual demographic trend called the Baby Boom that lasted from 1946 to 1964 as female fertility rates increased to the consternation of many researchers, whose population models predicted that rising wealth correlated with a lower birth rate because more affluent adults needed fewer children to meet their needs in old age. America's post-war baby boom, a rare exception to that overarching trend, was partly attributable to the decision of many couples to make up for lost time after fertility rates had dropped during World War II, when millions of men were separated from their wives and girlfriends. Moreover, the marriage age dropped by several years after the war so that the average family size increased from 3.1 children in 1950 to 3.8 in 1960. Child raising changed dramatically with the publication of the *Common Sense Book of Baby and Child Care* (1946) written by the paediatrician Benjamin Spock, who urged young mothers to replace the sometimes harsh methods of earlier generations with greater affection and attention to a youngster's particular needs. "Every time you pick your baby up, even if you do it a little awkwardly at first, every time you change him, bathe him, feed him, smile at him, he's getting a feeling that he belongs to you and you belong to him," Spock wrote. "Nobody else in the world, no matter how skilful, can give that to him." Sold more often than any book except the Bible, the *Common Sense Book* also discouraged the age-old practise of enforcing a strict sleep schedule and counselled mothers to hold their babies when they cried at night.

While Spock's approach was in many respects innovative, it also implied that a mother should be readily available to tend to her child's needs at all times, discouraging women from leaving the home to seek regular employment or pursue a career. This reinforced conventional gender norms that had been partly suspended in World War II, when women were encouraged to work in factories and shipyards in order to contribute to the war effort. During the 1950s, many women were happy as stay-at-home mothers and wives, but many others missed the sense of independence and camaraderie they had experienced while working in wartime factories, only to be told after 1945 to go home, raise children, wait for their husbands to come home, and be content with the material benefits of suburban life. The labour force participation of married women with school-aged children actually increased to almost 40 per cent in 1960 as mothers with school-age children took low-paying jobs in the service sector, but such choices were actively discouraged in mainstream culture. The hugely popular sitcom "Leave it to Beaver," for example, portrays a suburban family headed by white-collar employee and sole breadwinner Ward Cleaver whose conviction that "a woman's place is in the home" is shared by his wife June, who spends her days cleaning the house, cooking, and raising their sons. The fact that June's obvious contentment with her role often did not square with the reality of suburban life was revealed in author Betty Friedan's path breaking study *The Feminine Mystique* (1963). Aiming to explore "the problem that has no name," the book documents widespread discontent among stay-at-home mothers and wives who led emotionally and intellectually unfulfilling lives, often keeping busy just to avoid having to confront their feelings of boredom and emptiness. Friedan's elucidation of stifling gender norms was widely lauded in the American and Western European press, even if some commentators deemed her book exceedingly dour. Britain's *Economist* magazine noted that the case against gender inequality "needed to be made; women, like Negroes, have too often been given equal rights in name only. . . . Unfortunately, [Friedan] displays the same feminine failings as did [French feminist Simone] de Beauvoir in the Gallic version of the same case – humourlessness, righteousness and running on too long."

Critics of consumer society included members of the "Beat Generation," a group of bohemians who were influenced by Jean-Paul Sartre and other French existentialists. "Beat" literature broke with mainstream norms, explored Buddhist spirituality, and encouraged experiments with narcotics. Prominent writers included Allen Ginsberg, whose poem "Howl" (1956) denounced the materialism of American life while lionising jazz musicians, drug addicts, and mental patients as "the best minds of my generation." Jack Kerouac's novel *On the Road* (1957), a defining piece of beat literature, explores the friendship and adventures of two dropouts during their travels from New York City to San Francisco in search of meaning, music, sex, and drugs. Overseas, Ginsberg, Kerouac, and other beat authors received considerable attention in underground Dutch and West German literary magazines that republished their writings, which were often dismissed as lewd and obscene by mainstream culture.

Youth culture

Middle-class teenagers faced enormous pressures to conform to rigidly defined social and cultural ideals. Parents and schools imposed strict dress codes on young women, who were expected to wear buttoned-up blouses and calf-length skirts or dresses; approved hairstyles were limited to ponytails and permanent waves, while short haircuts were frowned upon as unladylike. Young women who were encouraged by parents and teachers to seek a college education enrolled on courses that prepared them for careers in teaching, nursing, and other "female" professions. Many attended all-women colleges that taught not only academic skills but also proper table manners, good posture, and conversation skills that would attract prospective husbands without conveying excessive cleverness. Teenage boys received instructions to wear trousers and button-down shirts along with crewcuts instead of jeans and long hair. Like their fathers who often attended institutions of higher learning under the GI Bill, middle-class sons frequently attended colleges that granted degrees in accounting, engineering, the sciences, and other disciplines demanded by prospective employers. Both sexes were told in no uncertain terms that premarital sex was out of the question.

While middle-class teenagers faced pressure to meet strictly defined notions of proper dress and comportment, they also enjoyed a degree of material comfort unheard-of by their parents who had grown up during the Great Depression. Thanks to parental generosity and part-time jobs, teens amassed enormous purchasing power that attracted the attention of publishers, advertisers, and film producers. *Life* magazine reported in 1959, "American teen-agers have emerged as a big-time consumer in the US economy. Counting only what is spent to satisfy their special teen-age demands, the youngsters and their parents will shell out about $10 billion this year, a billion more than the total sales of [General Motors]." Teenagers spent a staggering $1.5 billion a year on magazines, comic books, film and concert tickets, and records alone. Businesses that sought to profit from such largesse included *Seventeen* magazine, founded in World War II to promote values such as responsible citizenship and hard work among young women. Recalibrating its focus during the 1950s, *Seventeen* concentrated more on cosmetics and fashion advice, romance, and courtship, blazing a trail for dozens of new teenage magazines like *Modern Teen*, *Confidential Teen Romances*, and *Teen Today* that appealed to a similar readership. Male teenagers were drawn to superhero comic book series such as Superman, Batman, and Human Torch. Teenage car ownership soared over the course of the decade, precipitating the development of drive-in restaurants and cinemas, where young couples could find privacy. Hollywood film producers who began to lose adult audiences to television during the 1950s offered a broad array of big-screen productions specifically targeted at teenagers, including "Life Begins at 17," "High School Confidential," and "Teenage Zombies."

Adults often felt disconnected from youth culture and suspected the worst of teenagers who congregated outside of homes and schools beyond the reach adult supervision. The Federal Bureau of Investigation reinforced these fears with reports that 54 per cent all car thefts in the USA were committed by perpetrators 18 years or younger. The US Senate investigated the contribution of comics, films, and television to juvenile delinquency, and though its report took the media to task for idealising sex and violence, it was unable to establish a widely suspected link between comic book reading and teenage crime. As a result, the public's obsession with juvenile delinquency faded as quickly as it had emerged.

The existence of a semi-independent youth culture continued to trouble many parents and social commentators who were horrified by the perceived sensuality of rock 'n' roll music epitomised by Elvis Presley's hip gyrations and Ray Charles' suggestive moans when he performed his top hit "What'd I Say." Growing fears of premarital sex were reinforced by the widespread teenage practise of "going steady" with a single partner over a period of time, symbolised by "friendship rings," which were worn on a necklace and regarded as an pre-engagement emblem. This presumably blurred the distinction between teen love and marriage, opening the door wide for premarital sex in the minds of social commentators. Parent groups therefore discouraged the practise of going steady, as did film productions like "Unwed Mother" and "Diary of a High School Bride" in which intense teen love ends in emotional disaster, unwanted pregnancies, and even suicide.

The Americanisation of Western culture

Concerns that Hollywood films and rock 'n' roll corrupted teen morals were shared by parents and social commentators overseas who were confronted with the spread of American culture into many corners of the world. West German teenagers' imitations of Elvis Presley's hip gyrations at parties and concerts prompted commentators to call them "wild barbarians in ecstasy" and to decry the "sexualisation of 15-year-olds." Other critiques carried racist overtones that resembled white supremacist reactions to rock 'n' roll in the American South. When the premiere of the wildly popular film "Rock Around the Clock" featuring Bill Haley caused teenage riots in London, a West German teenage magazine reported that the film transformed "cool Englishmen into white Negroes" and surmised that Haley's performance was African ritual music in disguise while Britain's *Daily Mail* dismissed rock 'n' roll as a mixture of "African tom-tom and voodoo dance." Similar adult sentiments greeted the arrival of rock 'n' roll in Latin America during the late fifties, when Fats Domino, Little Richard, and other black American performers became popular among teens, quickly followed by homegrown bands like Cuba's "Los Llopis" and "Los Hot Rockets."

US exports that evoked conservative misgivings also included American cars that became popular among working-class youngsters, who used them as symbols of their cultural independence and upward social mobility. Swedish adults gasped when young men eschewed modest Volvos in favour of flashy Chevrolets to cruise Stockholm's quiet streets sporting leather jackets, with petticoated girls in the backseat and rock 'n' roll music blasting from the car radio. Swedish media called male youngsters who owned American cars "raggare," a denigrating noun derived from the verb "ragga," which means "to pick up women." In German, the similarly derogatory term "Halbstarke" ("half-strong") described unruly male adolescents who imitated American

Figure 14.3 Fashionably dressed British teens posing at a funfair, the young men sporting American-style pompadour haircuts popularised by rock 'n' roll stars Elvis Presley and Johnny Cash during the 1950s.

Source: Courtesy of Tim Ring/Alamy

styles, drank Coca-Cola, and idolised the actor Marlon Brando. The very rebelliousness of American rock 'n' roll culture that appalled their parents fascinated teenagers, including 15-year-old John Lennon of Liverpool, later of Beatles fame, who decided to make music his life's passion after watching "Rock Around the Clock." West German teens were thrilled when US Army Private Elvis Presley was stationed in an American base near Bad Nauheim and posed in front of the city gates to shoot a photo later used as an album cover of "A Big Hunk o' Love."

Other manifestations of consumer culture were greeted with great enthusiasm as American refrigerators, electric ovens, and washing machines entered many middle-class homes in the Western world. The Ohio-based Hoover Company's domination of global markets for electric vacuum cleaners prompted British homemakers to use the verb "to hoover," meaning "to vacuum the floor." Though Western Europe began to catch up, however, electric appliance ownership was less common than in the USA. In 1960, for example, almost all American households included refrigerators, but only half did in West Germany and less than one-third in Italy. American kitchen appliances that never made it to Europe astonished visitors during trips to the USA. British novelist Malcolm Bradbury received a practical demonstration of a kitchen waste-disposal unit from his American host, who fed a cooked chicken into the device just to show his guest how it worked. "I stared at the gurgling hole as it slowly ate the entire chicken and flushed it away," Bradbury later recalled. "I knew I had seen America, and it worked."

Mass-produced housing along the lines of the Levittown development garnered interest in France, Italy, and Spain in 1955, when America's Prefabricated Home Manufacturers' Institute organised a travelling exhibit called "Main Street, USA" that featured model suburban houses equipped with a dazzling variety of household appliances to provide "the people of Europe with a life-size picture of how Americans live." In 1959, Vice President Richard Nixon touted suburbia's virtues to Soviet Premier Nikita Khrushchev during their so-called kitchen debate, only to be told by Khrushchev, "Your American houses are built to last only 20 years so builders could sell new houses at the end. We build firmly. We build for our children and grandchildren." Though American-style suburbanisation proved unfeasible in Western Europe for lack of sufficient space, the concept of prefabricated housing became popular, particularly in Italy, where mass-produced apartment buildings rose on the outskirts of major cities. Some Western European critics disdained American suburbs: Britain's *Architectural Review* deemed them "a visually scrofulous wasteland" and a West German architect dismissed Levittown as a "modern slum."

Western European professors who had traditionally discounted American Studies as a subject of serious inquiry began to take advantage of the Fulbright Program and other government initiatives that funded conferences and academic exchanges. The British Association for American Studies, founded at Oxford in 1955, sponsored conferences attended by scholars from both sides of the Atlantic, provided funds for American Studies departments, and offered scholarships for British professors and students to visit American universities. Other programmes served anti-Communist propaganda purposes. The Congress for Cultural Freedom, established in West Berlin and secretly funded by the Central Intelligence Agency, organised conferences attended by leading American and Western European intellectuals and sponsored high-brow magazines like *Encounter*, published in London and edited by the American journalist Irving Kristol. Other institutions sponsored by the US government included cultural centres called America Houses, 27 of which operated in West Germany alone. In addition to showcasing American films, photography, and art, they treated audiences to performances of musicals, a distinctly American art form that was unfamiliar to Europeans.

Efforts to popularise American culture often collided with stereotypes held dear by many Europeans. Having sampled the opinions of Britons who were critical of the USA, the American humourist Art Buchwald reported, "if Americans would stop spending money, talking loudly in public places, telling the British who won the war, adopt a pro-colonial policy, stop chewing gum, move their air bases out of England, settle the desegregation problem in the South, put the American woman in her proper place, and not export Rock n' Roll, and speak correct English, the tension between the two countries might ease and the British and Americans would like each other again."

The liberal consensus and the politics of the 1950s

Politically, the 1950s and early 1960s were characterised by what historians call the "liberal consensus" that pervaded the Democratic and Republican parties. Eisenhower, elected in 1952 as a Republican, resisted calls from within his own party to dismantle large segments of the New Deal and instead maintained the viability of social and economic programmes instituted by Franklin Roosevelt in the 1930s. While Republicans learned to live with the New Deal state, most Democrats abandoned the critical attitude towards free-market capitalism many liberals had espoused in the 1930s, and instead embraced the enterprise system. Both parties claimed that American-style capitalism created abundance for all segments of society and rendered class divisions obsolete. Most Democrats and Republicans also agreed on the need to contain communism worldwide.

Eisenhower's election ended a 20-year period when the Democrats had controlled the presidency but hardly spelled doom for the New Deal order. Pondering whom to nominate for the presidential elections of 1952, many Republicans initially supported Robert Taft, a staunch opponent of Social Security and the regulatory state, proponent of isolationism, and critic of the North Atlantic Treaty Organization (NATO). The party's moderates meanwhile rallied around Eisenhower, a former NATO supreme commander who was fond of saying that he was "conservative when it comes to money, liberal when it comes to human beings." Eisenhower defeated Taft for the Republican nomination, beat Democrat Adlai Stevenson in the general election 55 per cent to 44 per cent, and helped his party win control of the US Senate and the House of Representatives. Consistent with his fiscal conservatism and social liberalism, Eisenhower initiated a major revenue reform that raised taxes on the rich and lowered them for the poor, making the fifties a period with the most equal distribution of wealth in American history. Eisenhower also expanded the New Deal's Social Security Act to include ten million new beneficiaries and placed the programme under a new cabinet-level office called the Department of Health, Education, and Welfare formed in 1953.

The Democratic Party, which regained control of both houses of Congress in 1954, worked closely with the Eisenhower administration and solidified the politics of the liberal consensus under the leadership of Senate Majority Leader Lyndon Johnson and Speaker of the House Sam Rayburn, both Democrats from Texas. Eisenhower, who was born in that state, quipped "There's no problem that three Texans can't solve." Frequently meeting the president over drinks to discuss policy, Johnson and Rayburn helped Eisenhower pass 80 per cent of his legislative agenda. The Republican administration, in turn, adopted countercyclical policies when a recession disrupted the post-war economic boom in 1955. Arthur Burns, the Chairman of the Council of Economic Advisors explained, "It is no longer a matter of serious controversy whether the government shall play a positive role in helping to maintain a high level of economic activity." Eisenhower told Democrats, "If we have to stress party differences, let us do it on relatively small matters."

The convergence of American political parties around a core set of values had parallels in Western Europe, where some countries developed their own brand of a "liberal consensus." West Germany's Social Democrats, for example, relinquished Marxist doctrine in favour of a belief in a "social market economy" and the conservative Christian Democratic Union abandoned some of its more extremist nationalist fervour. Post-war British politics were characterised by a liberal consensus called the "Attlee consensus" in which the socialist Labour Party government under Prime Minister Clement Attlee pursued an imperial foreign policy that differed little from that of its Conservative predecessors except in India, while Conservatives endorsed workers' rights and accepted the National Health Service that had been established by Labour, initially over right-wing objections that nationally financed universal health coverage reeked of state socialism.

Figure 14.4 President Eisenhower with Senate Majority Leader Johnson and House Speaker
Rayburn at a national security conference, 1958. All three strongly supported foreign aid to developing countries, a core aspect of the "liberal consensus."

Source: Courtesy of Everett Collection Historical/Alamy

Eisenhower and the cold war

In the USA, the two major parties found common ground in foreign and defence policies once Republicans accepted the Truman Doctrine, which became a vital element
of the liberal consensus. This was hardly a foregone conclusion as many conservatives held sharply divergent views of foreign affairs. While stalwart isolationists like
Taft objected to the NATO alliance and other forms of American global engagement,
radical interventionists deemed the containment of communism in the nations where

it existed morally bankrupt because it "abandons countless human beings to a despotism and godless terrorism, which in turn enables [communist] rulers to forge the captives into a weapon for our destruction," in the words of the Republican election platform of 1952. John Foster Dulles, Eisenhower's Secretary of State, proposed a new strategy of rollback to "liberate the captive peoples" from the iron grip of communist oppression. The more pragmatic Eisenhower remained committed to containment and sought an armistice in Korea that would end the fighting and re-establish the peninsula's division along the 38th parallel, signalling an implied US acceptance of North Korea's communist regime in accordance with the Truman Doctrine. Eisenhower's line of thinking gradually gained traction in the Republican Party, partly because large segments of the American public worried about the possibility of World War III if the USA embarked on a strategy of liberating Eastern Europe from Soviet control. In 1956, when a popular uprising in Hungary toppled the communist government and provided the USA with an opportunity to detach the country from the Eastern bloc, the Eisenhower administration did little to support the revolution, which was crushed by Soviet military intervention.

The cold war entered a new phase when Josef Stalin died in March 1953, less than two months after Eisenhower had been sworn in as president. Though the new Soviet leadership under Prime Minister Nikita Khrushchev moderated some of the most oppressive features of Stalin's rule, it also built up Soviet military strength with the deployment of thermonuclear weapons of unparalleled destructive power, development of missile technology, increase in troop strength from 2.8 million men (1950) to 5.8 million (1955), and establishment of a military alliance with Eastern Europe under the Warsaw Pact of 1955. These developments created serious dilemmas for Eisenhower, a critic of the military-industrial complex who told the American public during his "Chance for Peace" speech of 1953, "Every gun that is made, every warship launched, every rocket fired signifies, in the final sense, a theft from those who hunger and are not fed, those who are cold and are not clothed. . . . The cost of one modern heavy bomber is this: a modern brick school in more than 30 cities. . . . We pay for a single destroyer with new homes that could have housed more than 8,000 people." Evoking William Jennings Bryan's famous "Cross of Gold Speech" of 1896, Eisenhower concluded, "This is not a way of life at all, in any true sense. Under the cloud of threatening war, it is humanity hanging from a cross of iron." Though he understood the socio-economic consequences of military build-up better than most American leaders, Eisenhower found it difficult to rein in defence spending in the face of continued Soviet rearmament. Trying to escape this dilemma, he adopted the "New Look" defence policy of 1953 that introduced the strategy of "massive retaliation" in which Soviet aggression with conventional, non-nuclear forces anywhere in the world would prompt an American nuclear attack on the Soviet Union itself. Public announcement of "massive retaliation" by Secretary of State Dulles in 1954, it was hoped, would deter the Soviet Union from launching acts of aggression in the first place because its leadership sought to avoid an American nuclear attack at all cost.

The New Look required further build-up of the American nuclear arsenal and the Strategic Air Command (SAC) that was slated to carry out massive retaliation. As a result, Eisenhower reduced spending on conventional forces like navy destroyers and army artillery, and ramped up expenditures for B-47 and B-52 long-range bombers to equip SAC with sufficient capability to destroy the Soviet Union. To protect American cities from Soviet nuclear retaliation, the administration poured billions into air defences and nuclear fallout shelters, but in was widely acknowledged that millions of Americans would still perish in a nuclear war.

Massive retaliation unsettled America's allies who doubted that a president would risk the destruction of major US cities in response to Soviet aggression in a remote corner of the world. In the 1950s, the Soviet Union did not yet possess sufficient nuclear capability to destroy the USA entirely, but it was widely expected that an American first strike would trigger one-way suicide missions of Soviet bombers that could lay waste to New York and Chicago. Was the USA prepared to pay this price in order to retaliate for a Soviet invasion of Norway, for example? The number of American casualties to be expected in such a war would only grow as the Soviet Union acquired greater nuclear capabilities, casting further doubt on the credibility of massive retaliation. Moreover, leaders of Western European NATO members wondered why they should devote ever-increasing amounts to conventional armament if a future conflict was to be fought with nuclear weapons in any event (Britain spent as much as 7 per cent of its gross national product on weaponry and France 6.8 per cent).

The NATO partners occasionally exploited America's obsession with Soviet expansionism in order to further their own agendas. In 1951, for example, Britain suffered a setback when a progressive Iranian government under Mohammad Mosaddegh nationalised the Anglo-Iranian Oil Company, which had long been a symbol of European imperialism in the Middle East. The British government, which was desperate to regain control of Iranian petroleum, sought American assistance to topple Mosaddegh by portraying him as a communist, even though he was a widely respected democrat. A senior British intelligence officer later explained, "The Americans were more likely to work with us if they saw the problem as one of containing Communism rather than restoring the position of the Anglo-Iranian Oil Company." The director of America's Central Intelligence Agency (CIA) John Foster Dulles promptly swallowed the bait, explaining to Eisenhower that "if Iran succumbed to the Communists there was little doubt that in short order the other areas of the Middle East, with some 60 per cent of the world's oil reserves, would fall into Communist control." To forestall such an eventuality, the CIA helped the British overthrow Mosaddegh and install a government under Shah Reza Pahlavi, who consented to Western majority control of Iranian oil and became a loyal Western ally.

The Middle East was increasingly dragged into the cold war as the 1950s progressed. Egypt's nationalist government under Gamal Abdel Nasser alarmed the Eisenhower administration when it bought weapons from communist Czechoslovakia, prompting Secretary of State Dulles to cancel an American loan intended to finance the construction of the Aswan Dam on the Nile River. In response, Nasser sought Soviet financial assistance for the project and nationalised the British-French-controlled Suez Canal, another potent symbol of Western imperialism. A Franco-British attempt to attack Egypt and overthrow Nasser in collaboration with Israel had to be abandoned in 1956 as a result of Eisenhower's objections, but the episode heightened the president's fear that the Soviets sought to stake a claim in the Middle East, whose oil resources were critical to Western Europe's economic well-being. This prompted him to apply the containment doctrine to the Middle East by promising American financial aid and even military intervention to protect the region's newly independent states "against covert armed aggression from any nation controlled by international communism."

The cold war affected other regions as well when the Soviet Union supported nationalist independence movements in their struggle against Western European colonial powers. In Vietnam, armed guerrillas under the leadership of communist Ho Chi Minh inflicted a stunning defeat on French forces at the battle of Dien Bien Phu in 1954 despite long-standing American support of France's war effort (see Chapter 13). The defeat prompted the French government to commit itself in the Geneva Accords to a complete withdrawal. At Geneva, the USA, the Soviet Union, Britain, France, and the People's Republic of China also negotiated a temporary division of Vietnam along the 17th parallel that was scheduled to end with the election of a national government. The pro-Western politician Ngo Dinh Diem, however, rejected the agreement with the backing of the Eisenhower administration, which feared that the communists would win the democratic elections scheduled for 1956 (they never took place). While the communists took control of North Vietnam, the US-backed Diem ruled the South with an iron fist, provoking widespread dissatisfaction among the Vietnamese people that contributed in 1960 to the formation of armed resistance under the National Liberation Front. Thus America's effort to contain communism in Asia laid the groundwork for the Vietnam War that escalated in the 1960s (see Chapter 15).

Widespread beliefs that American technology was superior to its communist counterpart suffered a blow in October 1957, when the Soviet Union launched the Sputnik satellite, the first man-made object in Earth orbit. Officially labelled a contribution to the International Geophysical Year, the event demonstrated Soviet scientific prowess because Sputnik was carried aboard a rocket-propelled launch vehicle called the R-7. American scientists worked on similar technology at the time, but their hasty attempts to pull even failed when the rockets exploded before they reached orbit, adding shame to the humiliation of having been beaten in round one of the space race. Western Europeans who had long been impressed with American prowess were baffled: more than 80 per cent of Britons saw Sputnik as the beginning of America's slide towards second-class status in science and technology. In addition to producing a public relations disaster for the Eisenhower administration, Sputnik had serious military implications because the R-7 rocket was actually a ballistic missile designed to carry a nuclear warhead, raising the possibility that the Soviet Union could respond to an American nuclear bomber strike with a missile attack on the USA.

The Sputnik crisis contributed to growing criticism of the administration, which found itself accused by Democrats of permitting the emergence of a "missile gap" in favour of the Soviet Union that had to be closed with appropriations for more research, missiles, bombers, and nuclear submarines. Eisenhower knew better because he possessed top-secret intelligence gathered by U-2 spy planes that took photographs of Soviet military installations, showing only meagre missile production facilities and launch pads. Sputnik, it turned out, was little more than a Soviet publicity stunt. Rejecting calls from Jackson and others for major increases in American military spending, the most Eisenhower was prepared to do was accelerate existing missile programmes that produced the powerful Atlas intercontinental ballistic missile and a variety of smaller launch vehicles. Moreover, he supported Senate Majority Leader Johnson's call for the establishment of the National Air and Space Administration (NASA) to conduct non-military space research and development. Long eager to provide federal funding for higher education, Eisenhower also used the Sputnik crisis to promote the National Defense Education Act of 1958 that provided $2 billion annually to train hundreds of thousands of engineers, scientists, and mathematicians in American universities. These measures, which passed Congress with bipartisan support, soothed raw nerves in the wake of Sputnik and solidified the liberal consensus in American politics.

The civil rights movement

Proponents of the liberal consensus had preciously little to say about racial oppression, which had disfigured American life in the first half of the twentieth century and showed little signs of abating in the 1950s. The political leadership in Congress and the executive branch wilfully ignored civil rights to avoid "rocking the boat" and confront powerful Southern Democrats, most of whom remained committed to white supremacy. Only when grass roots civil rights activists began to challenge the widespread belief in Washington that racial discrimination was a marginal issue did mainstream politics even begin to address the problem.

The post-war boom largely bypassed African Americans, who found themselves excluded from the vibrant core of the US economy. At the beginning of the decade, the majority of blacks still lived in the South, where the technological transformation of agriculture deprived many of their livelihoods.

African American sharecroppers and farm labourers had traditionally earned most of their income in the cotton fields, but rapid mechanisation cost millions their jobs as the share of machine-picked cotton rose from 5 per cent (1950) to more than 50 per cent (1960). Since better-paid jobs in Southern steel mills and textile factories remained bastions of all-white labour, a growing number of blacks migrated to northeastern and midwestern cities. Here, all-white unions excluded them from the job market, forcing new arrivals into the low-wage labour market that usually lacked fringe benefits like pensions and health insurance. By 1960, a majority of African Americans lived in urban centres, precipitating the outmigration of white working class people who refused to live with black neighbours. Nine out of ten white Americans approved of laws prohibiting interracial marriage.

Bleak as Northern city life was for many blacks, it paled next to what African Americans endured under Southern white supremacy. Here, discrimination did not just reflect racist attitudes among whites as it did in the North, but also the Southern legal system of segregation where the law of the land forced whites and blacks to attend separate schools, use separate recreational facilities, sit in separate sections on buses, and even be buried in separate cemeteries. The *Plessy v Ferguson* decision of the US Supreme Court had upheld the constitutionality of legal segregation in 1896, provided that blacks had access to equal facilities and services, but in reality African Americans invariably attended the most overcrowded schools, travelled in the most dilapidated train cars, and spent their leisure time in the dirtiest parks. The ballot box provided no remedy because Southern states systematically denied blacks the right to vote through an insidious interpretation of the Fifteenth Amendment to the Constitution that prevented states from denying the right to vote only on the basis of "race, color, or previous condition of servitude." Since the amendment did not prohibit other forms of voter discrimination, Southern states felt free to introduce poll taxes (people too poor to pay them forfeited their right to vote), literacy tests (people who could not read and write had no right to vote), and other provisions that vastly reduced black constituencies. Literacy tests for blacks were far stricter than for whites, so that fewer than 7 per cent of eligible voters in Mississippi were admitted to the ballot box during the 1950s.

White supremacy emerged as a serious problem for American foreign policy during the early cold war. It received worldwide attention in 1947, when the prominent black intellectual W.E.B. Du Bois appealed to the United Nations on behalf of the National

Association for the Advancement of Colored People (NAACP) that branded race discrimination "not only indefensible but barbaric. . . . It is not Russia that threatens the United States so much as Mississippi . . .; internal injustice done to one's brothers is far more dangerous than the aggression of strangers from abroad." Pleas for racial justice did not fall entirely on deaf ears as Truman desegregated the armed forces by an executive order signed in 1948, but the core issues of legal segregation in the states and voter discrimination remained unresolved. Soviet propaganda exploited the issue for all it was worth. White supremacy tarnished America's image throughout the world, a Dutch diplomat told his American colleague: "the opponents of American policies possess one propaganda theme which is extremely effective throughout Europe and even more effective in Asia – criticism of American racial attitudes." Racial supremacy was "extremely difficult for friends of America to explain, let alone defend," he stressed. People around the globe were outraged in 1957, when an Alabama court sentenced the black farmhand Jimmy Wilson to death for stealing $1.95. Britain's Labour Party feared that the case handed communists "ammunition for their propaganda," a Norwegian housewife wrote to express her "sympathy for the Negro, Jimmy Wilson, and plead clemency for him," and Ghanaian labour activists proclaimed that the verdict "constitutes such a savage blow against the Negro Race that it finds no parallel in the Criminal Code of any modern State," pleading with US officials to "save not only the life of Wilson but also the good name of the United States from ridicule and contempt." The governor of Alabama commuted the death sentence under international pressure and Wilson spent 16 years in prison.

White supremacy suffered a major blow when the NAACP intensified its long-standing legal challenges to racial segregation in public education, a campaign spearheaded by its chief legal counsel Thurgood Marshall. In Kansas, Marshall filed a class-action lawsuit on behalf of black parents in order to force the Board of Education of Topeka to admit their children to the city's all-white primary schools, which were located closer to their homes than the all-black schools. When a district court sided with the Board of Education citing the *Plessy v Ferguson* decision, Marshall appealed to the US Supreme Court to challenge the constitutionality of the "separate but equal" doctrine itself. In 1954, a unanimous Supreme Court headed by Chief Justice Earl Warren ruled in the plaintiff's favour in its landmark decision *Brown v. Board of Education* that overturned *Plessy v Ferguson*, declaring that segregated schools were inherently unequal and therefore violated the Fourteenth Amendment to the Constitution, which prohibited states from denying any citizen the "equal protection of the laws."

The *Brown* decision unleashed a political firestorm as white supremacists vowed to resist desegregation. In Birmingham, Alabama, members of Ku Klux Klan kidnapped and castrated a black veteran, shouting "You ever heard of a nigger-loving communist Earl Warren?" One hundred members of Congress signed the so-called Southern Manifesto that accused the Supreme Court of misinterpreting the Constitution and claimed that its decision "has planted hatred and suspicion where there has been heretofore friendship and understanding" between the races. Majority Leader Johnson was one of only three Southern Senators who refused to sign the statement, which put a spanner in his works to keep racial politics out of Congress. US Senator Harry Byrd, Sr., one of the signatories, led a campaign of "massive resistance" in Virginia that entailed months-long school closures in entire districts until court rulings declared the practise unconstitutional. In the Deep South, Arkansas governor Orval Faubus deployed National Guard units to prevent black students from entering the central high school in Little Rock. Photographs of armed soldiers blocking nine well-dressed teenagers who were eager to learn went around the world, prompting particularly negative reactions in Western Europe, where opinion polls indicated that the events in Little Rock reinforced negative views of American race relations. The Soviets sneered that white supremacists "commit their dark deeds in Arkansas, Alabama, and other Southern states, and then these thugs put on white gloves and mount the rostrum in the U.N. General Assembly, and hold forth about freedom and democracy." Eisenhower, though hardly enamoured with the *Brown* decision, felt that he had no choice but deploy the US Army's 101st Airborne Division to Little Rock, where the paratroopers escorted the students to school jeered by a racist mob. Civil rights leaders who congratulated former general Eisenhower on his "last battle" included Martin Luther King, Jr.

A young Baptist minister from Atlanta, Georgia, King gained fame and notoriety as leader of a bus boycott in Montgomery, Alabama, a seminal event in the civil rights movement. Challenging a local segregation law that required a black bus passenger to make room for a white customer in the front of the bus, 15-year-old NAACP Youth Council activist Claudette Colvin refused to give up her seat to a white man in March 1955. The local NAACP chapter had already planned to mount a protest against bus segregation but decided that Colvin, a teenager who was falsely believed to be pregnant at the time, did not project the sort of respectability the organisation sought. Nine months later, NAACP member Rosa Parks also declined to vacate her seat for a white man and was arrested for violating the segregation ordnance. A 42-year-old

Figure 14.5 Members of the 101st Airborne Division escorting black teenagers to school in Little Rock, Arkansas, 1957.

Source: Courtesy of Science History Images/Alamy

married mother who had attended college and worked as a seamstress, Parks was considered a more presentable figure than Colvin, and the local NAACP chapter launched a boycott of the bus company the next day with the aim to have the segregation law removed so that blacks could sit where they wanted on the bus. Instead of taking the bus, boycotters carpooled to get to work, rode bicycles, or walked; asked if she was exhausted, a 72-year-old responded "My feets is tired, but my soul is rested." King, a young pastor at a local church, became the movement's leading spokesman, emphasising the nonviolent nature of the protest that resembled boycott movements organised by independence leader Mahatma Gandhi in India, one of King's personal heroes. Though white supremacists bombed King's house and the boycotters faced frequent harassment, the 381-day boycott forced the Montgomery city council to repeal the segregation law. The civil rights movement had staked an important claim, though white supremacists attacked integrated buses with guns, bombed five local churches, and lynched a black man after the end of the boycott. King subsequently became a co-founder of the Southern Christian Leadership Conference, an organisation of black ministers that placed greater emphasis of direct nonviolent action than the NAACP, which focused on court challenges and antidiscrimination legislation.

The Montgomery Bus Boycott inspired others to engage in direct action. In 1958, two members of the NAACP Youth Council conducted a sit-in at the lunch counter of a Dockrum drugstore in Wichita, Kansas, that refused to serve African Americans. When the entire Dockrum chain abandoned that policy after three weeks, a group of NAACP activists conducted another sit-in at Oklahoma City, which also met with success. These little-publicised actions were followed in 1960 by sit-ins in Greensboro, North Carolina, that attracted national attention when four well-dressed black teenagers sat down at a Woolworth lunch counter designated "all white" and asked politely to be served. Within four days, more than 300 people joined the sit-ins and the movement spread to other cities, sometimes attracting white supremacist crowds that attacked the protesters. Eisenhower took sides by stating that he was "deeply sympathetic with the efforts of any group to enjoy the rights of equality that they are guaranteed by the Constitution." As a result of the sit-ins, most Southern drugstore chains abandoned all-white and segregated lunch counters, while young activists formed the Student Nonviolent Coordinating Committee that played a major role in the civil rights struggle of the 1960s.

Chapter summary

This chapter examined the economic boom of the 1950s and its social and political consequences. It explained that economic growth was partly attributable to global institutions like the International Monetary Fund that were instituted and dominated by the USA and enabled America to double its exports during the fifties. Innovative technologies like microelectronics and business strategies such as product diversification contributed to domestic growth, which was sustained by consumer spending. Organised labour reaped rewards in the form of higher wages and improved benefits, enabling millions of workers to purchase suburban homes and afford household items that had previously been considered luxury items. The politics of the 1950s reflected a growing consensus among Republicans and Democrats that core elements of the New Deal were here to stay, notably Social Security and government intervention into the economy, and that the free enterprise system produced substantial benefits for society.

National leaders also agreed to extend the containment doctrine in the Third World while rejecting more radical strategies like the rollback of communism in Eastern Europe.

Many liberals were convinced that the fifties' consensus represented a triumph of their ideas over conservatism. Literary critic Lionel Trilling proclaimed that "liberalism is not only the dominant but even the sole intellectual tradition . . . there are no conservative or reactionary ideas in circulation." Such smug contentment ignored the persistence of white supremacy that disfigured the lives of most blacks and American society as a whole. Excluded from the core sectors of the post-war economy as a result of employment discrimination across the USA, African Americans rarely reaped the benefits of suburbanisation and consumer society. In the South, they experienced the worst forms of white supremacy in the form of legal segregation and exclusion from the ballot box, leaving them with no venues to articulate their grievances in mainstream politics. Since both parties usually ignored demands for racial justice, Southern blacks embarked on grass roots activism to attack legal segregation in education, transport, and at lunch counters. Though they occasionally forced mainstream political leaders and institutions to act in the 1950s, much remained to be done to dismantle white supremacy during the 1960s and beyond.

 ## Discussion questions

- What factors contributed to the economic prosperity of the 1950s?
- What were the most important benefits of consumer society?
- What were some of the downsides of suburban living?
- Why did most mainstream politicians ignore civil rights problems?
- What was the liberal consensus?

Further reading

American Cinema of the 1950s: Themes and Variations, ed. Murray Pomerance (New Brunswick, NJ, 2005). A collection of essays exploring the Hollywood film industry, major films, the impact of McCarthyism, and other important themes.

Borstelmann, Thomas. *The Cold War and the Color Line: American Race Relations in the Global Arena* (Cambridge, 2001). Examines the serious foreign policy problems that arose for America's cold war policymakers as a result of racial discrimination at home.

The Columbia History of Post-War War II America, ed. Marc C. Carnes (New York, 2007). Essays included in this collection introduce readers to post-war social structures, popular culture, gender, religion, sexuality, and more.

Cummings, Richard H. *Radio Free Europe's Crusade for Freedom: Rallying Americans Behind Cold War Broadcasting 1950–1960* (Jefferson, NC, 2010). An innovative study of American-European media campaigns and propaganda warfare during the early years of the cold war.

Dudziak, Mary L. *Cold War Civil Rights: Race and the Image of American Democracy* (Princeton, NJ, 2011). An important study of how race relations and foreign policy influenced one another at a time when the USA sought to attract global support for the containment of communism.

Galbraith, John K. *The Affluent Society* (New York, 1958). A classic study written by leading an economist explains the development of post-war middle-class life in a period of unprecedented economic growth and calls attention to income inequality and the impoverishment of public life and institutions.

Jackson, Kenneth T. *Crabgrass Frontier: The Suburbanization of the United States* (New York, 1985). The author, a leading urban historian, examines the development of suburban architecture, social structure, and culture from a critical perspective.

Johns, Michael. *Moment of Grace: The American City in the 1950s* (Berkeley, 2003). A nicely illustrated study of post-war urban culture that captures the vibrancy of American cities.

Leffler, Melvyn P. *For the Soul of Mankind: The United States, the Soviet Union, and the Cold War* (New York, 2007). A leading historian of American foreign relations provides a highly readable and balanced portrait of US-Soviet relations during the cold war.

Patterson, James T. *Brown v. Board of Education: A Civil Rights Milestone and Its Troubled Legacy* (New York, 2001). Written by a prize-winning historian, this critical study examines the origins and impact of the US Supreme Court decision that mandated the end of school segregation.

Putnam, Robert D. *Bowling Alone: The Collapse and Revival of American Community* (New York, 2000). A critical examination of American society and culture in the age of consumerism, suburbanisation, and television.

Rethinking Cold War Culture, eds. Peter J. Kuznick and James Gilbert (Washington, DC, 2001). This fresh look at post-war culture introduces students to the diversity of the American experience, including the making of American national identity, child rearing, literature, and the militarisation of everyday life.

Riesman, David. *The Lonely Crowd* (New Haven, CT, 1961). Written by a leading sociologist, this classic study examines emergence of social conformity among middle-class Americans.

Tyler May, Elaine. *Homeward Bound: American Families in the Cold War Era* (New York, 1988). This major study of post-war society and culture shows that the cold war played a role the lives of ordinary Americans at every turn, from work and leisure to childrearing and sex life.

15 The turbulent sixties

Timeline

1960   Students for a Democratic Society (SDS) founded
Democrat John Kennedy elected president
Establishment of the National Liberation Front for South Vietnam

1961   Bay of Pigs invasion of Cuba fails
Freedom Riders challenge segregation in interstate transport
Construction of the Berlin Wall
Alliance for Progress launched

1962   SDS issues Port Huron Statement
Cuban Missile Crisis

1963   Civil rights march on Birmingham
March on Washington
Nuclear Test Ban takes effect
Ngo Dinh Diem assassinated in South Vietnam
Kennedy assassinated in Dallas, Texas

1964   Civil Rights Act passed
Economic Opportunity Act launches War on Poverty
Free Speech movement at University of California at Berkeley
Gulf of Tonkin incident
Democrat Lyndon Johnson elected president

1965   March on Selma, Alabama
Launch of Operation Rolling Thunder against North Vietnam
Malcolm X assassinated
Deployment of US ground troops in Vietnam
Voting Rights Act passed
Medicare Act passed
Immigration Reform Act passed
Elementary and Secondary Education Act passed
Ghetto Riots in Los Angeles

1966   Establishment of Black Panther Party
Draft protests begin
National Organization for Women established

1967   Ghetto Riots of the "long hot summer"
March on the Pentagon

1968   Tet Offensive in Vietnam
Johnson announces he will not run for re-election

Martin L. King, Jr., assassinated; riots in many US cities
Robert Kennedy assassinated
Chicago Convention of the Democratic Party
Republican Richard Nixon elected president

Topics covered

- Kennedy and the cold war
- The new frontier and its limits
- From Kennedy to Johnson
- The Great Society
- The northern racial crisis and black power
- Johnson's escalation of the Vietnam War
- The anti-war movement and the new left
- 1968: the year of upheavals

Introduction

In a snapshot of the political unrest that gripped America in the late sixties, the chapter opens with the March on the Pentagon in October 1967, when tens of thousands of protesters converged on the Department of Defence in Washington DC to voice their opposition to the Vietnam War. The chapter then backtracks to the presidency of Democrat John F. Kennedy (1961–1963), whose hard-line anticommunism contributed to severe foreign policy crises and deepened American involvement in Vietnam early in the decade. Domestically, Kennedy sought to address major social problems from poverty to healthcare, but his most ambitious programmes remained incomplete due to his lack of political experience and influence. This changed dramatically under his Democratic successor Lyndon B. Johnson (1963–1969), a shrewd legislator who implemented wide-ranging reforms called the Great Society that had a major impact on social conditions and race relations in the USA. Their positive effects notwithstanding, the Great Society initiatives failed to solve America's proliferating racial and urban crises that contributed to the ghetto riots and the rise of the Black Power movement. In foreign policy, Johnson was committed an anti-Communist course in Vietnam and escalated US involvement with a massive air campaign against the North and the deployment of American ground forces to the South. The descent into the Vietnam quagmire coincided with the growth of student radicalism that fed the growth of the largest anti-war movement in American history. These developments culminated in 1968, when America's lack of preparedness for a massive communist offensive in South Vietnam swayed public opinion against the war, the Johnson presidency disintegrated, Martin Luther King and Robert Kennedy were assassinated, and the convention of the Democratic Party in Chicago descended into chaos. The chapter ends with the election of Republican Richard Nixon as president in November 1968.

The March on the Pentagon

On 21 October 1967, 70,000 demonstrators marched against the Vietnam War at the Lincoln Memorial in Washington DC. Attended by student activists, hippies, men in pinstripe suits, flower girls, war veterans, clergymen, Black Power militants, and bespectacled professors, the largest anti-war demonstration in American history to that date featured placards encouraging Americans to "Join the Draft Dodge Rebellion" next to posters of the Cuban revolutionary Che Guevara. Novelist Norman Mailer, poet Robert Lowell, and other prominent intellectuals marched under a banner urging Americans to "Support our GIs – bring them home." Featured speakers included Benjamin Spock, the soft-spoken child psychologist and author of the *Common Sense Book of Baby and Child Care*. Once the speakers had finished, tens of thousands of marchers headed across the Potomac River to the US Department of Defence in the Pentagon, where they encountered 10,000 policemen and soldiers. Some protesters adorned the troops' guns with flowers while others tried to break through the lines and get into the building. By the end of the day, police had arrested more than 600 people, including Mailer, who later recalled these events in his book *Armies of the Night*.

The March on the Pentagon marked a seminal moment in the history of the 1960s, when the cold war liberal consensus split under the weight of the Vietnam War. Like Spock, many people who took to the streets to protest the escalation of the Vietnam War had voted for Johnson in 1964 because they supported his Great Society programme of sweeping social reforms and his cautious approach to Vietnam at the time, causing deep anger when he deployed US forces to Vietnam shortly after the election. For the first time in history, Americans from all walks of life rose up in mass protest against US military intervention, shattering the core assumption of cold war liberals that militant anticommunism abroad could coexist with progressive reforms at home.

A new look at sixties America

The story of sixties America is often told as a drama that started with high hopes at the beginning of the decade and ended in despair. John F. Kennedy's election as president in 1960 and his ambitious plans for sweeping reforms were indeed symbols of a new era as liberals set out to eliminate white supremacy, enhance social justice, expand the welfare state, and reach out to the newly independent nations of the developing world. President Johnson implemented his predecessor's domestic reform agenda with his Great Society programmes that expanded the New Deal state, but his presidency eventually collapsed as a result of the Vietnam War.

Oftentimes portrayed as the "triumph and tragedy of American liberalism," this so-called declinist narrative has been questioned by recent historians who develop a critical perspective on Kennedy that emphasises his uneven record in foreign policy, failure to deliver key domestic reforms, and responsibility for America's growing involvement in Vietnam. The triumph of liberalism during Johnson's presidency, was never as complete it appeared, and his Great Society had many shortcomings. The liberal consensus, in short, was less dazzling and more fragile than its protagonists believed.

Kennedy and the cold war

Intelligent and handsome, John F. Kennedy cut a dashing figure in public. The scion of an influential Irish-American family from Boston that had long been involved in Democratic Party politics, he graduated from Harvard and Oxford Universities, distinguished himself as a lieutenant in the Pacific War, and was first elected to Congress in 1946. Six years later, he became a senator from Massachusetts and married the beautiful and sophisticated Jaqueline Bouvier, with whom he had several children.

In 1960, he defeated Democratic Senate Majority Leader Johnson for the nomination of the Democratic Party for president, picked Johnson as his running mate, and won the general election in a close contest with Republican Richard Nixon.

Behind the glamorous façade lurked a troubled man who remained largely hidden from public view. Already suffering from a variety of illnesses as a youngster, Kennedy sustained a back injury in World War II that caused him excruciating pain for the rest of his life. Jaqueline endured a miscarriage and other health problems that caused her to fall into a depression while her husband engaged in extramarital affairs. His Senate colleagues considered him a political lightweight who was frequently absent during important votes and failed to attach his name to major legislation.

Kennedy's foreign policy was off on a rocky start. Confronted with national liberation movements in developing nations that received Soviet support, he stated in his presidential inaugural speech, "Let every nation know, whether it wishes us well or ill, that we shall pay any price, bear any burden, meet any hardship, support any friend, oppose any foe to assure the survival and the success of liberty." Intended to showcase Kennedy's steely determination to contain the spread of communism in Latin America, Southeast Asia, and elsewhere, his rhetoric proved hollow when he passed up an early opportunity to follow words with deeds in Cuba. Here, a revolutionary movement headed by Fidel Castro and his associate Che Guevara had overthrown the corrupt, American-supported dictator Fulgencio Batista in 1959. A US economic embargo drove Castro into the arms of the Soviet Union, which assisted him with financial and military aid. During the last year of the Eisenhower administration, the Central Intelligence Agency (CIA) hatched a scheme to overthrow Castro by supporting anti-Communist Cuban exiles who had fled to Florida after the revolution. The plan called for the exiles to receive CIA-provided paramilitary training, invade Cuba, bomb Castro's forces with US-supplied aircraft, and instigate a popular uprising against his regime. After Kennedy had approved the operation, 1,200 Cuban exiles staged an amphibious landing at the Bay of Pigs and launched an air strike against Cuban positions in April 1961. Unfortunately for the exiles, Castro's men had been warned that the invasion was coming, enabling them to repel the assault and imprison the attackers. Kennedy, recognising the futility of further action, called off a second air strike as the operation collapsed and America's involvement became public knowledge. During a press conference in the aftermath, a grim-faced president acknowledged his responsibility for the fiasco.

The Bay of Pigs debacle had serious ramifications for Kennedy's foreign policy. First, it enhanced popular support for the Castro regime because ordinary Cubans were disgusted with what they regarded as American-sponsored aggression against their country. These sentiments were shared by many people in Latin America and triggered anti-American protests across the region as radicals in Bogota, Columbia, declared that they stood "with Cuba to the death" and Mexican volunteers flocked to Cuba to defend the Castro regime. Second, Kennedy's refusal to provide the Cuban exiles with direct US support made a mockery of his boast that America would "pay any price" to resist communist expansion. Concerned that Soviet Premier Nikita Khrushchev viewed him as a paper tiger, the President resolved to stiffen his spine in future cold war confrontations in Southeast Asia, despite warnings that such ventures courted disaster. French President Charles de Gaulle told Kennedy presciently, "The more you become involved out there against Communism, the more the Communists will appear the champions of national independence, and the more support they will receive. You will sink step by step into a bottomless military and political quagmire."

Cold war tensions increased in the wake of the Bay of Pigs fiasco. At a US-Soviet summit in Vienna in June 1961 where he suffered from debilitating back pain, Kennedy felt that Khrushchev "beat the hell out of me" in discussions of Cuba, Southeast Asia, and Germany. A gloating Khrushchev reached the same conclusion and authorised the construction of a heavily guarded wall that separated East Berlin from the West to prevent desperate East Germans from fleeing the communist dictatorship. Kennedy rejected suggestions to raze the Berlin Wall because he worried that such drastic action would lead to World War III, preferring to let it stand as a symbol of communist oppression. Meanwhile he tripled the military draft, asked Congress to raise defence appropriations, and expanded nuclear fallout shelters for civilians.

Kennedy's actions, combined with proliferating speculations by American military leaders about the feasibility of nuclear war, had profound effects on Khrushchev, who worried that the USA could exploit its missile superiority by initiating a nuclear attack on the Soviet Union. At the time, the Union of Soviet Socialist Republics (USSR) still lagged far behind the USA in the development of strategic capabilities that would enable it to strike the United States from missile sites inside the Soviet Union, but its scientists had made greater headway with intermediate and medium-range missiles. To level the playing field, Khrushchev proposed to station the medium-range missiles in Cuba, from where they could be launched against the continental United States, thereby creating a deterrent that would prevent the Americans from attacking the Soviet Union in the first place. The deployment would have the added benefit of protecting the Cuban regime from a possible American invasion, which was widely rumoured at the time. In September 1962, the Soviets secretly dispatched cargo ships laden with nuclear missiles and 40,000 Red Army forces to Cuba.

These events precipitated the Cuban missile crisis, the most dangerous episode in the cold war that could have ended in a nuclear conflict between the superpowers. When American spy planes detected Soviet missiles in Cuba, senior American military leaders urged Kennedy to authorise air strikes to eliminate the threat. Having learned from the Bay of Pigs debacle to mistrust the counsel of trigger-happy advisors, the president asked a series of pertinent questions: How would Khrushchev respond to an American attack on Cuba? He would most likely retaliate with Soviet military action against Western Europe, came the answer. How should the USA react in such an event? America would have to fulfil its obligation under the NATO treaty, defend Western Europe, and likely launch a nuclear attack on the Soviet Union. How would the USSR respond? By retaliating with a nuclear bomber strike against the United States. Confronted with the possibility of World War III, Kennedy shelved the attack on Cuba and opted instead for a quarantine to be enforced by the US Navy that would prevent additional Soviet cargo ships from sailing to Cuba. Simultaneously, he placed American forces around the world on heightened alert under Defense Condition 2, indicating that nuclear war was imminent.

The Cuban missile crisis proved difficult to resolve. Khrushchev explained that Soviet missiles in Cuba were no different from nuclear missiles the USA had already deployed in Turkey, from where they could strike targets in the Soviet Union. He was also furious at Kennedy for declaring a naval quarantine, calling it an authorisation of piracy that could not be tolerated by the Soviet Union, whose ships would remain on course for Cuba. Kennedy in turn insisted on the right to inspect any vessel bound for Cuba, raising the prospect of American sailors forcing their way onto Soviet ships bound for Havana. Back in Washington, the president's brother Robert Kennedy held secret meetings with the Soviet ambassador to find a peaceful solution. In the end, the Soviets agreed to withdraw their missiles in return for an American promise not to invade Cuba in the future, combined with a secret pledge to withdraw US missiles from Turkey within a few months.

The Cuban missile crisis had sobering effects on Kennedy and Khrushchev, precipitating a gradual relaxation of US-Soviet nuclear tensions. The Americans recognised that placing their forces on Defense Condition 2 was an extraordinarily dangerous exercise that raised the possibility of nuclear war by accident as a result of a single false move by a local commander (Defense Condition 2 was never declared again). Though the Soviets declared victory after the missile crisis because they had achieved their objective of safeguarding the Castro regime, they developed grudging respect for Kennedy and proposed a nuclear test ban treaty to prohibit tests of atomic weapons above ground, in space, and underwater that was endorsed by British Prime Minister Harold Macmillan. A chastened Kennedy responded positively in a speech of August 1963 that urged the Soviets to join the USA in pulling back from the precipice of nuclear holocaust, stating "Confident and unafraid, we must labor on – not towards a strategy of annihilation but towards a strategy of peace." Thus Kennedy inaugurated a process of détente, a lessening of tensions in direct relations between the superpowers that continued under his successors Johnson and Nixon.

His fine rhetoric notwithstanding, Kennedy remained committed to containing communism in the developing world, particularly in Vietnam. The situation in South Vietnam was already dire at the time of his inauguration because the US-sponsored dictator Ngo Dinh Diem's unpopular policies triggered armed resistance organised by the National Liberation Front (NLF, also known as the Vietcong). Faced with a steady expansion of NLF control of the South Vietnamese countryside, Kennedy resolved to escalate indirect US involvement in the aftermath of the Bay of Pigs fiasco, saying "Now we have a problem making our power credible and Vietnam looks like the place." Eschewing the deployment of American combat troops because he believed Diem's forces could defeat the NLF on their own as long as they received proper help, he raised the number of US military advisors from 900 to 16,000 in order to support South Vietnamese combat operations.

The results of Kennedy's escalation strategy were questionable. In 1962, for example, American advisors counselled the South Vietnamese to relocate 4.3 million peasants into fortified villages so as to remove them from NLF control and create free-fire zones outside these strategic hamlets, where helicopter gunships could kill Vietcong guerrillas at will. Peasants resented having to abandon their farms and ancestral lands, only to be forced into fortified villages that were run by corrupt South Vietnamese officials. As support for the NLF proliferated in the countryside, growing persecution of Buddhists by minority Roman Catholics led by Diem precipitated urban protests by Buddhist monks, one of whom committed ritual suicide by setting himself on fire in front of Diem's presidential palace in Saigon. These events convinced South Vietnamese generals of the necessity to overthrow the Diem regime and replace it with a military dictatorship. The plan received a sympathetic hearing from the US State Department, which assured the plotters that their planned *coup d'état* would not result a termination of American aid to South Vietnam. The generals struck in early November 1963, when they assassinated Diem and his brother, throwing the country

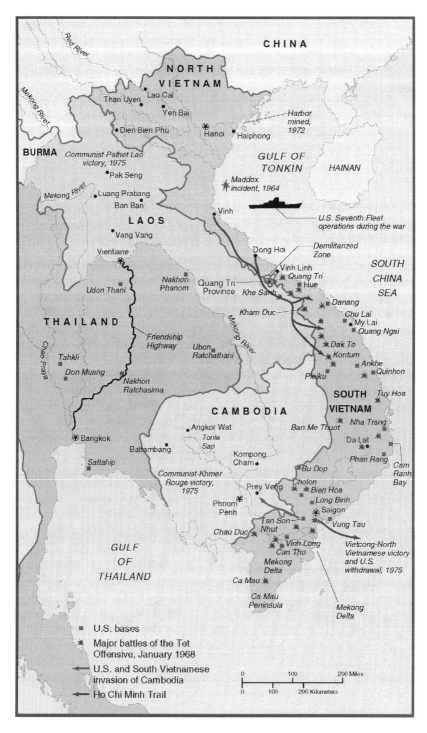

Figure 15.1 The war in Vietnam.

into turmoil as the military proved unable to establish a stable government and the Vietcong stepped up its assaults.

The containment policy that guided Kennedy's Vietnam War strategy was also evident in US relations with Latin America, notably a major new initiative called the Alliance for Progress launched in 1961. Latin America, which had long been regarded as a sideshow in US foreign affairs, received close attention as a result of Kennedy's fears that communists could exploit endemic poverty and political backwardness to establish a Soviet ally on the continent, much as Castro had in the Caribbean. The Alliance for Progress sought to improve US relations with Latin American countries by providing increased American development aid, as well as support for democratic reforms, literacy campaigns, and land redistribution. Though the Alliance scored some modest successes, notably its battle against illiteracy and support for land reform in Chile and Colombia, insufficient funding and growing US preoccupation with Vietnam contributed to failure to achieve its core political objectives, including democratisation campaigns that ran into determined opposition from national elites that supported authoritarian rule.

Kennedy's foreign policy produced a mixed legacy. His overconfident cold war rhetoric, combined with the Bay of Pigs fiasco, resulted in a credibility problem for the USA which he tried to resolve by ramping up American engagement in Southeast Asia, setting the stage for worst crisis in twentieth-century US foreign affairs as the Vietnam War spun out of control. His Alliance for Progress achieved only few of its main objectives. On the positive side, Kennedy's handling of the Cuban missile crisis averted World War III and paved the way for better superpower relations under his successors.

The new frontier and its limits

Kennedy's domestic record was equally ambiguous. During the presidential campaign in 1960, he challenged Americans to tackle New Frontiers of "unconquered problems of ignorance and prejudice, unanswered questions of poverty and surplus." Like the British Labour Party's "New Britain" campaign of the 1960s that borrowed extensively from American election rhetoric, Kennedy's New Frontier agenda envisioned a series of reforms to achieve full employment, expand of Social Security, improve health care for the elderly, provide federal aid to education, and intensify the space programme. Even though the Democrats controlled Congress, however, his reforms faced serious opposition because Kennedy and his team lacked legislative clout, conservative Southern Democrats often sided with Republicans to defeat his initiatives, and many seasoned legislators regarded the president as inexperienced.

Overall, Kennedy reforms that built on the New Deal fared better than ones that departed from political precedent. The former included Social Security initiatives that raised benefits by 20 per cent, expanded coverage to include five million new recipients, and encouraged early retirements. Redeeming Franklin Roosevelt's unfulfilled promise of a major public housing initiative financed by the federal government and Congress appropriated funds for 100,000 units. Lastly, Kennedy asked for and received a raise in the minimum wage, which had originally been established under the National Industrial Recovery Act of 1933. In these and other areas, the president sought the counsel of experienced legislators who helped him steer his reforms through Congress.

His more ambitious initiatives went down in defeat. For example, Kennedy failed to secure passage of a government-funded insurance programme called Medicare for

the elderly that was assailed as "socialised medicine" by the American Medical Association and other powerful lobbying groups. The same fate befell his proposals for
wide-ranging education reforms, tax cuts to revitalise the economy, and a civil rights
act. The administration's inability to secure passage of these "Big Four" pieces of
legislation demarcated the narrow limits of the New Frontier (all of them, plus many
others, were later navigated through Congress by Johnson, his successor as president
and far more experienced legislator than Kennedy).

Kennedy's failure to secure passage of a civil rights bill disappointed grass roots
activists who had initially attached high hopes to his presidency. Though he appointed
an unprecedented number of blacks to federal office, Kennedy was reluctant to move
forcefully on racial matters because he feared that doing so would further complicate
his relationship with Southern Democrats, who were already blocking his social programmes in Congress. Civil rights activists, confronted with the hard truth that the new
administration was disinclined to take the lead on racial justice, sought to force Kennedy's hand with the Freedom Rides of 1961 that challenged racial segregation in interstate transport. Some were arrested by South Carolina police, followed by mob attacks
in Alabama and Mississippi, where white supremacists firebombed the buses and beat
up the freedom riders. US Attorney General Robert Kennedy, who deemed the freedom riders unpatriotic because they allegedly besmirched America's image overseas,
announced that the Justice Department could not "side with one group or the other
in disputes over Constitutional rights." After hundreds of new activists had joined
the Freedom Rides in summer 1961, the Interstate Commerce Commission ordered
bus companies to remove "for whites only" signs from waiting areas and restrooms
throughout the South, but the conflict left a bitter aftertaste among activists and administration officials. Robert Kennedy told the prominent civil rights solicitor Thurgood
Marshall, "the problem with you people [is that] you want too much too fast."

The administration's hope that racial conflicts would subside were dashed in 1962,
when a controversy erupted over air force veteran James Meredith's attempt to gain
admission to the University of Mississippi in Oxford, which was at the time still segregated even though the US Supreme Court had ruled the practise unconstitutional
in Brown v. Board of Education eight years earlier (see Chapter 14). Encouraged by
the white supremacist governor of Mississippi Ross Barnett, the university refused
to admit Meredith despite his stellar academic credentials, triggering a series of legal
actions in which the federal courts backed Meredith. A racist mob prevented Meredith
from entering the university, killed a French journalist and another man, and injured
dozens. White supremacists chanted "Go to Cuba, nigger lovers, go to Cuba!" Kennedy finally dispatched thousands of soldiers to restore order and escort Meredith to
the university.

Overseas, the sight of massive troop deployments to secure the rights of a single
man was greeted with applause, particularly in Africa, whose newly independent
nations had been harshly critical of Kennedy's earlier inaction during the Freedom
Rides. A Kenyan newspaper compared his forceful intervention into the Mississippi
crisis to Eisenhower's use of federal troops to escort black pupils to the Central High
School in 1957 in Little Rock. "[T]he words 'Little Rock' and 'Oxford, Mississippi'
should be considered as a vindication of American democracy," it commented. "In
each case we have seen the federal authorities, working through the channel of the
decisions of the Supreme Court, pursuing honestly and fearlessly a policy aimed at
eradicating the taint of racialism from American life." These sentiments, which were

echoed in Morocco, Congo, and elsewhere, demonstrate that developing nations often took a keen interest American racial affairs.

Another major confrontation erupted in Birmingham, Alabama, in May 1963, when the city's police commissioner ordered attacks on peaceful demonstrators during a civil rights march. Birmingham, one of the most racially divided cities in the USA, was often compared to Johannesburg, where South Africa's white apartheid regime brutally enforced racial segregation. Birmingham's blacks endured crippling poverty, unemployment rates, and job discrimination. Calling attention to their horrendous conditions, the Southern Christian Leadership Council and other civil rights organisations launched a series of sit-ins, marches, and voter registration drives that resulted in the incarceration of hundreds of protesters, including King. At the initiative of Birmingham's police commissioner Eugene "Bull" Connor, an ardent racist, officers unleashed dogs on the demonstrators and firefighters used high-pressure hoses to knock down protesters, causing outrage around the world. African leaders discussed the Birmingham events during a conference in Ethiopia, where they issued a statement expressing "the deep concern aroused in all African peoples and governments by the measures taken against communities of African origin living outside the continent and particularly in the United States of America."

Events in Birmingham prompted Kennedy, at long last, to endorse passage of a civil rights bill in a televised speech of June 1963 that highlighted the impact of racial

Figure 15.2 Policemen with German shepherd dogs attacking civil rights demonstrators in Birmingham, Alabama, 1963. At the time, the photograph evoked memories of Nazi police forces assaulting Jews in World War II.

Source: Courtesy of Black Star/Alamy

incidents around the world and at home. He asked rhetorically, "Are we to say to the world, and much more importantly at home, to each other that this is a land of the free except for the Negroes; that we have no second-class citizens except Negroes; that we have no caste system, no ghettos, no master race except with respect to Negroes?" The Birmingham protesters demanded basic rights, but few of these rights were actually guaranteed by federal law, leaving the administration without a legal basis for intervention, Kennedy argued. Segregated lunch counters, job discrimination, and other forms of racialism practised by private parties were indeed a matter of state and local laws because existing federal law prohibited only discrimination by state authorities in areas such as education. To provide a wider range of legal protections, Kennedy favoured legislation that prohibited racial discrimination in employment, gave citizens equal access to private and public services, and protected voting rights. In autumn 1963, a bill to that effect wound its way through the House of Representatives with support from liberal Democrats and Republicans but was held up by white Southern Democrats. At the time of Kennedy's assassination on 22 November 1963, the civil rights bill seemed destined for defeat along with Medicare, federal education funding, and a tax cut.

From Kennedy to Johnson

The president's murder by Lee Harvey Oswald in Dallas, Texas, sent shock waves across the nation and the globe. Many people found it difficult to believe that a leader of Kennedy stature could be killed by a nobody like Oswald, giving rise to baseless conspiracy theories that suspected the involvement of the CIA, the FBI, the vice president, foreign governments, or a combination thereof. Khrushchev expressed his condolences to the American people, calling Kennedy a man "who realistically assessed the situation and tried to find ways for negotiated settlements of the problems which now divide the world." Cuban leader Castro was less forgiving, accusing Kennedy of having brought the world close to nuclear war, though he hastened to add that the Cuban people felt repulsed by the assassination "because we should not consider this method a correct form of battle." Others expressed greater sympathy. The British government established a Kennedy Memorial at Runnymede (where King John had signed the Magna Carta), the Columbian city Techotyna was renamed Ciudad Kennedy, and Nigeria christened the main crossing of the Niger River the Kennedy Bridge. At home, most Americans were grief-stricken. Republican House Leader proclaimed that "in this hour of tragedy, Americans stand together as one – shocked and grieved at this unbelievable news."

Johnson, sworn in as president aboard Air Force One during the flight from Dallas to Washington, moved swiftly to capitalise on the sense of national unity in order to promote the passage of the civil rights bill. The new president was in many ways the polar opposite of his predecessor. Born in modest circumstances in Texas in 1908, he entered political life during the New Deal and became a loyal disciple of Franklin Roosevelt, whom he regarded as his political role model. Elected leader of the Democrats in the US Senate in 1953, he was an unscrupulous and highly effective dealmaker who accumulated vast amounts of political capital by helping Senators from both parties pass legislation dear to their hearts, for example, federal funding for courthouses and motorways, public housing estates, and foreign trade bills. His years as vice president were the most unsatisfying of his career because he was usually side-lined by

Kennedy's close advisors, who regarded him as unsophisticated, rude, and a closet racist. Johnson's sense of frustration mounted as he watched Kennedy fail to get key elements of his domestic reform programme approved by Congress. Springing into action after the assassination, Johnson used the tragedy to coax legislators into passing the civil rights bill, telling a joint session of Congress during a memorial service only days after the assassination, "No eulogy could more eloquently honor President Kennedy's memory than the earliest possible passage of the civil rights bill for which he fought so long." Constantly on the phone with legislators, he called in some of his vast political credits, applying the "Johnson Treatment" of intimidation and promises to break the political logjam that had prevented passage of the civil rights bill during the final months of the Kennedy presidency.

Passed in 1964, the Civil Rights Act marked a turning point in American history because it ended legal segregation of public accommodations and prohibited employment discrimination based on skin colour, religion, national origin, and sex. In education, it greatly enhanced the ability of the federal government to enforce desegregation by empowering the Justice Department to sue noncompliant school districts. As a result, the percentage of black students enrolled in Southern majority white schools rose from less than 3 per cent in 1964 to 43 per cent in 1988 (though it decreased in subsequent years). Other enforcement mechanisms helped sweep away segregated hospitals, restrooms, lunch counters, cinemas, restaurants, and other facilities. To combat workplace discrimination, the Civil Rights Act created the Equal Employment Opportunity Commission (EEOC) to investigate complaints about unequal treatment of blacks, women, immigrants, and religious minorities, and to advise the federal government on specific antidiscrimination policies. These measures contributed to a decrease in African American unemployment from 10.8 per cent (1960) to 6.4 per cent (1969), and though appreciable gaps in black and white unemployment rates, wages, and benefits persisted, the civil rights act strengthened the black middle class. Prohibiting discrimination by private employers, the law went significantly beyond Britain's Race Relations Act, which was passed in 1965 to curb discrimination against non-white immigrants from Commonwealth countries, but covered only discrimination in public places.

African Americans also benefitted from rapid growth as a result of a tax cut that stimulated the economy with an injection of $14 billion, strengthening a decade-long boom. After Congress had rejected ambitious tax cuts when Kennedy proposed them, Johnson reintroduced the measure and used his legislative skill to get it passed only four months into his presidency, providing corporations with savings they could invest in fresh productive capacity that created jobs, and individuals with extra cash they could spend on homes and consumer items. Coming at a time when the economy had already recovered from a brief recession early in the decade, the tax cut contributed to one of the longest growth spurts in modern American history, when unemployment fell from 6.8 per cent (1961) to 3.8 per cent (1966).

In 1964, Johnson launched a series of antipoverty initiatives called the War on Poverty that was spurred by revelations that the poor constituted as much as 25 per cent of the population. America's infant mortality rate, which correlated closely with poverty, was twice that of Sweden's and higher than that of most industrialised nations. Having declared "unconditional war on poverty" in his first state of the union address, Johnson convinced Congress to pass the Economic Opportunity Act of 1964 that provided funds for a variety of programmes. The most important ones included Head Start, an early childhood education and health programme for disadvantaged children; Job Corps, which created vocational and academic training opportunities for young adults; and Volunteers in Service to America (VISTA) that attracted primarily young and educated Americans who worked in underprivileged communities. The War on Poverty failed to achieve Johnson's goal of eradicating indigence from American life, but the doubling of federal expenditures for the poor during the late 1960s played a major role in reducing the number of people living in poverty from 20 per cent of the total population (1965) to 12 per cent (1969), the single-largest decline in American history.

Having launched the War on Poverty and secured passage of civil rights reform and the tax cut, Johnson faced the voters in the presidential elections of 1964, when he confronted Republican candidate Barry Goldwater. An archconservative who alienated many moderates with his vote against the Civil Rights Act in Congress and reactionary rhetoric, Goldwater joked about the use of nuclear weapons ("Let's lob one into the men's room of the Kremlin"), sought to make Social Security voluntary, and urged abolishment of the graduated income tax. Johnson not only crushed him in the general election with 61.1 to 38.5 per cent of the popular vote, but also helped the

Figure 15.3 President Johnson in conversation with unemployed saw mill worker Tom Fletcher in Kentucky, 1964. The Fletcher family included eight children and lived in abject poverty, highlighting the ordeal of working-class and rural families. Johnson's War on Poverty was intended to alleviate their plight.

Source: Courtesy of Everett Collection Historical/Alamy

Democrats achieve one of the largest majorities in both houses of Congress in modern times. Simultaneously, however, Goldwater attracted a strong following in the South, where white voters turned towards the Republicans over civil rights during the 1960s with major implications for American politics in subsequent decades as the Deep South became a Republican bastion. Confounding liberal predictions that the conservative takeover of the Republican Party inaugurated its doom, moreover, many Goldwater supporters eventually led a conservative backlash, notably Ronald Reagan, who was elected president in 1980, and William Rehnquist, chief justice of the Supreme Court from 1986 to 2005. Young Republican activists who supported Goldwater's doomed presidential bid included the 17-year-old Hillary Rodham, who herself ran unsuccessfully for president as a Democrat in 2016 under her married name Hillary Clinton.

The Great Society

Johnson regarded his election victory as an endorsement of a more ambitious reform programme called the Great Society that combined elements of Kennedy's New Frontier with urban redevelopment, infrastructure improvements, consumer protection, health care reform, education, environmental protection, and many other initiatives. As a result of Johnson's relentless pressure on Congress, where the Democrats controlled both the House and Senate by large margins, the legislative session of 1965–66 produced more than 200 pieces of legislation that sought to improve the lives of ordinary Americans, more reforms than during any other period in American history. Indicative of Johnson's peculiar combination of braggadocio and political realism, he commented "Nothing has moved in this country since the New Deal ground to a halt in '38. The Fair Deal was small potatoes. Ike sat on his hands for eight years. Jack couldn't get the Congress to pass the time of day. I have two years to move the country into the twentieth century" before the political capital he had gained in the elections would run out.

Johnson persuaded Congress to establish the Medicare national health insurance programme for the elderly by amending the New Deal's Social Security Act in 1965. Funded by payroll taxes paid in equal parts by employers and employees, Medicare provided federally administered health insurance for anyone over the age of 65 who had paid into the system, covering elderly Americans who had heretofore remained uninsured because they could not afford the high premiums charged by private insurers. Johnson's reforms also included Medicaid, a health insurance programme that provided federal matching funds to states that insured the poor. In contrast to Germany and Britain, whose public health insurance systems had originated decades earlier and provided universal coverage after World War II, Medicare and Medicaid did not cover people under the age of 65 and the non-indigent, who remained dependent on private health insurance. Indeed, 30 per cent of the American population remained uninsured during the 1960s, making it difficult especially for the working-age population to access regular primary care. Because they saw doctors less frequently, American workers entered their retirement years sicker and with more undiagnosed chronic illnesses than their Western European counterparts, creating financial burdens for Medicare that paid on average nearly twice as much for hospital care than public health insurance programmes in other developed countries. Building on the Johnson reforms, the Republican George W. Bush administration added a prescription drug benefit to Medicare in 2003 and Affordable Care Act passed under

President Barack Obama in 2010 significantly expanded health insurance but still stopped short of universal coverage (see Chapter 17).

Congress also passed the Voting Rights Act of 1965 that demolished long-standing obstacles to black voter participation. Like the Civil Rights Act of 1964, the new legislation was the result of presidential initiative and of grass roots pressure. Activists in Selma, Alabama, long a hotbed of civil rights conflicts, organised a voter registration drive that triggered a violent backlash by local authorities. Known as "Bloody Sunday," the event caused King and other national leaders to join the proliferating protests in Selma that were met by further police violence. Johnson, who dispatched federal troops to protect the demonstrators, went on national television demanding that Congress pass the Voting Rights Act and ended his speech saying "We shall overcome," a reference to the civil rights movement's famous protest song. Enacted in August 1965, the Voting Rights Act suspended literacy tests and other tactics that had kept blacks away from Southern ballot boxes for decades. The act increased southern black voter registration dramatically from one million (1964) to three and a half million (1971). Considered the most successful anti-discrimination law in American history, the act was renewed and strengthened during subsequent decades. It suffered a debilitating setback in 2013, however, when a conservative majority on the Supreme Court ruled that the Justice Department could no longer review changes to election laws in nine Southern states.

Lastly, Johnson initiated major changes in immigration law with a reform package enacted in 1965. Kennedy, who deemed the existing quota system "nearly intolerable," had called for the equal treatment of immigrants regardless of their race and nationality. These principles became the building blocks of the Immigration Act of 1965, whose passage was spurred by the enactment of other antidiscrimination legislation, notably the Civil Rights Act. The reform deracialised American immigration policy and established an upper limit on the number of people to be admitted annually to 290,000. Reflecting widespread homophobia, it prohibited the immigration of gays and lesbians who were defined as "sexual deviants," a provision that was repealed only in 1990. Though Massachusetts senator Edward Kennedy (JFK's brother) and other supporters of the Immigration Act stressed that it would not "upset" America's ethnic mix, the reform resulted in a major influx of immigrants from Asia, Latin America, the Middle East, and Africa. From 1950 to 2013, the share of foreign-born Americans in the total population doubled to 14 per cent. Conservative critics often attributed a variety of social problems to the growth of the immigrant population after 1965, particularly the poor performance of American students compared to their European counterparts. In fact, however, by 2013 the populations of Western Europe and other developed parts of the world included a growing share of foreign-born persons, for example, Britain (12.4 per cent), France (11.6 per cent), West Germany (11.9 per cent), and Canada (20.7 per cent).

The northern racial crisis and black power

In the decade leading up to 1965, civil rights activism spawned one of the most successful social movements in American history. Relentlessly pushing the Kennedy and Johnson administrations to implement social justice here and now, the movement felled a system of state-sponsored white supremacy in the American South that had disfigured the nation's political and social life for generations. From a global perspective, this stunning achievement ranked with the defeat of European colonialism in the developing world after World War II and the overthrow of the South African apartheid regime in the late twentieth century. Victory came at a considerable price as large segments of the civil rights movement subordinated themselves to the anti-Communist imperatives of American liberalism to avoid offending their powerful allies in the white establishment. While legal segregation breathed its last during the mid-1960s, moreover, racism remained a potent force in American life that provoked the rise of the Black Power movement.

"ghetto"

To the surprise of many non-Americans, the use of the word "ghetto" is controversial in the United States, where it is colloquially often used in a pejorative sense. Analytically, it refers to racially homogenous, socially isolated neighbourhoods with high concentrations of unemployment, poverty, female-headed households, and welfare dependency. Historically, American ghettos emerged in the first half of the twentieth century during the "great migration" of African Americans from the rural South to the urban North. Here they frequently encountered racial discrimination in job and housing markets, and were forced to live in poor neighbourhoods with substandard housing whose previous (usually poor white) residents moved elsewhere in a process called "white flight."

Some studies like sociologist William J. Wilson's classic *The Truly Disadvantaged: The Inner City, the Underclass, and Public Policy* (1987) attribute the social characteristics of ghettos to class discrimination, primarily the lack of employment opportunities for young black males. His critics like historian Gerald Bennett respond that Wilson side-lines racial discrimination as a primary factor in ghetto development.

Racial segregation was a defining characteristic of ghettos in many northeastern, midwestern, and West Coast cities (see concept box). Though not officially written into law as it was in the South, it reflected discriminatory practises that channelled African Americans into all-black neighbourhoods like Watts in Los Angeles, the most racially segregated city in America. While the ghettoisation of African Americans in the early twentieth century had been created by informal policies in the real estate industry, the "second ghetto" of the post–World War II era stemmed from conscious decisions by urban planners to create vast public housing estates inhabited mostly by African Americans. This development was partly attributable to white working-class resistance against the influx of black residents during the 1950s. In Chicago, for example, whose black population tripled from 1940 to 1960, whites launched determined efforts to keep the new arrivals out of neighbourhoods, including frequent arson and bombing of black homes. White politicians and policymakers sought to defuse this situation with the construction of 28 identical high rises along a four-mile strip that concentrated 27,000 African Americans in the world's largest public housing estate.

Racially homogeneous and socially isolated from the rest of the city, second ghettos resembled South Africa's Bantustans, territories set aside by the apartheid regime in the 1940s for exclusive settlement by blacks. American ghettos typically suffered from disproportionate unemployment, poverty, inadequate public services, and crime. National leaders rarely acknowledged the sheer horror of ghetto life, with the notable exception of Robert Kennedy, who decried the racial "brutalities of the North . . . All these places – Harlem, Watts, Southside – are riots waiting to happen." Kennedy's dire prediction proved accurate as ghettos became the scene of social unrest in the 1960s. More often than not, they were triggered by police violence. In August 1965, two days after the passage of the Voting Rights Act, Watts erupted into a riot involving 30,000 people that lasted for almost a week. The unrest left 34 blacks dead, more than a thousand injured, and $40 million in property damage.

Against this backdrop, black militants argued that the tactics and goals of the civil rights movement – non-violent protest, alliances with white liberals, and racial integration – were woefully inadequate to tackle a racial crisis that was not confined to the American South. Radicals rallied behind the slogan "Black Power" introduced in 1966 by activist Stokely Carmichael, who defined it as follows: "It is a call for black people in this country to unite, to recognise their heritage, to build a sense of community. It is a call for black people to define their own goals, to lead their own organizations." Recognising one's black heritage usually entailed positive views of African American history and culture, often combined with an ideology that cast Africa as the common denominator of disparate groups of blacks in the diaspora. African leaders admired by Black Power proponents included Patrice Lumumba, the charismatic anti-imperialist prime minister of the Republic of Congo whose friendly relationships with the Soviet Union precipitated his ouster in 1961. Lumumba's death at the hands of his domestic opponents and Belgian soldiers was called a "lynching" by black militants who sought to draw parallels between American racism and European colonialism. Carmichael and others indeed portrayed American race relations as a form of "internal colonialism," claiming that American blacks, like colonised African people, confronted forcible subjugation, economic exploitation, destruction of indigenous cultures, and management of their social life by racist government bureaucracies. To combat these conditions, many Black Power proponents advocated the exclusion of whites from community affairs, combined with the development of independent black political and business structures. Malcolm X, the former spokesman of the radical Nation of Islam, told a crowd in Detroit in 1964, "The time when white people can come in our community and get us to vote for them so that they can be our political leaders and tell us what to do and what not to do is long gone." Important community organisations that emerged from the Black Power Movement included the Black Panther Party (see concept box).

Johnson's escalation of the Vietnam War

Johnson faced unsettled conditions in South Vietnam from the beginning of his presidency in November 1963. Diem's assassination by his own generals earlier that month inaugurated a chaotic period when senior military commanders spent more time outmanoeuvring each other for political advantage than fighting the guerrilla forces that controlled almost half the country. Simultaneously, the North Vietnamese communist government under Ho Chi Minh stepped up its support for the Vietcong and even authorised the secret deployment of regular North Vietnamese troops to South Vietnam. Johnson, lacking familiarity with foreign affairs generally and Kennedy's Vietnam policy in particular, developed several rationales for continued American involvement. Most important, Johnson shared Kennedy's and Eisenhower's belief in the domino theory, postulating that the fall of South Vietnam to communism would trigger a tidal wave of revolutions across Southeast Asia that would sweep away pro-American regimes throughout the region.

Black Panther Party for self-defence

Formed in Oakland, California, by activists Huey Newton and Bobby Seale in 1966 to combat police brutality, the Black Panther Party derived its name from a US Army tank battalion primarily comprised of African American soldiers who had fought in World War II under the motto "Come out fighting." Taking advantage of lax gun laws, members of the Black Panther Party brandished rifles and shotguns openly whilst monitoring the conduct of police officers in black neighbourhoods while chanting, "The Revolution has come, it's time to pick up the gun." In 1967, the Panthers adopted a ten-point programme that included demands for decent housing, an end to police brutality, and "the robbery by the Capitalists of our Black Community," "education that teaches us our true history," and the release of all black prisoners from jail. The party's radicalism soon attracted attention from the FBI, whose covert Counterintelligence Program COINTELPRO sought to disrupt, discredit, and neutralise domestic opposition groups, often by illegal means.

As the Johnson administration grappled for strategies to deal with increased guerrilla activity in South Vietnam, it began to focus on North Vietnam on the assumption that the strength of the rebellion in the South was attributable to presence of Northern communist forces. As a remedy, US policy advisors proposed a series of air strikes against North Vietnam that would force Hanoi to abandon its support for the Vietcong, stabilising the situation in the South. All that was needed to implement the plan was a trigger that would convince Congress to pass an authorisation for the use of military force. Such an event in fact materialised in early August 1964, when the US destroyer *Maddox* sailing in the Gulf of Tonkin on a reconnaissance mission was attacked by North Vietnamese torpedo boats, causing Johnson to warn Hanoi publicly that he would seek Congressional authorisation for military action if US forces were attacked again. Only days later, when frantic American destroyer crews off the coast of North Vietnam reported torpedo attacks on their ships, Johnson made good on his threat by asking Congress to pass the Gulf of Tonkin Resolution that authorised him to conduct military operations in Southeast Asia as he saw fit. Suspicions that these events were being stage managed by an administration looking for an excuse to implement its already-planned attacks on North Vietnam proved correct: The second attack on US naval forces that triggered the Gulf of Tonkin Resolution never occurred.

Shortly after reporting attacks of 4 August, the destroyer sent a corrected version of events that blamed the initial sighting of torpedoes on "overeager" sonar operators. Johnson was aware of the corrected report but failed to inform the American public because doing so would have jeopardised passage of the Gulf of Tonkin Resolution. Obtained under false pretences, the resolution was used by Johnson to order airstrikes against North Vietnam and remained the only legal basis for the deployment of US combat forces in Southeast Asia until its repeal in 1971.

The administration continued to prevaricate in order to justify the gradual escalation of direct US military involvement in Vietnam. Johnson, having portrayed himself as an opponent of deployment of American combat forces during his presidential election campaign in order to garner liberal votes, in March 1965 authorised a massive bombing campaign against North Vietnam called "Operation Rolling Thunder" that was officially described as retaliation for a Vietcong attack on American barracks in Pleiku, South Vietnam. In truth, the Pleiku incident was merely a convenient excuse to justify an expansion of the war that had been urged by Johnson's National Security Council months earlier to curb North Vietnamese support for the Vietcong. In addition to the air force, Johnson soon deployed ground forces as well to protect American air bases in South Vietnam from guerrilla attacks. Convinced that South Vietnamese troops totalling one million men were unable to fight 100,000 Vietcong effectively, the US Army and Marines gradually assumed most of the responsibility for fighting the guerrillas, putting the lie to Johnson's campaign promise that "We are not about to send American boys nine or ten thousand miles away from home to do what Asian boys ought to be doing for themselves." By the end of 1965, US troop levels had increased to 184,000 and more were on their way.

America's deepening commitment strained relationships in the North Atlantic Treaty Organization. The United Kingdom, America's closest ally, refused to send combat forces to Vietnam to join contingents from South Korea, New Zealand, the Philippines, and Australia, drawing heated reactions from frustrated American leaders. An infuriated Secretary of State Dean Rusk went so far as to question America's commitment to the defence of Britain, saying "When the Russians invade Sussex, don't expect us to come and help you." Some of the harshest criticism of came from French President Charles de Gaulle, who strongly opposed the Vietnam War and American domination of NATO and indicted the Americans for "threatening for the peace of the world." Growing US-French rifts culminated in de Gaulle's decision to withdraw French forces from NATO's military command in 1966. Ludwig Erhard, the West German Chancellor, by contrast, subserviently complied with American demands to extend financial aid to South Vietnam and rebuffed French attempts to enlist him in diplomatic attempts to establish Vietnamese neutrality, but refused to send combat forces. Like most NATO members, the West Germans worried that the US build-up in Southeast Asia would come at the expense of the American troop presence in Western Europe, weakening the alliance's ability to deter the Soviets. The USA in fact reduced its troop presence in West Germany from 366,000 (1966) to 300,000 (1968) as West Germany became the largest contributor of NATO troops in Europe.

Trained and equipped to repulse a Soviet attack on Western Europe, US troops were ill-prepared to fight guerrilla forces in the Southeast Asian jungle. Here, they confronted a lightly armed and highly mobile enemy organised into small units that were nothing like the Red Army's heavy combat divisions with their tanks, artillery, and air support. Indochina's jungle-covered, mosquito-infested countryside was a world apart from the Northern German plains where the US Army expected to defeat a Soviet invasion of Western Europe. Searching for new tactics that seemed more suitable for the unfamiliar combat environment, the commander of US forces in Vietnam General William Westmoreland adopted a "search and destroy" (S&D) approach that had been used successfully by the British in Malaya. Instead conquering large swaths of territory, S&D units identified enemy-controlled target areas, killed as many foes as possible, and then withdrew to their base camps. Though the Vietcong and North Vietnamese forces learned to evade S&D missions, Westmoreland insisted on the tactic long after its flaws had become obvious. In January 1967, for example, 30,000 US and South Vietnamese forces launched the massive "Cedar Falls" S&D operation against a Vietcong-controlled fortified village north of Saigon. The troops encircled and invaded the town after a heavy air strike, permanently relocated its 6,000 inhabitants, bulldozed the area, and pulled out; what little remained left standing was saturation bombed and torched with napalm to destroy the Vietcong's underground tunnel system. Westmoreland considered Operation Cedar Falls a success because it killed more than 700 Vietcong and presumably eliminated a strategic threat to Saigon, but the guerrillas quickly returned to the area, rebuilt their infrastructure, and created a

Figure 15.4 US and South Vietnamese forces escort women and children to a "central collection point for civilians" near the Cambodian border. The plight of civilians, two million of whom died during the Vietnam War, caused outrage around the world.

Source: Courtesy of Everett Collection Inc./Alamy

launch pad for an offensive against Saigon. Their perseverance occasionally elicited grudging respect from American commanders. One commented after a hard-fought battle with North Vietnamese forces, "Damn, give me two hundred men that well disciplined and I'll capture this whole country."

Operation Rolling Thunder meanwhile failed to break North Vietnam's determination to resist. From 1965 to 1968, the air force dropped close to one million tons of bombs, twice as many tons as the USA had expended during the entire Pacific War. The effect on North Vietnam, whose landmass was smaller than Britain's, was nothing short of catastrophic. By the end of 1967, the attacks had killed 100,000 civilians, left many more injured and homeless, and crippled the small industrial base. Dumbfounding the Americans, however, the bombing had little effect on North Vietnam's ability to support the Vietcong with weapons and materiel, most of which were imported from China and the Soviet Union. Hanoi also stepped up the infiltration of regular army forces into South Vietnam from 35,000 (1965) to 150,000 (1967). North Vietnamese President Ho Chi Minh said he was prepared to fight as long as it took to reunify Vietnam under communist auspices, explaining stoically, "If the Americans want to make war for twenty years then we shall make war for twenty years. If they want to make peace, we shall make peace and invite them to afternoon tea."

The anti-war movement and the new left

Anti-war activists challenged the core assumption of establishment liberals that progressive domestic reforms could be squared with military intervention on behalf of cold war anticommunism. Johnson sometimes portrayed the Vietnam War as a vital corollary to the Great Society because the former protected the latter from his right-wing opponents. If liberals "wished to pass progressive laws, [we] had to show that [we] were firmly committed against the ultimate 'progressives' – the communists," he explained. Unfortunately for Johnson, his calculations failed to account for the possibility that major liberal constituencies would contest the political and moral legitimacy of the war, shattering the cold war liberal consensus that sustained his presidency.

Students for a Democratic Society (SDS)

Formed in 1962 by activists at the University of Michigan led by Tom Hayden, the SDS adopted a political manifesto called the Port Huron statement on behalf of "this generation, bred in at least modest comfort, housed now in universities, looking uncomfortably to the world we inherit." Decrying the bureaucratisation of universities, poverty, the cold war, and white supremacy, the statement demanded greater student and faculty involvement in university governance, universal disarmament, and greater mainstream liberal support for civil rights activism.

Anti-war protests owed much to the emergence of the New Left, so called to distinguish it from the communist and socialist Old Left that been primarily concerned with labour issues prior to its suppression during the McCarthy era. Eschewing the Old Left's orthodox Marxism and preoccupation with formal organisations like trade unions, New Left organisations like the Students for a Democratic Society rejected impersonal bureaucracies and promoted participatory democracy (see concept box). Many SDS members initially participated in racial justice campaigns before turning to anti-war protest when the US Air Force launched Rolling Thunder, the bombardment of North Vietnam, in spring 1965. At the University of Michigan in Ann Arbor, SDS members organised the first anti-war teach-in where faculty discussed their objections to US involvement in Vietnam with 3,000 students. By the end of the spring term, similar teach-ins had been held at more than 100 campuses across the country and the SDS had organised an anti-war march in Washington DC attended by 20,000 protesters.

Student activists who participated in civil rights campaigns before engaging in anti-war activism included Jack Weinberg from the University of California at Berkeley. In 1964, Weinberg was arrested at Berkeley for distributing leaflets for the Congress for Racial Equality in violation of a university policy that prohibited political campaigning on campus, prompting 3,000 students to conduct a spontaneous sit-in to force his release. These events sparked the formation of the Berkeley Free Speech movement that demanded student rights in areas such as political activism on campus, curriculum development, and academic personnel decisions. Shortly after the start of Operation Rolling Thunder, Berkeley activists organised a massive teach-in against the Vietnam War where historian Isaac Deutscher (a prominent figure in Britain's New Left), child psychologist Benjamin Spock, and other luminaries lambasted Johnson's escalation policy before an audience of 30,000 students.

As the SDS membership reached 80,000 by 1968, it embraced radical forms of anti-war activism, including resistance against conscription as protesters publicly burned their draft cards. One explained "To cooperate with conscription is to perpetuate its existence, without which the government could not wage war. We have chosen to openly defy the draft and confront the government and its war directly." Congress and Johnson responded with the passage of the draft card burning law stipulating a maximum fine of $10,000 and up to five years imprisonment.

Students were soon joined by other radical opponents of the Vietnam War, including Black Power activist Carmichael who cast his anti-war stance in antiimperialist terms. Calling attention to the sordid history of US military intervention in the Philippines and American support for the South African apartheid regime, Carmichael told students at Berkeley in 1966 American foreign policy "means raping South Africa, beating Vietnam, beating South America, raping the Philippines, raping every country you've been in." Others cited political motives that echoed domestic racial conflicts. Muhammed Ali, the world heavyweight boxing champion, explained his refusal to serve in the armed forces by saying, "I ain't got no quarrel with them Viet Cong. No Viet Cong ever called me Nigger." Conspicuously absent from the ranks of early anti-war activists was King, who remained reluctant to abandon his close relationship with a president who had done much to enhance civil rights. By April 1967, however, even King had enough of Johnson's war, telling a crowd in New York City that he had often heard activists ask " 'What about Vietnam?' Their questions hit home, and I knew that I could never again raise my voice against the violence of the oppressed in the ghettos without having first spoken clearly to the greatest purveyor of violence in the world today: my own government."

Anti-war protests attracted Americans from all walks of life. In Washington DC, honourably discharged soldiers marched under a banner that read "Vietnam Veterans

Against the War." Christian ministers joined Jewish rabbis in an organisation called Clergy and Laymen Concerned about Vietnam. Suburban housewives sent Mother's Day cards to their Congressmen imprinted with the slogan "War is not healthy for children and other living things." Some protesters articulated their disdain for a mainstream culture they held responsible for the war by growing their hair long, wearing blue jeans and tie dye shirts, endorsing sexual promiscuity, and smoking marijuana, all of which became defining symbols of the hippie counterculture. Though often disdained as apolitical by the SDS and other New Leftist, hippies were enthusiastic participants in anti-war marches, which one regarded as "a great place to get laid, get high, and listen to some great rock."

Second-wave feminism

The civil rights and student movements that inspired anti-war activism also had profound effects on feminism, which entered a new phase in the 1960s when women began to challenge gender inequality and discrimination in many walks of life. To distinguish it from the first wave of feminist activism that focused on women's suffrage since the nineteenth century, historians have labelled the new movement "second wave feminism."

The movement's roots were planted in the early 1960s, when a handful of intellectuals questioned the belief that the vast majority of educated women were happy with their roles as wives and mothers, surrounded by material comforts of middle-class life. These notions were challenged by Betty Friedan's path-breaking study *Feminine Mystique* that revealed the deep sense of unhappiness many middle-class women felt with their lives as homemakers (see Chapter 14). The Presidential Commission on the Status of Women, established by Kennedy in 1961 at the initiative of former first lady Eleanor Roosevelt, revealed gender discrimination in almost every area of American life, notably in employment where women were often excluded from high-paying jobs and rewarding careers. Its findings motivated Congress to pass the Equal Pay Act of 1963 that mandated equal pay for equal work in a narrowly defined set of occupations, excluding professionals and administrators. At the initiative of Democratic Congresswoman Martha Griffith of Michigan, lawmakers included sex as a protected attribute in the Civil Rights Act of 1964 under Title VII, which prohibited employment discrimination against women among others. The Equal Employment Opportunity Commission that was tasked with enforcing the law, however, was almost entirely composed of men who exhibited scant interest in sex discrimination. Feminist activists, angered by the commission's neglect, in 1966 formed the National Organization for Women (NOW) whose most prominent members included Betty Friedan herself and other female intellectuals.

In addition to NOW, which was primarily active on behalf of female professionals, second wave feminism also included younger women who participated in the student and civil rights movements, where they often encountered the same sort of sexism that disfigured mainstream society. Carmichael of the Student Nonviolent Coordinating Committee (SNCC), for example, joked viciously "What is the position of women in SNCC? The position of women in SNCC is prone." Similar attitudes were evident in many campus organisations of the Students for a Democratic Society (SDS), whose male members reserved leadership roles for themselves and expected women to make coffee, take stenographic notes, and clean up after meetings. Outraged women drew parallels between sexism and racism, charging that assumptions of male superiority were "as widespread and deep-rooted and as crippling to the woman as the assumption of white supremacy are to the Negro." Withdrawing from what they perceived as male-dominated spaces, feminists began to establish all-female organisations to discuss gender-specific issues and engage in their own form of political activism. Members of a prominent "women's lib" group called New York Radical Women, for example, gained notoriety with a protest against the Miss America pageant in Atlantic City, New Jersey, where they set makeup, girdles, court shoes, and other "instruments of female torture" on fire in a trash can, earning them the sobriquet "bra burners" in the media.

The year of upheavals

1968 was among the most crisis-ridden years in American history. A massive Vietcong offensive in January called the Tet Offensive precipitated a collapse of public support for the Vietnam War, fatally undermining the Johnson presidency. Johnson's surprise announcement in March that he would not run for re-election was followed by the assassinations of King and Robert Kennedy, the slain president's brother. At a rancorous convention in Chicago, radicals and the Democratic Party establishment turned on one another. The year of upheavals ended with the election of Republican Richard Nixon as president.

In January, Vietcong guerrillas and North Vietnamese troops launched the Tet Offensive, the largest military operation of the war so far. Attacking urban centres in hopes to trigger a general uprising that would topple the South Vietnamese government, they made impressive gains in the first couple of weeks, when they invaded the capital Saigon, laid siege on the American combat base in Khe Sanh, and captured the ancient city of Hue. But they failed to spark a general uprising as American and South Vietnamese forces rallied, recaptured the cities, and killed more than 46,000 combatants, inflicting a defeat from which the Vietcong never recovered. North Vietnamese forces henceforth did most of the fighting in South Vietnam.

Though the Tet Offensive proved a military disaster for Vietcong, it produced a political and psychological defeat for the Johnson administration, which had done nothing to prepare the public for the sheer scale and ferocity of the fighting. Indicative of the rosy picture US leaders painted of Vietnam, the commander of US forces Westmoreland had told the American people in November 1967 that there was "light at the end of the tunnel." Having been lulled into complacency with misrepresentations and outright lies, war supporters were suddenly confronted with television footage of Vietcong battalions attacking the US Embassy in Saigon. Television anchor Walter Cronkite expressed the incredulity of many when he exclaimed, "What the hell is going on? I thought we were winning the war!" Opinion polls taken in February 1968 showed for the first time a majority of respondents agreeing with the statement that the war was a mistake. Footage of a Vietcong suspect being executed by the national police chief of South Vietnam in the streets of Saigon caused revulsion against the US-supported government around the world. When anti-war protesters in London, West Berlin, and Amsterdam demanded an immediate US withdrawal from Vietnam, Robert Kennedy commented, "Our best and oldest friends ask, more in sorrow than in anger, what has happened to America?"

The breakdown of political support for the Vietnam War left the administration unsure how to proceed. Clark Clifford, who had recently replaced the exhausted

McNamara as Secretary of Defense, asked the Joint Chiefs of Staff, in early March "What is the plan for victory in Vietnam?" to which they responded "There is no plan." Upon Clifford's advice, Johnson on 31 March announced a suspension of Operation Rolling Thunder against North Vietnam and asked the communists to commence peace negotiations. At the end of the speech, he stunned his audience by stating that he would not run for re-election.

Americans had barely caught their breath at the collapse of the Johnson presidency under the weight of Vietnam when King was assassinated in Memphis, Tennessee, on 4 April 1968, by a white supremacist. Having been instrumental in achieving the landmark civil and voting rights legislation in the mid-1960s, King had lost political influence as the Black Power movement gathered strength later in the decade and was derided by Malcolm X as "the Reverend Dr. Chickenwing." When he turned against the Vietnam War in 1967, King lost his close relationship with Johnson. A year later, he tried to regain political relevance with his support of black garbage workers in Memphis who were engaged in a two-month strike to protest wage discrimination and poor working conditions. The night before his assassination, he said presciently during his last speech with a Biblical reference to the land of Canaan promised by God to Abraham and his people, "I've seen the Promised Land. I may not get there with you. But I want you to know tonight, that we, as a people, will get to the Promised Land." The next day, King was shot in the head and died.

The King assassination triggered the worst urban rioting in the USA in decades. The unrest, which broke out in more than 120 cities and left 39 people dead, turned lawlessness into a major political issue that outranked even the Vietnam War as a matter of concern among voters. Opinion polls indicated that 81 per cent of respondents agreed with the statement "law and order has broken down in this country" and that 42 per cent believed blacks to be "more violent than whites." Conservatives, notably Nixon, the Republican candidate for the presidency, blamed the unrest on liberals who had allegedly mollycoddled radicals. Nixon embraced demands for law and order, harsher penalties for criminals, and more extensive incarceration, promising in a campaign commercial that showed screaming anti-war protesters, dope-smoking hippies, and burned-out inner-city buildings. "I pledge to you, we shall have order in the United States."

Robert Kennedy, who sought the nomination of the Democratic Party for president in spring 1968, had a different message in the wake of the King assassination. On the night of 4 April, he broke the terrible news to a largely black crowd in Indianapolis that was not yet aware of the fact that King was dead. In one of the most eloquent speeches of the twentieth century – delivered impromptu – Kennedy laid out the choices facing the nation generally and African Americans particularly at this crucial moment: to respond with bitterness and hate, or to muster "love and wisdom and compassion towards one another, and a feeling of justice towards those who still suffer within our country, whether they be white or whether they be black . . ., [and] to tame the savageness of man and make gentle the life of this world." Indianapolis was among the few major cities that remained quiet on the night of King's death. Kennedy's campaign was supported by young militants, veteran civil rights activists, liberal intellectuals, anti-war protesters, labour radicals, and ordinary Americans who saw him as the only beacon of hope amidst the turmoil of the late sixties. On 5 June 1968, he scored his greatest political victory when he won the California primary election that all but assured him the nomination of the Democratic Party for the presidency. The same night, he was shot to death by a Jordanian of Palestinian descent who objected to Kennedy's support for Israel. Coming as it did on the heels of the King assassination, his death left many Americans desperate and adrift. "I won't vote," said one young man. "Every good man we get they kill."

In August 1968, members of a counterculture group called the Youth International Party and the National Mobilization Committee to End the War in Vietnam appealed to anti-war activists to converge on Chicago, where the Democratic Party convened to select its candidate for the presidential election in November. Chicago's Democratic mayor Richard Daley, a beefy machine politician, vowed that no one "will come to our city and take over our streets, our city, our convention." He mobilised 23,000 law enforcement officers clad in riot gear who assaulted 10,000 demonstrators with billy clubs, tear gas, and pepper spray while shouting "Kill, kill, kill." Inside the convention hall, Connecticut Senator Abraham Ribicoff told delegates that the conduct of the Chicago police resembled "Gestapo methods," a reference to Germany's secret police that carried out anti-Semitic laws and oppressed political opponents of the Nazi regime. Mayor Daley yelled at Senator Ribicoff, "Fuck you, you Jew son of a bitch, you lousy motherfucker, go home." These events overshadowed the nomination of Hubert Humphrey, Johnson's vice president, as the standard bearer of the Democratic Party for the presidential elections.

In one of the most tumultuous elections in American history, Humphrey faced off against Nixon on the Republican ticket and white supremacist George Wallace for

Figure 15.5 Demonstrators and National Guard members in Chicago during the national convention of the Democratic Party, 1968. The protests were soon followed by large-scale police violence.

Source: Courtesy of RBM Vintage Images/Alamy

the American Independent Party. Though he managed to hold on to most elements of organised labour, Humphrey lost support among white Southern conservatives who had already begun to abandon the Democratic Party in the 1964 presidential elections over Johnson's civil rights reforms ("From Kennedy to Johnson", pages 440–43). Nixon sought to exploit these divisions in with his so-called Southern Strategy that emphasised his support for "states' rights" and "local control," which were code phrases for resistance against federally mandated desegregation. Republicans faced fierce competition from the Wallace campaign that targeted the exact same voters. A former governor of Alabama who had gained notoriety for saying "segregation now, segregation tomorrow, segregation forever," Wallace had personally tried to prevent four black students from entering the University of Alabama, earning his far greater racist credentials than Nixon could hope to achieve with his more subtle rhetoric. Unlike Nixon, moreover, Wallace was a die-in-the-wool Southern Populist who favoured national health insurance, labour rights, state-financed higher education, and other progressive causes that earned him the support of many trade union members and other voters who had previously supported Robert Kennedy. In the end, Nixon won with only a razor-thin margin of 43.4 per cent of the popular vote over Humphrey's 42.7 per cent and Wallace's 13.5 per cent.

Chapter summary

The chapter developed a critical perspective on the Kennedy and Johnson years, when liberals embarked on anti-Communist crusades in Cuba, Vietnam, and other parts of the world while marshalling the powers of the federal government to tackle social and racial problems at home. In foreign affairs, the Bay of Pigs debacle of 1961 contributed to subsequent crises, notably the Cuban missile crisis and America's growing involvement in Vietnam. Domestically, Kennedy managed to build on the New Deal but faced difficulties bringing his New Frontier programmes to fruition, leaving the task to Johnson. Though the Great Society achieved much in areas such as health care for the elderly and the poor, immigration, education, and above all civil rights, it suffered from a variety of shortcomings, notably its inability to solve the proliferating urban and racial crises particularly in the North, where socially isolated ghettos repeatedly exploded in violence. The passage of the Civil Rights Act of 1964 and the Voting Rights Act marked major victories for the civil rights movement, but its leaders – Martin Luther King included – found it difficult to respond to the racial crisis in Northern cities, where the Black Power movement gained influence. The escalation of the Vietnam War meanwhile provoked the rise of the anti-war movement as students and many other Americans questioned the legitimacy and sincerity of the Johnson administration. Johnson's prevarications and lies about Vietnam finally caught up with him during the Tet Offensive whose domestic fallout prompted him to abandon his re-election plans. Shortly afterwards, public revulsion at the King assassination riots strengthened conservative calls for law and order at the very moment when the murder of Robert Kennedy deprived liberals, progressives, and leftists of a leader who could have rallied the New Deal coalition once more to achieve a Democratic victory in the presidential election. Instead, various elements of that coalition turned against each other at the Chicago convention and at the ballot box, enabling Nixon to achieve a narrow election victory in November 1968. Unbeknownst to most Americans who were preoccupied with political and racial problems, a crisis of an entirely different sort was brewing deep inside the bowels of the US economy, whose strength was quietly eroded by inflation and lack of competitiveness in key industries at the dawn of the 1970s.

Discussion questions

- What were the consequences of the failed Bay of Pigs invasion for American foreign policy in the 1960s?
- Why did some of Kennedy's New Frontier programmes succeed while others failed?
- What were the most important differences between Kennedy and Johnson as presidents?
- What were the major achievements and failures of Johnson's Great Society reforms?
- What were the differences of the civil rights movement and the Black Power movement?
- Why did many Americans oppose the Vietnam War?
- What was the relationship between feminism and other social movements of the 1960s?
- Why was 1968 a crisis year in American history?

Further reading

Austin, Curtis J. *Up Against the Wall: Violence in the Making and Unmaking of the Black Panther Party* (Little Rock, 2006). A balanced account of the Black Panthers that examines the origins of their self-defence ideology, its impact on black politics, and the demise of the Panther leadership.

Branch, Taylor. *The King Years: Historic Moments in the Civil Rights Movement* (New York, 2013). Selections from the author's prize-winning, multivolume study of Martin Luther King's role in the civil rights movement from the 1950s to King's death in 1968.

Dallek, Robert. *Flawed Giant: Lyndon Johnson and His Times, 1961–1973* (New York, 1998). This prize-winning biography by a leading historian of the twentieth century examines Johnson's foreign and domestic policies, personal life, and impact on American politics, foreign affairs, and society.

Farber, David R. *The Age of Great Dreams: America in the 1960s* (New York, 1994). A magisterial survey of how the period's political, social, and cultural conflicts transformed American consumer society.

From Camelot to Kent State: The Sixties Experience in the Words of Those Who Lived it, eds. Joan Morrison and Robert K. Morrison (New York, 2001). First-hand accounts by American soldiers in Vietnam, Peace Corps workers, student rebels, and many others.

Fursenko, Aleksandr, and Timothy Naftali. *One Hell of a Gamble: Khrushchev, Castro and Kennedy, 1958–1964* (New York, 1997). A deeply researched study of the origins and escalation of the Cuban missile crisis that gives equal weight to American and Soviet perspectives.

Herring, George C. *America's Longest War: The United States and Vietnam, 1950–1975* (New York, 2001). The fourth edition of a Herring's classic study of US involvement in Vietnam from the French Indochinese War until the fall of South Vietnam.

Hoefferle, Caroline. *British Student Activism in the Long Sixties* (London, 2013). A path breaking study of student unrest, anti-war protest, and countercultures at British universities and their relationship with American radicalism.

Imagine Nation: The American Counterculture of the 1960s and '70s, eds. Peter Braunstein and Michael William Doyle (New York, 2002). A collection of essays exploring the multifaceted aspects of the period's counterculture, including communal living, drugs, the sexual revolution, and feminism.

Klimke, Martin. *The Other Alliance: Student Protest in West Germany and the United States in the Global Sixties* (Princeton, NJ, 2010). Based on deep archival research and interviews, the book explores the transatlantic interconnectedness of anti-war protests, West German perceptions of the American Black Power movement, and the responses of the American and West German governments.

Lytle, Mark H. *America's Uncivil Wars: The Sixties Era from Elvis to the Fall of Richard Nixon* (New York, 2006). Examines three phases of domestic conflict: From the 1950s cultural upheavals to Kennedy's death, civil rights and Vietnam War protests, and the social movements of the Nixon era.

Manchester, William. *The Death of a President: November 20–25, 1963* (New York, 1967). A classic and highly readable study of the Kennedy assassination by a leading historian and journalist.

Oppenheimer, Mark. *Knocking on Heaven's Door: American Religion in the Age of Counterculture* (New Haven, CT, 2003). A provocative account of how sixties counterculture transformed mainstream religion and churches, from female ministers to the religious pop music.

Reeves, Thomas. *A Question of Character: A Life of John F. Kennedy* (New York, 1991). A provocative biography that highlights Kennedy's personal flaws and their impact on his presidency.

The World the Sixties Made: Politics and Culture in Recent America, eds. Van Gosse and Richard Moser (Philadelphia, 2003). Thirteen essays explain the New Left's long-term impact on American politics, society, and culture.

16 Economic turmoil and conservative triumph, 1969–1988

Timeline

1969	Nixon announces Vietnamisation policy
1970	National Guardsmen kill Vietnam War protesters at Kent State and Jackson State universities
	Environmental Protection Agency established
1971	Nixon terminates the Bretton Woods system of fixed currency exchange rates
	US domestic oil production peaks and declines afterwards
1972	Nixon visits China
	Nixon visits the Soviet Union and signs the Strategic Arms Limitation Treaty
	Beginning of Watergate scandal
	Nixon re-elected in a landslide
	US Air Force conducts Christmas bombings of North Vietnam
1973	The first oil crisis triggers worldwide recession
	United States withdraws last combat troops from South Vietnam due to Paris Peace Accords
	US productivity stagnates
	Roe v Wade decision of the US Supreme Court legalises abortion
1974	Nixon resigns from the presidency; succeeded by Ford
1975	South Vietnam falls to communism
	Inflation reaches 11.8 per cent, unemployment 9 per cent, highest in decades
1976	Jimmy Carter elected president
1977	Carter's National Energy Policy defeated in Congress
1978	Carter brokers Israeli-Egyptian peace agreement at Camp David
1979	Islamic Revolution in Iran
	Second oil crisis
	Iranian hostage crisis
	Soviet invasion of Afghanistan
1980	US attempt to rescue hostages fails
	Republican Ronald Reagan elected president
	Inflation reaches 13.5 per cent
1981	US hostages in Iran freed
	Attempted assassination of Reagan
	Reagan tax cut passed by Congress
1982	Unemployment reaches 10.8 per cent

1983   US economy recovers
       Deployment of US missiles in Western Europe
       US invasion of Grenada
       Reagan proposes Strategic Defence Initiative
1984   Reagan re-elected in a landslide
1985   Reagan meets Soviet leader Gorbachev in Geneva, Switzerland
1986   Iran-Contra scandal becomes public
1987   The USA and the Soviet Union negotiate the Intermediate Nuclear Forces
       treaty
1988   Soviet withdrawal from Afghanistan

Topics covered

- Economic crisis: the 1970s
- Domestic reforms
- Détente
- Watergate
- Gender, race, and class
- The Carter interlude
- Reagan's domestic policies
- The second cold war, the Iran-Contra scandal, and nuclear arms control

Introduction

The era of long-term economic growth that underwrote America's superpower status, the rise of a prosperous middle class, and ambitious social reforms came to a screeching halt in the 1970s, when the country entered a period of economic turmoil, retrenchment, and shrinking opportunities for millions of Americans. Following a look at these developments in Cleveland, Ohio, the chapter traces the roots of the crisis to a transformation of post-war capitalism that had drastic consequences for cities, the working class, women, and minorities. When the administrations of Republican Richard Nixon (1969–74), Republican Gerald Ford (1974–77), and Democrat Jimmy Carter (1977–81) proved unable to tackle the crisis during the 1970s, voters flocked to conservative Republican Ronald Reagan, whose tenure from 1981 to 1989 coincided with a deep recession followed by an uneven economic recovery that benefitted some groups and regions more than others.

America's foreign policy unfolded in the shadow of its defeat in Vietnam that prompted Nixon's attempt to tone down the cold war by negotiating diplomatic agreements with the Soviet Union and the People's Republic of China. Carter and especially Reagan, by contrast, adopted a more confrontational approach after the Soviets invaded Afghanistan in 1979. Reagan's massive rearmament effort escalated the cold war to a level where the Soviet Union could no longer compete, setting the stage for a de-escalation of the nuclear arms race at the end of his presidency.

Cleveland

In 1978, the midwestern city of Cleveland, Ohio, became the first big American municipality to declare bankruptcy since the Great Depression of the 1930s. Public expenditures had risen for years while tax revenues stagnated due to a sluggish economy, setting the stage for a showdown as Cleveland's creditors tried to force progressive mayor Dennis Kucinich to raise money by privatising city-owned assets. When Kucinich refused, the banks backed conservative mayoral candidate George Voinovich, who defeated the incumbent in a hotly contested election, served as a Republican mayor in a working-class city for nearly a decade, and eventually became influential in conservative state and national politics.

Though Voinovich touted it as "the comeback city," Cleveland continued to suffer economic decline during his tenure. Once called the "heart of the industrial revolution," it lost scores of industrial employers and more than 100,000 jobs. Real estate values plummeted in once-prosperous working-class neighbourhoods as unemployment and poverty soared and local businesses collapsed, leaving behind vacant housing and boarded-up storefronts. Mayor Voinovich offered tax breaks and other incentives to corporations like BP America and Key Bank that brought white-collar professional jobs to the city, prompting the revitalisation of some neighbourhoods that thrived alongside decrepit slums.

Cleveland was in some respects a microcosm of American society in the late twentieth century. Seismic economic shifts on a global scale set adrift US industries especially in the Midwest and the Northeast, regions that acquired the sobriquet "rustbelt" whose major employers closed shop, relocated to low-cost labour markets in America's so-called sunbelt farther south and overseas, or shifted their investments into the service sector. These economic shocks reverberated in social structures as old industrial centres like Cleveland suffered job losses, erosion of their tax base and public services, impoverishment, and population declines. The shift from manufacturing to a service-sector economy, combined with the effects of antidiscrimination legislation, created job opportunities for some groups, but the simultaneous deterioration of working-class life contributed to a growing wealth gap that became a salient characteristic of American society.

Political leaders did little to cushion the impact of the socioeconomic crisis. The inability of liberals to reverse the decline convinced a majority of voters to support conservatives like Reagan, who attributed America's economic woes to excessive government regulation. The US economy rebounded after a sharp recession in the early eighties, but its benefits were distributed unevenly. Tax cuts went disproportionately to the wealthy and corporations, whose share of national income grew precipitously. Indifferent to the social plight that engulfed urban ghettos and factory towns, Reagan cut billions from social programmes in a futile attempt to balance the federal budget as defence expenditures skyrocketed.

A Triumph of conservatism?

Some scholars credit conservatives with instigating a revolution in American life. John Chubb and Paul Peterson wrote during the eighties, "The American political system, during the presidency of Ronald Reagan, has been transformed to an extent unknown since the days of Franklin Roosevelt. The terms of political debate, the course of domestic and foreign affairs, and the dominant line of partisan cleavage have all been fundamentally changed." Political scientist Larry Schwab disagrees: "While conservative Republicans made gains in public opinion, elections, and policymaking, Republicans never became the dominant party, and there was no historic conservative shift in either public opinion or government policies."

The Reagan presidency indeed marked a transformative moment as faith in deregulated capitalism, distrust of government, and acceptance of deep social inequality became widely shared by many Americans. More than that, the "Reagan Revolution" constituted the opening chapter in a rightward turn of Western nations as liberal and socialist parties lost power to conservatives who shared Reagan's core beliefs. "Ronald Reagan's two terms [as president], and even more the events that led up to them, do constitute a major turning point in American politics," journalist Godfrey Hodgson posits. "After Reagan, liberal ideas were on the defensive for more than twenty years."

Economic crisis and decline: the 1970s

Long-term prosperity ended in the late 1960s and 1970s as a result of major changes in the US economy. Inflation grew due to a mounting federal debt and as a result of rising oil prices, making it impossible for the USA to sustain the Bretton Woods system of international monetary cooperation that had provided the framework of post-war economic prosperity in Western industrialised countries. Entire sectors of the US economy succumbed to foreign competition, precipitating slow growth and rising unemployment.

Inflation was partly triggered by deficit spending to finance the Vietnam War, whose annual cost soared from $5.8 billion (1966) to $26 billion (1968). President Lyndon Johnson asked Congress to raise taxes, but conservatives insisted that revenue increases go hand in hand with cutbacks to his beloved Great Society programmes. Instead of choosing between guns and butter, Johnson financed the war largely with deficit spending, in effect force-feeding an economy that was already growing at a rapid pace of 6.6 per cent in 1966. Two years later, when inflation in the overheating economy reached 4.2 per cent, Johnson finally agreed reduce Great Society appropriations in return for a tax increase, resulting in the last balanced budget in American history for more than a quarter century. But it was too late: the tax increase failed to hold down inflation, which rose to 5.7 per cent in 1970 while unemployment grew to 4.9 per cent – grim numbers indicating that the economy headed in the wrong direction.

Growing inflation contributed to the collapse of the Bretton Woods system of fixed currency exchange rates. Under Bretton Woods rules, a country whose economy suffered from high inflation had to cut government expenditures so that its currency maintained its value in global trading, but the Republican Nixon administration refused to reduce spending. Moreover, Bretton Woods made dollars convertible to gold at $35 per ounce, enabling foreigners could turn in greenbacks and receive bullion in return. As Western European countries, particularly France, took advantage of this option to unload their bulging dollar holdings, the US Treasury's gold reserves began to shrink, raising the spectre that the USA could soon no longer meet its obligations. These developments prompted Nixon to terminate dollar convertibility into gold in 1971. Called the "Nixon Shock," the abrupt end of the Bretton Woods system destabilised a global economy that had long depended on fixed exchange rates but was now confronted with wild fluctuations in currency values. From 1971 to 1973, the dollar lost 25 per cent against the Japanese Yen and 30 per cent against the West German Deutschmark. Western Europeans worried about global currency instability experimented with a variety of mechanisms to replace Bretton Woods. In 1979, they adopted the European Monetary System that permitted only slight rate fluctuations among member currencies, triggering a chain of events that eventually led to monetary union with the adoption of the Euro in the late twentieth century.

The troubled US economy received another blow in 1973, when Arab members of the Organisation of Petroleum Exporting Countries (OPEC) raised oil prices. Four developments contributed to the crisis. First, American oil petroleum consumption had more than doubled in the previous decades because manufacturers introduced a range of petroleum-based products, drivers bought petrol guzzlers, and developers built suburban homes that consumed vast amounts of heating oil and electricity. Second, domestic oil production declined after 1971 as a result of depletion and environmental regulation, rendering the USA increasingly dependent on imports. Third, petroleum exporting countries formed the OPEC cartel in 1960 to gain independence from American and British oil companies that controlled petroleum markets at the time. Since petroleum traded in dollars, OPEC members were unhappy when Nixon devalued the American currency in 1971, so they slowly raised oil prices in the next two years. Fourth, some OPEC members were outraged with Nixon's Israel policy. In 1973, when an Arab coalition attacked Israel, Nixon ordered a strategic airlift to resupply the beleaguered Israeli armed forces with ammunition, tanks, and artillery. Arab OPEC members retaliated by raising petroleum prices 70 per cent and terminating their oil shipments to the USA and the Netherlands whose governments supported Israel during the war. The embargo was lifted in March 1974 after the USA had pressured Israel to negotiate with its foes.

The oil crisis had a disastrous effect on Western economies. In 1973, petrol shortages led to long lines at refilling stations, governments discouraged the use of Christmas

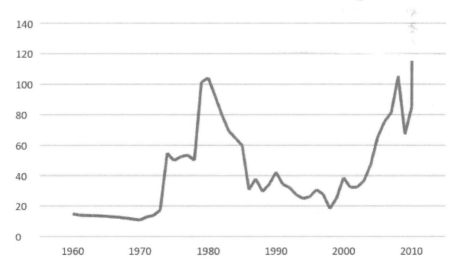

Figure 16.1 Oil price per barrel in 2016 dollars.

Source: Data sourced from the World Bank

lighting, and some countries banned car travel on Sundays. For the next two years, the oil crisis triggered the worst recession in post-war history as consumers saved money everywhere to fill up their cars and heat their homes. Housing starts in the USA slumped by more than half, causing the construction industry fire workers as unemployment doubled from 1973 to 1975, rising to 9 per cent. The Federal Reserve, trying to keep unemployment from spinning out of control completely, encourage borrowing, contributing to a rise in inflation to 11.8 per cent in 1975, the highest level in almost three decades.

The oil crisis triggered an unprecedented contraction of the US automobile industry, which lost market shares to fuel-efficient imports, especially from Japan. American carmakers still controlled the market for larger vehicles in the early 1970s, but imports like Toyota dominated in economy-sized saloons that achieved better fuel efficiency than cars manufactured by General Motors, Ford, and Chrysler. The market share of imported cars increased during the oil crisis to 20 per cent in 1975 as American consumers began to prize fuel efficiency. Car buyers quickly realised that Japanese automobiles were not only less expensive to buy and operate than American ones, but also possessed distinct quality advantages: the average Japanese car cost $2,000 less and had far fewer defects than a comparable American-made automobile.

Foreign competition also cut deep into the market shares of other American industries, partly as a result of successful capital investment strategies by overseas competitors. Japanese steelmakers, for example, benefitted from cutting-edge technologies like basic oxygen furnaces that enabled them to produce high-quality steel at a lower price than American firms, resulting in an increase of Japan's share of world steel production from 6.4 per cent in 1960 to 15.5 per cent in 1980, when it surpassed that of the USA. By then, one-quarter of American steel mills were completely outdated, partly because companies like U.S. Steel spent their profits on acquisitions such as shopping malls, oil companies, and golf courses instead of better furnaces. *Time* magazine commented, "Like an aging heavyweight gone to flab, US industry has fallen behind some of its world-class competitors. Many steel, rubber, auto and other essential plants have become outmoded because not enough capital has been invested in them." Japanese electronics companies like Sony, Toshiba, and Sharp made inroads into American consumer markets with low-cost, high-quality home entertainment products, crowding out American firms like Emerson Radio Corporation and Zenith. The post-war era of widely shared prosperity came to an end. Hourly income, which had grown 2 per cent annually from 1948 to 1973, flat lined for the rest of the decade while discretionary income fell by almost one fifth because workers spent more of their earnings on basic needs like housing and food. Productivity in manufacturing slowed from 3.4 per cent annually before 1973 to a snail's pace of barely 1 per cent, inaugurating a trend that continued into the twenty-first century. What was once known as America's "industrial heartland" in the Midwest and the Northeast was now called the "rust belt," areas where deindustrialisation hollowed out entire regional economies. Bethlehem Steel shuttered its giant works in Lackawanna, New York, and Johnstown, Pennsylvania, while U.S. Steel closed more than a dozen plants in the Northeast and Midwest. In many instances, the wave of plant closings was caused by management's search for low-wage non-union labour especially in Southern states that were hostile to trade unions. General Motors, for example, closed seven plants in heavily unionised midwestern states and opened eight new ones in the South where the United Auto Workers Union played no role in labour relations. The deindustrialisation of the Northeast and Midwest contributed to a decline of organised labour as trade union membership fell from 28 per cent (1970) to 15 per cent (1989) of the non-agricultural workforce, inaugurating a downward trend that continued into the twenty-first century. Workers who lost well-paid industrial jobs often faced major problems. Many joined the ranks of the long-term unemployed and more than half saw their occupational status, wages, and benefits sharply reduced. In Youngstown, Ohio, a worker who had earned $8.60 an hour in the steel plant found a job as a shoe salesman that paid him one-third that amount. Workers who experienced steep wage declines often had trouble paying their home mortgages, car loans, and other debts, and many had to cut expenses for clothing, food, and recreation.

Working-class Americans shared their woes with Western Europeans who experienced deindustrialisation and regional decline. This was especially obvious in Britain, whose old industrial heartlands of Yorkshire, Manchester, the West Midlands, and Clydeside recorded steep declines in industrial employment when the bottom fell out from underneath steelmaking, engineering, and shipbuilding as a result of foreign competition (in 1971, Japan boasted twice of Britain's GNP). On the continent, deindustrialisation was evident in France's Lorraine region and West Germany's Ruhr area that had formed the throbbing core of the Western European steel industry until the 1970s, when Japanese firms began to dominate the world steel market.

Nixon's domestic policies

Against the backdrop of a growing socioeconomic crisis, Nixon rarely demonstrated interest in domestic affairs, telling his advisors "This country could run itself domestically without a president. You need a president for foreign policy." His administration nevertheless initiated substantive reforms in areas such as welfare policy and environmental protection. Despite his right-wing rhetoric, Nixon was at heart a political opportunist who was quite willing to compromise conservative beliefs if it earned him a "place in history" (one of his favourite phrases). After reading a biography of Benjamin Disraeli, a conservative British prime minister who instigated electoral reforms in the nineteenth century, Nixon commented "Tory men and liberal policies are what have changed the world."

Welfare reform received close attention. A guaranteed minimum income programme for the working and nonworking poor was defeated in Congress, but proposals to expand the Food Stamp Program that was part of the Great Society reforms received broad political support from conservatives, liberals, and the farm lobby whose clientele expected to benefit from government-subsidised food purchases. Under the programme, millions of nonworking and working poor people could redeem government-issued coupons at groceries, contributing to drastic reductions in hunger during the late 1970s. Simultaneously, the number of recipients of federal welfare benefits almost doubled from 1969 to 1974 under Aid to Families with Dependent Children (AFDC), a New Deal programme expanded in the Great Society. Nixon also initiated sweeping reforms of Social Security (established by President Franklin Roosevelt) that raised government benefits for the aged and established a pension programme for the blind and disabled regardless of age.

Though the American welfare state alleviated the suffering the poor and disabled, it was more tight-fisted and restrictive than most Western European systems. In contrast to West Germany's welfare programme, for example, AFDC failed to lift a majority of recipients above the official poverty line. The American practise of terminating AFDC benefits if a recipient refused to seek employment was illegal elsewhere. Fiscal responsibility for the American welfare system was shared by the federal and state governments, resulting in vast regional differences unheard-of in Western European countries. In 1976, New York state paid eight times as much in average AFDC benefits as Mississippi.

In addition to recalibrating the welfare system, Nixon presided over the most important environmental reforms since the New Deal with the establishment of the Environmental Protection Agency (EPA). Throughout the 1970s, EPA enforced environmental regulations far more aggressively than its Western European counterparts, prohibiting the use of cancer-causing dioxins that were only mildly regulated in Britain, for example. The agency quickly attracted the ire of businessmen who had to spend billions of dollars on pollution control systems to comply with EPA standards, prompting intense lobbying by industry groups to curtail or abolish the agency.

Nixon's foreign policy

Nixon undertook a major recalibration of American foreign policy in a global environment where the USA was no longer the unbowed leader of the Western world as it had been during the early cold war. Defeat loomed in Vietnam, calling into question US preparedness to contain communism in other corners of the globe. Worries about communist expansion in the developing world proliferated because the Soviet Union supported left-leaning movements in Africa at a time when the USA was ensnared in Vietnam. The People's Republic of China meanwhile sought influence in Southeast Asia. Amidst these alarming developments in a multipolar world, Nixon and his National Security Advisor Henry Kissinger sought opportunities to preserve American power and influence.

Nixon was painfully aware that attempts to force a communist surrender in Vietnam were not an option when he took office in 1969. The best he and Kissinger could hope for was a negotiated settlement that left a non-communist government in South Vietnam in place for a few years while the USA withdrew its forces. The president was brutally honest about South Vietnam's long-term prospects. "Call it cosmetics or whatever you want," he told a senior advisor behind closed doors. The extraction of American forces "has got to be done in a way that will give South Vietnam a chance to survive. . . . It's got to survive for a reasonable time. Then everybody can say 'goddamn, we did our part,'" and the USA could wash its hands in the matter.

A key component of Nixon's disengagement strategy was to hand responsibility for fighting the communists to the South Vietnamese army as US ground forces withdrew, a policy known as "Vietnamisation." Between 1968 and 1972, when American troop presence shrivelled from 540,000 to 24,000, South Vietnam received enormous amounts of weapons and materiel from the USA, including planes and helicopters that equipped South Vietnam with one of the world's largest air forces. Attempting to shield American withdrawals from North Vietnamese interference, Kissinger ordered the secret bombing of communist sanctuaries in Cambodia along the border with South Vietnam. The effects on North Vietnamese offensive capabilities were negligible, but the raids destabilised neutral Cambodia, which collapsed into chaos. When civil war erupted in 1970, Nixon ordered a ground invasion of Cambodia by American and South Vietnamese forces, triggering a wave of protest at home, where the Ohio

National Guard shot and killed four students at Kent State University. Moreover, the invasion backfired on Kissinger's secret talks with the North Vietnamese, who boycotted the negotiations until American and South Vietnamese forces withdrew from Cambodia, which they did only three months after the operation had started.

Ceasefire negotiations between Kissinger and his North Vietnamese counterpart Le Duc Tho in Paris finally began to bear fruit in October 1972, when the Americans pledged to withdraw all their forces from South Vietnam without demanding the same of the North Vietnamese. Tho agreed to leave the non-communist South Vietnamese government in place and to release American prisoners of war, mostly combat pilots who had been shot down over North Vietnam. Nguyen Van Thieu, the president of South Vietnam, objected strenuously because he had not been informed of the negotiations and because the proposed deal allowed North Vietnam to keep its troops in the South, enabling them to resume their offensive at will. Nixon tried to force North Vietnamese concessions with a savage air offensive that rained 15,000 tons of bombs on the capital Hanoi and the port city of Haiphong in December 1972, killing more than 1,600 civilians. Internationally, the "Christmas Bombings" further tarnished America's battered image. Swedish Prime Minister Olof Palme condemned them as "a form of torture" and West German chancellor Willy Brandt called them "disgusting." In the end, the Christmas Bombings resulted in only token changes to the US-North Vietnamese agreement, which was signed in January 1973. The peace accords enabled the USA to terminate its direct involvement in Vietnam, but the agreement did not hold: In April 1975, North Vietnamese and Vietcong forces conquered Saigon as American helicopters and ships evacuated the last US personnel along with more than 100,000 desperate South Vietnamese refugees.

America's first military defeat in history had a profound impact at home and abroad. Its armed forces, which had been unable to vanquish a poorly equipped enemy despite their vast material superiority, were no longer regarded as invincible. The US Army emerged from the conflict as a mere shadow of its former self: dispirited, wracked by rampant drug use, and demoralised by reports of war crimes like the massacre of more than 500 South Vietnamese civilians in the village of My Lai in 1968. The searing memory of defeat in Vietnam, often called the "Vietnam War Syndrome," diminished Americans' appetite for an interventionist foreign policy. Defeat in Vietnam also shocked American allies: The West German newspaper *Frankfurter Allgemeine Zeitung* ran an editorial entitled "America – A Helpless Giant."

Nixon and Kissinger worried that the Vietnam debacle would embolden communists to challenge America's containment policy elsewhere, particularly when it became clear that the Soviet Union possessed as many strategic missiles as the USA. The result was a stalemate called Mutually Assured Destruction, guaranteeing that the Soviets had sufficient nuclear capability to destroy the USA even after they had suffered a strategic attack on the Union of Soviet Socialist Republics (USSR) itself. This development, combined with communist successes in Vietnam, was likely to boost Soviet self-confidence, raising the spectre of Soviet-sponsored aggression elsewhere, American policymakers argued. To uphold containment, Nixon and Kissinger developed a policy of détente (French for "relaxation of international tensions"). At its core, it constituted American diplomatic outreach to the Soviet Union and the communist People's Republic of China (PRC). Nixon's background as a hard-core cold warrior made him well-suited for such overtures because few doubted his anti-Communist credentials, leading many Americans to believe that he would drive a tough bargain.

Figure 16.2 Evacuees from South Vietnam of the US Aircraft Carrier *Midway*, 1975.
Source: Courtesy of Signal Photos/Alamy

America and the USSR had good reasons to seek a thaw in the cold war. While Washington wanted to prevent the further build-up of Soviet nuclear forces, Moscow was eager to improve its relations with the West, whose assistance was necessary to stabilise the sclerotic Soviet economy. In 1972, Nixon and Soviet premier Leonid Brezhnev signed the Strategic Arms Limitations Treaty (SALT I) that capped the number of strategic missile launchers. Nixon and Brezhnev also initialled a trade agreement that provided US-government credits for American grain exports to the Soviet Union, whose inefficient agricultural economy was vulnerable to harvest failures (unfortunately for Americans, soaring Soviet demand for US wheat contributed to inflation and shortages at home).

Nixon's outreach to Brezhnev went hand in hand with his China policy, which was primarily intended to curb Soviet expansionism. Relationships between the USSR and the PRC had deteriorated during the 1960s as a result of ideological differences to a point where the communist superpowers considered each other greater dangers to their respective interests than the USA. Shooting erupted during a border conflict in 1968 that claimed almost 1,000 lives. Nixon sought to fuel the Sino-Soviet split so that Moscow would have to focus on a resurgent China instead of spreading Soviet communism in the Third World. "We're doing the China thing to screw the Russians," Nixon told his advisors. His visit to Beijing in February 1972 resulted in the reopening of diplomatic relations after the USA had refused to recognise the PRC at the beginning of the cold war and had considered non-communist Taiwan the official representative of China in world affairs. During Nixon's visit, the PRC promised to seek a peaceful solution to its troubled relations with Taiwan in return for an American commitment to support the transfer of China's permanent seat on the United Nations Security Council from Taiwan to the PRC. American allies welcomed these initiatives and benefitted considerably from the Sino-US thaw: British exports to China more than tripled from 1972 to 1973.

The 1972 elections and the Watergate scandal

During his 1972 re-election campaign, Nixon sought to deepen the political realignment that had begun in the previous decade. He did so by appealing to constituencies that had historically voted for the Democrats but felt increasingly alienated by their party's liberalism. Disrupted by the Watergate scandal, the conservative ascendancy continued in the late seventies and eventually enabled Reagan to win the presidency in 1980.

Southern whites, who had sustained the grip of segregationist Democrats on the region since Reconstruction, were key to Nixon's strategy. George Wallace, a former Democrat who ran as an independent in 1968, attracted almost ten million votes of southern whites and disaffected northern working-class voters with a campaign that emphasised white supremacy, law and order, and populist economic demands. To woo Wallace voters, Nixon adopted the so-called Southern Strategy that played on their racial resentments. In 1969, Nixon's Justice Department supported a petition by the state of Mississippi to the US Supreme Court to delay school integration and his administration asked Congress to weaken the Voting Rights Act. Though both initiatives failed, they helped establish Nixon's credentials with white southerners, as did his successful nomination of conservative Warren Burger as chief justice of the US Supreme Court. These tactics contributed to his overwhelming electoral victory in the South, where Nixon received almost 70 per cent of the popular vote.

Nixon gained the same percentage of the white working-class vote, a stunning achievement for a Republican candidate given the fact that blue-collar workers had long been a core constituency of the Democrats' New Deal coalition. He received the official endorsement of the International Longshoremen's Association, whose leaders were grateful for his support of the US merchant marine. Construction workers were delighted when Nixon released federal funds for major building projects that created new jobs just in time for the election, coupled with cutbacks to a controversial plan to increase minority representation in the construction trades that appealed to white working-class voters. These tactics enabled Nixon to crush Democratic nominee George McGovern in the general election with 60.7 per cent of the popular vote, one of the biggest landslides in American history.

Nixon's spectacular re-election could have ushered in a triumph of conservatism had it not been for the Watergate scandal that wrecked his presidency. What began as a minor break-in at the headquarters of the Democratic National Committee in the Watergate Hotel in Washington DC, in June 1972 snowballed into one of America's most serious constitutional crises of the twentieth century. When it became clear that the burglars had been hired by the president's re-election campaign, Nixon personally ordered his subordinates to sabotage an FBI investigation of the break-in because he feared that an official inquiry would uncover a wide variety of illegal activities by White House officials. Confronted with extortionist threats by the burglars that they would reveal the involvement of presidential aides unless they received substantial sums in "hush money," the president of the USA responded like a petty criminal, telling an aide, "You could get it in cash. I know where it could be gotten." The key was to prevent his confidants from cooperating with investigators, Nixon stressed. "I don't give a shit what happens," he told his aides. "I want you all to stonewall it, let them plead the Fifth Amendment [against self-incrimination], cover up or anything else if it'll save it – save the plan."

The cover-up unravelled when Nixon's aides began to cooperate with FBI and Congressional investigators in spring 1973. Keen to avoid a lengthy prison sentence for obstruction of justice and other crimes, Nixon aide John Dean became a star witness of televised Senate hearings where he exposed the president's involvement in the conspiracy. The hearings also revealed the existence of a secret taping system that had been installed in the Oval Office at the start of the Nixon presidency. The recordings were seen as important evidence by the Senate investigators and by the special prosecutor, who led a broad-based investigation into Watergate-related matters, but Nixon refused to turn over the tapes citing "executive privilege." The spiralling scandal worried American allies, particularly Britain, where senior cabinet members told the press that they were "finding Washington paralysed. . . . President Nixon's authority is simply gone."

The scandal entered its final phase in spring and summer 1974, when Nixon was confronted renewed demands for access to his tapes. Heavily edited transcripts released in March discredited a president who claimed to speak for the "moral majority" of decent Americans but behind closed doors used obscene language in discussions of political enemies and friends, blacks, Jews, and ethnic groups that appalled even his most stalwart defenders. In July, a US Supreme Court ruling in *United States v. Nixon* forced the president to release tapes to the special prosecutor that documented his involvement in the cover-up, followed a few days later by the approval of articles of impeachment (see concept box). On 9 August 1974, he became the first president in American history to resign from office.

Impeachment

A process in which a legislature brings charges against a high-ranking government official for potential removal, federal impeachment procedures are defined by Article 1 of the US Constitution. It stipulates that drafting formal impeachment charges is the responsibility of the House of Representatives while the Senate serves as a jury with the Chief Justice of the US Supreme Court presiding. In President Nixon's case, the House Judiciary Committee drafted impeachment charges for obstruction of justice, abuse of presidential power, and contempt of Congress. Nixon resigned before the full House of Representatives could pass a formal vote. The only presidents who were formally impeached by the House were Andrew Johnson (1868), Bill Clinton (1998), and Donald Trump (2020). All three were acquitted by the US Senate.

The Watergate scandal produced a multilayered legacy. Domestically, Nixon's misdeeds further eroded Americans' trust in government, which had already suffered as a result of Johnson's brazen lies about the Vietnam War. In the long run, disgust with government benefitted the Republicans, Nixon's own party, whose conservative wing came to dominate American politics in the 1980s. In foreign affairs, conservatives cleverly exploited the Watergate scandal by associating the policies they detested with Nixon's tarnished image, notably détente with the communist powers, which began to die slowly after he left office. Many European commentators gave the American political system credit for its ability to deal with a profound constitutional crisis. The West German weekly *Die Zeit* editorialised that a less energetic people "would have been totally demoralised" by the scandal. "Who knows what would have happened in Bonn [the West German capital], Paris or London if a situation like Watergate had occupied their attention for two years?" Over the long haul, however, Nixon's downfall confirmed Western European beliefs that an America beset by economic problems, defeat in Vietnam, and a diminished presidency was no longer able to exercise strong leadership in the transatlantic alliance. Western Europeans, troubled by the oil crisis and other problems, entrusted their fortunes to the pragmatic leadership of French President Valéry Giscard d'Estaing and West German chancellor Helmut Schmidt, whose foreign policies turned increasingly self-assertive and independent of the USA as the 1970s progressed. Unlike American leaders, Western European ones persisted in détente and improved trade relations with the Soviet Union, which became the continent's largest oil and natural gas supplier in the late 1970s.

Gender, race, and class

The 1970s and 1980s marked a period of rapid social change for women and African Americans who began to reap the benefits of civil rights activism that brought them important gains. While middle-class women and blacks made significant strides, however, the less fortunate faced increasingly precarious socioeconomic conditions.

White middle-class women benefitted from civil rights legislation, notably the Civil Rights Act of 1964 an policies that gave special consideration to social groups whose employment opportunities had suffered as a result of past injustices (see concept box). Called "positive discrimination" in Britain, affirmative action required an employer to hire a female or black applicant if her or his qualifications were equal to those of a white male job seeker. White middle-class women made significant strides as a result of antidiscrimination legislation and affirmative action because their high rate of college education enabled them to enter professions that had historically been dominated by men once gender discrimination declined. From 1970 to 1980, the proportion of female solicitors more than doubled and women made headway in science and engineering occupations as well. White women of childbearing age joined the labour force in disproportionate numbers, so that more than half of all white women with children worked for wages or salaries by 1980. Though the shift in gender roles was partly driven by women's desires for rewarding careers and their ability to take advantage of new opportunities, male wage stagnation played a significant role as well because many wives felt compelled to seek paid employment when their husbands' earnings no longer sufficed to sustain middle-class lifestyles. Even though dual-earner families became much more common during the 1970s, however, women's earnings often failed to produce significant increases in total household incomes.

Middle-class family life began to change dramatically against the backdrop of growing female labour force participation. Demographically, the post-war baby boom gave way to a "baby bust" as the total fertility rate declined from its post-war peak of 3.6 (1964) to 1.7 (1976) when women took advantage of the birth control pill, which was first commercialised in 1960 despite massive opposition from the Roman Catholic Church. Especially middle-class women in the USA, Scandinavia, and Britain who entered the professions and spent years building their careers began to postpone marriage and childbearing. Their growing financial independence enabled many women to leave failing marriages, contributing to steep rise in the US divorce rate from 24 per cent of all marriages (1964) to 48 per cent (1976).

Affirmative action

Building on New Deal initiatives, most affirmative action programmes were instituted during the 1960s to ameliorate the effects of discrimination. They included the Civil Rights Act of 1964, whose Title VII prohibited discrimination based on race, skin colour, religion, sex, or national origin in firms with more than 15 employees, in addition to excluding government contractors found guilty of discrimination from tax-payer funded public works like defence contracts. President Johnson's Executive Order 11246 of 1965 required private businesses to institute non-discriminatory hiring and promotion policies to reach targeted goals. Though affirmative action did not require quotas or preferential treatment of minorities and women, its conservative critics claimed that it did precisely that and resulted in reverse discrimination, especially of white men.

In higher education, Harvard University encouraged recruiters to consider race and ethnicity in admissions to enhance the diversity of its student body, which had historically been dominated by white male students from wealthy backgrounds. The policy served as a model for many other universities and was declared constitutional by the US Supreme Court in the case *Regents of the University of California v. Bakke* (1978).

Middle-class blacks made major socioeconomic gains as well. The Civil Rights Act of 1964 helped many to pry open the doors of labour market segments that had historically been the provenance of whites, notably in professional, skilled craft, administrative, and clerical occupations. The proportion of blacks classified as middle class increased from 27 per cent (1970) to almost 40 per cent (1980) and black professionals' average earnings grew by 38 per cent over the course of the decade, even though blacks still earned only 60 per cent of whites' salaries. Like their white counterparts, black middle-class women greatly increased their labour market participation and recorded lower fertility rates. Growing numbers of black middle-class families left the ghettos and moved to suburbs by taking advantage of fair housing legislation that prohibited racial discrimination in the real estate industry. Buttressed by rising incomes, the black suburban population grew 5.2 per cent annually in the 1970s, almost as fast as the white suburban population had in the post-war era. Many middle-class African Americans moved to majority-black suburbs, usually as a matter of personal choice rather than housing discrimination. A resident of Prince George's County in Maryland, a black-majority suburban area near to Washington DC, explained, "Many families see themselves creating their own kind of promised land, bringing the good life with them and expecting even more. This is the classic American suburban dream, this time filtered through the lens of a history forged by inequality and the struggle to overcome."

In the inner city, the outmigration of middle-class blacks often left behind an impoverished, socially isolated ghetto population. The economic downturn of the 1970s diminished the employment prospects for unskilled black males who were looking for the sort of mass-production jobs in the steel and automobile industries that had sustained the white working class during the prosperous post-war years. In a cruel irony, the Civil Rights Act of 1964 opened employment opportunities by reducing job discrimination, but now the opportunities themselves began to disappear, often making it impossible especially for unskilled young black males to find jobs that could feed a family. The limited number of jobs available to unskilled young black men were concentrated in the low-level service sector and often located in suburbs beyond the reach of the ghetto poor, while well-paid, union-protected jobs in manufacturing and construction withered in many urban areas. Bereft of conventional employment opportunities and yet often eager to participate in consumer society, many earned money in the underground economy. By the end of the 1970s, more than half of all violent and property crimes in the USA were committed by young black males, who were also victims of violence as murder became the leading cause of death among African American men aged 25 to 34, often as a result of gang activity. The latter was fuelled by the introduction of inexpensive and highly addictive crack cocaine in inner-city neighbourhoods during the 1980s.

The scarcity of conventional employment and the growth of the underground economy had a devastating effect on family structures among the ghetto poor. Early death, incarceration, and lack of stable employment shrank the pool of marriageable black males, contributing to a steep decline in the marriage rate of young black women from 56 per cent (1970) to 21.6 per cent (1980). Female-headed households, which were more vulnerable to impoverishment than two-parent families, became the norm in many inner-city neighbourhoods as the share of black babies born to unmarried mothers grew from 38 per cent (1970) to 55 per cent (1980). Often growing up without fathers and other male role models who had stable jobs and went to work in the morning, many black inner-city youngsters lacked basic community support structures, received substandard education, and drifted into petty crime and gang activity.

Many Europeans initially viewed the emergence of ghetto poverty as a peculiarly American phenomenon, the result of a unique combination of deindustrialisation, suburbanisation, urban decay, and racism that was unlikely to materialise elsewhere. By the end of the 1970s, however, some began to worry that similar developments were evident in parts of Britain whose deindustrialisation rates resembled that of northeastern and midwestern American cities. Old urban-industrial centres like Liverpool and Manchester experienced staggering unemployment when the shipping and textile industries, respectively, disappeared in the 1970s. In contrast to America's ghetto poor, Britain's consisted primarily of underprivileged whites as well as immigrants of Afro-Caribbean, Pakistani, and other minority backgrounds who clustered in hollowed-out centre cities. Similar trends were evident in West Germany, where some inner-city neighbourhoods became ethnic enclaves inhabited by impoverished "guest workers" of Turkish descent. In France, ghetto poverty emerged primarily in dilapidated suburban housing developments like Sarcelles near to Paris, home to North African immigrants who received more generous welfare payments than British and American recipients but experienced even greater racial discrimination in employment and housing. European ghetto poverty in the 1970s and 1980s also differed from its American counterpart due to lower rates of gun violence as a result of more restrictive legislation. In later decades, British gangsters' growing use of firearms was promptly blamed on "an Americanisation of violence . . . whereby gunmen are blasting away to sort out a minor dispute as if they are playing the part in a gangster movie. Firearms have replaced forearms," the *Guardian* newspaper editorialised in 1997.

The Carter interlude

The election of Jimmy Carter as president in 1976 marked the return of a Democrat to the White House for the first time since Johnson had left office. A born-again Christian who promised voters "I will never lie to you" in order to distinguish himself from Johnson and Nixon, Carter defeated incumbent Republican Gerald Ford, who had disgraced himself by pardoning Richard Nixon from possible prosecution for his role in the Watergate scandal. The failure of the Carter presidency due to his political ineptitude, inability to tackle the economic crisis, and foreign-policy setbacks paved the way for the triumph of conservatism with Reagan's election as president in 1980.

Casting himself as a Washington outsider, Carter was notoriously aloof in his dealings with Congress, often refusing to meet with Democratic leaders to discuss his agenda. His ambitious National Energy Policy, introduced in 1977 to reduce consumption and encourage conservation in the wake of the first oil crisis, fell victim to senior Democrats who had not been consulted on Carter's plans for a petrol guzzler tax, price controls, and regulatory reforms. The thrashing of his energy policy was soon followed by defeat of other presidential initiatives like hospital cost controls, consumer protection, and tax reform. Carter further enraged Democrats with his retreat from core principles of the New Deal and the Great Society when he announced in 1978, "Government cannot eliminate poverty or provide a bountiful economy or reduce inflation or save our cities or cure illiteracy or provide energy," which sounded like a wholesale surrender to conservative ideology.

Economically, the greatest challenge confronting Carter was "stagflation," an unusual combination of high inflation, high unemployment, and slow growth that contributed to his political undoing. Its emergence initially confounded economists because unemployment and inflation were assumed to be inversely related instead of rising simultaneously. Market mechanisms were unhinged by the adverse supply shock of the 1973 oil crisis that triggered inflation as a result of a political OPEC decision, not because confident consumers who were flush with money made more purchases. Other causes of stagflation included an increase in the money supply by central banks, price hikes by companies that exploited their oligopolistic market control, and large government budget deficits. When pollsters asked Americans if they were more worried about unemployment or inflation, most picked the latter for fear of inflation's debilitating impact on the housing market. One analyst commented, "For the public today, inflation has the kind of dominance that no other issue has had since World War II." Carter responded with an anti-inflation programme of reducing the federal deficit, capping federal hiring, instituting wage-price guidelines, and deregulating interstate transport to encourage competition that would lower cargo rates. In a televised address to the nation of July 1979 called the "Crisis of Confidence Speech," he also castigated excessive consumerism and encouraged Americans to dedicate themselves to energy conservation. Unfortunately for the president, his initiatives failed to achieve their goal as inflation continued to rise from 7.6 per cent (1978) to 11.3 per cent (1979). Seeking stronger measures to flush inflation out of the economy, Carter sought the counsel of Paul Volcker, an economist who advocated steep increases in interest rates. In autumn 1979, Carter appointed Volcker as chair of the Federal Reserve Board, where he promptly implemented anti-inflationary measures that were bound to raise unemployment to levels not seen since the Great Depression.

Events in the Middle East precipitated more economic and political turmoil due to another oil crisis that exacerbated Carter's inflation problem at home. His diplomacy began on a hopeful note when he met with Egyptian President Anwar Sadat and Israeli Prime Minister Menachem Begin in 1978 at the Camp David presidential retreat in Maryland to negotiate an end to the 30-year state of war that existed between the two countries. In a tit-for-tat, Egypt recognised Israel's right to exist in return for a generous American aid package and Israel's evacuation of the Sinai Peninsula to Egypt that had been occupied by its army in 1967. Carter's hope that the Egypt-Israel Peace Treaty would be followed by a broader Middle Eastern settlement remained unfulfilled, however, and Sadat was assassinated in 1981 by Islamic fundamentalists who opposed the treaty. Elsewhere in the Middle East, the Shah of Iran Reza Pahlavi, who had long been America's most loyal ally in the region, was overthrown in 1979 during an Islamic revolution spearheaded by the fiercely anti-American Muslim leader Ayatollah Khomeini who called the USA "the number-one enemy of the deprived and oppressed people of the world." Revolutionary turmoil brought Iranian petroleum production to a near-standstill, precipitating a doubling of oil prices that drove inflation from 11.3 per cent (1979) to an unprecedented 13.5 per cent (1980). To make matters even worse, the Soviet Union invaded Afghanistan in December 1979 to prop up a tottering client regime there, stoking unfounded Western fears that Moscow's real intention was to gain control of the Middle East that controlled more than 40 per cent of global petroleum reserves. Carter responded by extending President Truman's containment doctrine to the Middle East, warning the Soviets "An attempt by any outside force to gain control of the Persian Gulf region will be regarded as an assault on the vital interests of the United States of America, and such an assault will be repelled by any means necessary, including military force." In response to the invasion, Carter suspended American grain exports to the USSR, declared an American boycott of the 1980 Olympic Games in Moscow, and reinstituted draft registration.

Wracked by rampant inflation, growing unemployment, sky-high interest rates, turmoil in the Middle East, the second oil crisis, and a major accident at the Three Mile Island nuclear power plant in Pennsylvania, America suffered yet another indignity when radical Iranian students occupied the US Embassy in Teheran and took 52 American diplomats hostage. With Khomeini's blessing, the hostage takers demanded the repatriation of Shah Pahlavi from the USA, where he had fled to in 1979, so he could face prosecution in Iran for crimes committed by his repressive regime. Carter responded with economic sanctions against Iran and in April 1980 ordered a secret rescue operation to extract the hostages by military force that ended in a humiliating failure. Though many Americans initially gave Carter credit for trying to get the hostages out, a majority turned against him when he failed to resolve the crisis by other means. European observers were dumbfounded by America's mounting fiascos. The West German weekly *Der Spiegel* commented that the great superpower was "unable to wrest the hostages from Ayatollah Khomeini's Iran; unable to meet the Soviet aggression in Afghanistan; unable to bring the world economic crisis under control."

Reagan's domestic policies

Republican Ronald Reagan's defeat of Carter in the 1980 presidential contest marked a major step in conservatism's rise to dominance. Propelled by constituencies that had historically voted for the Democratic Party but shifted their allegiance to the Republicans, Reagan instituted deep tax cuts primarily for the wealthy, deregulation, reductions in welfare spending, and massive increases in defence spending that reshaped American politics on a scale not seen since President Franklin Roosevelt's New Deal.

Reagan profited from an electoral shift that had been in the works since the late 1960s as majorities of white southerners, northeastern and midwestern working-class voters, and middle-class suburbanites began to vote for the Republican Party. In the 1970s, these voters often felt sickened by growing crime rates and drug use, the leftward drift of the Democratic Party, and the federal government's inability to solve festering economic problems. Many joined forces with traditional Republican supporters like businessmen keen on rolling back the regulatory state and Christian conservatives who were appalled by federal court decisions that prohibited prayers in schools and protected abortion rights. Reagan's ascendancy was further buttressed by conservative intellectual publications like William Buckley's *National Review* and think tanks like the American Enterprise Institute that helped Republicans shed the image of "the stupid party" (philosopher John Stuart Mill's epitaph for Britain's Conservatives). Reagan's political genius lay in his ability to speak to the concerns of disaffected Democrats and hard-core Republicans alike, coupled with his projection of inner strength and supreme confidence that America's problems were soluble.

Reagan's background served him well in these endeavours. Born to poor parents in 1911, he became a self-made sports announcer and accomplished B-movie actor. Initially a registered Democrat and screen actor union president, he switched to the Republicans in 1962 but maintained a sentimental attachment to Franklin Roosevelt. After a spirited endorsement of arch-conservative Republican Barry Goldwater during the presidential elections of 1964, he successfully campaigned for the governorship of California in 1966 with the slogan "send the welfare bums back to work." Upon completion of his tenure as governor in 1975, he failed to win the Republican nomination for president after a vigorous campaign against incumbent Gerald Ford but won the support of hard-core conservatives who shared his aversion to détente, the welfare state, and high taxes. In 1980, Reagan launched a feisty campaign for president that showcased his rhetorical skills and deft sense of humour. "A recession is when your neighbor loses his job," he told voters. "A depression is when you lose your job. And recovery is when Jimmy Carter loses his." Reagan won more than 50 per cent of the popular vote to Carter's 41 per cent (the balance went to a third-party candidate), inflicting the first electoral defeat on a sitting president since Roosevelt beat Herbert Hoover in 1932. Reagan's presidency began on a high note when the Iranian government announced its acceptance of a deal negotiated by Carter that freed the hostages only minutes after Reagan had been sworn in on 20 January 1981.

During its first two years in office, the new administration focused on economic policy, implementing major changes in tax policy. Reagan's proposal for a massive tax cut that primarily benefitted corporations and the wealthy was based on a theory of supply-side economics promulgated by economist Arthur Laffer who proposed that growth could be achieved by lowering taxes on companies that would invest the money they saved in better production equipment, enhancing their ability to compete. Increased production would create more jobs and more intense competition would result in lower prices for consumers, thus reducing unemployment and inflation, the twin scourges of the 1970s that had triggered stagflation. Some supply siders went so far as to claim that the economic growth that would result from the tax cuts would actually increase the government's revenue intake even if corporations were taxed at a lower rate. Reagan's proposed $280 billion tax cut over three years was passed by the Senate, which was controlled by the Republican Party since 1980, but ran into trouble in the House of Representatives, still under Democrats' control. In the middle of tough negotiations, a mentally unstable shooter nearly killed Reagan, generating a wave of public sympathy for the wounded president that facilitated the passage of his tax cut with the help of Republicans and conservative Democrats.

Reagan's tax policy was incompatible with the Federal Reserve's continuing attempts to battle inflation under the leadership of Paul Volcker, who maintained exceptionally high interest rates that made it prohibitively expensive for corporations to borrow money for new productive capacity. While the Federal Reserve's interest rate policy sought to control inflation with high interest rates, Reagan's tax policy fuelled inflation by putting money in corporations' pockets. One observer commented, "Reagan's tax cuts pushed on the accelerator as Volcker's tight money pushed on the brakes. The brakes won." By 1982, unemployment reached 10.4 per cent, the highest percentage since the Great Depression, while the dollar came in high demand on global currency markets as foreigners sought to take advantage of high US interest rates.

Reagan's attempts to resurrect the US economy included the deregulation of business by cutting government "red tape." Building on Carter's liberalisation of the airline and trucking industries, Reagan pursued deregulation with a vengeance that reflected his oft-repeated mantra "Government is not the solution to our problems. Government is the problem." Adopting a strict pro-business approach, he froze hiring at regulatory agencies and ordered federal departments to conduct cost-benefit analyses of all new rules. Regulations scheduled to go into effect were rescinded, including mandatory airbags in cars. The Environmental Protection Agency, a target of corporate fury since its inception under Nixon, relaxed the implementation of clean water rules, enabling polluters to discharge cyanide and lead into rivers and lakes. Starved of staff, agencies were increasingly unable to enforce regulations, sometimes with lethal consequences: Deaths in coal mining increased by more than 50 per cent after budget cuts had sharply reduced the number of mine inspectors. Democrat Albert Gore commented, "This Administration's No. 1 priority is to make certain that no industry is in any way displeased or even slightly disconcerted by any action of Government." Congressional Democrats pursued similar policies when they relaxed federal regulations that had hitherto forced savings and loan associations to restrict their lending to the home mortgage market at low interest rates. Combined with sloppy government oversight, the reforms enabled associations to make high-risk investments that flung one-third of the industry into insolvency over the next decade.

Supply side economics failed to achieve some of its core objectives. Savings derived from corporate tax cuts were rarely invested in physical capital like new machine tools that could boost productivity. Total fixed non-residential investment actually fell from 11.8 per cent (1980) of GNP to 10.9 per cent (1986). Instead of boosting their spending on physical capital, corporations spent substantial amounts on mergers and acquisitions, whose worth quadrupled from $44 billion (1980) to $180 billion (1986). Annual nonfarm productivity growth rose from -0.4 per cent to 0.7 per cent during the same period. This moderately encouraging statistic was largely attributable to the fact that employees worked harder. Hourly earnings did not rise correspondingly because the Reagan administration pursued a stridently anti-union policy that weakened organised labour's ability to extract better wages and benefits from management. The federal government itself launched a frontal assault on organised labour in 1981, when Reagan fired 11,000 striking air traffic controllers, replaced them with non-union employees, and destroyed their union, encouraging employers to follow suit.

Reagan's fiscal policy reflected conservatives' dissatisfaction with the liberal welfare state. Some right-wing critics of the Great Society like Charles Murray argued that welfare harmed the poor because it rendered them dependent on public assistance and disincentivised work, entangling them in a cycle of poverty that was passed down over generations. Others suspected widespread fraud, abuse, and mismanagement. (Reagan was fond of citing the case of Linda Taylor, who illegally collected welfare cheques under several names and defrauded the government of hundreds of thousands of dollars.) Determined to institute draconian cutbacks, his administration and Congress reduced appropriations for Aid to Families with Dependent Children and the Food Stamp programme by 14 per cent, and community service grants and employment training by 38 per cent during the first half of the 1980s. Hunger, which resurfaced as a serious problem after having been nearly eradicated in the previous decade, reached "endemic proportions" among the poor, a physician task force reported. Cuts in programmes for the poor accounted for more than 70 per cent of total budget savings Reagan achieved in his first term in office.

Simultaneously, his administration conducted the largest peacetime military build-up in history. Defence spending, which had already increased after the Soviet invasion of Afghanistan in 1979, grew 50 per cent in the first half of the 1980s as the cold war arms race reached new heights (see the next section). Fiscally, the increase had to be financed with debt because the revenue shortfall due to the tax cut left no other options. Under Reagan, who had lambasted his predecessor during the presidential campaign of 1980 for a budget shortfall of 2.5 per cent of GDP, the deficit reached 5.7 per cent in 1983. Given the simultaneous decrease in the US savings rate, most of the money had to be borrowed overseas, driving up the value of the US dollar and hurting American exports. Fortunately for Reagan, this enormous infusion of money, combined with a steep fall in oil prices, helped end the recession that had gripped the economy during the first year of his presidency. In 1984, he won re-election in a landslide with 58.8 per cent of the popular vote, leaving Democrat Walter Mondale with a paltry 40.6 per cent.

Most Western governments initially viewed US economic policies with trepidation. America's skyrocketing debt and high interest rates attracted vast amounts of foreign capital, leaving Western European economies starved of investments. In 1981, West German chancellor Schmidt denounced the "highest real interest rates since the birth of Christ" that were "absolutely unacceptable" because they ruined European economies. Even British Prime Minister Margaret Thatcher, Europe's most outspoken proponent of supply-side economics, worried that the dollar's rapid appreciation threatened her anti-inflationary crusade at home, admonishing Reagan to return to fiscal discipline. The tide turned when US inflation and interest rates subsided in 1983, coupled with American economic growth rates twice as large as those of its leading competitors. Western European politics followed the Anglo-American rightward turn: The West German Christian Democrat Helmut Kohl replaced Social Democrat Schmidt as chancellor in 1982, followed by the appointment of conservative supply sider Ruud Lubbers as Dutch prime minister. In France, Francois Mitterrand, the socialist president, made a dramatic U-turn from progressive economic policies to an austerity programme that entailed liberalisation of labour markets and reduced subsidies for state-owned enterprises. At the G7 summit meeting of major industrial nations in 1985, the leaders of the USA, Canada, Britain, France, West Germany, Italy, Japan, and the European Economic Community confirmed their commitment to deregulation, low inflation, and labour market flexibility. Though Western Europeans did not embrace supply-side economics to the same extent as Americans, deregulation, tax reductions for the wealthy, cuts in social programmes, and income inequality made their presence felt in many parts of the continent.

In the USA, recovery from the recession of the early 1980s produced uneven benefits. On the positive side, stagflation had been replaced with low inflation and unemployment coupled with strong economic growth. Per capita GNP increased at the respectable rate of 3.3 per cent from 1982 to 1988 in the USA, compared to only 2.4 per cent in West Germany. Moreover, the US economy posted a net gain of 15 million jobs during Reagan's tenure. More problematically, many of the new jobs clustered at the lower end of the service sector like retailing and fast food that did not pay nearly as well as the millions of manufacturing jobs lost during the recession. Britain's *Guardian Weekly* reported in 1987, "Over half the jobs created since 1980 pay less than the poverty level, and the number of working poor grew by half between 1978 and 1986. Of all those officially living in poverty, 41 per cent have jobs." White-collar occupations stood transformed. After millions of mid-level managers had been fired during the recession, demand for their services resumed in the mid-1980s, but their jobs became less secure and remunerative. "Ask a middle manager about life on the frontlines of the corporation these days, and you're likely to hear a bitter story," one analyst reported. "The ranks have been so decimated by the corporate trend to 'downsize' that some middle managers feel as if they are an endangered species." The gap between the rich and the rest of society increased: The top 1 per cent of Americans increased their share of the national income from 8.1 per cent (1981) to 14.7 per cent (1986), inaugurating a trend that continued in subsequent decades. American poverty rate remained shockingly high even after recovery had settled in: In 1985, the percentage of US families living in poverty was three times as high as in Norway, Sweden, and West Germany.

Poverty rates

West Germany	5.2
Netherlands	8.0
Norway	5.1
Sweden	5.4
United Kingdom	11.4
USA	17.2

Source: Luxembourg Income Study

The second cold war, the Iran-Contra scandal, and nuclear arms control

Reagan escalated the cold war to new heights with anti-Communist rhetoric, massive increases in defence spending, and aggressive initiatives in the developing world that earned the era the label "second cold war." Though a disastrous scandal involving secret US arms deliveries to Iran and illegal support of anti-Communist guerrillas in Nicaragua threatened his presidency, Reagan ended his tenure on a high note by negotiating an end to the nuclear arms race that terminated the Second cold war

A zealous anti-Communist throughout his career, Reagan castigated the Soviet Union as an "empire of evil" that threatened freedom and democracy everywhere. In the late 1970s, he joined the Committee on the Present Danger, a group of conservatives who warned that "The ultimate Soviet objective is . . . the worldwide triumph of 'socialism.'" Soviet foreign policy was accordingly designed to sow discord between the USA and Western Europe in order to weaken NATO, spread communism in the developing world by political and military means, and achieve strategic superiority over the USA with a colossal arms build-up. Norman Podhoretz, a founding member of the Committee on the Present Danger, warned of the "political and economic subordination of the United States to superior Soviet power," echoing post-war conservatives who argued "World Communism has as its sole purpose the establishment of a totalitarian dictatorship in America" (see Chapter 13). Though Reagan agreed with most of this, he also argued that a determined Western response would eventually defeat the Soviets, announcing at the beginning of his presidency, "The West will not contain Communism, it will transcend Communism. We will not bother to denounce it, we'll dismiss it as a sad, bizarre chapter in human history whose last pages are even now being written." In practical terms, this meant a major American arms build-up, including Trident nuclear submarines, land-based MX strategic missiles, B-1 and B-2 bombers, and a vast expansion of the American surface navy. Reagan was convinced that his $2.8 trillion military build-up would raise the cost of the arms race to levels the Soviets could no longer afford, "They cannot vastly increase their military productivity because they've already got their people on a starvation diet," he explained. The Soviets "know our potential capacity industrially, and they can't match it." In addition to expanding their own arsenal, the Americans encouraged the expansion of British and French nuclear forces to a size comparable to the entire Soviet arsenal of the early seventies, including Britain's formidable nuclear submarine force that was equipped with US-made Trident missiles.

The transatlantic alliance remained intact even though many Europeans disliked Reagan's simplistic attempts to divide the world into good and evil. James Callaghan, Britain's former prime minister, posited that "the Europeans have a better understanding of the complexities of the present world difficulties than the United States" and a retired French foreign secretary hoped for "a real American foreign policy which takes realities into account." Most Western European governments were broadly supportive of Reagan's rearmament efforts, however. In addition to raising their own level of defence spending, they promoted the deployment of a new generation of land-based American intermediate-range nuclear missiles that could threaten the Soviet Union from Western Europe. When opponents staged mass demonstrations, the British, West German, Italian, and Dutch governments cracked down hard to ensure the successful deployment of the new missiles. Anti-Americanism proliferated at the grass roots, the

US ambassador to Britain reported: "America the violent, America the crass, America the inept have all become everyday images in Europe." Dutch pollsters reported that "almost half the population shows a more or less negative attitude toward the United States." The US State Department feared that "the latest swell of anti-Americanism in various parts of Europe may even surpass that of the Vietnam era." From 1982 to 1987, positive views of the United States in France declined from 68 per cent to 51 per cent, and in West Germany from 71 per cent to 50 per cent, significantly lower than in Britain and Italy.

In 1983, Reagan announced a new programme called the Strategic Defence Initiative (SDI, popularly known as "Star Wars" in reference to a popular science fiction movie) that envisioned a space-based defence system capable of shooting down incoming strategic missiles. Though its technical feasibility was questionable, SDI greatly worried Soviet leaders because it could theoretically render their missile arsenal obsolete and undermine the logic of Mutually Assured Destruction that had heretofore made nuclear war unthinkable: In a worst-case scenario, the USA could launch an attack on the Soviet Union and use SDI to defeat Soviet retaliation. Concerns that American strategic planners actually considered nuclear conflict a viable option multiplied when the Pentagon publicly acknowledged the possibility of an atomic war lasting six months, in the course of which "American nuclear forces must prevail and be able to force the Soviet Union to seek earliest termination of hostilities on terms favorable to the United States." Reagan added fuel to the fire when he tested a microphone by joking "My fellow Americans, I'm pleased to tell you today that I've signed legislation that will outlaw Russia forever. We begin bombing in five minutes."

Reagan's foreign policy buttressed anti-Communist forces in parts of the developing world, sometimes in active collaboration with authoritarian pro-Western regimes. Intensifying Carter's efforts to fund Islamic warriors who fought the Soviets in Afghanistan, the CIA worked with Pakistan's military government to provide jihadists with training, weapons, ammunition, and logistical support, contributing to such heavy losses in life and materiel among Soviet forces that they withdrew in 1989. In Angola, the CIA worked with the South African apartheid regime to support anti-Communist rebel forces in their struggle against the Marxist Angolan government that received Soviet assistance. In Latin America, US forces invaded the tiny Caribbean island of Grenada in 1983 to dispose of a revolutionary regime, infuriating the British government because Grenada was a Commonwealth member. Nicaraguan anti-government forces called the Contras (short for counterrevolutionaries) that fought a protracted struggle against the country's left-leaning government received extensive American aid. The so-called Boland Amendment of 1982 that prohibited all US military assistance and training for the Contras was covertly violated by the CIA and members of the White House staff, including one Lieutenant Colonel Oliver North.

Reagan's Nicaragua policy intersected with a secret arms deal between the USA and Iran, resulting in the Iran-Contra scandal that nearly destroyed his presidency. From 1980 to 1988, Iran was embroiled in a war with Iraq, whose dictator Saddam Hussein received official American backing. Unofficially, however, members of Reagan's White House staff sought Iranian assistance in freeing American hostages in Lebanon who had been kidnapped by an Iranian-backed group, despite Reagan's public pledge never to negotiate with terrorists. When the Iranians asked for US-made weapons they could use against Iraqi forces, White House aide North arranged for the secret sale of American antitank missiles to Teheran. After Reagan secretly approved the transfer even though two of his cabinet officers told him it was illegal, the deal produced a multimillion dollar profit that was transferred to the Nicaraguan Contras by North with active participation of senior White House aides. These transactions were patently illegal because they violated the Boland Amendment and encroached upon Congress's authority to appropriate funds for the conduct of American foreign policy.

When the Iran-Contra scandal broke in 1986, Reagan made things worse by denying initially that he had authorised the Iran deal, only to admit later, "A few months

Figure 16.3 Reagan and Gorbachev during the Moscow summit of 1988, when they finalised the Intermediate-Range Nuclear Forces Treaty that eliminated an entire class of nuclear weapons and inaugurated the end of the cold war.

Source: Courtesy of ITAR-TASS News Agency/Alamy

ago I told the American people I did not trade arms for hostages. My heart and my best intentions still tell me that's true, but the facts and the evidence tell me it is not." The conclusions of an independent commission reinforced the impression of a president dangerously out of touch with the realities of governing and incapable of understanding even basic foreign policy principles; one panel member thought of Reagan as "a man who sometimes inhabited a fantasy island." European observers worried about the scandal's global ramifications. In Britain, a senior Member of Parliament opined that it was "certainly not in our interest to have a broken-backed U.S. President" and the *Independent* newspaper editorialised, "Either [Reagan] must simply go or he must act intelligently to preserve what little is left of his Presidency."

The possible meltdown of his presidency over the Iran-Contra scandal encouraged Reagan to take bold initiatives to improve US-Soviet relations because he did not want to be remembered as another failed leader like Johnson, Nixon, Ford, and Carter before him, coupled with his genuine dread of nuclear war. Luckily, his determination to seek reductions atomic weaponry was shared by Mikhail Gorbachev, the energetic new leader of the Soviet Union who embarked on ambitious reforms of the political system called *glasnost* ("openness") and economic changes named *perestroika* ("restructuring") when he came to power in 1985. Encouraged by Thatcher's verdict "I like Mr. Gorbachev. We can do business together," Reagan met the Soviet leader in 1985 at Geneva, Switzerland, where they discussed the arms race and human rights. During a follow-up meeting at Reykjavik, Iceland, in 1986, they came close to an agreement that would have eliminated their *entire* nuclear arsenals by the year 2000, but the deal collapsed when Reagan refused to meet Gorbachev's demand that he terminate SDI. Reagan became more conciliatory in 1987 as the Iran-Contra scandal took its toll on his presidency, quietly acquiescing when Congress sharply reduced SDI funding and prohibited system tests in space. This paved the way for the Intermediate Nuclear Forces Treaty of 1987, the first cold war arms agreement that eliminated an entire class of atomic weapons. When Reagan was asked during his last meeting with Gorbachev whether he still thought of the Soviet Union as an evil empire, he responded, "I was talking another time, another era."

Chapter summary

The two decades from the beginning of Nixon's presidency in 1969 to Reagan's departure from the White House in January 1989 witnessed enormous changes. Large segments of the American manufacturing sector lost their erstwhile vigour while the rest of the economy struggled with rising inflation, unemployment, slow economic growth, and the end of the Bretton Woods system. Trust in government declined in the wake of the Watergate scandal, and the USA suffered setbacks in world affairs from its defeat in Vietnam to the Iranian hostage crisis. Socially, well-educated men and women of the middle class, largely regardless of their skin colour, took advantage of employment opportunities in the expanding white-collar sector, in contrast to the working class especially in the rust belt whose fortunes declined. Disappointed with the failed Presidencies of Johnson, Nixon, Ford, and Carter, a majority felt enticed by Reagan's conservatism that promised a return to prosperity, affluence, and global dominance. Following a sharp recession in the early eighties, the economy indeed performed significantly better, but federal deficits and social inequality increased. In foreign affairs, Reagan initiated a second cold war with his massive arms build-up and support for anti-Communist forces in many parts of the world. Diverting attention from the Iran-Contra scandal that nearly crippled his presidency, he ended his tenure with the first nuclear arms reduction agreement in history.

Looking back on America during the Reagan years, *Newsweek* magazine editorialised, "The last years of his presidency had been soiled by scandal and stained with red ink; his Shining City on a Hill was $2.4 trillion in debt and heavily mortgaged to bankers in Tokyo, Frankfurt and Riyadh. . . . But Reagan remained the largest single figure in the sad recent history of politics, the first president since Dwight Eisenhower even to last out two full terms and arguably the best since Franklin Roosevelt at making the office serve his ends. The welfare state unsurprisingly survived the Reagan Revolution, but his tax cuts and his military build-up put a choke hold on its funding; no one was proposing new social programmes anymore. The business of America was business again, and the president's policies bought five unbroken years of good times and fast bucks. The benefits were unevenly shared, and Reagan had to pawn tomorrow's treasure to pay for today's. . . . The long Reagan spring had been a holiday . . . from leaders who talked about malaise and sacrifice and what the country couldn't do. But his hour was passing, and at the dawn of the campaign, Americans for the first time in years were apprehensive about tomorrow again."

Discussion questions

- What were the most important causes of the economic crisis of the seventies?
- How did the administration of Nixon, Carter, and Reagan respond to the economic crisis?
- What was the relationship between the economic crisis of the seventies and social developments of the period?
- Why did Nixon have to resign from office?
- How did defeat in Vietnam impact American foreign policy in the seventies and eighties?
- Was Reagan a strong leader?
- How did middle-class life change during the seventies and eighties?
- Why was Reagan not impeached in the Iran-Contra scandal?
- Why do many conservatives have positive memories of the Reagan years? Why do many liberals dislike him?
- Do you agree or disagree with the concept of a conservative triumph?

Further reading

Berman, William C. *America's Right Turn: From Nixon to Clinton* (Baltimore, MD, 1993). This broad overview explores the triumph of conservatism in American politics.

The Cambridge History of the Cold War, Vol. 2: Crises and Détente, eds. Martin Leffler and Odd Arne Weststad (Cambridge, UK, 2008). A collection of essays written by leading historians of international relations that cover cold war grand strategies, economics, and culture from John F. Kennedy to Richard Nixon.

The Cambridge History of the Cold War, Vol. 2: Crises and Détente, eds. Martin Leffler and Odd Arne Weststad (Cambridge, UK, 2010). A collection of essays written by leading historians of international relations that cover major aspects of the second cold war from the Soviet invasion of Afghanistan to the end of the Soviet Union in 1991.

Cannon, Lou. *President Reagan: The Role of a Lifetime* (New York, 1991). A classic and amazingly detailed biographical study by one of America's leading journalists.

A Companion to Richard Nixon, ed. Melvin Small (Chichester, UK, 2011). Essays provide introductory overviews of major aspects of the Nixon presidency, including his early career, domestic policies, and foreign policy.

Hodgson, Godfrey. *More Equal Than Others: America from Nixon to the New Century* (Princeton, NJ, 2006). An overview of economic development, new technologies, politics, and society by a renowned British journalist and commentator on American affairs.

Kutler, Stanley I. *The Wars of Watergate: The Last Crisis of Richard Nixon* (New York, 1992). Best study of the Watergate scandal by a leading Nixon scholar.

The Shock of the Global: The 1970s in Perspective, eds. Niall Ferguson, Charles S. Maier, Erez Manela, and Daniel J. Sargent (Cambridge, MA, 2010). This collection of essays explores the economic and political history of the 1970s with a primary focus on the USA and Western Europe, including these rise of stagflation, the end of the Vietnam War, the oil crisis, human rights, and environmentalism.

Stein, Judith. *Pivotal Decade: How the United States Traded Factories for Finance in the Seventies* (New Haven, CT, 2011). An insightful study of economic policy, deindustrialisation, and the rise of corporate finance during the 1970s.

The Strained Alliance: US-European Relations from Nixon to Carter, eds. Matthias Schulz and Thomas A. Schwartz (Cambridge, UK, 2010). The essays in this volume explore transatlantic relationships from the era of détente to the Soviet invasion of Afghanistan and the Iranian hostage crisis.

Tygiel, Jules. *Ronald Reagan and the Triumph of American Conservatism* (New York, 2004). A solid and balanced biography that examines Reagan in the context of American political culture.

Wilentz, Sean. *The Age of Reagan: A History, 1974–2008* (New York, 2008). A leading American historian surveys the Reagan era, including its origins in the 1970s and its consequences for American politics and society in the early twenty-first century.

17 The age of neoliberalism, 1989–2016

Timeline

1989 Fall of the Berlin Wall
1990 Iraqi invasion of Kuwait
1991 US and Allied forces defeat Iraq in the Gulf War
      Breakup of the Soviet Union
1992 Los Angeles riots
      Democrat Bill Clinton elected president
1993 US peacekeeping mission in Somalia fails
1994 US intervenes in Haiti
      North American Free Trade Agreement (NAFTA) takes effect
      Elections give Republicans control of Congress
1995 US airstrikes against Serbian regime
      Establishment of the World Trade Organisation
      US government shutdown
1996 Bill Clinton re-elected president
1997 Asian financial crisis
1998 Sex scandal tarnishes Clinton presidency
      Russian financial crisis
1999 Impeachment of President Clinton fails
      US and Allied air campaign against Serbia
      Repeal of the Glass-Steagall Act deregulates US financial markets
      Anti-globalisation protests in Seattle
2000 Republican George W. Bush declared winner by US Supreme Court in contro-
          versial presidential election
2001 US and Allied invasion of Afghanistan
      Patriot Act authorises expanded surveillance
2002 Bush administration adopts preventive war doctrine
2003 US and Allied invasion of Iraq
2004 George W. Bush re-elected president
2005 Hurricane Katrina kills nearly 2,000 people
2006 Democrats regain control of US House of Representatives and Senate
2007 Start of economic recession
2008 World financial crisis
      Democrat Barack Obama elected president
2009 Congress passes $800 billion economic stimulus package
2010 Dodd–Frank Wall Street Reform and Consumer Protection Act regulates financial
          services industry

2011   Withdrawal of US combat forces from Iraq
2012   Barack Obama re-elected president
2013   Black Lives Matter movement formed
2014   US forces re-enter Iraq to fight Islamist terrorists
2015   US Supreme Court decision legalises same-sex marriage
2016   Donald Trump elected president

Topics covered

- End of the cold war
- Clinton and neoliberalism
- The nineties' boom
- Clinton's foreign policy
- Race, ethnicity, and social conflicts
- 9/11 and the global War on Terror
- The Great Recession
- Obama and the persistence of neoliberalism
- Obama's foreign policy
- Sociocultural conflict and conservative resurgence

Introduction

The chapter opens with statements by Democratic President Bill Clinton (1993–2001) and others who advocated fiscal austerity, free trade, deregulated markets, and other neoliberal policies. After the end of the cold war in 1991, many Americans hoped for a future when the world's embrace of democracy and free markets would produce tangible benefits at home. Technological innovation indeed boosted productivity and growth in the nineties, but the new millennium brought an economic slowdown as social inequality grew. Attempts to solve international problems by force often failed, most spectacularly after the invasion of Iraq in 2003 that discredited the USA and destabilised world affairs. Technological change created poorly paid jobs for low-skilled workers and well-remunerated for highly skilled ones but decimated opportunities for the broad middle. Financial deregulation helped unleash a real estate buying binge which was followed by a financial collapse in 2008 that contributed to the election of Barack Obama as president. Though Obama's policies mitigated the recession's impact and reformed the US health insurance system, opposition against his administration proliferated. In 2016, Republican Donald Trump defeated Democrat Hillary Clinton in the presidential elections.

Explaining the "golden nineties"

Clinton's supporters often credited him with unleashing the nineties' economic boom. Economists like Lawrence Summers argued that a major problem bedevilling the US economy early in the decade was the bloated federal debt of the Reagan years that presumably "crowded out" private investments by absorbing funds that could otherwise have been borrowed by corporations to finance productive improvements. According to economist Lawrence Summers and others, Clinton's deficit reduction gradually eliminated the "crowding-out" phenomenon, thus enabling private investors to obtain low-interest loans to finance productivity enhancements that boosted economic growth. "The result has been a virtuous cycle, in which the right policies in 1993 kicked off a chain reaction of smaller deficits, lower costs of capital, higher investment, increased technology in the workplace, and faster economic growth," the President's Council of Economic Advisors reported in 2001.

Others disagree. "Why was the Clinton economy so good?" economist Paul Krugman asks. "It wasn't because Mr. Clinton had a magic touch, although he did do a good job of responding to crises. Mostly, he had the good luck to hold office when good things were happening for reasons unrelated to politics." Those who share this view attribute the 1990s boom to the successful exploitation of information technologies, which in turn led to higher productivity rates and economic growth.

On the threshold of a new era

The dawn of the third millennium found the USA's elite in celebratory mood. Columnist Thomas Friedman explained in 1991 that "America's triumph in the cold war was not a territorial victory but a victory for a set of political and economic principles: democracy and the free market." President Bill Clinton agreed that the world was on the verge of a new era, pledging at the UN General Assembly in 1993 that his administration "will work to strengthen the free market democracies by revitalising our economy here at home, by opening world trade through the [General Agreement on Tariffs and Trade], the North American Free Trade Agreement and other accords, and by updating our shared institutions, asking with you and answering the hard questions about whether they are adequate to the present challenges." The Clinton presidency marked a high point of neoliberalism (see concept box).

Neoliberalism

A set of economic concepts that sought to resurrect nineteenth-century notions of limited government, deregulation, trade liberalisation, balanced budgets, and a market-based society, neoliberal ideas were promulgated by the economic thinkers Friedrich Hayek, Milton Friedman, and Ayn Rand. They rejected the economic theory of John M. Keynes, whose advocacy of a regulatory state, anticyclical deficit spending, and demand-side economics had inspired economic policy in developed countries after World War II. Deregulation and other neoliberal economic policies were implemented in the 1980s by British Prime Minister Margaret Thatcher and President Ronald Reagan, but Reagan's large deficits and occasional forays into protectionism were inconsistent with neoliberalism. Austerity budgets, trade liberalisation, and financial deregulation became hallmarks of President Clinton's economic policy discussed in this chapter.

The end of the cold war

The nineties began auspiciously with the end of the superpower confrontation that had dominated world affairs since World War II. Though US leaders claimed credit for themselves ("By the grace of God, America won the cold war," Republican President George Bush proclaimed in 1992), the cold war's end was largely the result of political activism of valiant protestors and reformers in Eastern Europe and the Soviet Union.

The end of the cold war came on the heels of a historic nuclear arms control treaty signed by President Ronald Reagan and Soviet leader Mikhail Gorbachev in 1987 (see Chapter 16). Determined to reform the Soviet Union's sclerotic economy and authoritarian political system, Gorbachev sought to reduce Soviet military expenditures and strategic commitments. Milestones along the way included the withdrawal of Russian troops from Afghanistan, cessation of Soviet support for communist regimes in Eastern Europe, and the Strategic Arms Reduction Treaty (START) signed by Gorbachev and Reagan's successor George Bush which eventually reduced strategic arsenals significantly. Eastern European activists took advantage of Gorbachev's reforms by toppling communist regimes throughout the region, culminating in the demolition of the Berlin Wall in 1989, the end of communist party control of East Germany in 1990, and the unification of Germany a year later.

By then, Gorbachev's domestic reforms had thrown the Soviet Union into chaos. State-owned enterprises released from the control of central planning authorities were often unable to manage their operations, triggering a contraction of national income by one fifth, a rate that exceeded America's 1930s' economic meltdown. Skyrocketing poverty and crime rates undermined the entire system, prompting the embittered population to turn to nationalists who shredded what little remained of Soviet unity. In December 1991, the 15 member republics dissolved the USSR and Gorbachev handed power to Boris Yeltsin, the president of the Russian Republic who had successfully resisted a failed *coup d'état* by communist hardliners. Yeltsin administered an economic "shock therapy" devised by Harvard University Professor Jeffrey Sachs and other US advisors. Abolishing price controls and state subsidies, he liberalised trade and privatised state-owned enterprises, most of which fell under the control of former Communist Party officials and others who comprised Russia's new elite called the "oligarchs." Ordinary Russians who had managed to put aside a few roubles watched their savings evaporate as inflation and poverty rates reached catastrophic levels.

Simmering Russian resentment towards the West over botched economic reform was reinforced by a US policy of admitting former Soviet allies in Eastern Europe to the North Atlantic Treaty Organisation (NATO) in violation of President Bush's earlier pledge to refrain from such initiatives. Clinton's claim that NATO expansion was necessary to buttress democracy was contested by experts who doubted that membership in a US-dominated military alliance was relevant to the democratisation of the former Soviet satellites. George Kennan (the architect of containment, see Chapter 12) considered NATO expansion a "tragic mistake" that did not produce tangible benefits for the USA, the alliance, or Eastern Europe and would likely mark the "beginning of a new cold war" Combined with Yeltsin's American-sponsored economic shock therapy, NATO expansion laid the groundwork for renewed US-Russian tensions in the early twenty-first century.

The George Bush interlude

Republican George Bush's one-term presidency (1989–1993) yielded important departures in American foreign affairs. Though he scored successes with the defeat of the Iraq during the Gulf War of 1991, however, his tenure was overshadowed by domestic economic problems.

Bush was a skilled foreign policymaker. Initially reluctant to develop a cordial relationship with Gorbachev, he reached out to the Soviet leader at the urging of French President François Mitterrand and British Prime Minister Margaret Thatcher. When the Soviet Union entered its death throes, moreover, Bush refrained from gloating at the time even though he later engaged in a bit of triumphalism ("America won the cold war"). The Gulf War marked a high point of his presidency. In August 1990, Iraqi dictator Saddam Hussein ordered his army to invade Kuwait, precipitating fears that he sought control of the region's oil reserves. Bush assembled a broad coalition of allies, including Britain, France, Egypt, Syria, and Pakistan which deployed forces to Saudi Arabia for an assault on Iraqi positions in Kuwait. Codenamed Operation Desert Storm, the campaign showcased the formidable technological superiority of the USA, whose ground forces defeated the Iraqi army in four days. Though it resulted in a resounding victory and the liberation of Kuwait, the war had dire consequences. To safeguard against the possibility of further Iraqi aggression in the region, the USA maintained several thousand troops in Saudi Arabia, raising the ire of Muslims who resented the presence of Western military forces in the home of Mecca and Medina,

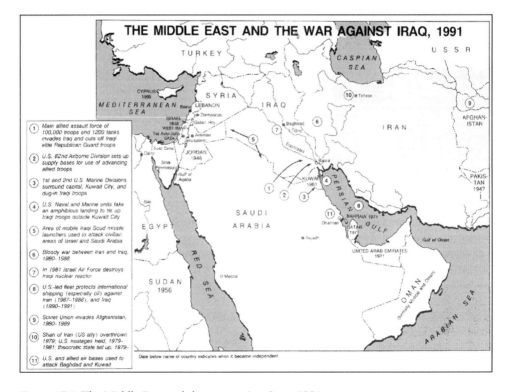

Figure 17.1 The Middle East and the war against Iraq, 1991.

two of the holiest places in Islam. Osama bin Laden, leader of the fundamentalist al Qaida terrorist organisation, used the continued presence of US troops to justify the terrorist attacks on the USA in September 2001 ("The 9/11 attacks and the 'Global War on Terror'").

Though Bush received high marks for his foreign policy, his failure to address economic problems cost him the presidency during the 1992 elections. Trying to tackle the outsized fiscal deficits of the Reagan era (see Chapter 16), Bush abandoned his campaign promise "Read my lips: No new taxes" and signed a deficit reduction bill that included tax increases and spending cuts amidst a recession. Reductions in military expenditures worsened unemployment in states with large clusters of defence-dependent industries. Fears that Bush's economic policies would cost American jobs proliferated when his administration negotiated the North American Free Trade Agreement (NAFTA) which abolished tariff barriers between the USA, Canada, and Mexico, raising concerns that American employers would relocate south of the border to take advantage of low Mexican labour costs. Whilst Bush and Democratic presidential candidate Bill Clinton supported NAFTA, independent candidate Ross Perot opposed the treaty. Enfeebled by economic woes and lacklustre Republican support, Bush achieved only 37 per cent of the popular vote to Clinton's 43 per cent and Perot's 19 per cent.

Bill Clinton and the ascent of neoliberalism

A pragmatist who questioned political principles the Democratic Party had long espoused, Clinton adopted a variety of neoliberal positions which had been pioneered by his Republican predecessors, including deregulation and trade liberalisation, and added new ones, notably a balanced budget and welfare reforms.

Clinton's economic programme prioritised fiscal austerity. Though his campaign had promised a middle-class tax cut and public works to hasten economic recovery, his administration quickly discarded such plans. His *volte face* occurred during a December 1992 meeting with Federal Reserve Chairman Alan Greenspan, who told Clinton that large federal deficits sucked credit markets dry, boosted interest rates, discouraged businesses from borrowing money to finance capital expansion, and raised the spectre of inflation. Though Clinton instituted cuts in military and domestic spending, interest rates actually *increased* slightly at the exact time when the administration began to balance the budget, much to the amazement of neoliberals who had predicted that fiscal austerity would result in an interest rate decline. Further dumbfounding proponents of federal belt tightening, rising interest rates did not prevent businesses from borrowing money to finance productivity enhancements, casting further doubt on the validity of the "crowding out" theory. Progressives and organised labour who had looked forward to a public works programme and other federal spending initiatives Clinton had promised during his election campaign were disappointed. On the plus side, the USA achieved a budget surplus in 1997 which enabled it to pay down some of its national debt.

Labour organisers, environmentalists, and many Democrats were also dismayed at Clinton's support for the North American Free Trade Agreement (NAFTA). Clinton defended his position as follows: "NAFTA will provide more jobs from exports. It will challenge us to become more competitive. It will certainly help Mexico to develop. A wealthier Mexico will buy more products. As incomes rise there that will reduce pressure for emigration across the border into the United States which depresses wages here." Congressional majorities which included more Republicans than Democrats ratified the treaty in 1993. As its proponents had predicted, trade between the three member countries increased precipitously. Ominously, however, Mexican exports to the USA increased faster than *vice versa*, turning a modest American trade surplus with Mexico prior to NAFTA into a 20 per cent deficit by 2014. American consumers benefitted from lower prices for manufactured goods, but the US economy lost almost 600,000 jobs from 1994 to 2014 as businesses relocated manufacturing plants to Mexico to take advantage of cheap labour and lax enforcement of environmental laws. Car production in Mexico grew significantly at the expense of its American and Canadian counterparts.

Light vehicle production share

	2005	*2020 (projected)*
USA	73.2% (11.5 million vehicles)	63.7% (12.2 million)
Canada	16.7% (2.6 million)	9.9% (1.9 million)
Mexico	10.1% (1.6 million)	26.4% (5.1 million)

Source: *Wall Street Journal*

Contrary to Clinton's claim that NAFTA would enrich Mexicans so that they could buy more American-made goods, Mexico experienced one of Latin America's slowest growth and wages rose a miniscule 2.4 per cent in the two decades after NAFTA went into effect. Highly mechanised US farms exported inexpensive agricultural products to Mexico, where two million peasants found themselves jobless as a result. Many crossed the border into the USA illegally in search of employment, depressing wages among American agricultural labourers. NAFTA, in short, was more of a mixed blessing than Clinton had predicted.

Clinton scored another controversial victory when he supported a crime bill that solidified his image as a "New Democrat" who embraced "law and order," traditionally a Republican campaign slogan (see Chapter 15). Sensationalist television coverage convinced a majority of Americans that violent crime was out of control, even though the rate had actually begun to decline in 1992 and remained on a downward trajectory in subsequent decades. Responding to public opinion which favoured punitive measures, Clinton introduced the largest crime bill in American history which provided $30 billion for law enforcement and prison construction, introduced mandatory life sentences for repeat offenders, and required other draconian measures. Passed in 1994, the law contributed to a doubling of the federal inmate population to more than 200,000 in 2016, when the United States accounted for more than 25 per cent of the world's prison population.

Clinton's embrace of fiscal austerity and trade liberalisation set the stage for the midterm elections of 1994, when Republicans gained control of both houses of Congress for the first time since 1946. Led by Representative Newt Gingrich, they rallied around an election platform called "Contract with America" which promised to cut taxes and spending, balance the budget, pass stringent welfare reform, and enact other conservative policies. In contrast to the Republicans' unified campaign and coherent message, the Democrats and their constituencies disagreed over major policies, notably NAFTA, which remained a thorn in the side of organised labour, the party's most important campaign contributor. (One union president told Democrats who had voted for NAFTA "we're gonna whip your ass and throw you out of office.") The party suffered particularly heavy losses in the South, enabling Republicans to gain a majority of seats in the region for the first time since Reconstruction. The South henceforth remained a Republican Party bastion.

The Democratic president and the Republican Congress clashed over fiscal policy in 1995, when the conservative majority demanded cuts in non-defence spending which triggered a Clinton veto. The ensuing impasse resulted in a partial shutdown of the federal government. Though Gingrich expected to ride a wave of popular sentiment which favoured a balanced budget, Clinton emerged victorious as his approval ratings increased and many people blamed the Republicans for the impasse. Afterwards, however, Clinton made a sweeping concession to conservatives when he announced in January 1996 "The era of big government is over," distancing himself from the legacy of Franklin Roosevelt, much as President Jimmy Carter had in the late 1970s.

Seeking to redeem his campaign promise to "end welfare as we know it," Clinton worked with Republicans to abolish the Aid to Families with Dependent Children (AFDC) programme which had originated in the New Deal. Long a *bête noire* of conservatives who argued that it ensnared poor people in a cycle of welfare dependency, AFDC was replaced with the Temporary Assistance for Needy Families (TANF) programme which slashed benefits, limited lifetime eligibility to five years, and allowed states wide latitude in managing the programme. The reform was criticised by the left, including Clinton's long-time friend Marian Wright Edelman, the founder of the non-profit Children's Defense Fund who commented "Today marks a tragic end to our nation's legacy of commitment to our most vulnerable children – this is truly a moment of shame for all Americans." Though senior administration officials resigned in protest, Clinton stood by welfare reform in 1996, when his successful re-election bid was buoyed by economic prosperity. The boom and shrinking unemployment contributed to a decline in welfare dependency for the remainder of the decade, but hard times eventually revealed TANF's shortcomings: The caseload dropped from five million families (1996) to three million (2016) even though the number of families living in poverty reached nine million (2016), indicating that only one-third of poor families received TANF assistance.

Clinton's neoliberal economic policies included the deregulation of the financial industry, which had long complained about the separation of commercial and investment banking instituted under the Glass-Steagall Act of 1933. British banks operated under similar restrictions until 1986, when Conservative Prime Minister Margaret Thatcher's so-called Big Bang reforms removed the firewall between investment and commercial banking to the envy of US bankers. The Federal Reserve gradually relaxed regulations, permitting Citicorp, J. P. Morgan, and other bank holding companies which controlled commercial banks to form investment banking subsidiaries. Republicans and Democrats in Congress meanwhile passed the Riegle-Neal Act of 1994 which abolished long-standing restrictions on interstate branching, hastening the growth of mega banks like Bank of America. What little remained of Glass-Steagall was repealed by Congress in 1999 at Clinton's urging.

Clinton's neoliberal turn intersected with similar developments in Western Europe, where leaders of centre-left parties embraced a pro-market orientation. In Britain, the Labour Party abandoned its commitment to the nationalisation of industries at the urging of Tony Blair, elected prime minister in 1997. In office, Blair's Labour government maintained the Conservatives' fiscal and tax policies, attacked trade unions for making wage demands which ostensibly threatened economic growth, and rejected pleas to spend more on education. Anglo-American neoliberalism inspired Germany's Gerhard Schröder, the leader of the Social Democratic Party. Elected Chancellor in 1998, his government lowered corporate taxes, reduced unemployment benefits, and cut welfare. To plot further departures from left-wing politics, Clinton, Blair, and Schröder met the Netherlands' Prime Minister Wim Kok of the Dutch Labour Party and Italian Prime Minister Massimo D'Alema of the Democratic Party of the Left who shared their proclivities. Their policies, they explained, were based on a "public ethic [of] mutual responsibility. Its core value is community. Its outlook is global. And its modern means are fostering private sector economic growth."

Anatomy of the nineties' boom

Though Clinton took credit for the US economy's good performance, the combination of economic growth, productivity gains, low unemployment, and low inflation was largely the result of other factors, especially major changes in information technology (IT). Problems soon became evident as income inequality increased, prosperity was interrupted by financial crises, and resistance against neoliberalism proliferated.

Statistics indicate significant gains in US economic performance during the 1990s. Once the economy had emerged from a short recession at the beginning of the decade, GDP growth averaged 3.5 per cent from 1995–2001 compared to 3 per cent in Britain and 1.9 per cent in Germany, whose post-unification problems earned it the sobriquet "sick man of Europe." US unemployment averaged 4.8 per cent during the same period compared to 6.6 per cent in Britain and an appalling 8.7 per cent in Germany, whilst inflation remained low in most developed countries. The USA's good economic performance was largely attributable to increasing business use of information technology (IT). Computers evolved from large mainframe machines of the 1950s to personal computers (PCs) pioneered in the 1970s whose low price enabled small and medium-sized businesses to automate data processing. Apple, a major player in the IT industry founded in 1976, developed spreadsheet software which completed complex calculations heretofore performed by accountants and bookkeepers with electronic calculators. International Business Machines introduced PCs using a disk operating system developed by Microsoft founder Bill Gates which emerged as an industry standard in the 1980s. These changes intersected with the rise of the internet, which evolved from a government-owned computer network into a publicly available system in 1994, enabling businesses and consumers to exchange information faster and cheaper than the use of the postal service and fax machines had in the past. Consumers increasingly bought goods from online retailers like Amazon and ebay, and investors took advantage of online brokerages like E-Trade Financial Corporation which used electronic trading systems to buy and sell stocks. Productivity growth during the second half of the 1990s clustered in wholesaling, retailing, semiconductors, computer manufacturing, and telecommunications, but none rivalled financial services, where the average trade was now completed in milliseconds. The IT boom began to fizzle in 2000, when GDP growth began to slow down amidst a stock market slump.

Analysing the nineties, Federal Reserve chairman Greenspan noted "the American economy was experiencing a once-in-a-century acceleration of innovation, which propelled forward productivity, output, corporate profits, and stock prices at a pace not seen in generations, if ever." Conspicuously absent from Greenspan's list were hourly wages, whose growth rate was anaemic even though worker productivity improved (see chart). The boom's financial rewards went disproportionately to corporations and shareholders as social inequality proliferated: In 1980, the average chief executive earned 40 as much as the average worker; by 2005, the ratio was 500:1, compared to Germany's 11:1 and Britain's 25:1. The half-dozen heirs of the Walmart retail imperium owned more wealth than 40 per cent of the entire US population combined. Workers' inability to achieve significant wage gains reflected the weakness of trade unions, whose efforts to organise workers in the IT sector often failed as a result of extreme hostility of employers who sought competitive advantages by controlling their labour costs. Average hourly wages stagnated while productivity increased, much as they had since 1973.

The decline of US unemployment during the boom was accompanied by a trend towards job polarisation as demand for unskilled and highly skilled labour increased whilst employment of middle-skill labour stagnated. In the latter category, many routine jobs in the clerical sector, services, and manufacturing were susceptible to automation. Bank tellers, for example, who had long been a fixture of retail banking, were increasingly replaced by machines which dispensed cash more cheaply and reliably than humans. Whilst job opportunities for these middle-skill workers decreased, the need for more highly skilled professionals like loan specialists and investment advisors increased, as did demand for janitors and security guards. The gradual hollowing-out of job opportunities for middle-skill workers continued in the twenty-first century, when the availability of artificial intelligence and big data permitted the computerisation of non-routine tasks like medical diagnostics, translation, and software engineering. Job polarisation created enormous pressures on middle-class Americans to acquire advanced cognitive skills in colleges and universities, whose substantial expense created economic woes for heavily indebted graduates even in the best of times.

Despite these drawbacks, the nineties' boom produced tangible benefits for ordinary Americans. Price declines in imported commodities like oil, combined with slow wage

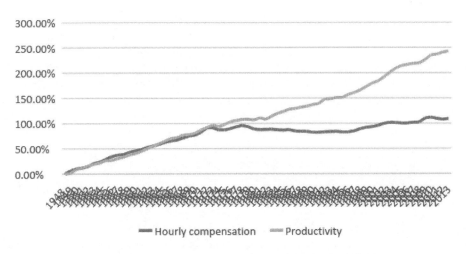

Figure 17.2 Hourly wages and productivity: cumulative change, 1948–2012.

growth, produced only moderate inflation and caused the Federal Reserve to lower interest rates during the late nineties, enabling consumers to borrow money for home purchases and goods. Many people expected the good times to last, the *Wall Street Journal* reported in 1996: "A new consensus is emerging from boardrooms, trading floors, government offices, and even living rooms: 'The big, bad business cycle has been tamed.'"

In truth, growing interdependence made the world economy more vulnerable to financial crises. A series of disasters unfolded after neoliberal policymakers at the US Treasury Department, the International Monetary Fund (IMF), and the World Bank encouraged developing countries to adopt the so-called Washington Consensus of fiscal austerity, tax reductions, free trade, privatisation of state-owned property, and deregulation. These policies enabled developing nations to become more active participants in the global economy, but also rendered countries dependent on foreign investors in government securities who often reacted nervously to sovereign debt problems. In 1997, the Thai government's possible default prompted investors to liquidate their holdings in that country as well as South Korea and Indonesia, turning a local calamity into an Asian financial crisis. The IMF and the US Treasury provided a $120 billion rescue package (the largest in history) that required recipient countries to reduce tariff barriers further and open their markets even more to foreign investments. Though it stabilised the financial industry, the rescue programme also fomented slower economic growth and sharp increases in unemployment. Economic slowdown in Southeast Asia, in turn, led to lower demand for oil which affected Russia, whose economic fortunes depended on petroleum exports. The loss of revenue forced the Russian government to default on its sovereign debt in 1998, jeopardising US, European, and Asian holders of Russian bonds. In the USA, potential casualties included the hedge fund Long-Term Capital Management, which was bailed out by Wall Street banks in collaboration with the US Treasury. In these and other instances, the Clinton administration received high marks for its successful crisis management which prevented a global financial meltdown, but the chain reaction linking the Asian and Russian financial crises also highlighted the pitfalls of an increasingly deregulated and interdependent global economy.

The social hardships imposed on developing countries by the Washington Consensus, combined with the uneven distribution of the boom's benefits in the developed world, produced backlashes against the neoliberal order. In Mexico, a NAFTA-mandated privatisation of collectively owned land sparked an armed uprising by the left-wing Zapatista Army of National Liberation when the treaty went into effect in 1994. The Organisation for Economic Co-operation and Development's (OECD) draft proposal to curtail countries' ability to regulate the financial industry had to be abandoned in 1998 after huge protests by trade unions, environmental groups, and human rights activists in the USA, France, and other developed countries which coordinated their resistance with groups in developing nations. In 1999, a similar coalition mobilised for massive demonstrations against a meeting of the newly formed World Trade Organisation (WTO) which assembled in Seattle, Washington, to negotiate a fresh round of trade liberalisation.

Race, ethnicity, and social conflicts

Economic change affected American society in areas such as immigration and race relations which produced new challenges. Social conflicts flared as Hispanic and Asian immigration increased.

The arrival of large numbers of immigrants raised the share of foreign-born Americans from 8 per cent (1990) to 13 per cent (2016), percentages that were roughly comparable to Western Europe. Legal immigration fell under a 1965 landmark law (see Chapter 15) that was amended by Congress in 1990 to double the quota of persons allowed to immigrate. Though the reform's major objective was to make more skilled and educated workers available to US employers, most immigrants were immediate relatives of US citizens who could claim legal residency status. Immigrants settled disproportionately on the West Coast, the Southwest, and the Northeast, largely bypassing the Midwest. In 2015, California became the first state whose Hispanic population exceeded that of non-Hispanic whites. Some immigrant groups, notably from the Indian subcontinent and Northeast Asia, achieved higher average incomes than whites, whilst others, including many Hispanics, clustered at the bottom of the economic hierarchy.

Growing ethnic diversity contributed to ferocious conflicts. America's Voice and other immigrant rights organisations argued that foreign-born Americans were important net contributors to American society because they paid more in taxes than they obtained in public services. Claims of immigration critics who charged that immigrants facilitated a "race to the bottom" among unskilled US workers proved correct; however, research by respected scholars like George Borjas documented that unauthorised immigrants in fact depressed wages in low-skill occupations by 8 per cent in the late twentieth century. Liberal economist Krugman concluded reluctantly "you'd be hard pressed to find any set of assumptions under which Mexican immigrants are a net fiscal plus," though he added that one would be "equally hard pressed to make the burden more than a fraction of a percent of G.D.P." Immigration opponents scored a victory in 1994, when California voters passed a referendum on Proposition 187 that denied public education and other tax-payer funded services to unauthorised immigrants. Proposition 187 was eventually declared unconstitutional, but it set the tone for other campaigns which thrived on fears that immigrants threatened traditional American values: ProEnglish, a group founded in 1994, lobbied for legislation to make English the nation's only official language and require English-only instruction in public schools.

Blacks made significant headway but racial tensions remained a fact of life. African American unemployment declined during the nineties in tandem with that of Hispanics and whites, but the black rate remained significantly higher than that of other groups. Black-white disparities were partly attributable to racial biases among employers who were more likely to invite job applicants with "white-sounding" Christian names for interviews than those with "black-sounding" ones. Blacks' poverty rates, which were three times as high as those of whites, declined from 32 per cent (1990) to 23 per cent (2000) but then increased to 26 per cent (2014) as the economy slowed. On the other end of the spectrum, African Americans with college degrees made gains in the managerial sector, and many left the Northeast to head for faster-growing Southern states like Texas, Georgia, and North Carolina, reversing the South-North migration pattern of earlier decades (see Chapter 14).

Racial tensions flared up repeatedly. In 1991, four Los Angeles police officers inflicted a savage beating on black motorist Rodney King which was recorded on videotape. The officers' subsequent acquittal triggered protests and lootings during the Los Angeles riots of 1992 by African Americans and members of the city's rapidly growing Hispanic population. The unrest featured new dimensions of interracial conflict: after rioters attacked Korean-American owned greengroceries, gun-toting members of that community lined up in front of their neighbourhood stores to protect them.

Figure 17.3 Man injured during the Rodney King riots being led to safety, 1992.

Source: Courtesy of Glasshouse Images/Alamy

Humanitarian interventions

The sole surviving superpower, the USA embarked on several foreign interventions under Clinton. These initiatives usually combined the use of force with "nation build-ing" efforts to create stable political and economic structures as well as peaceful socio-political conditions, most of which failed.

The Soviet Union's collapse in 1991 created a unique situation when the USA could dominate global affairs like few other powers in history. Clinton's America spent as much on its military as the rest of the world combined, sailed a vast navy into all corners of the globe, stationed more than 250,000 troops in 700 military bases world-wide, and maintained unmatched military technology. Clinton deployed this military might to conduct humanitarian interventions in countries that had little or no direct relevance to American national security. In Northeast Africa, he inherited a mission to Somalia from his predecessor George Bush, who had deployed 25,000 US troops to spearhead UN attempts to feed civilians amidst a civil war. The operation saved many lives but also encountered resistance from local guerrillas. When an abortive attempt to capture a rebel leader cost the lives of 18 US servicemen and several hundred guerrillas, Clinton ordered a withdrawal in summer 1993 and the country imploded. Failure in Somalia impacted subsequent operations. During an attempted intervention in the Caribbean island of Haiti in autumn 1993 to replace a military junta with the elected President Jean Bertrand Aristide, US forces pulled out when hostile demonstrators chanted "Somalia, Somalia" – a surreal humiliation of the world's only superpower by a handful of thugs. The subsequent occupation of Haiti by 20,000 US troops managed to install Aristide, but attempts to rebuild Haiti's shattered economy and political institutions failed.

The USA also intervened in southeastern Europe, where the formerly communist country of Yugoslavia collapsed in a series of ethnic conflicts. The first erupted in 1991, when the Serb-dominated central government in the capital Belgrade tried to prevent the Croatian Republic from breaking away from the Yugoslav federation, followed by vicious fighting in Bosnia between Serbs, Croats, and Muslims which cost more than 150,000 lives from 1992 to 1995. After Western European efforts to halt the bloodshed failed, the USA bombed Serbian forces in Bosnia which were responsible for a genocidal massacre of Muslims in Srebrenica. US-sponsored peace talks in Dayton, Ohio, finally terminated the fighting in 1995, when Yugoslavia's Serb-run government agreed to end its military involvement in Bosnia and recognise its sovereignty in return for a Muslim-Croat pledge to respect the quasi autonomy of a Serbian province in Bosnia. The USA and other countries deployed 60,000 troops to enforce the peace agreement and support reconstruction, but their efforts did not prevent the de-facto breakup of Bosnia into ethnic enclaves. The latter development encouraged Kosovar nationalists in rump-Yugoslavia to seek independence from the Serb-run central government in a guerrilla campaign which received US support. Rumoured Serb atrocities against Kosovar civilians prompted US and Western European air forces to bomb Belgrade in 1999, forcing the Serbs to withdraw from Kosovo. Atrocities subsided as Kosovo achieved de-facto independence, but NATO intervention remained controversial. Critics noted that the USA and its allies had intervened militarily into the domestic affairs of sovereign Yugoslavia without a UN mandate. Law professor Jonathan Charney commented, "The NATO actions, regardless of how well-intentioned, constitute an unfortunate precedent for states . . . to justify intervention for less laudable objectives." The George W. Bush administration indeed cited the NATO attack on Yugoslavia as a precedent when it tried to prove the legality of the US attack on Iraq in 2003 ("The 9/11 attacks and the 'Global War on Terror'").

From Clinton to Bush

Clinton's chequered presidency ended in 2001, when he was succeeded by Bush after a contested election. A conservative who was especially critical of Clinton's personal conduct, Bush became one of most controversial presidents in American history as a result of his foreign policy after the terrorist attacks of 11 September 2001.

The last two years of Clinton's presidency were consumed by a sex scandal which led to his impeachment. Long known for his extramarital affairs, Clinton secretly had sex with a 22-year-old White House intern and then publicly denied having done so. Taken up by conservatives who despised Clinton's questionable morals, the scandal was investigated by independent counsel Ken Starr, a Republican solicitor who recommended that Clinton be impeached for perjury and obstruction of justice. The Republican-controlled House of Representatives passed articles of impeachment, but the Democratic majority in the Senate (the president's "jury" according to the Constitution's impeachment rules) voted against Clinton's removal from office. His moral failings constituted a core theme of Republican presidential candidate George W. Bush's campaign, which promised to "restore honor and dignity" to the White House. His Democratic opponent, Vice President Al Gore, distanced himself from Clinton, making it difficult to capitalise on the president's economic record. The close election hinged on the Florida results, which were tainted by broken voting machines and other irregularities. Bush was declared the winner after a conservative majority on the sharply divided US Supreme Court ruled against a complete recount.

In office, Bush retreated from fiscal austerity, which had been a hallmark of Clinton's neoliberalism, and instead proposed tax reductions which dwarfed the Reagan cuts of the early 1980s. Claims by the conservative Heritage Foundation that the tax cuts would not only pay for themselves but spur economic growth to such an extent that they would actually increase the government's revenue intake echoed Reagan-era rhetoric. They also proved incorrect: combined with Bush's increases in military spending ("The 9/11 attacks and the 'Global War on Terror'"), his tax cuts accounted for almost half of the federal debt in the new millennium. Clinton-era projections that the entire federal debt would be paid off by 2008 gave way to an expansion of net debt that reached 87 per cent of GDP in 2016, compared to Britain's 82 per cent and Germany's 74 per cent. Further distancing himself from Clinton's fiscal austerity, Bush endorsed an expansion of Medicare drug benefits for elderly Americans which cost $400 billion in the first decade. Britain's *Economist* labelled Bush "the most profligate president since Vietnam" whose "self-proclaimed party of small government has turned itself into the party of unlimited spending."

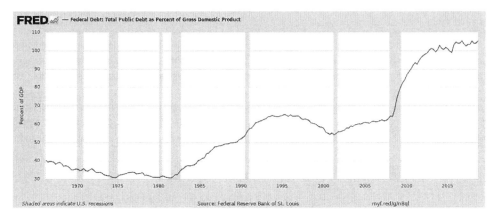

Figure 17.4 Federal debt: total public debt as a percentage of gross domestic product.

Source: Federal Reserve Bank of St Louis

Bush's environmental and social policies reflected a peculiarly American brand of religious conservatism and wariness of science. In 2001, his administration cut federal funding to stem cell researchers whose use of cell clusters was deemed morally objectionable by religious groups. The US Conference of Catholic Bishops and others insisted that the tiny specks of tissue (which could not evolve into a viable foetus) constituted life which had begun at inception and should not be used for scientific research to develop cures for heart disease and other ailments. As a result of the cuts, biotechnology research in the USA fell behind its counterparts in Britain, Switzerland, and elsewhere. In another setback for research science, the Bush administration pulled out of the Kyoto Protocol of 1997 which obligated signatory countries to limit their greenhouse gas emissions, citing polluter-funded research claims that man-made global warming was a chimera. The Cornwall Alliance, a coalition of religious groups, explained that Earth, "created by God's intelligent design, [is] robust, resilient, self-regulating, and self-correcting, admirably suited for human flourishing, and displaying His glory. . . . Recent global warming is one of many natural cycles of warming and cooling in geologic history."

The 9/11 attacks and the "Global War on Terror"

On 11 September 2001, hijackers crashed two passenger jets into the twin towers of New York's World Trade Center, followed by a similar attack on the Pentagon in Washington DC. Orchestrated by the terrorist organisation al Qaida, the atrocities claimed nearly 3,000 lives and destroyed $55 billion in physical property. In response, the Bush administration declared a "Global War on Terror" and invaded Afghanistan and Iraq.

Al Qaida (Arabic for "base") espoused a fundamentalist Islam that became popular among radical Muslims in the late twentieth century. Rejecting America's autocratic client regimes in the Middle East, al Qaida embraced Sharia law and the concept of jihad (Arabic for "striving") to justify its violent struggle against secularism. Formed in the 1980s to fight the Soviet occupation of Afghanistan (see Chapter 16), the organisation was led by the Saudi millionaire Osama bin Laden. Though al Qaida's contribution to the guerrilla war was negligible, bin Laden claimed credit not only for the Soviet withdrawal from Afghanistan in 1989, but also for the subsequent collapse of the USSR, solidifying his confidence that al Qaida could defeat the remaining superpower. Incensed by the deployment of US forces in Saudi Arabia, bin Laden declared war on the USA in 1996 and al Qaida staged terrorist attacks on US embassies in Kenya and Tanzania, followed by the bombing of the US Navy destroyer *Cole* in 2000. By then, bin Laden had found refuge with the fundamentalist Islamist Taliban regime in Afghanistan, whence al Qaida planned the 9/11 attacks on New York and Washington. Its goal was to inflict indiscriminate mass casualties, in contrast to other terrorist organisations which targeted specific individuals.

The Bush administration, which had paid scant attention to al Qaida prior to September 2001, quickly deemed the organisation an existential threat to the USA. To deprive it of its sanctuary in Afghanistan, Bush ordered an air offensive in 2001 which routed the Taliban regime in collaboration with local guerrilla forces. Assisted by the European members of NATO, which invoked the alliance's treaty clause that an attack on one member was an attack on all for the first time in its history, the USA installed a pro-Western government and supported reforms which improved the lives of many ordinary Afghans. The new government, however, was wracked by corruption and in 2005 faced a resurgent Taliban guerrilla that embroiled the country in a civil war. Bush's nation building efforts in Afghanistan failed just like Clinton's had in Somalia and Haiti.

Bush's response to the 9/11 attacks shared other features with Clinton's foreign policy, notably the belief that "rogue states" threatened US national security because they supported terrorism, pursued weapons of mass destruction (WMD), and oppressed their own people. Such rogue states included Iraq, Iran, and North Korea, Clinton's National Security Advisor Anthony Lake enunciated. In 2002, Bush labelled these same countries more colourfully an "axis of evil" whose replacement with democracies and capitalism would presumably remove the underpinnings of 9/11-style terrorism, even though there was no evidence that any of these countries actually supported al Qaida. The Bush administration nevertheless contended that the Iraqi dictatorship of Saddam Hussein had ties to bin Laden and sought WMD, raising the spectre of Iraq handing al Qaida atomic weapons to attack the USA. These conjectures provided the basis for the Bush doctrine of preventive war which sought the elimination of such risks "before they are fully formed." The fact that preventive war was illegal under international law and that Iraq had neither WMD nor ties to al Qaida failed to impress Bush, who in 2002 received Congressional authorisation for military action against Iraq from Republicans and many Democrats. Neoliberals who endorsed Bush's strategy included columnist Thomas Friedman, who predicted that Saddam's ouster would puncture the "terrorism bubble." Internationally, the looming confrontation caused rifts among America's European allies: whilst Britain, Portugal, Poland, Spain, and Denmark pledged troops, the French and German governments criticised the endeavour, earning them the sobriquet "axis of weasels" from US Defense Secretary Donald Rumsfeld. Millions took to the streets in New York, London, Berlin, and elsewhere to protest against the invasion.

The Iraq War turned into an unmitigated disaster. US forces quickly routed the Iraqi army and Saddam's regime collapsed in March 2003, but the invaders found no evidence for WMD or ties to al Qaida. An interim government called the Coalition Provisional Authority was largely staffed by inexperienced Americans with little understanding of the historic enmity between Iraq's minority Sunni Muslims and the Shia majority. The dissolution of the Iraqi army idled hundreds of thousands of soldiers, many of whom joined religious groups which fought each other and the Americans. Lacking sufficient troops to quell a growing Sunni insurgency, US forces became embroiled in fighting which killed more than 100,000 Iraqis and nearly 5,000 Americans by 2011. Graphic evidence that US troops tortured prisoners at the Abu Ghraib prison contradicted Bush administration claims that American initiative turned Iraq into a beacon of freedom and democracy in the Middle East. In 2004, opinion polls revealed that bin Laden enjoyed a higher favourability rating than Bush in Pakistan and elsewhere in the region. Europeans, many of whom had expressed solidarity with the USA in the wake of the 9/11 attacks, began to reject US claims to global leadership by sizable margins. Philosophers Jürgen Habermas of Germany and Jacques Derrida of France explained that Europe "sees itself challenged by the blunt hegemonic politics of its ally" epitomised by "the illegality of the unilateral, pre-emptive, and deceptively justified invasion."

The Iraq debacle, combined with domestic developments, eroded support for Bush at home. Though he was re-elected in 2004, domestic opposition to the war proliferated when it became clear that the US-sponsored election of Shia Prime Minister Nouri al-Maliki in 2006 brought Iraq closer to the Shia government of Iran, the USA's arch enemy in the region which emerged as the war's greatest beneficiary. Conservatives disliked Bush's stance on immigration, particularly his support for a proposed guest worker programme that would have legalised many of the four million unauthorised immigrants who arrived in the USA during his tenure (the initiative failed). The left criticised Bush's indefinite detention of terror suspects at the Guantanamo prison which was widely deemed a violation of the US Constitution and international law. His inept response to Hurricane Katrina, one of the worst storms in American history which killed nearly 2,000 people in 2005, meanwhile solidified the impression that Bush cared little about the lives of ordinary Americans. In the midterm elections of 2006, the Democrats regained control of both houses of Congress for the first time in more than a decade.

The great recession

In 2007, the US and world economies descended into the worst recession since the Great Depression of the 1930s which was followed by the weakest economic recovery on record. Called the Great Recession, the downturn contributed to considerable hardship and Democrat Barack Obama's election as president in 2008.

The Great Recession was preceded by an ever-worsening US trade deficit which had major long-term repercussions. In addition to Japan, whose trade surplus with the USA dated to the 1970s (see Chapter 16), key players included the Peoples' Republic of China (PRC), whose leadership sought to combine a communist dictatorship with a capitalist economy. By the turn of the century, Chinese factories employed virtual armies of low-wage workers and became the USA's leading suppliers of textiles, footwear, computers, and other consumer items. Controversial side effects of the USA's growing reliance on the PRC included the net loss of more than three million American manufacturing jobs from 2001 to 2008 and a rapidly growing trade deficit that reached $270 billion in 2008. Its burgeoning exports left the PRC with vast amounts of dollars which were entrusted to American banks for investment in US real estate.

The USA's financial markets underwent a massive transformation at the time. First, its trading partners and wealthy Americans accumulated a "giant pool of money" – $70 trillion by some estimates – in search of profitable returns. Second, the giant pool of money attracted investment banks like Goldman Sachs and other "shadow banks" which were not subject to strict regulatory regimes. Third, Citibank and other commercial banks took ever-greater financial risks after deregulation enabled them to pursue investment banking aggressively, generating enormous bonuses for bankers. Fourth, earners of middle and lower incomes who watched their paycheques grow anaemically sought funds to finance purchases that would otherwise have been beyond their means. In response to these developments, commercial and "shadow" banks offered new financial products like "Collateralised Debt Obligations" (CDOs) and other mortgage-backed securities which seemed to meet investors' demand for safe and profitable returns as well as borrowers' need for loans (see concept box). European banks like Britain's Northern Rock and Germany's Dresdner Bank soon joined the fray.

Collateralised Debt Obligation (CDO)

First offered by the investment bank Drexel Burnham Lambert in 1987, a CDO was an investment vehicle that was at the heart of the 2008 banking crisis. The typical CDO was structured as follows: a commercial bank issued mortgage loans to homeowners and then sold them to an investment bank; the latter bundled thousands of loans into a CDO and sold "tranches" (slices) to an investor. Though CDOs usually received "safe" AAA grades from credit rating agencies like Standard & Poor, investors often discovered that the tranche they had acquired was not backed by sufficient assets: the investment bank had combined low-risk loans to borrowers who were likely to pay off their mortgages with unsecured loans that were unlikely to be repaid.

Once markets for conventional mortgage loans were saturated, banks began to target "subprime borrowers" with spotty credit histories, baiting them with teaser rates which were set to increase a few years down the road. Ignorant borrowers often obtained loans at low introductory rates, only to realise later that they could not afford the eventual adjustment. Though warnings of a potentially catastrophic collapse by IMF economist Raghuram Rajan were dismissed in 2005 as "misguided" by neoliberal economist Summers, financial managers often admitted behind closed doors that their presumably rock-solid investment vehicles were deeply flawed. Bank of America, a prestigious megabank, fraudulently repackaged substandard loans as prime securities under a programme known internally as "The Hustle;" a Bear Stearns investment bank trader called the investment he had just sold to a client a "sack of shit;" and an executive at the Standard & Poor's rating agency confided, "Let's hope we are all wealthy and retired by the time this house of cards falters."

The moment of truth arrived in 2007, when a rise in interest rates punctured the boom in housing markets which were overvalued by 50 per cent and more. Shadow banks that had financed long-term investments in mortgage-backed securities with short-term loans faced a perilous "maturity mismatch" as lenders withdrew their loans. Investment banking imploded in 2008, when it came under siege from investors seeking to liquidate their assets: Bear Stearns and Merrill Lynch were acquired by Bank of America and JPMorgan Chase, respectively, Goldman Sachs and Morgan Stanley turned themselves into commercial banks to avail themselves to US Treasury funds, and Lehman Brothers went bankrupt. Simultaneously, the giant American International Group (AIG), which had sold investors credit protection on more than $400 billion in securities, became unable to meet its obligations.

The financial crisis caused an economic contraction on a scale not seen since the 1930s. A credit seizure made it impossible for consumers to sustain debt-financed consumption which had been a salient feature of US economic growth for a decade. Lack of sufficient credit for automobile purchases caused a massive contraction in automobile sales which plunged General Motors and Chrysler into bankruptcy. The automakers' crisis affected collateral industries from electronics to metals (U.S. Steel's sales fell by half in 2009). The same year, US unemployment approached 10 per cent, the highest rate in more than a quarter-century, and US household wealth dropped 22 per cent. The crisis reached deep into Europe, whose banks had borrowed vast sums for investments in American mortgage-backed securities, $1 trillion of which had to be written off. Severe liquidity problems caused many to prune credit lines with disastrous effects on consumption and industrial production across the continent.

Obama and the perseverance of neoliberalism

The Great Recession triggered an unprecedented government intervention into the economy under President Bush and his successor Barack Obama (2009–2017). Though Obama's presidential campaign of 2008 signalled departures from the policies that were widely held responsible for the Great Recession, however, his administration remained committed to core assumptions of neoliberalism.

Deregulation, trade liberalisation, regressive taxation, and other neoliberal policies came under blistering attack even from some of capitalism's staunchest supporters. France's conservative President Nicolas Sarkozy charged, "The idea of the absolute power of the markets that should not be constrained by any rule, by any political intervention, was a mad idea." *Financial Times* economics editor Martin Wolf agreed: "Another ideological god has failed. The assumptions that ruled policy and politics over three decades suddenly look as outdated as revolutionary socialism." Presidential candidate Obama remarked during the financial meltdown of September 2008, "What we've seen in the last few days is nothing less than the final verdict on an economic philosophy that has completely failed."

Initial policy responses to the financial crisis abandoned market-based solutions in favour of government intervention. By September 2008, the entire banking industry was on the brink of disaster due to the proliferation of "toxic assets" – mostly mortgage bundles which could not be sold at any price – that led to a credit freeze throughout the private sector. To forestall total collapse, the Federal Reserve relieved the banks of such assets at a cost of $800 billion and the Troubled Asset Relief Program (TARP) passed by Congress empowered the US Treasury to purchase hundreds of billions in illiquid securities from the private sector. TARP also enabled the Treasury to buy bank stocks, effectively making the US government a major shareholder in Bank of America, Citibank, Goldman Sachs, JPMorgan Chase, and other large institutions. Similar rescue packages were enacted by Britain's Labour Prime Minister Gordon Brown – formerly a devotee of financial deregulation – to forestall the imminent collapse of the Royal Bank of Scotland, and by Germany's conservative Chancellor Angela Merkel, whose government bought a large share of the troubled Commerzbank. Presidential candidate Obama supported TARP, though he later told Congress "We all hated the bank bailout. I hated it. You hated it. It was as popular as a root canal." Opinion polls at the start of his presidency indicated that 59 per cent of the public opposed the policy.

The first black man to be elected to the presidency, Obama seemed to symbolise a fresh departure in American politics. Supported by a broad coalition of young voters, women, independents, African Americans, and Hispanics, he outperformed recent Democratic candidates for president among white working class voters and Roman Catholics, resulting in a decisive popular vote victory of 53 per cent to 45.7 per cent over Republican John McCain. Having seized the executive branch of government, Democrats retained control of both houses of Congress.

To the surprise of some of his supporters, Obama's economic policies had much in common with those of his predecessors. Summers, a champion of financial deregulation

Figure 17.5 President Obama with Vice President Joe Biden, Senate Majority Leader and New
York Senator Chuck Schumer, and House Speaker Nancy Pelosi during the presidential inauguration, 20 January 2013. At the time, Democrats controlled the
presidency and majorities in the Senate and the House of Representatives.

Source: Courtesy of Military Collection/Alamy

under President Clinton, became Obama's Director of the National Economic Council. Favouring tax cuts over public works, Summers objected to leftist proposals of
major infrastructure initiatives to repair bridges and highways, update electrical grids,
and provide unemployment relief especially to construction workers ("Larry Summers
hates infrastructure," a frustrated Democrat commented). The Treasury Department
was entrusted to Timothy Geithner, a Summers protégé and former head of the New
York Federal Reserve who had asserted in 2007 "Financial innovation has improved
the capacity to measure and manage risk." Instrumental in a $180 billion bailout of the
stricken AIG insurance company, Geithner was widely regarded as a Wall Street advocate who prevented an outright nationalisation of Citibank and government-mandated
limits on bank executives' compensation. Economist Simon Johnson compared Geithner to the French statesman Charles Talleyrand, "who served the Revolution, Napoleon and the restored Bourbons – opportunistic and distrusted, but often useful and a
great survivor."

Anti-recessionary policies included economic stimulus, low interest rates, bank
bailouts, and regulatory reform, all of which were controversial. First, the American Recovery and Reinvestment Act (ARRA) passed by Congress in 2009 provided
$500 billion for investments in infrastructure, education, energy efficiency, and other
programmes, as well as $290 billion in tax cuts. The stimulus was deemed too little

by economists like Princeton University's Krugman, who argued that a package at least three times ARRA's size would be necessary to compensate for the decline in private-sector spending during the recession. The relatively small size of the stimulus package reflected the influence of deficit hawks, notably Budget Director Peter Orszag, who worried that a larger debt-financed stimulus would result in the "crowding out" effect cited by neoliberals to justify fiscal austerity in the 1990s ("Bill Clinton and the ascent of neoliberalism"). Second, the Federal Reserve cut interest rates to zero in order to stimulate borrowing, a move which reflected Chairman Ben Bernanke's determination to avoid the monetary policy mistakes of the 1930s, when high interest rates contributed to the length of the Great Depression (see Chapter 11). Simultaneously, however, Bernanke opposed a larger fiscal stimulus which would raise inflation above his target rate of 2 per cent whilst critics like economist Laurence Ball argued that a 4 per cent target was necessary to combat unemployment effectively. Third, the Treasury Department devoted $250 billion in TARP funds to relieving banks of toxic assets, but only $50 billion to foreclosure relief, prompting a federal regulator to comment that Secretary Geithner "consistently put the interests of the banks over those who were supposed to be helped, like struggling homeowners." Simultaneously, however, Geithner helped launch an $80 billion bailout of bankrupt General Motors and Chrysler which saved both companies. Fourth, Congress passed the Dodd-Frank Wall Street Reform and Consumer Protection Act of 2010, the most comprehensive financial reform since the 1930s which sought to protect borrowers from predatory lending, restrict commercial banks' ability to engage in investment banking, regulate shadow banks, and control credit rating agencies. Assaulted by the American Bankers' Association and other lobbying groups which sought to prevent its passage and weaken implementation for fear that the Dodd Frank Act would reduce bank profits, the reform was backed by Americans for Financial Reform, a coalition of labour and consumer groups that supported limits on executive pay and increased capital requirements.

The recession's global reach prompted efforts to coordinate recovery policies internationally. At a meeting of developed nations in 2009, leaders agreed on a $1 trillion package to supplement individual countries' $5 trillion stimulus programmes. Monetary policies diverged, however: whilst the Bank of England adopted the US Federal Reserve's 0 per cent interest rate, the European Central Bank maintained higher rates which contributed to a slower recovery in most Eurozone economies. The recession had a particularly devastating effect on Portugal, Italy, Greece, and Spain whose enormous public debts raised the spectre of sovereign defaults. The stronger economies of Northern Europe refused to provide support unless their southern neighbours shrank their budgets, cut social benefits, and reduced labour rights: German Chancellor Merkel ordained that "fiscal austerity is the only right way to deal with the Euro debt crisis." Lacking sufficient funds to finance effective economic stimulus packages, many European countries remained in recession longer and experienced even higher unemployment rates than the USA.

The USA's Great Recession ended officially with the resumption of GDP growth in June 2009, but the labour market did not recover for years. The *Wall Street Journal* reported in 2012 that "many American companies have emerged from the economic crisis – the worst recession since World War II – leaner, more productive, and more profitable." Job growth was evident in retailing, fast-food preparation, and other low-skill areas, but employers continued to eliminate middle-skill jobs in administration and manufacturing which often fell victim to automation and outsourcing. Wage growth remained lopsided as the top 1 per cent earners accrued more than 90 per cent of aggregate income gains. Adding insult to injury, financial institutions on life support from the federal government awarded enormous bonuses to executives, including the stricken insurance giant AIG, which issued more than $200 million in executive bonuses in 2009 after having lost $62 billion. Business analyst Karim Bardeesy commented "Sometimes the internal workings of a society are so rotten that it takes a complete outsider to come in and change the culture." Obama was not that sort of outsider: "My administration is the only thing between you and the pitchforks," he told bankers at the start of his presidency.

Foreign affairs

Obama entered office in 2009 at a time when the wars in Iraq and Afghanistan had stalled, the Bush administration's tacit embrace of torture had tarnished the USA's image overseas, and multiple crises unfolded in the Middle East. Seeking to avoid his predecessors' rush to precipitate action, Obama often told his foreign policy advisors to avoid "stupid" mistakes. His more cautious approach to world affairs produced mixed results.

An early opponent of the war against Iraq, Obama gradually reduced the US troop presence in the war-ravaged country while increasing deployments to Afghanistan. At the start of his presidency, when the level of violence had been reduced thanks in part to the presence of 140,000 US soldiers in Iraq, Obama ordered the withdrawal of forces by 2011. Some of the combat forces previously deployed in Iraq were stationed in Afghanistan, where troop levels more than doubled to 68,000 by 2013. The subsequent drawdown left a counterterrorism force on the ground which assisted Afghan regulars in their fight against Taliban guerrillas, echoing the situation in South Vietnam in 1973, when the USA had transferred combat operations to government forces in 1973 (see Chapter 16). Like South Vietnam and Somalia, moreover, Iraq and Afghanistan remained on the brink of collapse – a far cry from Bush's 2003 prediction "The establishment of a free Iraq at the heart of the Middle East will be a watershed event in the global democratic revolution."

Instead of spreading democracy, the Iraq invasion fomented the growth of the terrorist organisation Islamic State of Iraq and the Levant (ISIL), whose significance was initially underestimated by the Obama administration. Founded by a Jordanian Islamist radical who pledged allegiance to al Qaeda leader bin Laden in 2004, ISIL gradually took control of western Iraq and in 2011 intervened into an escalating civil war in Syria to establish a "caliphate" by means of extreme violence. In January 2014, Obama labelled it al Qaeda's "junior varsity" team, even though ISIL's influence had already surpassed that of al Qaeda partly due to its clever use of social media to attract jihadi recruits. The administration took the new threat more seriously when ISIL terrorists launched suicide attacks which eventually claimed hundreds of lives in North Africa, Turkey, France, Belgium, and Germany, in addition to thousands who died in ISIL-controlled territory in Syria and Iraq. In response, US forces re-entered Iraq in mid-2014 to conduct airstrikes and limited ground offensives against ISIL in collaboration with Iraq, Britain, France, Germany, Canada, and other allies. By the time Obama left office in 2017, ISIL had been dislodged from key positions in Iraq but remained ensconced in Syria, where its last strongholds finally collapsed in 2019.

Obama's attempts to repair America's battered image especially in the Middle East proved largely unsuccessful. His election promise to close the USA's controversial detention centre in Guantanamo, where hundreds of Islamist terror suspects were held indefinitely without trial, ran afoul on Republican opposition. In 2011, the Obama administration was caught off guard by a wave of protests called the "Arab Spring" that swept away the authoritarian regimes of Tunisia and Egypt which had long enjoyed tacit US support. In an ill-conceived intervention into domestic unrest in Libya which erupted during the Arab Spring, the USA and Britain bombed government forces loyal to dictator Muammar Gaddafi. Obama considered his unpreparedness for the subsequent Libyan civil war the "worst mistake" of his foreign policy. Another controversy erupted in 2011 when US special forces killed bin Laden in his hideout in Pakistan without informing that country's leadership beforehand for fear that government authorities sympathetic to al Qaida would warn the terrorist leader of the impending operation. Though celebrated in the USA as revenge for the 9/11 attacks, bin Laden's killing strained the US-Pakistan relationship, which many considered vital for future anti-terrorism operations. Obama's Middle East policy was further complicated by his objections to the construction of Jewish settlements in the majority-Palestinian West Bank, which raised the ire of the Israeli government. The latter also objected to a nuclear treaty framework signed by Obama in 2015 that limited Iran's ability to develop atomic weapons in return for the lifting of some US sanctions.

Obama's national security policy was equally controversial. Using provisions of the Patriot Act of 2001 which had permitted extensive surveillance in the aftermath of the 9/11 attacks, the National Security Agency (NSA) conducted secret global reconnaissance of internet and phone communications that was criticised by candidate Obama in 2008, when he pledged to revisit the Patriot Act and "harness the power of technology to hold government and business accountable for violations of personal privacy." Citing the need to prevent future acts of terrorism, however, he endorsed an extension of the Patriot Act in 2011 and authorised mass surveillance of communication by the NSA in collaboration with private internet and phone providers as well as the British, German, French, and other foreign intelligence services. Surveillance activities which were revealed by former NSA contractor Edward Snowden in 2013 included the wiretapping of foreign leaders like German Chancellor Merkel, whose mobile phone conversations were monitored by the NSA. Though Obama promised to rein in the NSA in the aftermath of the Snowden revelations, its mass surveillance programme continued to the end of his presidency.

Sociocultural conflict and conservative resurgence

The Obama years marked a period of social activism by sexual and racial minorities, and by conservatives who rejected core aspects of his domestic policy agenda. These developments contributed to the election of Republican Donald Trump as president in 2016.

Lesbian, gay, bisexual, and transgender (LGBT) Americans gained substantial rights. Activism in the 1970s and 1980s had sought decriminalisation, acceptance of LGBT identities by straight family members, friends, and colleagues, and greater public awareness of the proliferating HIV/AIDS crisis. This was followed in the 1990s by efforts to gain rights to marry, adopt and raise children, and receive legal protection from hate crimes. These campaigns bore fruit after the turn of the century, when state courts and legislatures began to legalise same-sex marriage. In 2009, Obama signed a reform of the US Federal Hate Crime Law that extended hate crime protections to LGBT people. Six years later, the Supreme Court legalised same-sex marriage, with opinion polls indicating that more than 60 per cent of Americans supported same-sex marriage while a majority of Republicans opposed it. Opposition clustered among conservative Christians who – citing Biblical prohibitions of same-sex relationships – resisted the court ruling and sought legal rights for Christians to discriminate against LGBT people in businesses and churches. Ronnie Floyd, head of the influential Southern Baptist Convention explained, "The Supreme Court of the United States is not the final authority nor is the culture itself. The Bible is God's final authority about marriage and on this book we stand." In contrast to the USA, where courts played a key role, some European countries introduced same-sex marriage rights by parliamentary law or public referenda, including the Netherlands (2001), France, England, and Wales (2013), Scotland (2014), and Ireland (2015); Germany extended legal recognition to same-sex civil unions in 2001 but stopped short of legalising marriages between partners of the same sex.

Expectations that Obama's election in 2008 marked the beginning of a post-racial era in American history faded quickly as blacks suffered disproportionate rates of unemployment, poverty, and loss of homeownership in the aftermath of

Figure 17.6 A male couple kissing during an LGBT pride parade in Los Angeles with conservative protesters in the background, 2012.

Source: Courtesy of Hayk Shalunts/Alamy

the Great Recession. Racial profiling was evident among many police forces which stopped and frisked African Americans more frequently than whites (more than half of all New Yorkers who were stopped and searched by police in 2012 were African American). Fatal police shootings of blacks, which had often been ignored, garnered increased attention when video footage captured by bystanders with their mobile phones sometimes disproved police claims of threatening conduct by suspects. These developments contributed to the growth of Black Lives Matter (BLM), a grass roots movement whose members protested police violence directed at racial minorities. In 2014, for example, the shooting of black teenager Michael Brown by police in Ferguson, Missouri, prompted local rioting and nationwide BLM demonstrations.

The early twenty-first century marked an upsurge in mass killings by gunmen who murdered Americans in schools, offices, stores, houses of worship, factories, shopping malls, and other venues. The worst occurred in Newtown, Connecticut, where a gunman killed 20 first-graders in 2012. Obama, deeply shocked by the Newtown shootings, called for an assault weapons ban that was defeated in the Senate by a bipartisan coalition of Republicans and Democrats. Per capita civilian gun ownership, which was higher in the USA than in any other country, was safeguarded by influential lobbying groups like the National Rifle Association (NRA). In the aftermath of the Newton shootings, the NRA and similar organisations claimed without evidence

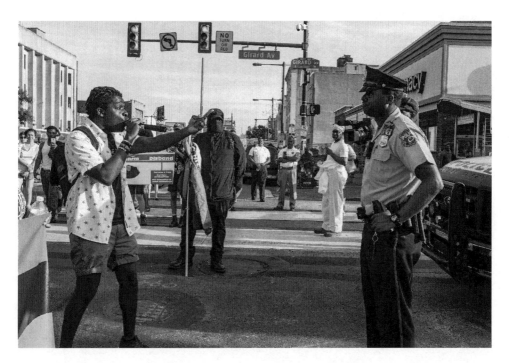

Figure 17.7 Black Lives Matter protest in Philadelphia, 2017. Demonstrators assembled in response to a police officer who had shot and killed a bicycle rider trying to evade arrest.

Source: Courtesy of Christopher Evens/Alamy

that Obama sought to duplicate a British law passed in 1997 that effectively outlawed private handgun ownership after a school massacre in Dunblane, Scotland (statistics indicated that the USA had the highest rate of gun-related homicides among developed countries whilst Britain had one of the world's lowest rates).

The Affordable Care Act (ACA), Obama's most important legislative achievement that reformed the USA's health insurance system, was portrayed as European-style socialism by conservative critics. Passed in 2010 despite massive Republican opposition, the ACA was in fact modelled after a Massachusetts health care law signed by Republican governor Mitt Romney in 2006 that required individuals to obtain health insurance or pay a fine. Many people received government subsidies which were financed through taxes on the rich to help low-income Americans pay their premiums to private health insurance companies. The latter could no longer cap lifetime benefits, drop policyholders who became sick, or implement similar policies which had been used routinely by insurance companies to safeguard their profitability. The ACA also relaxed eligibility requirements for Medicaid, the government-run health insurance programme for the poor. Unlike a more comprehensive reform attempt proposed by Clinton that failed in 1995, the ACA imposed no limits on premium raises at the urging of insurance companies, most of which supported the Obama reforms. After a difficult start, the ACA enrolled 30 million people who had lacked health insurance of any kind. Michael Cannon of the conservative Cato institute objected that the ACA encapsulated "everything that's wrong with the European-style democratic socialist state" and Republican Party chairman Reince Preibus claimed "Americans don't want European style Socialism."

Critics who portrayed the ACA as un-American were moderate compared to Obama opponents who claimed that he planned to establish Democratic Party re-education camps to indoctrinate American youngsters (a theory promulgated by Republican Congresswoman Michele Bachman), had attended a Muslim fundamentalist madrassas school in Indonesia (*Insight Magazine*), and ordered the murder of right-wing blogger Andrew Breitbart (activist Jim Garrow). Though most of these conspiracy theories remained on the radical fringes, false claims that Obama was not born in the USA and therefore ineligible for the presidency were believed by more than 40 per cent of Republicans polled in 2010. Chief among those who doubted Obama's citizenship was businessman Trump, who noted in 2011 "if [Obama] wasn't born in this country, which is a real possibility, then he has pulled one of the great cons in the history of politics."

Republican Trump's 2016 presidential election win over Democrat Hillary Clinton reflected widespread voter dissatisfaction with conventional politics. Backed in the general election by traditional Republican constituencies like Southern whites, cultural conservatives, and pro-business groups, Trump attracted crucial support from working-class voters, many of whom had voted for Obama in 2008 and 2012 but were disappointed with the president's failure to deliver the fundamental change he had promised. Often clustering in rural communities and small towns whose social structure had been undermined by deindustrialization, poverty, drug epidemics, and unemployment in the wake of the Great Recession, these voters felt ignored by conventional Democrats and Republicans who were perceived as representatives of big business, "Washington insiders," or urban elites. Many of Trump's working-class supporters felt abandoned by a government that seemed to spend their tax dollars to bail out megabanks, shower racial and ethnic minorities with benefits, and defend foreign countries while leaving ordinary Americans struggling with inadequate incomes, mounting debts, and a declining standard of living. Trump appealed to these voters with his campaign slogan "Make America Great Again," a promise to bring back jobs in the steel and coal industries, and an unapologetic embrace of the phrase "America First," which had long been taboo in American politics because it had been used by pro-Nazi isolationists in the early 1940 (see Chapter 9). Clinton, the competent but uninspiring Democratic candidate, committed the worst blunder of her poorly managed campaign when she told attendees of an LGBT fundraising gala in New York City "you could put half of Trump's supporters into what I call the basket of deplorables. The racist, sexist, homophobic, xenophobic, Islamaphobic – you name it." Though she later apologised for the remark, it confirmed the widespread impression that she was an arrogant and entitled elitist who looked down upon ordinary Americans. Left-wing activist Michael Moore, one of the few commentators who predicted Trump's victory, compared the lives of America's midwestern working class with those of their counterparts in Britain's old industrial heartland: "From Green Bay to Pittsburgh, this, my friends, is the middle of England – broken, depressed, struggling, the smokestacks strewn across the countryside with the carcass of what we used to call the Middle Class. Angry, embittered working (and nonworking) people who were lied to by the trickle-down of Reagan and abandoned by Democrats who still try to talk a good line but are really just looking forward to rub one out with a lobbyist from Goldman Sachs who'll write them nice big check before leaving the room. What happened in the UK with Brexit is going to happen here." As Moore predicted, the electoral votes of the rust-belt states Wisconsin, Pennsylvania, Michigan, and Ohio provided Trump with a comfortable margin of victory over Clinton as the Republican Party took control of the presidency, the US Senate, and the House of Representatives for the first time in nearly a century.

Chapter summary

The 1990s began with high hopes for a new era of growth and affluence after the end of the cold war. Neoliberals sought to achieve these objectives by combining Reagan-style deregulation and free trade with austerity budgets which would reduce fiscal deficits and unleash the potential of the US economy. More importantly, the nineties' economy benefitted from the adoption of new information technologies like personal computers and the internet which improved productivity. Though these developments contributed to swift growth and low unemployment, they also produced growing social inequality, employment polarisation, and financial instability whose effects became more apparent when the nineties' boom fizzled and the Great Recession struck in 2007. Internationally, the USA embarked on a series of military interventions which were ostensibly undertaken to replace in rogue regimes with democratic ones which were unlikely to support terrorist organisations like al Qaida that attacked the USA on 9/11. These attempts at "nation building" largely failed, undermined international relations, and provoked widespread dislike of the USA especially in the Middle East. President Obama's effort to repair America's image overseas, rein in mass surveillance, and tackle the Great Recession began with high hopes, but many of his supporters were disappointed when he entrusted economic policymaking to neoliberals who were held responsible to creating the crisis in the first place. Persistent income inequality and the agonisingly slow recovery from the recession contributed to Trump's election in 2016.

Discussion questions

- Why did the cold war end?
- What were neoliberalism's effects on the U.S. economy and society?
- How did the attacks of 11 September 2001, affect US foreign policy?
- What were the similarities of the Clinton, Bush, and Obama Presidencies?
- Who or what was responsible for the Great Recession?
- Which short- and long-term developments contributed to the election of Donald Trump as president?

Further reading

Alexander, Michelle. *The New Jim Crow: Mass Incarceration in the Age of Colorblindness* (New York, 2010). This provocative study argues that the modern criminal justice system replicates the functions of legal segregation and other traditional forms of racial control.

Greenwald, Glenn. *No Place to Hide: Edward Snowden, the NSA, and the U.S. Surveillance State* (London, 2014). Written by a journalist who assisted Snowden in revealing the NSA's mass surveillance programmes, this book examines the recent history of global spying and its violation of US constitutional law.

Levinson, Marc. *An Extraordinary Time: The End of the Postwar Boom and the Return of the Ordinary Economy* (New York, 2016). A former senior editor of the *Economist* magazine argues that the post-war period until 1973 constituted a unique chapter in history whose strong productivity growth rates are unlikely to be replicated in the twenty-first century as the US and world economies return to "normal" – i.e., slower – growth rates.

Mandelbaum, Michael. *Mission Failure: America and the World in the Post-Cold War Era* (New York, 2016). A leading diplomatic historian examines troubled US attempts at nation building in the wake of military interventions after the end of the Cold War.

Pinketty, Thomas. *Capital in the Twenty-First Century* (Cambridge, MA, 2014). Written by a leading French economist, this best-selling study examines the growth of income inequality primarily in the USA and Western Europe.

Romano, Flavio. *Clinton and Blair: The Political Economy of the Third Way* (London, 2006). This useful comparative study examines the historical background, policies, and impact of Anglo-American neoliberalism.

Steger, Manfred, and Ravi Roy. *Neoliberalism: A Very Short Introduction* (New York, 2010). This useful survey introduces readers to the assumptions and policies of neoliberalism in a global perspective.

Tooze, Adam. *Crashed. How a Decade of Financial Crises Changed the World* (New York, 2018). A leading economic historian examines the 2008 financial crisis and its aftermath.

Troy, Gil. *The Age of Clinton: America in the 1990s* (New York, 2015). Written by a presidential historian, this critical study examines how the 1990s political culture shaped President Clinton and vice versa.

Index

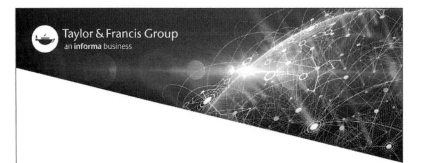